BETRAYAL

Other books by William Hoffer:

Caught in the Act
Midnight Express
Every Other Man
Saved!
Volcano
The Book of Granville
Not Without My Daughter
Mort! Mort! Mort!
Freefall
Cop Hunter
Victor Six
Adams v. Texas
Inside Out
The Senator

BETRAYAL

THE UNTOLD STORY OF THE KURT WALDHEIM INVESTIGATION AND COVER-UP

ELI M. ROSENBAUM
with WILLIAM HOFFER

ST. MARTIN'S PRESS
NEW YORK

A THOMAS DUNNE BOOK

Designed by Chris Welch

Library of Congress Cataloging-in-Publication Data

Rosenbaum, Eli.
Betrayal : the untold story of the Kurt Waldheim investigation and cover-up / Eli Rosenbaum and William Hoffer.
p.   cm.
"A Thomas Dunne book."
ISBN 0-312-08219-3
1. Waldheim, Kurt.   2. Presidents—Austria—Biography.   3. World War, 1939–1945—Atrocities.   4. War crimes—History—20th century.   5. Austria—Politics and government—1945–   6. World politics—1945–I. Hoffer, William.   II. Title.
DB98.W28R67   1992
943.605′3′092—dc20

[R]   92-24718

First Edition: September 1993

10   9   8   7   6   5   4   3   2   1

For our parents.

E.M.R. and W.H.

And to the memory of my friend and colleague
Michael S. Bernstein
Assistant Deputy Director
Office of Special Investigations
United States Department of Justice
—murdered by terrorists, December 1988.

E.M.R.

For many of those affected by the
Second World War, life is easier and
better.

—*Kurt Waldheim (1980)*

C O N T E N T S

ACKNOWLEDGMENTS

Numerous persons have contributed unselfishly to the production of this book, and several must be singled out for special mention.

Special thanks are due to: Marilyn Hoffer, who was totally involved in every phase of the composition; our agents, Jay Acton of Acton and Dystel, Inc., and Mel Berger of the William Morris Agency, Inc., and our editor, Thomas Dunne, for their professional advice and encouragement; and Dan Dietz and Joseph Friedman for their invaluable comments and guidance. We are grateful as well for the support and very capable assistance of John Murphy, Patty Rosati, Reagan Arthur, Joshua Marwell, and Eric Meyer of St. Martin's Press.
—E.M.R. and W.H.

The exposure of the Waldheim cover-up and conspiracy would have been impossible without the extraordinary efforts and assistance of a great many people. Although several of those individuals continue to insist on anonymity, others may be acknowledged here. Special thanks are due Willi A. Korte (Washington), the late Stephen S. Katich (Library of Congress), Dr. Lavoslav Kadelburg (President, Federation of Jewish Communities in Yugoslavia), Hans Safrian (Vienna), Philip Rubenstein (Office of the Hon. Greville Janner, House of Commons, London), Michael May (Institute of Jewish Affairs, London), Dr. David Crown (formerly Chief, Document Laboratory, Central Intelligence Agency), Ernest Goldblum (New York), Ralph Blumenthal and John Tagliabue (the *New York Times*), Dusko Doder and John M. Goshko (the *Washington Post*), and Hubertus Czernin (*Profil* magazine, Vienna).

More than anyone else, it was the men and women of the World Jewish Congress who made possible the systematic destruction of Kurt Waldheim's life lie. A special expression of gratitude is owed to the three principal leaders of the WJC, who had the courage and fortitude to press on despite the long odds, the enormous costs (financial and otherwise), and the constant threats: WJC President Edgar M. Bronfman, Secretary General Israel Singer, and Executive

Director Elan Steinberg. Thanks are in order as well to other gifted and dedicated WJC professionals in New York (Hella Moritz, Sidney Gruber, Sharon Cohen, Emily Rubin, Nelly Harris, Bessy Pupko, the late Benjamin Weiss, Rose Zeiman, and Ruth Shamansky), Jerusalem (Dr. Avi Beker), Geneva (Daniel Lack and Dr. Gerhart Riegner), Paris (Serge Czwaigenbaum), and London (Dr. Stephen Roth, Antony Lerman, and Avriel Butovsky). A brief, but significant, research effort was undertaken for the WJC by a historian I engaged several weeks after we broke the Waldheim story, Professor Robert E. Herzstein of the University of South Carolina. Important assistance was also provided by two members of Edgar Bronfman's management team at Joseph E. Seagram & Sons, Inc., William K. Friedman and Anna G. Resnik.

At the United States National Archives, valuable assistance was provided by Robert Wolfe, the late John Mendelsohn, George Wagner, and Amy Schmidt. In Vienna, cooperation was freely given by Silvana Konieczny-Origlia, Erhard Loecker, Ariel Muzicant, Dr. Georg Zanger, and Professor Dr. Leon Zelman. Appreciation must be expressed as well for the assistance generously rendered by several present and former officials of the Government of Israel; those who can be named are the Honorable Benjamin Netanyahu and Isser Harel.

Support and assistance were provided by a large number of people associated with the United States Congress. Special mention must be made of Rep. Gary Ackerman, Rep. Stephen Solarz, Rep. Hamilton Fish, Jr., Rep. Tom Lantos, and a number of talented Congressional staffers: Richard Goodman (Senate Governmental Affairs Committee), Nicholas Hayes (Office of Rep. Hamilton Fish, Jr.), Wayne Simmons (Office of Rep. Joseph J. DioGuardi), Mark J. Tavliarides (Office of Rep. Gus Yatron), and Alexander Wohl and Bob Hathaway (Office of Rep. Stephen Solarz).

Among the many other individuals whose contributions need to be gratefully acknowledged are the following: former U.S. Secretary of State George P. Shultz, Frederick Chapman (International Law Library, Harvard Law School), the late Joseph Lovinger (Athens), the late Justice Arthur J. Goldberg, Dr. Alexander Kitroeff (*Journal of Modern Greek Studies*), Peter Lubin, Rabbi Arthur Hertzberg, George Dardavilas (Consulate of Greece, New York City), Genya Markon (U.S. Holocaust Memorial Council), Tom Bower, Gerald Posner, Dr. Vesna Najfeld, the Honorable Greville Janner, M.P. (House of Commons), Simon Nusbaum, Peter Lerner, David "Dubi" Bernstein, Ayall Schanzer, Alan Oirich, Kim Danish, David Newell and Andrew Nagorski (both of *Newsweek* magazine), Ed Saltman and

Ed Braman (Thames Television PLC, London), Diane Wallerstein, Ira Silverman, and James Polk (all of NBC News), Susan Birnbaum (Jewish Telegraphic Agency), Ana Marija Bešker (Embassy of Yugoslavia, Washington), David Kahn, Ambassador John D. Scanlon, Robert B. Cave, Susan M. Hoffman, Jennifer Kirkpatrick, Rabbi Marvin Hier of the Simon Wiesenthal Center (especially for his assistance in obtaining a copy of Waldheim's doctoral dissertation), Mark Wurm, Dusan Tatomirovic, Michael Wutzel, Shelly Zima Shapiro, Dr. Michael Neiditch (B'nai B'rith International, Washington), Sarabeth and Sten Lukin (the *Boston Jewish Times*), Isi J. Leibler, C.B.E., Jeremy Jones and David Bernstein (Melbourne, Australia), Professor Jozo Tomasevich (Stanford University), Professor John Louis Hondros (College of Wooster), James Demos (Hellenic Freedom Foundation), Sam Beller, Admiral Stansfield Turner (United States Navy, Ret.), the late Wim van Leer, former Nuremberg prosecutor Theodore Fenstermacher, Julian O'Halloran (British Broadcasting Corporation), John Ranz (The Generation After, New York), Sanford J. Hausler, Margot Munk, Katherine M. Valyi (Adams & Reinhart, New York), Mike Beckham (Granada Television, London), Zivko Gruden, Uros Lipuscek, and my brother, Daniel Rosenbaum. As on so many other occasions in my life, I benefited enormously from the wise counsel of my father, Irving M. Rosenbaum, who, in this case, must be specially thanked for sharing with me the important insights he gained while questioning Nazi officials and other German prisoners during his World War II service in the U.S. Seventh Army's Psychological Warfare Branch in North Africa and Europe.

I am grateful as well to the United States Department of Justice, which rehired me in May 1988 despite my prior criticism of the manner in which the Reagan Administration responded to the Waldheim revelations—and notwithstanding my disclosure of the pendency of this book project. Neal M. Sher and Patrick J. Treanor of the Justice Department's Office of Special Investigations played central roles in the investigation of Kurt Waldheim's war record. Although my first act upon returning to the Department was to recuse myself from anything even tangentially relating to the Waldheim affair, false accusations will perhaps be made by Waldheim supporters that I "must have" subsequently gained access to information and evidence in the Department's possession. My federal service has always been a source of great pride to me, and I deeply appreciate the confidence that the Department, and especially the Criminal Division, has had in me.

My wife, Cynthia, suffered the seemingly endless torments of this project with me, never once wavering in her support or her love. I will never be able to repay my debt of gratitude. To my daughters, Karina and Alissa, who had to cede so many hours that they might have spent with their daddy to the demands of finishing this book, I can only say that all of this will make sense to you—one day. I promise.

—E.M.R.

A U T H O R ' S   N O T E

This is a true story. Quotations have been re-created either from documentary material or from my personal notes, recorded during or immediately following the referenced conversations. In order to protect informants, it was necessary to change minor circumstances in a few passages. This was done, however, without materially altering the record of their actions, and the only pseudonym used is the one that is expressly identified as such.

The views expressed in this work are solely those of the authors and do not necessarily represent the views of the United States Department of Justice or any other component of the United States Government.

—E.M.R.

PREFACE

On June 21, 1991, Austrian President Kurt Waldheim went on nationwide television to announce a decision over which he had plainly agonized for some time. Solemnly facing the camera from behind a large desk inside the sumptuously appointed Hofburg Palace in Vienna, the obviously weary former United Nations Secretary General brought an end to the suspense that had gripped his country for months. Dogged ever since the 1986 election campaign by sensational allegations that he had covered up an appalling Nazi past for more than forty years, Waldheim disclosed that he would not seek reelection in 1992.

In so doing, the seventy-two-year-old self-proclaimed former "chief human rights officer of the planet Earth" at last bowed to a painful reality: The torrent of shocking revelations that began five years earlier during his hate-filled but successful presidential election campaign had taken its toll. He had been transformed into an international pariah, a virtual prisoner of the presidential palace, shunned by visiting dignitaries and celebrities and by nearly all of the world's non-Islamic governments. Even his supporters now recognized that Waldheim had become an onerous liability to his country, one whose personal travails continued to bring a most unwelcome foreign media focus onto the role played in the Nazi machinery of oppression and mass murder not just by this one-time Wehrmacht intelligence officer, but also by the many thousands of his fellow Austrians who had eagerly embraced Adolf Hitler's malignant vision. The reputation he had so carefully built over four decades now lay in ruins, and along with it the methodically cultivated image of his country as a "victim" of the Nazis.

In the hope that Kurt Waldheim's belated withdrawal from political life may at last make possible a chronicling of "the Waldheim affair" that is as free as possible from the distortion introduced by electioneering and political maneuvering, we have attempted to present the first comprehensive "inside" account of the investigation that exposed the unprecedented Nazi cover-up that dominated world headlines during much of 1986 and 1987. With Waldheim's recent withdrawal from reelection contention, the story can finally be told without provoking renewed Austrian charges of "foreign interference in our domestic political affairs" and "election campaign mudslinging."

Such charges dogged us during the investigation. We have sought to re-create the electrifying political atmosphere in which the exposure of Waldheim took place, especially in Austria, where the reaction of Waldheim's handlers was to fight back by launching the first overtly anti-Semitic election campaign attempted by a major political party in Europe since the Nazi Party of Germany horrified the civilized world in the 1930s. This is arguably the most important, and least told, aspect of the entire affair: the breaking of the postwar European taboo on the open use of anti-Semitism as a political weapon. Waldheim as an individual is not especially important; he presided over a relatively impotent United Nations, and his wartime misdeeds hardly rivaled those of Eichmann and the other architects of Nazi bestiality. What *is* important is what Waldheim represents: the cynicism, selective memory, and outright dishonesty that still pervade many Europeans' views of their countrymen's role in the horrors unleashed by Hitler.

Although the story is told initially from my perspective as the former U.S. Justice Department war crimes prosecutor who directed the Waldheim probe for the World Jewish Congress, we have attempted to recount as faithfully as possible the painstaking efforts of the other members of the tiny band of Waldheim pursuers—historians, researchers, lawyers and journalists—to piece together an almost impossibly intricate puzzle. However much Waldheim's Nazi past is today taken for granted, it will be recalled that, at the outset of the investigation, the proposition that the proudly "anti-Nazi" Kurt Waldheim, one of the world's best-known public figures, could have been hiding such a past was nothing short of preposterous.

As a federal prosecutor, I had been involved in some of the most difficult and sensitive investigations ever undertaken by the United States Department of Justice. Never, however, had I encountered anything like the Waldheim investigation. Working together at times and laboring individually at others, all of us who were at the center of the maelstrom faced some of the most daunting odds in the history of criminal investigation. We knew that the bulk of Waldheim's wartime activities would never have been recorded in written documents. In any event, the Axis-created documents of the period had been largely destroyed, either inadvertently during and after combat or else intentionally by the Nazis themselves when they saw that the war was soon to be lost and realized that incriminating evidence had to be obliterated. The documents that somehow survived the conflagration were scattered among archives throughout Europe and the United States, and many of those collections were still deemed so sensitive by the governments possessing them (most especially the then–Soviet Union and its satellites) that we were barred from them. The collections to which we could gain access were poorly (if at all) indexed and many, if not most, of the documents required one to be able to decipher Nazi parlance and coding, thus reducing much of the Waldheim probe to a "needle-in-a-haystack" search. Moreover, the potential witnesses most likely to have accurate knowledge of Waldheim's wartime activities—namely, his erstwhile comrades-in-arms—were surely going to oppose our efforts to get at the truth, since any proof of criminal activity on Waldheim's part was likely to implicate them as well. Of course, we lacked subpoena power to compel them (and, for that matter, Waldheim himself) to testify. And the fact that Waldheim (who declined to be interviewed for this book) unashamedly changed his alibis to fit each new disclosure complicated our detective work enormously. These changes—which frequently took the form of dramatic retractions of prior admissions or recantations of prior denials—caused his pursuers to chase numerous false leads and to shift investigative direction repeatedly, even to ascertain the broad outline of his whereabouts and unit assignments during the war. The complex mystery unfolded in piecemeal fashion, a fact that left most of the free world's media hopelessly confused.

Given the subject of our probe and the intricacies of the task, I could never have imagined that so few people, working with such meager resources, would succeed in documenting so much of Waldheim's well-hidden Nazi past. Nor would I have believed that the results would be so startling. Our astonishment was probably exceeded only by that of Kurt Waldheim and his advisers.

If the barriers to uncovering the truth about Waldheim's war activities were intimidating, they were modestly sized in comparison with those that lay in the way of discovering who had helped Waldheim pull off what many observers came to call the international political cover-up of the century. As trail after investigative trail seemed to lead to the intelligence services of various governments—on *both* sides of the former "Iron Curtain"—we found ourselves almost completely blocked. Hence, the greatest challenge of all became that of answering the single most-asked question in the Waldheim affair: How had Waldheim been able to get away with such a brazen cover-up for as long as he did, and as successfully as he did (to the point that even the *Israeli* delegation at the United Nations had vouched to the media for Waldheim's non-involvement with the Nazis)?

The solution to that mystery, presented here for the first time, is one that causes me considerable anguish. But the billions of people who were so cruelly deceived by Kurt Waldheim are entitled to know just who it was who made it possible for the deception to succeed. Allowing the explanation to remain secret forever would be both unwise and unjust. For only by painful confrontation with reality will we come to understand fully the grave consequences that can result from unquestioning acceptance of the credentials and professed good intentions of those who would purport to champion the interests of justice and humanity.

—E.M.R.

1

January 29, 1986. Without warning, a hand clamped down on my shoulder from behind, wrenching me away from a conversation in midsentence. "I have to talk to you," said my boss, Israel Singer. "Right now."

Tall and angular, wearing his ever-present black knitted *yarmulke,* the forty-three-year-old Secretary General of the World Jewish Congress (WJC) sported, this day, one of his tailored, wide-lapel Italian suits. Singer seemed perpetually en route to an encounter, whether in another room or another country. Invariably, he conveyed the impression that he was running late. In part, he did this by speaking in loud, concise, rapid-fire bursts and expecting—demanding—that the listener assimilate the words immediately. When Singer said he had to talk, you frequently had just one quick chance to hear his message before he became a blurry memory.

He hustled me across an expanse of institutional carpet toward an unoccupied corner of the Jerusalem Hilton's lower lobby. This was the "Global Plenary Assembly" of the WJC, held only once every five years, always in Israel. Hundreds of delegates were here to represent the Jewish communities of dozens of nations. For many of them, the gathering provided a rare opportunity to speak with the frenetic Singer and, as we strode through the hall, several of the conferees spotted him and sought a brief word. The expression on his face warned them off.

I assumed that Singer had yet another, probably minor, conference-related assignment for me, until he announced, "You're going to Vienna. You'll leave as soon as we finish here."

I was nonplussed. "*Vienna?* Why?"

"I don't know exactly what's going on," he confided, "but there's something important that has to be checked out." He added in an uncharacteristically quiet tone, "It has to do with Kurt Waldheim."

"*The* Kurt Waldheim?" I asked. I suggested that the man was ancient history; he had served two rather undistinguished terms as Secretary-General of the United Nations (where some of his associates called him "The Headwaiter," and others, viewing him as spineless, dubbed Waldheim "Mr. Pudding") and then disappeared into obscurity, much like his predecessor, U Thant. I had heard that he was running for president of Austria now, but that was a largely ceremonial post. Why was he of any concern to the WJC?

"This is very sensitive," Singer responded. He leaned forward, speaking in a whisper made hoarse by the nonstop hours of speech-making and politicking of the past few days. "Do you know who Leon Zelman is?"

I shook my head.

"He's the executive director of something called the 'Jewish Welcome Service' in Vienna. He's a survivor of the camps, by the way. He had a terrible time during the war. Horrible." Singer told me about the time at the infamous Mauthausen concentration camp when Zelman's unconscious body was loaded onto a cart containing corpses, and he awoke to find himself among the dead. "But look," Singer continued, "he just showed me some papers. Believe it or not, it looks like our Dr. Waldheim may have been a Nazi. A *real* one."

I presumed that Singer used the term "real" to signify something more sinister than the simple, well-known fact of Waldheim's service in the German armed forces—the Wehrmacht—during the invasion of the Soviet Union in 1941. "Real" surely denoted a more substantial indictment than the vague epithet "that Nazi Waldheim," which was often hurled in a cavalier fashion behind the back of the man who had displayed such open hostility to Israel during his years at the U.N. helm.

Singer *can't* be serious, I thought. Could he be joking? The earnest expression on his face assured me that he was not employing his sometimes caustic sense of humor. Singer did not take such matters lightly; his parents had fled Vienna to escape the Nazis.

"I want you to speak with Zelman right now," he commanded. "And on Tuesday, fly back with him to Vienna. I told him about the work you did when you were at the Justice Department, and I told him you're the guy to handle this."

Just recently, I had left a job with a large Manhattan law firm to become the General Counsel of the New York–based WJC. The new position occasioned a painful pay cut, but I had been raised in a home where charity—in contributions of time as well as money—was a central theme. When I told my father—already retired from a successful business career—that I was considering the job change but did not know if I was wise to accept the dramatic income reduction, he had placed an open palm over his chest and counseled me, "Follow your heart."

In the few months I had held my position, I had come to see the wisdom of my father's words. The work was consistently interesting, and almost always meaningful. At least once a week I traveled uptown to the headquarters of the United Nations to monitor developments there that had relevance to Jewish interests around the world. In recent years, the U.N. had turned ever more hostile to Israel, and its activities required constant scrutiny. I also wrote *amicus curiae* ("friend of the court") briefs in U.S. court cases of interest to the WJC.

It was exciting and challenging work, but I certainly could not have anticipated that one of my assignments would be to investigate the former Secretary-General of the United Nations.

Before my stint near Wall Street, I had worked for three years as a trial attorney in the U.S. Justice Department's Office of Special Investigations (OSI), the federal government's sole agency charged with investigating and prosecuting alleged Nazi war criminals. I had no desire to return to that frustrating task, but before I could demur, Singer cut me off.

"That's it," he decreed. "I want you in Vienna on Tuesday. Now let me introduce you to Zelman."

Singer dragged me back through crowded halls and anterooms until we located our man. Then, using the proper European appellation "doctor" for "attorney," he presented *Herr Professor Doktor Zelman* to *Herr Doktor Rosenbaum,* and was gone.

Zelman, I would later learn, had played a leading role in achieving a rapprochement of sorts between the Jewish world and the people of Austria. He had helped secure Austria's agreement to serve as a transit point for Soviet Jewish emigrés, and he had been quite successful in promoting Jewish tourism to Austria. His face bore the archetypal pink, puffy-cheeked look of the kindly European uncle, but his eyes betrayed something much more portentous. Unusually large, they appeared almost to bulge forward from their sockets and seemed never far from tears. I had seen eyes such as these before, in the faces of other elderly Holocaust survivors, and I sensed that, even as Zelman cautiously sized me up, dire memories were taking hold of him.

"You have investigated the Nazi cases for the American government?" he asked.

"Yes. But I gave that up two years ago, back in '84. Too frustrating."

"*Zinger,*" he said in a thick accent, "wants me to talk to you about"—he nearly spit the words—"*zis Vahl-l-l-dheim.*" The survivor's disdain for the former U.N. chief was unmistakable.

Zelman explained that his nation was currently enveloped in a scandal involving an Austrian military academy in the city of Wiener

Neustadt. Academy administrators had installed a marble memorial plaque in honor of General Alexander Loehr, eulogizing him as the founder of the modern Austrian Air Force. But there was much more to Loehr's military career than the plaque disclosed, Zelman advised. He had been *hanged*—as a Nazi war criminal—by the government of Yugoslavia in 1947.[1] Pulling a newspaper article from a soft plastic portfolio, Zelman adjusted his metal-rimmed spectacles and read aloud: ". . . for his supervisory role in the Luftwaffe's 1941 bombing of Belgrade, Yugoslavia."

It was a notorious episode, to be sure. Hitler had intimidated the Yugoslav monarch into signing a pact with the Third Reich, but when a military coup toppled the ruler, the Fuehrer deemed himself betrayed. He vowed that Yugoslavia would be crushed with "unmerciful harshness." Not even bothering to issue a formal declaration of war, he ordered a massive aerial bombardment "to destroy Belgrade in attacks by waves." In the early morning hours of April 6, 1941, Luftwaffe bombers surprised the Yugoslavs, methodically reducing their capital to ruins, even strafing columns of Yugoslav citizens— many of them women and children—as they fled. More than seventeen thousand civilians died in the ninety-minute downpouring of thousand-kilo bombs.[2]

Forty-five years later, Austrian officials now wished to venerate the commander of that attack. His face registering disgust, Zelman told me that the Austrian Defense Minister had refused to order the removal of the plaque, and his decision was supported by a number of Austrian newspaper columnists. The scandal was spreading abroad, Zelman said. Both the Soviet and Yugoslav media had denounced the Loehr honor in strident terms.[3]

The episode was hardly surprising to me, given what I knew of the darker side of modern Austrian history. This was the latest in a continuing series of postwar Nazi scandals in a country that, unlike Germany, had never been forced to confront its wartime past. But what did it have to do with the former Secretary-General of the U.N.? "Excuse me," I interrupted, as politely as I could, "but as far as I know, Kurt Waldheim was never in the Luftwaffe."

Zelman lifted his palm and slowly extended his forefinger skyward, requesting patience. He explained that sometime in 1942, Loehr had transferred out of the Luftwaffe—into the German army. From a sheaf of press clippings, Zelman produced a half-page article published the previous Sunday in the liberal, small-circulation Viennese weekly *Profil*—he pronounced the name in proper German, "Profeel." Written by reporter Otmar Lahodynsky, the piece attempted a summary of Loehr's war record, relying, for the most part, on statements by Manfried Rauchensteiner, head of Vienna's Institute for

Military History. In the final three lines of the article, Lahodynsky mentioned a "rumor" that "presidential candidate Kurt Waldheim" had once been Loehr's "personal adjutant in the Wehrmacht." But the rumor, Lahodynsky wrote, was refuted by Rauchensteiner, who explained that "Waldheim was only an *Ordonnanzoffizier*" on the staff of Army Group E, "whose *Kommandant* Loehr was."[4]

I struggled with the German text of the article, and with my thoughts. If the rumor was true, the designation *Ordonnanzoffizier* meant that Waldheim was an aide of some kind, but I could not determine from this brief mention how important, or unimportant, he was to Loehr. "It's interesting," I conceded. "But if Waldheim really did serve on the staff of a man who was hanged for war crimes, I'm amazed that it was never disclosed before."

To myself I said, interesting, yes, but not necessarily significant. A German army group ordinarily contained hundreds of thousands of men, and even if Waldheim had worked at Loehr's headquarters, there could have been a hundred or more other officers insulating him from the commander. In any event, Loehr was hanged for what he did in the *air force,* before transferring to the army. Yes, it was common knowledge that Waldheim had been a low-level Wehrmacht officer during the war—he had never denied that. Millions of other Germans and Austrians had served in the German army without involving themselves in Nazi crimes. The simple fact of Waldheim's service in the Wehrmacht, even in an army group commanded by Loehr, was not grounds for condemnation. Moreover, the matter-of-fact tone of this published "rumor" suggested its insignificance. Perhaps he had been assigned there only briefly, for a few weeks. If there was anything sinister in Waldheim's past, certainly the press would have sniffed it out during his decade at the U.N. Indeed, if there was even a hint of substance here, where was the shark-pack of journalists—especially inside Austria—circling the prey?

"Has there been any follow-up on this 'rumor' by the Austrian press?" I asked.

"No," Zelman admitted, "but you must understand the Austrian newspapers. They do not care to dig up the past. And the readers, they do not wish to have it dug up either."

"Has Dr. Waldheim issued a denial?"

"No, but—"

"Okay, I'll—" I was going to add "look into it, but don't expect me to find that there's much to this," but Zelman would not allow me to finish.

"There is yet another fact, my dear friend," he interjected. "And the papers don't seem to know of it. Or if they know, they don't want to publish it. You might call it the . . . ah . . . missing ingredient." There was a hint of a smile on the old man's face, his deep, distant eyes seeming to say: I see you need the last piece of the puzzle. Very well, here it is.

He quizzed me, "Do you recall, when Waldheim was at the U.N., that questions were asked about his military service?"

At the time, I was in my last year of law school at Harvard, but I had followed the news as best I could, especially when it related to the Second World War. I always had a special fascination for the war and devoured news items about the Nazi period and the postwar fate of former Nazis. I told Zelman what little I remembered. During his two full terms as U.N. Secretary-General (covering the years 1972–81), Waldheim had provided observers with considerable evidence that he was hostile to Israel in particular and to Jewish interests in general. For example, while making an obligatory official visit to Israel's Yad Vashem Holocaust memorial, he caused a furor by refusing to cover his head during a remembrance service for the six million Jewish victims of Nazi genocide (the only official visitor ever to have spurned this gesture of respect). In the mid-seventies, Waldheim was blamed for allowing Palestine Liberation Organization chief Yasir Arafat to address the General Assembly seemingly armed with a pistol—the frightening symbol of PLO terrorism—on his hip.* Waldheim maintained a passive posture when the U.N. issued its infamous 1975 resolution denouncing Zionism as a form of racism. The following year, he stood dramatically alone among the leaders of the civilized world when he declared Israel's daring hostage-rescue raid at the airport at Entebbe to be a violation of Uganda's territorial sovereignty.[5]

The cumulative effect of all these events, I recalled, was behind-the-scenes bickering that finally boiled over publicly in 1980, when an exasperated (and intemperate) few dared to hurl the epithet "Nazi" at the U.N. Secretary-General. Waldheim's aides blamed Israel's U.N. staff for spreading the Nazi rumors. For a time, innuendo flew about, but the rumor mill was silenced in 1981 when Israel's U.N. representative, Yehuda Blum, declared publicly that he and his government rejected those suspicions.†

This appeared to constitute the definitive exoneration. After all, Israel possessed what many believed to be the world's most effective foreign intelligence service, the Mossad. If *the Israelis*—the people with the strongest interest in discrediting former Nazis (and in sham-

---

*Waldheim and others at the U.N. later asserted that, unbeknownst to the delegates and the media, Arafat's holster was empty. Even if true, it did not soften the awful symbolism.
†Blum said that, while his government had "many differences" with the Secretary-General, "We don't believe Waldheim ever supported the Nazis and we never said he did."[6]

ing Kurt Waldheim)—had cleared the U.N. chief, was this not—
should it not be—the end of the matter?

I put that question to Zelman: "If I remember correctly, Waldheim
answered all the questions about his past and satisfied even the
Israelis."

"Do you know what Waldheim said about his war record *exactly?*"

"No, I guess I don't," I admitted.

"I checked with *Zinger*," Zelman said, "and he remembers it quite
clearly. Waldheim said he was wounded in 1941 in the fighting in
Russia, and he went into some hospitals, and then his injuries got
him out of the army. He said he came home to Vienna and went
back to law school. Do you see?"

I really did not.

"He said he left the army in 1941," Zelman emphasized. "But then
something is very wrong, you see. If he left in 1941, how could he
ever have served with Loehr in the army? Loehr did not even arrive
from the Luftwaffe into the army *until 1942!* There must be a . . ."
he lingered over the word, ". . . *de-zep-shun.*"

A deception? It still seemed farfetched, notwithstanding Zelman's
dramatic presentation. How could Waldheim have managed, for so
many decades, to hide behind a false description of his personal
history, eliminating a whole period of military service that could
probably be verified quite easily by checking Wehrmacht personnel
records in Berlin? "Are you absolutely sure that Waldheim said he
left the army in '41?" I asked.

"Ja, Ja, I am sure of it. Absolutely." Only moments ago, Zelman
explained, Singer had double-checked his recollection with Elan
Steinberg, the WJC's executive director, who confirmed the facts as
Zelman and Singer recalled them.

The permutations raced through my mind as Zelman waited pa-
tiently: The former Secretary-General of the U.N. contended that
his military service ended in 1941:

> . . . which seemed impossible if he served under Loehr.
> . . . which meant that the rumor that he served under Loehr was
> false.
> . . . or that Zelman was wrong about Loehr transferring to the
> German army in 1942.
> . . . or that Waldheim was lying.

If Waldheim had reinvented his wartime history, the only logical
explanation was that he had something to hide. But there was almost
certainly a mistake here, I told myself. The odds of someone of such

global prominence maintaining that kind of cover-up for forty years—especially during his ten years at the helm of the U.N. in the media capital of the world—were ridiculously slim.

Still, Zelman's presentation had piqued my curiosity. If Waldheim had pulled off such a deception, what was it that he needed to hide?

As Singer had led me to expect, Zelman invited me to accompany him to Vienna at the end of the WJC conference, so that I could make inquiries—*discreet* ones, he urged emphatically.

I did not want to go. Not right away, at any rate. My mental state was bordering on depression. Only the day before, the space shuttle *Challenger* had exploded shortly after lift-off, killing the entire American crew. It was a national, yet somehow very personal, disaster, much as President Kennedy's assassination had been, and I wanted to be back home in Manhattan as soon as possible. I wanted to speak with my family and friends. I needed to share the anguish, which was made worse by my distance from home. But despite my impatience to return to the United States and my continuing skepticism that the former U.N. Secretary-General could have covered up a connection with Nazi misdeeds, Singer had made the decision for me. I accepted Zelman's invitation, doing my best to conceal my reluctance.

Zelman thanked me. Then he added, "It is all very crazy, no?"

I made my way back through the hotel hallways, which were beginning to empty as delegates assembled in the ballroom for the next session. Up ahead, I spotted my former boss at the Justice Department, Office of Special Investigations Director Neal Sher. Still very close friends, we had been seatmates on the flight to Israel a few days earlier. Sher was here to take part in a panel discussion with war crimes prosecutors from other countries.

In the seven years of its existence, OSI had investigated more than a thousand cases involving allegations of Nazi atrocities. As a result of those investigations, the office had successfully prosecuted citizenship revocation and deportation lawsuits against several dozen Nazi criminals living in the U.S. In addition, thousands of nonresident aliens suspected of complicity in such crimes had been placed, at OSI's behest, on the "watchlist" of the Immigration and Naturalization Service, barring them from entry into the country.

From the sight of my friend's Cheshire-cat grin, I knew immediately that Singer had already briefed him.

"So, you're going to Vienna, eh, Roosevelt?" he said with a half-smirk, employing his favored nickname for me.

"I guess so," I replied without enthusiasm.

"Maybe there's something to it."

"Not bloody likely, Chief." Two years after leaving the Justice Department, I still found myself addressing him that way.

"Well . . ." With a shrug he communicated the message: It's worth checking out.

I had enormous respect for Sher. An almost-Hollywood-handsome former Army drill sergeant turned federal prosecutor, he had taken me under his wing when I served a summer law internship in 1979 at the then brand-new Justice Department war crimes office. One of his private passions was basketball; a master at the shorter-man's game of ball-handling and improvisational playmaking, he approached the task of prosecution with the same toughness, careful preparation, and ability to spot and immediately exploit a new opportunity. I had seen him, on more than one occasion, risk his career for a principle. He had a well-deserved reputation as the most tenacious and dedicated war crimes prosecutor in the world.

I could guess his line of reasoning: Nobody likes Waldheim. So if there is any substance to this "Nazi" charge, the chance to verify it and make it public was a war crimes prosecutor's fantasy.

"I guess, considering the Rudolph case, anything is possible, Neal," I conceded. Sher nodded in agreement. The reference was to Arthur Rudolph, the former director of NASA's Saturn V rocket program. As the result of an investigation that I had initiated and directed a few years earlier, OSI had uncovered conclusive evidence of Rudolph's involvement in war crimes. I had handled most of the documentary phase of that investigation, delving into captured German war documents, postwar U.S. Nazi prosecution materials, and American and British intelligence reports. Sher and I jointly interrogated the brilliant Rudolph in a hotel room in San Jose, and managed to trap him in a series of damning admissions. It remained one of the most complex and sensitive investigations in OSI's history.[7]

"Anything is possible," Sher repeated. "Especially with a fox like Waldheim."

Here we go again, I thought.

Sher had been disappointed to see me leave OSI and had phoned me frequently in the past two years, to talk shop. Now the grin on his face told me he was pleased to see me back in the hunt.

2

I exited the new Marriott Hotel in Vienna's First District, needing
a walk to clear my head before my scheduled 11 A.M. meeting with
Zelman, here in his home city. Almost immediately, I found myself
cursing the thin sweater and light trench coat that did little to shield
me from the piercing cold of this bleak fifth day of February; I had
packed for a trip to Israel, not for this surprise journey north. To
keep warm, I ducked into shops and public buildings every few
minutes.

The First District encompasses both Vienna's commercial hub and
the fabled "Old City." Winding streets run past meticulously pre-
served Baroque and Gothic buildings, remembrances of an era when
Vienna was the imperial capital of the Hapsburgs.

Perhaps no major European city lives as much in the past as does
Vienna. Reminders are everywhere of the glory days of the Austro-
Hungarian Empire and of Vienna's turn-of-the-century status as a
premier center of artistic and intellectual expression, the days when
men like Freud, Trotsky, and Kafka held court in smoke-filled cafés.
The cafés still flourish, but the cream of the artistic and intellectual
elite either fled soon after Austria became part of Hitler's Reich or
perished in the concentration camps.

Following the war, the nation was rebuilt, creating a curious mixture of the old and new. Modern concrete, steel, and glass buildings
now stand alongside majestic granite and marble structures dating
from the reign of Emperor Franz Josef. Antiseptic department stores
stand across the street from quaint shops that evoke images of *Heidi*.
The people reflect some of the same duality. Thus, while most of
the Viennese I encountered this morning were dressed in conventional business attire, I noticed a man in a rustic Austrian jacket,
and, moments later, another in a Tyrolean hat with upraised feath-
erbrush. For many Austrians, this mix is perfect. They want the world
to remember the glories of the distant past and the occasional, mostly
economic, accomplishments of recent years. They relish the image
of an Alpine *Wunderland* of Strauss and Schubert, of Lippizaner

stallions and Sacher tortes, of oom-pah-pah bands and cherubic choirboys.

The average Austrian wishes the world to see his country as it was depicted in the earlier portions of *The Sound of Music,* with its sumptuous vistas and Catholic aristocrat hero. However, Austrian censors would undoubtedly prefer to snip out the last half hour of the film. That final portion—when German and Austrian Nazis dispel the myth of the Alpine paradise—depicts what so many Austrians do not wish the world to recall: the country's disproportionate role in the atrocities of World War II.

Hitler himself was Austrian, and he recalled fondly in *Mein Kampf* that it was in Vienna where, for "a few pennies, I bought the first anti-Semitic pamphlet of my life." Indeed, Hitler said, "I came as a seventeen-year-old to Vienna . . . and left it as an absolute anti-Semite." Adolf Eichmann, the architect of Hitler's genocidal "final solution" to the "Jewish question," was raised in Austria, and 80 percent of his staff was Austrian, as were about 75 percent of the concentration camp commandants.

There exists in Austria a seven-year memory gap that borders on collective amnesia. Many—perhaps most—Austrians welcomed the *Anschluss* (literally "connection," the country's annexation by Nazi Germany in 1938). Soon thereafter, Vienna's avenues, bedecked with swastika flags, were packed with a sea of jubilant citizens cheering the Fuehrer's triumphant return to his native country. The percentage of the population that joined the Nazi Party was actually greater in Austria than in Germany itself. Yet a modern Austrian is likely to assert with a straight face that the Allies "liberated" his country. Austrian histories tend to glorify the resistance movement, but, in fact, opposition to the Germans was almost nonexistent until late in the war, when it became apparent that the Third Reich was destined to lose. Some have quipped that the country's greatest single accomplishment has been convincing the world that Hitler was German and Beethoven was Austrian.

Before the *Anschluss,* 200,000 Jews lived in a thriving community in Vienna, constituting nearly 10 percent of the city's population. Soon after the *Anschluss,* elderly Jewish men were forced to scrub the city streets on their hands and knees, while crowds jeered at and spat on them. Today, only about 8,000 Jews can be found in the entire country. And to those who survived, the Austrian government paid virtually nothing in reparations. The late Nahum Goldmann, the longtime WJC president who led the reparations negotiations with West Germany as well as unsuccessful negotiations with Austria, recalled in his memoirs that Vienna justified its refusal to follow Germany's example on the basis that Austria "considered itself just

as much a victim of Nazism as the Jews." When the rebuffed Goldmann then pleaded with the German government to appropriate
relief funds for the surviving remnant of Austrian Jewry, Bonn, too,
refused, "on the grounds that Austria was at least equally guilty of
Nazi crimes."[1]

Austria thus lives a great national lie, officially presenting itself as
Hitler's first victim when, instead, it was his homeland and enthusiastic ally.

Such thoughts helped me resolve to see this episode through to
its conclusion, which I presumed would be swift. It seemed to me
that Waldheim might even welcome an investigation into vague suspicions of wartime misconduct. He enjoyed, at least within Austria,
an impeccable reputation and he had every reason to cooperate in
efforts that might avert an unjustified attack on his honor. His giant,
full-color campaign posters, displayed throughout the city, showed
him in the company of many other world leaders, calling to mind
his well-known boast that, as U.N. Secretary-General, he had been
"the chief human rights officer of the planet Earth." Unarguably, his
election in New York had brought Austria its greatest postwar honor.
He was, ironically, the best-known Austrian since Hitler.

Simply by counting political posters and placards, one could determine that the major presidential aspirants were Kurt Steyrer, of
the liberal *Sozialistiche Partei Oesterreichs,* the Austrian Socialist Party,
and Kurt Waldheim, the heavily favored candidate of the conservative *Oesterreichische Volkspartei,* the Austrian People's Party.* On
the latter posters, Waldheim's smiling visage peered out through
narrowed eyes. As always, his thin hair was combed straight back,
close to the skull, from a deeply recessed hairline, and his eyebrows
were positioned in exaggerated arches. On one poster, Waldheim's
photo was superimposed over an impressive evening view of Manhattan, featuring the twin towers of the World Trade Center, resplendent in moonlight. The poster carried a giant legend:

DR. KURT WALDHEIM
AN AUSTRIAN THE WORLD TRUSTS

Leon Zelman arrived at my hotel at the precise moment of our
appointment.

"Come, let us walk," he suggested, gesturing toward the door.
"First we shall have some *Kaffee* and some cake. I know just the
excellent place. And then we talk in my office, *Ja?* Okay, *gut!*"

He strode with a vigor surprising for his age, carrying himself with

---

*Also commonly referred to in English as the Conservative Party.

the assurance of a man who knows he is well regarded. As we walked toward Vienna's main square, the Stephansplatz, perhaps a half dozen elegantly dressed ladies rushed up to kiss him and at least as many men paused to engage him in conversation.

After a brief stop for pastry and coffee, we arrived at his office at Stephansplatz Nr. 10. The room was small, but the window offered a striking view of the magnificent St. Stephan's Cathedral. Suddenly, Zelman was markedly less animated than before; it was almost as though our previous roles were reversed. I was ready to talk business; he was apprehensive. Evidently, it was one thing to be a fearless old Jew in Jerusalem; it was quite another matter in Vienna.

I asked for his suggestions as to where I might begin to inquire into Waldheim's past.

Zelman's face grew pale; he seemed almost to age before my eyes. He clasped his hands together tightly and brought them to his lips, as if in supplication, before lowering them slowly. "You know, my situation in Austria is already a difficult one, my dear Eli," he said, as if confiding in a favored nephew. "I love this city, really, but also I know what is underneath the surface."

I was surprised by his reticence, and waited for him to continue.

"Israel Singer has, I believe, given you all that you will need."

"You mean the list of his contacts here?" Before I left Jerusalem, Singer had thrust a short, handwritten note at me, containing the names of a few expatriate Israelis, one junior Western diplomat and a couple of Viennese—people he trusted. He supplemented this with a longer, verbal list of people to "avoid at all costs." Chief among these were former Austrian Chancellor Bruno Kreisky, whom Singer knew personally and characterized as "a perfectly charming snake."

"Singer has good contacts," Zelman pleaded. "*They* will help you. And you also know a few people here and in Germany, no? From when you were with the American Justice Ministry, *Ja?*"

I knew that Zelman could save me a great deal of work, but I also realized that he had already risked much simply by inviting me here. In the few days since we first met I had grown fond of this gentle, kindhearted man. I had no right to seek more from him. Doing my best to conceal my astonishment—and disappointment—that the man responsible for my compulsory detour to Austria was leaving me to fend for myself, I asked, "Do you want me to keep you informed of what, if anything, I find out?"

"Please, no. No, I don't think so. You please must keep me out of this. Perhaps you can just tell me later whether you have been successful or no."

I nodded in agreement, and immediately sensed Zelman's relief. Quickly he added, "But I want you to know that if you really need me, if you will get into any sort of trouble, I will help you, my dear Eli. I promise you that."

Singer's list was more productive than I dared hope. All I had to do was drop his name in order to receive assurances of both cooperation and discretion. Within twenty-four hours, I found myself on the fringes of a tiny but well-connected network of Austrians who were busily digging into Waldheim's past. Not surprisingly, most of them were associated with the ruling Socialist Party; they had, after all, a vested interest in discrediting the opposition's presidential candidate. In fact, I learned that the *Profil* item linking Waldheim with Loehr had been planted by the Socialists as a trial balloon. To their chagrin, it had seemed to attract no "outside" interest. Hence, my visit was viewed as a most welcome development.

These contacts led me at last to Karl Schuller,* the one person who, I would soon learn, probably knew more about the former U.N. Secretary-General than anyone outside of Waldheim's inner circle. On the phone, Schuller seemed hesitant to trust me, notwithstanding the assurances he had received from two of Singer's acquaintances. He finally agreed to speak with me, on the condition that I promise never to reveal his identity. He said he would meet me at 4 P.M. that very day, beside the Johann Strauss monument in the Stadtpark, one of Vienna's best-known landmarks. He would wear a dark blue overcoat and carry a rolled-up newspaper in his left hand. The arrangement struck me as contrived, rather like a scene in an old spy movie. But Schuller was apparently the man I needed to see, and so I agreed to his plan.

Even as I waited for the rendezvous with Schuller in Vienna, the WJC's talented executive director, Elan Steinberg was back at the WJC offices in New York, conducting his own research.

Steinberg was, in some ways, the antithesis of Israel Singer. Singer, in his early forties, was orthodox (a graduate of a Rabbinical seminary) and observant; Steinberg, in his mid-thirties, had no patience for religious ritual. Singer was a happily married family man; Steinberg was divorced and childless. Singer was tall, slender, suave, and smooth; Steinberg was round-faced, rough around the edges, and frequently fighting a minor weight problem. Yet in other ways, Steinberg was Singer's alter ego. Each a brilliant political strategist in his own right, both viewed their mission—through similar dark-rimmed eyeglasses—as vital to the protection of Jewish lives and interests, and both believed in the importance of remaining on the offensive.

*A pseudonym.

They were the "bad boys" of organizational Jewish life; often, when others were afraid to do more than wring their hands privately, Singer and Steinberg were ready to, as is said in Yiddish, give a *geshrei,* "to scream."

If I dared to criticize Steinberg for one of his occasional hyperbolic statements, he would respond, as often as not, with the curt retort *"You're* the lawyer. I'm not." But at the moment, he was uncharacteristically cautious. Refusing to trust his near-photographic memory, he dug back into the WJC files and unearthed the details of some 1980 correspondence between U.S. Congressman Stephen J. Solarz and U.N. Secretary-General Kurt Waldheim. Solarz had inquired about Waldheim's activities in the German army during the 1941 invasion of the Soviet Union and about a vague, undocumented allegation published in *The New Republic* that Waldheim had been "active," before the war, in what the magazine referred to, inexactly, as the "Nazi Youth Movement."[2] Solarz's primary question to Waldheim was precise: What were the names and numbers of the units you served in during the years 1939–1945?[3]

Waldheim's response, dated December 19, 1980, was unequivocal. He declared that he was "never associated in any way" with the Nazi youth organizations and he added that his family was known to be *anti*-Nazi, both before and after the *Anschluss.* Despite his political leanings, he said, he was drafted into the Wehrmacht like so many other young Austrian men and forced to serve. He noted that he was assigned to the 45th *Aufklaerungs-Abteilung* ("45th Reconnaissance Branch"), where he served as a horse-mounted cavalry officer. "I myself," Waldheim wrote to Solarz, "was wounded on the eastern front and, being incapacitated for further service on the front, resumed my law studies at Vienna University where I graduated in 1944."[4]

Steinberg compared this with another 1980 letter to Solarz, also unearthed from the WJC files. Dated a dozen days after Waldheim's, it was written by Frederick P. Hitz, legislative counsel of the Central Intelligence Agency, and it presented the CIA's response to the congressman's similar inquiry:

> We believe that Waldheim was not a member of the Nazi Youth Movement, nor was he involved in anti-Jewish activities.
>
> We have no intelligence reporting in detail on Waldheim's military service. However, we have gleaned the following from German open source materials. Upon the outbreak of war in 1939, Waldheim was drafted at age 20 into the German Army. He served as a staff intelligence officer with the rank of lieutenant, assigned to the 45th Infantry Division. This Division saw

action in the Polish Campaign (September 1939) and the assault on France (May 1940). It was sent to the eastern front in June 1941 to take part in the invasion of the USSR. Waldheim's service with this Division ended in 1941 when he received a leg wound. There is nothing in the files to suggest that while in this unit Waldheim participated directly or indirectly in anti-Jewish activities.

His recuperation from the leg wound required almost a year; he was discharged from military duties following his recovery and returned to study law in Vienna. He received his doctorate in law in 1944 and in 1945 began his diplomatic career in the Austrian Ministry of Foreign Affairs.[5]

The information in both of these letters confirmed the recollections of Singer, Steinberg, Zelman, and myself—that Waldheim long claimed to have been separated from German military service after his 1941 combat injury. And it meant that *somebody* was not telling a straightforward story. But was it Waldheim and his echoer at the CIA, both of whom asserted that Waldheim ended his military assignment in 1941—or was it instead *Profil,* which placed Waldheim as a junior officer on the staff of Loehr's Army Group E sometime later?

At a minimum, the CIA response raised the stakes. Now we were dealing not merely with the seemingly fanciful notion that the former U.N. Secretary General had misled the world for forty years, but with the possibility that the CIA had lied to a congressman. And if the CIA had been a party to such a mammoth deception, what could its motive have been? The implications were of potentially immense—and far-reaching—significance.

Steinberg phoned me in Vienna, where it was midafternoon. Over a static-plagued international connection, he read the two letters to me and voiced his conclusion. "The CIA backs him up completely," he said. "If Waldheim's story isn't true, I want to know what the hell's going on. Find out."

As I walked toward the Stadtpark, doubts seized me once again. It was wildly implausible that a public figure of Kurt Waldheim's stature could pull off a hoax of such magnitude and duration. Was the whole thing a mistake? The *Profil* paragraph offered no proof; the historian it quoted might simply have erred in stating that Waldheim once served under Loehr. For all I knew, the entire affair was nothing more than a phony story put out by Socialist Party operatives to discredit the opposing candidate; after all, Waldheim was well ahead in the polls and the Socialists were desperate. The last thing I wanted was to find myself (and my current employer, the WJC) in the midst of a political burlesque in a foreign country.

Nor did I relish the thought of returning to the job of investigating war crimes. My years at the Justice Department had been fraught with the frustration of trying to reconstruct decades-old crimes from the few surviving shreds of evidence. Moreover, if there really *was* any substance to this Waldheim allegation, it was a matter for government agencies to pursue. They alone possessed the all-important power to subpoena witnesses and the personnel to conduct the necessary worldwide search for documents, and they alone could obtain unfettered access to the appropriate archives. At most, I thought, the role of an organization like the World Jewish Congress might be to alert or, if necessary, prod the proper authorities to delve further; war crimes investigation was not an activity for dabblers and dilettantes.

I recoiled at the thought of being categorized as a "private Nazi-hunter." That field, in my opinion, had always been populated primarily by incompetents, charlatans, and even outright crooks—and by countless journalists who entertained their readers with phony accounts of cloak-and-dagger exploits. From my perspective at OSI, some of these self-styled Nazi-hunters had proved harmful to the cause they espoused, bogging us down with "leads" concerning people who were long dead, or accusing with little or no evidence one or another former refugee from Europe.

To be sure, the WJC had a long history of involvement in Nazi cases, ever since it helped to formulate the principles that governed the Nuremberg war crimes trials. But its role had always been a responsible one. Its major task since Nuremberg, insofar as war crimes probes were concerned, was to aid government prosecutors in Germany and the U.S. in their attempts to locate survivor-witnesses. It certainly had never claimed to be a "Nazi-hunting" organization.

In short, shivering in the frigid February weather as I entered the nearly deserted Stadtpark, I wanted nothing more than to wrap up this pseudo-investigation with dispatch. In the unlikely event that there really was a cover-up here, we could expose it and move on; pursuing the matter further would be a task for the authorities.

Ahead of me, beside the Johann Strauss monument, a solitary figure in a dark blue overcoat waited. He was tall and skinny, much, it occurred to me, like Waldheim. He carried a rolled-up newspaper in his left hand. I glanced at my watch. It was two minutes past four.

"Herr Schuller?" I inquired tentatively.

"Ja, und Sie?"

"Rosenbaum."

"Ja." He extended a gloved hand in greeting, shifted into excellent English, and said, "Good to meet you." He wasted no more time in small talk, but led me quickly out of the park and into a small building nearby.

There, standing in a darkened, deserted hallway, as he fumbled with an unfamiliar key, he explained that this office suite belonged to a friend who had agreed, without asking any questions, to let him use it for this afternoon and evening. As we entered, I was surprised to find the lights off, even though the workday had not quite ended. What appeared to be a secretary's station was vacant.

From a closet, Schuller withdrew a large briefcase, but before he proceeded, he announced, "I think I shall have a drink. Will you join me?"

I declined.

He produced a vodka bottle from a desk drawer, poured a glass for himself, and gulped it down. I interpreted this as a sign of nervousness, and his next words added to the impression. "I am told that you are interested in the case of our . . . most distinguished citizen," he began. "I can tell you what I know, but do you understand the"—he groped for the English word—*"sensitivities?"*

I reassured him that I would never reveal his identity. When I recapitulated my background as a federal prosecutor of Nazi war crimes cases, and reminded him that I was accustomed to dealing with informants who required anonymity, he nodded approvingly.

Having accepted my warranty and taken a second gulp of vodka, Schuller gestured for me to sit in a comfortable, leather-upholstered chair. He settled into a companion chair and set his vodka glass and briefcase on a coffee table between us. He took a few moments to fill and light his pipe, allowing the smoke to billow toward the ceiling, adding to the nascent sense of intrigue. Finally he removed a large cache of books and documents from his overstuffed briefcase. He was about to open one of the books when his hand paused in midair. He offered the preamble that he had been probing Waldheim's past for some time already, with the assistance of what he called "helpers," some of them inside the Austrian government. He described a convoluted chain of events that had led to our meeting on this winter afternoon:

The preceding year, after Kurt Waldheim had announced his candidacy for the presidency, an Austrian historian named Georg Tidl began a routine background study. Before long, Tidl discovered what appeared to be serious discrepancies between official records and Waldheim's autobiographical accounts of his wartime activities. Waldheim had always asserted that he was wounded on the Russian front in 1941 and, thereafter, resumed his law studies in Vienna.

But what Schuller referred to cryptically as "certain documents" now indicated that Waldheim, after recovering from his wounds, had returned to active duty.

The news had ultimately reached Schuller and, with a group of associates, he launched a very private inquiry. At first, he admitted, the motives of his group were unabashedly political. But some of the investigators, notably Schuller himself, claimed a genuine sense of righteous indignation. There were still too many Nazi ghosts in the Austrian closet and somehow, Schuller announced, it had to be swept clean.

Were these his true sentiments? I wondered. Or was this an act, performed to establish credibility with me?

Schuller's people made discreet inquiries at the Berlin Document Center (operated by the U.S. State Department, it is the free world's largest repository of captured Nazi personnel records), but they found nothing there concerning Waldheim's wartime activities.

The amateur investigators then enlisted an unwitting ally. "It's really crazy," Schuller said with a chuckle. "The man who is making these inquiries doesn't even know he is doing research about Waldheim. He is just getting unit records—documents about the membership of units as a whole—for someone he thinks is sympathetic to these guys. This old fellow is a veteran himself, a pathetic little man with one arm and one leg. He looks like this." Schuller closed one eye and manipulated his arms and fingers into a contorted pose to illustrate his description of the gnarled old man, then added, "He works for the 'Black Cross.' "

My face must have telegraphed my unfamiliarity with the term.

"That's the organization that looks after the graves of Austrian soldiers who died in the war," Schuller explained.

One of Schuller's comrades had convinced the old man to make inquiries in Berlin at the *Wehrmachtauskunftstelle* and the *Krankenbuchlager,* the two main archives of military personnel and medical records in West Germany. The veteran believed that he was contributing to military research that would rekindle what he considered to be glorious memories. In reality, however, his work was helping those who hoped to establish that Waldheim had returned to the Wehrmacht after 1941.

Meanwhile, Schuller and his people haunted bookshops and libraries, snapping up publications about the war. In Austria as well as Germany, one can find a multitude of books that venerate the military exploits of Hitler's forces. Schuller hastened to assure me that he found these writings repulsive. However, he added with a smirk, they could be "useful" on occasions such as these.

By late 1985, Schuller said, he was certain that he had evidence—

in the form of documents that he said he was about to show me—
that Waldheim had distorted the account of his Wehrmacht service.
But Schuller was unsure of how to use the information. Much more
research remained to be done, in archives around the world, and he
knew that the task was far too formidable for his tiny group. Beyond
that, the 1986 presidential election was now just three months away.
He decided that he had to get the story outside Austria, to interest
others who would have more resources and better access to potential
evidence. Schuller had concluded only recently that it was time to
detonate the powder keg.

But how?

Taking his story directly to the Austrian news media was out of
the question, he lamented. He complained that all of the major
newspapers were controlled by conservative business and agricultural
interests, and Waldheim was, in Schuller's words, "their candidate."
Beyond that, he claimed that his nation's media were just as affected
as other segments of society by the collective amnesia concerning
the role of Austrians as copractitioners of Hitler's villainy.

Finally, he and his comrades had decided: They would feed a
solitary appetizer to *Profil* and see if anyone came in search of a full-
course dinner. He arranged, through several layers of protective
cover, to dangle the tidbit in front of *Profil,* which published the
"Loehr" story that piqued the interest of Leon Zelman, who in turn
alerted Singer, who then ordered me to Vienna.

Having concluded this lengthy preface, Schuller now opened the
first book in his stack of materials and launched into a methodical
presentation, much in the style of a learned professor tutoring a new
student.

It quickly became apparent that he had mastered an extraordinary
jumble of documents and books; not once did he find it necessary
to refer to notes or other memory aids during the ensuing hours of
his presentation.

3

With a flourish, Schuller pulled from his briefcase a German-language edition of Waldheim's latest book, *Im Glaspalast der Weltpolitik* ("In the Glass Palace of World Politics"—a reference to the U.N. Secretariat headquarters building*), and deftly turned to his target page. Here, Waldheim wrote of how his father opposed Hitler's annexation of Austria, and of the consequences of that opposition. His father, Waldheim said, was briefly detained by the Gestapo and subsequently lost his job, rendering the family "almost penniless." To help out, the young Waldheim tutored Greek and Latin. Waldheim wrote that he, like his father, had been a supporter of Chancellor Kurt von Schuschnigg, who opposed unification. He claimed to have suffered cuts and bruises in an attack by Nazis who caught him and others "distributing pamphlets encouraging people to resist" annexation.[1]

"So he writes that he was—," Schuller chuckled, lingering with mock pomposity, "—a proper Austrian." My host had a surprisingly hearty laugh for such a slim man, but there was, underneath the facade of bemusement, an unmistakable air of solemnity that communicated his contempt for Waldheim.

I laughed with Schuller, understanding that Waldheim was boasting of his supposed choice of one totalitarian dictator over another. Von Schuschnigg and his reactionary Fatherland Front government, in promoting an Austrian brand of semi-fascism, curbed individual liberties and imprisoned thousands of political opponents. Although von Schuschnigg's right-wing authoritarian government had indeed opposed annexation, it had many of the Fascist trappings of the Hitler and Mussolini regimes, with the notable exception (and this fact certainly seemed to speak in Waldheim's favor) that it was not anti-Jewish.

Schuller continued to chortle as he placed several sheets of paper

---

*The English-language editions of the book are entitled *In the Eye of the Storm: A Memoir.*

on the table and sorted through them. These, he claimed, constituted a partial copy of Waldheim's military service record. The originals were locked away in a sealed file in the Austrian State Archives, inaccessible to the public. Almost no one had access to this material, he declared, downing another shot of vodka. He handed the papers across the coffee table and confided, "A friend of mine who works in the government succeeded in getting copies of these few pages."

I took the papers from his hand and felt a mixture of excitement and apprehension. As I examined the documents, it was clear that Schuller was not exaggerating their sensitivity. These were the intimate records of Austria's most honored statesman, obviously obtained without the subject's permission.

The first sheet was a photocopy of Waldheim's *Wehrstammkarte* ("Military Locator Card") dated June 2, 1939. It began with basic, and wholly innocuous, information:

> *Familienname:* Waldheim.
> *Vornamen:* Kurt.
> Born: 21 December 1918.

Then, under the section "Memberships," was a most surprising notation: S.A. N.S.D.S.B. 1938.

I was dumbfounded. The N.S.D.S.B. was the Nazi *Studentenbund,* the Nazi student organization. In his letter to Solarz, Waldheim said he was "never associated in any way" with any of the Nazi youth organizations, and the CIA had similarly reported, "Waldheim was not a member of the Nazi Youth Movement."

But this was a minor matter in comparison to the "S.A." notation, which appeared to denote membership in the *Sturmabteilung* (literally, "Assault Department")—the infamous brown-shirted storm-trooper detachment of the Nazi Party!

Schuller laughed again, enjoying my astonished reaction. This, he declared, was the one document that he could not allow me to copy, for he feared that its disclosure would compromise—or even endanger—his sources.

He fed my curiosity with a second, even more remarkable, document, handing me a photocopy of a page from Waldheim's Austrian Foreign Ministry "Conduct Journal," prepared after the war. It quoted from a questionnaire purportedly filled out by Waldheim himself on April 24, 1940.* According to this second document,

---

*The original questionnaire has mysteriously "disappeared."

Waldheim verified that he had enrolled in the *Reitersturm,* a mounted unit of the S.A., on November 18, 1938.[2]

Schuller pointed out (and I later verified) that official questionnaires ordinarily had to be signed under oath; thus, Waldheim presumably had sworn to the fact of his S.A. membership. If this document was genuine, it meant that Waldheim had either lied to the Nazis (a life-threatening and hence unlikely act) or lied later to Solarz.

The November 18 date was particularly intriguing. Schuller did not have to remind me that, little more than a week earlier, on the night of November 9–10, 1938, the S.A. helped lead vicious pogroms throughout both Germany and what had been Austria. This was the infamous *Kristallnacht* ("Night of Shattered Glass"). Throughout the now-unified Reich, synagogues were torched, Jewish-owned businesses were looted and wrecked, and thousands of Jews were beaten in the streets and hauled off to concentration camps. After that, no one could have doubted the sinister agenda of the S.A. Yet it appeared from this document that Waldheim had enrolled in this already notorious Nazi organization little more than a week later. This was an incendiary revelation, if true. And unless Schuller was feeding me skillfully crafted forgeries, it certainly seemed to be true.

Other explosive items lay like landmines on this single page. There was a 1940 explanation of why Waldheim was not a member of the Nazi Party: "Not yet possible, since in the military." Wehrmacht officers, Schuller reminded me, were not supposed to join or remain in the Party while on active duty.

Citing Waldheim's *Personalbogen* ("Personnel Sheet"), the document referred to Waldheim as an *S.A. Mann* and verified his membership in the Nazi *Studentenbund,* listing the date of his enrollment as April 1, 1938.

The April 1 date was a shocker. "Just two weeks after the *Anschluss,* and already he was in a Nazi organization?" I asked.

"*Ja,*" Schuller said with a nod. "I thought you would notice the date. It looks like the great 'anti-Nazi' had a change of philosophy as soon as the Germans arrived."

Further indication of the rapid shift in Waldheim's political allegiance was here in the document's quotation from a wartime Nazi Party "political assessment" of Waldheim. It noted his pre-*Anschluss* "hostility to our movement," but added that Waldheim had subsequently "proven his worth as a soldier of the German Wehrmacht," so that the Party did "not oppose" his professional advancement.[3] This seemed a lukewarm endorsement at best, but I knew that the Nazis were chronically mistrustful. They often penned such dubious recommendations for men who soon thereafter rose to power in Hitler's hierarchy.*

There was, in this extraordinary document, a postwar "defense" statement as well, dated January 1946. Once the war had ended in a Nazi defeat, Waldheim, like countless other Austrians, evidently needed to disassociate himself from earlier affiliations. The "defense" statement asserted that Waldheim's only involvement with the brownshirts had been "in sporting activities."[4]

I struggled to keep a record of Schuller's high-speed presentation, scribbling notes in a soft-covered binder. Schuller paused to refill his glass yet again from the vodka bottle. I felt suddenly and strangely removed from the scene, as if watching from a distance while a hard-drinking, middle-aged Viennese man whom I hardly knew dragged me on an implausible journey through the distant and dark past. Schuller's composed manner and the bass-timbred laugh that frequently punctuated his presentation only heightened the sense of unreality.

Almost to the point of paranoia, I was wary of a trap. I could not risk having the World Jewish Congress lured into making public accusations that might prove baseless—especially in a case like this. I peppered Schuller with the toughest questions I could devise. He fielded them without evidencing any of the subtle signs of discomfort or reluctance that my years as a prosecutor had trained me to discern. He readily acknowledged that there were huge gaps in the record. Key pieces of the puzzle were still missing.

Nevertheless, there was much more ground to cover. With an index finger upraised for emphasis, Schuller announced that we would next concentrate on Waldheim's role in the Nazi invasion of the Soviet Union, the one portion of his military service to which the former U.N. chief had always freely admitted. Again Schuller began with Waldheim's own words, penned in his memoirs. He directed me to a passage in the second chapter of *Im Glaspalast . . .* , in which Waldheim wrote that he and his brother Walter were called to serve in the Wehrmacht "just as the Second World War began." The book was silent about the initial years of the war, picking up its narrative in mid-1941 when Hitler launched his fierce surprise attack upon his erstwhile ally, the Soviet Union. Waldheim recounted that he was serving as a lieutenant in Reconnaissance Branch 45 in the "Upper Austrian Division" when the unit was ordered to the Eastern

---

*One example was Heinrich Mueller (a.k.a. "Gestapo Mueller"). A 1937 internal memorandum of the Munich Nazi Party Headquarters referred to Mueller as "an odious opponent of the Movement" who had referred to the Fuehrer as an "immigrant unemployed house-painter" and "an Austrian draft-dodger." Despite this early negative assessment, Mueller later became chief of the Gestapo and was the immediate superior of Adolf Eichmann.

front. Schuller read the relevant paragraphs aloud, detailing Wald-heim's description of how the mechanized equipment became mired in mud whenever the rains came. At such times, the call went out for the cavalry. Waldheim said that he was part of a unit forced to ride forward on horseback to attract enemy fire in order to locate Soviet positions. He characterized this as "desperate work, a *Him-melfahrtskommando,* as we called it." Schuller repeated for emphasis: *"Himmelfahrtskommando."* His translation of this as a "Passage-to-Heaven" unit stretched the limits of my modest grasp of the language, but it sounded correct.

By December, Waldheim's memoir continued, when the Wehr-macht had advanced to an area southwest of Orel, "I was wounded in the leg by a grenade splinter." Although the wound was not es-pecially serious, it soon became infected. Waldheim was taken to a field hospital, where he was examined by a Viennese surgeon who remarked, *"Mein leiber Freund,* another day and your leg would have been gone." Waldheim wrote that he was sent to a convalescent center in the mountains, where several months passed before his wound responded to treatment.[5]

"And that," Schuller concluded, closing the book and returning it to the coffee table in front of us, "was the *end* of our friend's war experience in the Soviet Union."

"That's not exactly what I would call a detailed account," I inter-jected, noting that Waldheim, in precious few sentences, had glossed over six months of the fiercest fighting in the history of warfare. "He doesn't even say where in the Soviet Union he was, except for the ending point in Orel."

Schuller responded with a smile, adding, *"Ja,* but we have some additional . . . ah, research . . . on this period. First, however, we must understand what was this 'Reconnaissance Branch 45.' "

Schuller and his "helpers" had pieced together more of the story by consulting several German-language histories, and he exhibited them to me to prove his point. The first book he turned to was a small, hardbound volume with a garish, amateurishly drawn cover, *Mein Weg mit der 45.Inf.Div.* ("My Way with the 45th Infantry Di-vision"), by one Rudolf Gschopf. The author was a veteran of the division, and his 1955 book made it clear that Reconnaissance Branch 45 was a part of that unit. Schuller rolled his eyes as he expressed his disgust that "such books" were being published in Germany to recall "the heroic days."

"Look at this," he requested, pointing to a passage on page 152. "He writes here that Reconnaissance Branch 45 was ordered *zu saeubern* the city of Brest-Litovsk at the beginning of the invasion, in late June 1941. Do you know that expression, *zu saeubern?"*

"To cleanse," I replied with a nod. Schuller's mouth opened to amend my answer, but I continued, explaining that I knew it was one of the Nazis' more infamous euphemisms, used to signify the immediate liquidation of resistance fighters and/or Jewish populations in captured territories. I knew that thousands of Jews were rounded up in Brest-Litovsk in the first weeks of the invasion, marched outside the city, and executed. But in fairness, I cautioned, the Nazis did not always use the expression to indicate mass executions. It was also used to describe the legitimate securing of an area after conquest and could be equivalent to the U.S. military term "mopping up."

Schuller cut me off with the comment, "Gschopf, of course, does not give specifics on this 'cleansing.' I am not surprised." Unflustered by my caveat, Schuller leafed through the book and said, "Look where else this unit went."

The curious little volume was full of hand-drawn maps, depicting the route that Waldheim's detachment took through Russia. The names of the localities sent a shiver up my spine: Gomel, Kiev, Pinsk. All were the sites of well-known massacres.

"Yes, it is all very suspicious," I admitted. "But it's really not hard evidence."

"Then let us continue with Herr Doktor Gschopf's memoirs," Schuller suggested. He plunged ahead, and it was obvious from his confident manner that he had much more to show me. "Here, at pages 160 to 177, he talks about the division's march through the so-called Pripet Swamps in the area of Pinsk, in July and early August 1941." Schuller called my attention to an obscure reference on page 160, in which Gschopf wrote that the division created a motorized advance detachment, composed of Reconnaissance Branch 45—Waldheim's unit—and two other units. It was denominated "V.A. 45" and was commanded by a certain Lieutenant Colonel Helmut von Pannwitz.[6]

Schuller placed the Gschopf book aside and picked up a thick paperback collection of photographic reproductions of captured SS documents. Its German title, *Unsere Ehre heisst Treue,* translated to "Our Honor Is Loyalty," a pluralization of the inscription on the standard-issue SS belt buckle: "My Honor Is Loyalty." The book reproduced wartime German documents that were made public by Czech authorities in 1965.

Schuller's fingers raced through the pages until he located a particular document dated July 19, 1941, wherein SS chief Heinrich Himmler ordered several mounted SS units to go to the Pripet Swamps "for a systematic search."

Without pausing, Schuller located another document in the book, this time a report by one SS-*Scharfuehrer* Fassbender, which stated that, on August 6, 1941, the SS, "in cooperation with V.A. 45," had attacked "Hof Buda" and "Hof Repplof," killing two hundred enemies and taking four hundred prisoners.

"Keep this place 'Buda' in mind as we look through the other papers," Schuller requested.

I found myself restless, but fascinated. The names and unit numbers were new to me and difficult to order in my mind. The German military text was forbidding. I hoped that the disjointed components of Schuller's discourse would somehow fit together in the end, like the tiles of a mosaic, to reveal a coherent design.

He located yet another report in the book, written to Himmler by a certain SS-*Standartenfuehrer* Fegelein. The report summarized six "major battle engagements" between August 4 and 7, 1941. One of these was a confrontation at Buda-Andrejewka, for which Fegelein reported "our losses" as "one wounded." For the six operations together, German losses were one killed and thirteen wounded. Schuller pointed out to me the reappearance of the place name "Buda." "Now we shall see what kind of 'battles' these really were," he declared, uttering the word "battles" with exaggerated derision. He flipped ahead to the concluding paragraphs of Fegelein's report. "Look here," he instructed.

I leaned forward toward the coffee table. Just above Schuller's fingertip, I saw the enemy casualty report of the Pripet Swamp operation. The brief statement, a classic example of the SS lexicon in its most perverse form, declared: "10,844 plunderers and soldiers in civilian clothing shot."

"Good Lord!" I exclaimed. *One* German fatality against nearly eleven thousand Soviets? That final phrase was especially shocking. "Plunderers and soldiers in civilian clothing" was clearly a euphemism for unarmed victims. Obviously, this was no "battle"; it was a mass liquidation of human beings.

"By the way," Schuller added, "Fegelein uses an unusual word to describe the men who took part in the Pripet Swamp operation." He pointed it out: *Himmelfahrtskommandos.*

It was the very word Waldheim had used to describe his own assignment, and I could tell from the look on Schuller's face that he was savoring the crowning moment of his evidentiary striptease. Was it not clear now, he asked rhetorically, what the term "Passage-to-Heaven" unit really meant?

I agreed that the analysis seemed very damaging, but I vowed to myself to defer judgment until I studied these documents on a word-by-word basis.

Schuller was not about to give my spinning mind a moment's rest.

There was yet one more document he wanted to show me from this depressing book. It was entitled "Report on the Course of the Pripet Swamp Operation from July 27 to August 11, 1941," and it was penned by an SS-*Sturmbannfuehrer* Magill of the 2nd SS Cavalry Regiment.

Magill added a modifier to the word "plunderers" that gave it an unambiguous definition. "Jewish plunderers," he wrote, "were shot." The Germans had spared only a few Jewish workers, whom they consigned to labor in the Wehrmacht repair shops. The author wrote unabashedly about the most defenseless of the victims:

> The driving of women and children into the marshes did not have the expected success, because the marshes were not so deep that one could sink. After a depth of about one meter, there was in most cases solid ground (probably sand) preventing complete sinking.[7]

Magill's easy prose showed how confident the Germans had been of ultimate victory. Such accounts would never have been committed to paper if the Nazis believed that the reports could ever fall into enemy hands. The written legacy of their brutality had helped make war crimes prosecutions possible.

I sat back in my chair for a moment, trying to digest what Schuller was telling me. I wondered how many scores—perhaps hundreds— of books he and his "helpers" had studied to come up with this information. I asked, and he responded with a wave of the hand. "*Ach,* it *was* terrible, reading so many of these terrible books."

Stealing a glance out the window, I realized that the sun had nearly vanished beneath the horizon. Schuller noticed, too, and he rose to switch on an extra lamp.

He was ready to press on, and turned to the subject of Lieutenant Colonel von Pannwitz, Waldheim's commander in V.A. 45. I had never heard the name before. Schuller dove again into his collection of obscure books and emerged with *General von Pannwitz und seine Kosaken* ("General von Pannwitz and His Cossacks"). Small strips of white paper had been thrust into the volume at various points, identifying relevant pages. According to this book, von Pannwitz, who was once described as "a 1,000 percent Nazi," served in 1938 as commander of the 11th Cavalry Regiment, headquartered in the Vienna suburb of Stockerau. "Let us return for a moment to the page we have from Waldheim's military service record," Schuller said. "Look what it says for that year: '*Kav. Rgt. 11, Stockerau.*' It was the very unit commanded by von Pannwitz! So Waldheim and von Pannwitz obviously served together for a number of years."

Von Pannwitz's adoring biographer noted that his subject was awarded the Iron Cross on September 4, 1941, which, Schuller pointed out, was just three weeks after the Pripet Swamp operation. The book said that von Pannwitz was the first officer in the entire division to receive such high commendation. Eventually attaining the rank of general, he went on to command several of the Cossack units in Yugoslavia. Tactfully, the book did not mention that the Cossacks, peasant-soldiers who rode into battle on horseback, brandishing oversized swords as their loose robes billowed in the wind, were known as some of the most brutal of Hitler's volunteers.* Late in the war, the Cossack units under von Pannwitz were transferred to the Waffen-SS and redesignated the 15th SS Cossack Cavalry Division.

Most interesting, Schuller continued, was how von Pannwitz's career ended. The British captured him and thousands of his men in Austria, then turned them over to the Soviets in May 1945. Von Pannwitz was held in the Lubianka prison. "But look how very long it was before the Russians hanged him!" Schuller exclaimed. The biography dated von Pannwitz's execution as having been carried out on January 16, 1947.[9] "For one and a half years they held him in Lubianka, no doubt questioning him every single day, in a very . . . ah, unpleasant . . . way. Now, do you suppose that von Pannwitz never *once* mentioned to the Soviets his longtime associate, Lieutenant Waldheim?"

It was intriguing, but quite speculative. I pointed out that the young Waldheim was probably low on the totem pole and might never even have had direct contact with von Pannwitz. Nonetheless, the possibility that the Soviets held undisclosed, and perhaps damaging, information about Waldheim's war record was worth bearing in mind. The Red Army had captured millions of German war documents that, to this day, the Soviets shared only selectively with the rest of the world. If Waldheim had participated in wartime misdeeds under von Pannwitz, the Soviets might have known of that fact long ago. Indeed, I theorized, they might have had the information in their files during Waldheim's two five-year terms as Secretary-General of the U.N. If so, what awesome leverage they would have had!

Schuller disclosed that his "helpers" had succeeded in locating one of von Pannwitz's former colleagues, living in the Vienna area. "He does not like to talk, I'm afraid," Schuller said. "And it is all quite strange, actually. This 'gentleman' has not worked a single day since

---

*I had once seen a captured document in which a *German* officer complained to his superiors about atrocities committed by Cossack units. The grandson of the Cossack general Pyotr Krasnov later admitted that "bad elements" within the Cossack forces "robbed like bandits. They raped women and set fire to settlements."[8]

the war ended. Some guess that his silence has been purchased; others say that maybe he succeeded in getting his hands on some of the Cossack treasure before the Cossacks were handed over to the Soviets. According to legend, you know, their gold and jewels were given over to some German officers to hide until they got back from Russia. But of course they never returned. . . ."

Schuller shifted in his chair, ready to move on to another topic. He announced that we would next inquire into Waldheim's military record *after* 1941, during the time he claimed to have been a student in Vienna. Schuller searched through his briefcase, emerging at last with a collection of papers that he referred to as "Waldheim autobiographies." He handed me a copy of a campaign brochure issued in 1971 when Waldheim first ran, unsuccessfully, for Austria's presidency. A capsule biography of the candidate on page 4 mentioned briefly that Waldheim was wounded and sent home to Vienna in 1942 to resume his studies. This was the by-now familiar line. But the brochure added, "After his graduation in 1944, he marries and then must go back to the front."[10]

Cryptic though it was, here was the first admission I had seen that Waldheim returned to active military service following his leg injury, albeit not until the closing months of the war. This, apparently, was the homegrown version of his autobiography; as I already knew from Waldheim's 1980 letter to Solarz, the rest of the world received a markedly less complete story. Schuller wanted to be sure that I understood that the wording compelled the impression that Waldheim did not go back to war until 1944 or 1945. "Here he is *lying*," my guide snapped.

But Schuller was not yet ready to elaborate. First, he wanted to take me through all of the autobiographical accounts that he had been able to find, to assure me of Waldheim's unfailing insistence that he had been on home leave during the middle years of the war.

After losing the election in 1971, Schuller recalled, Waldheim, accomplishing one of the great rebounds in political history, was elected to the top U.N. post later that same year. From that point on, he seemed to have conveniently "forgotten" about his return to Wehrmacht service. "His official U.N. biography is actually silent about what he was doing during the entire war," Schuller advised. "Here is the U.N. official statement from 1971." He read aloud:

> Mr. Waldheim was born on 21 December 1918. He graduated from the University of Vienna as a Doctor of Jurisprudence in 1944. He also graduated from the Vienna Consular Academy. From 1948 to 1951, Mr. Waldheim served as First Secretary

at the Austrian Legation in Paris. He was head of the personnel department of the Ministry for Foreign Affairs in Vienna from 1951 to 1955.[11]

"And on and on it goes," Schuller said. Then, with a laugh, he added, "Something *does* seem to have been omitted, no? What happened to the Second World War?"

Next, Schuller pulled out a brochure from Waldheim's current presidential campaign. The slick booklet was packed with glossy color photos from Waldheim's glory days at the U.N., showing him hobnobbing with world leaders. Now that he was again addressing his native audience, Waldheim appeared willing to admit his return to duty late in the war. The candidate's first-person account declared that he was stationed in Trieste in 1945. These were harrowing days, near the end of the war, and Waldheim's bride, the former Elisabeth Ritschel, whom he called "Sissy," took refuge in western Styria, in the area of Ramsau bei Schladming. Waldheim said he "managed" to link up with her there and, "on the day which the war ended, our first child, Liselotte, was born."[12]

"Let us return to his recent *Im Glaspalast* autobiography," Schuller announced. He quickly found the key passages in the new book. Waldheim wrote that he was stationed in the Trieste area—during the final phase of the war. He continued, "Under difficulties which are unimaginable today, I found my way via Udine to Carinthia, and finally reached the area of Ramsau near Schladming."[13]

Schuller stressed the obvious: Waldheim once again had led the reader ever-so-carefully to the conclusion that he was home on study leave from 1941 until the war was nearly over.

Just as I was about to inquire about this "study leave," Schuller conceded that Waldheim had, in fact, studied law on and off during the middle years of the war. According to Schuller, Waldheim had received several leaves of absence to do so, but the key fact was that Waldheim wanted everyone to believe that he was absent from military service throughout the entire midwar period.

But where, I asked, was any proof to the contrary? It would have to be something considerably more impressive than the Army Group E "rumor" reported by *Profil*. Nothing Schuller had shown me demonstrated any military service by Waldheim during the midwar years.

Schuller smiled and paused for several seconds. Speaking softly, slowly, and precisely, relishing the moment, he asked, "What if I would tell you that there is a photograph from May 1943 showing our friend in uniform, far from Austria—in fact, in Yugoslavia?"

His question stunned me. A photograph, I allowed, would be

sensational. May 1943 was smack in the middle of the period when Waldheim—according to all of his own accounts—was home, studying law.

"Yes, all right, then, look at *this*," Schuller said. He pulled a large black-and-white print from his briefcase and announced, "This, by the way, is the *original* photo, from 1943."

As I watched him grasp the photograph, I was at once fascinated and mortified. Here, at last, was the ostensible proof that Waldheim was covering up his wartime service record. But I knew from experience that although authenticating *any* photograph represented a significant forensic challenge, an original photograph in private hands (rather than official archives) was especially difficult to authenticate. To make matters worse, the private hands that held it—Schuller's—ran roughshod over both the front and back surfaces, even as we spoke.

Schuller placed the photo on the table in front of me. I picked it up gingerly, raising it by the edges. The glossy, eight-by-ten, black-and-white, well-focused image was printed on heavy stock and was in excellent condition; the only sign of serious mishandling was a small crease in the lower left corner. It showed four uniformed officers, in an obviously posed shot, standing on a grassy airstrip. Two parked airplanes were visible in the distance. The officers stood next to another plane, the left wing of which extended most of the way across the top of the picture. In the background, a small group of soldiers marched in formation, with rifles upraised. In the foreground were two automobiles from the late thirties or early forties. Three of the officers wore German uniforms of the Nazi period; the fourth wore a uniform unfamiliar to me.

"The tall fellow," Schuller said, "the second from the left, *that* is our friend."

The stiff, slim, hawk-nosed *Oberleutnant* was glancing to one side. The profile did, indeed, appear to be a young version of Waldheim.

"Turn it over," Schuller suggested.

The reverse side bore what looked like an original black-and-red stamp of the photographic branch of the Prince Eugen Division of the Waffen-SS, along with identifying information, typed in German: the date (May 22, 1943) and location ("landing strip at Podgorica") of the picture, the photographer's name, the film roll and frame number, and, finally, the legend, in German:

> From l. to r.: Excellency Roncaglia Escola, Italian Commandant of Montenegro, *Oberleutnant* Waldheim, Adjutant of the Colonel, Col. Macholz, and *Gruppenfuehrer* Phleps.

There it was, then, literally in black and white: Waldheim in a Wehrmacht uniform on duty in the late spring of 1943, at a time when he insisted that he was a law student in Vienna! If this photograph was genuine, it also offered a clue as to *why* Waldheim felt obliged to cover up this period of his life: The photo showed him posing with a full-fledged SS-*Gruppenfuehrer* (major general)—and not just any SS-*Gruppenfuehrer* either! I had read enough history to know that Artur Phleps's Prince Eugen Division was perhaps the most notorious of all of Hitler's Waffen-SS units.

Schuller fidgeted with his empty glass. When, at last, I lifted my gaze from the photograph, a trace of a smile was visible as he posed a single sarcastic question: "It *is* a very *nice* picture, don't you think?"

4

Schuller told me that the extraordinary photo had been discovered the previous year by "an amateur historian, in a curio shop in Innsbruck."

That was difficult to believe, but I was not particularly concerned with how Schuller had obtained the photograph nor with any precautions he might be taking to protect a source. What I really needed to know was whether it was authentic. How could we prove, or disprove, the legitimacy of this improbable picture?

Schuller related what he had been able to determine thus far. After some difficulty, he had located Podgorica, the site purportedly depicted in the photo. "I finally found it in an old atlas from before the war," he said. "After the war, you see, the place was given a new name. Now it is called Titograd."

He searched further through his collection of books, strewn about the coffee table. "Ah, yes, here it is," he mumbled. "We learn a lot from this book here." *Vorwaerts Prinz Eugen!* ("Forward Prince Eugen!") was yet another Nazi memoir published in West Germany after the war, a glorified and thoroughly laundered "history" of the Prince Eugen SS Division. The author was former SS General Otto Kumm, one of Phleps's successors as division commander.

I was familiar with Kumm's postwar activities. In 1951, he established the first above-ground organization in Germany for former SS troops. *Hilfsgemeinschaft auf Gegenseitigkeit* (HIAG) was ostensibly a "mutual aid association," but its real mission was to combat "defamation" of the Waffen-SS. Several writers have characterized it as "the real ODESSA," charging that HIAG helped spirit fugitive Nazi war criminals to havens in South America and the Arab world. What, I wondered, could Kumm's book possibly tell us about Kurt Waldheim?

Ignoring the question I imagined was written on my face, Schuller riffled past pages of photographs depicting SS troops at work and play until he reached a chapter entitled "The 'Black' Operation." It recounted an "antipartisan" campaign waged in Montenegro, Yu-

goslavia, from May 15 to June 15, 1943, under the overall command
of a Wehrmacht general surnamed Lueters. Kumm's version painted
a picture of fierce but conventional combat with the Yugoslav
resistance.

Schuller handed the book to me, open to page 76. He helped me
with the occasional German word I did not understand. In the middle
of the page, I read:

> On May 22, Gen. Phleps travels to Podgorica and welcomes the
> Commanding General at the landing strip, with an honor com-
> pany of unit III/2, which presents a faultless rifle drill—the C.G.
> is very pleased. A discussion follows with the Ital. Army-Gen.,
> who claims the overall leadership of the operation for himself,
> which Gen. Lueters refuses.[1]

I read the paragraph twice. Then I stared at the photo, and shifted
my gaze back and forth between it and the book's text. The paragraph
might as well have been the caption for the photo. It was a perfect
match, from the date to the rifle-equipped honor guard! Or, I wondered, was it perhaps *too* perfect? This was either one of the greatest
feats of detective work I had ever seen, or an extremely bold hoax.

"Can you really be sure that this photo is genuine?" I asked
nervously.

Schuller parried. "Let us wait one more minute on that. First, we
must look at precisely what was this 'Black Operation' which was
being discussed." He placed *Vorwaerts Prinz Eugen!* down, and spoke
solemnly. "Our Mr. Kumm depicts it as a major offensive against
the Tito partisans, just a series of regular battles." A flash of pain
crossed Schuller's face as he added, "Yugoslavia is our neighbor, and
a great many Austrians were sent there during the war. Every Austrian who was alive then *knows* what it meant to have fought the
partisans in Yugoslavia. Do you know what such 'battles' usually
were like?"

I had some idea. Comparatively little had ever been published in
English about wartime atrocities in Yugoslavia. Western historians
tend to concentrate on Nazi crimes committed against the Jews,
Hitler's most viciously targeted victim group. And since the Western
allies were not fighting in the Soviet Union and Yugoslavia, English-
speaking writers of popular military histories have assumed that British and American readers would rather learn about Normandy or
Bastogne or Okinawa. This tendency to ignore the war in Eastern
Europe was compounded by the fact that so many of the primary
research materials fell into the hands of the Soviets and the Yugoslav
partisans, and those archives remained largely closed. Despite this

failure of Western historians, much is known about the Soviet aspects of the war, partly because the Soviet government had long used reminiscences of "The Great Patriotic War" as a national rallying device. By comparison, very little is available in the West concerning the war in Yugoslavia, and most of what is obtainable is written in Serbo-Croatian. Yet anyone with a rudimentary knowledge of the war there is aware that brutal crimes occurred in the Balkans on a large scale. There had been no real "Yugoslav army." Hence, the Germans' opponents were various ragtag partisan groups, primarily the rival units led by Tito and Mihailovich. I knew generally that the German effort against the partisans in Yugoslavia, as well as in Greece and throughout the Balkans, entailed some of the most savage episodes in the history of armed conflict. I knew that the Germans and their feared Croatian Ustashi allies were involved in mass killings of women and children, prisoner executions, and wholesale destruction of villages suspected of "supporting the partisans" or even merely of having failed to report the presence of resistance fighters in the area. Mass reprisals were standard practice for Wehrmacht and Waffen-SS forces in the Balkans.* But I confessed that I had not heard specifically of the "Black Operation."

Schuller replenished his glass with vodka and reached for a well-worn copy of an old Yugoslav government document. Entitled *Report on the Crimes of Austria and the Austrians Against Yugoslavia and Her Peoples,* it had been issued in English in 1947 by the Yugoslav War Crimes Commission. The report asserted that one hundred and twenty thousand Axis troops had been concentrated in the relatively small geographic area of Montenegro in the spring of 1943, under the immediate command of General Lueters, who reported directly to General Alexander Loehr, the man who, according to *Profil,* was rumored to have been Waldheim's commander.

The report contained page after page of frightful detail about the Black Operation: Prisoners were routinely executed by gunfire or, when the captors were Croats, often burned alive or hacked to pieces with knives and hatchets; innocent hostages were shot and hanged by the thousands; villages were destroyed, often with their entire

---

*In his landmark work *German Rule in Russia 1941–1945* (London: Macmillan, 2nd ed., 1981, pp. 210–12), Alexander Dallin wrote of the "startling brutality" of German anti-partisan operations in the East, in which "[w]hole villages suspected of harbouring sympathizers were burned down" and "in other instances the entire male population was evacuated." Historian Juergen Foerster, referring to the German army's similar campaign against partisans in Russia, cited, as proof of the "ruthless reprisal policy," the "considerable discrepancy between the number of 'partisans' killed and German casualties on the one hand, and the minor difference between the numbers arrested and those later executed on the other. . . ." Juergen Foerster, "The German Army and the Ideological War Against the Soviet Union," in Gerhard Hirschfeld (ed.), *The Policies of Genocide: Jews and Soviet Prisoners of War in Nazi Germany* (London: Allen & Unwin, 1986).

populations trapped inside. Schuller pointed out one chilling example in the report:

> German troops broke into the village of Bukovac in the district of Savnik; the villagers, having heard of atrocities committed by German troops in the vicinity and in the rest of Montenegro, tried to save their lives by escaping into a mountain cave. The Germans, however, found them, took them to a hillside and set to work to shoot them at once. A survivor, witness Mrs. Marica Blagojevic, described the above crime as follows:
> "The Germans immediately opened fire from machine guns and tommy guns on the people herded on the slope. One could hear the horrible cries of the women and children and the shouting of men. A couple of Germans tore from my hands my six-year-old child and slaughtered it in front of me. Then they cut it to pieces and forced me to take the pieces into my hands. I also saw a group of people being shot in front of a house after they had been bestially ill-treated; afterwards, their bodies—and I saw some were still alive—were thrown into the house, and the whole thing set on fire."

The report also contained a photographic reproduction of an order from General Lueters, concerning an inhabited area in which a group of partisans had been trapped. "Not one able-bodied man is to come out of the valley alive," he commanded. And: "Women are to be inspected, to make sure that they are not disguised men."[2] The date of the order was May 29, just six days after the Podgorica photograph, and it indicated that strategic—and plainly criminal—decisions were still being made by the Germans regarding the "Black Operation."[3] If, as Schuller's photograph indicated, Waldheim was in the area at a time when "operational" planning was well under way, just what was it that he was discussing with two generals and a colonel?

"*This*, you know, was the *real* 'Black Operation,' " Schuller said loudly, jabbing his finger at the text for emphasis. "And here, in the middle of it all, in the company of Phleps and Lueters, the leaders of the slaughter—a most rarified atmosphere, I think you would say in English—we find our *Mister* Waldheim." Schuller's use of the term "Mister," rather than the genteel *Doktor,* was yet another signal of his contempt for Waldheim.

I repeated my previous question, with urgency this time. "Are you sure that this photograph is genuine? Because anything short of certainty is going to be inadequate." Without proof, I continued, how could one ever publicly accuse anyone, much less the former U.N. Secretary-General, of a cover-up of such apparently monumental dimensions?

Schuller fell strangely silent. Apprehension seemed to seize him. No, he admitted, he could not be certain. A friend had performed some preliminary analyses, but he could not gain access to a sophisticated laboratory without attracting undue attention. Schuller admitted that he could not rule out the possibility that the photograph was a clever forgery, left in a curio shop to be "discovered." He could not even be sure that the man in the picture and identified in typescript on the reverse as "*Oberleutnant* Waldheim" was really *Kurt* Waldheim; perhaps it was someone else, even his brother, Walter. "I am, unfortunately, at a dead end with the photograph," he conceded. "In my heart, I *know* that it is our friend. On the other side, my head says we cannot be positive. In this country, only the Austrian police might have the technical ability to analyze such a photograph. But I can't go to them with *this,* of course. Can you imagine what would happen to me?"

So this, I realized, was why Schuller had not gone public with his extraordinary scenario; his case was not quite airtight. And his next words suggested the reason why he was willing to meet with me.

"Can you take the photo to the States and have it checked there?" he asked.

The room seemed to grow cold. This was no simple request. I would first have to get the photo through security at the Vienna airport. If I was caught, it would be difficult to explain to Austria's notoriously short-tempered police what I was doing with a compromising photograph of the country's leading citizen, especially if it turned out either to have been stolen from some archive or, perhaps worse, to be a defamatory forgery. Thinking in terms of the worst-case scenario, I did not want to be a foreign Jew in an Austrian prison.

I was an attorney, I reminded myself, not some sort of covert agent. This was dangerous business, more so than I had contemplated. Danger was not completely unknown to me; I had been the first federal prosecutor to conduct "drop-in" interviews of suspected Nazi war criminals, and I had seen a gun drawn during one such encounter. But I had left the federal government two years ago, and I had hoped that those days were behind me.

Yet, with all my reservations, I found myself energized. I knew of a few topflight forensic experts in the U.S. who could attempt to authenticate the photograph. And here, dangled in front of me, was an opportunity to recapture the excitement of working on a sensitive international investigation. Already I found myself making plans. For starters, I thought, I want to have the typewriter ink analyzed to make sure that the text on the back is not of recent origin. Then the stamps will have to be checked. Someone will have to perform an image analysis, to test for superimpositions or other alterations. Schuller had hooked me, no doubt about it. I accepted his proposal, and told him simply, "Yes, I will try."

"Excellent!" he shot back. Schuller even authorized me to have a limited amount of so-called destructive testing done, if necessary. (Destructive testing entails the extraction of ink and paper samples from a questioned document.)

He handed me the photograph, and I placed it carefully inside my portfolio.

Without missing a beat, Schuller moved on, reciting what was known of the men who had commanded the "Black Operation." Although Phleps had disappeared and was still a wanted man, the best guess was that he died in combat near the end of the war. Loehr, of course, was hanged by the Yugoslavs. But, like von Pannwitz in the USSR, Loehr was not executed until 1947. Indeed, the Yugoslav War Crimes Commission quoted extensively from Loehr in its reports, indicating that he talked at some length. Several of his top aides ended up in Yugoslav custody and, after extensive periods of interrogation, they, too, were executed. Schuller served up another rhetorical question: "So who, then, should have known the most about our friend, Mr. Waldheim? The Soviet and Yugoslav intelligence services, no? I would bet money on it."

Schuller seemed determined to show me everything that he had stuffed into his big briefcase. There was, for example, a photocopy of the front page of the December 3, 1944, edition of a Wehrmacht newspaper, *Wacht im Suedosten* ("Watch on the Southeast"). "I think that this will shed some light on the question of where Mr. Waldheim went after the 'Black Operation' was finished," Schuller declared.

Beneath the newspaper's masthead was a photo taken in Sarajevo, Yugoslavia. It showed General Loehr, described in the caption as the Supreme Commander of Wehrmacht forces in the Balkans, poring over situation maps in the Bosnian capital with some of his senior officers. Next to the commander of Army Group E was a young officer, shown full-face.[4] And although the text did not identify him by name, there was little doubt that it was the same young man depicted in one of the Waldheim campaign brochures Schuller had shown me. It suddenly occurred to me that the young *Oberleutnant* seemed to have had a penchant for getting himself into official photographs with Nazi war criminals—first Phleps and then Loehr! More importantly, if this new photo was what it appeared to be, then there really was a verifiable link between Waldheim and General Loehr.

There was more to learn about Loehr. Schuller explained that although the Yugoslavs hanged Loehr for his commanding role in the Luftwaffe's bombing of Belgrade, and although that was the focus of the current publicity surrounding the Austrians' attempt to memorialize him, an examination of the record revealed another major historical theme. At Loehr's trial, there was much talk of other crimes committed *later,* during Army Group E's retreat from Greece and Yugoslavia.* Indeed, said Schuller, this newspaper photo was published at precisely the time when Loehr's troops were said to have been involved in atrocities against local populations. It must have been "quite an honor," Schuller sneered, to appear in this posed shot with the commanding general for the front page of a newspaper circulated to hundreds of thousands of men under Loehr's command. "I wonder how Waldheim 'distinguished' himself to gain this honor," he added, once again in a contemptuous tone.

Responding to his own question, he noted with a rueful chuckle, "Loehr cannot tell us any longer, and I do not suppose that our Mr. Waldheim will do so either."

My mysterious Viennese source asserted that he had come across one curious connection between the two men. He had wondered why Waldheim, at the end of the war, had instructed his wife to leave Vienna and wait for him in Ramsau, a picturesque Alpine resort town in the Enns River valley. It was logical enough to leave Vienna, for the Soviet army was pushing nearer. But did the Waldheims just "happen" to choose Ramsau? Neither of them, said Schuller, had any family there. Schuller believed that he might have found an answer in a fawning biography of Loehr published by one of his former men in 1964, which noted that the general's staff had prepared for him "a precise escape route to the Enns River valley."[5] "Loehr, of course, never got to use this escape route," Schuller observed dryly. "The Yugoslavs captured him before he could get to it, you see. But perhaps his trusted aide, this *Oberleutnant* Waldheim, used it instead." Schuller had also learned that von Pannwitz's wife had waited for her husband in the same vicinity, not leaving until 1947, when the Soviets announced his execution.

I recalled that this was the same area in which many of the most-wanted Austrian Nazis were holed up in the months after the German surrender. Eichmann, Kaltenbrunner, and Globocnik were among those who had fled to the so-called Alpine Redoubt.

"*Ja, Ja,*" Schuller replied. "They were all there, all of them."

I was relieved that Schuller's numbing tour through Waldheim's past appeared at last to be nearing its end. He had given me a great deal

---

*Otmar Lahodynsky's original piece in *Profil* had mentioned these allegations in one sentence, followed immediately by a quotation from an Austrian journalist calling this charge "disgraceful" and a statement by an Austrian historian that Loehr was, in actuality, "an example to be followed."

of information to assimilate in one session, and even if only part of it was true and verifiable, its import appeared startling. Not really expecting an answer, I exclaimed, "How in God's name did this man get approved by the superpowers for the top U.N. post?"

Schuller saw it as an easy pitch, and he took a hard swing at it. He again expressed his belief that the Soviets had known about Waldheim's wartime record all along. In addition to whatever information they might have obtained from captured Wehrmacht officers and records, they could have counted on a full briefing on anything learned by the Yugoslavs, at least until an angry Marshal Tito parted ways with Stalin in 1948.

But if they really possessed a wartime dossier on Waldheim, why had the Soviets kept their own counsel? Why had they not exposed him, or at least vetoed his nomination for the top U.N. position?

Schuller noted that the very first postwar newspaper published in Austria was *Oesterreichische Zeitung,* the official journal of the authorities in the Soviet occupation zone of the country. The paper routinely featured exposés on ex-Nazis and possible war criminals who had obtained official positions in "liberated" Austria. "Even one sentence in that paper about 'Waldheim and Loehr' would have been enough to force our friend out of the civil service," Schuller contended. But the Soviets never did expose Waldheim in this manner and, in Schuller's mind, this was evidence suggesting that they maintained a quiet leverage over the man.

"Do you know how it happened that our friend came to be elected as U.N. Secretary-General in the first place?" Schuller asked.

That I *did* know. The Security Council's 1970 deliberations were supposedly secret, but Waldheim's U.N. predecessor U Thant and others subsequently divulged the details. The Soviet Union had repeatedly vetoed the other two "finalists,"* resulting in Waldheim's de facto election. In other words, Moscow virtually installed Waldheim in his U.N. post.[6] Schuller added his recollection that the Soviets had even tried to win a third term for Waldheim in 1980, but failed when China withdrew its support.

But what could the Soviets have hoped to accomplish by "compromising" Kurt Waldheim? I wondered aloud. As Secretary-General, Waldheim could not dispatch armies to serve Soviet interests. Nor could he offer anything important in the way of intelligence data. Equally beyond his power was the delivery of even a single General Assembly or Security Council decision.

---

*These were the U.N. representatives of Argentina and Finland. Finland's foreign policy had long been effectively directed by the Soviets, but their candidate, the distinguished Finnish U.N. Ambassador Max Jacobsen, had, to Soviet eyes, the singular disadvantage of being a Jew.

Schuller listened impatiently and then acknowledged, "*Ja,* all of that is true. That, you see, is why I prefer to look at the period in our friend's life when he actually had something that one perhaps might call 'power,' or at least 'authority'—when he was Foreign Minister of Austria, from 1968 to 1970." Schuller suddenly appeared skittish. "What I am about to show you is quite sensitive," he said. "But I think you must see it if you are to understand the position that this man Waldheim found himself in . . . vis-à-vis the Soviets."

Schuller directed my attention to Czechoslovakia, recalling the tragic events of the so-called Prague Spring of 1968. Their dominance threatened by the liberal policies of Czech leader Alexander Dubcek, the Soviets mounted a full-scale invasion. Blood flowed freely as Soviet tanks rumbled through the streets of Prague. Dubcek and his allies were spirited to Moscow, where they were compelled to cancel their reform measures.

I nodded; it was a justly notorious episode in modern European history.

Schuller jumped back to Waldheim's *Im Glaspalast* . . . memoirs, pointing out the section that dealt with the Czech crisis of 1968. As Foreign Minister, Waldheim recalled, he was part of the emergency group formed within the cabinet to handle Austria's response. "It is most interesting to compare Mr. Waldheim's words in this book with his actions at the time," Schuller said. "Look what he writes here: 'A spontaneous wave of goodwill helped the large numbers of refugees to overcome their first misery.' You might expect from such touching words that Foreign Minister Kurt Waldheim had instructed the Austrian Embassy in Prague to assist those people who were fleeing from the Soviets, no? Our embassy, as the legation of the neighboring neutral country, was the most logical place for those poor people to seek refuge, of course. And Czechs who were being hunted by the Soviet security forces actually did come there in large numbers. Now notice what Waldheim writes in his memoirs about how 'Moscow became very concerned' about the pro-Dubcek reaction in Austria. The government in Vienna, he writes, was 'under pressure' and 'had to tread something of a tightrope.' "[7]

Schuller told me that, four months ago, *Profil* reported that Foreign Minister Waldheim had ordered the embassy in Prague to turn away the would-be refugees.[8] But the reporter had no documentation to back up his claim, and Waldheim denied it. In fact, Schuller pointed out, his denial had the ring of truth, for the embassy had remained open and had issued visas to thousands of Czechs.

Schuller paused, searched for another document, found it, and handed it over to me. "This," he declared proudly, "has never been published."

The piece of paper I now held was further proof of Schuller's ability to gain access to sensitive government documents. It was a photocopy of a cable from the Austrian Foreign Ministry to its legation in Prague, dated August 21, 1968, the first day of the Soviet invasion. Entitled "Treatment of Requests for Asylum," it instructed:

PLEASE HAVE LEGATION BUILDING CLOSED AND ALLOW ADMITTANCE ONLY TO AUSTRIAN PASSPORT HOLDERS. CZECH CITIZENS ALREADY FOUND IN THE BUILDING SHOULD BE INDUCED TO LEAVE THE BUILDING THROUGH POLITE INSISTENCE, WITH REFERENCE TO THE FACT THAT THE LEGATION MUST BE RESERVED TO OUR OWN CITIZENS.

The cable's cover sheet contained a handwritten notation: the letters *HBM,* followed by a larger, loosely scrawled *W.*

Schuller explained: "HBM stands for *Herr Bundesminister,* 'Mister Federal Minister.' I assume that you do not need me to tell you who 'W' is." He added, with a seemingly habitual grimace of disdain, "This order to the embassy was *inhumane,* especially by our standards. Fortunately, the Austrian ambassador in Prague simply disregarded it—at great risk to his own career, of course. What a great champion of human rights our Mr. Waldheim is!"

I pondered the significance of this episode. It would be ludicrous to suppose that Waldheim was ever a Soviet spy, in the conventional sense of the word. But if he knew (or even suspected) that the Soviets possessed compromising information about him, it would certainly have been in Waldheim's interest to "oblige" them. From the Soviet perspective, the "proper" use of such a resource would be to reserve it for the most important favors. Was this cable to Prague the result of such Soviet pressure? It did seem to be precisely the sort of "big favor" the Soviets might expect from one of their "assets."

By now it was past 8 P.M., and Schuller readily accepted my suggestion that we break for dinner. He stuffed his research materials back into his briefcase, and we left in search of a restaurant.

My head was spinning by now, and not just from inhaling Schuller's pipe smoke. We were discussing one of the world's senior diplomats, a veteran statesman known by name and by sight to hundreds of millions of people. He was as far removed as possible from the run-of-the-mill Nazi suspect. For a decade he had headed the closest thing the planet Earth had ever seen to a world government. Was it really possible that he had, in earlier and decidedly more savage times, cooperated with the likes of von Pannwitz, Phleps, and Loehr, and managed to maintain that secret throughout his two U.N. terms?

In the span of just a few hours, my informant had taken me on a journey from Austria to the Soviet Union to Yugoslavia to Czechoslovakia and back again, a journey that purported to place a former U.N. Secretary-General in the company of notorious Nazi criminals, serving in units that perpetrated horrible war crimes in the Balkans and in the Soviet Union. He hypothesized a cover-up of unprecedented magnitude and supported the thesis with some of the subject's most personal records, two nearly incredible photos, and a high-level government cable of extraordinary sensitivity.

I had come to Vienna a skeptic. Now I did not know what to believe.

As Schuller and I walked through central Vienna, the Waldheim campaign posters touting "An Austrian the World Trusts" now seemed part of a demoniacal joke. For the first time, I noticed a second slogan in smaller print: "His Experience for Us All."

At dinner, Schuller switched to scotch, ordering for both of us, so that I had little choice but to join in. I sipped at my drink and asked quietly, "So we don't know precisely when 'our friend' recovered from his war injuries and returned to active duty, right?"

"Ja. All we can do so far is place him at Podgorica with Phleps on May 23, 1943, and in Sarajevo with Loehr around December 1944." Schuller's voice was surprisingly loud in so public a place. I was amazed at his lack of concern over security.

"I can try to do some research back in the States," I offered, "beginning, of course, with a professional examination of the Podgorica photograph. There's also the National Archives in Washington, which has an enormous collection of captured German documents. The problem is that the records are poorly organized and hardly indexed at all."

"What about U.S. intelligence?"

"I can file some Freedom of Information Act requests when I get home. Do you have any particular reason to think that there's something important in American intelligence files?"

Schuller told me that, almost immediately after the war, Waldheim went to work for Foreign Minister Karl Gruber, who was especially close to Allen Dulles, head of the Office of Strategic Services bureau in Switzerland and, later, the first CIA director. Late in the war, Gruber had joined the Austrian resistance, which worked closely with the OSS. Schuller conjectured that Gruber would not have hired the young Waldheim to be his principal assistant without having him checked out in advance by his friend Dulles; hence, the U.S. files might well have some pertinent information.

It was a long shot, and I told Schuller so. The CIA had inherited most of the OSS records, so that was the logical place to look. But that agency was notoriously slow in responding to Freedom of Information Act requests and, when an answer did come back, it was usually a refusal to release any information. Furthermore, I told Schuller, the CIA had cleared Waldheim six years earlier in a letter to a U.S. congressman; it was therefore quite unlikely that the Agency would admit to having any contrary information today.

"Ah, I see," Schuller said with a disappointed sigh.

I turned to a pragmatic question. If the suspicions about Waldheim were verified, what did we plan to do then? Certainly we should go public, but how? It was the first time either of us had spoken of "we," but Schuller seemed quite comfortable with the implication of ongoing cooperation. "What about the Austrian press?" I asked.

"No!" Schuller shot back. "No, no, they would never publish such a story. They especially do not like to dig into anyone's 'brown' past," he said, using the vernacular term for former Nazi affiliation.

"If there really is something here, I think I could interest an American newspaper in the story," I said. "I've worked with the *Times* before, and I think they would pursue this, at least if I gave it to them as an exclusive."

"That is an interesting possibility, *Ja.*"

For special reasons, I explained, it could be important in this case to join forces with a reporter. It would be unfair to accuse Waldheim publicly concerning irregularities in his past without giving him a chance to respond privately and, perhaps, explain. But neither Schuller nor I could accomplish that. Schuller was tied to Waldheim's political opposition, and I was an attorney for the WJC and a former war crimes prosecutor. Waldheim would naturally be suspicious, and the crucial element of surprise would likely be lost. However, if a reporter from a major American newspaper requested an interview in the midst of a presidential campaign, Waldheim would undoubtedly agree to talk. During his U.N. days, Waldheim seemed obsessed with seeing his name in the *New York Times*. I knew Ralph Blumenthal there. He was an experienced and talented reporter who spoke fluent German, and one of his areas of expertise was the postwar activities of former Nazis.

Schuller gave his approval to my suggestion and gestured broadly to our waiter, ordering another round of drinks.

But the waiter scowled and caught the eye of the maître d', who pointed out to us that we were the last two diners, and it was late.

"Let us go to your hotel," Schuller suggested. "We can finish our discussion over there."

It was past midnight and the scotch I had consumed was sounding a painful drumbeat in my head when I asked Schuller what seemed like a logical question: "Have you shown the photographs and documents to Simon Wiesenthal? I could call him and—"

"Oh, God no!" Schuller interrupted. "He doesn't know you are in Vienna, does he?"

"Not yet, but—"

"Good. He must not find out what you are doing. He would go straight to Waldheim."

"You *can't* be serious," I retorted. Wiesenthal was, by anyone's account, the most famous Nazi-hunter of all time. He was a Holocaust survivor himself, and a resident of this very city, which was the headquarters of his "Jewish Documentation Center." *Of course* he should be brought into this investigation.

Perhaps, I thought, scotch-on-vodka makes Schuller paranoid. True, working in this field had given me a disconcertingly realistic view of Wiesenthal. He was, in fact, more of a figurehead and publicist than a true investigator. Insiders knew that he had happily accepted credit for the spectacular achievements of others; but prosecutors of Nazi cases yielded to the apparent desire of the media—and a good part of the world's Jewish population—to focus upon a single personality as Jewry's tireless "Avenger of the Six Million." I reminded Schuller that, at least from a public relations standpoint, Wiesenthal's clout was impressive. His imprimatur on any disclosure would guarantee that the press would take it seriously. How could we ignore Wiesenthal in what, if Schuller's information panned out, would likely be the greatest Nazi exposé ever? "This is Vienna," I continued. "We are right under Wiesenthal's nose. If we don't involve him from the start, it'll be very difficult to ask him for help later. He's anything but perfect, I know that. Still, if I carefully explain to him the sensitivity of this thing, I'm sure he'll understand."

"You are not seeing Wiesenthal in his political context, my friend," Schuller argued. "He is loyal to the People's Party, and Waldheim is their candidate. If you wonder why that should be so, just think about what happened in the Peter affair."

The episode had occurred a decade earlier. I knew the case generally, but Schuller reminded me of the details. It was the culmination of a longstanding feud between Wiesenthal and Chancellor Bruno Kreisky. The dispute had turned ugly. For example, when Wiesenthal accused Kreisky, a Socialist, of cozying up to the Palestine Liberation Organization, Kreisky, himself born Jewish, had called Wiesenthal a "Jewish fascist." Later, Kreisky, believing that no party would achieve a majority in the Austrian elections, had openly contemplated a coalition government between his Socialist Party and the small Freedom Party, headed by Friedrich Peter. Wiesenthal thereupon disclosed that Peter had been a tank commander in a Waffen-SS infantry brigade that was implicated in the deaths of thousands of civilians. Wiesenthal admitted at the time that there was no proof implicating Peter in the actual crimes; but he declared that serving in a criminal unit (Wiesenthal used such expressions as "murder brigade") was enough to disqualify the man from public office. Instead of breaking with Peter, Kreisky and his party counterattacked. Kreisky accused Wiesenthal of employing "political Mafia methods" and threatened to close down Wiesenthal's Vienna office. Kreisky even asserted that he had evidence to back up old unsubstantiated claims made by the Polish and Soviet governments that Wiesenthal had collaborated with the Gestapo during the war,* charges long denied by Wiesenthal. All in all, it was probably the dirtiest public feud in postwar Austrian history.

Even though Kreisky had retired years ago, Wiesenthal, in Schuller's view, "will never forget how the Socialists tried to destroy him. Thus, his only important political ally is the People's Party, even though they are the ones who really have been the most closely linked to the ex-Nazis. The Socialists are still in control of the government, and you just cannot imagine how much Wiesenthal is thirsty for revenge."

There were so many ironies at work here. Schuller recalled that it was Kreisky who gave Waldheim his big break in international politics, appointing him to the post of Austrian U.N. representative shortly after Waldheim lost the 1971 presidential election. Wiesenthal, it seemed to me, might take some delight in exposing Waldheim and thereby discrediting Kreisky.

Schuller contended that Wiesenthal's longtime association with the People's Party was even more ironic, and he provided a brief sketch: Only months after the end of the war, one of the People's Party leaders, Leopold Kunschak, publicly announced that he had long been an anti-Semite; he was subsequently elected president of Austria's parliament. One of the party's most tenaciously waged postwar campaigns was to win back voting rights for former Nazis. In 1949, the *New York Times* exposed a series of meetings between People's Party leaders and former SS and S.A. members, held for the purpose of forming a political alliance. At about the same time, the editor of the People's Party newspaper denounced hundreds of thousands of forlorn displaced persons still living in camps inside Austria as "these foreign incorrigibles," and another party official was bemoaning what he saw as the U.S. government's obsession with

---

*I have seen two affidavits from purported witnesses to Wiesenthal's wartime activities. However, both are from former soldiers in Hitler's army whose motives must therefore be considered suspect.

chasing down former members of the Nazi Party. In 1953, the party published an appeal by the founder of the Austrian Nazi Party for ex-Nazis to vote for the People's Party, touching off a fevered battle with the Socialist Party for the "brown vote."[9]

Most Austrian Jews traditionally supported the Socialists; but Wiesenthal had been in the People's Party camp at least since his long-ago feud with Kreisky. Indeed, an organization known as the "List Simon Wiesenthal"—one of several groups that put forward "political" candidates for election to the central leadership council of Vienna Jewry—is commonly described in Austrian parlance as "close to the People's Party."[10]

It was all very confusing. Wiesenthal's conservative politics, however strange, had never before seemed to be a cause for serious concern. Schuller saw the skepticism still on my face.

"I will tell you how I see Mr. Wiesenthal," he said. "He is in his late seventies, *Ja?* Until last year, he had only three remaining life goals. The first one was to win a Nobel Peace Prize. But he probably knows he is too controversial for that. His second goal was to see Dr. Mengele [the notorious Auschwitz "death doctor"] brought to court. But he became an international laughingstock last year when Mengele's bones were found in Brazil. So that leaves only his third goal as a real possibility: a People's Party victory at the polls. And Waldheim is the best chance that his party has had in a generation."

It was preposterous. In fact, for the first time in this long session with Schuller, I felt the stirrings of what some of my friends refer to as "the legendary Rosenbaum temper." For decades Wiesenthal almost singlehandedly kept alive, especially through his statements in the media, the issue of unpunished Nazi war criminals. To suggest that he would play politics with the horrors of the Nazis was beyond belief. Schuller's analysis was logical enough, but it ignored the emotional aspect. Wiesenthal was a Holocaust survivor himself. He would be—I was sure of it—the first to demand an explanation for any misrepresentation of Waldheim's war record.

But Schuller was adamant. If I went to Wiesenthal, he would cooperate no further. The choice was mine. Swallowing my reservations, I at last acceded.

"Good," Schuller replied with obvious relief.

A few minutes later, he excused himself to make a phone call. I was alone with my thoughts, and I found them racing wildly about my head. The scotch was taking effect, too. Who was this fellow Schuller? I asked myself. He was an old-line Socialist who had obviously been assisted in his inquiries by other Socialists, evidently including some within the Austrian government. His interest in discrediting Waldheim was blatantly political. Certainly, the Socialist Party too had its share of ex-Nazis within its ranks.

Still, the man had convinced me over the past hours that there was more than political motivation behind his quest. He seemed genuinely appalled by Waldheim's apparent cover-up. But be careful, I warned myself. We will have to double- and triple-check everything. There is no room for error here. With a shudder, I remembered how the venerable London *Times* had been embarrassed a few years earlier by its acceptance of the phony "Hitler Diaries."

If this Waldheim story was true, I wondered, how would Schuller feel about playing a major role in disgracing his own country? I posed the question when he returned.

"Austria will survive," he responded softly. "The truth about this man is the most important thing. And perhaps the fact that some Austrians have participated in revealing the truth will be counted in my country's favor one day."

5

Manhattan was buried in a Friday night snowstorm. From my one-bedroom apartment in Battery Park City, overlooking the Hudson River, I telephoned Elan Steinberg to report what I had found in Vienna. My immediate superior at the WJC was intrigued by what little I was willing to tell him over the phone, and eager to see my entire stockpile of evidence, especially the Podgorica photograph. But neither he nor Israel Singer could meet with me before Monday morning.

That left me facing a seemingly interminable weekend. I collapsed onto my sofa, exhausted.

A mere half day ago I had braced myself for the task of confronting the airport security agents in Vienna. I had packed copies of Schuller's materials into my luggage on the theory that a checked suitcase was far less likely to be searched than a carry-on bag. But the most damning piece of evidence was the one that I could not risk consigning to the baggage handlers. The Podgorica photograph was *the original* and a "lost luggage" episode would be an irreparable disaster. Thus, the key photograph remained stashed inside a book and tucked into my briefcase. My sense of apprehension was at a peak as I approached the security checkpoint. The encounter was brief and without incident, but it nonetheless left me drained.

For once, I had thought, I was tired enough to be able to doze on an airplane. Instead, I spent most of the eight-hour transatlantic flight staring out the window, into vacant airspace, haunted by Schuller's presentation.

Now safely ensconced in my own apartment, I wondered how long it would be before my brain would allow me to sleep.

Humankind is a strange and terrible creation, I said to myself. We have wars—perhaps that is inevitable. Then we have rules for how we may kill and maim in wars, codified in the Geneva Conventions of 1929 and 1949 and the 1907 Hague Convention on Land Warfare, among other accords. Except under the most limited, unavoidable circumstances, the laws of war do not permit a soldier to execute a military or civilian prisoner. In any protracted war, there are likely to be violations of those international laws, but there is a vast difference between isolated acts of brutality and the systematic program of atrocities carried out by the Nazis.

History contains many examples of genocide conducted under the banner of a despotic leader. Certainly the most well-known of these tragedies occurred during World War II, when the Nazis violated the laws of warfare and the basic norms of civilized behavior on an unprecedented scale. They executed prisoners. They routinely annihilated entire villages of blameless civilians. They methodically set out to remove an entire religious group from the face of the earth. All told, they slaughtered approximately eleven million innocent civilian victims, six million of them Jews. And as it was happening, they recorded much of their evil handiwork in war diaries and reports.

The impetus for this barbarity came directly from the demonic mind of Hitler himself, whose edicts filtered through countless layers of subordinates. This made possible the classic "I was only following orders" defense, which was rejected categorically at the Nuremberg war crimes trials—and thereafter—for several major reasons. Most fundamentally, the discovery of the eleven million civilian murders perpetrated by the Nazis reaffirmed the principle that society cannot afford to excuse obedience to criminal orders. Hitler could not have imposed his will without the active assistance of his generals, their staff officers, and thousands of lower-level acolytes. The Nuremberg trials reminded the world of the precept that it is immoral to carry out—or to cause to be carried out—an immoral order. And although those who helped to perpetrate the Third Reich's crimes contended, all the way down the chain of command, that they had had "no choice," in fact, no defendant had ever been able to prove that the Nazis imposed serious penalties on anyone who refused to obey a criminal order. Individual men and even entire units had refused without suffering dire consequences.

But believing that someone was significantly involved in Nazi crimes and actually proving that fact are two very different matters, especially in court. The difficulties facing war crimes prosecutors and investigators have long been recognized. On January 22, 1945, the U.S. Attorney General and the Secretaries of State and War reported, in a joint memo to President Franklin D. Roosevelt:

> . . . the crimes to be punished have been committed upon such a large scale that the problem of identification, trial, and punishment of their perpetrators presents a situation without parallel in the administration of criminal justice. In thousands of

cases, it will be impossible to establish the offender's identity or to connect him with the particular act charged. Witnesses will be dead, otherwise incapacitated, or scattered. The gathering of proof will be laborious and costly, and the mechanical problems involved in uncovering and preparing proof of particular offenses is one of appalling dimensions. It is evident that only a negligible minority of the officers will be reached by attempting to try them on the basis of separate prosecutions for their individual offenses. It is not unlikely, in fact, that the Nazis have been counting on just such considerations, together with delay and war weariness, to protect them against punishment if they lost the war.

At the moment, thoughts of such obstacles weighed heavily on my mind.

I glanced at the hundreds of books that cluttered my small apartment. They constituted my private research library, what some of my friends called "Rosenbaum's Nazi books," a legacy of my work at the Justice Department. Most of them were in English or German, and they included some of the official Nuremberg document compilations. I wondered whether they might reveal something about the matter at hand. It was a long shot but, I reminded myself, this entire affair was, to put it mildly, an unlikely one.

"Might as well try a little research," I said to myself with a sigh. "I can't sleep anyway."

There would surely be no direct references to Waldheim in these books—or his game would have been lost long ago. Where, then, should I begin? As I scanned the book spines, my thoughts flipped back and forth in time, trying to formulate the beginnings of a chronology: Russia in 1941, Austria in 1942, Podgorica in 1943, Sarajevo in 1944, Trieste in 1945, and then back to Austria. If Schuller's suspicions were correct, Waldheim had been all over the place. Could we pin down the specifics?

I decided to see what more I could learn about the single most compelling piece of evidence, the Podgorica photograph. Following this tack, I searched for references to General Phleps, the Prince Eugen Division commander pictured in the photo, and to the "Black Operation" that was the topic of discussion. I could find no specific mention of the campaign, but I did locate a few grisly accounts of practices employed by German forces against Yugoslav partisans. One book quoted what a British official had written in a 1947 internal Foreign Office report:

There seems little doubt that taken by and large, the Germans behaved worse in Yugoslavia than almost anywhere else and that the atrocities committed by them and on their behalf were too appalling to imagine.[1]

In another of my books, historian George H. Stein characterized the Nuremberg disclosures concerning the Prince Eugen Division as "perhaps the most shocking" of all charges lodged against the Waffen-SS. He reported that the evidence included descriptions of the torture and murder of partisans and the indiscriminate destruction of villages in reprisal raids. He mentioned specifically a photograph taken from a P.O.W., a Waffen-SS soldier, "showing a Yugoslav being decapitated with a woodsman's axe" as other SS men from the Prince Eugen Division watched in obvious enjoyment. The U.S. indictment at Nuremberg of General Wilhelm List described how the Prince Eugen Division raided "numerous" Yugoslav villages and "burned the inhabitants alive," with the assistance of the 369th "Devil's" Division.[2]

Another historian wrote that during the summer of 1943, the Prince Eugen Division had "liquidated" the entire population of one village because German troops had " 'apparently' been fired on from the church." One page later, he related an officer's attempt to explain a subsequent atrocity as an "error." That prompted a retort from a certain SS-*Oberfuehrer* Fromm: "Since you arrived, there has unfortunately been one 'error' after another."[3]

Like Schuller, I had found it necessary to amass a number of what could only be described as repulsive works. One of these was a volume devoted to those Waffen-SS men who had won the Third Reich's Knight's Cross medal during the war. It contained a seven-page tribute to *Obergruppenfuehrer* Phleps, complete with photographs of the great man himself. Most important for my purposes, it gave Phleps's date and place of birth—information that I could use to file a Freedom of Information Act request to see whether U.S. agencies held any relevant files concerning the man.

None of this implicated Waldheim himself, of course, nor did it necessarily implicate the Wehrmacht, which was operating in the same area at the same time but was distinct from the Waffen-SS. However, my suspicions grew concerning the activities of Wehrmacht soldiers stationed in Yugoslavia when I came upon a translation of a "Top Secret" directive dated December 16, 1942, from Wilhelm Keitel, chief of staff of the Wehrmacht High Command. The frightful order was introduced into evidence at Nuremberg and was partially responsible for Keitel's subsequent hanging. It read in part:

Subject: Combatting Partisans
. . . This struggle has nothing to do with soldierly chivalry or with the obligations of the Geneva Convention.

If the most brutal measures in this struggle against the partisans in the East and in the Balkans as well are not applied, our forces will fail to eradicate this plague in the near future. Accordingly, the troops are obliged and have the right to apply in this struggle any method without restriction, stopping at nothing, even as regards women and children, when this guarantees a success . . .[4]

The words "even as regards women and children" were unusually explicit, even by Nazi standards.

Shifting gears after a few hours, I leafed through some of my basic reference books concerning the Nazi campaign against the Jews of Europe. Schuller had not suggested any connection between Loehr's Army Group E and this subject, but I had consulted these volumes almost daily during my tenure at the Justice Department, and force of habit drove me back to them. I began with the first comprehensive English-language study devoted solely to the crimes of the Holocaust, Gerald Reitlinger's landmark *The Final Solution: The Attempt to Exterminate the Jews of Europe 1939–1945.* What I found sent a chill up my spine. Reitlinger cited Nuremberg documents that reflected General Loehr's responsibility for carrying out, in close cooperation with the SS, the deportation of tens of thousands of Greek and Albanian Jews, primarily to Auschwitz, during 1943 and 1944. The survivors of the deportations "can be numbered on one's fingers," he added. A footnote stopped me cold. It charged that Loehr *"was perhaps more implicated in Jewish deportations than any other Wehrmacht commander . . ."* (Emphasis added.)[5]

This raised the stakes yet again, rather dramatically. Was it possible that Waldheim, apparently photographed with Loehr in December 1944 and described in *Profil* as "only" having been an *Ordonnanzoffizier* on Loehr's staff, had been involved in Jewish deportations to Auschwitz? Nothing I had learned in Vienna had prepared me for such a stunning possibility.

Comparing Reitlinger's book with the other principal reference work on the Holocaust, Professor Raul Hilberg's *The Destruction of the European Jews,* I found that the two historians were in full agreement concerning Loehr's complicity in the deportation of more than 54,000 Jews from Greece between May 1943 and July 1944. Both historians cited captured German war documents in which the Nazis meticulously recorded the details of these crimes. According to the footnotes, many of the documents came from Army Group E headquarters and from component units of the army group, and this meant that copies of these documents were likely to be available at the U.S. National Archives in Washington.

One of my Nuremberg evidence volumes contained a document that disclosed why so few of the deportees had survived. It was an affidavit from a top Eichmann deputy, SS-*Hauptsturmfuehrer* Dieter Wisliceny. Wisliceny recounted their fate in matter-of-fact fashion:

> Altogether, 60,000 Jews were collected from Greece and shipped to Auschwitz. . . . In July 1944, Hoess, Commandant of Auschwitz, told Eichmann in my presence in Budapest that all of the Greek Jews had been exterminated because of their poor quality.[6]

Reading on, I learned that Loehr, whom Hilberg described as the "military overlord" of all Greece, had not merely "gone along" with what the SS wanted; he had been an enthusiastic participant, an initiative-taker. He had personally implored the ranking Italian general in occupied Greece, Carlo Geloso, to assist the Germans in removing the Jews (only to be rebuffed by Geloso). According to one Nuremberg document cited by Hilberg, Loehr's Army Group E headquarters had specifically authorized the allocation of ships to transfer Jews from the Greek islands of Corfu and Crete to the mainland, from whence they were deported eastward in railroad boxcars. The islands, Hilberg wrote, were under Loehr's "complete control."[7]

One of the more obscure volumes in my collection was an index to Holocaust-related evidence assembled for the main Nuremberg trial. Researchers in Israel and the U.S. had labored over the unwieldy mass of Nuremberg paperwork for years, reviewing and categorizing the thousands of documents collected by the prosecution teams (including many that were never actually introduced into evidence). I pored over the tiny print in this index of references to a litany of horror: evacuations, deportations, mass killings. Each of these entries was accompanied by a Nuremberg document number, which also indicated its likely availability at the National Archives.[8]

Most intriguing—and appalling—were the references to the destruction of the Jewish community of Salonika. Before the war, Salonika was the center of Sephardic culture in Europe. Between May 1943 and March 1944, the Germans deported nearly forty-six thousand Jews from this one city, fully two-thirds of the Jewish population of Greece. I was almost certain that Schuller had said something in passing about Loehr having been based in Salonika sometime during the war. Was he there at the time of the deportations? Was Waldheim on his staff there? I realized with a start that the Salonika deportations occurred during the very middle of the period that Waldheim was apparently concealing.

My eyes and fingers raced through books, searching for more specific information on the locations and dates of Loehr's assignments. Finally I found proof of what I had suspected: Loehr's Army Group E was headquartered in Arsakli, a town in the hills overlooking Salonika, from late 1943 until the autumn of 1944. According to Professor Hilberg, from mid-March through May 1943, *Wehrmacht* trains departed Salonika nearly every day, carrying thousands of Jews to Auschwitz. During this entire period, Loehr had been the senior Wehrmacht officer in Greece.

I checked my notes. The Wehrmacht newspaper photo purportedly linking Loehr and Waldheim was dated December 3, 1944. By then, Army Group E had pulled out of Salonika and was in retreat, back across Yugoslavia. How long, I wondered, had the two men been deployed together? And what had they been doing?

Could it be that it was really *this* connection that Waldheim was hiding—*had* to hide?

As the weekend wore on, realities gnawed at me. I worried that we might never be able to prove anything about Waldheim's personal actions during the war. Much of the evidence concerning Nazi crimes was never recorded on paper. Much more was intentionally destroyed before war's end in German bonfires. What remained was fragmentary at best. Some of the available documents were accessible to the general public, but many were not, and I was no longer a governmental insider. Furthermore, there was little doubt that Waldheim, if and when we confronted him, would be less than enthusiastic about filling in the blanks.

As I dropped down onto a living room chair, with dozens of books now scattered on the floor nearby, I wondered whether I—and the WJC—had the resources and the resolve for the job.

As a younger man, expatriate Canadian Edgar Miles Bronfman was a reluctant darling of the scandal sheets. He was rich, ruggedly handsome, and had a penchant for what *Time* magazine called "young models and society girls." Even the family fortune had a checkered history. Bronfman's father, Sam, had built it during Prohibition partly by shipping liquor from his Canadian distilleries to border points where such customers as Lucky Luciano smuggled it into the U.S.

Edgar was in his early forties when his father died in 1971 and he became the billionaire chairman of the family business, Joseph E. Seagram & Sons, Inc., the world's largest distillers. Over the years, he had expanded his family's business empire to include enormous stakes in chemical and oil companies, and he had mellowed. Gradually, he developed an increasing interest in his faith and in humanitarian causes, especially Jewish ones. In 1979, he was elected president of the WJC, no doubt partly in recognition of the large infusion of Bronfman family funds that had saved the organization from financial ruin, but also because of his considerable intellectual gifts and his ability to move smoothly among the world's political and corporate elite. Upon his election, he began to study Hebrew with a private tutor, and he built on that symbolic act with a growing record of responsibility as a Jewish leader. By 1986, at the age of fifty-six, Edgar Bronfman was most definitely the "here" where the WJC buck stopped.

On Monday morning, after listening stone-faced to my initial report, Israel Singer rushed to see Bronfman in his office in the Seagram Building at Park Avenue and Fifty-fourth Street, in an attempt to persuade Bronfman to authorize me to commence a full-scale investigation into Waldheim's past. Seated amidst a Miró tapestry, two heroic-sized Rodin sculptures, and other priceless artworks, Singer presented a memo from me referring to "certain questions that have arisen" about Waldheim's "war record" and prewar "affiliations." The wording was purposely vague. Singer preferred to brief Bronfman orally on the specifics. As the final dramatic act of his presentation, he showed Bronfman the extraordinary Podgorica photo.

Bronfman sized up the problems quickly. The timing was both interesting and disturbing. This year marked the golden anniversary of the WJC, which was founded in 1936 primarily to counter the then-growing threat of Nazism. Despite a number of successes, the inescapable bottom line was that our organization, along with the rest of the Jewish world, had failed miserably. Six million Jewish men, women, children, and infants had paid the price for their coreligionists' collective inability to convince the world to confront the Nazis before it was too late. If any lesson had been learned, it was that the word "silence" had to be banished from the Jewish lexicon.

Yet there were major pragmatic concerns that argued against our pursuing this matter. "You know," Bronfman cautioned, "we're not in the Nazi-hunting business. That's for government prosecutors—they've got the resources, and the access to closed records."

In response, Singer pointed out the obvious: Every major government in the world had already embraced Waldheim; they could hardly be expected to carry the investigative ball now. He reminded Bronfman that the WJC had on its staff someone who "knew the ropes," who had handled investigations "just like this one" for the U.S. government.

Bronfman countered that there had never been a case "just like this one." The subject of the proposed investigation was the former

Secretary-General of the U.N., who was now running for the presidency of Austria! This latter fact posed a particularly delicate problem. If the WJC attempted to expose the candidate prior to the Austrian election, the move might be seen as political mudslinging on the part of Jews who held a grudge because of Waldheim's past actions on Middle East issues. As a result, it might well backfire. On the other hand, if we waited until after the election, we could be accused of being party to a cover-up. The issues were sticky and Bronfman needed time to think about them.

Singer left the memo with Bronfman and, disappointed with the lack of an instant decision, sped off to other business.

There was little for me to do but wait. Back at the WJC offices at Thirty-third Street and Park Avenue, I found the delay excruciating.

Three hours passed before a courier arrived with an envelope containing a single slip of paper. It was my memo. Below the typed text was a terse notation, in Bronfman's hand: Do it. —EMB.

My first move was to fire off a Freedom of Information Act request to the U.S. Army's Intelligence and Security Command, asking for copies of "all records, documents, and materials in the possession of the Department of the Army referring or relating to" Artur Phleps and Kurt Waldheim.

Next I turned my attention to the Podgorica photograph and the photocopy of the Wehrmacht newspaper. Who could be trusted to test these materials thoroughly and professionally, and at the same time safeguard our secret? I called Neal Sher at OSI, to pick his brain. To do so, I had to tease him with a bit of information regarding my finds in Vienna. He was fascinated. What I needed right now, I said, was someone to authenticate a photograph.

He suggested David Crown.

"David Crown *of the CIA?*" I asked. "He's not allowed to take private work." I knew Crown as the longtime chief of the CIA's Questioned Document Laboratory.

"He retired a while back," Sher explained. "He's been in private practice for a couple of years now. And he's the best there is, Roosevelt."

Within minutes, I had Crown on the phone at his laboratory in a Virginia suburb of Washington. I gave him a summary of the task: We had some wartime Nazi photos purporting to show a man who later became "a major European politician." Could he authenticate the photos, certify that they were unaltered, and perhaps even establish that the subject in question was the man we suspected? He responded with immediate interest. I sensed that his private work was not nearly as intellectually satisfying as his CIA assignments had been.

He asked how the subject was facing in the photos.

"In one, his face is basically in profile," I replied. "In the other, he's facing the camera."

"Okay, fine. Can you get some confirmed shots of the man, preferably including some profiles, to make a comparison?"

"I've got some confirmed photos of our subject from before and during the war, and I'm sure I can track down some pictures of him from the seventies."

"Excellent," Crown said. "How soon can you get the stuff to me?"

I told him that it would take a few days to put together a package. When it was ready, I would arrange for it to be hand-delivered.

I was delighted when, on his own initiative, Crown promised to set aside the rest of his work and concentrate on my project until he had results, he said, "one way or the other."

When I reported to Singer, he made it clear that, in light of the WJC's precarious financial situation, we would have to have a "darn good reason" to pay Crown for more than two days' worth of work.

I added to the boss's budgetary worries. "If we intend to continue to be a global organization in the modern world," I said, "we need to enter the twentieth century."

"What do you mean?" he asked.

"We need a computer."

Singer grimaced. He was not a creature of the electronic age. Our major concessions to technology, thus far, were a telex, a copying machine, and a modest supply of aging IBM Selectrics. But Singer almost always bowed to reality, even if he did not like it. "Okay," he said with a sigh of resignation.

"And we need a fax machine, too."

"A what?"

I explained that the device was an improved version of the old, justly despised telecopier.

Singer exhaled deeply. Perhaps because the WJC had that word "World" in its letterhead, listing offices in New York, Paris, Geneva, London, Buenos Aires, Rome, and Jerusalem, outsiders often had the mistaken impression that it had a giant staff and global resources. In fact, our headquarters office in New York consisted of but a dozen people (most of them support staff) toiling in cramped, rather dingy, fourth-floor quarters well away from the fashionable districts of Manhattan. The bulk of our resources came from Bronfman's beneficence. Singer had to watch the pennies with care. He stared at the ceiling for a moment, then said softly, "Go get what you need."

* * *

The next day, Tuesday, I visited the New York Public Library, where I tracked down a copy of an interview that Waldheim gave to editors of the West German newsweekly *Der Spiegel* shortly after his election to the top U.N. post. The magazine's editors expressed their surprise that the Soviet Union had not vetoed his election, since he had participated in the Nazis' bloody 1941 invasion of the USSR.

Waldheim had brushed the issue aside with typical aplomb. His war record was irrelevant, he told the magazine. His military service was involuntary, and he had come from an anti-Nazi family. He hastened to add his standard disclaimer: "I was wounded already in 1941, and from then on was unfit for military service." I labored over the German text and finally realized that Waldheim had made an interesting selection of words. He declared that he was rendered *Nichts Kriegsdienstverwendungsfaehig,* "unfit for military service." He had not used the narrower term *Nichts Frontdienstverwendungsfaehig,* "unfit for service at the front."[9] More clearly than ever, he had claimed that he was out of the military altogether after 1941.

Waldheim gave an even more categorical account in an interview with the *New York Times* in 1981 when the newspaper was preparing a profile of the then U.N. Secretary-General. I found the article in the library's microfilm collection of *Times* back issues. "Fortunately, I didn't last long," Waldheim told the paper in answer to a question about his World War II service in the Wehrmacht. "My unit moved to the Russian front in the winter of 1942. I was badly wounded in the ankle, I couldn't walk, and they gave me a medical discharge."[10]

While I worked at the library, Steinberg struck pay dirt at New York's legendary Strand Bookstore, returning to the office with copies of two earlier Waldheim books, *The Austrian Example* (1971) and *The Challenge of Peace* (1977).

In the 1971 book, Waldheim made a single, low-key reference to the Holocaust, specifically to Austrian Jews who had waited too long to emigrate. These unfortunate Jews, he said, eventually realized an "uncertain fate."[11] Ever the circumspect Austrian, he did not spell out what that fate was, but he did append a superscript numeral referring the reader to a back-of-the-book note. Steinberg flipped to the endnotes and read aloud: "See Gerald Reitlinger, *The Final Solution: The Attempt to Exterminate the Jews of Europe 1939–1945.* London, 1953."

Steinberg threw back his head and laughed. Waldheim was referring his readers to the very book that characterized his apparent wartime commander, General Loehr, as "perhaps more implicated in Jewish deportations than any other Wehrmacht commander," and contained ten pages of gory text detailing the involvement of Army

Group E, Waldheim's apparent unit, in the deportation to Auschwitz of fifty-four thousand Jews.

In *The Challenge of Peace* we found a slightly more complete self-description of Waldheim's activities after his leg wound. He wrote of the difficulties of completing his law school studies during wartime, asserting that the police were "suspicious" of his "civilian status." He detailed how he had met and married Elisabeth and how, near the end of 1945, she "sought refuge in the countryside of Styria to await our first child. . . ."[12]

I shook my head in dismay at the pattern of his accounts. "Elan," I said, "either we're on the trail of one of the great deceptions of all time or else we're completely wrong, and the guy spent all of '42 through '44 back in Vienna."

Steinberg responded without a missed beat: "For that to be true, the Podgorica photo would have to be a forgery."

6

The telephone woke me from a stuporous sleep. Karl Schuller was calling. It was Wednesday, February 12, 1 P.M. in Vienna and 7 A.M. in New York.

"We just got the results from the West Berlin archives, and they are marvelous documents, really," Schuller gushed.

Sleep left me. "Yes?"

"They tell some very interesting things about our friend. You know who I mean, okay?"

Of course I knew, and I also knew that Schuller did not want to mention Waldheim by name during a transatlantic call. "What have you got, Karl?" I asked.

"We have obtained the medical records from the Wehrmacht 45th Infantry Division on which is recorded our friend's medical leave at the end of 1941. He has at least told the truth about one thing. He did go into the hospital in December 1941—on December 18, to be precise."

"And then?"

"The same archives have the medical records of the 12th Army. And there we find the date on which our friend's medical leave *ended*. The document says that our friend, who wants us to think that he was away from the war at least until late 1944, finished his medical leave on March 14, less than ninety days after he was injured! And he became a staff member of the 12th Army by June 1942." Schuller explained that the Wehrmacht's 12th Army was one of the predecessors of Loehr's Army Group E.

"Are you sure, Karl?"

"One hundred percent. Now he is trapped!"

Waldheim's 1977 claim that he returned to "civilian status" following his 1941 leg injury suddenly came to mind. I had not expected the truth to be so definitively documented, nor so easily obtained. "Karl," I shouted into the phone, "that means that he was back in uniform a *full year before* the May '43 meeting in Podgorica, right?"

"*Ja,* that is correct. It means that our friend was never away from the Wehrmacht for more than a few months! It is almost unbelievable that he could have gotten away with such a deception for so long, is it not?" Schuller did not wait for an answer, for he had more information to impart. He said that he had obtained two documents from the Austrian archives that confirmed Waldheim's membership in the S.A. One of them disclosed another important fact. "It looks like our friend actually managed to distinguish himself in the Wehrmacht. I am looking at a document now that says he won four medals during the war, in 1941 and 1942. I am going to try to find out what those medals were usually awarded for."

At the office later that morning, I returned a call from Pat Treanor, a brilliant young historian and former colleague of mine at OSI. I had phoned him earlier to ask a question concerning a friend-of-the-court brief I was writing for the WJC in support of the government's position in an OSI case that was on appeal. As long as I had Treanor on the phone, I decided to ask him whether he knew anything about *Unternehmen Schwarz,* the "Black Operation," the apparent subject of discussion at the Podgorica meeting. Abruptly, Treanor put me on hold. He returned only a few minutes later and advised that in one of his histories of the war in Yugoslavia, he had located a pertinent reference. Professor Jozo Tomasevich of San Francisco State University wrote that the chief aim of *Unternehmen Schwarz* was the annihilation "of all partisans in Montenegro and Sandjak." The campaign had pitted 117,000 Axis troops, under the command of General Lueters, against a mere 19,000 partisans. The author noted that the summary execution of partisans "probably reached its peak during Operation *Schwarz."* He cited Lueters's order of May 5, 1943:

> The troops must move against the hostile populace without consideration and with brutal severity, and must deny the enemy any possibility of existence.[1]

The professor summarized another captured Wehrmacht document, which reported twelve thousand "communists" killed and fifteen hundred taken prisoner. In one month's time, the Axis troops wiped out 70 percent of the resistance fighters in Montenegro.[2]

So the operation really had been aptly named. What we did not know, however, was what role Waldheim might have played in it.

The next few days were crowded with activity. I labored to put together the package of materials Crown needed for his photo analysis. Meanwhile, with Singer's approval, I implemented the next phase of our plan, contacting Ralph Blumenthal of the *New York Times.* He reviewed my materials, discussed them with his editors, and reported that they, and he, were "very interested." I promised the *Times* access to all of our evidence on the condition that he protect Schuller's identity. Blumenthal agreed readily. He told me that he would pursue the story on this side of the Atlantic and turn the European end over to the paper's Bonn bureau.

Here, we ran into a serious problem. James Markham, chief of the Bonn bureau, was enthusiastic about the story, but balked at protecting Schuller. He did not like the fact that the attack on the People's Party candidate emanated from a Socialist, and saw no reason to withhold the identity of the source, even though his newspaper would verify the authenticity of any evidence prior to publication. A series of phone calls and meetings ensued. In the end, Markham's New York editors required him to go along with my stipulation, but the episode aroused my concern. Once Schuller overcame his early reticence, he had bared himself to me, arguably placing his life in my hands. It was a responsibility that weighed heavily on me.

Markham assigned reporter John Tagliabue to the story. He was currently in Rome, covering the trial of Mehmet Ali Agca, the would-be assassin of Pope John Paul II. As soon as he could break free from that assignment, Tagliabue promised, he would rendezvous with Schuller and me in Vienna. Until then, we would continue to search for more evidence.

Exhaustion overtook me as the weekend approached. I looked forward to a few quiet days with Cynthia. She was an attorney whom I had met when I worked in Washington at the Justice Department. We had fallen in love and now, separated by a one-hour shuttle flight between National and La Guardia airports, we saw each other as frequently as we could.

Cynthia flew to New York on Friday evening. Expecting a social weekend, she instead found me working on the floor amidst an assortment of World War II histories, engrossed in the texts. Small talk was beyond me.

I swore her to secrecy and told her everything that had happened. Within minutes, she too was enmeshed in the intrigue.

In the early afternoon hours of Monday, February 17, a taxicab sped from Washington's National Airport to a private home in Fairfax, Virginia. Following my instructions to the letter, Cynthia delivered a small package to the man awaiting her arrival, jumped back into the cab, and was gone.

David Crown, retired chief of the CIA's Questioned Document Laboratory, examined the contents of the package he had just received: the original Podgorica SS photograph, a copy of the photo in the Wehrmacht newspaper *Wacht im Suedosten,* and several confirmed photos of our subject, taken from various angles. He was astonished to realize that the "European politician" we were investigating was none other than Kurt Waldheim.

Crown set to work, knowing that there was no room for error. Almost immediately he ruled out any possibility of authenticating the newspaper photograph, for its image was imprecise; the original newsprint would be difficult enough to work with, and this was only a photocopy.

But the Podgorica print held potential. Examining it under magnification, Crown found no evidence of retouching or substitution. Comparison of the right ear, nose, and facial outline of the man identified as *Oberleutnant* Waldheim with known photos of our subject showed a clear correlation in anatomical structure, and not a single apparent inconsistency.

Studying the caption on the reverse side of the photo, Crown was able to determine that the typewriter was of German origin, probably an Olympia, but possibly a Rheinmetall, Diplomat, Kappel, Erfurt, or DM. His reference works told him that all machines with this typeface were manufactured between 1931 and 1949. A cloth ribbon was used. The paper did not fluoresce, and this was reassuring; fluorescent paper was not used until after the war.[3]

But there was one major problem. The paper was imprinted with the manufacturer's logo "Agfa Brovira." Crown knew Agfa as a giant German photographic firm that was in business before and during the war, but he had never encountered the "Brovira" designation. He telephoned several of his colleagues and inquired discreetly, but none of them had heard of it either. His reference books did not mention "Brovira."

Crown called me with the mixed news. "The typing looks good," he advised. But unless and until he could answer this nagging "Brovira" question, he could not, in good conscience, vouch for the authenticity of the photograph. "Listen, Eli," he asked, "what about your contacts in Austria? They've got more on these wartime photographic papers than we've got over here."

It was a major problem, I replied. Perhaps police labs in Austria or Germany *could* tell us about the "Brovira" brand of photographic paper, but they were sure to ask the one question we had to avoid: What was the reason for the inquiry?

I was treading water, hoping that Crown could come up with something, waiting to hear from Tagliabue in Europe, wondering what more Schuller might unearth.

In the meantime, I turned my attention to the speculative subject of whether Waldheim might have been compromised by the Soviet and/or Yugoslav intelligence services. If there was a connection, how far back did it go? Waldheim's own *Im Glaspalast* . . . memoirs provided the first clue. He wrote that four months after the end of the war in Europe, he moved with his wife and baby daughter from the province of Styria to rejoin his parents in Baden. In the process, he crossed from the American occupation zone to the Soviet sector.[4] Thus, immediately after the war, he was subject to Soviet authority—and scrutiny.

I knew that the Soviets had actively recruited ex-Nazis during this period, in Austria and elsewhere. An American diplomat named Hugh Gibson complained bitterly in 1947 about the U.S.'s "bungling denazification procedure" which made it possible for ". . . any former Nazi, no matter how obnoxious," to "obtain absolution by walking into the Russian zone and applying for registration as a Communist . . . no questions."[5] Individuals implicated in some of the most heinous Nazi crimes had become KGB agents and assets.

Even after the occupation ended, the Soviets maintained a strong covert presence in Austria. In a biography of the late West German intelligence chief Reinhard Gehlen, I read of Vienna's transformation into a major operational base for Soviet intelligence (a status that the city still retained in 1986). The authors wrote that KGB operations were facilitated there by the fact that "the communists had a foothold in the Austrian police." So thorough was the Soviet penetration of the Austrian *Staatspolizei* that Gehlen's U.S.-backed agents in Vienna were warned that they were "threatened with danger" not only from the Soviets, but also from the Austrian police.[6]

What was Waldheim doing during these years? I knew from his memoirs and his *Who's Who* entry that he had already joined the Austrian Foreign Service as confidential secretary to the Foreign Minister and almost immediately became a member of the team that was negotiating with the Allied forces—including the Soviets—to forge the terms of the treaty that would restore Austria's sovereignty. While not the head of the Austrian team, Waldheim was an important player. In the process, he visited Moscow for more than a month during the spring of 1947. The Austrians fought fiercely against proposals calling for them to pay compensation to Jews. Austrian Foreign Minister Karl Gruber explained gamely in 1955 that this was because the Arab nations had threatened to oppose Austrian interests at the U.N. if the Austrians agreed to make such payments.*[8]

---

*Later in 1986, Gruber would be quoted as stating that the real reason for his opposition was that reparations would create "a danger of arousing afresh the embers of anti-Semitism."[7]

The multinational negotiations dragged on for years. One of the biggest snags was that both the Soviet Union and Yugoslavia coveted chunks of Austrian territory. Tito, for example, vigorously pressed Yugoslavia's claim to portions of Carinthia and Styria. The Yugoslav booklet Schuller had shown me, detailing the war crimes of "Austria and the Austrians," was issued in 1947, during the height of this diplomatic battle. The fact that it was published in English, rather than German, suggested that it was intended to be part of the negotiation strategy. I could visualize Waldheim's horror at seeing that booklet and its descriptions of grotesque crimes attributed to men with whom he had (evidently) served.

Did the Yugoslavs know of a link between the infamous Loehr and the confidential secretary of the Austrian Foreign Minister? If they did, it was almost a given that the shrewd Tito would have used that knowledge to his advantage.

But who knew what about Waldheim? It was a question that brought easy speculation, but no hard answers. In 1948, after Tito split from the Eastern Bloc, the Soviets withdrew their support of Yugoslavia's territorial claims and, one year later, backed off from their own demands. Why? In one of his books, Waldheim explained that the turning point came when Austria agreed to a package of "economic concessions," originated through American mediation, which included a payment of $150 million to the Soviet Union, plus the rights to 60 percent of all crude oil production as well as certain other mining rights and petroleum refining facilities.[9]

It was a steep price. How had the Soviets managed to drive such a hard bargain? Had they, perhaps, enjoyed the priceless advantage of knowing—from a "friend" inside the Austrian negotiating team— precisely how far Vienna was willing to go?

And what about the later years, when Waldheim rose to international prominence? If Waldheim had been compromised in the early postwar years, he would be unlikely to be allowed to slip off the hook later. Schuller had already provided dramatic evidence that Waldheim might have caved in to the Soviets during the "Prague Spring" of 1968. But was there evidence that the Soviets and/or the Yugoslavs had improperly influenced Waldheim during his decade as U.N. Secretary-General?

On this subject, I found a few tidbits in Waldheim's most recent memoirs, beginning with an account of his professed surprise that the Soviets would support his candidacy. According to Waldheim, the first clue came during a luncheon at the Soviet Mission in Manhattan, on Sixty-seventh Street, hosted by longtime Soviet U.N. representative Jakob Malik. To his amazement, wrote Waldheim, "I found myself placed at his left hand." Malik noted Waldheim's surprise at this honored position and said with a smile: "You see, I put you nearer to my heart."[10]

Later, Malik made a special point of expressing his enthusiasm over Waldheim's election. He declared to the General Assembly:

> To succeed U Thant is not an easy task. But I am confident that Mr. Kurt Waldheim, our new Secretary-General, will do so with credit and honour for himself, his country, and for the entire United Nations system. I would like to . . . assure him that we will do our utmost to lighten his burden and to work closely with him . . . [11]

If the Soviets were determined to be friendly with Waldheim, the Yugoslavs, it seemed, would not be outdone. Reflecting upon his association with Tito, Waldheim reminisced that he was a "frequent guest" of Tito's at Brioni, the Yugoslav leader's impressive two-island vacation complex in the Adriatic. Waldheim found the Marshal to be a "frank" host who "always impressed me with his straightforwardness."[12] How frank? I wondered. How straightforward? What did the two men talk about?

Elan Steinberg, himself an experienced U.N. hand, told me that Waldheim's longtime press spokesman—and virtual shadow—at the U.N. was Rudolph Stajduhar, one of Tito's partisan fighters during the war!

Perhaps the most fascinating view of Waldheim during these years was contained in the memoirs of Arkady Shevchenko, the former U.N. Under Secretary-General, who, in 1978, became the highest-ranking Soviet official ever to defect to the West. Shevchenko wrote of receiving his instructions from the KGB when he was first posted to the U.N. in 1973. His contact reminded him that the U.N. "is our best watchtower in the West," a place where Soviet agents "collect valuable information." Shevchenko's first responsibility, the agent said, was to promote the advancement of KGB officers within the U.N. Secretariat, and to protect them in the event they came under suspicion.

According to Shevchenko, before his departure to New York, he suggested to Boris Ivanov, head of the KGB's foreign operations directorate, that he might try to exert influence on Waldheim. The KGB official grinned and told him not to spend too much time at that task, declaring that it was impossible to "reeducate" Waldheim. "He's no ally of ours," Ivanov reportedly said. "He never will be."

Shevchenko claimed that the Soviets simply viewed Secretary-General Waldheim as "the best they could expect" in the post.[13]

The purported Ivanov comment raised myriad questions. Was Ivanov leveling with Shevchenko? If the Soviets already "owned" Waldheim, it would be enough for Malik and/or the KGB's New York station chief to know. Perhaps Shevchenko had no "need to know." Or perhaps he knew more than he reported. Or perhaps there was nothing to know.

On the surface, Waldheim, like the majority of his countrymen, was Western-oriented—he had even taken up arms against what Hitler called "the Bolshevik devil." But was there something else here, far beneath the surface? The Soviets could never have allowed such an asset (if, indeed, that was what Waldheim was) to swing overtly to their side, lest his cover be blown. *If* they worked him, it would have to have been done with the greatest subtlety.

What did the record show? It seemed to me that Waldheim, as U.N. Secretary-General, had possessed one special power that Moscow coveted: significant authority over filling staff positions at Secretariat headquarters. Shevchenko admitted in his book that his primary task was to install and protect KGB agents within the Secretariat. It was an open secret that U.N. headquarters was the KGB's principal outpost of operations in the United States. U.N. staffers were not subject to the mobility restrictions placed on Soviet Embassy and consular personnel, and could travel freely about the country in cars bearing American license plates.[14] A U.N. Secretariat post was a KGB agent's fantasy. Article 100 of the United Nations Charter requires all U.N. employees to sign a document pledging "not to receive instructions . . . from any government or other authority external to the Organization," but there was no real prescreening of prospective personnel. The result was that many Soviet employees of the U.N. were caught engaging in acts of espionage.

Further research revealed that the percentage of U.N. positions in New York filled by Soviet nationals grew dramatically during Waldheim's two-term tenure as Secretary-General, a phenomenon that led to embarrassing problems.[15] According to some critics, Waldheim had been personally responsible for turning the U.N.'s Russian Interpretation Section and Russian Translation Service into important Soviet espionage cells, by authorizing an exception to the settled U.N. practice of hiring personnel for these units solely on the basis of ability. After the change, new hires were exclusively Soviet nationals—even though a huge number of qualified Soviet émigrés lived within the New York metropolitan area.[16]

During the Waldheim regime, Shevchenko wrote, the Secretary-

General's "willingness to help the Soviet Union" brought "substantially increased numbers" of Soviets into the Secretariat. Waldheim "readily agreed" to the Soviet's "five-year plan" to fill professional posts in the Secretariat.[17]

As time passed, the Soviets expressed growing satisfaction with Waldheim's soft position on human rights questions—as Shevchenko put it, "displaying caution and trying to avoid complications with us." Harsher critics preferred the adjective "spineless." Once, Waldheim went so far as to require the removal of Soviet dissident Aleksandr Solzhenitsyn's works from the bookshops at the U.N. building in Geneva.[18] Shevchenko quoted a Soviet Foreign Ministry report on Waldheim, prepared for the Politburo, that concluded: "Waldheim listens to our demands and advice."[19]

My reading suggested that the symbolic culmination of the Waldheim/Soviet relationship might have occurred in 1977, when Waldheim journeyed to Moscow at the invitation of the Soviet government. He held talks with Foreign Minister Andrei Gromyko, who noted that he "was pleased" with how the U.N. was carrying out its mission. According to a Soviet report, Waldheim said that he considered it to be a great honor to visit the Soviet Union in the year of the sixtieth anniversary of the October Revolution. At Moscow's Lomonosov State University, Waldheim was presented with an honorary Doctor of Science degree. Finally, on September 12, Waldheim presented ailing Soviet dictator Leonid Brezhnev with the gold United Nations peace medal, along with a citation that praised the brutal Brezhnev for his "considerable and fruitful activities in favor of universal peace and peoples' security." Shevchenko wrote that Brezhnev accepted this honor "with childlike delight."[20]

The German-language edition of *Im Glaspalast . . .* carried a photograph of the event. To me, it seemed that Brezhnev had a most unusual smile on his face as he gazed into Waldheim's eyes—part conspiratorial, part condescending. Perhaps it was just my overactive imagination that made me laugh out loud when I saw it.

The high point of the Shevchenko book was the account of his defection. He recalled that, on hearing of this decision, Waldheim summoned him for a private meeting. The defecting Soviet described his boss as "noticeably tense" until Shevchenko gave a negative response to Waldheim's plaintive query, "No one pressured you into this, did they?"

Shevchenko's account of Waldheim's tenure had a suspicious smell to it, and I suggested to Blumenthal that he try to interview Shevchenko, now living under a CIA-arranged identity, to see what more he might be willing to say about Waldheim. Blumenthal accepted the challenge.

Then I turned my attention to Waldheim's activities on the Russian front in 1941. I saw this as back-burner work, principally because Waldheim had never concealed this aspect of his war service; despite the tantalizing items Schuller had found concerning the *Himmelfahrtskommandos,* I doubted whether we would discover any additional damaging evidence in this arena. In his own writings, Waldheim had even provided us with the name of the small unit in which he served, "V.A. 45."

Indeed, a closer look at Schuller's materials now revealed serious conflicts. One document placed Waldheim's unit at "Hof Buda," but it made no reference to any possible war crime. Another document reported the annihilation of eleven thousand "plunderers and soldiers in civilian clothes," but it did not mention Waldheim's unit; this second incriminating document further confused the issue by referencing a locale called "Buda-Andrejewka." Neither of the two "Budas" was listed in my atlases, so it was impossible to determine whether they might be the same place, but there was reason for doubt. "Hof Buda" translates as "Buda estate," and it was common to name estates after their owners. "Buda-Andrejewka" seemed to indicate one or more villages. Key links were missing here.

An attack of nerves hit me. We had too many blind alleys. We needed a break—and soon.

A medium-sized one came on Thursday in the form of a welcome phone call from John Tagliabue, who announced that he was ready to get started. I placed another transatlantic call and set the details. On Saturday, two days hence, Schuller would meet with the *Times* reporter and me in Vienna.

In the meantime, I addressed a very basic question: Who was this man, Kurt Waldheim? I had already begun to develop a dossier of sorts.

At the U.N., obsessed with protocol and known for his explosive temper, the haughty Waldheim had been decidedly unpopular with the staffers. Shevchenko characterized him as a man who presented a "stiff and dry" appearance, one who loved to be the center of attention, driven by an amalgam of "personal ambition" and dedication to U.N. goals. The Soviet defector's view of Waldheim was that of an autocratic workaholic who had difficulty delegating authority; he would agree with the periodic suggestions of his "charming, intelligent wife" to trim his workload, then "inevitably go right on as before." Shevchenko said it was the norm for his associates to wait "half an hour or more" for scheduled meetings to begin, whereupon Waldheim would enter the room with "a self-important expression . . . a half-smile," and a polite apology.[21]

Author Shirley Hazzard, one of the few to raise suspicions about Waldheim's past during his U.N. tenure, had characterized him as obtuse, self-interested, and untruthful, with an insensitivity to human rights issues that made him the "consummate expression" of the world body's preference for leaders distinguished by their "lack of moral courage and independent mind."[22]

Martin Mayer, in his 1983 book *The Diplomats*, had charged that Waldheim was "universally loathed" by U.N. personnel, and characterized him as a man who turned the lives of his coworkers into "a special hell" every autumn as he awaited the announcement of the winner of the Nobel Peace Prize. Each winter, Mayer added, Waldheim was in "a state of fury" over not receiving the award. Mayer wrote that Waldheim "was a dour and self-important presence" in the general manager's box of the Metropolitan Opera.[23]

The descriptions painted a partial, enigmatic portrait. Waldheim was known throughout the world, yet he was a shadow. A British magazine characterized him as "colorless," and observed that the most telling fact about Kurt Waldheim "is that there are no stories about his past."*

---

*Later, after the facts of Waldheim's cover-up were made public, former colleagues came forward with additional reminiscences, most of them decidedly unflattering. For example, Brian Urquhart, former U.N. Under Secretary-General, described Waldheim as "an energetic, ambitious mediocrity" who demonstrated determination and courage, but lacked "vision, integrity, inspiration, and leadership." Urquhart said that he and his colleagues saw Waldheim as a man of two distinct personalities. One was a "scheming, ambitious, duplicitous egomaniac." The other was a "statesmanlike leader."[24]

Robert Rhodes James, who served in Waldheim's executive office from 1972 to 1976 and subsequently became British Member of Parliament, remembered the Secretary-General as a man whose moods varied severely, from "charming, kind, and even amusing" to "hysterical, bullying, boorish, and brutal." According to Rhodes James, Waldheim was quick to claim credit when things went right and equally quick to blame others for problems and failures. "His vanity was colossal," he reported. Rhodes James drafted Waldheim's speeches, and learned never to make a reference to the late U.N. Secretary-General Dag Hammarskjöld, lest he arouse the jealous wrath of the boss. Rhodes James added later, "I've never met anyone who actually liked him."[25]

A few other glimpses of the man came through. Waldheim was "a stiff, angular, and solitary figure" with "the hide of a rhinoceros." He was a man with "a rubber hose instead of a backbone." His Manhattan home was adorned with works of art. One Austrian diplomat, writing anonymously, mentioned that when Waldheim was U.N. Secretary-General, he sent shipments of American toilet paper home to Austria in diplomatic pouches; later, he continued to import the material to Vienna, so that he would not have to use the rough, Austrian-made product. A UNESCO official opined that Waldheim was elected to his U.N. post because the important nations "wanted a nobody."[26]

7

Karl Schuller's home in the Vienna suburbs could have been a middle-class residence almost anywhere in the United States. On this Saturday morning, bright sunlight glared off white snowdrifts and streamed inside through large windows. Over coffee, in this cozy setting, Schuller, *New York Times* reporter John Tagliabue, and I sat down to discuss Waldheim.

I found Tagliabue to be a personable fellow, and I was pleased to discover that Blumenthal had briefed him well.

Schuller was disappointed to learn of my doubts concerning the usefulness of the 1941 Russian front information, but he was even more worried about David Crown and the "Brovira" question. He expressed little hope of learning anything about wartime photographic papers through his own contacts. And if we could not authenticate the Podgorica photo, our only hope was that Waldheim himself would certify it (as well as the Wehrmacht newspaper photo) as genuine, if and when Tagliabue confronted him. But how likely was it, we wondered, that Waldheim would admit that he posed with an SS general in the middle of the "Black Operation"?

Despite these setbacks, Schuller was excited, for he had many new documents to show us. His "helpers" had somehow obtained, from the *Wehrmachtauskunftstelle* (abbreviated "WASt" in German), the French-run Wehrmacht Information Bureau in West Berlin, copies of certain pages of the central personnel rosters of the 45th Infantry Division and Army Group E. Tagliabue and I were suitably impressed; WASt records are ordinarily unavailable to the public.

The first page revealed that, as of August 1939, Waldheim was already a noncommissioned officer in the 45th Infantry Division. The second page documented his assignment to Reconnaissance Branch 45. The information, by itself, was unimportant, for Waldheim admitted these facts. But both Tagliabue and I were mesmerized by three handwritten notations on the documents, each consisting of a series of initials accompanied by a date, recorded in the customary fashion of European archives. The notations, written as 5.6.72; 5.10.72; and 20.3.79, indicated that someone, or, more likely, several persons, had inspected Waldheim's military records on June 5, 1972, and October 5, 1972—during his second year as U.N. Secretary General—and, many years later but still during his U.N. tenure, on March 20, 1979.

Who was checking on Waldheim's WASt files during those years? And why? Schuller had been unable to get any answers. It was yet another frustrating mystery.

Schuller then showed us the documents that he had told me about over the phone. A 45th Infantry Division report confirmed that Waldheim was hospitalized on December 18, 1941. Interestingly, other soldiers were listed as "wounded," while Waldheim was reported only as "ill." This was consistent with his statement that his leg wound became serious only when infection set in; on the other hand, it did not convey any sense that the condition was serious enough to keep him out of the remainder of the war.

The next document disclosed that Waldheim was transferred to the 12th Army on March 14, 1942. Here it was, then, in black and white: He was reactivated less than three months after his hospitalization. We could now say with absolute certainty that the former U.N. Secretary General had indeed been engaged in a cover-up. He was hiding *something*.

This page, too, had been inspected three times, on dates corresponding closely to the entries we had seen on the other pages. Handwritten notations in the margins indicated that the records had been checked on May 24, 1972; October 3, 1972; and March 20, 1979. If these unknown researchers were aware of Waldheim's longstanding claim that he was out of the war after 1941, they must have discerned the significance of this data, all of which was contained in a single short paragraph on a single page. This document was political dynamite, unequivocally exposing the falsity of Waldheim's standard autobiographical accounts. Who was it that had obtained this information fourteen years ago? And why had they not disclosed it to the world?

We now knew that Waldheim had returned to military service some fourteen months before we found him pictured at Podgorica. What duties had he performed for the Wehrmacht during that time? The personnel records did not indicate his specific assignments, but Schuller was ready with an educated guess.

"I had not focused on 1942 until I saw these documents," he explained. "It wasn't necessary before. But now that we know that our friend was serving in the 12th Army as of the spring of 1942, I decided to see what was the biggest operation going on in the region at that time."

He reached for a war history written by Yugoslav historian Vlado Strugar. "Here at page seventy-seven," Schuller said, "we read about what was going on when Waldheim arrived in the Balkans in March '42. Strugar writes that the Germans, the Croatian Ustashi leaders, and the Italians had agreed to combine their efforts against the Yugoslav resistance." In eastern Bosnia, the Germans and the Italians would work together. In western Bosnia, the Germans and the murderous Ustashi would join forces. In central Croatia, the Croats would handle the partisans by themselves. In Montenegro, the Italians and the Serbian Chetniks would work together.

It was all very confusing, but Schuller, in his methodical style, attempted to clarify things. He continued, "You can see what kind of a 'war' was being fought against the partisans from a Wehrmacht order of March 19, 1942: Mass executions were to be carried out by Wehrmacht troops whenever a single German soldier was killed by the resistance. The most horrible—and the biggest—operation was carried out, Strugar writes, in June and July 1942 in western Bosnia, in the area of Prijedor. Many villages were completely destroyed in reprisals. He also reports that after the Germans finished their armed struggle with the partisans, they rounded up all of the inhabitants—more than fifty thousand people—including all of the children—and sent them to the Croatian death camps. Many of them died on the long marches. Most of the rest were executed after they arrived, or else they eventually died from starvation or disease."[1]

Schuller shivered noticeably as he concluded, "It must have been horrible, really horrible."

Could *this* be what Waldheim was trying so desperately to hide? Once more, we had no way to prove our suspicions. It was simply not enough to know that he was an officer with the 12th Army and/or Army Group E "somewhere in the Balkans." Without ascertaining his specific unit assignments, we could not even place him in the vicinity of known atrocities.

Schuller had still more to show us. The most interesting item was a copy of Waldheim's *Standausweis,* his postwar Civil Status Certificate, which declared him to be the recipient of four wartime medals. The dates of the first three—the Iron Cross, 2nd Class, the Cavalry Assault Insignia, and the Eastern Medal—coincided with Waldheim's Russian front service. But the fourth medal was very different. According to the certificate, Waldheim had received something called the "Zvonimir Medal, in silver with oak leaves," in July 1942, near (Schuller reminded us) the end of the bloody western Bosnia operation. Neither Tagliabue nor I had ever heard of this particular decoration.

Nor had Schuller, until he dug out some information from an old book of Nazi regalia that he now held open. As it turned out, the "Medal of the Order of the Crown of King Zvonimir" was not a German award at all, but rather a Croatian decoration.* According to this directory, the Zvonimir Medal came in three ascending classes: iron, bronze, and silver. And it did not always come with oak leaves. Thus, Waldheim had received the most prestigious version. Schuller jabbed his finger at two lines in the book and declared, "Here it says that the Croatian Hitler, Ante Pavelic, awarded the Zvonimir Medal with oak leaves only in cases in which the honoree had 'served under enemy fire.' "[2]

Schuller slammed the book closed and threw it down on the table in front of us. "So now," he announced, "our Mr. Waldheim, who was not even in the war in '42 and '43, has received a medal from the Croatian war criminal Pavelic right at the time of a big atrocity carried out by Croatian and German troops in western Bosnia. And he has even received it for distinguished service 'under enemy fire'!"

Waldheim's Civil Status Certificate noted that he was fluent in German, Italian, English, and French and had a "slight" knowledge of Serbo-Croatian. Any ability to communicate in Serbo-Croatian raised the possibility that he might have worked directly with the dreaded Croatian Ustashi forces. The theory tallied nicely with his receipt of the Zvonimir Medal, but we knew that we were only speculating.

Schuller could not resist pointing out a humorous element in an otherwise ugly, depressing story. The Civil Status Certificate noted that, in 1968, shortly after he became Austria's Foreign Minister, Waldheim was awarded the "Great Cross of the Yugoslav Flag Order," conferred by Tito himself. With a broad smile, Schuller pointed out that Waldheim was probably the only man ever to receive medals from both Pavelic *and* his archenemy Tito.

It was my turn now. I filled Schuller and Tagliabue in on what I had learned from my own research about the involvement of Loehr and Army Group E in Jewish deportations from Greece. Schuller's eyes widened as he thought through the implications. "This must be researched," he declared. "Right away."

Throughout the conversation, Tagliabue asked incisive questions, often reverting to fluent German. The reporter scribbled detailed notes, for it was he who would attempt to confront presidential candidate Waldheim with our evidence, and with our suspicions. Waldheim, like any other "suspect," would have no way of knowing what evidence we did or did not have. What would he say?

Schuller speculated. He had learned that a reporter from *Profil*

---

*Zvonimir was king of Croatia during the latter part of the eleventh century.

had worked his way into the state archives and examined Waldheim's military locator card, discovering the evidence of the candidate's prewar memberships in the Nazi Student Union and the S.A. Already, the magazine had confronted Waldheim on these matters, which, from what we now knew about the rest of Waldheim's cover-up, could almost be considered minor. Waldheim had stonewalled *Profil*, insisting that the recorded information was simply wrong. On that basis, we had to expect that he would try to deny our even more damaging discoveries, too.

Clearly, Tagliabue had a tough job ahead of him. We were matching wits with someone who was not easily shaken by the evidence of official documents. More ominously, the *Profil* probe had to have put Waldheim on alert. Now he might be suspicious of the *New York Times*'s sudden interest in the Austrian presidential election, and refuse an interview altogether. At the very least, he could be prepared for what we had hoped would be "surprise" questions.

Tagliabue flew back to Rome, to cover the resumed proceedings of the Agca trial. He would try to get an interview with Waldheim later in the week.

I spent two more days in Vienna, photocopying Schuller's latest research findings and trying, unsuccessfully, to unearth additional pertinent data in the local libraries, as Schuller searched for information about "Agfa Brovira" photographic paper. He, too, struck out, and we were left in a tight spot. Our hopes of authenticating the photograph now hinged on a tricky, last-ditch scenario. If Waldheim agreed to an interview with Tagliabue, the reporter would present a copy of the photo and try to get him to concede that it was genuine. How would Waldheim respond to the ambush? Would he continue to play hardball, denying the authenticy of the Podgorica picture? Or would he, suspecting that we were able to prove more than we really could, actually verify the photo for us?

Before I left for home, Schuller dropped one last tidbit in my lap. He had heard "a rumor" from one of his contacts that Waldheim "was supposed to have served in the intelligence unit, the so-called Ic branch, at Army Group E headquarters."

If it was true, if Waldheim had been not merely a run-of-the-mill lieutenant but an intelligence officer, it would potentially place him in the very eye of the Nazi hurricane.

My return flight arrived in New York early on the afternoon of Wednesday, February 26, and I rushed to the office to see if there was word of any new developments.

On my desk I found a pile of paperwork: memos, routine mail, and telephone message slips—much of it having to do with my regular duties. I sighed at the memory of my recent days as a Wall Street attorney, when I had a legion of support personnel to back up my work. Things were very different here at the WJC.

I caught sight of a thin brown envelope in the middle of the stack. Pulling it free, I ripped it open to find the response to my Army FOIA request. A cover letter from Thomas F. Conley, chief of the Freedom of Information/Privacy Office of the U.S. Army's Intelligence and Security Command, reported:

> . . . we have been unable to identify any Army intelligence investigative records about Artur Phleps. However, we have located the enclosed Army intelligence investigative records concerning Kurt Waldheim. A review of the information contained in these records has determined that it is releasable to you.

Enclosed was a copy of Army file number XA 161 471, containing a mere three pages. Page 1 was simply a photocopy of the outside of a manila folder bearing the file number. Page 2 was a photocopy of a routine postwar "personality" file card prepared by the Army's 430th Counter-Intelligence Corps Detachment, which stated that Waldheim was listed, as of June 23, 1948, as "Austrian Representative in Paris, France." In the upper right corner of this card was the designation "S.I. File." Shorthand for "Special Investigation File," it was, despite its significant-sounding name, nothing more than the designation routinely given by the 430th CIC Detachment to entries in its biographic files. Page 3 was a photocopy of a similar file card reporting that Dr. Kurt Waldheim had been born on 21 December 1918 in St. Andrae-Woerdern, Austria.

That was it? I was flabbergasted. Could this really be all the information that the Army Intelligence and Security Command had on file concerning Waldheim? Anyone could learn far more in ten minutes at the tiniest local library.

But there was an additional passage in Conley's cover letter that bore scrutiny:

> During the processing of your request, information was disclosed which originated with another government agency. This office has no authority to release these records and they are being referred, along with your request, for appropriate action under the Freedom of Information Act, and direct reply to you.

My request, the letter continued, had been forwarded to the State Department. This was an invocation of the so-called Third Agency

Rule. Only the originating agency (in this case the State Department) was empowered to release these records—whatever they were. Why, I wondered, did the Army have custody of State Department documents? Had State and the Army been involved in discussions concerning Waldheim? If so, why, and when?

I knew from experience that the answers to those questions might be a long time coming. I had seen FOIA requests languish at the State Department for two years and more. In a week or so, I could expect to receive a form letter from someone at State, advising me that my request had been added to the bottom of its lengthy FOIA processing list.

The "Agfa Brovira" question continued to torment David Crown—until he suddenly remembered one of his own experiences. Near the end of World War II, Crown's Army unit had commandeered a castle in Austria, and there Crown had chanced upon a box of original Nazi photographs, including shots of Reich Armaments Minister Albert Speer and other Nazi VIPs. Crown had kept the photos as souvenirs. Perhaps, he thought now, they could provide some useful points of comparison with the Podgorica photo.

But Crown could no longer recall where he had stored the material. He began a scavenger hunt through the basement, garage, and attic of his Virginia home. At last he found the photographs, and his fingers raced through the stack. He paid no attention to the subjects on the front; he was interested, first, in what was imprinted on the reverse.

Suddenly the "Agfa Brovira" logo leaped out at him, and it was absolutely identical to the imprint on the Podgorica photograph! He turned the print over and found that it was a picture of SS chief Heinrich Himmler inspecting the Mauthausen concentration camp.

He called me immediately to report that he could now verify that every aspect of the Podgorica photo was consistent with a genuine SS product.

I was elated. But I had one question. Was it possible that someone had a stock of old Agfa Brovira paper and was able to print a phony photo on it?

"That's nearly impossible to imagine," Crown replied. "You see, the paper itself goes bad after a while, and then you can't use it for photoprocessing anymore."

"Excellent."

"I'm sending you my final report, along with your originals and my own photos. The bottom line is that I don't detect a single indication that this photograph is anything other than what it purports to be: a 1943 photo of a group of German and Italian officers, one of whom is *Oberleutnant* Kurt 'W.' You're home free, Eli!"

More good news came on the following day, Friday, the last day of the longest February in my memory. Tagliabue telephoned from Rome to report that Waldheim had agreed to an interview on Sunday. I told him, in turn, about Crown's serendipitous find. My news armed the reporter with a strategy. He would first confront Waldheim with the photograph. If Waldheim, for whatever reason, denied that it was real, or that he was the *Oberleutnant* depicted in it, Tagliabue would then disclose that it had been authenticated by the former chief of the CIA's Questioned Documents Laboratory.

We discussed additional issues that should be raised with Waldheim. In particular, I urged the reporter to ask questions about the role of Loehr's Army Group E in the deportation of Jews from Greece, especially those from Salonika. Tagliabue agreed.

If all went well, the *New York Times* planned to run a story on Tuesday, four days from now, along with a reproduction of the sensational Podgorica photograph. Tagliabue asked me to make copies of the most important supporting documents and have them hand-delivered to his editor in New York, along with the original Podgorica photo.

Finally, Tagliabue promised to call me from Vienna on Sunday, immediately after the interview.

"It is already Saturday night here in Vienna, Eli." Schuller's excited voice boomed over the hissing and clicking noises on the phone line. "The new issue of *Profil* goes on sale tomorrow, and certain members of the press have received advance copies of the featured article. You would love it."

"What have they done?" I asked.

"As I predicted, they have revealed our friend's membership before the war in the brownshirts and the Nazi Student Union. They have reproduced his military card in which this was recorded. And, in the same article, they quote their interview with him in which he denies that he belonged to either organization. It is marvelous, really. He looks quite ridiculous!" Schuller burst out laughing.

Recovering his composure, Schuller said that Waldheim had provided *Profil* with a short written statement that supplemented his interview. This, too, denied membership in any Nazi organization. According to Waldheim, the entry on his military identification card "does not agree with the facts." He conjectured that it somehow grew out of his having "participated in a few horsemanship programs sponsored by the Consular Academy." With a guffaw, Schuller added, "So, you see, only his *horse* was a Nazi."

Waldheim also told the magazine's editors that these charges were known as long ago as 1946. He said that his boss at the time, Foreign Minister Karl Gruber, had the anonymous allegations checked by the Austrian State Police, which found them to be "without merit."

This was an unexpected confirmation of the possibility that Schuller had raised during our first meeting, that Gruber had known of his young associate's past. Gruber was close to the U.S. occupation forces. If Gruber knew, the Americans presumably knew too. Yet the skimpy batch of material the Army had just sent to me did not reveal a hint of suspicion of Nazi affiliations. And the CIA, in 1980, had assured Congressman Solarz's office that Waldheim had never belonged to the "Nazi Youth Movement."

The possibilities were enough to make one's head spin. I thought out loud on the phone: "If we take our friend's statement at face value, we can assume that Gruber, and probably the Americans, became suspicious. If, then, Gruber's fears were calmed by a report from the Austrian *Staatspolizei,* this could be further evidence, Karl, of what we have read about the Soviets' strong influence inside the Austrian police."

It was, Schuller shot back, much more than "strong influence." He explained that the chief of the state police from 1945 to 1947, Heinrich Duermayer, was a communist, as were many of his subordinates. So if the state police knew, in 1946, of allegations that Waldheim was involved with the Nazi student movement and had joined the S.A., you could be sure that the Soviets knew. Just as assuredly, they were capable of withholding the information from Gruber and the Americans, if they had a "good reason" to do so.

We moved on to other topics that, to us, were more important. I asked what *Profil* had to say about Waldheim's whereabouts during the war.

"The title of the article refers to our friend's ties to the S.A. brownshirts—and this is what they emphasize for nearly all of the five pages in the story. There is a very short section on the war, and it is just too funny, Eli, really."

"What do you mean?"

"You see, the author—it is this fellow Hubertus Czernin—obviously doesn't understand the full importance of what the magazine has walked into." The article, Schuller explained, mentioned Waldheim's war injury and hospitalization, and then noted that he was transferred to the 12th Army on March 24, 1942. Czernin had unearthed the same 1972 interview that I had found in the West German magazine *Der Spiegel,* the one in which Waldheim had spouted his standard cover story, that he was declared "unfit for military service" after 1941. Czernin contrasted this with the 1942 transfer information, and concluded, in matter-of-fact fashion, that Waldheim's 1972 statement was "false." With that, the *Profil* journalist dropped the cover-up issue. He apparently knew nothing about Waldheim's similar statements over the years, to Solarz, to numerous reporters, in his autobiographical sketches and books, and in his old campaign brochures. Czernin had nailed Waldheim on the comparatively minor offense of concealing his Nazi memberships, but missed the big issue. Or perhaps it was simply that such life-lies were so common among Austrians of Waldheim's generation that this one seemed barely newsworthy.

As Schuller read the highlights of the piece to me, I realized that Waldheim, perhaps believing that Czernin and *Profil* were no match for him, had dropped his guard, allowing some valuable information to slip out. For example, Schuller's people had been trying for weeks to determine Waldheim's assignment within Army Group E. Through *Profil,* the former U.N. chief simply told us. Partially confirming the "rumor" Schuller had heard, Waldheim disclosed that he had served as an *Ordonnanzoffizier* and interpreter in the "Ic" section of Army Group E. He said that his assignment had been to analyze reports "for the Chief" of the "enemy picture," especially as it concerned "combat against the partisans." Waldheim emphasized that he had been "just a lieutenant." *Profil* did not seem to realize it, but Waldheim had just admitted that he had served as a staff officer in the *Intelligence* Branch at the headquarters of an army group of more than four hundred thousand men who occupied nearly all of the Balkans!

"This 'Ic' business is very, very important, I believe," Schuller stressed. "I have spoken this evening with some of my contacts, and they believe that it was the Ic section that was in charge of the selection of hostages—the people who were shot during reprisal actions. But I have not seen any actual documentation of this yet, so we must be cautious."

Another remarkable part of the *Profil* account was the tacit assumption by the author that Waldheim, and Army Group E, were simply involved in traditional combat activities. There was no hint that some of these Wehrmacht troops, under Loehr, committed well-documented atrocities.

"It is also very interesting what *Profil* mentions about our friend's fate after the war when he was near Trieste," Schuller related. According to the article, he spent four weeks in an American P.O.W. camp in the town of Bad Tolz, near Munich.

Here then was an addition to our list of concealments. In his *Im Glaspalast . . .* book Waldheim wrote, ". . . I endeavored to escape being made a prisoner and to reach the homeland."[3] He recounted how he was reunited with his wife and how, some four months later, they and their infant daughter managed the arduous trip back home. The reader was left with the logical impression that his "endeavor" to escape was successful. But what reason would Waldheim have had to conceal a few weeks in a P.O.W. camp? Furthermore, if *Profil's* report of Waldheim's confinement by the Americans was correct, why was it not mentioned in the material I had received only a few days ago from the U.S. Army? True, I knew from experience that such matters as P.O.W. status often (in fact, usually) are innocently omitted from Army intelligence files, but viewed in the context of Waldheim's forty-year cover-up, this generated still more suspicion.

By now I was accustomed to Schuller's penchant for the dramatic; he almost always saved the best for last. In the *Profil* piece, he reported, "our friend identified the city in which he served when he was assigned to Army Group E headquarters. You will love this. It is exactly as we suspected: Salonika! Our friend says he was there in 1942 and then again after he returned—on March 31, 1943, he says—from a study leave. Now it looks like he really might have been in Salonika during some of the Jewish deportations. The *Profil* people didn't even realize that anything bad happened in Salonika, so they didn't ask him about it!"[4]

"Karl, we desperately need to pin him down on the specific dates in Salonika," I said. "And our only chance for that lies in Tagliabue's interview tomorrow. We'll just have to keep our fingers crossed."

On Sunday, Tagliabue became the first member of our tiny team to confront the subject of our research face-to-face, spending three full hours in a bizarre verbal fencing match with Kurt Waldheim. As promised, Tagliabue phoned me immediately afterward with his blow-by-blow account.

The Austrian presidential candidate admitted that he spent most of the period between 1942 and 1944 in Wehrmacht service in the Balkans.

When Tagliabue asked why he had hidden this information for so long, Waldheim boldly denied that he had covered up anything. His recent book, he explained, had never made any claim to be a complete account of his life, and he had not bothered to detail what he termed the "boring" facts concerning his military service. "No one would have read it," he quipped. He quoted from the Foreword to *Im Glaspalast* . . . : "This is not a book of memoirs in the ordinary sense . . ."

Tagliabue was not so easily put off. It was not just a matter of the new book, he replied. It was the consistent pattern of concealment and misrepresentation that ran throughout the years—in, for example, his letter to Solarz, his interviews as Secretary-General with Tagliabue's own newspaper and other publications, and his 1971 Austrian campaign literature.

Waldheim responded that any claim of a cover-up was just pre-election mudslinging.

Tagliabue countered that, with all due respect, Waldheim was not answering the question.

The Socialists were behind any such accusations, Waldheim grumbled. The timing, he added sarcastically, "is perfect."

The source of the allegations was not the issue, Tagliabue repeated.

At that point, Waldheim closed the subject, declaring that such matters were not "relevant" to the current election campaign or to discussions about his postwar record.

Having run into a brick wall on the subject of a cover-up, Tagliabue turned to a discussion of Waldheim's prewar affiliations with the Nazis. Waldheim said that he had learned—only *after* the war—that he had been enrolled in both the S.A. and the Nazi Student Union, but that he had never received membership cards, or any other kind of notification, and he had never considered himself a member. He said that student groups were only involved in social gatherings, coffee parties, and similar innocent activities. He repeated his defense that he had merely taken part in a few riding exercises, and he added that he had done so only to shield his family from political harassment and to be able to complete his studies at the Consular Academy. He repeated what he had told *Profil:* that he had been the subject of an anonymous denunciation in 1946, which caused Foreign Minister Gruber to check out the allegations, and to clear him.

Waldheim's responses to Tagliabue's questions about the war provided the most fascinating material. Yes, he said, he had been in Yugoslavia, but only as a simple interpreter between German and Italian commanders. "The German command gave orders to the Italian units and the Italians gave messages back, and they needed an interpreter," Waldheim protested. "I was not chief of the liaison staff. There was a whole group of interpreters." He asserted that none of the orders he translated involved atrocities, or even major combat operations.

If Waldheim was nothing more than an interpreter in Yugoslavia,

Tagliabue asked, why had he been awarded the King Zvonimir Medal, conferred with oak leaves for "valor under fire"?

It was meaningless, Waldheim replied. The medal was given by the Croatian regime to virtually all German staff members "as a matter of routine."

Waldheim admitted that he served in the 12th Army, and in its successor, Army Group E, under Loehr, as an interpreter and *Ordonnanzoffizier*. But he said it was "absolutely absurd" and "pure nonsense" to attempt to link him to Nazi war crimes. He declared that he was wholly unaware of any atrocities committed by the units in which he had served.

The presidential candidate seemed to be denying too much, and Tagliabue decided that it was time to unleash the heavy artillery. He showed Waldheim a copy of the Podgorica photograph.

The reaction was not quite what we had expected. After our herculean efforts to authenticate the photograph, Waldheim simply admitted that, yes, it was genuine, and that he was the *Oberleutnant* Waldheim pictured with SS-*Gruppenfuehrer* Artur Phleps and the others. But, he insisted, he was merely at Podgorica as an interpreter and, anyway, this happened to be the only time he was ever in Podgorica and the only time he ever met the SS general.

What about the "Black Operation"? Tagliabue asked, the brutal antipartisan "cleansing operation" that was under way at the time of this meeting, terrorizing the towns and villages surrounding Podgorica even as the men posed for the photo?

Waldheim shrugged off the question, denying that he had ever heard of *Unternehmen Schwarz*.

What about General Lueters? Tagliabue asked. Were not Waldheim and the others at the airstrip waiting for Lueters's arrival?

Waldheim said he had never heard of General Lueters.

This was beyond ludicrous. Lueters was the German commander for all of Croatia, and we knew that he was the senior participant in the airstrip meeting.

Tagliabue continued to press. He showed Waldheim the photo we had copied from the front page of *Wacht im Suedosten,* the Wehrmacht newspaper.

Yes, Waldheim admitted, he was the young lieutenant in the photograph with General Loehr. Yes, it was the same Loehr who was later hanged for war crimes. But his own job for Loehr, he said, involved only innocent desk-bound duties. He analyzed reports on enemy troop movements, nothing more.

Tagliabue asked whether Waldheim had been stationed in Salonika when he worked for Loehr.

Yes, Waldheim admitted. He had already said as much to *Profil*.

As I had begged him to do, Tagliabue pressed for the dates. And when Waldheim answered, he backed himself into a corner. He said he was officially assigned to Salonika from April 1943 onward.

Tagliabue jumped on the answer. He asked if Waldheim knew of the Jewish deportations from Salonika that occurred during that very period.

For the first time during the interview, Tagliabue thought his subject appeared agitated. Waldheim maintained that at Salonika he merely sat in an office charting enemy troop movements. He denied even knowing that Jews were deported, much less being involved in the crime, and claimed that this was "really the first time" he had ever heard of "such things."

Tagliabue's account infuriated me. The Salonika episode was one of the most notorious of the Holocaust. Fully a fifth of the city's population disappeared in a short span of time. A huge portion of the merchant class was gone, their stores boarded up. Salonika's distinctively dressed Jews were nowhere to be seen. The leadership of Army Group E had to have been deeply involved in the removal of the Jews, and Waldheim was an intelligence officer in the headquarters branch. Yet he knew nothing about it? The subject never came up during conversations with his colleagues, either then or during the succeeding two years of war? Had he never bothered even to read about it after the war?

Tagliabue had one last issue to address. He asked Waldheim whether any governments had ever used knowledge of his prewar activities or his war record to pressure him.

Angrily, Waldheim denied that any blackmail attempts had ever been made.

His narrative completed, Tagliabue informed me that the *New York Times* had confirmed its intention to go with the story on Tuesday, March 4, based on the findings of our joint investigation. It would be a bigger scoop than we had thought, for the *Profil* disclosures had gone virtually unnoticed outside Austria.

Finally, some five weeks after we began to probe Waldheim's past, the world would learn that the man who once headed the world's most important international body had concealed for more than four decades a Nazi past that included membership in the "Brownshirts" as well as wartime duty in both Greece and Yugoslavia, where he served under some of the most notorious of all Nazi war criminals during periods of unparalleled infamy.

8

On Monday morning, March 3, 1986, the U.N. Commission on Human Rights met at the Palais des Nations in Geneva to debate the sole item on its agenda: "Measures to be taken against all totalitarian or other ideologies and practices, including Nazi, Fascist, and neo-Fascist, based on racial or ethnic exclusiveness or intolerance, hatred, terror, systematic denial of human rights, and fundamental freedoms, or which have such consequences." In their addresses, all of the delegates paid lip service to the fact that the U.N. had been established forty years earlier as a direct response to the world's postwar revulsion at discovering the full magnitude of the Nazis' crimes, and nearly all condemned the apartheid policies of South Africa as well. But much of the discussion was undeniably tragicomic.

The Soviet delegate, Mr. Bykov, bemoaned the fact that the specter of Nazism was still alive. He cited a statistic that only thirty of the thousands of guards at Auschwitz had ever been brought to justice. Too many of the guilty parties, he complained, lived under the protection of Western governments. He lectured his colleagues that harboring war criminals was immoral, inhumane, and contrary to the principles and decisions of the United Nations, adding that the U.N. would not be fulfilling its duty toward the millions of war victims if it did not make every effort to eliminate all manifestations of Nazi ideology. This laudable rhetoric was merely preamble, however, to the delegate's main point. The present-day embodiment of Hitler's evil ideology, he declared, was Zionism. Bykov charged that there was a spiritual, political, and ideological relationship between fascism and Zionism, both of which advocated the Hitlerian ideas of racial purity and expansionism.*

In the midst of this surreal scene, Efraim Dowek, the official Israeli observer, rose to protest. He complained bitterly that the recently

---

*Those of us who monitored the U.N. were accustomed to such slanders on the part of the Soviet government. For example, two years earlier a *Pravda* story had leveled the venomous charge that Zionists had collaborated with the Gestapo in sending Jews to their deaths.

elected vice-chairman of the very commission conducting this meeting, an East German diplomat, had once been a member of the Nazi Party. The Israeli deplored the fact that an ex-Nazi could rise to such a position of prominence within the U.N. infrastructure.[1]

The assembled delegates had no way of knowing that a much more important U.N. figure—a former Secretary-General, in fact—was less than twenty-four hours away from being the subject of a far graver Nazi exposé.

There was a full Monday of calm to wait out before the storm broke on Tuesday. It was important for me to remain within shouting distance of my secretary, in case the New York Times called with a last-minute question or request, but it was nearly impossible to concentrate on my regular work.

I checked the wire services by computer and found a short wire-service dispatch concerning a controversy in Vienna, sparked by the Profil story regarding Waldheim's prewar Nazi affiliations, but the piece said nothing about Waldheim's role during the war. The story quoted Waldheim spokesman Gerold Christian as saying that Profil was simply mistaken: He explained that Waldheim "became incorrectly associated with the S.A." because "he occasionally rode horses" belonging to the group.[2]

There was one "operational" disappointment this day as well: An afternoon call from New York Times reporter Ralph Blumenthal, who informed me that Arkady Shevchenko, the Soviet defector who had been Waldheim's assistant at the U.N., was "unavailable" for an interview.

Shortly after 10 P.M., I emerged from the Times Building, clutching two copies of the early edition of the next day's newspaper. Multi-colored flashes of light from Times Square's colossal neon displays shimmered across the windows of Elan Steinberg's waiting car.

I hopped inside and made no attempt to conceal my excitement from Steinberg and his assistant, Sharon Cohen. "Here it is!" I exclaimed. "It's the front page!"

The headline declared: FILES SHOW KURT WALDHEIM SERVED UNDER WAR CRIMINAL.

John Tagliabue's bylined "Special to the New York Times" story disclosed to the world that the former U.N. Secretary-General had served in a Wehrmacht unit that engaged in "brutal campaigns against Yugoslav partisans" and engineered "mass deportations of Greek Jews." Tagliabue also presented evidence, similar to what had been published in Profil two days earlier, that Waldheim had been a prewar member of two Nazi organizations.[3]

Accompanying the lengthy article was the Podgorica photograph that, even without the rest of the evidence, was enough to prove Waldheim's forty-year deception. The photo credit, printed in tiny letters below what was, of course, an official SS photograph, seemed absurdly incongruous. It read: "World Jewish Congress."

I had visualized this moment for weeks, and now that it had arrived, I discovered that my major emotion was relief—I no longer had to live with the secret. I was particularly glad to see that the *Times* had yielded to my warning about the questionable reliability of the evidence that Waldheim's reconnaissance unit was involved in the 1941 "Buda" massacre in the Soviet Union. We could not afford to give his supporters the opportunity to accuse us of leveling so much as a single unsupported charge.

As Steinberg headed the car south on the F.D.R. Drive toward my apartment, we debated the impact of the story. Perhaps the most obvious point was that the WJC had finished its role in the investigation. The reporters of the free world, having been given the scent, would surely move in and finish the job now. The international media—including the Austrian press, which despite Schuller's pessimism had played a major role in unearthing previous governmental and financial scandals within the country—would badger Waldheim until he at last answered the most basic question, the one he had studiously evaded in his interview with Tagliabue: What was it about your Wehrmacht service that made you so determined to conceal it? Or, put more concisely: Why did you lie?

Continuing our conjecture, we reasoned that the Austrian people, having learned of the cover-up, would demand Waldheim's withdrawal from the presidential race. Steinberg and I compared the situation to Watergate. In that affair, the leader of the world's most powerful nation had been forced to resign his presidency in disgrace after the American people learned that he had lied to them in denying any role in the cover-up of the Watergate burglary.

What, after all, had Richard Nixon really covered up? Steinberg asked, launching a colloquy that we had repeated so often in the past several days that it was beginning to sound like a stage routine.

"After-the-fact knowledge of a fumbled burglary," I replied from the back seat.

"And Waldheim?"

"Service under the Nazis on the headquarters staff of a war criminal."

Steinberg and I knew that many Austrians would sympathize with the circumstances of Waldheim's war experience. But we were also convinced that the electorate would find the forty-year cover-up of those experiences intolerable in a candidate for the presidency.

*   *   *

A few hours later at the Palais des Nations in Geneva, apparently unaware of the *New York Times*'s revelations, a certain Mr. Ogourtsov of the Byelorussian Soviet Socialist Republic delegation rose to address the morning session of the U.N. Commission on Human Rights, which was continuing its discussion of Nazism, Fascism, and neo-Fascism. Remembrance of the Nazi victims, he declared, could not be erased. As long as one Nazi war criminal or one of his protectors walked the earth, he would be accountable "to the court of memory." Ogourtsov charged that evidence was emerging that many war criminals were holding responsible positions in the service of the governments that protected them. The punishment of Nazi war criminals, he asserted, was the world's solemn duty.[4]

If ever there was a mouse that roared, it was the World Jewish Congress, especially in the days after the Waldheim story broke. By Tuesday afternoon, we found our small staff greatly outnumbered by reporters and TV crews.

Outside, street vendors hawked the tabloid *New York Post,* with its screaming front-page headline: EX—UN CHIEF HID NAZI PAST.

Beneath that banner, an enlarged reproduction of the Podgorica photograph filled the balance of the page. Thanks to the wire services, copies of the photograph were now on their way to thousands of newspapers, magazines, and television stations throughout the free world. The powerful image of young *Oberleutnant* Waldheim, standing on the airstrip with Phleps, Roncaglia, and Macholz, had already become a sort of logo for the Waldheim story.

Inside our cramped offices, pandemonium was the order of the day. Reporters descended upon us in search of documentation, especially copies of the *Wacht im Suedosten* photo of Waldheim with General Loehr; it was a powerful companion exhibit to the Podgorica print.

Singer and Steinberg were old hands at coping with press mania. They set up shop in their respective offices, so that they could handle the inquiries two at a time. Over and over, they fielded the same questions.

Who were your sources in Europe?

We are not at liberty to say, they replied.

Are you accusing Waldheim of being a Nazi war criminal?

No, we are accusing him of lying, of perpetrating one of the greatest deceptions of the century.

What does the WJC want from Waldheim?

Singer repeated his practiced answer to this question in front of countless television cameras: "We want him to tell the world why he lied; why he engaged in this cover-up." Singer had questions for others, also. Did the CIA knowingly give false information to Congressman Solarz about Waldheim's Nazi-era past, and if so, why? If the CIA did not know of Waldheim's war record, how could it explain its ignorance? And the most mind-boggling question of all: How could the superpowers have approved such a man to head the U.N.— not just once, but twice?

During the interviews, Singer made no attempt to hide the fact that he was especially offended by Waldheim's statement to Tagliabue that he had never even heard of the Jewish deportations from Salonika until the *New York Times* reporter had informed him—a mere two days ago. "Every dog in Salonika knew what was happening to the Jews," Singer bellowed, working himself into a near-frenzy. "How is it that Lieutenant Waldheim didn't know what every dog knew?"

Singer was further infuriated by something implicit in Waldheim's denial. To believe that he had been unaware of the Salonika deportations, Singer pointed out, one had to conclude that the former U.N. chief had not bothered to read any of the serious works on the Holocaust or even the portions of those works discussing the Nazi crimes of his own army group command. If true, it indicated a numbing callousness.* Singer noted that Waldheim had often boasted of his devotion to the study of history and to the search for its lessons. Yet the former U.N. chief now expected the world to believe that he had ignored the extensive body of literature on the unprecedented Nazi crimes in which his own army group had played so large a role. Surely, Singer asserted, the self-styled "chief human rights officer of the planet Earth" had an obligation to educate himself, at least superficially, about the most notorious human rights violations of the century.

One media question would not go away: Was it the WJC's aim to force Waldheim's withdrawal from the Austrian presidential race? Steinberg formulated a stock answer, designed to prevent Waldheim from accusing us of interfering in Austrian domestic politics: "The only elections we're interested in were those held in 1971 and 1976, when this man somehow was elected and reelected to the position of U.N. Secretary-General."

Singer, Steinberg, and I recited this litany to the press so often that it began to sound, to us, almost like a mantra. But it was so obviously disingenuous that it convinced no one. We very much wanted Waldheim to quit—or be forced from—the race. It was

---

*But, of course, it was not true; Steinberg had already discovered that Waldheim had cited Reitlinger's book in his own writings.

inconceivable to us that any country, and especially one with Austria's history of enthusiastic participation in Hitler's "Final Solution," should have a president who covered up any portion of his German war service—for whatever reason. We saw this as an overt and indecent affront to the memory of the millions who had been murdered by the Nazis.

The election campaign still had two months to go. If Waldheim pulled out now, we felt, the People's Party would have ample time to replace him with another candidate. Certainly the WJC had no sympathy for the ruling Socialist Party. Ever since the days of Chancellor Bruno Kreisky, the Socialist Party's Middle East policy, highlighted by a high-profile relationship with Yasir Arafat's Palestine Liberation Organization, was anathema to most Jews. During the Socialists' long reign in Austria, prosecution of Nazi war criminals in that country had ceased. We would not be displeased if the Socialists lost; only if Waldheim won. In sum, we had no interest in who became Austria's next president, so long as it was not Kurt Waldheim.

While Singer and Steinberg parried with the press, I spent much of my day worrying over the copying machine. The reporters were hungry for documents, and we had been unprepared to service so many requests. I did not trust anyone else to handle our irreplaceable materials, so I supervised the copying myself.

When I finally returned to my office, I flipped through the collection of newspaper articles and wire-service reports that had piled up on my desk, to see what the rest of the world's journalists had to say. Most of them simply reworked Tagliabue's exposé. But my jaw dropped in surprise when I came upon a brief item in the *Financial Times,* the London-based business daily. It was too soon for this paper to have a report on Tagliabue's story, but it did carry a piece by its Vienna correspondent, Patrick Blum, concerning *Profil*'s two-day-old disclosures. There was nothing new in the article, except for the final paragraph, in which Blum wrote that famed Nazi-hunter Simon Wiesenthal had "expressed doubts" about the allegations concerning Waldheim's prewar Nazi affiliations, contending that neither the Soviets nor the Israelis would have allowed Waldheim to become U.N. Secretary-General if there was "any evidence" linking him to the Nazis.[5]

"Has to be a misquote," I muttered to myself. Despite Schuller's warning, it was impossible for me to imagine that Wiesenthal would do anything but join us on the front lines—at least in calling for an explanation from Waldheim. Moreover, the statement attributed to Wiesenthal by the British newspaper was simply inane. Obviously, Simon has been misquoted, I assured myself again. Wiesenthal surely knew that it was hardly a point in Waldheim's favor that the Soviets had pushed for his U.N. election; the Soviets had a long record of exploiting information on the prior Nazi affiliations of Westerners in order to secure their "cooperation." Indeed, in the sixties, Wiesenthal had written entire books on the subject of ex-Nazis, Nazi collaborators, and prewar Fascists whom the Soviets had permitted to rise to positions of power in their East German and Polish satellites. I wondered how Wiesenthal could profess to trust anything the Soviets said or did. This was, after all, the same government whose state-controlled press once "reported" that during the war "Wiesenthal had made a secret deal with the Nazis and had entered their service."[6]

As for Israel's so-called agreement to the Waldheim election, Wiesenthal had to know how that had worked. At the time, Israel was represented in the General Assembly, but not on the Security Council. As was customary, the Security Council presented its nomination as a *fait accompli* and the General Assembly elected Waldheim by acclamation. There was nothing Israel could do about it. Despite this, the Israeli delegation had made no secret of its disappointment that the top U.N. post was entrusted to a former Wehrmacht soldier.

I was prepared to deal with Wiesenthal's ego. I expected him to be furious at us for not contacting him at the outset of our probe. Certainly he would be embarrassed that he had missed a Nazi scandal of international proportions arising in his very own city. And, yes, he had his reasons to hate the Socialist Party. Notwithstanding all of this, Wiesenthal was well acquainted with the first commonsense tenet of criminal investigation: *An individual who conceals something does so because he believes that the truth is damaging.* I was sure that Wiesenthal would demand an explanation from Waldheim. My confidence on this point was bolstered by my knowledge that Wiesenthal was, at this very moment, involved in a major campaign to force Werner Hoefer, popular moderator of the West German television program "*Fruehschoppen*," to respond to what Wiesenthal referred to as "grave charges" that Hoefer had been a member of the Nazi Party and had written for Nazi periodicals during the war.[7] It was obvious that the Waldheim allegations were far more serious. Moreover, Wiesenthal's condemnation years earlier of the Socialist Party for allying itself with Friedrich Peter had been based solely on Peter's service in a *unit* that had committed atrocities; Peter himself had never been personally implicated. I could only conclude that the *Financial Times* correspondent must have swallowed a clever piece of disinformation, perhaps handed out by some People's Party functionary.

Managing to catch Steinberg between television interviews, I showed him the piece. To my surprise, he did not seem especially concerned. "Look, Wiesenthal's a petulant guy," Steinberg offered, "and we've stepped onto 'his' turf. He's just reacting to the *Profil* piece from the weekend, not the story in today's *Times*. Simon'll be with us. Don't worry."

Upon reflection, I had to agree. I had forgotten that, at this point, we knew so much more than Wiesenthal did. All he had to go on was the relatively insipid *Profil* article.

But as Steinberg stepped in front of yet another television camera and I walked back to my office, misgivings returned. To be sure, the *Profil* piece was nowhere near as damaging as Tagliabue's article, but *Profil's* disclosure that the former Secretary-General of the U.N. had lied for forty years about his membership in Nazi organizations was damning enough. I headed for my computer, to scan the wire services for any additional comments from Wiesenthal.

To my chagrin, I discovered that Reuters was carrying quotes that paralleled what I had read in the *Financial Times*. Wiesenthal told Reuters that he had seen no evidence that Waldheim had joined a Nazi organization, and he said again that if the Soviets had any such information, "they never would have agreed" to Waldheim's elevation to the high U.N. post.[8]

Already our fax machine was spitting out a stream of stories sent by our contacts abroad. Many of the pieces were from the Austrian press. I rushed the German-language articles to Hella Moritz, Singer's remarkable assistant. Often, during the course of one or another frenetic WJC meeting, I had seen her surrounded by a crowd of people, each person chattering out his request or advice in his own particular language. She could somehow manage everything at once, switching from English to Hebrew to Yiddish to German to Italian or French without, to my ears, missing a beat. Now her language skills proved invaluable as she was able to type quick translations for me.

The giant Vienna daily *Neue Kronenzeitung* quoted Wiesenthal rejecting the charges, and added that, according to the Nazi-hunter, not only was Waldheim guilt-free, but so were the units in which he served. Wiesenthal was quoted as saying that German officials had assured him that the units to which Waldheim was assigned had no connection with reprisals or deportations, but were simply "pure combat troops."[9]

I felt sick to my stomach. Wiesenthal was one of the shrewdest men I had ever met. He could not have turned suddenly stupid. Why, then, was he so quick to defend Waldheim? Had we bruised his ego so very badly, or had we simply underestimated his thirst for political revenge against the Socialists? Was this my fault, for acceding to Schuller's demand that Wiesenthal be kept in the dark?

Late in the day, the newswires brought us the first responses to Tagliabue's story from Waldheim's office. The candidate's spokesman, Gerold Christian, angrily denied what he claimed was an implied charge in the *New York Times*/WJC revelations: that Waldheim had been personally involved in war crimes. Tagliabue had made no such accusation, but Christian's statement seemed calculated to lead the uninitiated to believe otherwise. For me, this evoked a Watergate-era memory of President Nixon's infamous "I am not a crook" denial. Here was Waldheim's representative raising the stakes in a big way—from concealment of service in criminal units to personal involvement in Nazi crimes. I worried that we might have been hit with a dastardly masterstroke: The aggressive defense against a nonexistent charge could well divert attention from the simple allegation of a cover-up. Christian had sounded the first notes of what was to become a familiar Waldheim refrain: They call me a war criminal, but where is their proof?

This "straw man" defense proved remarkably successful; to my dismay, countless reporters rose to the bait, clamoring for the WJC's response. Steinberg tried to explain: "We're not saying that Waldheim is Eichmann or Himmler. But no one ever gave Eichmann or Himmler the keys to the United Nations."

I heard the tone of my voice betray my exasperation as I offered my own explanation to another reporter: "We haven't called Kurt Waldheim a Nazi war criminal; we *have* called him a *liar,* and we call on him to explain *why* he lied."

9

Jolted from my early morning drowsiness, I put down my coffee mug and stared at the television screen.

For weeks I had encountered Waldheim only as a name on documents and in the pages of books, magazine articles, and newspaper stories. I had seen static images in old photographs. But now, there he was, on the screen in my apartment. I was transfixed. Waldheim appeared weary to me. Undoubtedly, the rigors of campaigning, compounded by the stress of the past forty-eight hours, had exacted a physical toll. Perhaps it was my imagination, but his features seemed more exaggerated than I remembered them. The nose seemed longer and more pointed. The ears were extended, like antennae. The hairline was disappearing. An attack of facial wrinkles had set in.

But Waldheim was an experienced fighter, whom no one could accuse of a lack of intelligence, intensity, and tenacity. He was ready for the tough questions put to him by Jane Pauley during a live-via-satellite interview on NBC's "Today" show.

Pauley drove straight to the point, asking Waldheim to reply to Bronfman's charge that he had engaged in "one of the most elaborate deceptions" of our time.

"The whole story is invented," Waldheim responded, speaking in adequate, but thickly accented, English. He said that yes, he had served in the Balkans, but as "an interpreter" for the German High Command, "and that was it." He offered an analogy: Surely no one would blame a United Nations interpreter for the content of statements that he translated.

I muttered to myself, "It's the living reincarnation of Goebbels's 'Big Lie.'" Only a few days earlier, Waldheim had admitted to Tagliabue that he was both an interpreter *and* an *Ordonnanzoffizier*.

Pauley reminded Waldheim that he had "always maintained" that his military service ended when he was wounded in 1941.

The response was audacious: "I never said that I wasn't in the German army until the end of the war." Waldheim repeated the old story of his return to Vienna for treatment of a leg wound, then added that, since he was "disabled" from combat, someone had asked him what languages he spoke. When the Germans realized that he was fluent in English and French and spoke some Italian, they shipped him to the Balkans because Italian units were stationed there, alongside German troops.

Pauley approached from another angle, asking Waldheim why the facts of his later military service were "in fact omitted" from his autobiographical accounts.

"Isn't that interesting?" Waldheim snapped. He pointed a long finger at the camera and shook it angrily. "For forty years nobody cared about all this." Not only Austrian intelligence, he said, but "probably the whole international intelligence" community had checked his background carefully and found nothing sinister. But now, because he was a political candidate, someone had made "accusations which are completely untrue."

Apparently deciding that she would not get a straight answer to the cover-up question, Pauley moved on to the subject of the deportation of the Salonika Jews.

"I definitely didn't know anything about the whole thing," Waldheim declared. He repeated his preposterous statement that the first time he had heard of Jewish deportations from Salonika was when Tagliabue raised the issue during their interview the previous Sunday.

Pauley asked the question I wanted to ask: How could he *not* have known?

"Well, it's very simple," Waldheim answered. He was an interpreter in a low-level position. Deportations were not handled by the army. "Those things," he said, were done by "the secret police and other organizations. So I assure you that I had nothing to do with this, and I had no knowledge of it."

The logistical realities of commercial television forced Pauley to end the brief segment. "Well, Mr. Waldheim, thank you for sharing your side of the story with us this morning."

With that, the network cut to a commercial.

I waited impatiently for the break to end. What was next? I wondered. Whom did the show have ready to refute Waldheim's denials? Would Pauley and cohost Bryant Gumbel comment on the absurdity of what they had just heard?

Ninety seconds later, Gumbel's face reappeared on the screen. "Sitting here looking to the half hour ahead," he said, "and I certainly mean no disrespect, but every time you see Ron Howard's name, don't you still think: *Opie?*"

Frustrated, I flipped to the local CBS affiliate where, minutes later, Waldheim appeared for another live interview. "I had not the slightest idea" about deportation of Jews from Salonika, he insisted. He had never been involved in any "cruelties" during his Wehrmacht service in the Balkans. "All I did was to interpret between Italian and German commanders. That was all."

When I reached the office, I found a wire-service dispatch on my desk quoting Waldheim: "There was no reason, is no reason to hide anything. Whatever I had done during the war is an open book."[1]

"Where's Singer? Where's Singer?" demanded Nelly Harris, the WJC's matronly bookkeeper, as she poked her head into room after room, searching desperately for the boss. Her face appeared in my office doorway. Breathlessly she asked, "Do you know where he is?"

"No. Sorry."

She screamed in frustration, *"Kurt Waldheim* is on the phone! He wants to speak to Israel."

I ran into the hallway and helped her track down Singer. Then we raced to his office and huddled around the phone.

The two men had met on a number of occasions during Waldheim's U.N. days, so the conversation retained a veneer of gentility. As they spoke, Hella Moritz listened on an extension, and scribbled notes in shorthand.

Waldheim said he was on a campaign stop in a city near Vienna and had only a few moments to talk. But he wanted to assure Singer, "so that you know it from me personally," he said, that "there is absolutely nothing behind this story, and it is not true that I was a member of a Nazi organization." He offered Singer what he considered the best possible reference to his integrity: "Dr. Wiesenthal made a statement yesterday that he was checking my file thoroughly, and had not found anything which would indicate any sort of actions."

Waldheim confirmed that he had, indeed, been assigned to the Balkans during the middle years of the war, "because of my knowledge of languages." He added, "Not being able to be sent back to the front, they sent me to staff, not with fighting troops but with the High Command of the Germans in Salonika, where I did nothing but interpret and do some work in the offices there. . . . I am deeply worried about the assumption that I could have been involved in any sort of Jewish deportation or cruelties against . . . guerrilla troops."

But Salonika was not the only place in question. Singer wanted to know about Waldheim's other assignments during the latter years of the war.

"I was the interpreter for a German liaison officer in Tirana, Albania," Waldheim recalled, "and from there I drove to Podgorica, Montenegro." He described the meeting wherein he was photographed with General Phleps, and insisted that he was there only as an interpreter "between the Italian commander and the German commander, that SS man whom I saw for the first time in my life and never again."

Singer asked what the subject of the discussions at Podgorica had been.

"Troop movements," Waldheim replied cryptically.

Singer asked whether Waldheim would send the WJC a telex formally summarizing his wartime whereabouts and activities.

"I shall do so," he promised. "I will tell my office in Vienna to send you this information immediately."

After the call, we studied Moritz's notes carefully. Waldheim had admitted to being stationed in Salonika and Tirana, and his description of the Podgorica meeting, although terse, was consistent with our belief that it was a strategy session for the deployment of troops in the "Black Operation." Although we had indications that he had been a full-fledged intelligence officer, we had, as yet, nothing solid to contradict his claim that his responsibilities had included only interpreting and "office work." Nevertheless, that latter term seemed general enough to cover just about anything. We hoped that his telex would provide greater detail.

Over the course of the next few days, we had some surprising visitors at the WJC. First, Javier Perez de Cuellar, Waldheim's successor as U.N. Secretary-General, dispatched a trusted U.N. emissary to our offices. The Secretariat official asked to view our evidence, and as I took him on a document-by-document tour of my files, he made no attempt to hide his astonishment. My visitor volunteered the personal recollection that, during his tenure as Secretary-General, Waldheim had always responded to questions about the war with his stock story: He was injured in 1941 and out. The unambiguous message he saw in my files was that Waldheim was a liar.

The Greek Consulate in New York sent a senior representative for a similar briefing. The Israeli Embassy sent Eliyakim Rubenstein from Washington. Both men were stunned. In turn, I was shocked at how little the Israelis apparently knew about Waldheim's past. It appeared that the 1981 statement of Israel's U.N. ambassador, Yehuda Blum, that his government did not believe Waldheim had ever "supported the Nazis," represented their honest state of knowledge at the time. Here, I decided, was an obvious failing of the vaunted Israeli foreign intelligence service, for even a cursory check of the WASt archives in West Berlin would have disclosed the rudiments of the cover-up. Had the Israelis really failed to spot the sensational information that lay in Berlin, or, worse yet, did the intrigue instead run all the way to Tel Aviv and Jerusalem?

*   *   *

I pored again over my rapidly growing stack of newspaper articles. What the press had quickly dubbed "the Waldheim affair" was a top news story, worldwide. Everyone—on both sides of the Iron Curtain—was covering it, with the notable exception of the Soviet press; there was not a mention of Waldheim in *Pravda, Izvestia,* or the Tass news service reports. This was, on one hand, quite bizarre, for the Soviets never seemed to miss a chance to evoke memories of "The Great Patriotic War." On the other hand, I reminded myself, the man had been installed atop the U.N. hierarchy primarily by Moscow, and the Soviets had been so very pleased with his "performance."

The *Times* of London placed its initial Waldheim story at the top of its front page, under the lamentable title: EX–UN CHIEF ACCUSED BY JEWS.

The bulk of the story was a repeat of the disclosures we had made through the *New York Times* and Waldheim's by-now standard denials, but here also was our first glimpse of Simon Wiesenthal's response, not to the early *Profil* story, but to our much more serious allegations. To our dismay, Wiesenthal repeated his assertion that the charges were "without foundation," and once more relied upon the argument that Waldheim had been cleared "by the secret services of every major power" prior to his election as U.N. chief.[2]

It was the Austrian press, however, that was most important to us; the viability of Waldheim's continued candidacy would depend solely on what his countrymen learned. To our horror, nearly every Austrian newspaper rushed unabashedly to Waldheim's defense. Great play was given to the candidate's denials, while readers were given little information concerning the evidence that was now being circulated, reprinted, and quoted throughout the rest of the free world's media. To the extent that there was any "investigative journalism" involved in these Austrian reports, it was in the form of attempts to ferret out the WJC's sources.

The Vienna daily *Die Presse* buried its initial story on page 4, under the headline: WALDHEIM DEFENDS HIMSELF ON THE WAR: "I WAS SLANDERED."

Another Vienna daily, the giant-circulation *Kurier,* chose to cover the story on the front page, but its headline reassured: WAR COMRADE CONFIRMS: WALDHEIM HAD NOTHING TO DO WITH DEPORTATION OF JEWS.

The text of this story, however, actually provided us with a useful piece of new information. To Singer, Tagliabue, and others, Waldheim had admitted to service only in Salonika, Greece, and Tirana, Albania, from where he embarked on his one and only trip to Podgorica. This was his sole reference to an assignment in Yugoslavia. But *Kurier* quoted him as saying that he had been "an interpreter of Italian on various liaison staffs" in "the areas of Croatia and Dalmatia," both in Yugoslavia.

Almost immediately, the Yugoslav theme assumed greater dimensions. It was Wednesday afternoon when a man who identified himself as Zdravko Tuvic called me from the Manhattan-based Yugoslav Press and Cultural Center, an official bureau of the Yugoslav government. He informed me that he had just received a dispatch from Tanjug, the Yugoslav news agency, which would be "of interest to the WJC."

The mere fact of the phone call—*any* phone call from a Yugoslav official—was extraordinary. The Yugoslav government was closely allied with the Arab nations and maintained no diplomatic relations with Israel; yet, suddenly, one of its press representatives chose to tip the WJC to a story breaking from Belgrade. Sounding at least as mysterious as helpful, Tuvic would say only that the story "should be" self-explanatory to me. If I could send a messenger over, he would be happy to furnish a copy.

A short time later, I held a manila envelope from Tuvic in my hands and stared at it, momentarily succumbing to skepticism. Would the Yugoslavs, of all people, really send anything of importance to the WJC?

The Tanjug report previewed an exclusive story that it said was scheduled to appear in the next day's edition of *Vjesnik,* a daily newspaper in Zagreb, capital of what was then Yugoslavia's Croatian republic. According to the story, *Vjesnik* reporters had picked up on the *New York Times*'s reference to Waldheim's receipt of the King Zvonimir Medal, and had tracked down the records of that award in the Croatian State Archives in Zagreb. They had found the precise date of the award, September 9, 1942. However, the medal had been presented for service not in Croatia or Dalmatia, but in western Bosnia, where some of the worst atrocities of the war had occurred.

The story confirmed that the medal, "King Zvonimir's Crown with Oak Leaves," was conferred on Waldheim by Ante Pavelic, Tito's archenemy, whom the report described, quite accurately, as a "war criminal, founder, and leader of the quisling puppet state." Schuller had already deduced the Pavelic connection, but the Yugoslavs added an important detail: the name of Waldheim's commanding officer. The report said that the medal was awarded on the recommendation of Major General Friedrich Stahl, whose command was located in western Bosnia, where the Wehrmacht "took part in military operations against partisan units. . . ." Stahl had recommended Waldheim for the medal on July 22, 1942. That was consistent with the date

(July 1942) attributed to the award on Waldheim's Civil Status Certificate. Waldheim's name, the story claimed, "is third on the list of nominees."

Here was a new character in the drama. Who, I wondered, was General Stahl, and how did Waldheim come to the attention of yet another Wehrmacht commander? I made a mental note to find out what I could.

The Tanjug report said that a document from the Zagreb archive, identified as "Wehrmacht call number 1228," listed Waldheim as "the 916th officer of German and Pavelic units" to receive highest honors from the Ustashi forces during 1942. That was the year, the story said, that Nazi military units, along with "quisling forces," conducted a fierce antipartisan offensive in the area of Mount Kozara, resulting in "unprecedented crimes against the civilian population of western Bosnia." The toll was listed as nearly seventy thousand people, "predominantly women and children," who were killed or deported to Jasenovac, an infamous death camp, where "barely a few survived."[3]

Why was Waldheim decorated immediately following such a brutal campaign? No facts were offered about Waldheim's individual actions; thus we could only make wild guesses as to what role he might have played. The story noted that, based upon Waldheim's self-description as an interpreter, he was most likely assigned to an intelligence unit, for that was where interpreters served in the Wehrmacht's customary organizational scheme. This tracked our own theories rather well.

I knew about the Jasenovac camp, but the Mount Kozara area was unfamiliar to me. Using the WJC's new computer, I accessed NEXIS, the largest publicly available general information database. The NEXIS files only went back to the mid-seventies, so they did not cover wartime events on a contemporaneous basis. But the computer kicked out several references to "Kozara" in connection with annual war remembrance ceremonies in Yugoslavia, and they sufficed to brief me on the basic details. During the spring of 1942, the partisan forces of Marshal Tito were concentrated in two areas. The Germans first directed their attention to the vicinity of the town of Foca, along the Drina River. By midyear, the action moved north to the town of Prijedor and the nearby Kozara Mountains, in western Bosnia. The partisans stung the invading Germans by disrupting bauxite mining operations and threatening the security of the railways that serviced the mines. The Germans launched a major offensive against the partisans and, in the process, swept the Prijedor area clean of villagers, who they feared might assist the partisans.

Prijedor! That was the very locale that Schuller had found described by Yugoslav historian Vlado Strugar as the site of a massacre and mass deportation of civilians to the Jasenovac camp. Prijedor, I realized now, was but one vicious episode of the Kozara campaign.

In each news story I read, the "Kozara massacres" were recalled vividly as emblematic of the bestial crimes perpetrated by the Nazis against Yugoslav civilians. Special mention was always made of the twenty-three thousand children reportedly deported to the Croatian camps during the "cleansing operation" that followed the Wehrmacht's victory over the partisans there. It seemed that the word "Kozara" carried nearly the same emotional impact for Bosnians and many other Yugoslavs that the word "Auschwitz" did for Jews.[4]

Something essential was still missing from all of this. Assuming that the *Vjesnik* story was true—and I was extremely uncomfortable with the notion of accepting the Yugoslavs' unverified account at face value—it still contained no hard proof of a sinister role for Waldheim. Undoubtedly, he would continue to claim that he was merely an interpreter. The article did not directly allege any involvement on Waldheim's part in the Kozara nightmare.

Nevertheless, there was a significance to these unexpected "discoveries" that went beyond the obvious. In the arena of political reporting, Yugoslavia's press was strictly controlled and the news story therefore carried an implied message that the Belgrade government was suddenly prepared to make public some or perhaps even all of the information that it held on Waldheim. It was an exciting prospect. But if this damning information was available all along, why had Yugoslavia twice voted to elect the man as U.N. Secretary General? Was it not additional evidence suggesting that the late Marshal Tito had sunk his hooks into Waldheim?

I telephoned Schuller in the early evening. It was already very late in Vienna, but I knew he would still be awake. Things were undoubtedly as hectic for him in Vienna as they were for me in New York.

He passed on a vague tip: "There should be an English-language book about Loehr, or possibly Phleps, with a photograph of our friend. But I don't have the details yet. I have also heard that [the German magazine] *Stern* will publish next week a photograph of our friend in the uniform of either the S.A. or the Nazi Student Union. But that is just a rumor so far."

Schuller spoke at length of the regrettable accuracy of his prediction that the Austrian press would take Waldheim's side, and he noted that local reporters had used Simon Wiesenthal's statements as the centerpiece of their accounts. "Here, he is positively *killing* the effort to expose our friend," Schuller moaned. "The newspapers are all quoting him like he is a god. You know, it is funny in a way. Here is a guy who has always been very much disliked in my country. He worked too hard, you see, to remind Austrians of what so many had done during the war. And now, after all these years, Mr. Wiesenthal has achieved popularity overnight! He is portrayed as coming to the defense of an Austrian national treasure—that is our friend—and through him, to the rescue of the national reputation." Schuller was extremely upset, almost despondent. "Honestly, I don't think our friend has really been damaged here," he lamented. "With the help of the Austrian press, he has succeeded in transforming this affair into an 'attack on an honorable gentleman.' "

When copies of Vienna's major newspapers arrived at our office, I saw what Schuller meant. The *Die Presse* headline for March 6 blared: ENCIRCLEMENT AND EXTERMINATION OF KURT WALDHEIM PRODUCES TOTAL UNITY NOW IN THE PEOPLE'S PARTY.

Whereas nearly every newspaper in the free world reprinted the Podgorica photo on its front page, *Die Presse* chose to run one of Waldheim being interviewed in his own defense. Farther down the page was a companion story, entitled: MATERIAL CAME FROM THE WORLD JEWISH CONGRESS.

Kurier's headline for the same day was a brazen disclaimer: NOTHING TO DO WITH TRANSPORTATION OF JEWS.

Wiener Zeitung (literally "Viennese newspaper") carried an extraordinary interview in which Wiesenthal declared that he did not believe that Waldheim was personally implicated in any Nazi crimes. He spoke specifically to the Salonika episode, proclaiming that in all of the postwar trials pertaining to Salonika, only the SS had been implicated, not the Wehrmacht. Wiesenthal admitted, however, that he found Waldheim's denial of knowledge about the deportations incredible. Wiesenthal, reported the newspaper, conceded that the Wehrmacht might possibly have played a role in the Salonika deportations, but he wanted to reserve judgment until he could inspect the documents upon which the *New York Times* had based its story.[5]

On the campaign trail, meanwhile, Waldheim played overtly to his nation's favorite fantasy. "Austria was never involved in the Second World War," he declared. "Germany was. The Nazis were not in Austria, the Nazis were in Germany."[6] He dismissed the new Yugoslav allegations as a "smear campaign."

Waldheim was taking quite a gamble, I thought. Now he was not only fighting the WJC, but also attacking the integrity of the Yugoslavs. We at the WJC could not prove that Waldheim was a war criminal, and we had said as much. But the Yugoslavs, along with the Soviet Union, held comprehensive files concerning German activities in the Balkans. The candidate was wagering that the Yugoslavs did not have true "smoking gun" evidence against him—*or* that if they had it, they would not release it, perhaps for fear of implicating the still-revered Tito in Waldheim's cover-up.

But already there were indications that Waldheim's Yugoslav prospects were fading. For example, when the Yugoslav paper *Vjesnik* published its Waldheim exposé, the story covered nearly the entire first page. It was accompanied by a dramatic reproduction of a September 9, 1942, Croatian document listing nine German officers who were being awarded the King Zvonimir Medal. The third name on the list was: WALDHEIM, KURT. To the right of the name was a valuable piece of information: FUERUNGSTAB WESTBOSNIEN— "Command Staff West Bosnia." Here was documentary evidence that Waldheim had, indeed, served in western Bosnia.

The *Washington Post* carried a report, meanwhile, on the personal dilemma faced by James and Esthy Adler, a Jewish couple living in suburban Washington. Esthy Adler was a concentration camp survivor. Her husband was on the board of the local chapter of the American Jewish Committee. It was their small publishing house, Adler & Adler, that had issued the U.S. edition of Waldheim's most recent memoirs. "We are absolutely shocked," Esthy Adler told a reporter. She said that she and her husband were considering withdrawing the book from sale.

The same *Washington Post* story quoted Simon Wiesenthal declaring that there was "nothing at all incriminating" in the charges against Waldheim.[7]

"Roosevelt, remember the long battle we fought with the U.N. Secretariat for access to the files of the U.N. War Crimes Commission?" The question came over the phone from Neal Sher, my old boss at OSI.

I had not, until he reminded me. For years, OSI had struggled with the U.N. Secretariat, trying to gain access to the forty thousand suspect and witness files of the long-defunct war crimes investigating agency. Those files were housed right here in New York, in some dusty archive near the U.N. complex, but a stubborn bureaucracy had consistently refused OSI permission to scan for information potentially of value to its war crimes investigations and prosecutions. Then, shortly before I had joined the Department of Justice, OSI had finally received permission to review at least some of the UNWCC files.

"Do you recall the Civiletti letter?" Sher asked, referring to former U.S. Attorney General Benjamin Civiletti.

I tried to remember the details. After the Secretariat's initial promise of partial access, OSI had drafted a letter for Civiletti to sign, thanking the U.N. for its cooperation. "Oh, my God, Chief!" I blurted out. "It was addressed to *him!*"

"You got it. Small world, isn't it?" Sher said, roaring with laughter.

But we both knew that it was not really a humorous story. The Civiletti letter had been a simple courtesy. But after it was sent to Waldheim, OSI obtained only modest cooperation from the U.N.; all that we ever received was a photocopied set of a few selected suspect lists and access to two suspect files—not the thousands that OSI had been promised.*

On Friday, March 7, the *Jerusalem Post* published a report based on an interview with an obviously embarrassed Heinrich Duermayer, chief of the Austrian State Police from 1945 to 1947. He contested Waldheim's statement to *Profil* that the *Staatspolizei,* under his leadership, had checked into allegations that the then-secretary to Austrian Foreign Minister Karl Gruber had a Nazi background. "We had no reason to investigate Waldheim at the time," Duermayer asserted, "because he was not an important man."[8]

This characterization of Waldheim was difficult to accept. Waldheim might not have been important to other countries, but as Gruber's assistant he was privy to highly classified information, and therefore had to be "an important man" from the standpoint of the Austrian security services. It was interesting to note that the Austrian State Police was purged a few years after the war to bring an end to communist domination of that organization. Duermayer, a communist, was himself forced out as police chief in 1947. Had the police performed a service for the Russians by not investigating Waldheim? Had they disingenuously "cleared" Waldheim at the Soviets' behest?

The WJC's ancient telex roared to life, spitting out a "Dear Mr. Bronfman" message, the report that Waldheim had promised to send to Singer. The March 7 cable was devoted mostly to a repetition of the defenses we had heard so often in the past few days: Allegations of Waldheim's membership in Nazi organizations were apparently based upon his "occasional participation in riding exercises"; his activities in the Wehrmacht were just "normal" army duties; the entire controversy was designed to damage his presidential campaign; and, anyway, the intelligence agencies of Austria and the superpowers had checked his past long ago and had pronounced him clean.

The final paragraph addressed the allegations that he had served in criminal units. These charges were "equally unfounded," Wald-

---

*Waldheim's successor, Peru's Javier Perez de Cuellar, had been no more accommodating, at least until March 1986.

heim declared, adding, "I wish to state categorically that I had nothing whatever to do with such atrocities." He claimed that unspecified "independent sources" confirmed that his assignments "as an interpreter and staff officer" did not involve him in "such tragic and deplorable events." He asserted that he had "never been informed" about Jewish deportations from Greece, which, in any event, were not conducted by regular army units. Perhaps emboldened by Simon Wiesenthal's statements of support, Waldheim continued to attempt to remove the Wehrmacht from the history of the Holocaust.

At one level, Waldheim's flirtation with historical revisionism was a low-risk undertaking. He could count on the fact that most people still think of the Holocaust only in the context of the SS-operated concentration camps. To be sure, some of the better informed also know of the mobile killing units, the *Einsatzgruppen,* set up by the SS to track down and annihilate Jews and suspected communists in the towns and forests of the Soviet Union. Comparatively little known, however, is the fact that the Wehrmacht too was a major perpetrator of Nazi atrocities against both civilians and opposing combatants. The German army followed on the heels of the SS liquidation squads, and often cooperated with both vigor and lethal effectiveness. Captured SS documents I had seen at the Justice Department contained frequent expressions of appreciation for the assistance rendered by the German army. Other documents conveyed explicit requests from Wehrmacht units for the *Einsatzgruppen* to dispose of Jewish communities. In many cases, army units actively participated in the mass killings. Wehrmacht forces also took part in the liquidation of the Warsaw Jewish Ghetto.

Waldheim's telexed historical rewrite was directly contradicted by the plethora of evidence we already had on hand demonstrating the direct participation of Army Group E itself in the Jewish deportations. Numerous captured German documents introduced into evidence at Nuremberg and cited in authoritative history texts belied Waldheim's claims. Evidence of Wehrmacht involvement in the Holocaust in Greece was also made public during the 1959 Greek trial of Max Merten, who had been chief of military administration in Salonika. Merten, a Wehrmacht employee, had been one of the principal villains in the process of destroying Salonika Jewry. Tens of thousands of Jewish men, women, and children of Salonika were hauled off to Auschwitz on Wehrmacht trains.[9]

Singer read Waldheim's telex, slammed it onto his desk, and shouted, "The man is a *pig,* you know? He really is!"

"What the hell did you expect Waldheim to do?" one of my friends asked me. "Did you really expect him to say, 'Okay, ya got me—

I've been lying to the whole goddamn world for half a century'?"

I had been asking myself the same question for days. Actually, I was not sure what I had expected, but I thought I knew how I would have handled the situation had I been Waldheim. I would have gone on Austrian television, I told my friend. Suddenly I was acting, playing the role of Waldheim. I realized with a start that I was almost able to replicate his scarecrow-like posture. There were traces of a poorly contrived Viennese accent as I said the words that I felt Waldheim should have spoken:

"My dear countrymen, the revelations of the past few days have been very painful for me. Because of them, the time has come for me to relieve myself of a terrible burden. I was a young man during the war. I was drafted into military service. I did not choose to be assigned to Army Group E, but because I was fluent in languages, they made me an interpreter and put me into this intelligence unit. No one was more horrified than I to see what the Wehrmacht was doing, but there was no possibility that I could stop it. I did not participate in any of the bad things perpetrated by some of those with whom I served. And whenever possible, I arranged to get home leave, either for medical treatment or to complete my studies.

"After the war, I wanted nothing more than to resume my quest to serve the people of Austria, to make Austria a better place. But I knew that in the atmosphere immediately following the war, anyone who had had even the most tenuous connection with the Nazis was disqualified from government service. If I said that I had served with Loehr and with others from Army Group E who were prosecuted by the Allies, it would have been impossible for me, *ever*, to serve you.

"And so I made a mistake. I did not disclose the details of my war service. I ask you to understand this as the error of a young man who was blinded by his burning desire to be of use to his beloved people, the people of Austria.

"It became worse for me as I rose in the Austrian government because, having once told the fundamental lie, I had to remain consistent. Whenever the subject came up, I had to tell the same story. Of course, this became increasingly awkward. Occasional questions were raised at the U.N., and I had to stick to my story. Even in this current campaign I had to stick to my story.

"But I realize now that this course is no longer viable, no longer possible. It is a disservice to my country and an embarrassment to Austria internationally. So it is time now for the truth and it is time to get this unpleasant episode behind us. I will leave it to the people of Austria, in the upcoming election, to decide whether I am a suitable candidate for the presidency, and whether any of my good works since the war have atoned for the unfortunate misrepresentation that I made in haste, so foolishly, right after the war, as a young man.

"Good night. And thank you."

"Good speech," my friend said. "But he hasn't said that."

"He hasn't even come close," I admitted. "But it would win him a lot of sympathy in Austria. The country is full of voters whose fathers and grandfathers lied in exactly the same way. It probably would earn him a good deal of sympathy throughout the world, in fact."

I realized, however, that my Waldheim discourse, more or less patterned on Richard Nixon's "Checkers" speech, was something that an American might compose, but probably not a European, and especially not an Austrian. The attitude that politicians should always tell the truth is, if not an American invention, a uniquely American obsession. Europeans are much more inclined to forgive an elected official who lies in order to achieve his ends; they frequently prefer to judge him on the basis of what those ends are, and whether they are in fact achieved.

I confessed to my friend that I feared that proving the fact of Waldheim's prevarications might therefore accomplish nothing inside Austria, especially in light of the challenge that he had now thrown back at us. "It looks like Waldheim and his friends have pretty much dared us to prove that he was 'not just a liar' but a war criminal," I lamented.

But was he? And if so, could we prove it?

10

Waldheim, as a presidential candidate with an ambitious schedule of campaign appearances, could hardly take a vow of silence. He was vocal and visible in his own defense and, although most of his comments appeared repetitious and even innocuous, they often revealed incremental clues to the mystery of his past.

Profil seemed to be the only publication in Waldheim's country that was interested in following up on our revelations. The March 10 issue carried a transcript of an interview of Waldheim, conducted by publisher Peter Michael Lingens, who asked the candidate, "Do you know anything about a 'Black Operation'?"

"It is not in my memory," Waldheim replied. When pressed about the agenda of the Podgorica meeting, he recalled that there had been a difference of opinion between SS General Phleps and the Italian commander, but said that there was nothing sinister about it.

My eyebrows rose when I read that. I wondered whether the Italian general was arguing against the brutal tactics of his German allies. I recalled that the book by Phleps's second-in-command, Otto Kumm, asserted, without explication, that the Italian general had "claim[ed] the overall leadership of the operation for himself."

Regarding Waldheim's later assignment with Army Group E, Lingens asked whether Waldheim was aware of an order to execute suspected partisans.

"I have never seen such an order," Waldheim protested, adding that he "certainly" was not involved with such matters. He insisted that his duties were merely "to analyze the enemy picture." He said that reports came to his section from the divisions and he routed them to operations personnel, designated as the Ia Branch. "I translated, and I was poring over maps," Waldheim demurred. "You must believe me on this."

That was a difficult request for Lingens to grant. He was incredulous of the claim that Waldheim, as a staff officer at army group headquarters, could contend that he never saw, or even heard of, the infamous orders to shoot suspected partisans.

"Nothing like this" came to his notice, Waldheim repeated.

When Lingens asked about the deportation of the Salonika Jews, Waldheim replied that he had been sitting in an office in the hillside community of Arsakli, overlooking Salonika, and never learned about the deportations until John Tagliabue had told him.

Lingens countered with the information that his magazine had interviewed Colonel Roman Loos, a former German military police officer in Greece, who declared that the deportations were "known to everybody."

Waldheim held his ground, repeating that he knew nothing of mass deportations.

Had Waldheim not noticed all the people wearing the yellow Star of David patches, which the Germans required Jews to sew onto their clothes? Lingens asked.

No, Waldheim replied. He noted that Arsakli was a few kilometers outside Salonika, and added, "I hardly ever came into the city."[1]

In the same issue of *Profil*, Hubertus Czernin reported on Waldheim's previous admission to the magazine that, during his service with Army Group E, he was assigned to the Ic (Intelligence) section. Czernin asserted, without referencing any proof, that one responsibility of Ic was *Vernehmung* ("interrogation") of P.O.W.'s, deserters, and civilians.

Profil also published a second Podgorica photograph, snapped either moments before or moments after the one Schuller had supplied to me. A magazine staffer had found it in a 1983 West German "coffee table" book that attempted to glorify the infamous Waffen-SS Prince Eugen Division.[2] No one had noticed Waldheim in the photograph previously, but it was obviously a near duplicate of the now-famous one Crown had authenticated.

The conservative Vienna weekly *Wochenpresse* came to Waldheim's defense the following day. It had sent its reporter Lucian Meysels—accompanied by Ferdinand Trautmannsdorff, a People's Party official and high-level Waldheim campaign staffer—to the German military archives in Freiburg to review the surviving records of Army Group E. Meysels titled his piece "The 14th Man," and began by asserting that it had been "implied" and "hinted" in Tagliabue's *New York Times* article "and in Eli Rosenbaum's statements" that Waldheim was linked to some "awful things." But, he reported with ill-disguised relief, the archives revealed nothing incriminating in Waldheim's war-service records, other than his flight to Carinthia at the war's end, one step ahead of the German military police—which, Meysels concluded sarcastically, "people who live in the past may blame him for."

The reporter wrote that he had found some maps and "situation reports" prepared by Waldheim, which indicated that Waldheim was "fully informed on the war against the partisans . . . but there is no mention anywhere of deportations of Jews." Meysels contended that the King Zvonimir Medal was nothing more than a "corn award" given out by the Nazi puppet state in Croatia "to each and every staff officer" who worked with the Ustashi troops.

Included in the *Wochenpresse* story was a reproduction of portions of an Army Group E High Command staff list from July 1, 1944. Loehr's name appeared at the top as commander-in-chief, and the staff officers were listed below him in descending order of rank. The fourteenth name on the list was that of the future U.N. Secretary-General (hence the title of Meysels's article). To the Austrian reporter, the significance of the roster was that "not a single SS officer is listed" on it.

The more I studied the *Wochenpresse* story in the ponderous (to me) German text of the original, the more tempted I was to thank the Austrian reporter. There were important disclosures here, despite Meysels's obviously defensive reporting. For example, one of the Freiburg documents published with the story showed Waldheim listed as the "O3" officer (Wehrmacht shorthand for third *Ordonnanzoffizier*) in the Ic/AO Branch of the High Command of Army Group E. This was the Intelligence/Counterintelligence Branch. Here, at last, was documentary proof that Waldheim was assigned to a unit that encompassed potentially more sinister *counter*intelligence duties as well.

Meysels quoted from the German army's *Handbook for the General Staff Service in War:*

> Ic is responsible for the collaboration of all posts and units whose purpose is the gathering of information. . . . Ic will maintain the maps of enemy positions, on which the results of reconnaissance at specific times are listed. This is in order to provide a foundation of current data for the making of important decisions. [Ellipsis in original.]

This was an innocuous-sounding delineation of responsibilities, which supported Waldheim's public statements. But Meysels added that, as "O3," Waldheim was "the first assistant to the Ic officer." Thus, Waldheim was not merely "assigned" to the Intelligence/Counterintelligence Branch; one could properly infer that he was the primary aide to the chief of intelligence for all of Army Group E, a force of more than four hundred thousand troops having dominion over nearly the entire Balkans.

And here in the same story was a new addition to the geographical mix, another location for Waldheim at another date. The newspaper had tracked down a certain Waldemar Fend, who claimed to be an old war comrade of Waldheim's. Fend described Waldheim as someone who had neither influence nor authority. He conceded that "rumors were plentiful in the Wehrmacht" about what was happening to the Jews, but it seemed, to him, "ridiculous" to suggest that Waldheim might have played a role in the deportations. However, Fend admitted that he had no way of knowing what Waldheim did in Arsakli/Salonika, for he did not know him then. Rather, they had met in *Athens,* where Waldheim was working as an interpreter after the Italian surrender to the Allies on September 8, 1943.

Waldheim had never mentioned Athens. Perhaps, I speculated, he had met Fend only on a brief visit to the Greek capital. But maybe there was more here, yet another part of his war record that he felt the need to conceal. Or perhaps Fend's report was erroneous. I noted the Athens allegation on a memo pad and dropped the page into a folder marked INTERESTING BUT STILL UNCLEAR.

A second document reproduced in the *Wochenpresse* article was a copy of the November 7, 1944, "Daily Report" of Army Group E.[3] Meysels's manifest purpose was to confirm Waldheim's claim that he served in a relatively unimportant capacity. At the bottom of the document was what appeared to be Waldheim's signature. Just above that was the abbreviation: "F.d.R.," signifying *Fuer die Richtigkeit,* evidently indicating that Waldheim was signing "copy certified correct," that is, simply to verify the accuracy of the text.

Meysels did not comment on the substance of the "Daily Report" and I struggled with the tiny German text for some time to decipher what it was that Waldheim was verifying. The report contained a long section entitled "Enemy Losses October." The first entry read:

Englaender: 4 *Gefangene* ["prisoners"]

This was an intriguing notation, for it indicated that Waldheim might have encountered British prisoners. *Profil* had asserted that prisoner interrogation was a responsibility of the Ic section. Waldheim claimed to have been an interpreter, and we knew that he was already fluent in English at this time. It was another item for the INTERESTING BUT STILL UNCLEAR file.

But it was the second entry on the "Daily Report" that made me shiver. Here, wholly unmentioned in Meysels's article, was a scorecard of casualties suffered during the preceding month (October 1944) by the "bandits," a derogatory expression employed by the Germans as a euphemism for partisans:*

739 dead, 94 prisoners. Materiél: 13 machine guns, 49 rifles, 1 sub-machine gun.[4]

The numbers were wildly imbalanced. According to this report, the Germans and their allies killed or captured 833 partisans, but confiscated a total of only sixty-three weapons. It was tempting to subtract the latter number from the former and conclude that 760 of the victims were unarmed—in all likelihood, civilians. The problem with that analysis was that partisans often buried their weapons in order to keep them out of German hands. Still, the variance in the casualty and equipment totals seemed too wide to be explained by buried weapons. I dubbed this a "disparity document," similar in its sinister potential to some of the "Buda" materials Schuller had shown me. But how could we ascertain whether this document actually signified that Waldheim had signed a report on the massacre of civilians? I had no ready answer.

The frustration of being unable to answer so many questions about Waldheim's war record was magnified by my growing realization of just how much proof the world was demanding. Thus, although an editorial in Britain's respected Manchester *Guardian* criticized Waldheim for "omitting" parts of his war record from his past statements, it offered the opinion that if there was anything truly worth hiding in his past, it was difficult to believe that it could have eluded discovery all these years. The editorial closed with the observation that Simon Wiesenthal, "the indefatigable Nazi hunter," had declared that there was "nothing of substance" in the charges. Such a testimonial, the editorial concluded, "should be enough to settle the matter."[5]

Elan Steinberg ordered me into Israel Singer's office. All three of us had just read the *Washington Post*'s March 12 story, which, to our chagrin, declared that the Waldheim campaign appeared to be turning the charges "to political advantage." The *Post* cited polls indicating

---

*The Nazis generally eschewed the proper German word for "partisans" (*Partisanen*) in favor of either *Banden* (literally "bands" or "gangs") or, less often, *Banditen* ("bandits" or "brigands"). The usage, in either case, had an unmistakable pejorative intent, much as we might today employ the word "terrorists" to describe certain persons who call themselves "freedom fighters" or "resistance fighters." In order to convey this derogatory flavor, the authors of the present book have translated both *Banden* and *Banditen* as "bandits," as was commonly (if inconsistently) done in the official Nuremberg translations (see, for example, Nuremberg document NOKW-155). Some historians prefer translating the former expression as "bands" or "bands [partisans]."

that his lead over Socialist candidate Kurt Steyrer had actually doubled in the week following our revelations. The allegations appeared to have produced, according to the newspaper, a "wave of sympathy" among Waldheim's fellow Austrians. Waldheim was now firing up crowds on the campaign trail with attacks against the WJC and denunciations of "outside interference."[6]

Singer crushed the stub of his cigarette in an ashtray before addressing us. "Waldheim has turned this whole thing around, hasn't he? It's unbelievable. The man is dead and buried in most of the world, but in Austria, suddenly, he's Arnold Schwarzenegger. And he did it by challenging us to prove he's a war criminal." Singer paused for effect and aimed his best "we-*will*-manage-this-missile-crisis" gaze at me. I had the uneasy feeling that marching orders were on the way. "So what do you think of his challenge?" he asked.

"It's certainly been a clever one so far," I replied.

"And?"

"What do you mean, 'And?' "

"Can we prove he took part in war crimes?"

"Not so far," I replied. "That he served in one or more criminal units—that we can do, at least if you're prepared to call the High Command of Army Group E a 'unit.' Loehr's staff was certainly involved in the Greek deportations. But proving that Waldheim personally took part in Nazi war crimes, that's another matter, Israel. You know that."

"Yes, of course. But *could* we prove it? I mean is there anything that could be done that hasn't been done?"

The question elicited a deep moan of exasperation from me, and then a lecture. I told Singer of the thick manila folder on my desk, marked RESEARCH TO DO, and its equally thick companion folder, INTERESTING BUT STILL UNCLEAR. I reminded Singer that the average person has little understanding of the painstaking nature of this sort of investigative work. He "knows" that the Germans had a reputation for having recorded "everything" on paper; more than forty years have passed, and we have entered the electronic age, so, he presumes, all the documents captured by the Allies have been entered into computer databases that one can access at the touch of a button. But it simply is not so. Such databases do not exist. Nor are the files nearly as complete as the public seems to assume. The Germans did not document "everything" and, furthermore, they consigned many of their records to huge bonfires once they realized that the war was lost. Other documents were accidental casualties of war. Still others were removed by Allied soldiers and taken home as souvenirs, much as David Crown had stashed a box of Nazi photographs in his attic. Who knew what secrets were held in the nooks and crannies of the homes of World War II veterans? As the years passed and the veterans succumbed to illness and old age, their survivors undoubtedly relegated invaluable "mementos" to the trash.

What remained, I reminded Singer, were fragmentary, largely un-indexed records lying in dusty archives scattered in a dozen countries, some of which were very reluctant to provide public access. Archives in the USSR, East Germany, and, most likely, Yugoslavia would be completely closed to us, I advised Singer. If I tried to go to Austria or even West Germany and attempted to question Waldheim's for-mer colleagues, I risked being arrested for engaging in unauthorized "police work." And without the subpoena power enjoyed by gov-ernmental law-enforcement agencies, we could not compel any of Waldheim's ex-comrades to speak with us. We could attempt to secure access to the relevant archives in Greece and Italy, but there was no guarantee of success. In any event, the task would be time- and resource-consuming beyond Singer's worst budgetary nightmare. As Edgar Bronfman had suggested to him during their first meeting on the matter, this was properly a matter for governments to pursue.

Singer understood that we were talking about a needle-in-a-haystack proposition, but it was clear to me that he still did not comprehend the logistical difficulties. Again he pressed me for an answer. Where could we go to get *something*?

"Our best bet," I replied with studied nonenthusiasm, "is probably the U.S. National Archives' collection of captured German docu-ments, in Washington." I explained that the Archives held an enor-mous microfilm collection of surviving Wehrmacht and SS records, more than 15,000 rolls. Even now, Pat Treanor and some of my other former colleagues at OSI were exploring that collection almost every day, searching for evidence concerning other cases.

"What about Freiburg?" Singer asked.

I explained that the Freiburg archives had, for the most part, the originals of what we could find much closer to home, in the National Archives microfilm collection. There was a good deal of duplication.

"How many documents are we talking about?"

"I can only guess. We're talking not only about the records of the High Command of Army Group E, but also the records of its pre-decessor army command, its subordinate units, and all of the com-mands that were superior to Army Group E. And that's not all. You've also got to look at the other military, SS, diplomatic, and civilian units and organizations that Army Group E and its component units had dealings with. Israel, you're talking about tens of thousands of pages. Maybe hundreds of thousands. And there aren't any name indices."

"I want it done. Do it."

I was dumbfounded. Singer did not comprehend. Or else he simply was not interested in comprehending. "Israel, it could take *years!*" I protested. "If Waldheim had served in a concentration camp or in some small Wehrmacht unit, the records search would be more or less manageable. But Waldheim served in the High Command of a full-fledged army group. The relevant documents are going to be scattered all over the damn building."

Singer listened with a benevolent expression on his face. He lit another cigarette and allowed his eyes to follow the upward spiral of the smoke. His silence beckoned me to continue.

"If I go to Washington, who'll take care of my other responsibilities here?" I asked. "It could take months. And I'm not really the right person to do this anyway. I'm an attorney, not a historian." Singer raised his eyebrows skeptically. "Okay," I conceded, "I'm an amateur historian. And I've worked with these kinds of documents for a good few years. But I'm still not the right guy for the job. My German isn't good enough for a huge project like this. It's crazy, Israel."

Singer allowed a few seconds of silence to pass. Then, when he sensed that I had calmed down, he inquired simply, "Are you finished?"

"Yes." What I really meant was that I had given up trying to persuade him.

He flashed a half-grin. "Good," he said. "Now tell me what you need."

What I needed most was help from a professional military historian specializing in the study of Third Reich documents. Outside the government, there were probably no more than fifteen qualified people in the entire United States, and most of them were occupied with university teaching assignments. Singer authorized me to try to hire one of them.

My first call was to Professor Raul Hilberg of the University of Vermont, author of *The Destruction of the European Jews* and probably the top authority in the field of Holocaust studies. When I reached him by phone in Burlington, Hilberg was interested, and gracious in declining; he was inescapably busy with teaching obligations.

Three hours and numerous rejections later, I was down to my last scholar, Professor Robert Edwin Herzstein, a historian at the University of South Carolina at Columbia. I did not know him personally, but he was a full professor at a major university, and he did have experience in the field. He was a prolific writer, and although his books on Hitler and the Nazis were targeted for a mass-market readership, rather than academics, he was well regarded by his colleagues. He had also testified as an expert witness in one of the

Justice Department's Nazi cases. Herzstein had actually met our subject briefly in 1979, when his university awarded Waldheim an honorary degree.

Although Herzstein, too, said that his teaching obligations precluded his involvement in the project, his refusal seemed somewhat less resolute than the others I had received that day. Singer pressed me to offer him the equivalent of several months' university salary for little more than a week of research work. I phoned Herzstein again. "Wow, that's a pile of dough," the professor exclaimed moments before agreeing to plunge into the mass of aging National Archives records that might hold some keys to our mystery. We made plans to meet in Washington on Friday evening, two days hence.

"Bring whatever documents you can," Herzstein requested. "So far, all I've got to go on is what I've seen in the press."

It rained steadily all day Friday in Washington.

I arrived at the Capitol complex early and had a chance to visit the Library of Congress to pursue a tip from Peter Lubin, a writer in Massachusetts who was working on a Waldheim piece for *The New Republic*. I had shared our information with him and he, in turn, had pointed out an interesting reference in Hilberg's book; it concerned the German newspaper *Donauzeitung*, published in Belgrade during the war. If Waldheim, as he insisted, had been stationed in Croatia and Dalmatia during 1942, this, Lubin observed, was the German-language newspaper he was most likely to have read. According to Hilberg, two issues of *Donauzeitung* dealt candidly with the treatment of the Salonika Jews eight months before the beginning of the deportations to Auschwitz.[7]

Studying the Library of Congress microfilm copies of *Donauzeitung*, I found that Hilberg was correct, as usual. Page 3 of the newspaper's July 14, 1942, edition carried an article headlined: WORK INSTEAD OF THIEVERY—STRONG MEASURES AGAINST THE JEWS OF SALONIKA UNANIMOUSLY WELCOMED.

The story reported unabashedly that, on the previous morning, between six thousand and seven thousand Jewish males, ranging in age from eighteen to forty-eight, were forced to assemble in Salonika's Liberty Square to be registered for forced labor. Those deemed "fit" were sent to work in the swamps (where, according to Hilberg, many perished from malaria).

The third page of *Donauzeitung*'s July 26 issue contained a heartrending photograph of twelve thousand Jews lined up in Salonika's harbor area "in order to be registered and to be transported to useful work."

My Justice Department experience notwithstanding, I found the blurred microfilm image of this tragic moment unnerving. Here were twelve thousand doomed human beings, oblivious to the fate that awaited them. It was galling to see once more how audaciously the Germans had publicized some of their anti-Jewish measures, and it was doubly maddening to remember that Waldheim claimed never to have heard about them.

I copied the pages from the microfilm, then rushed out into the rain and flagged a cab, directing the driver to Cynthia's apartment, where Herzstein had agreed to meet me later in the afternoon. With a bit of time to kill, I phoned my office. Steinberg filled me in on the latest news from Austria.

"AP and UPI are both reporting that Waldheim's personnel file at the Austrian Foreign Ministry is missing," Steinberg said. "Vanished into thin air!"

"Why is it that I'm not surprised, Elan?"

"Get this, though. The file is missing, and Waldheim's people are telling every reporter within a thousand miles of Vienna that *that's* the file that would show that he never belonged to any Nazi organizations."

Bob Herzstein appeared to be in his late forties. He had a ready smile framed by a small, closely trimmed beard and mustache. He spoke at a fast clip, and this was fortunate, for we had much to discuss. I took him on a journey through the piles of photocopies I had brought with me, and gave him a handwritten partial chronological summary of what we knew, so far, about Waldheim's military assignments. It was an updated and streamlined version of Schuller's initial discussion with me.

Herzstein's eyes widened by degrees; what we had learned was so very much more extensive than what he had read in the newspapers. He asked the question that so many of my friends had asked: In light of these disclosures, what did I think presidential candidate Waldheim would do? I responded with my Waldheim impression, the "I made a big mistake in covering up my service and now it is time to come clean" speech. The historian laughed at my parody, but then grew serious. We both knew that levity was necessary to ease the tension, but the bottom line was that this was solemn business. He was ready to get to work.

Happily, Herzstein's fresh enthusiasm was invigorating and infectious, for the roller-coaster ride of the past few weeks had exhausted me. He was pleased that I could provide specific information on some of Waldheim's unit assignments, and expressed confidence that the National Archives would yield at least a few more secrets.

He would begin his week's work at the Archives the following morning, Saturday, and he would spend Sunday back home in Columbia, conducting research at the university library before he returned to Washington on Monday. I suggested, for background, that he study Professor Jozo Tomasevich's book on the war in Yugoslavia, and I passed on a recommendation from another historian: I had been told that a verbatim translation of a captured German account of the war against the Yugoslav partisans during 1941 and 1942 had been published by Professor Paul Hehn of the State University College at Brockport, New York.[8]

Most importantly, I set Herzstein on the trail of the activities that brought Waldheim the dubious recognition of the King Zvonimir Medal. I asked him to see what he could learn about General Stahl and the Kozara massacres. I mentioned that I had found a footnote in Hilberg's book indicating that Stahl had been questioned on June 10 and 11, 1947, by investigators from the U.S. Office of Chief of Counsel for War Crimes. Hilberg quoted Stahl's interrogation in reference to the general's role in the roundup of Serbian Jews in 1941. "But who knows what else Stahl might have talked about," I said. "Here's the citation, Bob: Nuremberg document NOKW-1714. The transcripts should be on microfilm series M1019."

"Great," Herzstein said, scribbling notes. "I'll check it out."

Herzstein clearly had a daunting research task ahead of him. But he was eager to begin.

I returned to New York, equally eager to hear his report.

11

Studying the background materials I had recommended, Herzstein quickly learned that Stahl had commanded the West Bosnia Combat Group, known as "The Steel Division," in honor of its commander, Major General Albert Gottfried Friedrich ("Hard as Steel") Stahl.*

In Hehn's book, Herzstein found a Wehrmacht report concerning the operations at Kozara that boasted, "Wherever the insurgents tried to break through, they were thrown back with bloody losses." The Wehrmacht report disclosed that the number of partisans caught or killed was 10,475, while German/Croatian casualties were a mere 185. Another document reported: "dead 1,626, wounded 273, prisoners 8,849, *shot in reprisal 431.*" (Emphasis added.)[1] When we discussed the report on the phone, Herzstein conceded that guerrilla warfare is always brutal; but, he opined, the numerical imbalances in these figures suggested "not so much warfare as mass murder." This was, to use my lay terminology, still another "disparity document."

At the Archives on Monday, Herzstein paid a courtesy call on Robert Wolfe, Chief of the Modern Military Branch, and senior staff member John Mendelsohn. Both men expressed their immediate willingness to help. A refugee from Nazi Germany (he was classified as what the Nazis called a *Mischling,* with both Jewish and Aryan blood in his veins), Mendelsohn was an expert on captured Third Reich documents and on the postwar U.S. trials of Nazis. He was a gentle older man, portly and gray, with a waggish sense of humor, but he approached this, like all of his work, with the seriousness it demanded.

It did not take the team long to pick up the paperwork trail of *Oberleutnant* Waldheim, but it took them several days to absorb what they were finding and collate it into an understandable chronology that traced what could now be documented of his assignments.

They found the formerly classified postwar interrogation reports

Stahl is the German word for "steel."

of General Stahl exactly where Hilberg's book indicated, and they validated my suspicion that Stahl had been questioned about numerous campaigns, including Kozara. Stahl confessed to U.S. officials that he was under orders to suppress partisan activity in western Bosnia by the use of what he conceded were "extreme" measures. Specifically, he said, he was ordered to murder scores of hostages for every German soldier killed by the partisans. The official interrogation summary continued:

> Subject states that while a ratio of 1:100 is out of the question, executions at a ratio of 1:1 up to 1:100 were performed by his division. Stahl bases the legality of such steps on the fact that it was an order and therefore had to be executed . . .[2]

Scanning through the surviving German documents regarding the 1942 Kozara campaign, Herzstein found one "progress report" that was particularly chilling. It stated that a total of 4,364 prisoners were deported to Germany and Norway for slave labor; presumably they were the able-bodied men in the group. This was followed immediately by the ominous notation: *3000 Kinder und Frauen.*[3]

That, sickeningly, was all it said. There was no verb included to describe exactly what had been *done* to three thousand children and women.

Next, Herzstein came upon a Wehrmacht document with a whimsical style that belied its ghastly contents. The title translated to *History of the Division in Verse,* and it was morbid poetry indeed. The chronicler detailed in free verse how the partisans at Kozara, surrounded by German and Croatian forces protected by barbed-wire entrenchments, had tried desperately to break out. The report described the partisans as "wild figures" and unkempt *Untermenschen* ("subhumans") who screamed and attacked like a "primeval horde." Dozens of them had been left to rot, lying stiff and lifeless "on the wire and in our lines."

These operations were candidly described as "cleansing actions" conducted "without mercy, without pity." Why were such harsh tactics employed? The report explained:

> . . . because harshness alone can give peace to the country, and only a cold heart can command what needs to be commanded, in order to make this fertile garden of Bosnia bloom again for everyone. . . . That which is necessary has already been done.

The report referred to the "purification" of the area and, even more ominously, to the achievement of "the final liquidation of the bandit plague."

The Kozara "poetry" was accompanied by a sort of table of honor, elegantly typeset, listing, in large capital letters, thirty-four Germans and Croats. Not surprisingly, General Stahl's name was at the top of the list. As Herzstein's eyes made their way down the roster of unfamiliar names, they stopped at honoree number twenty-five: "*LEUTNANT WALDHEIM.*" Herzstein was shocked by the import of what he had just found: The future U.N. Secretary-General was one of only thirty-four men singled out for "special mention" among perhaps twenty thousand German and Croatian soldiers involved in one of the grisliest Axis operations of the war.[4]

Suddenly, Waldheim's King Zvonimir Medal seemed more significant than ever. According to Yugoslav press reports, Stahl recommended Waldheim for the medal on July 22, 1942—only four days after the completion of the Kozara "operation." Now there was little doubt that Waldheim's honor had been conferred specifically in recognition of his performance in that notorious episode.

Continuing his research, Herzstein found a captured German *Activity Report for July 1942* that summarized the medals awarded in connection with the Kozara operation. It reported that 139 decorations, including the "wounded badge," were handed out among the twenty thousand troops who took part. And only *two* German soldiers were awarded the Zvonimir Medal "with oak leaves."[5]

Although we still did not know Waldheim's precise function in the West Bosnia Combat Group, it was now beyond doubt that his actions received special recognition from Stahl himself.

Exploiting what few details we had of Waldheim's assignments, Herzstein moved on to May 1943 and found additional information that bore directly on the Podgorica photo and the "Black Operation." The very day after the photo was taken, Loehr had ordered Phleps's Prince Eugen Waffen-SS Division to conduct a massive "cleansing" operation just a few miles east of Podgorica. This confirmed my suspicion that logistical planning for the operation was still under way at the time of the airstrip meeting. It was hard to believe that such planning was not among the subjects discussed at the airstrip meeting.

Herzstein followed the paper trail further, away from Yugoslavia now, and into Greece. He learned that the National Archives held an entire microfilmed series of captured personnel rosters of the High Command of Army Group E. These listed Waldheim as serving on General Alexander Loehr's staff beginning in August 1942, initially as an interpreter, later as "O3" officer in the Ic/AO Branch. This branch combined the duties of military intelligence-gathering (designated Ic) with the counterintelligence and political intelligence work of the Abwehr officer and his staff (designated AO). The Abwehr officer normally functioned as the Wehrmacht's liaison with the dreaded SD (*Sicherheitsdienst,* the Security Service of the Reich, originally set up as the intelligence service of the SS and Nazi Party) and the GFP (*Geheime Feldpolizei,* the Secret Field Police). We knew from the Hilberg volume and other books that Secret Field Police units were deeply implicated in the deportations of Greek Jews.

The thirty-four–page "secret" *Arbeitseinteilung* ("Work Allocation Table") of the High Command of Army Group E confirmed that Waldheim reported directly to the chief of the Ic/AO Branch, Lieutenant Colonel Herbert Warnstorff, and that Waldheim was important enough to have his own deputies, two first lieutenants, named Poliza and Krohne. Most importantly, the table listed "O3" Waldheim's duties. The first responsibility listed for Waldheim was in the form of a handwritten addition, but the microfilm copy was poor, and the text was indecipherable. However, Waldheim's other responsibilities were typed, and quite legible: "Enemy situation; morning and evening intelligence reports; enemy situation judgments; activity reports; prisoner interrogation; personnel matters of the Ic/AO Branch"; interrogation of prisoners from "Great Britain and the U.S.A."; and also *Sonderaufgaben* ("special tasks"). In Nazi parlance, this last expression was unforgettable: it sometimes served as a euphemism for killing operations. What did it mean here? There was, for now at least, no way to tell. But one thing was abundantly clear: Kurt Waldheim had been a senior intelligence officer, not merely an "interpreter."

The job description of Waldheim's boss, Colonel Warnstorff, was also intriguing. Among other duties, he was responsible for disciplinary matters and for giving technical and activity orders to Secret Field Police detachment 621. He was also responsible for "cooperation with SD" and similarly for "cooperation" with the Security Police. Finally, the chart confirmed that Warnstorff supervised both intelligence and counterintelligence activities, the latter largely through his position as the immediate superior of the headquarters Abwehr officer, Major Friedrich Wilhelm Hammer.[6]

Herzstein next found a directive dated December 22, 1943, signed by General Loehr himself, ordering that prisoners found to have assisted partisans in acts of sabotage were "to be shot." But, the order continued, if such "co-culprits cannot be found, punishment must be imposed upon people who can be considered partners in responsibility, particularly those who admit to being communists." For this purpose, Loehr suggested, "It might be advisable to take hostages preventively." Such hostages were to be selected by the SS and the "counterintelligence department of the affected unit."[7] Herzstein was confident that reports on such reprisals would normally be routed to Waldheim's Ic/AO Branch, since that branch held counterintelligence responsibility for Loehr's entire Army Group. Once again, however, a key question could not be answered: Had Waldheim's branch ordered or authorized specific reprisals? And if so, had Waldheim been personally involved?

Concentrating on the latter period of the war, Herzstein documented some of Waldheim's duties from the period of March 1944 through September 1944. Herzstein found some reports signed by Waldheim that summarized information that had been extracted from prisoners. It was well known that torture and execution were common features of German interrogation in the Balkans. Was Waldheim involved in the actual questioning or "disposition" of any of these prisoners? Or had he only received and collated the *results* of those interrogations? Once again, the answer was frustratingly elusive.

Herzstein found that Waldheim had signed a number of intelligence reports referring to "cleansing" operations, but it was unclear whether any of these actions went beyond the permissible bounds of military conduct. Herzstein advised that it would take an enormous amount of additional research, especially in Greek and Yugoslav archives, to learn what had occurred in the obscure Balkan towns and villages referenced in these reports.

Herzstein also found records disclosing that Waldheim routinely delivered oral briefings to Loehr's chief of staff, General August Winter. Waldheim briefed Winter on the enemy situation in a broad geographical arc, spanning much of the Balkan Peninsula. Summary notations in the minutes of these meetings referenced such matters as the "efficient" use of hostages to secure rail lines (by tying them to the fronts of locomotives in order to assure the safe passage of Wehrmacht trains) and the utilization of civilian slave labor. One meeting discussed talks that Winter held with Heinrich Himmler on the coordination of security measures. Finally, there was an unexplained reference to something called "Operation Viper."[8]

In sum, the paperwork trail of Lieutenant Waldheim painted the picture of a young man who, when he first returned to duty in the spring of 1942, may have been a mere interpreter, but who appeared to have risen rapidly to the post of senior intelligence officer. Regardless of his personal responsibilities and actions, Waldheim had to have been one of the best-informed German officers in the Balkans.

Herzstein called me at home each evening throughout the week to report his findings. He was mining gold. However, my instincts were to hold off on going public with his findings. Who knew what other secrets were still buried in the Archives? But after studying my summaries of Herzstein's research, Singer and Steinberg scheduled a press conference for Tuesday, March 25, with Herzstein slated to be our star witness, to present his research results to the world. Publicly, the WJC continued to deny any interest in influencing Austrian politics. But privately, Singer responded curtly to my concerns over a too-hasty press conference with the stern reminder, "This is an election campaign, Rosenbaum."

The professor had only a few more days to dig through the captured documents at the National Archives, and I wondered whether that was enough time for him to find anything else of major significance.

Perhaps the most startling feature of the material he had already found—quite apart from its often extraordinary content—was that these documents, many bearing Waldheim's name or signature, had been available to the public for decades, yet no one had found them. Or had they? The questions of who knew what, and why none of this was revealed earlier, gnawed at me. Who had helped Waldheim pull off this enormously improbable cover-up?

I wondered, in particular, how much the Yugoslavs had known about Waldheim's role at Kozara and later on in the war. Was it not possible that Yugoslav partisans had salvaged at least a portion of the same records housed in Washington, or even more damaging reports? If so, we could not necessarily count on Belgrade to release them. Serbian officials might be prepared to cooperate, but at some point, they would probably begin to appreciate the negative impact the disclosures were having on Tito's posthumous reputation. And most of their Croatian colleagues would likely be aghast, fearful of additional public reminders that the short-lived "independent" state of Croatia had been a Nazi ally. The fact that the Yugoslavs had disclosed nothing further after the single snippet of information was released by the Yugoslav press the day after the initial *New York Times* story was suggestive of internal struggles underway within the government. The wild card here was the importance of Tito's memory. Lionizing the late dictator seemed to be the government's best hope of preserving enough federalist sentiment to hold the country together. The Yugoslavs could not make additional disclosures about Waldheim without undermining Tito's honor, for it would be a tacit admission that Tito participated in the cover-up, or at least that he had befriended a Nazi. Already, journalists were asking the Yugoslav government the embarrassing question: Why had it never before released information on Waldheim?

And how much did the Austrian public know—even now—about the presidential candidate? I found myself pondering the organizational tables that Herzstein found, detailing the duties of Waldheim and his Army Group E boss, Colonel Warnstorff. They seemed so much more extensive than the description of Ic responsibilities that was published in the Austrian press only a week earlier. I searched through the materials that I had with me at home and at last found the piece. It was just as I had remembered: *Wochenpresse* had quoted directly from the *Handbook for the General Staff Service in War,* and mentioned nothing about "special tasks," prisoner interrogations, or the Secret Field Police. I could not help but wonder, in light of Herzstein's discoveries at the Archives, whether the magazine's editors had left out something important.

Sure enough, when I tracked down a facsimile reprinting of the complete Wehrmacht handbook and compared it to the quotation printed in *Wochenpresse,* I discovered that the Austrian magazine had engaged in some outrageous "selective editing." From the magazine's bland excerpt of the listed duties of Ic, the reader could never have guessed that it had neglected to quote certain passages, such as:

> Ic must also maintain close links with the troops. . . . The Abwehr Officer will be responsible for counterintelligence according to the instructions of Ic. . . . On behalf of Ic, AO will issue orders to any Gestapo personnel active in the operational area. . . . At Army High Command, Ic is the command office for the interrogation of prisoners, renegades, and inhabitants . . .[9]

Here as well was confirmation of Herzstein's find. The Ic section was the "command unit" for prisoner interrogations. Whatever that expression meant, it certainly carried significant responsibility. Here, too, was evidence that Gestapo units took orders from Waldheim's branch.

Wochenpresse's deceptive editing of the passage stunned me; it proved a powerful object lesson on the level of journalistic responsibility we could expect from the Austrian press.

Unfortunately, the attitude of growing numbers of Austrians seemed to be summed up by Harry Sauerkopf, the People's Party leader in Burgenland, who asked belligerently, "What business is it of the World Jewish Congress whom we elect as president?"[10]

Meanwhile, the West German news magazine *Stern* turned up the heat on Waldheim by publishing a photo (the one about which Schuller had heard rumors) of a 1938 Nazi student rally in Vienna. One of the students in the picture looked very much like a young Waldheim. He was standing directly in front of a swastika-emblazoned banner. A magazine reporter had shown the photo to Josef Tasler, one of Waldheim's Consular Academy comrades. Tasler responded, "Yes, that is Kurti. No doubt. It can only be him or a *Doppelgaenger* [a 'double']."[11]

The disclosure was of only modest importance, but the fact of its publication bolstered my spirits, for it was evidence that a major German media outlet was willing to dig, and willing to publish what it found. How different the situation was in Austria, where only tiny *Profil* was engaged in genuine investigative journalism. There was also a comical aspect to the episode: It reminded me that, however much most Germans dislike having to recall the Nazi era, they delight in puncturing Austria's "victim of the Nazis" balloon.

Waldheim wasted no time in responding to the *Stern* story. No, he insisted, the young man in the photograph was not him.

I spent part of Thursday, March 20, studying a telex that Waldheim had sent to his Washington publishers, Adler & Adler, trying to avoid the humiliation of having his book removed from their list. The Adlers sent me a copy of the four brief paragraphs in which Waldheim purported to "set my military record straight."

Waldheim told the Adlers that he was sent to the Balkans in April 1942 as a liaison staff officer at the headquarters of the Wehrmacht's 12th Army (later reorganized into Army Group E), initially based in Belgrade and later in Arsakli/Salonika, Greece. His tasks in Belgrade, he said, included German/Italian interpreting and "liaison duties to the Italian Army in Croatia." He continued: "As of the summer of 1942, I was transferred to AOK12 [12th Army] headquarters in Greece as an interpreter." He added that, throughout the period from mid-November 1942 to April 1943, he was on leave in Vienna, working on his doctoral thesis.

I was thunderstruck at the realization of the man's audacity. He wanted the Adlers to believe that he had spent the summer of 1942 in Greece. But this was contradicted by evidence cited in the Yugoslav press as well as by the Kozara documents Herzstein had discovered this very week. Waldheim could not know about our U.S. National Archives find, but he certainly knew that the Yugoslav press placed him in the West Bosnia Combat Group, under General Friedrich Stahl, in the summer of 1942. He was either growing more brazen in his lies or was having difficulty keeping them organized in his mind. Here, he appeared to be gambling that his U.S. publishers were unaware of the Yugoslav revelation, and that they would not share his telex text with any of his pursuers. On the latter count at least, he had wagered poorly.

The Adler telex made our National Archives material even more hard-hitting. If Waldheim had no blood on his hands from Kozara, why was he pretending to have been in Greece at the time?

Waldheim was somewhat more truthful in the final paragraphs of his telex, which concerned the period from April 1943 until the spring of 1945. He described his assignment as that of an *Ordonnance* officer for Army Group E in Arsakli, Greece. During 1943, he said, he was also given "several interpreting tasks with the then-allied Italian forces, such as in Tirana, Athens, and Podgorica." Those assignments, he said, were "based upon my language skills and involved no other functions, powers of command, or combat duty." He contended that there were "sufficient witnesses alive to testify to this," but he provided no names. This first mention by Waldheim of an Athens assignment sent my antennae up. I had been wondering about Athens ever since Wehrmacht veteran Waldemar Fend told *Wochenpresse* that he recalled meeting Waldheim in Athens in the autumn of 1943, when the latter man was serving as an interpreter there. In his telex to the Adlers, Waldheim was now confirming that he had performed interpreting tasks "and no other functions" in the Greek capital.

Waldheim spelled out the dates of his service and his extended periods of leave, and here he made what looked like a slip, for, in listing his only absences from Salonika on extended home leave in 1943 as having taken place in November and December of that year, he seemed to confirm that he was on duty in the Salonika area in August 1943. It was in that month, we knew, that the last Jews were deported from the city. Yet he still claimed to know nothing of the deportations.

Our office was closed early on Friday, in order to respect the beginning of the Jewish Sabbath, so I was home by 5 P.M., thoroughly exhausted and naive enough to believe that my long week was over.

The phone rang at 5:20.

Herzstein's voice put me on alert. He was ordinarily a rapid talker, but his words this evening were slow, precise, hushed. "I hope you're sitting down, Eli," he said. "What I have to tell you now, you're not gonna believe."

I waited, but I was skeptical. I had already been surprised by so many elements of this convoluted affair that such a preamble had lost the power to excite.

"It's a tip from John Mendelsohn," Herzstein said softly. He explained that Mendelsohn, on a lark, had decided to see if Waldheim's name might have been placed on the CROWCASS list. CROWCASS, which I had encountered during my Justice Department work years earlier, is an acronym for the Central Registry of War Criminals and Security Suspects. Administered for the Allied Control Authority by the U.S. Army in the immediate postwar years, its purpose was to coordinate efforts throughout Europe to apprehend the thousands of Nazi war criminals and security suspects who remained at liberty after the collapse of the Third Reich.

Herzstein sputtered, "Eli, now get this: Mendelsohn *found* Waldheim's name on the list!"

"Bob, are you kidding me?"

"Look, Mendelsohn showed it to me on the microfilm reader. I've seen it with my own eyes. Waldheim is listed on a June 1948 CROW-CASS list."

"CROWCASS? Oh my God!" I was shocked nearly beyond words. A CROWCASS listing ordinarily meant that the Allies had concluded that there was a substantial basis to suspect involvement in Nazi crimes. In effect, it was an arrest warrant. If Allied forces located someone on a CROWCASS list, he was supposed to be arrested and turned over to the nation that listed him. Was it possible that Waldheim's name could have been on the list for thirty-eight years *without anyone having noticed?* "Are you sure it's the *same* Kurt Waldheim?" I asked.

"No doubt about it, Eli. There's no date of birth listed, and there's a question mark after the first name 'Kurt,' but the rest of the entry makes it clear that it's our man. They list him as a lieutenant in the 'Ic' Branch of Army Group E in Yugoslavia during 1944–1945. It matches perfectly."

Calm yourself, Eli, I thought. There were many reasons why an Austrian national could land on a CROWCASS list. The original intentions behind CROWCASS were laudable—to facilitate the apprehension and prosecution of Nazi war criminals—but it soon was watered down by the inclusion of thousands of "security suspects" who had no connection with war crimes. Neal Sher's predecessor as OSI director, Allan Ryan, once wrote that CROWCASS eventually became "widely regarded in the field as an undiscriminating repository of politically motivated charges."[12] The significance of Mendelsohn's discovery would depend on why Waldheim's name was placed on the list, what the charges were, and how well they were documented.

Herzstein roared on: "The CROWCASS entry says that Waldheim is wanted by Yugoslavia and the crime he's wanted for is—get this—*murder.* And that's not the end of it. You know that column on the CROWCASS lists entitled 'UNWCC List/Serial Number'?"

I interrupted, "Bob, you don't mean to tell me that there's an entry for Waldheim in the *United Nations"*—I could barely get the words out—*"the United Nations War Crimes Commission* suspect number column?"

"That's *exactly* what I mean. The microfilm print I have is a bad one, and I'd need a magnifying glass to make out the number, but he does have one. Unbelievable, huh?"

We live in a strange world, I thought, but this disclosure was as close to "beyond belief" as I had ever encountered. The former Secretary General of the United Nations was listed as a wanted man, for murder, and by whom? The United Nations War Crimes Commission! This meant that a multinational panel had examined evidence provided by the Yugoslavs and had arrived at the conclusion that enough proof existed to arrest Waldheim on charges of being a Nazi war criminal! I shouted into the phone, "I've got to have that document up here as soon as possible, Bob!"

I called Cynthia in Washington and began our conversation, much as Herzstein had done with me, with "You're not going to believe this." I told her the news that, only minutes earlier, I would have found impossible to believe. I recruited her to pick up a copy of the document from Herzstein at the Governor's House Hotel in Washington and bring it to New York on a late Friday night shuttle flight. "The silver lining is you get a free trip up here," I said. "The WJC will cover the ticket."

She agreed at once, and I sensed that she savored the intrigue. Her own legal work, for a trade association, was pretty mundane stuff. About a month earlier, she had delivered the Podgorica photo to David Crown. Now she would handle a document that was even more explosive.

After speaking with Cynthia, I immediately called Neal Sher to tell him the news. At OSI, we had long had a partial set of CROW-CASS lists in our library, and on occasion I had waded into them to see if a particular name was listed. Usually this involved a case I was working on at the moment. Staffers sometimes idled away a few spare minutes by checking the names of well-known Germans. But neither I nor anyone else had ever come up with the bizarre idea—or so it surely would have seemed at the time—to see if the former U.N. Secretary-General's name might appear on the list alongside those of thousands of suspected Nazi war criminals.

I paced relentlessly as I waited out the hours in my apartment, contemplating the implications of Mendelsohn's discovery. We now knew with certainty that the Yugoslav government had conducted an investigation of Waldheim shortly after the war. Thus far, Belgrade had allowed the release of only bits of material, all concerning the Kozara massacres of 1942, but Herzstein said that the CROWCASS document referred to criminal activities in *1944 and 1945*. That meant that the Yugoslavs had to have a separate cache of evidence on Waldheim, as yet unseen—except, that is, by the U.N. War Crimes

Commission. Could we pressure Belgrade into releasing the rest of its evidence? Armed with the CROWCASS document, perhaps we could.

I also realized that we now had the definitive answer to a critical question: Had the Yugoslavs known about Waldheim's past? Most certainly, yes. It was possible to conjecture that the military files referencing Waldheim's 1942 role at Kozara had been buried in dusty archives and overlooked by the Yugoslavs. But listing him formally with the UNWCC in London was quite a different matter. When the wily Marshal Tito was negotiating Yugoslavia's territorial claims to parts of southern Austria, the Yugoslav leadership could hardly have missed the fact that a member of the Austrian Foreign Ministry's team was wanted by their own government—for murder. Yet Tito had subsequently befriended Waldheim, maintained the friendship when Waldheim became Austria's Foreign Minister, and, still later, supported him at the U.N. And now it was clear that throughout all the years of supposed cooperation and friendship, Tito could have destroyed Waldheim instantly, simply by whispering the single word "CROWCASS" or the phrase "U.N. War Crimes Commission" to just one reporter. It was hard for me to believe that Tito had failed to exact a *quid pro quo* for his government's otherwise inexplicable silence. Suddenly it seemed obvious why, during his years at the U.N., Waldheim had found so many ways to promote Tito's surprisingly successful claim to be the spokesman for the world's "nonaligned" nations.

I was struck, too, by the thought of how Waldheim must have panicked two weeks earlier when the Yugoslav press linked him with Kozara. He had likely reached an "understanding" (spoken or otherwise) with the Tito government that the Yugoslavs would keep his secrets. But now Tito was gone. Waldheim must have been—must still be, I realized—living in fear that Belgrade would hang out more of his dirty laundry. His only remaining hope would be that Tito's posthumous reputation was now tied inexorably to his own current one.

Where did the Soviet Union fit in? The USSR had not participated in CROWCASS or the UNWCC. It was therefore important to learn whether Yugoslavia developed its compromising information on Waldheim prior to June 28, 1948, when the Stalin–Tito rift exploded with Yugoslavia's expulsion from the Cominform, the Soviet-run international organization of communist parties. The answer was likely to be yes, since the U.N. War Crimes Commission had already completed its work by the end of 1948. And if the answer was yes, then the Yugoslavs almost certainly would have shared the information with the Soviets. In any event, the Soviets could have obtained access to the relevant files on Waldheim through either the Polish or the Czech government; both were participants in the CROWCASS program and both were represented on the UNWCC.

More troubling to me, as an American, was the question of U.S. knowledge. If Waldheim was listed on CROWCASS, U.S. intelligence, particularly Army intelligence, should have a record of the fact. Yet, only one month earlier, in its response to my FOIA request, the U.S. Army provided no hint of anything incriminating. Something is very wrong here, I said to myself.

There were only two plausible explanations on the American side: cover-up or foul-up.

I thought it highly unlikely that anyone in the Army's Investigative Records Repository had tampered with the files, at least in recent years. I had worked with these people before and was convinced of their integrity. But I could not discount the possibility that someone might have altered the records sometime during the past thirty-eight years. Waldheim's "clearance" by the CIA in its 1980 letter to Congressman Solarz argued further for the cover-up explanation. Was Waldheim, like Klaus Barbie and others, one of the lucky ex-Nazis who had been able to peddle his services to our own government?[13] I recalled that in 1977, U.S. military intelligence veteran William R. Corson had charged that CROWCASS "operated on two distinct levels . . . to catalog war crimes and the locations of war criminals; and to recruit former Nazis to serve as U.S. intelligence agents and sources."[14] His charge had never been substantiated, however. Still, it was impossible to rule out the possibility of a U.S. cover-up.

But, as I pondered the possibilities, the "foul-up" scenario seemed more likely. If Waldheim had been an American "asset," why was he so extraordinarily accommodating to the USSR during the "Prague Spring" of 1968, the Soviets' most serious foreign policy crisis during his tenure as Austrian Foreign Minister? Moreover, he had been the Soviets' candidate for U.N. Secretary-General, not ours. If Waldheim had been covert "U.S. property," one would have expected the United States—and its closest ally in the intelligence arena, the United Kingdom—to push Waldheim for the top post. They had not done so. Indeed, the U.K. *vetoed* Waldheim's nomination during the first round of deliberations. And once Waldheim achieved the top U.N. post, he continued to be enormously helpful to the Soviets and a frequent disappointment to the United States. Where, then, was the *quid pro quo* for the U.S.? If the U.S. had received anything from Waldheim, it was certainly well concealed.

It seemed far more plausible to conclude that the U.S. had not checked Waldheim very carefully in the years immediately following the war. His Wehrmacht rank of first lieutenant probably seemed comparatively insignificant at the time. There was no obvious evidence connecting Waldheim with the SS or the Gestapo, the notorious organizations that were the focal point of postwar Allied hunts for Nazi criminals. Nor had he been a member of the Nazi Party. Moreover, if the U.S. had placed any stock in a "clearance" of Waldheim by the Austrian State Police, Washington might have fallen into a KGB trap.

It was easy to imagine how inquiring American authorities could have come up empty-handed. The past four weeks had reacquainted me with the difficulties of dealing with wartime German military records. Often, I was amazed that we ever found anything. And if the records were in disarray now, the situation in the first months and years after the war was far worse. Harried American military clerks usually lacked even a rudimentary knowledge of German military practice. Few could speak or read German. They had neither copying machines nor computers. Record-keeping was a hit-or-miss proposition. Thus, I calculated, the Army's (supposed) current lack of information concerning Waldheim, CROWCASS, and the UNWCC could be the result of a colossal clerical error, a cross-filing oversight from the precomputer age.

Beyond these considerations, I was also aware that the American occupation authorities had been desperate to find "respectable" Austrians to help run the new government. When someone like Waldheim, with a degree from the Consular Academy and a wartime doctorate in law from the University of Vienna, appeared at the Foreign Ministry in search of a job, the fact of his service as a junior Wehrmacht officer probably seemed of minor consequence. By the end of 1947, the American occupation forces had completed their war crimes trials, and it was possible that Waldheim had not been listed either on CROWCASS or in the UNWCC files until the following year. Decades later, when he was a candidate for U.N. Secretary General, it was difficult to imagine that the U.S. government, which had come to view the U.N. as an impotent and increasingly irrelevant entity, would have seen any need to run an emergency background check on the well-known candidate. He had completed years of capable service as a representative of neutral-but-Western-oriented Austria, and had served as that country's Foreign Minister. If my suspicions were correct, it meant that U.S. intelligence had failed not only in neglecting to ferret out details of Waldheim's war record, but also in failing to appreciate how the communists could score an espionage triumph by exploiting compromising information in the nominee's past.

Thus, as far as discovery by the Americans was concerned, it appeared likely that Waldheim had simply lucked out.

Until now.

Shortly after 9 P.M., Cynthia arrived at my apartment with an envelope containing two large, heavy sheets of shiny, gray-white microfilm printout paper. Like all such fresh copies, they smelled faintly of formaldehyde. Knowing that I would be preoccupied, Cynthia went off to visit her brother at his Manhattan apartment.

I felt a rush of adrenaline as I sat down to examine the material. The first page was a cover sheet, printed in large capital letters, announcing:

THE CENTRAL REGISTRY
OF WAR CRIMINALS
AND SECURITY SUSPECTS

FINAL
CONSOLIDATED WANTED LIST
PART 1
M–Z
Germans Only
Note: All Previous Crowcass Wanted Lists
Should Be Destroyed
JUNE 1948

The June 1948 date was important, for it confirmed that Yugoslavia had assembled its Waldheim dossier prior to the Tito–Stalin split.

On the second page of the CROWCASS printout, in black type, along with dozens of names of SS men, Gestapo officers, and concentration camp personnel, was the name "WALDHEIM, KURT?" identified as a lieutenant in the Ic section of Army Group E. The dates of his alleged crimes were entered as "4.44–5.45" (April 1944 to May 1945). In the "Reason Wanted" column, Waldheim's entry contained but a single word: MURDER.

How would history have been changed, I asked myself, if this had become public knowledge back in 1971 or, for that matter, at any time in the succeeding decade? Waldheim's U.N. career would have crashed; at the very least, he would have returned to Austria in disgrace; it was even possible that he would have stood trial, although this was unlikely, given Austria's history of minimal interest in prosecuting Nazi war criminals.

It took me nearly twenty minutes to decipher the UNWCC file number from the blurry microfilm print. I had to resort to a magnifying glass and a strong light. It was difficult to make out every number, but I dared not make a mistake. A few fuzzy digits proved impossible to read, but I compared these with clearer numbers printed elsewhere on the page and, by process of elimination, at last identified every numeral. I wrote the digits on a notepad and stared at them: 79/724.

The numbers were etched into my memory immediately, because of what they meant. Incredibly, Kurt Waldheim was the 724th entry on wanted list number seventy-nine of the United Nations War Crimes Commission.

My exhausted mind painted the improbable picture of Secretary General Waldheim, sitting contentedly amidst the ornate trappings of his prestigious office on the forty-second floor of the Secretariat Building overlooking the East River while, somewhere else in the U.N. complex, there reposed a carefully guarded folder bearing his name, accusing him of being a Nazi murderer.

A sudden thought stopped me cold: *The file should still be at the U.N.—right here in Manhattan!*

12

Elan Steinberg drove over to my apartment early the next morning to satisfy himself that I was not, as he put it, "hallucinating." He stared at the photocopied pages for a few moments before deciding that the information was too important to be held back until our scheduled Tuesday press conference. Steinberg wanted to break the news immediately and I agreed, but we dared not do so without Singer's approval. The problem was, this was the Sabbath; Singer, an orthodox Jew, would not answer a phone call.

We hopped into Steinberg's car and, as he drove toward Queens, we discussed the "Civiletti letter" of April 1980, in which U.S. Attorney General Benjamin Civiletti thanked Waldheim for his staff's assistance in facilitating the Justice Department's examination of the UNWCC's files, only to find that the access was suddenly and severely curtailed. The episode now carried a whole new significance. Had Waldheim known that *he* was listed in those files? We amused ourselves with impressions of a panic-stricken U.N. Secretary-General reading Civiletti's thank-you letter and then calling in his staff to shriek at them for not clearing the matter with him first.

We saw this day as the end of Waldheim's campaign for the presidency of Austria. He now had to be considered a formally accused Nazi war criminal, and would surely have to withdraw from the political race. As a technical matter, he was still a fugitive, subject to arrest and extradition to Yugoslavia. It was, for both of us, a heady feeling to know that the investigation that had drained us was now over.

"You know," I declared jubilantly, "now even Wiesenthal will have to abandon him." I told Steinberg about an incident from a few years earlier, when Wiesenthal had cited similar Yugoslav charges as he exposed a Croatian immigrant who became a prominent member of Australia's New South Wales Liberal Party as a "war criminal."* The

---

*"[O]ur revelations struck like a bomb," Wiesenthal had boasted, adding, "Finally [he] had to resign from all his political functions."[1]

charges in that case—writing pro-German and anti-Semitic articles—
were obviously far less serious than murder. And there were other
cases in which Wiesenthal had cited CROWCASS listings as reason
enough to investigate and/or prosecute.

Wiesenthal was already under a great deal of pressure from Jewish
groups, especially outside Austria, to denounce Waldheim, or at least
to demand that the candidate explain his cover-up. Steinberg and I
concluded that, no matter how much he hated the Socialists, no
matter how angry he might be that we had exposed a giant Nazi
scandal in his backyard, Wiesenthal, finally, would be smart enough
to cut his losses.

Waldheim would be on his own now. We were sure of it.

Steinberg found a parking spot and we rushed up to the front
door of Singer's house. We did not want to offend him by using the
electric bell on the Sabbath, so Steinberg pounded on the door.
Singer's wife, Evelyn, answered and said with a shrug, "He's not
here."

"It's important," Steinberg said.

"He's at *shul*," Evelyn replied. She gave us directions.

It was about 10:30 A.M. when we stepped into the neighborhood
house that served as the *shul* for a small congregation. Even from
the back, as one of a few dozen *yarmulke*-covered heads bobbing
above rhythmically swaying shoulders, Singer's height and the dark
tan he had acquired on a recent vaction in Florida made him easy to
spot. We edged our way forward, to the end of the row where he
stood. Steinberg caught his eye and gestured. An expression of shock
registered on Singer's face.

He excused himself quietly, took me strongly by the arm, and
quickly ushered us outside the room, to a narrow hallway. "You,"
he said to both of us in mock derision, "are the last people I expected
to see in *shul*."

"Israel, you are not going to believe this," Steinberg said. It was
a popular choice of words these past twenty-four hours. "We have
the ultimate bombshell. Brace yourself. Guess who was wanted—
by the U.N. War Crimes Commission—for murder?"

"No!" Singer exclaimed. "You *have* this? You have it *here?*"

Steinberg reached into the inner pocket of his suit jacket, pulled
out the damning page and handed it over. Singer studied it slowly.
His eyebrows raised. His hand stroked his chin. "Amazing . . .
amazing," he muttered.

"We want to release it right away," Steinberg said. "Do you have
any objection?"

The question was not as simple as it might appear—not to Israel
Singer. We were a Jewish organization. It was, after all, the Sabbath.

For several moments, Singer's hand remained on his chin as he deliberated silently. Where was the proper balance amid the conflicting considerations? Was it more important to denounce to the world a man who—according to the Yugoslav War Crimes Commission—played an active role in the sins that led to the deaths of eleven million innocent men, women, and children, or to insist that two nonorthodox Jews adhere to the orthodox interpretation of God's law? Was it more important, on this quiet, otherwise unremarkable Saturday morning, to do battle with man's evil or to celebrate God's goodness? These were questions that had, perhaps, no correct answers.

Finally, Singer thrust the document back at Steinberg, communicating with the slightest of nods his willingness to let us make the decision for ourselves.

Steinberg and I raced for the doorway.

Singer returned to his prayers.

We summoned Hella Moritz into the office to help us prepare a press release. Steinberg and I decided that this story was so explosive that it required no hype. Some of our previous releases had to communicate complex and confusing facts and thus needed to be placed in context; this one was straightforward. "Elan, you could write this one up in *My Weekly Reader* and the kids would understand it," I joked. "It's a 'no-brainer.'" Our release simply laid out the facts without embellishment.

By early afternoon, we telexed the news to the major wire services, and we waited for a mob of reporters and camera crews to descend upon us. We knew that every journalist would have the same questions: How could a man listed in U.N. files as wanted for murder get himself elected to head the very same organization? Which governments might have known about the charges and voted for Waldheim anyway? And how had this remained secret when the wanted lists were sitting in the U.S. National Archives for so many years, available to anyone who wished to look?

For hours, Steinberg, Moritz, and I waited by the phones. I felt like a teenage girl hoping that *he* would call. It was an otherwise slow day for news, so we expected our revelation to be the headline in every newspaper and the lead on every newscast.

But we learned a sobering lesson that day: Never release a major story on a weekend. Who could imagine a more dramatic disclosure than this? But the top editors and the best reporters were not on the job. The result: The story was little noticed and poorly reported.

It was not until the next day that Diane Wallerstein, a producer for WNBC-TV in New York, spotted a brief mention of the story in a wire-service report and began to prepare a feature for the Sunday night news. She persuaded Singer, Steinberg, and me to come into the office on Sunday to tape interviews.

Wallerstein, meanwhile, tracked down the U.N.'s chief archivist, Alf Erlandsson, before he had even heard the news, and asked bluntly, "Do you know that there is a war crimes suspect file at the U.N. on Mr. Waldheim?"

The old Swede was shocked. "Do you mean *our* Mr. Waldheim?" he stammered. "*Kurt* Waldheim?" Erlandsson composed himself and declared that he would not believe this report until he saw the file himself.

When Wallerstein inquired about the possibility of her reviewing the file, Erlandsson replied that he would need the permission of the Secretary General, Perez de Cuellar. He explained that even the member governments of the U.N. were barred from access without such permission. He reminded Wallerstein that in the past forty years, access had been granted only three times: in the cases of Eichmann, Mengele, and Barbie, to the Israeli, West German, and U.S. governments.

Erlandsson's shock seemed genuine to Wallerstein, for had it been widely known at U.N. headquarters that there was a war crimes file on Waldheim, someone almost certainly would have leaked that fact to the press long ago.

At noon every Monday, U.N. press spokesman François Giuliani traditionally conducted a press conference. As a rule, these were tedious events, but not so on this day. By now, our story had made the rounds, and one reporter voiced the question of the moment: Was it true that the U.N. had a war crimes file on Kurt Waldheim?

"It is a possibility," Giuliani responded coolly.

The logical follow-up question came next: If there was such a file, would it be made available to the media?

Giuliani was not prepared to give a definitive answer. But he said that the press ought to bear in mind that the UNWCC files were sealed. Not even the member governments of the U.N. had access to them.

Reporters howled their indignation, but Giuliani stood firm.

Our release of the CROWCASS/UNWCC story was immediately noticed in Austria. An exultant Karl Schuller reported to me that one of his informants told him that Waldheim's backers were in a panic, facing the devastation of their presidential plans. There was dissension in the ranks, and some campaign workers threatened to quit.

It quickly became apparent, however, that the political bosses had decided to hold to their previous strategy: Deny everything and denounce the WJC. They managed to keep the few disillusioned team members quiet.

People's Party spokesman Gerold Christian declared that the allegations "lack every foundation," and were simply an effort by the WJC "to continue the defamation campaign." The CROWCASS charges, he told reporters, had never been pursued because they had been seen as "untenable" from the start. To "prove" the absurdity of the charges, he employed a by-now old refrain: If they were true, why would Yugoslavia have voted—twice—for Waldheim as Secretary-General?[2]

Reuters quoted a similar response from an unidentified Waldheim spokesman, who added the observation that Waldheim had enjoyed "a positive and very friendly relationship" with Tito.[3]

Neither Christian nor the unnamed spokesman addressed the possibility that Yugoslavia might have *wanted* a U.N. Secretary-General with a secret Nazi past.

On Monday morning, the *Salzburger Nachrichten* became the first major Austrian newspaper to condemn the candidate. An editorial accused Waldheim of "lying to the whole of Austria," and called upon the People's Party to find another presidential hopeful. The central issue, said the editorial, was "the credibility of a man who wants to be President of the Republic."[4] Scores of similar statements had appeared in U.S. and British editorials for weeks, but it was a relief to see at least one Austrian newspaper follow suit at last.

Thus far, Austria's Socialist Party had allowed the WJC to take all the heat. But now a few Socialists found their voices. The party's deputy chairman, Karl Blecha, told a reporter: "We were prepared to believe him before. But the concealing of important parts of his past has completely undermined his credibility." An unnamed party official, mocking Waldheim's campaign slogan, declared that he was now "an Austrian mistrusted by the world."[5]

The remainder of Austria's press, however, was much kinder to Waldheim and much more hostile to us. *Die Presse* ran the CROWCASS/UNWCC story as its lead, with a subhead that declared: THE ENCIRCLEMENT AND EXTERMINATION OF THE PEOPLE'S PARTY CANDIDATE GOES FURTHER.

An editorial inside the paper fumed about the WJC's "international psycho-terror." The writer expropriated and inverted a famous anti-Nazi statement from the closing lines of Bertold Brecht's *Arturo*

Ui, wherein the playwright warned of the dangers of neo-Nazism "creeping out of a still-fertile womb." The editorial sent a clear warning to Austria's Jews that the WJC's "attacks" could bring "dangerous consequences." "From this egg," the writer warned, "could be hatched anti-Semitism."[6]

Even *Profil* joined the counterattack. Its March 24 issue carried a story by reporter Peter Sichrovsky, based on interviews granted to him by Singer and Steinberg before we knew of the CROWCASS and UNWCC listings. Frustrated with our inability to get the Austrian press to take the Waldheim accusations seriously, Singer had spoken intemperately during his *Profil* interview. He warned that if Waldheim were elected, his first year in office would be "no honeymoon." The accusations, he said, would "haunt and follow" not only Waldheim, but every Austrian. Tourism and foreign trade would suffer, Singer predicted. "Who," he asked, ". . . will still want to deal with a country whose representative was uncovered as a liar?" On the other hand, Singer said, if the electorate spurned Waldheim, it would show the world the face of a "new Austria." In either event, Singer proclaimed, "we will go on searching." Waldheim's allies cited these statements as "proof" that the WJC was "threatening tiny Austria." The *Profil* piece was accompanied by unflattering photos of Bronfman and Singer, both shown—quite inappropriately—smiling, and of a virtually unrecognizable Steinberg, whom the camera somehow caught looking disquietingly like a caricature of a shifty-eyed, thick-lipped Jewish schemer. The photos almost seemed to confirm the calumnies that Austrians were being continuously fed about the three principal WJC "functionaries." A companion photograph meanwhile, depicted Waldheim as genteel, distinguished, and definitely statesmanlike.*[7] *Profil*, it seemed, needed to tell its readers that, even if it was leading the home-front attack on Waldheim, it was, by no means, a friend of the WJC. (In the months ahead, *Profil* would make a habit of selecting photographs of Singer and Steinberg that caught them with smug and/or seemingly conspiratorial expressions on their faces.)

Instead of digging into the substance of the charges, other Austrian press outlets launched a renewed effort to determine who had initially tipped off the WJC and the *New York Times* about Kurt Waldheim's Nazi-era activities.

I received numerous transatlantic calls from Austrian reporters who were desperate to ascertain our "first source." My standard answer remained, "No comment." One insistent reporter badgered

---

*The authors requested a copy of the Steinberg photograph for reproduction in this book. Although *Profil* forwarded other requested photographs, this one was not provided.

me for several minutes before I snapped, "You can ask me if Kurt Waldheim was my source and I'm not going to confirm or deny it." Forcing a civil tone, I added, "You know, your investigative efforts are really misdirected here. Why don't you look into the background of the presidential candidate instead of trying to question the messenger? The issue is, what substance is there in the accusations?"

"*Ja,*" the reporter said, "but why won't you tell us who is the source—"

"No comment!" I fired back, slamming down the phone.

I sat at my desk and allowed my mind to wander. The American press, I thought, for all of its faults, aggressively investigates and exposes even the most pedestrian political scandal. It came as an enormous shock to realize that the largest circulation newspapers and magazines of another free country would, with few exceptions, attempt to aid in the Waldheim cover-up and thereby promote his election.

I was in this frame of mind when I learned of the latest comments from Michael Graff, General Secretary of the People's Party. On Austrian radio, he denounced the WJC disclosures as "overexcited attacks" and warned ominously that such further "meddling" in the presidential campaign could provoke "feelings that we all do not want to have." His words terrified many Austrian Jews, and some concluded that he intended to do just that, hoping that the country's Jewish leadership would pressure the WJC to back off.

On Tuesday, March 25, *Wochenpresse* published an editorial cartoon depicting the candidate's pursuers as masked weasels rifling through a file drawer labeled "Waldheim."[8]

Meanwhile, *Die Presse* columnist Ilse Leitenberger charged that the WJC "never misses an opportunity" to exploit the "dismal past." Whatever Waldheim might have done during the war, she wrote, "is his own business; judging it is the business of the electorate." Finally came the dire warning that the WJC must bear responsibility for a resurgence of anti-Semitism in Austria, with consequences that "we cannot yet conceive."[9]

"What kind of evidence will satisfy them that, at least, he's unqualified to be president?" I bellowed in a phone conversation with Cynthia. "Do they want us to come up with film of him strangling babies? And how much do we have to discover before the Austrian government announces its own investigation?"

Shortly before our scheduled press conference to disclose Bob Herzstein's findings, an unexpected letter came into our offices from Dr. Lavoslav Kadelburg, president of the Federation of Jewish Communities in Yugoslavia, and the WJC's principal contact in that country. He enclosed copies of nine documents pertaining to Waldheim's receipt of the King Zvonimir Medal. Each bore on its reverse the official seal of the state archives in Zagreb. One, dated August 6, 1942, was Major General Stahl's formal proposal that Waldheim and nine other men receive the Croatian medal. Stahl's signature was at the bottom of the document, which listed Waldheim as a lieutenant in the Command Staff West Bosnia.

We were surprised to receive these materials and we could only conclude that if Kadelburg had been permitted to forward them to us, someone in the Yugoslav government wanted us to have them. I wondered what more we could expect to see.

As it happened, Yugoslav Prime Minister Milka Planinc was on an official visit to Vienna at the time. After meeting with Austrian Chancellor Fred Sinowatz, she met with the press. When questioned by a reporter, she insisted that she and Sinowatz had not discussed Waldheim's wartime activities; that, she demurred, was a matter purely for Austria to consider.[10]

Hours after Planinc's statement, a spokesman for the Yugoslav Foreign Ministry told an Associated Press reporter that the ministry had "no comment" on the latest Waldheim disclosures.

It was not only Kurt Waldheim and his handlers who found it necessary to deal with the UNWCC revelation. To our astonishment, Simon Wiesenthal called a press conference to address our disclosure. Since he had already declared publicly that he doubted that the Yugoslavs would have voted for Waldheim at the U.N. had they possessed evidence of his having committed war crimes, I was apprehensive about what the press conference might bring. "The truth lies with the Yugoslav government," Simon Wiesenthal declared at the hastily convened press briefing in Vienna. He called upon Belgrade to explain why it had submitted Waldheim's name to the UNWCC in 1948.

Then, Wiesenthal boldly suggested a number of defenses still available to the People's Party candidate. He speculated that Waldheim's name had been on an early Yugoslav list but was perhaps subsequently dropped for lack of evidence. "These lists were continually being supplanted," he lectured the press. "If he is not on a later list, that means they dropped it, they did not follow it up, or they did not have the documentation to support it." Left unmentioned was the fact that Waldheim's listing by the UNWCC meant that the documentation submitted by Belgrade—whatever it was—had been sufficient to satisfy the Commission's Fact-Finding Committee.

Even if Waldheim's name was on the final list, Wiesenthal continued, this was not conclusive, for there must be some reason why the

Yugoslavs "never asked for his extradition." Once again, Wiesenthal relied on the dubious notion that Marshal Tito was a man of integrity: He repeated his earlier statement, mimicking the standard Waldheim refrain, that he found it hard to believe that Tito would have befriended Waldheim if he had considered the charges to be true.

Wiesenthal's third line of defense for his countryman was the contention that some of these Yugoslav war criminal lists had simply included the names of *all* members of Wehrmacht units in certain areas.

Wiesenthal also wanted the press to understand that he was not caught off-guard by the continuing disclosures about Waldheim. He recalled, "Some people came to me in the fall of 1985 and they were looking for material against him, without knowing what one could reproach him with. I told them I had nothing of the sort, and they claimed I was covering up for Waldheim. I have nothing to be silent about."

Wiesenthal disclosed that he had spoken directly with Waldheim on the current matter and that the candidate had assured him "there is not a word of truth in the things that are being stated against him." Wiesenthal threw us one tiny crumb, acknowledging that the Salonika deportations "must have been the daily subject of conversation," and, hence, "I do not believe that Waldheim knew nothing."

But still he did not call upon Waldheim to explain why he had lied about his war record for forty years. Nor did he lash out at the anti-Semitic tone of the *Die Presse* editorial or the broadcast comments of People's Party General Secretary Graff, both issued earlier in the day. Instead, he reserved his harshest words for the WJC. "In its first statement," Wiesenthal declared, "the World Jewish Congress said that Waldheim was with the unit that deported Jews from Salonika. I said that this is not correct. The deportation of Jews was entrusted by Eichmann to [SS-*Hauptsturmfuehrer* Alois] Brunner. The Greek government requested the extradition of Brunner for that reason."*[11]

I was stunned. We had just made one of the most shocking disclosures in postwar history, that the former U.N. Secretary-General was listed as a war criminal, listed as wanted for murder by CROWCASS and the UNWCC, and that this was kept secret for forty years—and Wiesenthal criticized *us!* From the standpoint of the Austrian presidential race, this was a make-or-break moment of the entire affair,

*At this writing, former SS-*Hauptsturmfuehrer* Alois Brunner is widely believed to be living in Syria, where the government of President Hafez el-Assad is suspected of having granted him sanctuary. An unconfirmed report of his death in Syria, attributed to French sources, made international headlines in December 1992.

ared that Wiesenthal's words had just elected the next Austrian president. As Schuller had predicted, he was playing politics
with the Holocaust—and it was sickening.

I marched into Steinberg's office with a pile of newspaper clippings
reporting on Wiesenthal's statements, threw them on his desk and
screamed, "That's *it!*"

The legendary Rosenbaum temper had full hold of me now. My
scalp burned. I could feel my face flush as I paced the floor and
raged, "I will *not* cover for him anymore. From now on, if anybody
asks me about him I'll say, 'I don't think much of Wiesenthal. He's
a faker. He's using the Holocaust for political reasons.' I'm going to
tell them that all the so-called information sent by Simon over the
years hasn't resulted in a single prosecution in the United States, but
that he's real good at publicly accusing innocent people. Remember
that case in Canada, Elan, where he exposed the wrong guy?"*

Steinberg allowed me to continue, for he knew that the subject,
for me, was filled with personal pain.

"Okay," I sputtered, "Jews have always needed an avenger and we
made him that. And I feel a little guilty myself for never exposing
that charade. But look what he's doing now. It's . . . it's . . . indecent!"
I grabbed the clippings and pointed out the most odious passages.

I railed at Wiesenthal's audacity to lecture us on the details of the
Salonika deportations. In placing the blame solely on Eichmann,
Brunner, and their SS cohorts, Wiesenthal was, like Waldheim, writing the Wehrmacht out of the history of the Salonika tragedy. It was
outrageous. Yes, the SS had launched the campaign to annihilate the
Salonika Jews, but the Wehrmacht had actively collaborated in the
perpetration of that crime, as the basic history books had long reported. Coincidentally, I had just come across Wiesenthal's 1968
annual report in which he boasted of testifying in a German trial of
Max Merten, the Wehrmacht official in Salonika who had worked
hand-in-hand with the SS to concentrate the Jews of Salonika
and then deport them, aboard Wehrmacht-provided trains, to
Auschwitz.[13]

---

*In 1971, Wiesenthal accused a Vancouver janitor, Ivan Chrabatyn, of participating in the
execution of ten thousand Jews in the vicinity of Stanislav, Ukraine, on October 12, 1941.
After a witness who Wiesenthal told reporters could identify Chrabatyn as a participant in
killings of Jews in 1941 and 1942 said that he knew nothing about the allegations, and did
not even know a Chrabatyn in Stanislav, Chrabatyn sued the newspaper that had reported
Wiesenthal's claim. The newspaper subsequently agreed to a cash settlement of Chrabatyn's
libel case and conceded that its investigations determined "that the allegations that were made
pertaining to you were untrue." In his 1989 book, *Justice Not Vengeance* (London: Weidenfeld
& Nicolson), Wiesenthal leveled unsubstantiated charges against Chrabatyn yet again. This
time, however, Wiesenthal could do so without fear of being sued, for as the Nazi-hunter
noted in the book, Chrabatyn (whom he calls "Hrabatyn" in the text) had been "dead since
1980."[12]

This was heresy, I raged. Jewish leaders speak so often of the obligation to guard against Holocaust "revisionism." Fidelity to the truth of those horrible events is always regarded as essential, even when the truth hurts; even awkward truths, such as the fact that a tiny minority of Jews collaborated with their Nazi overlords, must not be suppressed. Wiesenthal himself frequently made these points in interviews and speeches. Yet here he was, not content merely to make ludicrous statements in Waldheim's defense, but determined to distort history.

Steinberg's eyes seemed to plead, Are you finished?

Drained, I sank into a chair, suddenly mute.

Steinberg was usually the jocular one in the office, almost always ready with a quip or a joke to soften the edges of a harsh day. But there was a wary tone in his voice as he lectured me: "The Wiesenthal legend has been important for Jews all over the world. They needed to believe that there was a 'Great Avenger' exacting justice on behalf of the Six Million. Believe me, I know how you feel. He's hurting *me*, too. But we can't take the symbol away from our people. We won't do it. Besides, you can't do battle with a legend and hope to win."

I found my voice once more and countered by concentrating on Wiesenthal's disclosure that he had been asked about Waldheim's past by "some people" in the "fall of 1985," less than a year earlier. Who had asked Wiesenthal? Schuller's "helpers," perhaps? If we took at face value Wiesenthal's response that he had "nothing" on the man, we had to assume that, at the time, he did not know about Waldheim's service in the Balkans under Loehr. Why, then, had he apparently missed the significance of the *Profil* piece on January 27, the disclosure that had set us on our quest? It was only a brief notice, to be sure, but it had been published in Wiesenthal's own city. What's more, I had learned that *Profil*'s publisher, Peter Lingens, was a longtime friend and collaborator of Wiesenthal's. I refused to believe that the great Nazi-hunter had suddenly gone either senile or stupid. Once more I started pacing. Again I felt the skin of my face burning.

Steinberg quietly stated the question his eyes had asked earlier, "Are you finished?"

"Yeah, I guess so."

Steinberg suggested another visit to Singer's office. There, in a somewhat more composed manner, I repeated my tirade, and I pointed out how absurd it was for Wiesenthal to continue to issue a clean bill of health for Waldheim. I pointed especially to Wiesenthal's assertions that the units in which Waldheim served were "pure combat troops" unimplicated in atrocities and that there was "nothing at all incriminating" in the initial disclosures. If we had leveled a specific charge—say, that Waldheim had butchered twenty civilians on such-and-such date in a given town—Wiesenthal might be justified in saying, "No, I know who did that, and it was not Waldheim." "But we're talking about someone who lied about where he was during whole *years* of the war," I reminded my two colleagues. "There's a gigantic potential universe of crimes that Waldheim could have been involved in. We just don't happen to know what they all are. No one even knows for sure yet where the guy was really stationed during all of those months. What we do know, however, is that this was a man who, for several hundred days during the war, could well have been involved in any number of crimes perpetrated by the members of his units. Army Group E, for sure, was up to no good. And so was the West Bosnia Combat Group. Look, guys, unless Simon was *handcuffed* to Waldheim for all the years of World War II, personally observed everything he did, and looked over his shoulder at every document that he signed, there's just no way he is in any kind of position to declare that Waldheim was not a Nazi war criminal. He could say, 'It remains to be proven' or something like that, but he can't say, categorically, that Waldheim was not involved in crimes. It's baloney and he knows it. And I don't think he's ever issued an exoneration like that in his whole life."

I reminded Singer that there were a number of episodes in Wiesenthal's career where he had leapt to conclusions and accused people falsely. Why was he leaping so quickly to the opposite conclusion in this case? Was it not obvious that Waldheim would have risked such bold lies over the years only if he had something very important to hide?

How bizarre all of this had to appear to the average Austrian citizen, I pointed out. In Austria, Wiesenthal was regarded by many as an irresponsible accuser of innocent people. Now, he had come immediately to the defense of Austria's most famous citizen. "Simon's support must be a very comforting security blanket for Waldheim," I said in disgust.

Singer shrugged off my rhetoric. Maybe I made sense, he acknowledged, but crossing swords with Wiesenthal did not. In a tone obviously intended to remind me that *he* was the boss, Singer declared that a fight with Wiesenthal was a fight that we could never win. Beyond that, he detested the thought of prominent Jews arguing among themselves (though he himself had been party to several such feuds). A full-scale fight among factions of the Jewish community would be, he warned, the worst possible outcome of this entire affair.

The most Singer agreed to do was react privately. He fired off a cable to Wiesenthal in Vienna, pointing out that our evidence showed that "personnel under Loehr's command" cooperated with the SS during the deportations of the Salonika Jews, and that the victims "were transported on Wehrmacht trains." He closed his cable with a polite request for a clarification of Wiesenthal's remarks "purporting to correct WJC misstatements concerning Salonika."

Singer sent a copy of this telex to Rabbi Marvin Hier, founder and dean of the Los Angeles–based Simon Wiesenthal Center (an international Jewish civil rights organization named after the Vienna Nazi-hunter, but independent of him). He added the following comment:

> SHOCKED AT WIESENTHAL'S FURTHER BACKSLIDING. CANNOT FIGURE OUT WHAT THAT MAN IS DOING. FURTHER SHOCKING REVELATIONS ON WALDHEIM'S PARTICIPATION WITH HIS PERSONAL SIGNATURE ON THEM. TELL WIESENTHAL TO SHUT UP: ENOUGH IS ENOUGH.[14]

13

Our small conference room was packed to overflowing with reporters, klieg lights, and electronic equipment as we ushered Professor Robert Edwin Herzstein into the limelight to perform his last official act for us before he returned to his teaching duties. Herzstein reported only the highlights of his findings, but the assembled journalists were plainly stunned by them—as well as by the disclosure that this material had been sitting unnoticed for all these years in the publicly accessible collection of the National Archives.

Herzstein noted that Waldheim, as Loehr's "O3" officer, was responsible for preparing the morning and evening intelligence reports for the High Command of Army Group E in Arsakli/Salonika. Waldheim and his assistant, Lieutenant Poliza, reported on intelligence concerning Greece and adjacent territories, especially on Allied activity in the area. Waldheim often briefed Loehr's chief of staff on developments throughout the European Theater and the Middle East. Waldheim's summaries of intelligence obtained from prisoners, Herzstein said, very likely mandated cooperation with the SS and the SD. He noted that interrogation by the Germans often involved torture and frequently ended in death. "Prisoner interrogation" was explicitly listed among the responsibilities assigned to Waldheim and his subordinates on the Army Group E organizational table.

Turning his attention to Waldheim's earlier assignment in western Bosnia, Herzstein read from the Kozara document that enumerated 10,475 partisans caught or killed as compared with 185 German/Croatian casualties. "This was not a battle," Herzstein declared. "This was a massacre."

He presented the "honor roll" that singled out thirty-four German and Croatian soldiers for their contributions at Kozara; Waldheim, the press learned, was one of them.

There were audible gasps, first when Herzstein quoted from the macabre Kozara prose poem referring to the massacre of "subhumans," and again when he produced the report concerning *3000 Kinder und Frauen.*

We also released the documents that Lavoslav Kadelburg had sent from Yugoslavia, confirming earlier reports that Major General Stahl himself had recommended Waldheim for the King Zvonimir Medal after the Kozara massacres. Singer and Steinberg renewed the WJC's call for Waldheim to admit that he had covered up his Balkan military service, and then to explain why.

Finally it was my turn to deliver my prepared remarks. "In my experience as a federal prosecutor," I asserted, "rarely did I see documents of such devastating impact as those that we are making available today.

"I cannot imagine that there is a single prosecutor anywhere in the world who would reach any conclusion other than that this documentary evidence is of a character and weight that, at a minimum, compels the initiation of a major criminal investigation. As of today, the Waldheim affair is no longer a matter for idle speculation regarding Kurt Waldheim's elaborate deception, or even for the unofficial detective work of a private organization such as ours. Rather, the Waldheim affair is now a matter to be taken up at once by the proper law enforcement authorities—in Greece, in Yugoslavia, and in Austria."

The only tough question the reporters asked was one we had anticipated: "Are you saying that Kurt Waldheim is a war criminal?"

We had agreed in advance that I would tackle this one. "In the absence of a trial, I would call even Josef Mengele an *accused* war criminal," I explained. "Waldheim, too, is accused—by Yugoslavia and the UNWCC. In the end, only a court of law can decide the question of guilt." A reporter tried asking the question another way: Was Waldheim directly involved in atrocities? We could not answer that with certainty, I replied. It was even possible that he received his King Zvonimir Medal for services that had nothing to do with the Kozara crimes. But there was no question that he was an important part of the war machine that carried out the atrocities.

"What we are saying," I declared, "is that our still-preliminary investigation has already proven that Kurt Waldheim served in, and concealed his service in, at least two criminal units." One of these positions was as a staff officer in the unit responsible for planning and executing the gruesome Kozara operation in western Bosnia, for which service Waldheim was honored and, most likely, decorated. Moreover, I pointed out, the evidence presented by Yugoslavia in 1948 had been deemed of sufficient weight by the UNWCC to justify listing him as a Nazi murder suspect. I concluded by repeating, "The evidence compels the commencement of a major criminal investigation. We call on the government of Austria, in particular, to launch such an investigation with all deliberate speed."

An hour later, I phrased it somewhat differently to Cynthia over the phone: "Based on what we have, Cyn, we're not saying he should be prosecuted or go to jail. At least not yet. But he should go away. He should at least have the decency to disappear."

But that, we knew now, was a pipe dream.

Later that same day, we set our sights on more attainable results. If we could not get the Austrian government to investigate Waldheim, perhaps we could persuade the U.S. government to take on the task. From the beginning, the WJC was ill-equipped to pursue Waldheim. But the U.S. Justice Department had an office staffed specifically to investigate Nazi war crime accusations. If our new strategy worked, it would bring Neal Sher and Pat Treanor—as well as the full resources of OSI—into the hunt. I composed a letter to U.S. Attorney General Edwin Meese III:

> Dear Mr. Attorney General:
>   I hereby request that Kurt Waldheim . . . be placed as soon as possible on the watchlist of the U.S. Immigration and Naturalization Service as an alien excludable from entry into the United States under Title 8, Section 1182(a)(33) of the U.S. Code on the basis of his participation in acts of Nazi-sponsored persecution.

The applicable provision of law, commonly referred to as the Holtzman Amendment (in honor of its principal author, then-Congresswoman Elizabeth Holtzman), bars from entry into the U.S. any person who, in association with the government of Nazi Germany or any other Axis government, "ordered, incited, assisted, or otherwise participated in the persecution of any person because of race, religion, national origin, or political opinion."

In order to bar a "Nazi persecutor," the statute requires *prima facie* evidence of participation in Nazi crimes. Whatever the evidence submitted by Yugoslavia against Waldheim in 1948 had been, it obviously had been strong enough to persuade the UNWCC Fact-Finding Committee (which included two U.S. representatives) to, in effect, indict Waldheim nearly forty years earlier; it might well suffice, I calculated, to prove a *prima facie* case today. Moreover, U.S. courts had ruled consistently that the Holtzman Amendment could be applied to bar the entry of persons who had served in significant positions in criminal units, whether or not the individuals could be tied to specific crimes. The evidence uncovered during the past two months left no doubt that Waldheim had served as an officer in units involved in sending thousands of civilians and partisans—Jews and non-Jews, men, women, and children—to concentration and death camps.

Privately, I gave the Meese letter little chance of succeeding. The Reagan Administration would have little to gain by involving itself in the Waldheim affair. The ex–U.N. chief was almost certain to be elected president of Austria despite—or, some claimed, even because of—our disclosures, and no head of state had ever been placed on the watchlist, not even longtime U.S. nemeses like Fidel Castro and Muammar Qadaffi.

But if we could somehow get Meese to agree to take up the matter, he would undoubtedly assign the investigation to OSI and, in that event, my talented ex-colleagues could officially join us in the search for the truth about Waldheim. OSI might even take over the laboring oar, so that we at the WJC could get on with our other business.

Before he left us, Herzstein had supplied me with a list of micro-film citations to several hundred documents that he felt might be worth studying. "If so much could be found in just one week," he had remarked, "imagine how much more remains to be unearthed." I recruited three college students, swore them to secrecy, and sent them to the Archives in Washington to print out copies of the documents Herzstein had listed.

"Pure lies and malicious acts" is how Waldheim summarized our press conference disclosures during an interview later in the day on the Austrian radio program *"Abendjournal."*

Until now, he had not responded specifically to the Yugoslav reports that placed him in western Bosnia during the Kozara massacres. He had earlier claimed, however, that his Yugoslavia service had taken him only to the provinces of Dalmatia, Serbia, Montenegro, and Croatia. No mention had ever been made of Bosnia. But now that we had presented irrefutable evidence that he was assigned to a post in western Bosnia, he suddenly altered his story to correspond to the newly proven facts. To our astonishment, Waldheim now admitted that he had indeed served in Bosnia during the summer of 1942, not, as in his telex to the Adlers, in Greece. But he insisted to his radio interviewer that he was merely an interpreter routing messages between the German High Command and the Italian division that was stationed in the area. And he insisted that he had "nothing to do" with the war against the partisan forces there.

Later in the day, appearing on Austrian television, he was asked directly about the Kozara massacres.

"That's nonsense," he replied. "It was no massacre I took part in; there were at that time fierce battles—"

"It was a horrible war," his questioner interrupted sympathetically.

"A horrible war," Waldheim agreed, "and I say, yes, it was a very severe altercation."[1]

Reading accounts of these latest interviews, Steinberg could not resist a wry comeback. "What are they going to put on Waldheim's tombstone?" he asked sarcastically.

I shrugged.

He laughed in anticipation of his own punch line. "Here lies Kurt Waldheim."

Indeed, Waldheim's revised account of his service in Yugoslavia still did not ring true. Some quick research disclosed that the Axis combat group operating in and around Mount Kozara was composed of Germans, Croats, and Hungarians. No Italian forces were involved.* If Waldheim was there—and he now seemed to be admitting that fact—his duties were *not* those of the German/Italian interpreter he claimed to have been at the time.

I was pondering this glaring discrepancy when Steinberg's ashen face appeared at my office door. "I just got the strangest phone call," he said. "It's either the 'sting' of the century or else it's the real thing." I had never seen Steinberg, whom I regarded as virtually unflappable, look so unnerved.

The call purportedly came from Yugoslavia, from a man who gave his name as Pagic and identified himself as an employee of *Politika Ekspres,* a Belgrade newspaper. His English was poor and the overseas connection was dreadful, but his message was clear: He was calling to alert us that another Belgrade newspaper—*Vecernje Novosti* ("Evening News")—was publishing a story tomorrow following up on our revelation about the Central Registry of War Criminals and Security Suspects.

Steinberg clutched a small piece of paper in his hand. He glanced down at it, and read aloud from his notes: "He says that this other newspaper will publish the decision—that's what he called it—of the Yugoslav War Crimes Commission from 1947, finding Waldheim *guilty!*—his word again—of World War II crimes. Pagic read me the list of crimes. Listen to this, it's incredible: 'Murders and exterminations. Hostage executions. Deliberate destruction and devastation of property. Setting afire inhabited places.' "

We stared at one another in silence.

Finally, Steinberg spoke. "I hope this isn't a hoax."

"Was the call directly from Yugoslavia?" I asked.

---

*For example, one of the documents Bob Herzstein had found for us at the U.S. National Archives was a July 17, 1942, order of General Stahl (T315/2258/1495) praising the victories won, under his leadership, by the "German, Croatian, and Hungarian alliance."

"It seemed to be. It was a person-to-person call, through someone who sounded like an operator. And the connection sure sounded like an international call."

Steinberg ran off to ask his assistant, Sharon Cohen, to check with the phone company. Within minutes she reported that yes, we had received a call from Yugoslavia.

Now we worried that the call might be a setup, perhaps orchestrated by Yugoslav intelligence, for whatever reasons, premised on the hope that we might release the "news" prematurely, and wind up with egg on our faces, badly discredited. There was nothing to do but wait, to see if the story really would run the next day in Belgrade.

I winced when I saw the headline on the March 26 edition of the tabloid *New York Post,* reporting on our press conference with Bob Herzstein: PAPERS SHOW WALDHEIM WAS SS BUTCHER.

The exaggeration was picked up quickly in Austria, reprinted by the domestic press as "proof" that the Americans were overreacting and understood little about how the Nazis really operated. I wondered whether the *Post*'s editors knew that their screaming headline might actually aid Waldheim politically.

This same day, Austrian People's Party Chairman Alois Mock told the West German newspaper *Die Welt* that the World Jewish Congress was guilty of "despicable infamy." The WJC, he charged, was involved in a "barefaced interference" in Austrian domestic politics; Mock predicted that many Austrians would vote for Waldheim out of "patriotic duty."[2]

Die Presse, meanwhile, defended Waldheim on the subject of the CROWCASS listing, contending that his name appeared "only" on a list prepared by American forces in 1948 based on reports from U.S. allies. (In truth, it also appeared on the U.N. War Crimes Commission wanted list, of course, and that organization was obviously not an American one.) Citing no proof, Vienna's most respected newspaper reported as fact what Wiesenthal had only suggested as a possibility—namely that Waldheim's name did not appear on "later" Yugoslav lists.

Austria's Jewish community was increasingly alarmed about the atmosphere of overt hatred that had developed so suddenly after forty years of postwar quietude. Threatening letters, usually sent anonymously, were being received by Jewish leaders, and crude anti-Jewish and pro-Nazi slogans were showing up throughout the country, spray-painted on building walls and other outdoor spaces. The *Kultesgemeinde,* the central organization of Viennese Jewry, issued a formal statement in reply to People's Party General Secretary Graff, who had earlier warned the WJC not to provoke "feelings that we all do not want to have." The organization declared: "We condemn most forcefully this subconscious appeal by certain People's Party functionaries to emotions that were long ago cast aside." More directly, the group's president, Ivan Hacker, warned that "such unmistakable threats . . . could give ideas to Nazi nostalgists and anti-Semites."

Die Presse quickly published Graff's denial that he had intended to make any kind of threat. At the same time, the newspaper printed the results of a telephone survey which, Graff claimed, found that 80 percent of the Austrian population believed that the attacks on Waldheim "were made only to defeat him in the elections." In addition, 57 percent of the respondents "rejected any interference from abroad."[3]

Almost overnight, campaign workers plastered large stickers onto Waldheim's campaign posters. Each bore a legend that was shockingly reminiscent of the well-known prewar Austrian Nazi slogan: "Now More Than Ever!"* The omnipresent stickers—which seemed to say that the accusations were a reason to vote *for* Waldheim—were printed in bright yellow, the same color that the Third Reich had used for the Star of David patch that branded the Jews of Europe for destruction.[4]

Although *Profil* quickly reproduced in its pages a portion of a Nazi publication highlighting the frightening similarity of the slogans, the Waldheim campaign never dropped the phrase. Simultaneously, new Waldheim campaign posters appeared on the scene. Against a bright yellow background, red capital letters, designed to look like angry, spray-painted graffiti, broadcast an unambiguous message:

WE
AUSTRIANS
WILL ELECT
WHOM *WE* WANT!

NOW MORE THAN EVER
WALDHEIM

Erhard Busek, a leader of the tiny liberal wing of the People's Party, called for the withdrawal of this "poster with anti-Semitic overtones," but to no avail.[5]

Waldheim himself joined the assault. He told a Yugoslav reporter that "an unprecedented attempt" was being made to destroy him.

---

*The Waldheim stickers read *Jetzt erst Recht!*, an almost verbatim rendering of the old Nazi slogan *Nun erst Recht!* They have identical meanings.

As though *Profil* magazine and other pursuers simply did not exist, he placed the blame squarely on the World Jewish Congress and speculated that our motive was revenge for his Middle East policies when he was Secretary-General.[6]

As we studied the reports coming in from Europe, it was apparent that the Waldheim camp had decided to violate an unwritten but universally respected taboo. Since the end of the Nazi era, no major political party in democratic Europe had overtly resorted to appeals to latent anti-Semitic sentiments. Suddenly, the tradition was scrapped by the People's Party, aided by the Austrian press. It was a strategy obviously born of desperation. The haunting question was: Would it work?

Singer, Steinberg, and I agonized over this issue. We knew that it was the small group of Holocaust survivors now living in Austria who felt the terror most acutely; for them it was a flashback to hell. We considered the sobering question: Would it be better, for the safety of Austria's Jews, to drop the Waldheim inquiry? Any growth in anti-Jewish sentiment anywhere was an ominous development, but particularly so in a country that had figured so importantly in the crimes of the Third Reich. Our nightmare was that Austrian rhetoric would give way to physical violence.

We consulted with Jews in Austria, particularly the younger leaders. With some exceptions, and almost always with considerable hesitation, they advised us to continue our efforts to uncover the truth. One of these younger leaders explained to Steinberg, "This is not 1939. We will never again be trapped, with the doors of the rest of the world closed to us. Now there is an Israel." He and others cautioned us, however, to avoid a repetition of inflammatory language of the kind Singer had used during his *Profil* interview.

We decided to forge ahead; silence seemed so plainly wrong. But we remained haunted by concerns for the safety of those Jews who lived in the vortex of the storm.

A Reuters correspondent in Yugoslavia provided us with initial confirmation that *Vecernje Novosti* had published the story about which Steinberg had been tipped off in the mysterious phone call from Yugoslavia. On its front page, the paper carried an extensive excerpt from "War Criminal File No. F-25572." We anxiously awaited a copy, so that we could have it translated from Serbo-Croatian into English.

Perhaps the best news that filtered through from Yugoslavia was the announcement that one of the newspaper's reporters would fly to Vienna on Friday, March 28, bringing with him a copy of the *Odluka,* the actual Yugoslav indictment that formed the basis of the CROWCASS and UNWCC listings.

It also came as a happy surprise when, only forty-eight hours after I wrote to Attorney General Meese, we were notified that the Justice Department had agreed to have OSI examine the Waldheim matter to determine whether the former U.N. Secretary-General should be barred from entering the United States. This decision to involve the U.S. government in an "Austrian political matter" was reportedly made by Meese himself.

Elated, I grabbed a foot-high stack of paper and headed for the copying machine. By now, I had four file drawers packed with documents, and I wanted to make sure that every shred of evidence got to Neal Sher and his staff at OSI as quickly as possible.

Singer found me busy at the task and announced, "The *New York Times* is coming over. Give them everything you have."

"You're joking, right, Israel?" I responded. I motioned toward the mountain of paper around me and said, "This is only the beginning."

"Well, just give them the best stuff."

I resumed my labor with a groan. I had far more important work to do, but I still could not bring myself to trust anyone else with the documents I had meticulously filed and cross-filed. Buried somewhere within the mass of paper, I was sure, lay still more key pieces of this infernal puzzle. A word or a single numeral could speak volumes when placed in proper context. But with all of the demands on my time—from Singer and Steinberg, from the press, from our European and domestic contacts, and now from OSI—what I seemed least able to find was an uninterrupted block of time in which to study the materials we already had.

What's more, the files were growing larger and more unwieldy with every passing day. Each morning I could expect a deluge of mail on my desk, some of it from responsible journalists, archivists, and historians, but much more from well-motivated amateur sleuths reporting something like: "Uncle Josef, before he died in 1974, told me about a Nazi atrocity committed by someone who sounds like he might be Waldheim." On any given day, the materials on my desk might be written in any of a dozen different languages. It was nearly impossible to find the time and energy merely to sift the wheat from the chaff.

My frustration grew in proportion to the height of the piles of paper. I was exhausted and angry. I was still not quite sure how I had become so thoroughly enmeshed in this web.

I told my friends that I felt like the sorcerer's apprentice, the character created by composer Paul Dukas and brought to life in Disney's *Fantasia.* Whereas the apprentice, played in the Disney film by Mickey Mouse, was bedeviled by an endless procession of animated brooms and buckets, my scourge was a swelling sea of paperwork in a babble of languages.

On Thursday, two days after our press conference, Waldheim declared that our disclosures, coupled with the Yugoslav press reports, were evidence of "an almost incomprehensible conspiracy" against him.

Concurrently, Waldheim's campaign manager, Heribert Steinbauer, reminded reporters that Tito had invited Waldheim to visit Yugoslavia a dozen times, voted for his election and reelection at the U.N., and even conferred a medal on him. Waldheim, he said, had "a friendly relationship with President Tito that went beyond normal ties."[7] Karl Schuller was at first amused as he recounted the statements to me in a phone conversation. Then his voice turned somber as he asked, "Do you see what our friend is trying to do? He is sending a message to Belgrade: Stop what you are allowing your reporters to do, because if I fall I will not fall alone; Tito will go with me." As if to underscore the point, the Waldheim team promptly issued a campaign brochure that featured on its front cover a 1968 picture of Waldheim bowing as he shook the hand of a smiling Marshal Tito.

Already, conflicting signals were coming from Yugoslavia. On the same day that a Yugoslav Foreign Ministry official told a journalist inquiring about the Waldheim matter, "It's very delicate. We can't say more at this stage,"[8] *Vecernje Novosti* published the text of a telephonic encounter one of its reporters had just had with Waldheim. "I have no doubts," Waldheim said in the interview, "that the documents kept in the Yugoslav archives contain heavy charges against me. But I assure you that it is not the actual truth." Following up on Waldheim's admission two days earlier on Austrian television that he had indeed been stationed in western Bosnia during the summer of 1942, at the time of the Kozara massacres, the Yugoslav reporter asked him to explain why he had omitted this information earlier. Waldheim replied, "Who could remember everything from the war period?" He said that he had checked his personal files and confirmed that he was not directly involved in the details of the Kozara operation. "At that moment," he said, "I was with the Italians in the area between Banja Luka and the German units on Mount Kozara."[9]

The interview unleashed a firestorm of indignation and wrath inside Yugoslavia, especially in Bosnia. To them, Waldheim's belated admission that he was in the Kozara area during one of the largest mass deportations of World War II—coupled with his cavalier dismissal of his previous inability to remember his presence at Kozara ("Who could remember everything from the war period?")—was an unpardonable affront. The anger was exacerbated by publication of the news that Waldheim, on Austrian television, had said that it was "nonsense" to call what happened at Kozara a massacre.

Yet, on Friday morning, when Yugoslav Foreign Ministry spokesman Alexander Stanic provided his government's first official response to the controversy, his words were deeply disappointing. Stanic noted that although "some newspapers have tried to involve Yugoslavia in the presidential campaign in Austria," his government had no new facts on the case. The presidential campaign "in friendly and neighboring Austria," he reiterated, was purely an Austrian concern.[10]

In Vienna, the official People's Party newspaper, *Neues Volksblatt,* proclaimed news of its own "historical inquiry" under a perverse banner headline: THE BLOOD ON THE FINGERS OF THE ISRAELI POLITICIANS!

The accompanying story by reporter Manfred Maurer declared that the WJC's "feverish rummaging in the archives had inspired us" to follow "the bloody trail of Jewish terrorism." Characterizing the WJC as "allergic to every 'brown' stain on the vests of our politicians," the paper wondered why we were not equally concerned about "the blood-red stains" on Israeli politicians, such as Menachem Begin and Yitzhak Shamir.[11]

At my request, Robert Wolfe of the National Archives staff rechecked the CROWCASS lists, searching for the name of Waldheim's immediate superior at Army Group E, Lieutenant Colonel Herbert Warnstorff, chief of the Ic/AO Branch. He was not listed.

This was disappointing news, especially when it was followed by our receipt of word that Warnstorff had never been prosecuted. In fact, he was still alive, living a peaceful existence as a seventy-three-year-old retiree in Moenchen-Gladbach, West Germany, near Cologne. These disclosures lent a disquieting measure of credibility to speculation that the Yugoslavs might have trumped up charges against Waldheim in order to set him up for a blackmail attempt.

What was the truth of the matter? It would remain an unanswerable question unless we could gain access to the Yugoslav indictment file, or at least to the U.N. War Crimes Commission file based on the Yugoslav charges.

Even as these thoughts raced through my head, a crowd of reporters waited at the Vienna airport for the arrival of a *Vecernje Novosti* courier, who was supposed to hand-deliver from Belgrade a copy of the *Odluka* indictment file on Waldheim.

The reporters waited all day. The courier never arrived.[12]

14

Sunday, March 30, 1986. A *Kronenzeitung* editorial showed Austria's largest newspaper dropping even the pretense of civility. "Jewry often transgresses the limit of prudence when in power," it declared. Meanwhile, the front page of the paper blared a sensational headline: U.N. SECRETARY-GENERAL PEREZ: ACCUSATIONS AGAINST WALD-HEIM ARE ABSURD.

The accompanying story asserted that the current U.N. Secretary-General had risen to Waldheim's defense.[1] This was disturbing news, for Perez de Cuellar's support would aid Waldheim greatly, in Austria and elsewhere. I was wary of yet another distortion by the Austrian press, especially when I recalled the shocked reaction of Perez de Cuellar's emissary when he reviewed our initial evidence. But there was no way to check the account over the weekend.

As the day passed, I grew increasingly apprehensive. Had the U.N. bureaucracy adopted a damage-control strategy? Was all of our careful labor about to be destroyed by Waldheim's successor?

On Monday, we checked with Perez de Cuellar's office and were assured that the current U.N. Secretary-General had made no comments on the substance of the charges against Waldheim, much less issued a statement defending him. Perez de Cuellar later released a public statement to that effect. Sunday's *Kronenzeitung* story was thus proved to be completely invented, much like the earlier report in *Die Presse* that Waldheim's name had been dropped from the Yugoslav wanted lists.

We were forced, now, to confront the unimaginable: The major Austrian press outlets were allies of the Waldheim cover-up. Schuller's prediction, which had struck me as bordering on the clinically paranoid, had come true.

Later that day, I found myself on the phone with a man from Washington, a stranger who said he could help in the Waldheim case. I was skeptical. Over the past few weeks, I had fielded dozens of such calls, which almost invariably led to blind alleys.

This new caller identified himself as Dr. Stephen Katich. He was a Yugoslav-born lawyer employed as a legal specialist with the Library of Congress's European Law Division. He explained that he had once assisted OSI in the investigation of Andrija Artukovic, the wartime Minister of the Interior of the Nazi puppet state of Croatia. The case had remained in the courts after I left OSI, and a long battle ensued before Artukovic was finally extradited to Yugoslavia, just two months earlier. Katich said he had pored over dusty volumes of Croatian documents and newspapers in order to help prove Artukovic's role in the deaths of hundreds of thousands of Serbs, gypsies, and Jews during the war, and in the expropriation of their property. As we spoke, Artukovic was awaiting trial in Zagreb.

Katich's principal motivation in helping first OSI and now the WJC was personal. He was a Serb who had lost many family members to the Nazis and their Croatian collaborators.

"You must come to Washington and see me," he implored. "I can help you."

"In what way?"

"You are trying to obtain the Yugoslav dossier on that bastard Waldheim, right?"

"Yes." In fact, we were desperate for it, since the promised courier had failed to deliver it in Vienna three days earlier. "Go on."

"Well, I have connections in Yugoslavia. Very good ones. I know a prominent military historian there. But better than that, I'm very close to the U.S. ambassador to Belgrade, John Scanlan."

"Of course, we'd be grateful, Dr. Katich, for anything you could do, but the government over there is keeping the lid on its Waldheim file. They're not letting it out."

"I know. My friends there are telling me that the government is embarrassed. The Waldheim affair makes Tito look bad, and worshiping his memory is the only thing that holds the damn country together; it keeps the Croats and the Serbs from each other's throats. So they've closed the archives."

Katich pointed to other motives also. Yugoslavia was beset by a punishing 90 percent inflation rate and owed $20 billion in foreign debt. The money sent home by tens of thousands of Yugoslav "guest workers" in Austria was a major source of hard currency for Belgrade. Katich's sources told him that some Yugoslav officials worried that they could ill afford to upset the Austrians. "But listen to me," he said impatiently. "I can get the file on that fucking son of a bitch. The Croatians don't want to hear any more talk about the Second World War. But there are Serbs there who want the whole truth to come out about that fucking bastard."

The language caught me off guard. But his reference to the Artukovic case and his claims of access to Yugoslav government sources piqued my interest. I asked how he proposed to obtain the dossier.

"Scanlan can do it. I can talk to him about it. Scanlan's goddamn Billy-boys can do it, no question. They just need the go-ahead from him. Scanlan's Billy-boys can get it for you."

He had lost me momentarily. But after he repeated the expression several more times, I realized that "Billy" was CIA Director William Casey.

Katich continued. "I can introduce you to Scanlan. He's a good man, and he's coming to the States on a visit soon. But we have to talk first, and not over the phone. When can we meet?"

It seemed like a poor bet, but I was desperate for that Yugoslav file. I promised Katich that I would call him when I planned to visit Washington, probably sometime within the next three weeks.

After hanging up the phone, I called a friend at OSI. He confirmed Katich's assertion that the Library of Congress staffer had assisted the Justice Department in the Artukovic case. Katich, he said, was a superb researcher who, moreover, seemed to have excellent contacts in Yugoslavia.

On this same Monday, Waldheim released a "Dear Countrymen" letter, in which he denounced the charges that had been leveled against him "at home and abroad." During the war, he wrote, he simply did what "hundreds of thousands of other Austrians did, namely my duty as a soldier."

This choice of words had a special ring in Austria. Almost exactly one year earlier, Joerg Haider, an official of Austria's far-right Freedom Party, had applauded the release from an Italian prison of ex–SS-*Sturmbannfuehrer* Walter Reder, a convicted Nazi mass murderer. Haider had caused an international furor at the time when he characterized Reder as "a soldier who had done his duty."[2] This was, critics pointed out, a variation on the long-discredited Nazi plaint, "I was only following orders."

Now Waldheim had adopted the line as his own, and it was a stroke of genius insofar as the Austrian electorate was concerned. Tens of thousands of Wehrmacht and Waffen-SS veterans remained on the Austrian voting rolls (and if one counted their families, the total swelled to hundreds of thousands of voters). Of course, most had simply been ordinary infantry soldiers involved in conventional combat. Only a comparative handful of them ever occupied positions that put them in contact with Wehrmacht and SS generals (as Waldheim had been), but the candidate's statement cleverly put all the veterans on the same level, as if the WJC was attacking every Austrian who fought in the war.

A reporter called to get my reaction to the statement. "Sure, right," I said sarcastically. "It's as though thousands of people in Austria served as first assistant to the chief of intelligence of an army group that had four hundred thousand men under arms." I also questioned how Waldheim, an Austrian, could have seen his actions on behalf of Nazi Germany as his "duty as a soldier."

The cover story of the April 1 issue of *Wochenpresse* was about us. Its title: WALDHEIM'S ADVERSARY: THE WORLD JEWISH CONGRESS.

The magazine's cover was devoted to a drawing of a man's *yarmulke*-covered head, seen from behind. Inside was a profile of Singer, Steinberg, and me, whom their writer labeled the "Infernal Trio." The article described us as "the raving functionary-trio from the World Jewish Congress." The writer charged that with a "hate-filled voice," the "soul-poisoning Israel Singer" had made the "bizarre demand" that Waldheim be barred from the United States. Singer and his comrades "who live in the past" were seeking, he reported, "to make unsavory capital" from the Waldheim controversy.

Why was Waldheim receiving such unfavorable press in America? A second *Wochenpresse* article purported to disclose the answer. After asserting that only anti-Semites would contend that Jews dominate the American news media, the article quickly pointed out that the owners of "the two most important" U.S. newspapers, the *New York Times* and the *Washington Post,* "are of Jewish descent."

Two of the magazine's writers warned of dire consequences that might flow from the WJC's statements, noting, "Such remarks stir anti-Semitic emotions."

The magazine also carried a full-page campaign ad, featuring a large photograph of U.N. Secretary-General Waldheim being embraced by Pope John Paul II. A smaller photo showed him meeting with Mother Teresa.

Two other stories promoted on the magazine's cover were ill-disguised attempts to further Waldheim's candidacy. One was entitled, "Kurt Steyrer's War Years," and was a probe into the military background of the Socialist Party's presidential candidate.* The other Waldheim piece was entitled, "Simon Wiesenthal: Verdict Without a Court!"

Wochenpresse's lengthy interview with Wiesenthal amounted to a declaration of war. The Nazi-hunter had a rhetorical question for the WJC: "Since when do you represent Yugoslav citizens who are not Jews?"

---

*I found the article's attempt to raise questions about Steyrer's war record wholly unconvincing.

Wiesenthal's anger openly boiled over on the pages of the magazine. He dismissed our factual assertions and declared that Austrian state radio's decision to broadcast a portion of the WJC's press conference the previous week "was for me as a Jew a slap in the face."

The "Great Avenger" gave Austrian anti-Semites all the fuel they needed. Wiesenthal claimed that he had tried unsuccessfully to reach Edgar Bronfman. He had "pleaded with the people in America," he said, "not to increase the damage." He agreed with his questioner's assertion that the WJC's efforts were rekindling anti-Semitism in Austria.[3]

I was stunned. How could he say such things? What did it matter that the Kozara victims were not Jewish? Wiesenthal had always been the leading proponent of the "universality" approach to Nazi crimes: One should not speak only of Six Million Jewish victims, but also of Eleven Million civilian victims. Indeed, I had long admired Wiesenthal for his public campaign to see to it that Hitler's mass murder of the gypsies received proper attention and that the survivors among them received reparations from the West German government.

The Rosenbaum temper was unleashed once more as I showed Singer the comments. "The Jews of Austria are being terrorized by the specter of one of the two major political parties openly fueling anti-Semitism," I complained. "And Wiesenthal, this Jewish leader right there in Vienna, isn't saying anything about it. Instead, he's criticizing the WJC, claiming that *we* are the cause of anti-Semitism in Austria. I hate to say it, but that's the anti-Semites' line: 'The Jews are getting what they deserve.' It's appalling, Israel."

Singer, too, was possessed of a formidable temper. He stared in disbelief at the text I had thrust in front of him. Then he threw the page down on his desk and yelled. "The *World Jewish Congress* is the cause of anti-Semitism in Austria? What's *wrong* with Wiesenthal? Somebody oughta remind him: Jews don't cause anti-Semitism; *anti-Semites* cause anti-Semitism. Where is his denunciation of the anti-Semitic filth in the Austrian press? And the anti-Semitic tactics of the People's Party? And where is his call for an explanation from Waldheim of his cover-up? *U-u-u-c-h!* Wiesenthal is worse than I ever imagined. How can we expect the man in the street in Vienna even to question Waldheim's credibility if Wiesenthal says, every day, that the man is kosher? How can Simon stay in bed with those People's Party pigs?"

At last I had in front of me a translation of the March 26 article in the Yugoslav daily *Vecernje Novosti,* along with a follow-up published by the newspaper five days later, and I studied the texts carefully.

The two stories provided the world with its first glimpse of the evidence underlying the Yugoslavs' decision to submit Waldheim's case to the U.N. War Crimes Commission in 1948.

Although Steinberg's caller from Yugoslavia had spoken of a "decision," the document described in the article as "War Criminal File No. F-25572"—the *Odluka*—was in the nature of what Western legal systems would call an indictment, rather than a judgment. The newspaper claimed that it had only now received the file from the government sources. A summary of the crimes allegedly committed by Waldheim was presented on the cover page, and it was identical to those reported by the enigmatic Pagic in his phone call to Steinberg: "Murders and exterminations. Hostage executions. Deliberate destruction and devastation of property. Setting afire inhabited places."

According to the two articles, the Yugoslav State Commission for the Establishment of War Crimes, on December 18, 1947, "established that Kurt Waldheim, Austrian, Lieutenant, officer of Abwehr, was a war criminal." The dossier's seven single-spaced typewritten pages supposedly provided a detailed explanation for the decision. The use of the term "Abwehr" was of special interest to me. We had no proof that Waldheim was involved in counterintelligence activities (although others in his branch at Arsakli, including his immediate superior, clearly had been); either the word choice was wrong or else the Yugoslavs were claiming that Waldheim's position at Army Group E headquarters involved him in even more questionable activities than we suspected.

The seven incriminating pages, the newspaper said, began with "a description of the role of the Ic Branch of Army Group E, under the command of General Loehr." That role included "decision-making capabilities" concerning reprisals and the use of hostages.

The charges covered only the period from April 1944 onward, during the latter stages of the war when Army Group E withdrew from Greece and retreated through Yugoslavia. This was consistent with the notation on the CROWCASS list. But we knew that Waldheim had served with Loehr's Army Group E since the autumn of 1943, and we knew, further, that he had previously served in Yugoslavia, Albania, and Greece at various times during 1942 and 1943. It appeared that the Yugoslav commission either did not study the earlier years or was unable to find relevant documents. So, in making its "determination" that Waldheim was a war criminal, it had not even considered his possible role in the Kozara episode, the "Black Operation," or any of his activities in Greece.

The newspaper stated that the commission's report included "numerous testimonies of witnesses," but said that "it would be too much to quote all crimes committed. . . ." It ran an excerpt from the testimony in Yugoslav captivity of one Johann Mayer who, the paper said, had known Waldheim personally:

> Waldheim's task was to prepare drafts for his superior officer, Lieutenant Colonel Warnstorff, on all actions of branch Ic, concerning procedures for hostages, reprisals, prisoners of war, and civilians. I was informed that at that time, while the Group E was in transfer from Greece to Yugoslavia, that is, shortly after my arrival, a general order was issued that the decisions on reprisals, hostages, and etc., would not depend on the decision of the field marshal, or other troop commanders, but on the military Group E, that is, on their Ic officers.

If true, Mayer's testimony was devastating to Waldheim, for it accused him of drafting criminal orders, an action that was indisputably a war crime.

Testimony from another captured ex–Army Group E officer, Major Klaus Mellinghoff, vaguely, if not very convincingly, sought to implicate every man in Waldheim's Ic unit:

> I am aware that Hitler's initiative and his wish for cruel reprisal measures against civilians was referred from the German High Command all the way down to the level of the troops. Therefore, I believe that the atrocities committed by certain troops in Macedonia and Bosnia were carried out on the basis of those instructions. It is possible that Army Group E acted in accordance with those orders too. . . . The same goes for the area of work of the Ic Branch.

The most damaging evidence in the Yugoslav file seemed to be provided by a third witness, who linked Waldheim, however imprecisely, to an act of mass murder:

> According to the testimony of the war criminal Egbert Hilker, Kurt Waldheim was responsible for the reprisal committed on the road between Kocane and Stip in late October 1944, when three villages were burned and 114 people killed.

I studied the account carefully, for this report was our first connection between Waldheim and a specific crime. But there was precious little detail here. It was yet another subject that demanded further research.

War Criminal File No. F-25572, as quoted in the Yugoslav newspaper, stated that "many other similar acts could be listed which

Army Group E committed while withdrawing through Yugoslavia."
Examples were cited, involving killings and mass-destruction activities in seventeen listed villages between May 1944 and early 1945.
Here were seventeen more localities to research.

Although the Yugoslav articles offered few specifics concerning
evidence available to corroborate the purported witness testimony,
they did claim that the Waldheim indictment had been accompanied
by copies of several captured documents, including reprisal directives
issued by General Loehr. That disclosure made getting our hands on
the actual file a more urgent priority than ever.

The newspaper quoted the damning conclusion of the Yugoslav
War Crimes Commission:

> Above-mentioned evidence points out that these orders were
> worked out in detail in collaboration with Department Ic at
> headquarters of the Army group, and particularly in collaboration with Lieutenant Waldheim. The practical execution of these
> commands makes the responsibility of those who gave orders
> and put them through to the lower units even larger.

To me, the biggest surprise in the *Vecernje Novosti* articles was not
what was revealed about the contents of the Waldheim indictment
itself, but rather the disclosure of the text of an official memo that
accompanied it. The memo was dated December 12, 1947, shortly
before the indictment was sent on to the UNWCC, and was reportedly written to the Yugoslav Ministry of Foreign Affairs by one
Uros M. Bjelic of the Legal Bureau. It suggested that attention should
be paid to "registering Waldheim [with the UNWCC] since there is
strong evidence for this and the report is complete and sufficient."
The next sentence in Bjelic's memo was remarkable. It noted that
Waldheim "is today in Austria, not only as a free person, but as a
Secretary in the Ministry for Foreign Affairs." This was a fact, the
letter said, "of not minor importance."

Here then was our confirmation. The Yugoslavs knew precisely
that Waldheim was working in the Austrian Foreign Ministry when
they reported him to the UNWCC as a war criminal! If they had
really wanted to extradite and try him, why had they not gone public
with their knowledge, way back in 1947?

Other official Yugoslav correspondence quoted in the two *Vecernje
Novosti* articles provided an answer. In one, Dr. Dusan Nedljkovic,
president of the Yugoslav War Crimes Commission, informed the
Ministry of Internal Affairs, on Christmas Day, 1947, that the commission had "identified and proclaimed as a war criminal the former
Lieutenant Waldheim and . . . has today sent its report to have his

name registered with the International Commission for War Crimes in London."

Four days later, Nedljkovic wrote to the Yugoslav Embassy in London: "A special effort should be made to register Waldheim, first of all because the reasons are good and enough evidence was sup plied, and, on the other hand, for us it is politically opportune."

The understated words "politically opportune" forced a laugh from my throat. The Nedljkovic letters eliminated any possibility that Tito was unaware that the "Waldheim, Kurt ?"—whom the Yugoslavs quietly submitted to the UNWCC as wanted for "murder"—was an official in Austria's Foreign Ministry. And once the UNWCC agreed to list Waldheim, Tito had held the ultimate blackmail weapon in his hands.

If the Yugoslavs had decided that it was "politically opportune" to register Waldheim with the UNWCC, they had two choices. First, they could score propaganda points by exposing him. This was the time when Yugoslavia was locked in difficult treaty negotiations with Austria, and part of its strategy was to embarrass Vienna by exposing Austrian veterans involved in war crimes committed on Yugoslav soil. Tito had indeed opted to go public in some cases (including, most significantly, that of another member of the Austrian negotiating team) but—quite obviously—not in Waldheim's. That left only the second strategy: blackmail. How easy it was now to envision one of the Yugoslav negotiators sidling up to Waldheim, allowing him the tiniest peek at the file, or at a page of his UNWCC or CROW-CASS correspondence. Waldheim would have had to resign immediately or else consider himself, henceforth, Tito's property.

Waldheim had, of course, remained at his Foreign Ministry post. Yet Tito's government never exposed him. The explanation seemed to require no special brilliance to deduce.

Vecernje Novosti gave Waldheim an opportunity to respond to its story. Reached by phone, Waldheim ventured the guess that the Yugoslavs had once attempted to list as a war criminal "every" German soldier who set foot in Yugoslavia. "I am not responsible," he insisted, "not even for a single war crime committed in your country."[4]

What was the truth? Had the Yugoslavs indicted Waldheim on genuine and persuasive proof (notwithstanding their less than completely honorable motives), or were the charges wholly fabricated, issued in order to exert pressure on the young Austrian diplomat? It was too early to say.

It was still possible to construct at least one unremarkable scenario in which Tito could have abstained from using his Waldheim ammunition. Shortly after the Yugoslavs listed Waldheim with the UNWCC, Tito split with Stalin, and Soviet support for Yugoslavia's territorial claims collapsed almost immediately. At that point, Tito might have developed an additional reason for keeping silent about Waldheim. Now he desperately needed friends, and he therefore sought to establish good relations with neighboring Austria. Denouncing the assistant to Austria's Foreign Minister, the American-allied Gruber, would hardly have endeared him to Vienna.

As far as the Soviet angle was concerned, we now knew conclusively that the Yugoslavs had indicted Waldheim prior to the split with the USSR, and it thus seemed a likely, if not quite certain, bet that they had shared the information with the KGB.

It was interesting to consider this hypothesis in light of the Soviets' reaction to our ongoing Waldheim disclosures, or, more precisely, to the *absence* of a reaction. For the first time in postwar history, the Soviets were resisting the temptation to make propaganda hay out of a possible "CIA/Nazi cover-up." The Soviets could not have overlooked the opportunity; the CIA whitewash letter to Solarz had been mentioned in Tagliabue's original front-page story in the *New York Times*. Soviet commentators, I told myself, should be having a veritable field day accusing the U.S. of withholding vital information when Waldheim first ran for his U.N. post—especially since the Soviets could feign ignorance by pointing out that they did not participate in either the CROWCASS or the UNWCC operations. But Moscow was silent, from the Kremlin to the Foreign Ministry to the state-controlled media.

Moscow's unprecedented silence was indirect evidence that Waldheim skeletons might lurk in the USSR closet too, but the real surprise was Moscow's lack of subtlety in the affair. Soviet spokesmen responded to press inquiries by claiming not to have a shred of paper in their files concerning Waldheim's wartime service. How much more effectively they would have helped Waldheim, it seemed to me, if the Kremlin had released a few comparatively innocuous documents and left it at that. Instead, the Soviets virtually telegraphed the message that they remained in Waldheim's corner.

However fascinating these speculations were, they were intrusions into the most important matter at hand. Worse still, all of these ancient political machinations made it far more difficult to ascertain just what it was that "law student" Waldheim had done during his hidden war years.

For that matter, the current political environment was no more hospitable to our investigation. Clearly, the entire affair was deeply embarrassing to the Yugoslav authorities, even though some individuals inside the Belgrade government wanted to get the story out anyway. Looking back at the Yugoslav press "disclosures," it now seemed obvious that the Belgrade government was determined to release only those bits of information that world opinion compelled it to release, and not one iota more. It was the WJC that revealed that Waldheim had been awarded the King Zvonimir Medal; within twenty-four hours, Yugoslav authorities permitted the press to publish Croatian documents confirming the award. It was the WJC that revealed that Yugoslavia had placed Waldheim on the CROWCASS list and had submitted his file to the UNWCC; almost immediately, Belgrade allowed the disclosure of some details. The Yugoslavs had promised to release the full text of the *Odluka,* but the courier never arrived with the indictment. The Yugoslav government was clearly suffering from a serious case of ambivalence. The information flow from Belgrade remained a trickle that eased but did not slake the thirst.

We decided that one of our highest priorities was to trace the witnesses cited in the Yugoslav reports. Since Egbert Hilker was described by the Yugoslavs as a captured "war criminal," he had probably been executed. But what about Johann Mayer and Klaus Mellinghoff? If they were alive and we could locate them, would they—Mayer in particular—still finger Waldheim as an Ic officer responsible for drafting and transmitting reprisal orders?

Schuller was already at work on these tasks, but he was pessimistic about the prospects for success.

It was also vital for us to obtain an actual copy of "File No. F-25572"—especially the *Odluka* and the documents and witness statements purportedly underlying that indictment—so that we could perform a proper appraisal of the evidentiary basis for the forty-year-old Yugoslav charges. We needed to get as close as possible to the raw investigative information. Idly, I wondered whether Stephen Katich, the legal specialist at the Library of Congress, really could persuade Scanlan's "Billy-boys" to help us with this quest.

In its April 1 issue, the Yugoslav magazine *Danas* published the gruesome recollections of a survivor of the massacres on the road between Stip and Kocane, the one atrocity said to have been directly attributed to Waldheim in the *Odluka.* Eighty-two-year-old Rista Ognjenov recalled that he was in the village of Karbinci when the Germans arrived:

> They lined us up on the south side of the road and thirty or so soldiers directed by two German officers started to shoot machine guns. The moment the shooting started, I threw myself in the ditch next to the road, while the bodies of shot peasants

began to fall on top of me. From our group, thirteen individuals succeeded to run away from the shots, while among the dead bodies in the ditch, two other peasants from the village of Karbinci remained alive.[5]

Meanwhile, as indignation continued to mount in Yugoslavia over Waldheim's attempt to characterize Kozara as "a normal battle," he was forced to move quickly to diffuse the threat. *Vecernje Novosti* and *Politika Svet* now published interviews with Waldheim, in which he artfully acknowledged the horrors he had previously denied. "Now I have understood what Kozara means for Yugoslavia," he said apologetically.

And now that he "understood" that it had indeed been a cruel operation, he attempted to craft a completely new alibi. While he admitted to the Yugoslav newspapers that Kozara was indeed more than an "altercation,"—*voilà!*—he had not really been there at all. In fact, he had not been *anywhere* in western Bosnia. "I made a mistake when I said I was in the Kozara area," Waldheim said. He had now analyzed the situation with his son Gerhard, "and I came to the conclusion that I was in Plevlje at the time." Plevlje is in *Montenegro,* 120 miles away from Kozara. Waldheim insisted that the documents showing him assigned to the command staff in western Bosnia in 1942 reflected a mere "paper" assignment. Technically, yes, he had been a part of Stahl's staff, but in reality he was in Plevlje, where "I received radio reports that I passed on to the Italians."

Why, then, had Stahl recommended him for the King Zvonimir Medal? The medal, Waldheim replied, was simply given to every officer on Stahl's staff.*

Waldheim's new version of his 1942 war record had two big advantages over its predecessors. Most importantly, it removed him from the vicinity of the Kozara atrocities. And by placing him with the Italians in Plevlje, it overcame the fatal flaw in his previous claim to have been a German-Italian interpreter in the Kozara area— namely, the fact that no Italian forces had been engaged there.

Attempting to deal at the same time with speculation that he had been compromised by foreign intelligence services, Waldheim claimed in a discussion with a wire-service reporter that both the KGB and the CIA "established that I am clear."[6]

NBC's Diane Wallerstein located Theodore Fenstermacher, one of the Americans who had prosecuted Nazi war criminals at Nurem-

---

*In an interview published in the March 5, 1986, issue of the Vienna newspaper *Kurier,* Waldheim had made an identical claim: "The order was routinely conferred upon all staff members."

berg; his area of concentration had been crimes committed in Greece and Yugoslavia. He was now an attorney in private practice in Cortland, New York.

When I reached him by phone, Fenstermacher told me that he did not recall Kurt Waldheim's name surfacing during his own postwar investigations, but he certainly remembered the name of General Alexander Loehr. He related that his prosecution team had wanted to bring Loehr to Nuremberg, to stand trial along with some of his comrades who had been captured by American forces, but the Yugoslav government was uncooperative. At last, the Yugoslavs agreed to allow Fenstermacher to come to Belgrade to question Loehr. When he arrived at the American Embassy, he found a message waiting, informing him that there would be a slight delay. For several days thereafter he was repeatedly put off, until the Yugoslavs finally advised that Loehr would not be available for questioning. The reason: They had just executed him.

15

New York, Thursday, April 3. "Oh, my dear Eli, it is so *gut* to speak *mit* you again." The sound of Leon Zelman's gentle voice over the transatlantic connection was reassuring. The kindhearted survivor who had set me on this unlikely journey had called me at my office to make sure I heard that Waldheim's campaign team had just staged a bizarre press conference at Vienna's Ambassador Hotel. Zelman filled me in. Assembled for the media were five former Wehrmacht officers who had served with Waldheim at Army Group E headquarters. Senior among them was ex–Lieutenant Colonel Herbert Warnstorff, Army Group E's chief of intelligence and counterintelligence—and Waldheim's immediate superior from the autumn of 1943 until the end of the war. He had traveled from his home in West Germany for the occasion.

Warnstorff assured the assembled journalists that not only had Waldheim been uninvolved in any deportation of the Jews, but the candidate had not even been aware of such actions. Warnstorff could be certain of this, he said, because he himself had not known of the deportations.

The others repeated the same refrain. "There was never anything said about the deportation of Jews," claimed Waldheim's immediate subordinate, ex–Lieutenant Helmut Poliza.

"We knew nothing of the persecution of Jews in Salonika," said Wolfgang Sattman, who had worked in the radio communications office.

"All reports came across my desk, and nothing came by radio or telex about the deportation of Jews," declared Friedrich Wiebe, another former Army Group E officer.

"Ah, just like the good burghers of Munich, who knew nothing about what was going on at nearby Dachau," I told Zelman. "It sounds very familiar."

Also at the press conference was Fritz Molden, the Austrian publisher of Waldheim's 1971 book, *The Austrian Example*. Molden brandished impeccable credentials; he had been a valiant member of the Austrian resistance during the war, and his exploits had come to the attention of Allen W. Dulles, then chief of the Swiss office of the OSS and later the head of its offspring, the CIA. Molden and Dulles had developed both a professional and personal friendship. After the war, Molden married Dulles's daughter.

Molden recalled for the press corps how he was serving as secretary to Austrian Foreign Minister Karl Gruber late in 1945, when Waldheim was proposed for a position as Gruber's assistant. Gruber had ordered Molden to check Waldheim's political record, particularly to determine whether Waldheim had ever belonged to any Nazi organizations. Molden said he had inquired of the Interior Ministry, which reported that it had no indication of any Nazi ties on Waldheim's part and noted that Waldheim had, in fact, been hostile to the Nazis before the war. Molden asserted that he had also asked his American contacts at OSS and the U.S. Army Counter Intelligence Corps to check Waldheim's political record. Both organizations, he said, reported finding no evidence of membership by Waldheim in Nazi organizations.*

Molden stated, however, that Waldheim's military record was not checked at the time, either by the Austrian Interior Ministry or by the Americans. "The Austrian police," he said, "were not capable of collecting any intelligence data, and how should the Americans have known about such a minor man?" Molden said that he knew at the time that Waldheim had been a first lieutenant in the Wehrmacht, but added, "It did not occur to me to ask what he did." This seemed a foolish statement from a former intelligence operative, who surely knew that it was a common practice to keep certain officers, especially intelligence personnel, at a low rank, partly to protect them in the event of capture.

A young Austrian historian named Walter Manoschek was present in the audience for the media event. He was a member of a fledgling organization calling itself "New Austria," devoted to combating the open resurgence of anti-Semitic and xenophobic sentiments brought on by the Waldheim affair and, specifically, to forcing Waldheim and all Austrians to face unpleasant and long-repressed truths about the Nazi period. Manoschek and a colleague had been digging into the captured records collection at the German Federal Military Archives

---

*It was hardly surprising that neither the OSS nor Army CIC knew of Waldheim's Nazi affiliations. At the time, their standard procedure for inquiring about such affiliations was to check files at the U.S.-operated Berlin Document Center. That facility, however, has never possessed the membership records of the groups with which Waldheim was involved. Furthermore, those particular Nazi-affiliated organizations had not been considered "criminal" by the Allies. Waldheim, moreover, had been able to show that he came from an anti-Nazi family, had himself been beaten up before the *Anschluss* for distributing pro-Schuschnigg literature, and had spent portions of the war years studying law in Vienna.

in Freiburg. Another "New Austria" member, historian Hans Safrian, was studying materials on file at the Institute for Contemporary History, in Munich.

In Freiburg, Manoschek had decided to follow the WJC's lead in researching the role of Loehr's Army Group E in the deportation of Greek Jews to Auschwitz. He had unearthed several important captured German documents dealing with the deportation of Jews from the island of Rhodes and, here at the press conference, he attempted to confront Warnstorff with them. Warnstorff would not respond to specific questions; he instead repeated that he had had nothing to do with the Jews and did not even know that they were being deported. (Frustrated, Manoschek vowed that his documents would in any case appear soon in *Profil.*)

Zelman told me that, as Waldheim's comrades faced the press, a small group of demonstrators protested quietly outside the hotel, carrying signs bearing such slogans as: WE WANT HITLER AS A DEFENDING WITNESS; MEMORY GAP FOR PRESIDENT; ANTI-SEMITISM: NOW MORE THAN EVER?

The demonstrators were well behaved, but the Austrian police moved in, tore down the placards, and hauled the protestors away.[1]

It was the sort of police behavior one might expect in a totalitarian country, but not in a modern, supposedly free nation. I shuddered at the thought of what might have happened to me if I had been caught at the Vienna airport with the Podgorica photograph and a suitcase full of Waldheim materials.

A series of phone calls buoyed my spirits. The first was from Neal Sher, who wanted to know if I had any information on the press conference. I passed on what I had learned from Zelman. "Roosevelt," he quipped, "can you imagine what kind of 'high fives' Waldheim's friends gave each other?"

Michael May of the Institute of Jewish Affairs, the WJC's small research office in central London, called to report that a Viennese journalist was on the trail of Johann Mayer, the chief witness supporting the Yugoslav charges against Waldheim. Mayer reportedly was living in the Vienna area and still disliked Waldheim. May and I agreed that if Mayer could be located, we would catch the first available flights, rendezvous in Vienna, and attempt to interview him.

Another call was from my close friend and former boss, Martin Mendelsohn, the first chief of OSI. Now he was an attorney in private practice in Washington and one of his clients was the Simon Wiesenthal Center. Mendelsohn told me that he was about to fly to Yugoslavia to act as the Center's observer at the war crimes trial of Andrija Artukovic, and he had some exciting news. By fortuitous coincidence, another of Mendelsohn's clients was the government of Yugoslavia. Thus, he had high-level contacts, one of whom had confided to him that the Belgrade government was, as we suspected, holding back a trove of incriminating documents on Waldheim. The files were in the Croatian State Archives in Zagreb. That city happened to be the site of the Artukovic trial, and Mendelsohn's contact promised that he would be granted access to the documents during his visit. Mendelsohn assured me that he would call with a full report as soon as he returned.

Confirmation of the Yugoslavs' new willingness to open their files seemed to come from a new story in *Vecernje Novosti,* which took exception to Waldheim's altered chronology of events that placed him at Plevlje, far away from the Kozara massacres. His claim that his assignment to Stahl's staff in western Bosnia was a "paper assignment" was, the newspaper asserted, an invention. But perhaps the most tantalizing item in the story was a brief statement concerning the Yugoslav archives: "Kurt Waldheim's complete dossier is to be found there."[2]

Waldheim waged an active counteroffensive. The cover of a new campaign brochure was emblazoned with the now familiar combative slogans: WE AUSTRIANS WILL ELECT WHOM WE WANT and NOW MORE THAN EVER: DR. KURT WALDHEIM. The text was devoted entirely to what it called the *Verleumdungskampagne* ("slander campaign") against the former U.N. chief. Prominently featured, in the middle of denunciations of "psychoterror" and the "unscrupulous" manner in which "certain officials of the World Jewish Congress" had "dealt with the honor of an international statesman," was a photograph of Simon Wiesenthal, along with his statement that Tito would never have received Waldheim on official visits if he had believed that Waldheim had been involved in Nazi war crimes. Also featured in the campaign pamphlet was Wiesenthal's charge that the WJC had erred in attempting to link Waldheim to the Salonika deportations. The last page carried a reproduction of Waldheim's March 31 "Dear Countrymen" letter, in which he claimed to have done nothing but "my duty as a soldier."[3]

"I am innocent," he declared to a reporter. "There is no blood on my hands." Waldheim swore that he knew nothing about the deportations of Jews and that he "never saw a single partisan." He assured the journalist, "I never participated either in burnings of villages or, still less, in executions."[4]

During a lunch conversation, he explained to a reporter why he had allowed himself, before the war, to be "in the shadow" of Nazi groups. He had done so, he said, for "opportunistic reasons," in order to be allowed to finish his education. "It can't do any harm," he said he had told himself.[5]

Reading a report on the interview, I wondered whether this last comment did not reflect what, in some respects, was most terrifying about the horrors of the the Nazi era. Comparatively few Europeans fully shared Hitler's perverse ideology and goals. But millions of others had simply gone along for "opportunistic reasons."

U.N. Secretary-General Perez de Cuellar steadfastly refused to release the UNWCC file on Waldheim even to any U.N. member-nation delegation without the consent of the countries that made up the old commission. Most troubling was his declaration that the seventeen UNWCC member-nations would have to consent *unanimously* before the file could be released. In response, Jewish students staged an angry demonstration outside U.N. headquarters. A group of influential U.S. political figures, including former Congresswoman Holtzman and former U.S. Supreme Court Justice Arthur Goldberg, urged Perez de Cuellar to relent, and editorial opinion, at least in the West, strongly supported the demand. Within days, Perez de Cuellar gave in to the pressure and granted the Israeli, Austrian, and U.S. delegations permission to review the file, on the condition that the contents would not be made public. We could only hope that someone in one of the delegations would see fit to leak a copy to us or to the press.

Waldheim professed to be at peace with Perez de Cuellar's decision. "You know, when you have a clear conscience, things like that don't worry you," he declared. The man who claimed that he had only been doing his "duty as a soldier" now sought to identify with the war's victims, adding, "I bear the awfulness of this war on my own body. I was a victim."[6]

That same night, April 4, Waldheim was interviewed by BBC-TV reporter Julian O'Halloran. In his most recent interview with the Yugoslav press, Waldheim had belatedly conceded that terrible things had indeed happened during the Kozara operation (albeit, he contended, in his absence). But he was apparently unwilling to repeat the same admissions for Western viewers. On British television, he reverted to his description of Kozara as nothing more than "a very tough military confrontation."

O'Halloran countered with documented reports of atrocities, including details that Stahl himself had admitted at Nuremberg: 360 villages destroyed, 70,000 people—including 23,000 children—driven into concentration camps. O'Halloran pressed: "I am not talking about fighting, I am talking about reprisals—"

Suddenly red-faced with rage, Waldheim pounded his fist onto the coffee table in front of him, interrupting his questioner: "The *German soldiers* also had casualties, they had *thousands* and *thousands* of casualties, the Germans! So please be a little more—objective. Casualties were on both sides."[7]

As I watched a rebroadcast of this interview on PBS's "MacNeil Lehrer Newshour," Waldheim's remarks struck me as close to obscene. It was bad enough that he had the temerity to call himself a "victim" of the war. But now he was attempting to equate the deaths of Axis soldiers, who had invaded another people's homeland, with the deaths of thousands of innocent civilians. The comparison owed much to a favorite theme of neo-Nazi revisionism, the attempt to "explain" some of the Nazis' criminal acts with the argument that "these things happen in war, to both sides." Waldheim knew better.

In short order, Waldheim again refined his Kozara story for Yugoslav press consumption, offering an "explanation" of his earlier "confusion." He said now that he had learned that Plevlje was near a place known as Kozara, but it was a *different* Kozara! Furthermore, he said, there was a witness still living in Plevlje who remembered him.[8] He stuck to his "paper assignment" story: Despite the several documents placing him on Stahl's staff in western Bosnia during the Kozara operation, he simply had not been there.

The conflicting versions of Waldheim's Kozara story were part of an audacious—and at times brilliant—defense. Although Waldheim had played an awkward game of catch-up in tailoring and retailoring his stories to fit each new series of disclosures, to my chagrin, the Western media typically reported each new Waldheim explanation in a straightforward manner, and generally missed or ignored the fact that these were drastically altered versions of his previous accounts.

We protested that there remained a giant hole in Waldheim's "paper assignment" story: It failed to explain the matter of his medal. Waldheim's claim that every member of Stahl's staff received the King Zvonimir Medal was a lie, and we had the documentation to prove it. He had to have *earned* that medal somehow, and his listing on the "honor roll" appended to the shocking Kozara prose poem strongly indicated that he had done so by contributing—in some fashion—to the execution of the Kozara operation. A befuddled press corps scarcely heard our protests, however; this "foreign story," with its convoluted twists and turns, piecemeal disclosures, conflicting responses and retorts, was becoming too intricate either to understand or else to handle in a brief news story or wire-service report, particularly when the typical American reporter we encountered was doing only a one-day stint on the Waldheim beat; most of them were ignorant of all but a tiny portion of what had already transpired. But there was little I could do to simplify it for them. War crimes investigations rarely evolve in a neat, orderly manner, and the Waldheim case was certainly no exception. Key facts in one or another of the Waldheim subplots would typically come out long after the initial discoveries. To make our case publicly, therefore, we desperately needed at least one clear new example, running logically and inexorably from *A* to *B* to *C,* of Waldheim's involvement in a specific criminal episode.

"I want the rest," Singer told me solemnly from the couch in his cramped office. "I want every single piece of paper that survived the war and has anything to do with Kurt Waldheim."

"Israel," I replied, "there's no one to do the research. Bob Herzstein gave us the one week that he could take off from his university responsibilities." I reminded my boss of the dimensions of the task. We had only the sketchiest information concerning Waldheim's whereabouts during a few days, here and there, in a protracted war that had ended forty-one years earlier. Only a minuscule percentage of the relevant documents had survived. The subject of our investigation would not speak with us, and insisted on providing misleading, ever-changing information to the press. The few witnesses we could locate were all former cohorts of the man. What's more, there were false leads all over the place.

I reminded Singer that this bore no resemblance to a modern-day criminal investigation. I offered an example: The police find a dead body at the corner of Broadway and Forty-second Street with two gunshot wounds in it. They find a discarded gun nearby. They question witnesses. The medical examiner can tell them when the crime occurred, give or take a few hours. The police probably have some fresh leads to follow. And however difficult it may be to solve, the mystery can at least be stated simply: "Whodunit." But in the Waldheim case, we did not even know what the universe of crimes was. Certainly we knew that the German war machine committed atrocities throughout Europe. But we did not know which of these to focus on and we had only the murkiest of clues showing us where to look.

It was, in a sense, the flip side of Watergate: We had proved the fact of a cover-up; that was the easy part in this case. But we still knew little about precisely what it was that Waldheim had covered up. Had we already spotted the mass of the iceberg, or merely the tip?

I pleaded, "Israel, we still don't even know where he *was* during most of the war, much less what was happening in those places or what role, if any, he played in those events." This was the most complex investigation I had ever encountered, and it exhausted me even to think about pursuing it much further. We already had exposed Waldheim as a liar and an accused war criminal, the latter based upon the CROWCASS and UNWCC listings. The Kozara documents were especially damning. What more did we need? What more did we have to do?

I suggested to Singer, "Why not wait and see how the Justice Department's investigation turns out?"

"That's not the answer I want."

"I know. But there's no one left to go to the Archives for us."

"Then you go."

I could have put up more of a fight, but I suddenly realized that my attitude had undergone something of a transformation in the past several weeks. A few years earlier, I had resigned from OSI because the work of investigating and prosecuting Nazi cases had proved too frustrating and too depressing. Little more than two months ago, after my initial conversation with Zelman in Jerusalem, I had resisted the thought of flying off to Vienna to probe vague and implausible charges. But Schuller's disclosures and the events of the past few months had steadily restored my resolve. These cases—all of them— had to be pursued to their investigative endpoint, wherever that might be. Justice required it. And so did fidelity to historical truth and respect for the memory of those who had perished.

In any event, Singer's command that I go to Washington settled the matter, rendering any further protest on my part pointless. Suddenly, however, that fact ceased to trouble me. Because the truth was, I wanted to go.

16

I prepared for my National Archives expedition with some weekend reading. *Hitler's Spies,* David Kahn's authoritative 1978 book on German military intelligence during World War II, helped to clarify the duties of a German army group's Ic/AO Branch, and its "O3" officer. Kahn confirmed that, at the army group level, the chief of intelligence, "Ic," had the "/AO" appended to his branch's title in part because he also controlled the commitment of Abwehr (counterintelligence) units at the front. According to Kahn, the "O3" officer, the chief's principal assistant, was normally at least a major, often a lieutenant colonel. The fact that Waldheim was installed in the position while only a first lieutenant accordingly suggested to me that he must have performed very capably in earlier assignments.

According to Kahn, the total staff of a German army group's Ic/AO Branch "came to only thirteen officers and eighteen noncoms, for a total of thirty-one." Their principal function was the gathering and evaluation of enemy intelligence. Kahn pointed out, however, that they also had other tasks "to occupy their time." These additional duties ranged from propaganda to maintaining troop morale. "In a few areas," Kahn added, "this included cooperating with SS murder squads, telling them where Jews were hiding" and, on occasion, "ordering the delivery of Jews to the SS." The branch also collated reports on the numbers of Jews killed or deported by the SS or by the Secret Field Police units detached to them. Kahn noted that the morning, afternoon, and evening intelligence reports summarizing activities in the field were written by the "O3."

Herzstein had already found such reports containing numerous references to "cleansing operations" and to information obtained through prisoner interrogations. Waldheim's signature appeared on many of these, typically certifying the accuracy of the text. But Kahn's comments made it clear that, as the Army Group E "labor allocation table" found by Herzstein had seemed to indicate, the "O3" ordinarily was also the anonymous *author* of these reports.[1]

A declassified U.S. War Department study I had purchased in a military bookstore offered further details. The report cautioned that the Wehrmacht term "O3" was often misunderstood. A common mistake was to mistranslate *Ordonnanzoffizier* as "ordnance officer," indicating someone who was involved in procuring, storing, or issuing weapons and ammunition. In fact, the report stated, the term translated more accurately as "Third Special Missions Staff Officer." As the study explained, this was a designation indicating *far* more important responsibilities:

> The O3, usually a captain or major, was the deputy of the chief intelligence officer. He was responsible for all operational intelligence and the control of the intelligence staff. He superintended the keeping of the situation maps and the intelligence filing system, and was responsible for informing higher and adjacent formations of all items on enemy intelligence and for collating all intelligence emanating from OKH [Army High Command] or adjacent units.

The War Department study also noted that the interrogation of P.O.W.'s was ordinarily conducted for the Wehrmacht by interpreters:

> In every army prisoner-of-war cage, an interpreter section (*Dolmetschertrupp*) consisting of two to four interpreters was employed, whose mission was to interrogate in accordance with submitted intelligence briefs.

At the army group level, the report noted, "only important prisoners of war were interrogated."[2] This statement immediately brought to mind the Army Group E labor allocation table, which included "prisoner interrogation" matters in *Waldheim's* sphere of responsibilities. Waldheim himself, we knew, was a qualified and experienced interpreter.

Waldheim's involvement in prisoner interrogation matters had to be understood in the context of the grim documentation we were beginning to assemble about German interrogation practices, particularly as applied to captured partisans and Allied P.O.W.'s. One such document was found for us by Michael May of the WJC's London research unit. Entitled "Combat Directives for Anti-Bandit Warfare in the East," it was an April 2, 1943, report from the 2nd Army Command to the High Command Army Group Center. The document, which had been a prosecution exhibit at Nuremberg, left little to the imagination about the methods authorized for use in Wehrmacht interrogations of both male and female prisoners:

During interrogation of bandits, also women, all means have to
be employed to obtain the necessary statements; interpreters
are to be specially trained for the interrogation of bandits.[3]

I was also well familiar with the German policy on the treatment
of Soviet P.O.W.'s, whom they murdered, through starvation and
other means, by the millions. Their fate had been sealed by Hitler's
order of March 30, 1941, decreeing that German soldiers

. . . must dissociate ourselves from the principle of soldierly
comradeship. The Communist is a brother-in-arms neither before nor after the battle. This is a struggle for annihilation.[4]

Almost everything I read about the Germans' treatment of prisoners had an ominous undertone—or worse. I made a mental note:
Keep an eye out for documents from Waldheim's units regarding
prisoners.

As a final preparation for my trip to the Archives, I began studying
the thick packet of photocopied pages that my small army of college
students had retrieved, based on Herzstein's handwritten lists. But
there was so much here that I gave up in exhaustion after a few hours
and threw the more important-looking documents into my briefcase,
so that I would have them on hand if I needed to refer to them
during my work in Washington.

On Sunday, April 6, a reporter bluntly asked Waldheim why he had
not withdrawn from the presidential race.

"The world still respects me," the candidate responded.[5]

Later that day, the Waldheim campaign organization released a
formal, typewritten memorandum, in which the candidate responded
defiantly to his critics. He declared that allegations about his prewar
membership in Nazi organizations were "apparently based on occasional participation in riding exercises." He also denied any involvement with prisoner interrogations; not only had he personally
been uninvolved in interrogations, but questioning of prisoners had
been conducted only "at the corps and divisions levels and not at
the [High] Command of Army Group E . . ."

Concerning claims that he must have been aware of the deportation
of Jews from the Greek islands, he maintained, "I was definitely not
aware that they had taken place." This information, he wrote, had
perhaps gone to the Ic/AO Branch's *Abwehr* officer ("AO"), Major
Hammer. Waldheim insisted that the activities of the AO section
were completely separate from those of the Ic section, and even the
branch chief, Lieutenant Colonel Warnstorff, "was not usually in-

formed about them." He added that at Army Group E, he had been "occupied" gathering information from subordinate units, drafting reports for Warnstorff, "and signing 'copy certified correct' on the report authorized by my superior." Waldheim explained that the "operational decisions based on these reports and evaluations" were made by Loehr and his chief of staff.[6]

On Monday morning, before beginning my work at the Archives, I telephoned our office in New York. Steinberg told me excitedly about *Profil*'s latest disclosures, which had just arrived via fax. The magazine had published highlights from the captured German documents discovered by Walter Manoschek and the "New Austria" organization. Two of them, Steinberg said, were of momentous importance. One was an activity report "for the period from July 1– September 15, 1944," prepared by the intelligence staff (Ic) of the Wehrmacht *Kommandant* for the East Aegean islands, Lieutenant General Ulrich Kleeman, commander of the Wehrmacht's 999th Division. It devoted a brief paragraph to the deportation of seventeen hundred Jewish men, women, and children from the Greek island of Rhodes. The report placed responsibility for the crime not just at Army Group E headquarters, but specifically *at Waldheim's unit,* the Ic/AO Branch:

> Deportation of Jews: End of July 1944, deportation of Jews not having Turkish citizenship from the entire command territory, *at instruction of High Command of Army Group E, Ic/AO.* Implementation in hands of SD-Greece, which detailed special detachment to command territory for this purpose. [Emphasis added.][7]

A second document, signed by Lieutenant General Kleeman himself, was addressed precisely and solely to the Ic/AO Branch at the High Command of Army Group E. The report noted that the reaction of most of the inhabitants of Rhodes to the deportation of the Jews "seemed to be negative." It added candidly, "In some cases, the Germans were even called barbarians."[8]

I shared Steinberg's excitement over the publication of these documents, a reaction that I experienced again later when I was able to see the documents for myself and confirm their extraordinary contents. Now no one could deny that we were on target with our charges that Loehr and his minions were involved in the deportation of Greek Jews for liquidation in Poland. What's more, this new material brought the crimes to Waldheim's doorstep. Now we knew that the deportation of Jews from Rhodes to Auschwitz was at the "instruction" of "Ic/AO" at the High Command of Army Group E, and we knew that reports on the deportations came directly to the small Ic/AO Branch, where Waldheim was the special missions staff officer who served as principal assistant to the chief! The whole branch had no more than fifteen officers in it. The new documents clashed with everything that Waldheim and his supporters were saying. The thought of Waldheim (and his comrades at their press conference) repeatedly claiming to have "heard nothing" about these deportations was nauseating.*

Steinberg and I wondered whether this latest revelation might finally force Waldheim from the presidential race. Here, after all, were documents proving that his tiny Army Group E unit was involved in a major Nazi crime, this time against Jews. But I was becoming more of a realist concerning Austrian politics. In his homeland, Waldheim still seemed untouchable.

Indeed, in the same issue that carried the Manoschek material, *Profil* published a story that resorted to questionable methods in an attempt to exonerate Waldheim from the Yugoslav charges. The magazine disclosed that its reporter Hubertus Czernin had traced Johann Mayer, the man identified by the Yugoslav press as the key witness in Belgrade's 1947 indictment of Waldheim. He learned that Mayer had died in Vienna, of cancer, in 1972. Czernin's report was necessarily obtained from secondhand sources, but he claimed that the evidence revealed that Mayer's charges were bogus. Czernin reported that Mayer had worked in the *Personnel* Branch at Army Group E, not in the Ic/AO Branch. If so, Czernin wondered, how could he have been in a position to testify about Waldheim's activities? Czernin, however, was overlooking at least two key facts. First, Army Group E's organizational table disclosed that one of Waldheim's responsibilities was handling "personnel matters of the Ic/AO Branch." So it certainly was plausible that Mayer knew Waldheim. Moreover, anyone who has ever worked in a large organization knows that personnel office staffers usually have a broad knowledge of organizational activities, especially of the who-does-what variety.

Czernin interviewed Mayer's widow, Rosa Mayer, and cited her remarks as further reason to discredit his testimony. She claimed that her husband had told her that while he was in Yugoslav custody, he and his fellow prisoners had tried to "put the blame" on those of

---

*On Rhodes itself, not only was the fact of the deportation well known (of course), but so was the fate in store for the Jews. According to the Nuremberg affidavit (no. NOKW-1715) of a German soldier who happened to be visiting Rhodes on the day of the deportation, when he asked his comrades—guarding over a thousand men, women, and children in the sweltering heat—why the Jews had so little baggage, he was told that they had no need for baggage as they were not going to live very long.

their comrades who had either died or escaped. Frau Mayer further maintained that her husband had never mentioned Waldheim's name to her.

The story thus suggested that Mayer had fabricated his testimony to the Yugoslavs in order to protect himself and his comrades. But the tale made little sense. For how would Mayer, sitting in a Yugoslav cell, have known for a fact that Waldheim was one of those who had escaped? And even if he had possessed that knowledge, how could he have been certain that the object of his blame would be able to avoid arrest and extradition to Yugoslavia in the future?

Czernin reported, moreover, that Mayer had been ostracized by his comrades as a "stool pigeon" when he returned to Vienna.[9] But this, too, contradicted Czernin's conclusion, for if Mayer had implicated only those who were out of harm's way, would he not have been regarded as a hero by his peers? Instead, he became a pariah. It made more sense to view his purported explanation to his wife as a cover story contrived to explain to his family why he was being "unfairly" shunned.

I mulled over the situation. Yes, it was clear from the material already released in *Vecernje Novosti* that the Yugoslavs had wanted to nail Waldheim back in 1947. And they certainly were capable of using contrived evidence. But the tone of the Yugoslav internal correspondence—what little the world had been allowed to see of it—seemed to reflect official behind-the-scenes confidence in the validity of Mayer's testimony. I had in mind most especially the memo that stated that "there is strong evidence" that justifies registering Waldheim with the UNWCC.

Again my head was spinning. The Yugoslav angle—like so much of the rest of this affair—was growing more confusing every day.

"I'm going blind, unfortunately," Stephen Katich declared, as he took out a pocket magnifier so that he could read a quotation to me from a Yugoslav newspaper. "The doctors say they can't do anything. It's just a matter of time."

He spoke matter-of-factly, as though he had long since resigned himself to darkness. With his wavy white hair and his outdated three-piece suit, he was, by appearance, every bit the central casting version of an old Library of Congress staff research specialist. The shelves behind his desk on the second floor of the Library's Madison Building were filled with dust-covered Serbo-Croatian law books. Katich's professorial appearance and quiet demeanor made me wonder for a moment if he was really the same man I had spoken with on the phone, who had so furiously cursed Waldheim.

Speaking almost in a whisper, Katich beckoned me to accompany him to a private room. Leaning on a cane for support, he led me forward slowly. When at last we were alone, he elaborated on why he was so interested in the Waldheim case, why he had insisted that I see him in Washington at the first opportunity. "I know what this Army Group E is responsible for in my country," he said. "And as a senior intelligence officer in that fucking murder command, Waldheim had to have been involved." He repeated his offer to put me in touch with the U.S. ambassador to Yugoslavia, John Scanlan.

Although I remained somewhat dubious, I accepted the invitation.

Again Katich expressed his confidence that Scanlan's "Billy-boys" could get copies of whatever the Yugoslav government was holding back. "But it will be up to you to convince him to do it," he declared. "Scanlan is a good man, though, and I think he can be convinced."

I thanked Katich for his assistance, and he promised to call as soon as he obtained Scanlan's agreement to meet with me.

Katich walked me out into the sunlight. As he ushered me into a cab for the trip to the National Archives, he permitted himself a small smile. "You'll see," he predicted, leaning on his cane, "the embassy will take care of this for you. And if they don't, I'll go there and do it myself."

The splendor of Washington's springtime was lost on me, but the legend "What Is Past Is Prologue," engraved in the imposing granite façade of the U.S. National Archives building on Pennsylvania Avenue, seemed to leap out at me as I approached the building. I stepped beneath the words and through the enormous steel doors that guard the nation's official memory bank.

My first stop was the Modern Military Branch, to thank Bob Wolfe and John Mendelsohn for working with Herzstein and tipping us off about Waldheim's CROWCASS and UNWCC files.

Mendelsohn got up from behind his cluttered desk to extend his hand. He was pleased to learn that someone was prepared to continue the research where Herzstein had left off. "You won't believe how many reporters came up here all excited after your press conference, asking to see 'the Waldheim file,' " he related with a smile. "Of course, I told them there was no such thing, that they would have to do what the WJC did—look at thousands of captured documents from Army Group E and the other Wehrmacht commands. Most of them left when they heard that." Mendelsohn chuckled at the memory and added, "The few who weren't deterred by that information left as soon as I told them that the documents are in German."

My next stop was the Microfilm Reading Room on the fourth floor. It was a darkened cavern that often was populated mostly by elderly women engaged in genealogical research, many of them working on microfilmed copies of faded Civil War military records. The only other people here delving into the Waldheim case were OSI historian Pat Treanor and freelance researcher Willi Korte, working under contract from the West German magazine *Der Spiegel*. I knew Treanor well from my days at OSI. I had met Korte about six months earlier when he was researching the fate of Josef Mengele. He was an immigrant from Germany and appeared to be in his mid-thirties. The three of us were natural allies, working side by side with the same materials and the same goals; the closeness of the quarters meant that each of us could see a good deal of what the others were doing.

I settled in front of an aging microfilm reader, with a contemporary paperback German–English dictionary and a 1944 German–English military dictionary issued by the U.S. War Department at my side, and contemplated the task. Dog-eared indices provided minimal information on the thousands of scratchy microfilm rolls containing captured Axis records. The U.S. had long since returned the originals to the German and Italian governments.

To review every document with possible relevance to Waldheim was clearly out of the question; that task would take years. I would have to play some educated hunches, just as Herzstein had done for us, and as Treanor and Korte were doing now.

I selected first a roll of microfilm containing official war diaries from Army Group E, covering a two-week period when, I knew, Waldheim was assigned to the unit. Advancing the film by hand, frame by frame, I searched for—I knew not what. Some of the frames were out of focus, some too dark, some too light. I worked laboriously with my dictionaries to decipher the awkward military parlance. But there was, I soon realized, a good deal of useful information to be found, even if one searched almost at random.

The first important discovery was a gruesome August 10, 1943, order from General Loehr commanding the implementation of reprisal measures "with most severe means." In areas where Yugoslav partisans had carried out surprise attacks against the Germans, Loehr advised, "the arrest of hostages from *all* strata of the population remains a successful means of intimidation." (Emphasis in the original.) Loehr minced no words about what was to be done with the hostages:

> Surprise attacks on German soldiers, damage to German property, must be retaliated in every case with shooting or hanging of hostages, destruction of the surrounding localities, etc. Only then will the population disclose to the German headquarters offices the gathering points of the bandits, in order to prevent the carrying out of reprisal measures.

In territories that were "especially valuable" to the Wehrmacht, Loehr continued, "it may also be necessary to seize the entire male population" between the ages of fifteen and sixty and "insofar as it does not have to be shot or hanged on account of participation in or support of the bandits," transport it to Germany for slave labor. This was essential, said Loehr's directive, in order to comply with the July 1943 "Fuehrer order concerning the importation of *Menschenmaterial* [human material] into the Reich to ensure the necessary supply of coal." Captured partisans were to be transported to Germany "according to separate order of the *Oberquartiermeister*," the commander of the Quartermaster Branch of Army Group E. The same document noted that "Directives concerning deserter propaganda proceed through the Commander in Chief Southeast [that is, Loehr himself], Ic/AO Branch."[10] Ic/AO, of course, was Waldheim's Intelligence/Counterintelligence Branch.

A series of entries in Army Group E's war diary for the first half of 1944 made it clear that Loehr's orders were obeyed scrupulously. In page after page, the diary referred to the reprisal shootings of hundreds of hostages throughout Greece, as well as the destruction of scores of villages, many of which were expressly described as having been "burnt to the ground."

That same diary addressed the subject of Allied commando units. The diary noted that, because of increased activity by British and American commandos in the Dodecanese Islands, an order was issued in March 1944 that greater efforts be made to capture members of the commando units, so as to subject them to interrogation. The order continued, "For the treatment of the prisoners after interrogation, the Fuehrer order of 18 October 1942 is applicable."[11] The reference was to Hitler's infamous "Commando Order." I had known of it for years, but I had never seen the actual text. Now I hunted up a copy, and read:

> If the German war effort is not to suffer severe damages by such [commando] actions, then it must be made clear to the enemy that every sabotage unit will be exterminated, without exception, to the last man. That means that the chance to get away live is zero. It can under no conditions be permitted that a demolition, sabotage, or terrorist unit simply surrenders and is taken prisoner to be treated according to the rules of the Geneva Convention. Consequently, *they are to be exterminated in every case without exception.*[Emphasis added.][12]

The order was personally signed "Adolf Hitler," and it was bloodcurdling, even by Hitlerian standards. To ensure that the threatening message was received by the Allies, the Germans even used their radio broadcasts to announce that Allied "terror and sabotage troops" would be treated "not . . . like soldiers but like bandits" and "slaughtered ruthlessly. . . ."[13] The intent was to let the Allies know, ahead of time, what awaited their commando forces in the event of capture. To be sure, the average British or American P.O.W. was not treated gently; however, he generally remained alive and, in fact, could count on far better treatment than a Soviet soldier who fell into German hands. But the commandos were among the elite of the Allied soldiers, and the Germans feared them the most. I tried to imagine what kind of courage these men must have had, to carry on in the face of such hideous threats.

Hitler's Commando Order was, by its very text, an admitted violation of the Geneva Convention. At Nuremberg, it would later be adjudged patently criminal; compliance with the order was a war crime under international law.* And the Army Group E war diary declared that Loehr had made a special point of instructing the troops in the field to carry out the order.

Sitting in the quiet Archives reading room, I stared at the war diary entry for a long time, trying to fit the pieces together. In the Army Group E organizational table that Herzstein had found, Waldheim and his deputies, Lieutenant Poliza and Lieutenant Krohne, were the only officers with the listed duty of "prisoner interrogation."

A bell sounded in my head. I searched through the packet of papers in my briefcase until I found a document that I had reviewed only briefly over the weekend: The two-page July 1944 "Monthly Activity Report" for the Ic Section of Army Group E. The report noted that among the duties carried out that month was the "interrogation of prisoners from the Anglo-American military mission in Greece."[14] The report, I noted, was from "Ic" and not "Ic/AO," yet it bore the signature of the branch's ranking Abwehr officer, Major Hammer, as well as a handwritten *W* initial. Was it Waldheim's initial? It was a logical enough assumption, for one of Waldheim's other listed responsibilities on the organizational chart was the preparation of the *Taetigskeitberichte* ("Activity Reports"). On the other hand, it did not look like the *W* with which Waldheim began his full signature on other Army Group E documents, nor even like the *W* that so often appeared in the "O3" box in the "received stamp" on still other such documents. Did this *W* belong perhaps to Warnstorff?

I pondered the *W* problem. German officers sometimes signed a

---

*"This order was criminal on its face," declared the U.S. Military Tribunal at Nuremberg in *United States* v. *von Leeb*. See *Trials of War Criminals Before the Nuremberg Military Tribunals Under Control Council Law No. 10*, Washington, 1950: U.S. Gov't Printing Office, Vol. XI, p. 527.

full last name to documents, but often they simply scrawled an initial. On the microfilm screen in front of me were numerous documents from Waldheim's branch that might have been initialed by Waldheim or Warnstorff. Comparing the documents with one another, I identified two distinct initials. One *W* had rounded bottoms; the other had pointed bottoms. Which belonged to Waldheim, and which to Warnstorff? There seemed to be no way to tell.

At any rate, the activity report left little doubt that captured British and American soldiers had indeed been interrogated by (or at least under the direction of) Waldheim's section—in which he was the number-two man, the highest ranking officer having the specifically designated duty of prisoner interrogation. And he spoke English. I wanted to learn more.

Continuing, frame by frame, with the microfilms, I came across an "Activity Report" for September 1944, which disclosed that the branch's Abwehr officer, Major Hammer, had ordered that all papers relating to "Allied military missions and commando members" were *zu vernichten* ("to be destroyed").[15] This was very bad news indeed, for it meant that the odds of finding incriminating evidence linking Waldheim to the carrying out of Hitler's Commando Order had just plummeted.

Throughout the long day, I compiled a list of those microfilm frames I wanted to copy. There were only three printers in the reading room, and one of them had a hand-scrawled Out of Order sign taped to it. The other two were generally monopolized by the amateur genealogists. I waited until 8:30 P.M., a half hour before closing time, when the reading room crowd had thinned out. Functioning at snail-speed, the copiers produced faded, soaking-wet facsimiles that reeked of formaldehyde. Unhappy experience taught me to let the pages dry before I collated them, or else they would stick together. I wondered if I would ever be able to turn this hodgepodge of papers into something that resembled a chain of proof.

The day left me totally fatigued, and with a splitting headache.

Sleep was long in coming that night. I was visited by vague images of doomed partisan fighters, of innocent villagers taken as hostages and then executed or deported, and of the men of the "Anglo-American military mission in Greece."

On my second day at the Archives, I played a hunch, studying documents assembled by Nuremberg prosecutors for what was known as the "Hostage Case." It was the seventh of the twelve war crimes trials that were held at Nuremberg by U.S. authorities following the conclusion of the more publicized main trial of the central figures in the Nazi hierarchy. The defendants in "Case VII" were a dozen German officers charged with the mass murder of hostages and the reprisal destruction of hundreds of towns and villages in the Balkans. All but two were convicted.

I soon found myself perusing the self-serving testimony of Major Hammer himself, an unindicted cohort-witness who spoke of cruel reprisals in Greece, especially in the area administered by the Italian 11th Army, based in Athens. From everything I knew, it was the Germans who committed the atrocities and the Italians who often protested against such crimes. *Sure,* I thought, blame it all on the Italians, Hammer.

After several fruitless hours of staring at the screen, I was nearly ready to give up this line of inquiry when I suddenly did a double take. I was in the midst of scanning a group of Nuremberg documents that had been introduced by U.S. prosecutors as proof of Nazi war crimes in Greece. On the screen in front of me was a captured Army Group E evening intelligence report dated August 11, 1944.

In the document, a first lieutenant reported that several "Communists" had been "shot to death" by German forces in Athens. The report also detailed the progress of "Operation Viper," an operation to which Herzstein had seen a cryptic reference but which he had been unable to identify. This report, and several intelligence reports that accompanied it, provided the elusive answer: "Operation Viper" was a massive antipartisan "cleansing" campaign in which the Wehrmacht's 22nd Mountain Corps (directly subordinate to Army Group E) wiped several Greek villages off the face of the earth.

The lieutenant's report identified for his superiors several localities on the island of Crete in which partisans had been encountered or detected, including the areas north of Karpenission and south of Iraklion. Reports by other officers, simultaneously introduced into evidence at Nuremberg, disclosed what happened subsequently. Within forty-eight hours of this lieutenant's evening report, a "cleansing operation" was undertaken southwest of Iraklion, which resulted in "twenty shootings of hostages, numerous arrests and evacuations, two bandit villages destroyed." Another Army Group E report for the following day noted:

> "Viper": Continued cleansing without important contact with the enemy. Destruction of Karpenission and of other bandit villages.

Even though, as the report expressly noted, no "important contact" was made with the enemy, the villages were destroyed anyway! Was it merely coincidence, I asked myself, that these atrocities followed on the heels of the lieutenant's report? Or had the lieutenant, in fact, knowingly targeted the area for a bloody reprisal operation?

That August 11, 1944, evening intelligence report carried a full signature, rather than an initial. Back then, the Nuremberg translation team had only been able to attribute it to a "first lieutenant, signature illegible." The last name appeared, at first glance, to be "Warheimm." At the time of the Nuremberg trials, that would not have meant much to anyone. But by now I had seen enough old Waldheim signatures to recognize the scrawl.[16] This was mind boggling, I told myself. The image reproduced on the microfilm held me transfixed. Here on the screen in front of me were the words of the Wehrmacht officer who would later become the Secretary-General of the U.N.—words introduced at Nuremberg as evidence of Nazi war crimes!

In his March 10 interview with *Profil,* Waldheim had admitted that he had "passed on" his "analyses" to his army group's Ia (Operations) Branch, which, he noted, "had the operational duties." Indeed, one of the duties of the chief of intelligence (Waldheim's immediate superior) as listed in the Army Group E organizational chart was the responsibility to "draft operational orders." The clincher was Waldheim's admission in his April 6 "Defense Memo" that "operational decisions based upon [his] reports and evaluations" were made by Loehr and his chief of staff. And as I examined *Oberleutnant* Waldheim's report more closely, I saw that the distribution list typed at the bottom disclosed that it was, indeed, sent to Ia Branch, as well as to Major Hammer. The implications were potentially far-reaching. Waldheim, like any other military intelligence officer, expected the "operations" side to act on his reports. That, after all, is the whole purpose of intelligence gathering: to provide a sound basis for making operational decisions. Here, Waldheim had identified Iraklion and Karpenission as areas of partisan activity at a time when he had to know that the standard operating procedure for such situations, as Loehr himself had reiterated, was the "shooting or hanging of hostages, destruction of surrounding localities, etc." in *"every case."* In other words, Waldheim had to have known when he wrote his report that he might well be condemning civilian inhabitants of the Karpenission/Iraklion area to death.*

Later in the day, I pursued the microfilm trail of the Jews of the Greek island of Corfu. According to the history books, they had

---

*Although ordering such reprisals was ordinarily to be accomplished at the divisional (field) level, the involvement of headquarters officers (i.e., Loehr and his staff) in pressing for, facilitating, or approving these criminal operations was a possibility that required investigation in each instance.

been deported shortly before the Jews of the island of Rhodes met the same fate. Alternately peering at the images of captured documents on the screen and writing notes on a pad, I fashioned a makeshift chronology of the last days of Corfu's small Jewish community:

On April 21, 1944, a secret order was sent from Waldheim's Ic/AO Branch at Army Group E to a subordinate command, *Korpsgruppe* Ioannina, declaring that the sixteen hundred Jews believed to be residing on Corfu must be registered. Four days later, the registration was completed.[17]

On April 28, an intelligence officer from *Korpsgruppe* Ioannina requested "Ic/AO" of Army Group E to "bring about implementation measures" for "the purpose of settlement of the Jewish question" by contacting the SD and Security Police to handle "evacuating" the Jews from Corfu.[18]

On May 9, Waldheim briefed General Erich Schmidt-Richberg, Loehr's chief of staff at the time, on the "situation in the Mediterranean, Italy, and the Balkans." The meeting also featured a discussion of the strengthening of the German forces "on the islands, particularly Corfu." The report's one-line reference to the subject of Waldheim's briefing closed with a parenthetical note: "See enclosure." To my dismay, the enclosure had not survived.[19]

On May 12, General Loehr personally agreed to "furnish transportation for an accelerated evacuation" of the Corfu Jews.[20]

On May 16, Waldheim again briefed General Schmidt-Richberg. Once more, staffing needs on Corfu were discussed and a "see enclosure" reference to Waldheim's presentation was attached, but the enclosure was nowhere to be found. Another dead end.[21]

Within a month, the deportations were under way, and on June 17 the SS reported that the operation was completed: The 1,795 Jews of Corfu had all been "seized and transported from the island."[22] The destination was Auschwitz, where nearly all of them were murdered immediately in the gas chambers.[23]

On August 9, Waldheim attended another meeting with General Schmidt-Richberg and presented a formal briefing "on the Far East, Italy, France, and situation in the Balkans"; the minutes of that meeting included a notation, without elaboration, that the general "spoke about the situation on Corfu . . ."[24]

It was getting increasingly difficult to stomach Waldheim's frequent protestations that he knew nothing about Jewish deportations. Here, once again, was unimpeachable proof that his own small intelligence/counterintelligence branch was criminally complicit in a mass deportation of Greek Jews to their deaths in Nazi-occupied Poland.

My eyes focused intently on the screen and, as I struggled to translate the jumble of German text and follow the routing of the various orders, I realized that my concentration was, in part, a defense mechanism, to avoid having to think about the *reality* of what I was reading. The awareness immediately negated the defense. There, in the quiet of the reading room, the out-of-focus reports came to life. The documents were not discussing military procedures; rather, they were reporting matter-of-factly on the final disposition of human beings—living, breathing people. Men and women and children.

Suddenly, I was overwhelmed by the memory of *the picture.* I could see it, almost as if it were superimposed on the microfilm screen.

The picture was a photograph on the cover of one of my books. I kept it standing atop my bookcase in the office so that I would see it every day. It had been taken in a Jewish ghetto, during the Nazi occupation of Poland. Jewish parents had been forbidden to send their children to school, an edict that ran agonizingly counter to everything that parents want for their children and was especially tormenting to parents of the European Jewish tradition, which so passionately stressed education as an end in itself. At great peril, many Jews defied the Nazis by sending their children to clandestine school sessions very early in the morning. *The picture* showed a little boy, surely no more than five or six years old, toddling off to school on a deserted ghetto street. It was one of the most poignant sights I had ever seen. It was my chosen reminder of what had been.

And now the image of *the picture* burned in my mind's eye.

The Nazis murdered a million Jewish children; how many of them, I wondered, were taken from Corfu?

17

New York, Wednesday, April 9. After two fatiguing days at the National Archives, I returned to New York to find the international political world in turmoil yet again.

A story in the *New York Times* indicated that even the Soviets were beginning to feel the heat. The suspicion was now being openly voiced by many—among them New York Senator (and former U.S. representative to the U.N.) Daniel Patrick Moynihan—that the Soviets might have blackmailed Waldheim during his U.N. tenure. Queried by the *Times,* Soviet U.N. mission spokesman Anatoly N. Khudyakov denied everything: "No attempt was made to investigate Mr. Waldheim," he asserted. "The Soviet Union knew nothing."[1]

The claim could hardly be taken at face value, I knew, but it was the first formal Soviet utterance concerning the Waldheim affair, and it indicated that the Waldheim affair was now registering shock waves in political circles on *both* sides of the Iron Curtain.

In Austria, Waldheim's campaign was in disarray. During my second day of work at the Archives, his office had released a revised version of the candidate's official biographical profile sheet, and now I had a chance to study it and compare it with the first version, which had contained his once-standard "wounded/returned to law school" description of his wartime service.

The revised version offered the following chronology:

> December 1941, wounded on the Eastern Front.
> April 1942, assigned to the Army High Command in the Balkans.
> Summer 1942, assigned to Arsakli, Greece, as an interpreter.
> April 1943, assigned to Ic/AO of Army Group E as an *Ordonnanzoffizier.*[2]

This was certainly an improvement over his original bio sheet, but it also continued the cover-up, in a surprisingly clumsy manner. Waldheim had himself serving in Arsakli, outside Salonika, in the summer of 1942. This had the effect of removing him from western Bosnia before the end of the Kozara massacres. But it simply was not true; we knew from the personnel rosters at the National Archives that he did not arrive in Arsakli until the final days of August 1942, after the Kozara operation was completed.

What had he actually *done* at Kozara, I continued to wonder, that made him so desperate to absent himself from the episode?

And as I wondered, *Time* magazine was finally getting Waldheim to admit to knowledge of reprisals against the partisans:

> Yes, I knew. I was horrified. But what could I do? I had either to continue to serve or be executed.[3]

A telex came in from Austria concerning a press conference that had just been held by the Waldheim campaign for the purpose of discrediting the documents that had been reproduced in *Profil* linking Waldheim's intelligence unit to the deportation of the Jews of Rhodes. Unfortunately, *Profil* had badly mishandled the graphic reproduction of the documents. Segments of the two key captured reports were inadvertently presented as though they came from a single document, and Waldheim's handlers jumped at the opportunity to expose it as a crude forgery. Close examination, they pointed out, disclosed that two different typewriters had been used!

Telexes flew back and forth between New York and Vienna before we were able to obtain our own copies of the actual German documents, and before the truth of the matter was revealed. The documents were certainly genuine,* but the juxtaposition of two portions of separate documents made them seem patently spurious, and before the magazine could counter with an explanation, the Waldheim campaign had scored a propaganda coup. The Austrian dailies gleefully reported that at last the "entire defamation campaign" was exposed as a tissue of lies. To our astonishment, *Profil*'s unlikely gaffe had enabled Waldheim to escape the impact of some of the most potent evidence that had yet been found.

Mike Wallace, the "60 Minutes" correspondent, visited our office for a briefing. He was about to leave for Vienna, to interview Waldheim. Singer, Steinberg, and I agreed to help him prepare, and we stressed one point above all others: Don't let Waldheim get away with denying that he intentionally covered up his Wehrmacht service in the Balkans. "You can make an enormous contribution to history,"

---

*I later confirmed that they were, by locating duplicates at the National Archives.

I urged Wallace, "just by getting him to admit that he lied about his war record. Then he will finally have to explain *why* he lied."

I pleaded with the veteran CBS correspondent to prepare himself as thoroughly as possible. "With all due respect, you're not going to be able to study this case for two hours and go in there and beat Waldheim on the subject of his specific actions in World War II," I warned. "He's too good for that and the materials are complicated beyond belief. On the subject of the big lie, I know exactly what he's going to say to you. 'I didn't lie. In my book, I just didn't tell everything. People would have been bored. To me, the highlight of my military service was the invasion of the Soviet Union, because that's when I got wounded.' Or he'll say, 'My statement was simply misunderstood' or 'I didn't mean to mislead anyone' or 'The English-language translation of my book omitted key passages' or some such nonsense."

"You can respond," I suggested, "by showing him at least a dozen statements that he's made over the years, in which he lied very directly to cover up key dates of his service record. Don't let him get away with it. Just keep hitting him with, 'Well, what about this statement . . . and that one . . . and this one . . . and that one . . . until he finally has to admit it—in which case you can ask, 'Well, *why* did you lie?'—or he turns red-faced and throws you out of his office."

Wallace promised to try, and his assistants happily accepted my offer to supply copies of Waldheim's statements about the war. I was optimistic: I could hardly imagine a better interviewer for the task at hand than the legendary inquisitor Mike Wallace.

It was later, on this same Wednesday, as I labored at the WJC's copying machine, that Karl Fischer, the Austrian representative to the U.N., emerged from the nondescript midtown Manhattan office building that housed the U.N. archives. He had spent seventeen minutes inside studying the UNWCC file on Waldheim. He issued a bland statement saying that the file "consisted of only a few pages," and noted that he was sending a copy on to Rudolf Kirchschlaeger, the president of Austria.

His Israeli counterpart, Benjamin Netanyahu, spent a full hour with the file and came away obviously shaken. Dozens of reporters pressed the grim-faced diplomat with questions. Netanyahu said that what he had just seen convinced him that "it cannot be said that the matter can be laid to rest." He added, "There is here clear indication of a need . . . for further comprehensive investigation." He explained apologetically that the U.N. Secretariat had forbidden him to disclose any information about what he had seen, but he noted that he was sending a copy of the file to Israel for further study.[4]

Despite Netanyahu's forced reticence, someone else apparently dared to speak. An unnamed U.N. source confided to one reporter that the file was only a four-page summary of documents that the Yugoslavs had provided in 1947. The raw evidence underlying the UNWCC's decision to list Waldheim as a suspected war criminal had been returned to Yugoslavia many years ago, after the commission's Fact-Finding Committee had studied it.

But even the four pages had apparently been enough to shake up the usually imperturbable Netanyahu.

So much was happening in such a compressed period of time! Even as Netanyahu was reviewing the files, Wiesenthal was here in New York, huddling with U.N. Secretary General Perez de Cuellar. The latter's spokesman, François Giuliani, reported that the two agreed that it was "important to clear the air" about Waldheim.

Afterward, Wiesenthal met with the press and cautioned reporters not to jump to conclusions merely because Yugoslavia and the UNWCC had listed Waldheim as a war criminal. However, he did call on Yugoslavia to release its underlying documentation and to explain why it had never requested Waldheim's extradition.

Then he launched into yet another tirade against the WJC, charging that we had created problems for the Jews of Austria. He upbraided us for not understanding how to interpret basic German military parlance. For example, he said, the reason that Waldheim's signature appeared on Army Group E intelligence documents was that he was merely attesting to the accuracy of the text as a kind of cosigner; Waldheim had not been, as the WJC claimed, the author of those documents. His own files, he said, contained no evidence implicating Waldheim in Nazi crimes. Wiesenthal again cited Waldheim's relationship with Tito as something that discredited the Yugoslav charges.[5]

I found out that Wiesenthal also took the time to warn a New York Times editor, "You will lose your reputation" if the newspaper kept publishing its "accusations" against Waldheim. (A few weeks later, when another newspaper reported that Wiesenthal had issued such a warning, he denied it; the paper stood by its account, however.)[6]

After I heard Wiesenthal's comments, I "went ballistic" again, as Steinberg phrased it. Wiesenthal's machinations seemed to provoke my anger even more than Waldheim's denials. This troubled me momentarily, until I realized that I properly held Wiesenthal to a higher standard. He was someone who lectured the world about the importance of learning the lessons of the Holocaust and about confronting evil. He had made himself a symbol of justice. In contrast, Waldheim was a fellow-traveler of the Nazis, and concealments and false denials from such people were the rule rather than the exception.

I screamed out my frustrations and once again my unlucky audience was Singer and Steinberg. If Wiesenthal knew anything at all about Wehrmacht operations, I complained, he would have known that it was the responsibility of the "O3" officer to prepare the daily intelligence reports. This was clearly spelled out on Army Group E's organizational table and in authoritative works on German military intelligence. "Waldheim himself has already *admitted* it, dammit!" I exclaimed, waving a copy of his April 6 "Defense Memo." Waldheim wrote the reports and only then did he sign what had been typed, to attest "copy certified correct." In an interview published on March 27 in the giant circulation Vienna daily *Kronenzeitung,* Waldheim had gone even further, conceding not only that he collected the intelligence information from the field, but *evaluated (auszwerten)* it too. The reports went out under the signature of the boss, but it was Waldheim and other subordinates who actually composed them. "Surely, Wiesenthal knows that by now," I moaned.

Singer and Steinberg made it clear that they shared my anger, but they remained adamant in their refusal to challenge the renowned Nazi-hunter publicly.

Was this latest Wiesenthal performance the result of mere arrogance and/or stupidity, I wondered, or was it part of something less obvious?

As I pondered this question, John Goshko, a senior foreign correspondent for the *Washington Post,* dropped in to chat. He had just finished covering the Netanyahu visit to the U.N. archives. When the subject of Wiesenthal came up, he mentioned an incident that had taken place in 1971, when then–Foreign Minister Waldheim was making his first, unsuccessful, run for the Austrian presidency. Goshko had visited Wiesenthal in Vienna at the time. "I knew that Waldheim had served in the Wehrmacht during the war," the reporter related, "and I asked Wiesenthal whether it was worth looking into his background. Wiesenthal told me not to bother, that he'd already checked Waldheim out, and the guy was clean."

At the time, that had settled the matter for Goshko. Now, fifteen years later, he was wondering why Wiesenthal had put him off the trail.

Until now, I had assumed that Wiesenthal's apparent blindness to Waldheim's faults dated back to 1974 and his feud with Socialist leader Bruno Kreisky. But hearing this, I decided that, Singer and Steinberg notwithstanding, it was time to begin my own, very quiet, parallel investigation, to see what I could learn about Wiesenthal's protective embrace around Waldheim.

I speculated that Wiesenthal's bizarre behavior might have something to do with his postwar service as an investigator for the U.S.
Army's Counter Intelligence Corps. He had boasted of this service
many times, in print and in speeches,[7] and I wondered whether there
was some hidden connection among Waldheim, Wiesenthal, and
Army CIC. I fired off another Freedom of Information Act request
to the U.S. Army, this time asking for anything in its files "referring
or relating to" Simon Wiesenthal.

I also decided to raise the issue with Schuller. He was the one
who had first warned me about Wiesenthal. What more did he—and
his friends—know about the great Nazi-hunter?

On Thursday morning, I dug into a mass of material that I had
hurriedly photocopied at the National Archives but had not yet had
time to study. One of the first documents that captured my attention
was the formerly classified August 5, 1947, Nuremberg interrogation
of Colonel Franz von Harling. He had been Warnstorff's predecessor
as chief at the Ic/AO Branch, but was transferred in 1943 to the post
of Chief of Intelligence at Army Group F, to which Army Group E
was subordinate. Questioned by prosecutor Theodore Fenstermacher about Hitler's order to execute captured commandos, von
Harling responded that he had found it repugnant and even ordered
Ic at Army Group E to disobey the order:

> I can state the following with regard to the commando and
> sabotage authority. I was entrusted with that authority in 1944
> and, in full rejection of its content, I instructed by telephone
> both Ic of the subordinate Army Group E and the 2nd Panzer
> Army not to act in accordance with this authority until further
> order.

His Nuremberg questioner asked whether von Harling had discussed this subject with the generals. "Personally," he replied, "no,
I informed the Ic." Von Harling's self-serving claims were hard to
swallow. But what really caught my attention was an assumption that
remained unstated during the verbal jousting between the two men.
Why, I asked myself, would von Harling have to order Waldheim's
Ic section *not* to comply with Hitler's order, unless Ic was directly
involved with the handling of commandos and other prisoners? The
obvious answer was that Ic *was* involved, despite Waldheim's denials.

During a later point in his interrogation, von Harling claimed that
he "could not recall" any case in which the Commando Order had
actually been applied anywhere within the Wehrmacht's Southeast

command.[8] For someone in von Harling's senior position during the war, it was an absurd assertion indeed.

No *wonder* the Germans lost the war, I joked to myself. There wasn't a single Wehrmacht "intelligence" officer who knew what was going on around him. Not von Harling. Not Warnstorff (who, less than a fortnight earlier, told reporters that he had known nothing about the deportation of Salonika's Jews).[9] Not his comrades at the Vienna press conference. And, of course, not Lieutenant Waldheim.

Willi Korte, the freelance researcher working for *Der Spiegel,* continued to slave over the microfilms at the National Archives. The young German had drilled countless dry holes. But he refused to give up. At last, Korte struck oil. He found documents pertaining to the fate of two groups of Allied commandos captured off the coast of Turkey during the spring and summer of 1944. The reports that had survived the war yielded only fragmentary accounts, but the facts they revealed were jarring nonetheless.

One set of documents told the story of a team of seven young men from Britain's elite Special Boat Squadron who, along with three seamen from the Greek Resistance, were captured by the Germans in the early morning hours of April 7, 1944, while attempting to raid German positions on the Dodecanese islands of Alimnia and Khalki. The team was headed by Captain Hugh William Blyth, of the Scots Guards. Other members included Sub-Lieutenant Allan Lane Tuckey; radio operator R.F. Carpenter; Private L. G. Rice, an Australian, of the Bedfordshire & Hertfordshire Regiment; Private A. G. Evans of the Sherwood Foresters Regiment; Sergeant G.W.J. Miller of the County of London Yeomanry; and Gunner Raymond W. Jones of the Royal Artillery. Three Greek resistance fighters, Michele Lisgaris, Demetrio Triandafilu, and Nicolao Velisariu, were also captured, wearing British uniforms. All ten were taken to Rhodes for questioning.

The prisoners proved uncooperative. One of the captors wrote that Tuckey spoke in a "sometimes arrogant tone. . . . He belongs to the class of young English intellectuals who show their self-confidence through ironic and sarcastic superiority."

Blyth, the commander, was quickly separated from the others, flown to Athens and then to Germany, presumably because he was believed to have high-level knowledge of Allied plans.

On April 18, 1944, the Ic/AO Branch of Army Group F sent a classified cable to Army Group E regarding the remaining Alimnia prisoners. The text made it clear that Waldheim's intelligence section was to handle the matter. It read in part:

Army Group E shall submit documentation after completed interrogations as soon as possible, in order to appropriately inform
the Turkish Government concerning Allied posts within Turkish
territorial waters. It is necessary to keep prisoners for this
purpose.

Addition: Subject matter is now under the sole authority of
Ic. Ia [Operations Branch] is to be informed.[10]

A detailed interrogation report discussing the Greek prisoner Lisgaris was transmitted from the field to Ic/AO Branch at Army Group
E and stamped "received" on April 24. The standard rubber stamp
contained seven small boxes wherein officers of the branch were to
indicate their receipt and review of the report. The second box from
the left, designated "O3," contained the handwritten initial *W*. Only
one other box, reserved for the officer responsible for air defense
matters, contained an initial.[11]

Two days later, on April 26, the "O3" officer at the Ic/AO Branch
of Army Group F received the following fateful cable from Waldheim's Ic/AO Branch at Army Group E, requesting authorization to
deliver most of the prisoners to the executioners of the SD:

> Further interrogations of English Alimnia commandos fruitless.
> *Request decision whether prisoners now to be delivered to the SD.*
> Suggest excepting Greek sailors since compelled to participate.
> Apart from the instructions for the captains of the Greek ships
> and the diary of the English radio operator, no further evidence
> for communication to Turkey. The English radio operator [Car-
> penter] and the Greek sailor Lisgaris are possible suitable wit-
> nesses. Decision requested. [Emphasis added.][12]

Army Group F replied the following day, explicitly granting the
request to murder the commandos:

1. English radio operator and Greek sailor are to be held under
   strict guard, ready for possible required testimony.
2. Remaining prisoners are to be made available to SD for possible
   interrogation on matters of SD interest and *abschliessender
   Sonderbehandlung* ["final special treatment"] pursuant to the
   Fuehrer Order.[13]

The "Fuehrer Order" was, of course, Hitler's Commando Order
of October 1942. Ironically, Army Group F's reply condemning the
commandos to death was signed "copy certified correct" by none
other than Colonel Franz von Harling, the Ic/AO chief of Army

Group F, who would testify at Nuremberg three years later that he had instructed his subordinates at Army Group E to *disobey* Hitler's Commando Order and "could not recall" any instance in which the order had been carried out.

There could be little doubt as to the fate of most of the commandos; the cable not only made explicit reference to the "Commando Order," but also used the expression "final special treatment," one of the more infamous Nazi euphemisms for execution. But what about Carpenter and Lisgaris? Had they managed to survive? Korte found the apparent answer to this question in another document. In early June, the Ic/AO Branch at Army Group F cabled Waldheim's Intelligence Branch that the "English radio operator Carpenter and Greek sailor Lisgaris, captured near Alimnia, are no longer required." They, too, were to be "freed [sic] for special treatment in accordance with the Fuehrer Order."[14]

Korte found a second set of documents pertaining to a smaller commando group—two Britons and an American medic—who were captured three months later, after a battle on the Dodecanese island of Calino, in the Aegean Sea southeast of Greece, during the night of July 1–2, 1944. A report of July 18, 1944, from Waldheim's Intelligence/Counterintelligence Branch at Army Group E, identified the three commandos and provided some preliminary information on their fate:

1. Sergeant John Dryden, born 25 October 1919 at Newcastle, was wounded, was flown to Athens on 5 July, and will be handed over to the SD in compliance with the Fuehrer Order.
2. Private Fishwick, personal particulars unknown, was flown to Athens, where he died in a military hospital.
3. James Doughty, medic, born 26 March 1919, later living in Ipswich, Mass./USA. On 17.7 transferred to camp in Salonika, and subsequently sent to a prisoner-of-war camp in Germany, since he had not participated in the battle and was without weapons.

The original document noted that the interrogation reports on Dryden and Doughty were attached. Unfortunately, they were not included on the microfilm copy; in all likelihood, Korte said, the reports had not survived the war. There was, however, a fascinating single-sentence summary of Doughty's interrogation history:

James Doughty, interrogated on Calino and Leros on 2.7. *and by Army Group E* on 17.7 *in Salonika.* [Emphasis added.][15]

So much for Waldheim's protestations (most recently in his April 6 memo) that neither he nor anyone else "at the command of Army Group E" ever conducted interrogations!

I had given Korte access to the WJC's files on Waldheim, and the researcher returned the favor. He excitedly reported his findings to me over the telephone from Washington. He pledged me to secrecy, for he wanted the commando stories as an exclusive for *Der Spiegel*. But he agreed to provide me with copies of the documents via overnight courier.

Korte asked me for an update on what was known about the role of Waldheim or Army Group E's Intelligence/Counterintelligence Branch in the interrogation of prisoners. I reviewed for him the present state of our knowledge: Waldheim asserted that he had never performed "such duties as interrogations of P.O.W.'s or captured partisans" and that prisoner interrogations were never conducted by anyone at Army Group E headquarters. Nevertheless, the Wehrmacht's handbook specified that at Army High Command level, those duties were the responsibility of the Ic section. Furthermore, the 1943 organizational table for Army Group E listed Waldheim as the intelligence officer having principal supervisory responsibility for "prisoner interrogation." We also knew that interrogations were generally conducted by interpreters, that Waldheim and his immediate subordinates were, in fact, interpreters, and that Waldheim was fluent in several languages, including English. We had on hand the July 1944 "Activity Report" for Waldheim's Ic section that listed "Interrogation of prisoners from the Anglo-American mission in Greece," and that report bore a *W* initial that might be Waldheim's. Moreover, according to Yugoslav press reports, Johann Mayer's 1947 testimony included a claim that Waldheim was responsible for formulating proposals on "behavior regarding prisoners of war." Then too there was the March 1944 order I had found referenced in one German document at the National Archives, instructing Army Group E that captured Allied commandos should be "handled in accordance with the Fuehrer order of October 18, 1942." And the war diary entry about that order noted that top priority was to be given to capturing and interrogating Allied commandos operating in the Dodecanese Islands, where they had been particularly effective. Finally, there was von Harling's testimony that he had dealt with "Ic" at Army Group E on the subject of carrying out Hitler's Commando Order.

When I examined Korte's documents myself, I was at once fascinated, saddened, and cautious. The fascination came from the detailed nature of the information. Here were people with real names and, presumably, traceable stories. This same fact was also responsible for my sadness, for the gray-white pages of the photocopies almost certainly recorded the extirpation of promising young lives.

But the documents also left key questions unanswered. I expressed my concerns directly to Korte on the phone. As damning as the commando documents appeared at first glance—especially since the W initial in the O3 "received" block on one of the documents proved that Waldheim had played some personal role in the "processing" of the Alimnia prisoners—I worried that Waldheim and his supporters could attempt to exploit two weak links in the evidence. First, we had no proof that the commandos had actually been executed. We could not afford to speculate on what happened after Waldheim's unit received the authorization it sought to turn the prisoners over to the SD for "special treatment," for there were cases on record in which sympathetic Wehrmacht intelligence officers managed to subvert the process, thereby saving the lives of otherwise doomed prisoners.

The second problem was even more frustrating. I quizzed Korte carefully concerning the April 26, 1944, message requesting permission to deliver the "Alimnia" commandos to the SD. The copy Korte had sent to me was the printout of the telex as it had been received by Army Group F. Korte confirmed my fear that Army Group E's copy, from the transmission end, was not contained in the microfilm records. Without it, we could not ascertain who in Waldheim's branch had been involved in preparing and transmitting the message. Our frustration was heightened by the fact that Army Group F's copy was initialed as received only by the unit's "O3" officer, a fact that strongly suggested that the request had originated from his "O3" counterpart at Army Group E, Lieutenant Waldheim. But without the transmission copy, we could not prove it conclusively.

And I was pessimistic that we would ever be able to get a complete picture. I told a disheartened Korte about the September 1944 order from Major Hammer "to destroy all materials relating to Allied military missions and commandos."

I promised Korte that I would do what I could to try to determine the ultimate fate of the men in question.

Britain seemed the most logical place to begin the search, and I therefore enlisted the aid of Michael May in our London research office. Within days, May called back with news about the Alimnia commandos. Most of it, as I had feared, was bad news.

May had found the information in an obscure 1983 book, *Special Boat Squadron: The Story of the SBS in the Mediterranean,* by Barrie Pitt. On page 135, Pitt's book described the capture of Captain Blyth along with "the young commander of a caïque, Sub-Lieutenant

Tuckey," and their men as having ended the "only" mission on which the SBS was "the loser." Pitt related that Blyth had been flown to a P.O.W. camp in Germany, just as one of Korte's documents stated, and that he was treated throughout "in accordance with the terms of the Geneva Convention." But the other prisoners had enjoyed no such luck, as the slender volume made clear. They had never returned, and their bodies were never found. The author speculated that they had either died accidentally or else been executed by their German captors:

> It is impossible to say what happened to Tuckey, his crew or the noncommissioned men of Blyth's patrol, for no trace of their fate has ever been found. Perhaps the transport upon which they were traveling was sunk . . . but it is also possible that they died at the hands of the SS or the Gestapo, as did quite a number of Special Service troops before the end of the war.

With this dismaying confirmation in hand that Tuckey and the others had indeed died after capture, it was now beyond question that they had met the very fate implied in the Army Group E documents that Willi Korte had just found: delivery to the SD for "final special treatment." But we could only speculate, for now, as to the possible role played in this fatal episode by Kurt Waldheim—the man whose Intelligence/Counterintelligence Branch had sought (and received) permission to effectuate the "delivery" to the SD and who was listed in the Army Group E organizational table as bearing principal responsibility within that section for "prisoner interrogation" matters.

In Vienna, two renowned Austrians, longtime antagonists, were at loggerheads once again. Until now, former Austrian Chancellor Bruno Kreisky had joined in the chorus of Viennese voices defending Waldheim and condemning the WJC. Although Kreisky was the "grand old man" of the Socialist Party, he was also the man who sent Waldheim to the U.N. and later authorized his candidacy for the Secretary General post. Throughout 1984 and 1985, Kreisky had tried to sell the idea of running Waldheim as a joint candidate for president, representing both the People's Party and the Socialist Party. But now he had seen and heard enough. He was particularly alarmed to see the foreign media shine such an unflattering spotlight on Austria's Nazi-era history and its postwar failure to acknowledge that past. On Friday, April 11, Kreisky declared that the Waldheim affair was "a catastrophe" for his country's international reputation. He expressed his belief that Yugoslavia's Marshal Tito had known much about Waldheim's war-service record but had been "very cunning" and never disclosed the information publicly. "I was deceived," Kreisky complained. "The curriculum vitae that Waldheim gave me . . . was a lie." Waldheim, he added, "no longer had credibility, and neither would Austria if it elected him president."[16]

Simon Wiesenthal disagreed sharply. He even refused a reporter's entreaty that he offer an opinion on whether Waldheim was fit to serve as Austria's president. This, he said, was for Austrian voters to decide. And he used the occasion to attack the World Jewish Congress yet again. The WJC, he said, was running a "smear campaign" that "even the Socialists . . . regard . . . as an external interference in Austrian internal affairs." "To call someone a war criminal, you must have very, very hard evidence," he declared.[17]

Of course, we had done nothing of the sort. Although we had disclosed to the press the evidence we had found that proved that Waldheim served in criminal units under commanders (such as Loehr and Stahl) who were, without question, Nazi war criminals, and although we had disclosed the fact that Waldheim was accused of Nazi war crimes by Yugoslavia and the UNWCC, we had specifically (and repeatedly) declined to call him a Nazi war criminal. Instead, the WJC had called for the appropriate government authorities to investigate the matter and for Waldheim to explain at last why he had concealed for forty years the fact of his service in the Balkans.[18]

NBC-TV producer Diane Wallerstein called me at home on Sunday to pass on some news. "Something wild's just gone out over the Reuters wire," she advised. "An Athens newspaper is reporting that Waldheim was *there* during the war, and they've supposedly got a photo to prove it—showing Waldheim with senior German officers sometime in 1943." The story, she said, was in that morning's edition of the Athens daily *To Vima* ("The Tribune").

Athens? What was Waldheim doing there? I was intrigued. We had the statement of Waldheim's old war comrade, Waldemar Fend, that the two met in Athens, and Waldheim himself had admitted that he visited the Greek capital for occasional interpreting assignments, but we had nothing more. I wondered whether this new account referred to a brief visit, or instead whether the claim was that Waldheim was stationed in Athens for a longer period of time.

Wallerstein read me the full wire-service dispatch, but it provided little clarification. The brief report said that the *To Vima* article, written by Professor Hagen Fleischer of the University of Crete, said that Waldheim "was in" Athens "in July 1943 when a German command was set up there to operate alongside the Italian one." The wire-service report did not disclose the names of the "senior German officers" purportedly photographed alongside Waldheim. According to Reuters, Fleischer had termed Waldheim "one of the best in-formed officers in the entire Balkans."

We needed to obtain a copy of *To Vima*. Fortunately, the enter-prising Wallerstein was game for the challenge. "I'll call Olympic Airways," she suggested. "The big airlines are almost always happy to help the American television networks. I'll bet that one of the attendants on an incoming flight has a copy of *To Vima* that she'd be willing to part with. I may have to send someone over to Kennedy Airport, but I think I can do it."

Within hours that Sunday, we had a copy of *To Vima*, fresh from Athens. There, on the front page, was the photograph, provided by an old comrade who had felt slighted in later years when Waldheim, now an international celebrity, failed to respond to his letters. It showed a young Lieutenant Waldheim posing with fifteen other uni-formed German officers in Athens, relaxing in a luxuriously ap-pointed anteroom of the Hotel Grande Bretagne. Identified in the photograph, in addition to Waldheim, were three particularly im-portant Wehrmacht officers. The first was Lieutenant General Heinz von Gyldenfeldt, the chief of the German General Staff attached to the Athens-based Italian 11th Army. The second was Lieutenant Colonel Bruno Willers, described by *To Vima* as an officer who served under von Gyldenfeldt in Athens (he turned out to be the vexed former colleague). Finally, in a fresh white uniform, there was Lieutenant General Helmut Felmy, the commander of the Wehr-macht's 68th Army Corps, which was subordinate to Army Group E. Felmy, who was smiling broadly in the photo, was later convicted in the Nuremberg "Hostage Case" for his role in atrocities committed by the 68th Army Corps during its antipartisan operations in Greece.

So now we had three wartime photographs of Waldheim. Each was a posed shot, and in each, he was pictured with one or more men who later would be justly branded as Nazi war criminals. Wald-heim's ability to insinuate himself into such photos was yet another irony of this affair, for it was common knowledge that, during his time at the U.N., he had an obsession for getting himself photo-graphed with famous world leaders.

While the picture was the most dramatic part of *To Vima*'s front-page treatment, it was the Greek text of the accompanying story that was likely to be of the greatest importance, for it might disclose just what it was that Waldheim was *doing* in Athens in 1943. I sent it out to be translated.

That evening, still awed by the challenge of yet another new mystery to research, I watched as CBS's "60 Minutes" aired Mike Wallace's interview with Waldheim, taped this same day in Vienna. Wallace ably confronted his subject with evidence of his prewar affiliation with various Nazi groups. For months, Waldheim had claimed to have participated only in a few sporting events with the Nazi Rider Corps, but now he simply changed his story. He shrugged off the issue, and, without the slightest suggestion that he was charting new territory, explained that he had attended only a few meetings and "participated in some of the discussions." He did so, he said, "to finish my studies" and to "survive politically." Suddenly, he was not just riding a horse; he was involved in meetings.

Wallace pulled out a copy of Waldheim's 1980 letter to Congressman Solarz. Why, Wallace asked, had he given the congressman the impression that he no longer served in the Wehrmacht after 1941?

Waldheim responded that he was sorry if he "perhaps misled" Solarz and assured Wallace that "this was not my intention." He extended the apology to "all of my friends" in the United States.

I waited for the incisive follow-up questions that I had urged Wallace to ask. They did not come. Instead, like so many journalists before him, the usually tough-as-nails interviewer let Waldheim slide off the hook without challenging him to explain his many *other* false autobiograhical statements over the years.

Waldheim declared that the UNWCC accusations against him were based on the false testimony of two German P.O.W.'s in Yugoslavia, who were trying "to save their own skins."

Throughout the balance of the interview, Wallace asked what were, by now, standard questions and listened politely to Waldheim's, by now, standard replies.

To my consternation, key questions were never posed: Did you know that others refused to participate in criminal actions and suffered no dire consequences? Why did you not decline the promotion to "O3" (and the increased responsibilities that came with it)? Why did you not try to use the fact of continuing complications from your 1941 combat injury as an excuse to remain an interpreter?

These and other questions leapt to my lips, but remained unasked. Waldheim asserted, without challenge, that to refuse to follow his Wehrmacht orders "would have been to be executed." He said in an innocent tone, "I was sitting in that staff command, doing my paperwork—receiving reports and forwarding my analyses to the operational department. That was all."

That was *not* all! I knew what kind of reports Waldheim was handling—and what the Operations Branch was likely doing with his "analyses." I felt sick to my stomach. I felt like throwing a brick through the TV screen.

18

Monday morning, April 14. I leaned back in my office chair to study an updated version of Waldheim's "Defense Memo." It was dated April 12, indicating that in only six days' time he had found it necessary to revise his first effort.

This new edition was largely a reiteration of the denials Waldheim had issued since the story first broke: He had nothing to do with war crimes; he knew nothing about the deportations of Jews from Salonika or the Greek islands (although he conceded that he was in the area during the time of some of the deportations); he was not involved in prisoner interrogations ("To the best of my knowledge, there were no P.O.W.—or partisan—interrogations carried out" at Army Group E headquarters); he had no involvement in the "Black Operation"; the CROWCASS and UNWCC charges were without basis, as proved by Tito's continuing friendship; he was in distant Plevlje (as "witnesses have confirmed") with the Italian division "Pusteria" during the time of the Kozara massacres; he was at Army Group E headquarters in October 1944 and thus could not have been involved in the massacres on the road between Stip and Kocane, Macedonia; he had been spotted at such places as Podgorica and Athens only because of "periodic assignments" as a lowly interpreter. In sum, if something terrible had happened somewhere, then Waldheim was nowhere to be found, even if this represented an unexplained change from his previous story. It brought to mind the refrain of an old Beatles tune; Waldheim was "a real nowhere man."

The new defense memo reported that an expert hired by the Waldheim campaign had compared samples of Waldheim's current handwriting with the *W* initials that appeared at the bottom of so many of the pertinent Wehrmacht records, and had found no match, with either the pointed *or* rounded version of the initial. (The conclusion was nonsensical; *one* of the initials surely was Warnstorff's and the other Waldheim's.)

Waldheim dismissed Johann Mayer's testimony to the Yugoslavs as "fictitious." "I do not remember having ever seen him," he declared. Here, I thought, was a new item for Waldheim's amnesia logbook. Mayer, a fellow Austrian, worked in the personnel branch at Army Group E headquarters; Waldheim was in charge of personnel matters in the Ic/AO Branch of the same headquarters, and yet he could not remember the man.

Near the end of the memo, Waldheim addressed the question of his prewar affiliations, making, in writing, the same admission he had made on "60 Minutes." A dramatic alteration had been made in his written account less than a week after its initial issuance. Six days earlier, in his first defense memo, his documented links to the Nazi groups were "apparently based on occasional participation in riding exercises." Now, however, he had also "participated in a few evening discussions of the [Nazi] Students' Union."

The new issue of Germany's *Der Spiegel* hit the streets with a dramatic cover headline: AUSTRIA'S QUIET FASCISM: THE WALDHEIM CASE.

The title was superimposed over a luscious photograph of an idyllic Alpine village, which, in turn, was shadowed by a powerful arm outstretched in the Nazi salute. Inside, the magazine presented a caustic analysis of Waldheim as the perfect symbol of a country that still refused to acknowledge its embarrassing partnership with Nazi Germany, and that remained, four decades after the war, a hotbed of anti-Semitic and even neo-Nazi sentiment. Leafing through the pages, one could readily sense the German editors' glee at seeing the Austrians finally "get theirs." After nearly a half a century, the world was coming to understand that Germany was not alone in bearing the responsibility for Hitler's crimes.

In an interview published in the same issue, Waldheim offered yet another version of the Kozara episode. Most recently, he had contended that western Bosnia was solely a paper assignment for him and that he was, in fact, 120 miles away in Plevlje, in Montenegro, near another place that also happened to be called Kozara. Now he told *Der Spiegel* that, yes, he actually had been stationed in western Bosnia for the briefest of times. But, he insisted, he had been quickly reassigned to serve as an interpreter and liaison officer between German forces and the Italian Divison "Pusteria" in Plevlje. He said that he had in his possession a recent newspaper item in which a Yugoslav family from the area recalled that he was "a pleasant lieutenant" who gave them chocolates. He described his duties at Plevlje: "I was given a radio truck and the necessary instructions to translate reports of the Italians into German and to pass them on to my superiors." This was only a small modification of his Kozara story, but a slick one. Obviously, he was alarmed that we had found documents that placed him on Stahl's headquarters staff during the

Kozara operation. Waldheim's solution: He placed himself there as well, but too briefly to have had any significant function there.

Changing the subject, Der Spiegel pointedly asked Waldheim whether he could still lay claim to the title of "The Austrian the world trusts."

"Yes," Waldheim replied, since the attacks upon his character emanated from "a single interest group in New York." This, of course, was a pointed reference to the WJC, and it willfully ignored the fact that many of the major disclosures concerning his past had emanated from such obviously non-Jewish entities as Profil magazine, the Yugoslav press, the New York Times, the Athens daily To Vima, and the "New Austria" organization. Previously, the anti-Semitic assaults had come from campaign functionaries and some supporters in the Austrian press; the candidate himself had refrained. Now, however, it seemed that Waldheim had decided that if anti-Semitic barbs garnered votes in Austria, he too would employ them.

Asked about the effect that the revelations were having on Austria's world image, Waldheim exploded: "There is scandal everywhere." Noting that the war had, after all, ended forty-one years ago, he urged, "There should be an end to this."

Der Spiegel reporter Hans-Peter Martin jumped ahead to 1968 and asked Waldheim about reports that he had ordered the Austrian Embassy in Prague closed to Czech citizens seeking asylum from the Soviet crackdown. Waldheim denied that he had given any such order. But Martin had ammunition, in the form of a copy of the telex from Vienna to Prague on August 21, 1968, ordering just such a shutdown. It was the same secret cable Schuller had shown me during our initial discussion in Vienna, the one document that, because it might still be classified, I had considered too dangerous to carry out of Austria.

Faced with hard documentation, Waldheim suddenly did an about-face. The plainly embarrassed candidate denied neither its authenticity nor its authorship. Now contrite, he said, "Please, allow me to say that I consider the behavior of [the Austrian ambassador in Prague] as extraordinarily decent and extraordinarily courageous, and that he deserves my highest appreciation." What Waldheim neglected to explain, of course, was that the ambassador's courage lay in his willingness to risk his career by disobeying the direct order of his boss, Foreign Minister Waldheim.*

*In a March 6, 1988, television interview broadcast by England's Channel 4, Waldheim finally admitted that he had sent the by-now notorious telex, but he insisted that the instruction originated with another government official.

Finally, *Der Spiegel* reported that "every home in Austria" had received a brochure quoting Professor Hagen Fleischer of the University of Crete proclaiming Waldheim's innocence. The magazine disclosed that it had contacted Fleischer. It quoted his livid response: "That is a dirty trick." He repeated to the magazine the assertion he had made in *To Vima* that Waldheim was one of the "best informed" Wehrmacht officers in all of Greece.[1]

A hornet's nest of emotions had been stirred up in Austria; of that there was no doubt. A columnist writing in *Kronenzeitung* under the name "Staberl" (the *nom de plume* of one Richard Nimmerrichter) denounced the "unheard-of impertinence" of "young Mr. Singer" for declaring that Austria would be in for six tough years if it elected Waldheim. He described "the young gentlemen from the WJC" and three inquiring Austrian radio journalists as *Rotzbuben,* a term that translates loosely as "snot-nosed young brats." No longer, "Staberl" wrote, should Jews be immune from criticism just because they are Jews. One should not be forbidden to call a man stupid or dishonest, he raged, "just because he happens to be a Jew!" He declared that Austrians opposed the WJC "not because they are Jews, but because, at best, they are hollow-headed, and at worst they are vile schemers."[2]

Austria's Jewish community was witnessing the unleashing of the "emotions" of which People's Party General Secretary Michael Graff had warned. Anti-Semitic graffiti was again spray-painted on the walls of buildings in Vienna and other cities. The central Jewish organization and prominent Austrian Jews received a new avalanche of hate mail, threatening that Jews would be killed if the "smear campaign" continued, or if Waldheim lost at the polls. One memorable postcard, addressed to the "Jewish Swine Department," proclaimed, "Hitler should have gassed you all."

Some of the letters, most of them anonymous, were carbon-copied to our offices in New York.

I studied closely the English translation of Professor Fleischer's story in *To Vima*. Most of the article was devoted to an angry charge that Waldheim, as the "O3" officer at Army Group E headquarters, had to have at least "known about the persecution of the Greek Jews." The deportation of tens of thousands of Jews, Fleischer declared, "was commented upon even by the common soldiers." He pointed out that Waldheim had worked in Greece as an intelligence officer and served as an interpreter between the German staff and the Italian 11th Army. Since the Italian occupation forces in Greece had resisted the Jewish deportations, he reasoned, that "must have been one of the subjects of discussion." Thus, the professor charged, Waldheim's denials of knowledge "must be considered a provocation."

The article's real news was contained in Fleischer's brief discussion of Waldheim's activities while he was, in the scholar's words, "stationed in Athens" during the summer and autumn of 1943. He wrote that Waldheim, after the Italian capitulation in September of that year, "participated in the negotiation of the disarming of the [Italian] 11th Army." This information had come to Fleischer, he said, in a letter from Bruno Willers, whom the article described as Waldheim's "boss at the time."

Whether or not Fleischer realized it, he had identified yet another phase of the cover-up. Waldheim had scrupulously avoided any mention of Athens, until Waldemar Fend told a Vienna magazine that he recalled seeing Waldheim there. Waldheim had then quickly added Athens to his wartime itinerary, characteristically insisting that it was simply one more brief stop on his tour of "periodic assignments" as an interpreter. But Willers's letter to Professor Fleischer indicated that Waldheim was stationed in Athens for several months.

If this was true, it led inexorably to the same old question: Why was he hiding it? Perhaps, I thought, there was a clue in the Nuremberg testimony of Army Group E's Abwehr officer, Major Friedrich Hammer, who, by attempting to place the blame for atrocities on the Italian 11th Army, had at least acknowledged that atrocities occurred in the Athens area.

Calling from Vienna, Schuller provided a tip. He said his sources believed that Waldheim had served in Athens not only as a subordinate of Willers, but also from time to time as personal adjutant to the German commander, General von Gyldenfeldt.

The "New Austria" historians were the first to pursue this new line of research, quickly releasing their findings through *Profil* and in a small booklet of their own. And what they found about Kurt Waldheim's tour of duty in Athens was dramatic indeed.

In both his telex to his American publishers and his April 6 defense memo, Waldheim had said that his assignment in Athens was to "interpret at meetings" between the Germans and Italians, "since the Italians were at the time allies of the Germans." In the telex, he had added that his assignments in Athens were "exclusively" based on his "language skills" and had "involved no other functions, powers of command, or combat duty." But in the West German military archives in Freiburg, the "New Austria" group located the personnel chart of the Athens-based "German General Staff attached to the Italian 11th Army," and learned otherwise. The chart designated Waldheim as "O1" officer, the deputy of Bruno Willers, who, in turn, was the Chief of the Ia (Operations) Branch in Athens. The entire unit was made up of just three officers and four enlisted men; Waldheim was second-in-command.[3]

Waldheim's standard refrain included the claim that he had no role in "operational" matters; he admitted that he had prepared intelligence reports on which other officers made operational decisions, but said it was unfair to hold him accountable for what others did with his information. However absurd that assertion was when made in respect to his service at Army Group E headquarters in Arsakli/Salonika, it was a blatant lie in the context of his Athens assignment. As "O1" at Athens, Waldheim's duties would have included, at a minimum, helping to draft proposed tactical orders for Wehrmacht units in the field—this at a time when, as the "New Austria" researchers ascertained, many of those units were conducting criminal operations.[4] He could not have been merely "interpreting" at meetings between the Germans and the Italians.

Not only had Waldheim concealed his operational responsibilities at Athens, but, as the Freiburg personnel records revealed, his claim that "at the time" the Italians were "allies of the Germans" concealed the fact that he had remained in this job *after* the Italians left the Axis. The Italian departure from the alliance with the Third Reich in September 1943 was a turning point of the war. Overnight, the "German General Staff attached to the Italian 11th Army" became "Army Group Southern Greece." From this point on, the Wehrmacht headquarters in Athens was a full-fledged army task force; von Gyldenfeldt was replaced by the war criminal Helmut Felmy, and one of the group's key tasks was the disarming of the remnants of the Italian army.

Soon it was clear to the "New Austria" researchers why Waldheim had risked so much to cover up this period of his military career, for in Athens Waldheim had left a paperwork trail that tied him to some of the most gruesome aspects of Wehrmacht operations in Greece.

Typed on the first page of each volume of the Wehrmacht's Athens daily war diary were the names of the officers responsible for preparing that particular volume. In volume 7, the officer responsible from July 19 to August 21, 1943, was listed as *"Oberleutnant* Waldheim." On August 8, 1943, Waldheim wrote in the daily war diary that the Wehrmacht's 1st Mountain Division was "marching off . . . for the cleansing operation in the area of Gliki-Parga," set to begin two days later. In a second entry for the same day, he wrote about captured partisans and suspected partisans, using the standard pejorative term "bandits" *(Banditen)*. The 1st Mountain Division, Waldheim wrote, was being instructed to kill captured partisans and deport other suspects to slave labor in the Reich:

> Concerning treatment of bandits, appropriate instructions are
> being sent to the 1st Mountain Division. According to a new
> Fuehrer order, bandits captured in battle are to be shot. Others
> suspected of banditry, etc. are to be taken prisoner and sent to
> Germany for use in labor details.[5]

Here was Waldheim recording the transmission by his own headquarters of one of Hitler's most infamous criminal pronouncements.
Forty-two years later, in a *Profil* interview, he had maintained that
he knew nothing about such an order, but now we had the proof
that he *did* know. Indeed, he had recorded it in the official war diary!

Five days later, Waldheim initialed a document detailing the results
of the 1st Mountain Division's Gliki-Parga operation. Although en-
countering what the report described as "little enemy resistance,"
the division boasted of "numerous villages cleared of inhabitants."
The village of Kuklesi, Waldheim was informed, was "burned to the
ground." The report stated that the Germans took fifty prisoners
and counted eighty to a hundred enemy dead. It added, "Ten bandit
suspects shot." This also turned out to be yet another "disparity
document." Enemy casualties had numbered at least eighty, yet the
Germans captured only thirty weapons.[6] The conclusion was inescapable that most of the victims had been unarmed.

Several of the Athens documents showed that Waldheim's operations branch was notified *in advance* of specific atrocities; for example, one report from his branch listed three Greek villages that
had been "evacuated," and ended with the notation, "Villages are to
be destroyed."[7]

Clearly, the new "Fuehrer order" had been carried out, and just
as clearly, Waldheim knew it at the time; he personally recorded the
fact that the lethal order was sent to the troops and received subsequent notification of the atrocities that ensued. But the key question remained unanswered: Who had actually *transmitted* the order?
It was confirmed at Nuremberg that one who transmits orders (or
authorization) for others to commit war crimes is himself guilty of
a war crime. It was not at all unlikely that Waldheim had indeed
participated in transmitting this particular criminal order; it was an
"operational" order and Waldheim was the number-two man in operations. If he was involved in passing on the order, he was, at the
least, an accessory, aiding and abetting the Germans in their systematic destruction of innocents. But could it be proved that he was the
man who transmitted the message? The "New Austria" researchers
set to work on the question. They found a handwritten transcription
of the incoming radio message, reflecting the order's receipt by the
1st Mountain Division; the document had been introduced into evi-

dence at Nuremberg. It confirmed that the order was received from the *Operations Branch* of the German General Staff attached to the Italian 11th Army—in other words, from the seven-man unit in which Waldheim was the second-ranking officer.[8] But to ascertain whether Waldheim himself had sent the order, one needed to see the record of the transmission at its *originating* point. Here, however, the trail went suddenly, maddeningly cold; that document had not survived the war. The final piece in yet another puzzle had vanished.

Another major discovery made by the "New Austria" researchers was a transcription of a radio message that came into Waldheim's Athens headquarters on August 15, 1943. The typed report to the Athens unit's commanding general bore Waldheim's identifiable signature, attesting to the accuracy of the text. The message, from the Wehrmacht's 1st Mountain Division, disclosed the presence of "heavy concentrations" of partisans in the area southeast of the town of Arta. Thus, the message reported, "the cleansing operations scheduled for this area are deemed necessary." However, the division would not be content to rid the area of only suspected partisans; it wanted to go beyond even Hitler's instructions. The transcription included a terse plea: "Hope of success only if all male civilians deported." Here was another atrocity in the making, and any soldier would have known as much. The Charter of the International Military Tribunal would later affirm that the "deportation to slave labor or for any other purposes of [a] civilian population" was both a war crime and a crime against humanity. In its report, the 1st Mountain Division also warned Athens headquarters about a potential problem in the Greek town of Ioannina: "Ioannina and Jewish Committee operating there must be regarded as center of preparations for a resistance movement." The report fretted that Italian soldiers stationed there were ignoring the threat.[9]

The document inspired more questions than answers. Waldheim's signature attested to the fact that he received—and, more importantly, passed on to his superiors—what amounted to a request to carry out a criminal deportation and a warning that the Jewish leadership of Ioannina was at the heart of an incipient resistance movement. This occurred only seven days after Waldheim had recorded in the war diary Hitler's order that suspected resistance members were to be shot or deported to Germany for slave labor details. Thus, Waldheim fully understood the likely consequences of passing on the message. We did not yet know what happened to the partisans and male civilians in the Arta area. Although we knew from historical accounts that the 1,725 Jews of Ioannina were eventually shipped to Auschwitz, the deportations did not occur until March 1944, seven months after the division's report passed through Waldheim's hands.

It was nearly impossible to believe that the German authorities would have waited so long to deal with the "threat" that Waldheim helped identify. Had Waldheim's superiors taken any kind of action in direct response to this report about a Jewish threat? There was no hint of an answer.

The "New Austria" researchers succeeded in verifying—and expanding on—Professor Fleischer's charge that Waldheim, while in Athens, had participated in the negotiation of the disarmament of the Italian 11th Army. The delicate talks resulted in the agreement of the Italians to surrender their arms on the understanding that they would thereupon be permitted to return to Italy. But in reality, the Germans had no intention of allowing their onetime comrades-in-arms to return to their homes. Their previously prepared plan, codenamed "Case Axis," was to put the Italians to work as slave laborers, some in Greece and others in Germany. A September 22, 1943, report, marked "Secret," recorded a telephone conversation in which Waldheim, still in Athens, briefed an officer at Army Group E headquarters in Arsakli about arrangements for the transport of tens of thousands of Italian soldiers to labor camps. In the report, Waldheim stated that 27,147 officers and men had been assembled in Athens and thousands of others were being held in regional collection camps for deportation to Germany, while 4,598 men were to be kept behind in Athens "for use as labor."[10] Waldheim's information was crucial, for it enabled his superiors to calculate how many more trains were necessary to complete the deportations.

By October 1, General von Gyldenfeldt could report that his forces had deported more than one hundred thousand Italians. "With these actions," he boasted, "the Italian 11th Army has been liquidated."[11] The betrayal of the Italians was completed.

When I correlated the dates of the Italian deportations with my records, I suddenly began to understand what the celebration scene photo accompanying the *To Vima* article was all about. It had been taken in the lobby of the Hotel Grande Bretagne shortly after the completion of the disarmament and deportation of the Italian Army. Toasting the success of "Case Axis" had doubtless been a major (if not *the* major) purpose of the festivities. And Waldheim was one of the revelers.

The "New Austria" researchers also found some important documents pertaining to Waldheim's service in the Ic/AO Branch at Army Group E headquarters in Arsakli/Salonika, following his return from Athens. One, a classified November 10, 1943, report by the German Secret Field Police, was initialed by Waldheim in the "O3" box of his intelligence/counterintelligence branch's "received" stamp. The report communicated a plan to overthrow the Greek government and replace it with a pro-Nazi regime. The scheme was proposed by a Greek shipbuilder, Alexios Petrou, who had been referred to the Germans by an "acquaintance in the League of Friends of Hitler" and had "already done successful work for the Secret Field Police in Salonika." According to the report, Petrou was offering a deal. In exchange for his appointment as Interior Minister in the planned pro-Nazi government, he would utilize his contacts "to deliver the main officials of the Greek communist party . . . within the shortest time to the knife."[12]

Another captured document initialed in the same way as received by Waldheim read like a virtual catalog of horror. It transmitted a Greek report complaining about the slaughter by German troops of Greek women and children, the shooting of priests and teachers, and the setting afire of more than a hundred Greek towns. All of these atrocities were committed by Wehrmacht forces under Army Group E's control, as "reprisals" after partisans were spotted or engaged in combat. The report described some of the most ghastly incidents:

> The city of Kalavrita was set afire from one end to the other. The Cloister of Haghia Lavra . . . was set afire, the holy treasures in the cloister were destroyed, and the 13 elderly monks in the cloister were shot.
> The village of Kommana, near Arta . . . was the victim of a terrible decimation. Seven hundred and fifty inhabitants of this village were shot by German soldiers. In the village of Lyngiades . . . 82 inhabitants were shot, including 42 children under the age of 15. . . . Thus, in a very small area, more than 1000 Greek citizens were killed, without any differentiation between guilty and innocent, the proof of this being the fact that the victims included many women and children.[13]

The Wehrmacht official who transmitted the report complained to Waldheim's headquarters that such excessive measures were "regrettable, because they harm the relationship of the population with the Germans." But he did not propose that reprisal killings were to be removed from the Wehrmacht strategic arsenal, only that they be better tailored to each situation. "In the future," he recommended, "it will be necessary to give the troops clear instructions as to reprisal actions and capturing of hostages.[14]

As I read the depressing text of these reports, I thought again of Waldheim's role in helping identify areas of suspected resistance activity. Now it was beyond dispute that Waldheim had understood fully that the reprisal operations that ensued could include even the indiscriminate butchering of women and children.

In London, the WJC's Michael May was able to determine the fate of Sergeant John Dryden, the sole surviving Briton in the small group of commandos captured at Calino. Although the report found by Korte at the National Archives stated ominously that Dryden "will be handed over to the SD in compliance with the Fuehrer Order," May learned that Dryden had, somehow, survived the war. Unfortunately, however, he had died some years earlier, in England.

When May reported this news to me, we agreed that our best remaining hope of gaining firsthand information about the fate of the "Calino" commandos was to try to locate James Doughty, the noncombatant American medic whom the Germans had evidently spared. I phoned a contact at the Veterans Administration in Washington who agreed to conduct an off-the-record check of World War II P.O.W. rosters to see if there were any references to Doughty. He called back soon with the news: "Your man Doughty was a prisoner of the Germans, no doubt about it. Even though he was serving in the Royal Medical Corps, he's right there on our P.O.W. rolls, same date of birth and everything. It says he was a P.O.W. as of July 1, 1944."

The question was: Had he survived?

"I don't have any information on whether he's alive today," my V.A. contact said. "But the files do show one thing: he definitely survived the war."

My pulse quickened. "How—how do you know that?" I sputtered.

"Simple. There's a notation in one of the records here that something happened on January 22, 1947: Your Mr. Doughty applied for educational benefits under the G.I. Bill." As of that date in 1947, he informed me, Doughty's address was 18 Green Street, Ipswich, Massachusetts.

Please God, I begged silently as I dialed Massachusetts directory assistance, let Doughty be alive. Let him still be living in Ipswich. But New England Telephone had no listing for a James Doughty in Ipswich or in any of the neighboring towns. In desperation, I called every Doughty in the Ipswich area. There were several, but none recalled a young soldier named James who had come home from a German P.O.W. camp.

As I studied a copy of the April 15 issue of *Wochenpresse,* I could not help but note the obvious: The old saw "Truth will out" does not always hold. Lies often prevail over truth—even, as in Waldheim's case, for forty years or more. Still, if the pursuit of truth is relentless, the prevaricator rarely triumphs—in part, because the more a liar tries to "explain," the more he inadvertently discloses. That is one reason why every prosecutor yearns for the opportunity to question a suspect. Twenty minutes of skilled cross-examination can often fell even a skilled perjurer.

Here, in yet another attempt by *Wochenpresse* to bolster the candidate's reputation in his homeland, was a fresh lead on the path toward the truth. The Austrian weekly reported on an interview Waldheim had given to the Italian newspaper *La Repubblica*. A reporter had asked Waldheim about his liaison service in 1942 with the Italian 5th Mountain Infantry Division, the "Pusteria Division," in Plevlje, Montenegro. This was the assignment that was central to the current version of Waldheim's Kozara story, which kept him a respectable 120 miles away from the atrocities in western Bosnia. The Italian reporter wanted to know just what it was that Waldheim was doing in Plevlje, other than handing out chocolates to the locals. Waldheim shrugged off the inquiry with the comment that he spent much of his time "drinking tea in a candlelit coffee and pastry shop, and talking and playing cards with General Esposito."[15]

I was impressed. A general does not ordinarily spend his off-time rubbing elbows with a mere lieutenant. We had just gotten a full copy of the final CROWCASS list, and it took me only a few moments to locate this entry:

> ESPOSITO, Giovanni . . . General, Italian Army, Div. "Pusteria" . . . United Nations War Crimes Commission suspect number 15/276 . . . Wanted By: Yugoslavia . . . Reason Wanted: MURDER.

Just how many major Nazi war criminals cavorted with Waldheim during the war? I wondered. For a man who continued to contend that he had only the lowliest of responsibilities, he had certainly made some interesting acquaintances.

Asked about the Waldheim scandal, Simon Wiesenthal could not resist ridiculing the former U.N. chief's pursuers yet again. "*I* never accuse people without evidence," he huffed.[16]

The following day, Rabbi Marvin Hier, dean of the Los Angeles–based Simon Wiesenthal Center, wrote to U.S. Secretary of State George P. Shultz, denouncing Waldheim for having lied about his Nazi-era past and strongly supporting the Justice Department's decision to investigate Waldheim.

This was both a remarkable and encouraging development. Although the Center paid Wiesenthal annual consulting fees (reported a few years earlier to have exceeded $90,000 in 1982) and was the licensee of his name, it remained an independent organization. Now it was daring, if only tentatively, to break ranks with the man whose name it bore.

How severe the split had become was made further apparent when Steinberg handed me a copy of Simon Wiesenthal's letter to the editor in the April 7 issue of *Newsweek*. The Nazi-hunter complained that the newsweekly had misquoted him as saying of Waldheim: "I don't understand why he is lying."[17] Now Wiesenthal wished to correct the record. He explained, "I said that I don't believe that he knew nothing about the deportations of the Jews during the time when he was in Greece, but I did not intend to accuse him of lying."[18] Wiesenthal did not explain the supposed distinction, one that neither Steinberg nor I could fathom.

Singer was frustrated enough now to make what he considered to be an offer that Wiesenthal could not refuse. Reaching the Nazi-hunter via telephone, he said, "Simon, I don't understand this. Why are you saying we have no documents? Rosenbaum has documents up to the ceiling. Why don't you come to New York? Come to our office. Rosenbaum will show you everything. *You* can release whatever new documents we find. *You* be the hero, Simon."

Wiesenthal replied immediately: "I am not interested in your documents."*

"I was just a sort of clerk," Waldheim told *U.S. News & World Report,* during a three-hour interview in Vienna with the magazine's editor-in-chief, Mortimer B. Zuckerman, and Bonn bureau chief Douglas Stanglin. The newsweekly asked Waldheim about the "clear inference" in one of his early books that he had spent the war years, after 1941, in Vienna. Waldheim replied that the distortion resulted from the fact that the book was written by a ghostwriter, based on "a series of conversations with me."

When asked about the deportations of Jews from Greece, Waldheim admitted that he knew, in general, that the Nazis were deporting Jews. It was, said Waldheim, "the greatest tragedy in human history." But he maintained that he was unaware of the Salonika deportations—even though Army Group E headquarters was involved—because "I was not there during that terrible period."

His questioners returned to the subject of Waldheim's forty-year cover-up and tried to back him into a corner, noting that U.N. staffers

---

*Wiesenthal subsequently made several trips to New York and Washington, including what he described to one reporter as a three-week stint studying documents in the Waldheim case (Jane Biberman, "Wiesenthal Decries Waldheim War Crimes Charge," *Long Island Jewish World,* June 6–12, 1986, p. 10). At no time did he seek access to the WJC's Waldheim files.

recalled that he claimed no involvement in the war from 1942 to 1944. "I have no recollection of such conversations with U.N. associates," Waldheim answered.

What about the possibility, the magazine asked, that, because the Yugoslav government had lodged formal charges via CROWCASS and the UNWCC, "the Russians also knew" about the allegations, and that both of those nations might have used their knowledge "to exert leverage" during Waldheim's U.N. years? Waldheim dismissed the theory as "complete nonsense." But he added a surprising comment. "Why should the *fact* that they knew about it have been used to exercise pressure upon me?" [Emphasis added.] Was Waldheim simply being sloppy in his choice of words, or was he actually confirming our suspicions? It was impossible to say. In any event, he threw the Americans into the mix as well, stating that he "could very well imagine" that the U.S. government "also had the information."[19]

Our continued inability to get our hands on Waldheim's UNWCC file was supremely frustrating. The three governments that had obtained copies—the U.S., Israel, and Austria—were bound by U.N. rules to keep the file's contents secret, and they were abiding by those rules. Waldheim himself had received a copy from the Austrian government, and if it was as demonstrably bogus as he insisted, we reasoned, he surely would have made it public by now. The media were pressing U.N. Secretary-General Javier Perez de Cuellar to open the file, but he continued to refuse. I had feelers out everywhere. *Profil* had made it a top priority to obtain the file, but its reporters, too, were stymied. Schuller, with his estimable track record of gaining access to Austrian and German files, ran into blind alleys. Even Singer and Steinberg, who were on a first-name basis with Israel's U.N. representative Benjamin Netanyahu (whom they addressed by his nickname, "Bibi"), had no luck.

Finally, I remembered that there was one public source that might provide at least a tidbit of additional information. The National Archives annex in Suitland, Maryland, housed master UNWCC lists that could provide partial evidence of the file's contents. It took but a single phone call to have the records checked. The brief entry for Waldheim disclosed only one additional fact, but it was an important one. On February 26, 1948, a fact-finding committee composed of a Briton, a Norwegian, and two Americans had given Waldheim the UNWCC's "A" classification. This was a designation that the committee had reserved for suspected war criminals whose apprehension was considered to be of the highest priority. Only those persons against whom a *prima facie* case was presented were branded with this modern-day scarlet letter. Suspects with lower classifications were supposed to be arrested and subjected to comprehensive investigation, but "A"-level suspects were singled out as those who "should be delivered up for trial."[20]

One thing was clearer than ever: *We needed to see the complete file.* Even more, we needed to see the *Odluka,* the Yugoslav indictment that was the basis for both the CROWCASS and UNWCC listings.

April 17 began with good news. One of the wire services reported that unnamed "Yugoslav officials" were stating publicly what my former boss Martin Mendelsohn had told me in private: that when he went to Yugoslavia to observe the Artukovic trial, he would be permitted to examine documents concerning Waldheim.[21] If the report was accurate, it would eliminate the need for any action by Ambassador Scanlan and his "Billy-boys." Mendelsohn had been assured that the Zagreb archives, containing records of the activities of the Ustashi troops, held important material concerning Waldheim.

I double-checked and confirmed that each of the documents sent to us earlier by Dr. Lavoslav Kadelburg of the Federation of Jewish Communities in Yugoslavia was embossed on the back with the stamp of the Zagreb archives. If Mendelsohn's contacts honored their promises, we might soon see some of the Yugoslavs' best material.

Back at my desk, my eyes scanned the mountain of materials in front of me, searching for a landing site. There were newspaper clippings, notes, microfilm printouts, and photocopies of every description in numerous languages, and my senses rebelled at the task of trying to integrate what we already knew into the mass of information—and disinformation—that came from Waldheim this day.

The *New York Times* carried a story by James Markham, based on a new interview with Waldheim. The candidate told Markham that the fighting between the Germans and the partisans in the Balkans "was a nasty, dirty confrontation." He admitted again that he knew about crimes committed against Yugoslav partisans, but added, ". . . I was far away from these atrocities, and I just got the reports." Once more he attempted to equate Yugoslav civilian casualties with German losses: "I also knew that many German soldiers were trapped and executed in a similar way."

Waldheim now added his hometown to the list of atrocity sites about which he was uninformed. Even though he still claimed to have spent much of the war on military leave in Vienna studying law, he professed ignorance about the deportation of Vienna's Jews, which was begun under the direction of Adolf Eichmann in 1939, one year after the *Anschluss.* Waldheim said he had heard that Jews were taken away to an undisclosed location, "but I didn't know it was such a mass affair."

Asked by Markham about reports of a resurgence of anti-Semitism in modern Austria, Waldheim reassured the veteran *New York Times* correspondent, "It's no problem, really." If there was a backlash, he declared, it was because of Singer and his "interference" in Austrian "domestic affairs."[22]

Also on my desk this day was a Waldheim interview in the *Christian Science Monitor,* in which the candidate made it clear that he had no intention of reining in his overzealous supporters. And why should he? "There is no anti-Semitism" in Austria, he proclaimed. In the next breath, however, he disproved his own claim: "Of course, if you have a man like Singer" issuing "polemics" against him and also "against Austria," "that angers the people . . ."[23]

This day also saw the arrival in New York of Gerhard Waldheim, a youthful-looking banker who spoke impeccable, unaccented English (he had spent much of his youth in the United States). He was tall and gangly, but nattily dressed. Although the father had cut a handsome figure at Gerhard's age, the son, I thought, was a comparatively unattractive man, with protruding ears and heavy, dark-framed glasses framing a drawn face. He combed his hair straight back above a high forehead and greased it in the same style favored by his father. He was here to testify at a Congressional hearing on the question of whether or not his father should be barred from the U.S. In fact, he and I were both scheduled to testify at the same hearing, on April 22.

The younger Waldheim came armed with a press handout, the second version of the defense memo, which, he declared, would prove that his father was "neither a Nazi nor a war criminal." He also distributed a shorter document purporting to quote statements made in support of Waldheim by "leading politicians and witnesses." Most of the names were familiar and expected—Simon Wiesenthal, Karl Gruber, Fritz Molden. Hans Uteschill, a former member of the French Resistance, was quoted as saying that when Waldheim was posted to Paris in 1948 as the number-two man in the Austrian legation, he, Uteschill, had been assigned to conduct a "full security check on Waldheim's past for the French Intelligence Authority." He had concluded that Waldheim was "an Austrian patriot, low-ranking officer in the Wehrmacht, no Nazi involvement." If we took this statement at face value, we had to conclude that the French, who controlled the WASt archive in Berlin, had cleared Waldheim within three years after the end of the war. Another of the testimonials offered by Waldheim's son was as brash as it was amazing. The press handout quoted Waldheim's successor, U.N. Secretary-General Javier Perez de Cuellar, as saying, "The allegations brought forth against Dr. Waldheim are absurd."[24] This fabricated statement had worked wonders for the Waldheim campaign when published beneath a screaming headline in the Vienna daily *Kronenzeitung* two weeks earlier, but relying on it, without verification, in Perez de Cuellar's backyard seemed almost masochistic.

To his credit, Gerhard Waldheim had enough courage to seek a meeting with Steinberg, and to drop the Perez de Cuellar "quotation" when its falsity was brought to his attention. During their low-key conversation, Steinberg asked if Gerhard would supply the WJC with a copy of the UNWCC file pertaining to his father. The son promised to do so.

Gerhard promptly embarked on a whirlwind media campaign, guided by a top Washington public relations consultant. His efforts included an op-ed piece published in the *Washington Post,* in which he equated the actions of Nazi troops in the Balkans with those of American forces in Vietnam.

On April 19, former Yugoslav Vice President Mitja Ribicic became the first prominent Yugoslav to discuss the Tito–Waldheim relationship. Asked whether Tito had known that Waldheim had served on the staff of General Loehr, Ribicic replied, "If he did not know it personally, then people in his Secretariat did." Why, then, had Belgrade never demanded Waldheim's extradition from Austria? Ribicic answered, "After the liberation, Yugoslavia did not busy itself with retaliation. We let thousands of Italians and Germans go home."[25] What Ribicic said was less important than the fact that anything was said at all. We took it as a signal that the Yugoslav government might be ready at last to put the worldwide demand for information concerning Waldheim ahead of its obsession with protecting Tito's image.

But the very next day, as I prepared my testimony for the U.S. House of Representatives, I received a call from Martin Mendelsohn, who had just returned from Yugoslavia. "I was sandbagged," he reported with a deep sigh. The previous week, he had met with a senior Yugoslav Foreign Ministry official in Zagreb, who renewed his government's promise to open the Waldheim files. Mendelsohn had been scheduled to leave Zagreb for Belgrade on Thursday, and the official assured him that the documents would be delivered to him there. But not a single piece of paper had arrived, and the friendly Yugoslav Foreign Ministry official seemed to have vanished. I recorded this nonevent in my notes and closed with the Spanish notation "*Nada*"—nothing.

Now, it appeared that my hopes of obtaining the *Odluka* would have to rest with Stephen Katich, Ambassador Scanlan, and the ambassador's "Billy-boys." The prospects were anything but encouraging.

Meanwhile, we learned of some disturbing developments within the Israeli government. A confidential source provided us with copies of secret and highly sensitive cable correspondence between Michael Elizur, the Israeli ambassador to Austria, and his superiors at the Israeli Foreign Ministry in Jerusalem. Elizur was requesting that Israeli Prime Minister Shimon Peres speak with Edgar Bronfman, a longtime friend of Peres, about the "great and unnecessary damage" that the WJC's efforts were causing in Austria.

The Israeli Foreign Ministry's response was blunt:

DO NOT UNDERSTAND WHAT GREAT AND UNNECESSARY DAMAGE HAS BEEN CAUSED ACCORDING TO YOU. REGARDING YOUR SUGGESTION, THEREFORE, WE WILL NOT RECOMMEND THAT THE PRIME MINISTER CALL BRONFMAN.[26]

Elizur's request came as a shock to me. Although it did not startle Steinberg, who attributed it to the fact that Elizur and Simon Wiesenthal were close, he was incensed. "It's not bad enough that we have to do battle with Waldheim and his People's Party henchmen? We've got to fight *Jews*, too?"

19

Vienna, April 22, 1986. Austria's outgoing president, Rudolf Kirchschlaeger, made an eagerly awaited twenty-minute television address to his countrymen. It was his first direct speech to the nation since he became president, two terms and a dozen years earlier. The speech was a report on his examination of Waldheim's UNWCC file and a portion of the documents the WJC had released to the press during the past several weeks.

The balding Austrian president was a Wehrmacht veteran himself, but he was also a former jurist with a reputation for quiet integrity. He began his address with a complaint that the "uproar" surrounding the disclosures "has gripped the entire Western world." It had caused the world press to focus not merely on Waldheim's past, but on the past of the entire nation, and he cautioned his viewers that Austria's political reputation "is inseparable from our economic position." Kirchschlaeger boasted that he had worked hard "to inject a calmer note into the uproar," and noted what he believed to be his biggest accomplishment in that campaign: "At least the press conferences held by the World Jewish Congress in New York every day or every other day came to an end." He pleaded with his countrymen not to react with blind anger. "Anti-Semitic feelings," he said, "have never been a benefit or blessing to us in the past." To this practical consideration, he added, "They are also extremely inhuman."

The heart of Kirchschlaeger's address was his report on his review of the Waldheim documents. He prefaced his summary with a caveat: "Expect no judgment from me. I have no right to pass judgment, and no right to acquit." He allowed that there would remain some facts "that cannot be ascertained."

Having said that, Kirchschlaeger nonetheless proceeded to acquit. He declared that if he was a public prosecutor, he "would not dare bring charges before a regular court based upon the evidence presented to me." He said he could not believe that Waldheim ever had the power "to issue orders for reprisals," and he speculated that Johann Mayer, the witness whose testimony was key to the Yugoslav charges, might have "made accusations containing inaccuracies in order to improve his lot as a P.O.W." Thus did the Austrian president neatly dispose of the UNWCC file—without offering anything approaching a detailed analysis of its contents.

Somberly, he moved on to the subject of the WJC documents. These, he said, demonstrated that Waldheim had served first as an "interpreter" in General Stahl's West Bosnia Combat Group and later as *Ordonnanzoffizier* assigned to Army Group E's chief of intelligence. He conceded that in this latter assignment, Waldheim "must have been well informed," but the nearest he came to linking Waldheim with any dubious activity was to declare, ". . . one must assume that he knew about the reprisals in the war against the partisans." He made no mention of any specific atrocities committed by any of the Wehrmacht units in which Waldheim had served during the final four years of the war.

Referring to the December 1, 1943, organizational table of Army Group E, he reported that "the then–First Lieutenant Waldheim was in charge of keeping the daily log; assessment of enemy status; Ic morning, evening, and activity reports." Few of Kirchschlaeger's viewers could have guessed that the Austrian president had conveniently omitted mention of other, perhaps more important, duties listed in the same column on the chart, including "personnel matters of the Intelligence/Counterintelligence Branch," "prisoner interrogation," and "special tasks."

He concluded with a harsh reprimand to those who would dare to judge his country:

> I think I personally still have a good enough memory of the events in Europe starting approximately in 1930 and especially of those in the years 1938 and 1939. On the basis of these memories, let me make this statement: Every nation has to be careful when it comes to assigning guilt. In particular, the reopening of many old wounds that have only barely healed in the recent past leads me to think that probably none of the European nations—and most likely America as well—has fully come to terms with the past.[1]

Kirchschlaeger's performance delighted Waldheim's handlers. In response to the speech, the candidate himself exulted, "All the allegations against me have now collapsed."[2]

As I boarded a shuttle flight to Washington later that same day, I was loaded down not only with copies of the testimony I would present to Congress in the afternoon but with the morning's newspapers as well.

The *New York Times* reported from the U.N. that Waldheim's successor had again denied making the statement that Gerhard Waldheim's press handout attributed to him (that the allegations were "absurd"). A U.N. spokesman announced that Secretary-General Perez de Cuellar "has not passed any judgment on the Waldheim charges, nor will he."[3]

Also this day, *New York Newsday*'s tabloid-style front page featured a large color photograph of Senator Daniel Patrick Moynihan and the headline: MOYNIHAN: WALDHEIM IS A LIAR.

As the airplane soared off southward from La Guardia Airport, I studied the *Newsday* piece. It quoted the former U.S. representative to the U.N. as declaring that Waldheim "emerges as a liar" concerning "matters that are at the very heart" of the United Nations. Moynihan added that, as far as he was concerned, Waldheim "is not welcome in the United States—as president of Austria or as anything."[4]

There was considerable activity in the Congressional back rooms and antechambers prior to the opening of the hearing before the House Subcommittee on Human Rights and International Organizations. Gerhard Waldheim met with Representative Stephen Solarz, the congressman who was the recipient of Waldheim's 1980 letter that had effectively, if impermanently, covered up the U.N. Secretary-General's wartime service record. Solarz had recently written again to Waldheim, requesting an explanation for the misleading information he had received six years earlier. Today, Gerhard Waldheim hand-delivered his father's written response, which explained that he had not thought it appropriate to provide the "details" of his war service:

> The reason for this partial omission has nothing to do with my having to hide something, but rather with my hesitation in general to talk in detail about my military service. In my country, it is not usual to provide military details in one's curriculum vitae if one applies for a post in the civil service. . . . To mention the fact of one's military service is all that is expected.

The explanation did not satisfy Solarz, for in his 1980 letter, Waldheim had provided considerable detail pertaining to his service through 1941, and nothing thereafter.

As Solarz and Gerhard Waldheim spoke, I met with one of the subcommittee members, Representative Gary Ackerman; like Solarz, he was a New York Democrat. I advised him that I thought it possible that Gerhard Waldheim had brought with him to the United States a copy of the UNWCC file bearing his father's name. If not, he could certainly obtain a copy, since his father had already been provided with one. I confided to Ackerman that, during my testimony, I planned to challenge the younger Waldheim to fulfill his promise to Steinberg to provide a copy of the file. I was sure that Gerhard would find some way to refuse, but I enlisted Ackerman's assistance. He promised to press the point during the question-and-answer period.

Finally, just before the hearing began, one of the legislative aides to subcommittee chairman Gus Yatron mentioned to me that Simon Wiesenthal had been in Washington, a few weeks earlier, to meet with the congressman. The Nazi-hunter had directed considerable energy, I was told, into attempting to discredit the WJC's handling of the case.

I wondered how much headway he had made.

The large chamber on the second floor of the Rayburn House Office Building was packed to capacity as Chairman Yatron called the hearings to order. The subcommittee members sat behind an elegant arc of mahogany, elevated so as to place them several feet above everyone else in the room. Those of us who were to be witnesses sat at two large tables with our backs to the sea of spectators, facing the assembled congressmen and the bright, bluish-white lights of a dozen television cameras. The hearings were being telecast, live, to a nationwide audience, by C-SPAN.

The first to testify was the dapper, smooth-tongued Solarz. In discussing the ramifications of Waldheim's 1980 letter to him, Solarz observed that the fact that Waldheim had returned to active service after 1941 did not, by itself, constitute an impropriety. But, he pointed out, "his deception only serves to raise the possibility that he was engaged in activities that he did not want to become public." And, Solarz declared, "Mr. Waldheim has so far failed to provide any kind of a rational explanation for these actions."

Solarz noted that both Waldheim and his son had apologized, one publicly and one privately: "Gerhard, in a meeting with me in my office a short while ago, expressed his father's regrets for any misleading statements his father might have made. On a recent television interview, Mr. Waldheim apologized to me for misleading me in our earlier correspondence. I was pleased with these apologies, but I am more interested in a rational explanation for *why* Mr. Waldheim had misled me in the first place.

"The fundamental question remains the same: Why did Mr. Waldheim cover up his military service in the period from 1941 till the end of the war . . . ? The failure to provide a plausible explanation, Mr. Chairman, continues to suggest that he had a fear of the discovery of actions that he did not want known. Each day, as new information about his past has been learned, Mr. Waldheim has revised his defense.

"It is just this sort of moral blindness and selective amnesia that were indispensable elements in the tragedy that is the Holocaust.

"Having changed his story so many times, and only in response to emerging revelations in the press, Mr. Waldheim can hardly be surprised that his remaining defense, that he was not involved in war crimes, is not automatically accepted."

Rabbi Marvin Hier of the Simon Wiesenthal Center had come from Los Angeles to testify. I was pleased to learn that he intended to speak in favor of the WJC's request that the U.S. government investigate whether to place Waldheim on the watchlist. I sat next to Hier at the long table in front of the congressmen and we were joined by the Center's Washington counsel, Martin Mendelsohn, who still looked jet-lagged from his disappointing venture in Yugoslavia. We formed an improbable trio of, as it were, prosecution witnesses.

Hier held up a copy of the doctoral dissertation that Waldheim had submitted to the University of Vienna in 1944 and pronounced its contents deeply disturbing. He disclosed that it had taken the Center weeks to track down a copy. The Center's accomplishment was notable; *Profil* had tried, without success, to obtain a copy more than six months earlier, but the dissertation had mysteriously "disappeared" from the university's library. Its title, in English translation, was *The Reich Idea of Konstantin Frantz.*

"Frantz," Hier explained, "was a notorious anti-Semite, considered one of the spiritual forerunners of National Socialism." In Frantz's concept of a "greater Reich," encompassing all the German-speaking peoples, there was no room for Jews. He suggested, according to Hier, that the authorities either (1) chop off their heads or (2) send them to Palestine. Hier pointed out that Waldheim wrote his thesis at a time when any reasonable person would have concluded that Germany was going to lose the war. Nevertheless, Waldheim's writings extolled Frantz's ideology, leaving little doubt as to where the author's sympathies lay. The most that could be said in Waldheim's behalf was that he had neither praised nor rejected Frantz's anti-Semitism; the dissertation made no mention of Frantz's writings on the Jewish question. Hier quoted the final sentence of the 1944 dissertation, allowing the words to linger in the hearing room: "Europe fell because of Germany, and Europe will again be resurrected because of Germany."

Quite courageously, it seemed to me, Hier contested one of Simon Wiesenthal's key arguments in Waldheim's defense (although he scrupulously avoided mentioning the Nazi-hunter in this context). Whereas Wiesenthal continued to assert that the Wehrmacht had nothing to do with the deportation of the Salonika Jews, Hier refused to be a party to that distortion of history. "It is true," he told the congressmen, "that the SS generally carried out the daily deportations, but the commander, General Loehr, not only had knowledge, but was pushing the idea."

When, at last, it was my turn to speak, I looked momentarily at Congressman Solarz, who had left the witness table and joined his House colleagues. "We have the same question that Congressman Solarz has," I declared. "Why the grotesque lies? We have been waiting now, for nearly two months, for a simple explanation, if there is one, from Dr. Waldheim, and still we do not get it. Dr. Waldheim refuses to write his true autobiography, and so we are forced to write it for him."

After briefly outlining what had already been unearthed about his father's hidden past, I turned my attention to Gerhard Waldheim, sitting only a few feet away from me. I shot the younger Waldheim a sideways glance, leaned into the microphone, and hurled my surprise challenge. "Last week," I disclosed, "during a meeting in New York between Gerhard Waldheim and World Jewish Congress executive director Elan Steinberg, Mr. Waldheim stated that his father is in possession of a copy of the United Nations War Crimes Commission suspect file pertaining to his case. The younger Mr. Waldheim agreed to provide the World Jewish Congress with a copy. We have, as yet, received nothing.

"Gerhard Waldheim is here today," I continued. "He is scheduled to testify next. I have reason to believe that he may have a copy of the U.N. file with him now. If, as Kurt Waldheim asserts, he has nothing to hide, then let his son make that file available to this subcommittee now, or agree to provide it to the subcommittee within forty-eight hours."

I shared a conspiratorial glance with Congressman Ackerman, and sat back, awaiting questions.

Chairman Yatron had a query for Rabbi Hier. He pointed out that at a National Press Club press conference the previous day, Gerhard had quoted Simon Wiesenthal as having said that Waldheim had never belonged to the Nazi Party or any of their affiliated groups. "Did he say this?" the congressman asked.

It was a painful issue for the founder of the Simon Wiesenthal Center. Hier was walking a tightrope, and he knew it. It was inconceivable to him that the Center would be on the "wrong side" of the

Waldheim issue. The occasional references in the American media to Simon Wiesenthal's strange position threatened to alienate thousands of the organization's contributors around the country. On the other hand, Hier dared not enrage Wiesenthal; with one stroke of the pen, the Nazi-hunter could revoke his franchise and, as Steinberg quipped, force Hier to rename his operation "The Center."

Hier had anticipated Yatron's question. The rabbi told the subcommittee that, one hour previously, Wiesenthal had authorized the Center to issue a statement in his name, which Hier now asked Mendelsohn to place in the record.

Mendelsohn read from a sheet of paper:

> I do not believe what Mr. Waldheim is saying about his war status. He was the best informed man in Group Ic. His constant revisions leave me with questions. I have no evidence that Kurt Waldheim was a war criminal, but I do not believe him. I do not defend Mr. Waldheim and I do not endorse Mr. Waldheim. I remain unbelieving.

Listening to Mendelsohn's recitation, I allowed myself to imagine Wiesenthal changing course, agreeing at last to review our documents, and joining us in the search for the truth. My thoughts were interrupted as the hearing was unexpectedly commandeered by Congressman Tom Lantos. During the war, Lantos had risked his life in Hungary alongside the heroic Swedish diplomat Raoul Wallenberg, working to save Jews from deportation to the death camps. After the war, he moved to the U.S. and became a university professor. Now, the silver-haired orator from California held the distinction of being the only Holocaust survivor ever elected to the U.S. Congress. He chose to use this moment, not to ask a question, but to give voice to his feelings. Speaking in moderately accented English, he began so softly that one had to strain to hear him above the din of reporters and spectators carrying on whispered conversations. But as he continued, and the fervor of the words he spoke took hold of his listeners, the room grew silent. In a measured, relentless tempo, Lantos delivered an unforgettable lecture.

"I find it demeaning and sickening and repulsive and repugnant that a man to whom the international community has given its highest position, after having been found out as a shameless liar, continues this charade—" Here, Lantos paused. He looked directly down from the mahogany platform at Gerhard Waldheim, and he placed a palm across his heart as he continued with heightened volume. "—instead of saying to the world and the people of Austria, *mea culpa, mea maxima culpa,* 'I have sinned, I have sinned greatly. Forgive me.'"

The younger Waldheim stared back, finally averting his eyes in a symbolic admission that the weight of Lantos's denunciation was no longer bearable. The audience, filling nearly every inch of the hearing room, took in a collective gulp of air as Lantos's final impassioned words echoed off the walls: "To pretend that a German officer was stationed six kilometers outside of Salonika, where tens of thousands of people were beaten and killed and packed into freight cars and shipped off to the gas chambers—to pretend that he didn't know that this was going on, under his nose, is an insult and a disgrace."

Silence reigned for many moments. And it was amid this silence that Gerhard Waldheim made his way quietly from a front-row seat to the witness table. He was joined there by Karl Gruber, the man who had given the elder Waldheim his first postwar job.

Gruber testified first. An aging, but still distinguished-looking ex-diplomat who spoke elegantly accented, if occasionally mangled, English, he detailed his background as a leader of the Austrian resistance movement and, then, as his country's first postwar Foreign Minister. His top postwar aide had been Fritz Molden, whose ties with Allen Dulles and the OSS were well known. Gruber said that it was Molden, along with other former members of the resistance movement, who first suggested a position for Waldheim. A background investigation failed to uncover anything suspicious. "All four Powers" approved, he noted, and Waldheim was hired.

I was intrigued by the thought of the U.S., Britain, France, and the Soviet Union all clearing Waldheim just months after the war had ended.

Gruber grew nostalgic. He told the subcommittee that he had been the first Western politician to visit Tito after the Yugoslav leader broke with Stalin. The year was 1948, and he spent several days with Tito at the presidential retreat on the two-island complex of Brioni (the same spot where Tito later entertained Waldheim). Gruber's description of the atmosphere painted an idyllic picture. "We went fishing together, we went hunting together," he reminisced. "We had long, long talks about our future relations and about the reasons he broke with the Russians, and all these kinds of questions."

Those questions did *not* include Waldheim, however, Gruber testified. "He never raised, at this time, any question about Mr. Waldheim, whom he did know was my secretary."

Oh-oh, I thought. He's trying to help Waldheim, but he's actually digging him deeper into the dirt: He's disclosing that the Yugoslav president knew who his secretary was.

Gruber claimed that Tito had confessed to him that some of the indictments handed down by Yugoslav authorities in the aftermath of the war were hastily prepared during a time when the country lacked "the personnel to make a thorough investigation." According to Gruber, Tito had remarked, "I do not put too much into what was written in these documents at the time."

Gruber was trying his best to save his old friend Waldheim. And it likely was more than just friendship that brought him to the hearing: For if it turned out that Waldheim had been a Yugoslav or Soviet asset, it would reflect very badly indeed on Gruber. His entire postwar career would be viewed as compromised.

Gruber turned his attention to Waldheim's chronic misrepresentation of his war record: "He wrote a book. I was very much against his writing any book. And I have many friends as reporters, and they came to me and said, 'We have read his book and there are two years of the war, and suddenly this ends, and you can understand that we became very interested in what was in these other years.'

"So I told them this: He was a lieutenant already and he was shot down from his horse. And he was for a very long time—we established this—between death and life.

"And as his comrades brought him along, he obtained a very high opinion of comradeship and all those other things which make an army. Too high perhaps, but anyway, this was the reason. And I think he got a *fixation* there, a fixation with his wounding that ended practically his combat role." Because of this "fixation" with events on the Russian front, Gruber theorized, Waldheim considered the remainder of his military service uneventful. The ex–Foreign Minister allowed that Waldheim's incomplete description of the war years "was certainly a big mistake," but he pleaded for understanding. "When you think back to a real war criminal like this Eichmann— he had not five percent of the publicity that Waldheim has had for the last four weeks."

Gruber's thoughts returned to Tito, and he closed with a rather frightening warning. He and Tito, he said, had agreed on a very important point. According to Gruber, Tito had cautioned, "We must be very careful that we do not wed the Austrian wagon to the German train."

The ex–Foreign Minister implored the U.S. Congress to heed Tito's words: "If you do anything where you make to wed the Austrian wagon to the German train, you make the biggest disservice to Europe and the biggest disservice to the American interests. Because whether Austria is free depends on its own will, not on anybody else. Nobody could make Austria a free state if the Austrians . . . want to become German again. . . .

"You must carry in mind not only the man Waldheim. You must bear in mind the fate of Austria, the character of Austria. And you must be sure that you do not try to wed Austria in your thinking to the German wagon—that they finally think, well, after all, we are Germans anyway for the world."

After a ten-minute recess to permit the congressmen to go to the House floor for a vote on a military retirement amendment, the subcommittee turned its attention to the final witness.

Gerhard Waldheim launched into a prepared speech, systematically denying many of the most publicized charges against his father. He was not a member of any Nazi organizations; he was never an intelligence officer; he was not a senior officer; he was not a general staff officer; he was not, as the CROWCASS listing stated, an Abwehr officer.

As I listened, I silently conceded this last point. The Yugoslav assertion appeared to be incorrect. Although Waldheim had worked with Army Group E's Abwehr officer, Major Hammer, in the small Ic/AO Branch, he did not appear ever to have been formally designated an Abwehr officer himself. But he certainly *had* been an intelligence officer as well as a member of several Nazi organizations.

For some minutes, the dutiful son continued with his aggressive point-by-point defense, which was for the most part a reiteration of the "Nowhere Man" theme. "All misinterpretations about the war have been clarified," he then announced.

Turning to the subject of his father's penchant for changing the essential facts of his story, the younger Waldheim begged, "I would like to ask for understanding on this point. We are talking about a time which was forty to fifty years ago."

Next, he spoke directly and pointedly to Congressman Lantos: "I also, as a son, would have had severe problems in believing that my father had been unaware of deportations if he had been there. The fact is that the record now shows that my father left the Salonika area and Arsakli, where he was stationed, in the middle of November 1942 for his study leave. The pre-events of the deportations, beginning with the obligation to wear the Jewish star, began on February 6, the deportations themselves on sixteen trains ran from March 15 to May 15, and my father returned from his assignment in Tirana in July—the beginning of July. Therefore, for me as a son, and I can assure you that this was not an easy task, I am personally fully convinced that my father . . . said the truth when he was asked by a reporter for the *New York Times* . . . whether he was aware of these deportations."

Lantos was not buying it. "Did I hear you to say that in your view your father is completely exonerated?" he asked.

Gerhard Waldheim acknowledged that this was "my personal conviction."

"His credibility has been totally shattered," Lantos countered sharply. "I would think that you would do him a more useful service by counseling him to admit to some of these very serious mistakes, because no one else believes it. If you believe it, you and your father are the only two people who believe it. . . . It defies ordinary human comprehension for you to expect that we swallow this."

Once more the room fell silent.

All eyes fixed on Gerhard Waldheim, who tried to maintain a respectful-yet-proud bearing. But his body seemed to grow limp as Lantos delivered another lecture, in words filled with pain:

"You need to understand that your father was not the only person who lived in Europe during that period. There were several others, including myself, who lived there and who *knew* what was happening, who had conversations with people about what was happening.

"This was not an isolated event. This is not like a movie that you choose not to see. This was the *central fact of life* in the Balkans. This was the pivotal development. This was the focus of activity. And to say that he was too busy with his legal studies in Vienna—it boggles the mind that you would think, and he would think, that anybody believes it.

"When Senator Moynihan says that your father is a liar, he speaks for the American people. The American people feel your father is a liar. They know he is a liar. . . . It's very difficult if he, and as his representative, you, persist in the Big Lie. The Big Lie went out with Goebbels. . . . We would like to have you come clean for him. Because that's the way you can help him."

Gerhard Waldheim managed a quiet reply, in which he continued to maintain that his father knew nothing of the Jewish deportations from Salonika.

Other congressmen fired questions. When Chairman Yatron warned that the hearings were "running out of time," I worried that Congressman Ackerman either had forgotten his promise to me about the UNWCC file or else would never get the chance to make good on it. Finally, when Ackerman got the floor, he began by asking Gerhard again about his father's concealment of his war service in Yugoslavia and Greece.

Gerhard did not see it as concealment. He said that *he* knew all along about his father's service in the Balkans.

"*You* knew that he had perpetrated this falsehood?" Ackerman asked.

". . . at the time, I did not perceive that in such a way," the son answered. "Because I saw his narrative of key experiences in his life as those key events that he considered relevant."*

"Did you ever wonder why he was not telling the truth?" Ackerman asked.

"I do not think at that time it struck me as him not telling the truth. It was that he did not consider it relevant, because he was an interpreter." I was astonished. Under pressure, Gerhard Waldheim had returned to his father's totally discredited—and long since abandoned—defense, that he was "just an interpreter."

Ackerman pressed further on the subject of the cover-up, until Gerhard, a defeated look on his face, responded meekly, "I appreciate the fact that in today's situation this definitely must be considered a very serious mistake."

Without any warning, Chairman Yatron interrupted, declaring, "The time for the gentleman has expired." He recognized the next questioner, Solarz. I was mortified. Ackerman's questions had been good ones, but he had forgotten to press the witness for a copy of the UNWCC file!

The questioning continued, and none of the other congressmen followed up on my challenge. My pulse raced. I could feel perspiration forming on my scalp.

Finally, at 5:54 P.M., with only six minutes left for the tightly scheduled hearing, Yatron announced, "I would like to yield to Mr. Ackerman for one brief question."

"Thank you very much for your indulgence, Mr. Chairman," Ackerman said. "Mr. Waldheim, the committee has been advised that you have a copy of the U.N. report. Would you make that available to us?"

Gerhard Waldheim, who had now had more than an hour to think of a response, replied, "I, unfortunately, am not in possession of such a report. I will, however, see to it that we get this copy as quickly as possible so as to have it supplied to the congressional records."†[6]

Late that evening, back in New York, I checked the other news of the day.

Vienna's *Die Presse* had carried an interview in which Waldheim

---

*It is interesting to compare this contention, that Waldheim's Russian front service was, for him, the only memorable aspect of the war, with a later statement from Gerhard Waldheim, disclosing that his father routinely carried a gun. "When I asked about the pistol, he told me it was from Greece," Gerhard recalled. "He said, 'My God, those were the days,' but he would never expand on it."[5]

†When the official transcript of the hearings was issued some two months later, it contained a terse notation: "The material was not received by the time of publication."

asserted that he was being attacked by "only that single private institution, the World Jewish Congress—Mr. Singer, Mr. Steinberg, Mr. Rosenbaum."[7] The odious refrain was getting old, but Waldheim had obviously concluded that it still played well with the voters.

Also in the latest press clips was a further indication that the warnings directed to Belgrade by Waldheim and his campaign aides were having their intended effect. Yugoslavia's official Tanjug news agency, which had previously reported that the evidence in Yugoslav files was sufficient to "condemn Waldheim as a war criminal," suddenly changed its tune. The agency now editorialized that Waldheim's pursuers were mistaken if they believed that the key to the case lay in Yugoslav archives. "The data relating to the wartime past of Kurt Waldheim," Tanjug declared, "are contained complete in the captured German documents" in the archives of the victorious Allies and West Germany, "while Yugoslavia has only some of the documents."[8]

Tanjug's claim was in direct contradiction to what Martin Mendelsohn had been told in Yugoslavia. According to Mendelsohn, a Yugoslav official advised him that the Zagreb archives held a larger, more detailed file on Waldheim—one that no one in the West had ever been allowed to see.

The day after the Congressional hearing, the daily stress of the Waldheim affair was eclipsed by the pain of a dreadful loss when I learned from the obituary pages of my morning newspaper that John Mendelsohn (no relation to Martin), the affable archivist who had alerted us to Waldheim's listing with CROWCASS and the UNWCC, had died unexpectedly.

All of us were badly shaken. Mendelsohn's kindness, generosity, and mastery of his area of specialty had made him something of a legend at the Archives. He would be greatly missed.

But we pressed on. Because the alternative was unthinkable.

20

Even as the congressional hearings were drawing to a close, *Washington Post* reporter John Goshko was becoming the first person in the West—outside of a few privileged officials in the U.S., Israeli, and Austrian governments (and, of course, Kurt Waldheim)—to examine Waldheim's U.N. War Crimes Commission file. The *Post* published his exclusive story on its front page the next day, April 23, but unfortunately, much of the piece was devoted to excerpts from the testimony of Waldheim's former Wehrmacht comrades that had already been disclosed weeks earlier in the Belgrade daily *Vecernje Novosti.*

However, there were a few important new items in Goshko's article. The most significant revelation was a snippet of testimony from Johann Mayer that had not been mentioned in the Yugoslav press. According to Goshko, the file quoted Mayer as linking Waldheim to a November 1944 execution that followed the desertion of a group of Wehrmacht soldiers. Said Mayer:

> I remember certain persons having been murdered at Sarajevo in November 1944. They were executed according to the order given by Waldheim in retaliation for desertion from the German Army of some other persons.

Goshko was also able to confirm that Yugoslavia's original evidentiary submission to the U.N. commission had, as we suspected, been returned to the Yugoslav government long ago.[1] This was standard procedure for the UNWCC, but we had hoped against hope that Waldheim's case might prove an exception to the rule. At least we now knew with certainty that the original file was solely in the hands of the Yugoslavs.

A dramatic confrontation now took place during a closed session of the Yugoslav parliament. The story quickly leaked out. Delegate Lojze Skok demanded to know why the government was not making public its war crimes files on Waldheim. The response he received was that the files contained "information of interest for eventual criminal trials" and hence could not be released beyond traditional judicial and law enforcement channels.[2]

Meanwhile, I was increasingly concerned about the U.S. State Department's delay in responding to my Freedom of Information Act request that the Army had forwarded to them for action under the "Third Agency" rule. We remained in a kind of informational limbo, knowing that the State Department held some documentation regarding Waldheim's prewar or wartime activities, but without having any idea what it might be. By law, an agency had ten days to respond to the request, but more than two months had passed and we had received only a notification by form letter that the matter was "under review and assigned case number 86-00285." The fact that some of my previous FOIA requests on other cases had languished at State for more than two years heightened my anxiety.

In an attempt to force the bureaucratic hand, we brought a lawsuit in federal court in Manhattan demanding the immediate right "to inspect and copy the requested records."

"Roosevelt, have you heard the news about Waldheim?"

The afternoon of April 24 had been relatively quiet until Neal Sher called me from OSI.

"What news are you talking about, Chief?" I replied.

"It's unbelievable." Sher moaned. "It really is. And I can't even say anything about it. Okay? All I can do is tell you what happened two minutes ago. So just listen. I got a phone call from some reporter with the Knight-Ridder newspaper chain. The guy tells me that they're going with a story on Waldheim that he wants me to confirm. So I ask him what the story is. And then he tells me that their story is that OSI has completed the investigation you called for in your March letter to Meese and has sent a recommendation to the A.G. that Waldheim be put on the INS watchlist."

"What did you say to—"

"I told him that I couldn't go beyond what the Attorney General had said publicly in March—namely, that the matter is under investigation by the Department. But no sooner did I say that than the guy comes back and says he'd like to read me some quotes from what he called 'your'—my—report to Attorney General Meese. Next thing I know, he's reading a series of long quotes over the phone. And all I can do is sit there like an idiot and say that I can't go any further than what I'd already told him and that I can't confirm or deny anything else about the case."

The Knight-Ridder reporter knew, as well as I did, that Sher's "no-comment" was eloquent confirmation. If the basic story was false,

Sher would surely have asked to go off the record, then told the reporter that he had it wrong.

I replayed the brief phone conversation in my mind and realized that Sher had chosen his words carefully with me, too. He had avoided telling me directly whether or not the reporter's story was accurate.

The Knight-Ridder disclosure was quickly picked up by all the major media. The extensive quotes seemed to argue for the legitimacy of the reporter's information.* Follow-up stories by other reporters confirmed the Knight-Ridder account and added additional detail.

It was *big* news. OSI really had recommended that Waldheim be placed on the watchlist. The determination was reportedly based largely on the "criminal unit" theory, validated five years earlier by the U.S. Supreme Court in the citizenship revocation case of a Nazi death-camp guard whom the Justice Department had found living in Florida. The rationale was that Waldheim's service as an officer in small detachments that perpetrated Nazi war crimes was sufficient to render him ineligible to enter the United States. Another reported justification for OSI's recommendation was that no other individual known to be listed as wanted for war crimes, either on the CROW-CASS or UNWCC rosters, had ever been granted permission to enter the country. According to the press accounts, OSI's report concluded that Waldheim was a "special-missions staff officer in the Intelligence/Counter-Intelligence Branch" of Army Group E, which had taken part in the perpetration of war crimes and crimes against humanity in the Balkans. His "O3" position "meant that Waldheim was the third-highest-ranking special-missions officer on General Loehr's staff, no mean feat for a young lieutenant."[3]

At the WJC, we were both gratified and relieved. The fact that an arm of the U.S. Justice Department agreed with us and had arrived at the historic conclusion that a former U.N. Secretary-General should be barred from entry to the U.S.—forever—was a vindication of our efforts. But as encouraging as this disclosure was, we worried that it was premature. Ed Meese was not a man who took being backed into a corner with equanimity. Reportedly, he had not yet made his decision on the issue. And he would surely be infuriated by the leak. I could easily imagine him striking back by delaying his decision or even by rejecting OSI's watchlist recommendation—something that no Attorney General had ever done.

In Vienna, Waldheim's campaign office immediately issued a written response. Virtually ignoring the fact that OSI was a U.S. gov-

*The leak was soon traced, with near-certainty, to a State Department official.

ernment agency, the statement emphasized that the recommendation was based "on a request by the World Jewish Congress." People's Party General Secretary Michael Graff denounced the WJC for its "unserious, dishonorable, and hate-filled" accusations. We at the WJC, he declared, were "dishonorable fellows."[4]

Simultaneously Waldheim seemed to accelerate the rightward shift in his campaign strategy. Inside Austria at least, he decided that he could actually use the accusations to his advantage. Stumping throughout his country, he stirred up large crowds with inflammatory rhetoric: "Neither a Herr Singer in New York nor a Herr Shamir in Israel . . . has the right to meddle in the affairs of another state," he bellowed. He assured his listeners that he had done "nothing other than what a hundred thousand other Austrians did during this time. . . . And we, my friends, are not criminals because of that." His well-received finale was an impassioned plea: "Enough of the past! We have more important problems to solve."[5]

The enthusiastic response of Waldheim's campaign audiences to these themes seemed to confirm a disquieting observation made by columnist Flora Lewis in the *New York Times:* The more apparent it was becoming that Waldheim had lied about his wartime duties, she observed, the more popular he was growing in his native land. An American Jew living in Vienna later made a similar observation, employing imagery that struck me as eerily reminiscent of the youthful Hitler "clones" in Ira Levin's *The Boys From Brazil:*

> "To say he is a war criminal misses the point. He embodies the attitude of the typical Austrian. It is not a problem with a single person. There are 10,000 Waldheims, 100,000 Waldheims. There are Waldheims in every shop, every government office, every school. There are Waldheim grandfathers and Waldheim children. Waldheim is not a person anymore, he is a state of mind."[6]

Late night seemed the only time available to me to attempt to unscramble the jumble of dates, places, military units, and events in the ever-expanding labyrinth of documents. The mundane details of life, such as laundry and dishwashing and paying bills, fell by the wayside. Most nights, I studied until 2 A.M. or later—and then found my sleep disrupted by unanswered questions. I kept a notepad next to the bed and, on awakening, often found it filled with nearly illegible scribblings.

Morning frequently found me nursing a splitting headache, and it was usually well after 9 A.M. when I lugged my bulging briefcase onto the steamy, overcrowded Number 6 Lexington Avenue subway.

And when the loudspeaker crackled, "Thirty-third Street; Forty-second is next," I sometimes had to struggle to resist the temptation to ride on to the end of the line.

I dreaded what awaited me at the office. My daily routine almost always included meeting with one or another visiting reporter who had just been assigned to the Waldheim story. Each inquiring journalist would settle comfortably into a chair across from my desk and say, "Well, tell me: So what *do* we know about Kurt Waldheim?" My standard response was to ask them how many hours they had available for a briefing.

I was not, however, without sympathy for the plight of the men and women of the media. What we had already learned about Waldheim placed him all over Europe during the war: the Soviet Union, Bosnia, Montenegro, Tirana, Athens, Salonika, and Trieste—to name only a few assignments. Relevant documents were difficult to unearth and were written in German, Italian, Serbo-Croatian, Greek, and other languages. Most of the journalists assigned to cover the developing story were hopelessly lost in a sea of dates and places, accusations and denials, admissions and retractions of admissions. To make matters worse, no Western news organization assigned even a single reporter to the case on a full-time basis. Instead, they dispatched a succession of "dabblers" to handle the Waldheim story *du jour,* with the result that few members of the press ever had a grip on the "big picture." Where, I wondered, were the Woodward and Bernstein of the Waldheim affair?

When reporters asked me what aspect of the case they might concentrate on most profitably, I usually suggested that they probe Waldheim's whereabouts during the summer of 1942, during the time of the Kozara massacres. Waldheim had already provided us with several contradictory versions of his assignment during that period. His latest story—that he had reported to Stahl's headquarters in western Bosnia but was immediately reassigned to a liaison post with the Italian Division "Pusteria" in Montenegro—was wildly implausible, but it was difficult to disprove conclusively. I hoped that someone could find a way to do so.

A few reporters, some in the U.S. and some abroad, enjoyed the luxury of an extended (if still not exclusive) assignment to the Waldheim story, and we developed a symbiotic relationship with several of them. We shared information and kept each other's confidences. Other critical sources included Schuller, Korte, May, and—the newest "arrival"—a former colleague of mine from OSI who had moved on to other work, just as I had done, but who retained close ties to the mission and staff of the office. Bob Herzstein also continued to pursue the story, more or less on his own now.

A Jewish survivor from Austria, now living in New York, Ernest Goldblum (a genuine hero who had daringly rescued Jewish children in Europe during and after the war), put me in touch with a new and extremely important contact. He was Hans Safrian, the talented young researcher with the "New Austria" group in Vienna. Through him, I gained access to the key research findings that Safrian's group was making in Germany.

All of us compared notes as best we could, fired off copies of our discoveries to one another, shared local media stories, and spent endless hours on the phone. We studied every report we could unearth concerning each statement that Waldheim uttered, knowing that any one of them might contain a tiny slip, a kernel of truth that would set us off on another, potentially rewarding, investigative path. We had our individual agendas, to be sure, but we were united in the view that Waldheim's hidden past had to be fully uncovered, and in the belief that the cover-up rendered him unfit for public office. Each of us was after the same thing: the one final, irrefutable piece of evidence, the straw that would break the back of this lie-laden camel.

The Kennedy family compound in Hyannis Port, Massachusetts, was perhaps the last place in the United States where one would expect to see the latest episode of the Waldheim controversy played out. These were, after all, well-nigh hallowed grounds in the history of liberal democratic politics in America. But on April 26, they also served as the setting for the wedding reception of one of Kurt Waldheim's most prominent supporters, Austrian bodybuilder-turned-actor Arnold Schwarzenegger, and Kennedy family member Maria Shriver, a familiar face on America's TV sets as co-host of the "CBS Morning News."

The celebrity/society wedding of the year brought scores of reporters and television crews to Hyannis Port, along with hundreds of others who hoped for a peek at the visiting political and Hollywood aristocracy. The Kennedy family took extraordinary precautions to hold the curious at bay, and banned even their guests from bringing cameras to the reception. The Kennedys used their political clout to get the airspace over Hyannis closed throughout the day, in order to prevent press planes from spying from overhead, as they had done during the marriage of rock singer Madonna and actor Sean Penn months earlier.

The wedding ceremony, held in the small Church of St. Francis Xavier, had thrilled those who had been able to catch a glimpse. Celebrities were everywhere: Senator Ted Kennedy, Jacqueline Kennedy Onassis and her children, Sargent and Eunice Shriver (Maria's parents), Andy Warhol, Grace Jones, Tom Brokaw, Abigail ("Dear

Abby") Van Buren, and Oprah Winfrey were among those in attendance. The beautiful bride, resplendent in her Dior gown, and the larger-than-life groom, flashing a broad smile to the crowds pressing against police barriers, looked like something out of a fairy tale as they exited the church to the strains of "Maria" from *The Sound of Music.*

The wedding reception, held in two giant tents inside the Kennedy compound, featured a 425-pound wedding cake, music by the famed Peter Duchin band, and an extravagant luncheon prepared by Boston's finest caterers. Everything about the day had been perfect—at least until Schwarzenegger was presented with a remarkable gift from someone who had been unable to attend.

The present consisted of two life-size papier-mâché replicas of Arnold and Maria, created by a prominent Austrian artist. The groom's figure was attired in *lederhosen,* and he was carrying Maria, who was dressed in an Austrian *dirndl.* The gift had been sent by Kurt Waldheim.

Schwarzenegger, who had endorsed candidate Waldheim the preceding year (before the scandal broke), had invited Waldheim to the wedding. As the enormous figures were brought in, a clearly delighted Schwarzenegger rose to make a statement. What he said shocked his guests.

"My friends don't want me to mention Kurt's name," Schwarzenegger announced, "because of all the recent Nazi stuff and the U.N. controversy, but I love him and Maria does too, and so thank you, Kurt." Waldheim, the actor continued, had been treated unfairly by the press.

The reception fell suddenly silent. Jackie Onassis turned visibly pale. Recounting the incident later, author Wendy Leigh wrote that as Schwarzenegger spoke, the dolls took on "a slightly sinister air, as if they might suddenly open up to reveal the grinning specter of Kurt Waldheim lurking inside their shells."

After the wedding, Schwarzenegger permitted his name to be used on Waldheim campaign posters that went up throughout Austria, and he later visited Waldheim at his summer home outside Salzburg.*

The mystery of Waldheim's assignment in Plevlje, Montenegro, began to unravel on April 27, when the Yugoslav magazine *NIN* published the results of research that it said was newly completed in Belgrade on the subject of Waldheim's Kozara alibi. Ironically,

---

*Schwarzenegger has never repudiated his support of Waldheim. For a well-researched account of the Schwarzenegger-Shriver wedding and its aftermath, see Wendy Leigh, *Arnold: An Unauthorized Biography* (Chicago: Congdon: Congdon & Weed, 1990), pp. 239–49.

the key documents had been found there in a U.S. National Archives set of microfilmed German records that had been acquired from Washington by the Military Historical Institute in the Yugoslav capital. The captured documents established that, in early 1942, Waldheim was assigned to the "General Bader Combat Group" *(Kampfgruppe General Bader),* named after its commander, Lieutenant General Paul Bader. A March 22, 1942, order listed Waldheim "as an interpreter" in the combat group's liaison unit to the 5th Italian Mountain Infantry Division, known as "Pusteria." Waldheim's unit was denominated "D.V.K.-5," an acronym for the German Liaison Detachment to the 5th [Italian] Division.[7] All of this information actually appeared to support Waldheim's current version of his 1942 story. He had indeed been stationed in Montenegro with the Italians.

But, according to *NIN,* a second document completely destroyed Waldheim's alibi. It ordered the *disbanding* of the entire Bader Combat Group *on May 28, 1942,* and the return of headquarters personnel to the West Bosnia Combat Group.[8] If (as we soon verified at the National Archives) the document was as good as its billing, it meant that Waldheim was ordered *back* to Stahl's command staff in West Bosnia immediately *prior* to the Kozara operation, which took place in June and July. It would give the lie to Waldheim's claim, in his April 6 and April 12 defense memos, that he remained with the "Pusteria" Division in Plevlje "for three months, approximately from late April onwards." Waldheim had been caught in yet another bare-faced lie!

So what had Waldheim *done* upon his return to the West Bosnia Combat Group? The Yugoslav magazine tried to address that question too. Waldheim had initially claimed that he was a "mere interpreter" during the summer of 1942 and, indeed, Bob Herzstein had found a personnel roster showing Waldheim assigned, as of the end of June 1942, as a *Dolmetscher* ("interpreter") at Stahl's headquarters.[9] But *NIN* confirmed our belief that the Axis forces in West Bosnia were composed solely of German, Croatian, and Hungarian units. *No Italian forces* had been present. And since Italian was the only pertinent language Waldheim was qualified to interpret, he could not have actually functioned as an interpreter there, the magazine stressed. "We may never know what Waldheim was actually doing in Stahl's headquarters during the Kozara offensive," wrote *NIN* reporter Vojin Hadistevic. But "one thing is certain: Waldheim is not telling the truth about Kozara."[10]

Unfortunately, there were some weak links in the analysis. I recalled that at our March 25 press conference, Herzstein had mentioned that the Italians "never showed up" at Kozara. Perhaps Waldheim was sent to western Bosnia in the expectation that Italian troops would arrive. I could imagine Waldheim's next Kozara defense: "Oh, yes, I was there after all, but I just sat around waiting for the Italians." Or perhaps he would claim to have been busy with long-distance radio communications with the Italians.

I telephoned Willi Korte in Washington. He was finished with his freelance assignments for the German press and agreed to work, temporarily, for the WJC. We negotiated a modest fee schedule and I gave him his first assignment: to race over to the National Archives, locate and copy the two documents cited by *NIN*, and send them to me by overnight courier.

I had them the next morning.

The March 1942 order citing Waldheim's assignment to the Bader Combat Group's "German Liaison Detachment 5" to the Italian Division "Pusteria" was much more interesting than *NIN* had indicated. The *only* personnel listed for this unit were "Lt. Waldheim," as "interpreter," and, below him, a technical sergeant named Kohler as chief radio technician. The line above Waldheim's name was entitled "Fhr." (for *Fuehrer,* "leader"), but it had been left blank. By contrast, the "Fhr." line for another of the Bader Combat Group's liaison units had the name of a certain Colonel Rohrbach typed in. The tantalizing implication was that Waldheim might have been the de facto leader of the unit, serving as chief liaison with the Italians, in a position, moreover, appropriate for a full colonel. This, I realized, could be a landmark breakthrough, for it appeared that we might finally have identified a period in which Waldheim bore the *principal* responsibility for a Wehrmacht unit, and had not just served as someone else's deputy.

I riffled through my file cabinets, searching for all of Waldheim's recent statements concerning the "Pusteria" Division. A careful reading of them gave credence to my hypothesis: In his first defense memo of April 6, Waldheim wrote of serving in Plevlje as "as interpreter *and liaison officer*" to the "Pusteria" Division; similarly, in the April 14 issue of *Der Spiegel,* he spoke of being "assigned to the 'Pusteria' Italian Division, as an interpreter *and liaison officer.*"

But what had he actually *done* in Plevlje? I asked myself once more. The sole mission of the Bader Combat Group and the Italian divisions allied with it was to conduct antipartisan sweeps, and they operated under the by-now standard instructions concerning reprisal measures.* Waldheim had told *Vecernje Novosti* that in Plevlje, "I

---

*For example, a "secret" order of April 14, 1942, to troops of the 718th Security Division (a component of the Bader Combat Group) commanded that localities and houses in which munitions and weapons are found were to be "burned to the ground" (*niederzubrennen*) and that a special effort be made to identify families whose men have gone "into the woods" to join the partisans (U.S. National Archives T501/250/371–373).

received radio reports that I passed on to the Italians." And we knew that the commander of the "Pusteria" Division, the Italian General Giovanni Esposito, with whom Waldheim told *La Repubblica* he sipped coffee and played cards (a statement that supported the theory that Waldheim had *headed* the liaison detachment), had been charged with murder by the Yugoslavs after the war. Just what, I wondered, was in these "reports" that Waldheim transmitted to the Italians? I stuffed my notes into my bulging RESEARCH TO DO folder, and turned my attention to the second document.

Dated May 26, 1942, it stated that, pursuant to an order of the Wehrmacht Commander Southeast, "the Bader Combat Group is to be dissolved by May 28, 1942." The document went on to note that the planned antipartisan operations in the Kozara area would be directed by the West Bosnia Combat Group—General Stahl's task force—and that the "personnel and vehicles of the Bader Combat Group will be available for formation of Command Staff West Bosnia after departure of personnel being reassigned." The order stated that all of the liaison officers with the Italian divisions "are returning to their commands."

Thus, even if (as the first document indicated) Waldheim was telling the truth about having been detailed to Plevlje on an Italian liaison assignment, we could now prove that he was ordered to *return* to the West Bosnia Combat Group—assigned to the command staff of its leader, General Friedrich "Hard as Steel" Stahl—on the very eve of the Kozara massacres. Waldheim was not "120 miles away" from the massacres; he was right in the middle of them!

Each day, the fax machine brought a new batch of stories from the international press, which spanned the range from the intriguing to the outrageous. As April drew to a close, we finally heard something critical of Waldheim from inside the Soviet Bloc. *Polityka,* the Polish Communist Party weekly, declared that questions about Waldheim were "substantial and the answers still evasive." Likewise, the Warsaw daily *Zycie Warszawy* editorialized: "There have been too many misinterpretations, corrections, explanations and supplements. . . . What is the whole truth about the man?"[11] These were encouraging statements, and we could only hope that other Warsaw Pact nations would follow with their own criticisms and, better yet, disclosures. The holy grail remained the Soviet files on Waldheim, but the Soviet press stayed mute on the case. The man-on-the-street in Moscow did not even know that there was a Waldheim controversy.

Fritz Molden, Waldheim's Austrian publisher and the man who, forty years earlier, had proposed Waldheim for service in the Austrian Foreign Ministry, unwittingly offered an explanation for the

Soviet silence. The former resistance leader and OSS liaison was asked by a reporter about the possibility that Waldheim might have been blackmailed by foreign intelligence services. Molden at first disparaged the notion, but then he conceded, "They say now in Austria that Russia might have blackmailed him. That might have been the case in 1972 when he was Secretary-General."[12]

Meanwhile, Waldheim received an important boost from West German Chancellor Helmut Kohl. Kohl, the architect of President Reagan's controversial 1985 visit to the Bitburg military cemetery, publicly praised his "old friend" Waldheim as "a great patriot." Referring to Waldheim's critics, Kohl commented, "I sense an arrogance of the late-born, which I find hard to bear." The conservative West German chancellor added: "May I say quite openly that I would know how to vote if I did have to vote in Austria."[13]

Waldheim and most of the Austrian press rejoiced in Kohl's words, and I pointed out the irony to Singer and Steinberg. Waldheim, his campaign team, and Austrian editorial writers were denouncing the WJC on a nearly daily basis for "interfering in Austria's domestic politics," yet Kohl's statement was a far more overt intervention than anything we had said or done.

In Los Angeles, Rabbi Marvin Hier of the Simon Wiesenthal Center condemned Kohl's comments as "sinister and politically motivated."[14]

This same day, the *New York Times* carried James Markham's report from Vienna that "an ugly tone of anti-Semitism has crept into the campaign." He quoted Waldheim as declaring again that his woes were the work of "some interest groups in New York."[15]

Former OSI Director Allan A. Ryan, Jr., was avidly following the unfolding drama from Cambridge, Massachusetts, where he now held a position at Harvard University. He found an intriguing pattern in Waldheim's responses to the burgeoning allegations. That pattern, he declared in a *Washington Post* op-ed piece, was "startlingly similar" to one seen in the defenses put forward by Nazi criminals prosecuted by the Justice Department. He offered a useful categorization:

- *The flat and false denial,* such as Waldheim's statement to *Kronenzeitung,* "I was never a member of a Nazi organization."
- *The wrong place/wrong time disclaimer,* seen in Waldheim's attempts to distance himself from the Kozara campaign.
- *The claim that appearance is not reality,* such as Waldheim's assertion that the King Zvonimir Medal was doled out "like chocolates."
- *Preposterous naiveté,* as in Waldheim's contention that he had been unaware of Jewish deportations.

- *Taking the offensive,* as in Waldheim's tactic of accusing his accusers of conducting a "slander" campaign.

"What are we to make," Ryan asked, "of a defense that matches, in several important respects, a pattern developed in dozens of cases of men who have been proven in U.S. courts to have been Nazi war criminals?"[16]

In Vienna, *Profil* magazine still suffered from something of a split personality. On the one hand, the Austrian weekly sought to claim leadership of the campaign to expose the truth about Waldheim. On the other, it wished to demonstrate to its readership that it shared the collective distaste for "interference from abroad." In its April 28 issue, *Profil* carried this strange dance one awkward step further by finding a Jew who was willing to condemn the WJC. The magazine printed a German translation of a column by Chaim Bermant, originally published in London's *Jewish Chronicle.*

Bermant condemned the WJC for making "such a big noise" about Waldheim, which, he said, was unjustified and counterproductive. Bermant capped his charges against us by observing that Simon Wiesenthal, "who can recognize a Nazi when he sees one," had ascertained "that the available documents do not justify" the WJC's conduct.

Profil's editors did not seem to realize the irony in all of this: Bermant's criticisms might just as easily have been aimed at them, rather than us.

Adding to the irony, *Profil,* in this same issue, advanced the investigation that Bermant condemned, by publishing a facsimile of a single-page summary of Waldheim's wartime record, prepared by French military authorities in charge of the Wehrmacht Information Office in the French occupation sector of West Berlin. The "WASt" summary noted Waldheim's midwar service in the High Command of Army Group E. It thus clashed directly and dramatically with Waldheim's "I spent the war after 1941 studying law in Vienna" story. The date on the document was March 21, 1979, and it seemed to solve at least part of one old mystery. In Vienna, Karl Schuller had shown John Tagliabue and me some of the underlying WASt unit files, and the handwritten notations on them disclosed that Waldheim's records had been examined on at least three occasions, the last check occurring on March 20, 1979. The French summary was typed the very next day. We still did not know who had made the two previous checks, but, as *Profil* reported, it appeared that French authorities had conducted the third examination.[17]

Profil reporter Hubertus Czernin confided to me via transatlantic phone, "I am still unable to figure out two things: Why the French checked, and precisely who requested that it be done."

I wondered whether France, too, now had to be added to the list of suspected Waldheim blackmailers. For if France had discerned the longstanding Waldheim cover-up in 1979, the government of then–President Valery Giscard d'Estaing had certainly never disclosed the information. Indeed, the French government had supported—or at least had not attempted to block—Waldheim's unsuccessful bid for a third term as Secretary General two years later.

When I asked Czernin about the reference in the Bermant piece to Simon Wiesenthal's defense of Waldheim, the reporter opined that Wiesenthal was "behaving in a way he never has in his entire career." Czernin attributed this to the lingering acrimony from Wiesenthal's decade-old dispute with former Chancellor and Socialist Party leader Bruno Kreisky. Czernin joked that if Waldheim was the Socialist candidate, Wiesenthal would "of course" be leading the campaign to expose him.

21

Three days prior to the Sunday election, the *Neue Vorarlberger Tageszeitung* newspaper of Bregenz, Austria, published a story under the headline JUDENRAT WANTS SIPPENHAFTUNG!

"Judenrat" ("Jewish Council") was the title given by the Nazis to the leadership councils they approved to represent the doomed Jewish communities of occupied Europe; it eventually had become an epithet even worse than "Uncle Tom." *"Sippenhaftung"* was a Nazi expression for the infamous practice of holding an entire family or race accountable for the alleged misdeeds of one of its members.[1] In this obscene parody of the two Nazi terms, Waldheim's Jewish critics were the *"Judenrat,"* and they were attempting to hold the entire Austrian "family" guilty for the actions of a few during the Nazi era.

Die Presse joined the perverse word game the following day, labeling Waldheim's critics as *Ewiggestrige,* people "stuck in the past." It was a term ordinarily used in Austria to describe unreformed Nazis! The Vienna daily also accused the WJC of generating anti-Semitism in order to denounce it.[2]

During his final campaign rally this same day in St. Stephan's Square in central Vienna, surrounded by balloons, banners, and an array of flowers, Waldheim elicited cheers with a stock speech referring to fathers and respectable soldiers. As his wife, Sissy, sat rock-still on the platform, Waldheim reached an angry crescendo. "Young people will not allow their fathers and grandfathers to be dragged in the dirt!"

Supporters in the crowd brandished placards that screamed: "No to Singer!" and "No to Bronfman!" There were a few anti-Waldheim posters in evidence, but the Austrian police moved in swiftly and ripped them up.

A reporter, interviewing people in the crowd, found no one who believed the charges against Waldheim. In truth, there was little reason for them to believe the accusations. They had been assured by the Austrian media that the charges against Waldheim emanated from Socialists and foreign Jews. And the evidence had been rejected by President Kirchschlaeger, by Simon Wiesenthal, and, as far as the average Austrian knew, even by U.N. Secretary-General Javier Perez de Cuellar.

People's Party Chairman Alois Mock continued to stoke the fires of hatred by singling out officials of the WJC as "vengeful slanderers."[3] The candidate outdid him this time, however. During an interview granted to the Paris newspaper *Le Monde,* Waldheim remarked, "You know, this campaign was led only by the World Jewish Congress." Then, asked to explain why so large a portion of the international press seemed to be critical of him, Waldheim responded, "But it is dominated by the World Jewish Congress, that is well known!"[4]

One poll showed Waldheim with a seven-percentage-point lead over Socialist Party candidate Kurt Steyrer, his closest rival.

In these last days before the election, Simon Wiesenthal dashed the hopes he had raised by the statement Martin Mendelsohn had read in his behalf to the congressional subcommittee. I learned that he was bombarding OSI Director Neal Sher with phone calls, insisting that there was nothing to the Waldheim allegations and warning Sher that he "could get burned" by pursuing the matter.

The calls served only to shock and anger Sher, and to pique his curiosity. He too was puzzled by Wiesenthal's mysterious behavior.

A depressed Schuller reported to me by phone that he now believed that there was only a slim chance that Waldheim would fail to receive the majority of votes necessary to avoid a runoff election. "No one knows what will happen," he told me. "But you can't blame the poor people here, really. They don't know. They only see what our media reports. It is, for me, almost unbearable to live in this country now. It's like the Iron Curtain. . . . I never made the comparison before, but now I start."

On Sunday, May 4, Austrians went to the polls and gave the world a mild surprise. Waldheim finished first, but he narrowly failed to win the necessary majority. He garnered a total of 2.34 million votes, or 49.64 percent. Steyrer was a solid but distant second. Frieda Meissner-Blau, the standard-bearer of an ecology-oriented ticket, drew 5.5 percent of the vote. A two-man runoff was scheduled for June 8, five weeks hence, pitting Waldheim against Steyrer. It was bittersweet news, for Waldheim's victory in the runoff was virtually assured; Steyrer would probably get most of Meissner-Blau's votes, but Waldheim would almost certainly have little difficulty gathering the few additional votes needed to put him over the top. It seemed that the only thing we had accomplished, politically, was to prolong the battle.

Waldheim's supporters geared up immediately for the runoff campaign. They took to the streets, handing out thousands of plastic trinkets embossed with a message intended to call attention to the forthcoming runoff election. On one side, it read "Dr. Kurt Waldheim." The text on the reverse was as short as it was ironic: "Do Not Forget!"

As the election campaign started anew, we received disturbing reports that Yehuda Blum, the former Israeli representative to the U.N., who had told the *New York Times* in 1981 that "we don't believe Waldheim ever supported the Nazis," was privately criticizing our efforts to expose Waldheim's deception. Meanwhile, Waldheim was trumpeting the friendly relations he had enjoyed with Blum when they were at the U.N. together, pointing out that they had socialized in each other's homes.*

Coincidentally, we received in early May an unsolicited affidavit from a Holocaust survivor, a Polish Jew living in Des Moines, Iowa, who was furious that it had taken the world so long to discover Waldheim's hidden past. The letter described a November 24, 1980, speech by then-Ambassador Blum to a Jewish group in Des Moines in connection with a United Jewish Appeal charity fundraising campaign. During the speech, Blum commented that it was a "pleasure" to work with Waldheim at the U.N. The survivor wrote that, on hearing this, he had jumped to his feet and shouted that Waldheim "was a Nazi German." Now that Waldheim's Nazi-era activities were being publicly exposed, the survivor was angrier than ever at Blum.

Why, I wondered, had Blum, the representative of a country that Waldheim had so deeply offended time after time during his U.N. tenure, gone out of his way again to "exonerate" Waldheim? Was it just another example of the hypocritical civility that cloaks the daily back-stabbing at the U.N.? Were the Israelis simply trying to get in Waldheim's good graces? Had the famed Mossad really known nothing? Or had the Israelis, perhaps, blackmailed Waldheim? These questions tied in with a widely circulated rumor that one or more of the handwritten notations on the WASt records—the ones indicating that someone had quietly checked the Waldheim files in Berlin in 1972 and again in 1979—reflected Israeli inquiries. It was a dis-

---

*Waldheim repeated the claim that "we still saw each other privately in our homes," later in an interview with an Israeli newspaper. See Ilona Henry, "Calling Me a Nazi Is Grotesque," *Jerusalem Post*, July 11, 1986, p. 1.

concerting possibility; for whoever checked those records almost certainly had discovered that the documents revealed Waldheim's great secret, and yet the mysterious researcher had chosen to maintain a public silence. The Israeli delegation at the U.N. had repeatedly defended Waldheim against the "Nazi" rumors. Would the Israelis have done so if they had inspected the Wehrmacht records and seen the Army Group E references? What possible reason could Jerusalem have had for failing to expose Waldheim years ago?

On reflection, I could only discount the rumor. I remembered the shocked reaction of the Israeli Embassy official who came to review my then comparatively small collection of evidence, shortly after the Waldheim story had broken. I also recalled vividly the televised image of Benjamin Netanyahu's near-ghostly complexion after he reviewed the UNWCC file. Still, one could not completely eliminate the possibility, however uncomfortable it was to contemplate, that the Israelis had owned a piece of Kurt Waldheim.

Ever since the Waldheim scandal was first exposed, Singer, Steinberg, and I found ourselves in greater demand than ever on the lecture circuit, especially for Jewish audiences. During the question-and-answer period that normally followed my presentation, there was one question that never went unasked: If all of this information was "out there," how had Waldheim managed to suppress it for four decades, especially during his ten years as U.N. Secretary-General?

I had to confess that the complete answer was still elusive, but I tried to draw a thumbnail sketch of how Yugoslavia, almost certainly the Soviet Union, and perhaps even the U.S. and/or France had "the goods" on Waldheim but found it in their interests to remain silent.

Frequently, someone would ask a follow-up question: Why had the Israelis not exposed Waldheim?

I explained my assumption that, for all its legendary prowess, Israeli intelligence operated with extremely limited financial and human resources and had to apply those resources almost exclusively to the life-and-death mission of countering the Arab military and terrorist threat. Thus, I hypothesized, the personal background of a U.N. Secretary-General was probably a low-priority issue for Jerusalem. Perhaps the Israelis assumed that the U.S. had run all the necessary checks on Waldheim.

Such was my public response. Privately, I wanted better answers. The first question of our investigation remained: *What did Waldheim do during the war?* But the second question—*Who knew?*—was in some ways more provocative, because it led directly to the most sensitive question of all: *Who helped Waldheim pull off this nearly incredible cover-up?*

*   *   *

A few days after the inconclusive election, Israel Singer received an airmail letter from Silvana Konieczny-Origlia, an anti-Nazi activist living in Vienna. She began by noting that as a longtime "cooperator" with Simon Wiesenthal, she had always admired his work. She was, in fact, a member of his staff. But, the letter continued, his "attitudes" in the matter of the Kurt Waldheim affair, both currently and "years before," had caused her to become completely disenchanted with Wiesenthal.

Konieczny-Origlia's letter went on to disclose that she had decided against continuing to work with the Nazi-hunter, whose conduct in the Waldheim matter was, in her view, "terribly dishonest." She closed by urging the WJC to carry on in the "incorruptible style" it had demonstrated thus far in the Waldheim affair.[5]

The letter buoyed our spirits. It was comforting to know that we still had a few friends in Austria. The writer's reference to Wiesenthal's disappointing "attitudes" in the Waldheim matter "now and years before" fascinated me. What did she mean?

But there was no time to pursue such collateral issues now. Keep your eye on the ball, I reminded myself. There is much still to be done in the investigation of Waldheim's war.

The truth of that quiet reminder was soon driven home, when I received a tip from a reporter who had learned that James Doughty, who appeared to have been the lone survivor of the commando unit captured on the island of Calino and interrogated, according to one of the captured documents, "by Army Group E" on July 17, 1944, had used his G.I. educational benefits to attend Harvard University. Over the phone, a clerk at Harvard's Alumni Affairs Office confirmed to me that a James Appleton Doughty, born on March 26, 1918, was a Harvard graduate. What's more, the clerk supplied what she believed was a current address! "It's sort of an unusual one," she said, "but here it is: 'care of E.S. Merrill, Orange Springs, Florida.' "

A directory assistance operator in Florida gave me a number for E.S. Merrill in Orange Springs, near Ocala. I dialed and waited impatiently. A woman answered.

"I'm trying to reach a Mr. James Doughty—" I began.

"One minute," she interrupted. As I waited, I could barely contain my exhilaration.

Moments later, a man's voice came on the line. "Hello?" he said tentatively.

"Mr. Doughty?"

"No, this is Ernest Merrill."

I identified myself and told Merrill why I was trying to track down Doughty.

Merrill wanted to help. He explained that he and Doughty had been friends since their days as Harvard classmates. He described Doughty as exceptionally bright and articulate, a graduate of both Exeter and Harvard. Doughty had been a "big, strapping fellow" when he was captured, but weighed only eighty pounds by the time he was freed from a German *Stalag* at the end of the war. Eventually he had recovered his vigor. And even today, Merrill said, his friend had a superb memory.

Merrill rambled on, and it was all I could do to control myself and allow him to finish. Where *is* he? I wanted to scream. But I let Merrill take his time.

According to Merrill, I was the fifth person to call for Doughty. A Reuters reporter had been first. Merrill said he would give me the same explanation he had given the others. Doughty's profession was teaching, but his avocation was sailing, and now that he was retired, he and his wife spent their time roaming the world on a blue, thirty-five-foot homemade steel sloop, the *Bon Chance*. "It's kind of a gypsy life they lead," Merrill added.

In a way, I realized, this could make Doughty an even better witness, as it was theoretically possible that he knew nothing at all about the Waldheim controversy. He might therefore be "uncontaminated" by the media accounts (and photographs) that had already appeared.

Merrill said that the Doughtys returned to the U.S. for a few brief periods every year, and he guessed that they "might come back to Florida this month or next, but it's really impossible to say."

I asked where they were now.

"Probably around the Abacos Islands. Somewhere in the Bahamas, anyway." Merrill said that Doughty had an AM radio on board, but rarely listened to it. And the sloop had no ship-to-shore phone or two-way radio communications system.

I could hardly have imagined the predicament in which we now found ourselves: We had a witness of potentially critical importance who was cruising around somewhere in the western Atlantic, and we had no way to reach him! I asked Merrill if we might be able to locate Doughty by telephoning the marinas in the Abacos Islands.

"They rarely moor at marinas," Merrill replied. "It costs too much money. They just sail around for months at a time." As my frustration mounted, Merrill offered a suggestion. He remembered that Doughty sometimes phoned his attorney, who practiced in Titusville, near Cape Canaveral. "His name is L.A. Vance."

I called Vance at once. After listening to my tale, the lawyer said that he would be happy to help us track Doughty. He could think of three possible strategies. One, we could wait until he phoned in, but there was "no way of knowing" when that would be. Two, we could attempt to enlist the Bahamas Air/Sea Rescue Service in a search for the *Bon Chance*. Third, we could put a message on "Charlie's Locker," an early morning AM radio show broadcast out of Fort Lauderdale; the show aired free messages intended to reach yachtsmen at sea.

Vance offered to handle the radio station angle. I spoke with the *New York Times;* the newspaper began to make preparations to hire a pilot in the Bahamas to conduct an air search for the *Bon Chance*.

On May 8, Stephen Katich called me from Washington to report that the U.S. ambassador to Yugoslavia, John Scanlan, would be in town at the end of the month. Katich promised to try to arrange a meeting for us.

Katich wanted to come to New York to see for himself what I had in my files. The information, he said, would help him in persuading Scanlan to meet with me. I suggested that he visit on Saturday, in two days time, when I was scheduled to brief David Newell, a talented senior correspondent with *Newsweek*, as well as Cathy Valyi, a writer with a public relations firm that Bronfman had engaged to help me prepare a written summary of what we now knew about Waldheim.

While I was going off in ten different directions at once, Waldheim sat down for an interview with Steven Nemerovsky of the American Press Service/London Times Syndicate. Nemerovsky quickly honed in on a sensitive subject, the postwar treaty negotiations between Austria and Yugoslavia. In his own country, this was perhaps the subject that Waldheim had to handle most delicately. Nemerovsky asked directly, "Can you prove you were not being blackmailed?"

With a laugh, Waldheim replied, "This is the new version of the Jewish Congress." He laughed again and added, "This is an unacceptable allegation. . . . Thank you very much." To the reporter's surprise, Waldheim rose to his feet and announced, "I have given those answers repeatedly. I was not blackmailed—never in my life— and by nobody—by no member state, by nobody." Beginning to walk away now, Waldheim said, "And the rest of the interview, if you like, you can give it to me, but this is not the interview I had in mind."

Nemerovsky halted Waldheim's walkout by changing topics, asking, "What would you like to talk about? Do you think you have been misrepresented outside?"

"By the Jewish Congress," Waldheim replied. "Only by the Jewish Congress . . . this whole story was started by the World Jewish Congress . . . of course, the Congress has great influence on the media."[6]

In Vienna, Nemerovsky also managed to get Simon Wiesenthal to sit for an interview. The reporter had learned of the telephone conversation in which Singer unsuccessfully implored the Nazi-hunter to examine the WJC's documents. Nemerovsky asked Wiesenthal why he had refused the WJC's invitation. "Never," Wiesenthal replied angrily, had the World Jewish Congress offered him the opportunity to inspect its evidence. "*Never,*" he repeated for emphasis. "And when they say it, this is a *lie.*" In fact, the WJC had never even contacted him, Wiesenthal insisted. (The denials astounded me when I learned of them later, for I had sat in on Wiesenthal's telephone conversation with Singer.)

Wiesenthal's use of the word "lie" prompted another question from Nemerovsky. The reporter had brought with him Wiesenthal's letter to *Newsweek,* published in its April 7 issue, in which the Nazi-hunter reproached the magazine for writing that he had called Waldheim a liar. "I said that I don't believe that he knew nothing about the deportations of the Jews during the time that he was in Greece, but I did not intend to accuse him of lying," Wiesenthal had written.

The distinction that Wiesenthal was attempting to draw was as unintelligible to Nemerovsky as it was to everyone to whom I had shown the letter. If anything, the Nazi-hunter's answers to the reporter's questions made the purported distinction even more elusive. "Did Kurt Waldheim know at the time it was not a true statement that he was making?" Nemerovsky asked. "I am sure that he knows," Wiesenthal conceded. "To me that's a lie," the reporter replied. "To *you!*" Wiesenthal shot back. "To me, *not.*" The reporter tried in vain to get Wiesenthal to explain what the difference was. "I tried getting at it from several different angles," Nemerovsky later told me, "but he never answered." As Nemerovsky pressed the point, Wiesenthal's face turned crimson with rage. "I'd never seen anyone turn red like that," the reporter recalled. "I was afraid he was going to have a heart attack." Moments later, "he exploded, yelled that the interview was over, and got up." Nemerovsky's session with Wiesenthal had been terminated.

Friday, May 9, was my thirty-first birthday, and I vowed to take it easy. I treated myself to some extra sleep. By the time I strolled into the office, the place was in an uproar. Steinberg had just learned that, after failing to get his own government to pressure Bronfman and the WJC, Israel's ambassador to Austria, Michael Elizur, had made the same appeal to Rabbi Arthur Hertzberg of Dartmouth College, a scholar with longstanding ties to our organization. Elizur argued that the WJC's efforts were directed at a man whose war record could be matched by many other Austrians, and that we therefore were needlessly jeopardizing Austrian-Israeli relations. Singer, who was in Canada on WJC business, got the news over the phone from Steinberg, and immediately dictated the text of an angry cable to the Israeli Foreign Ministry in Jerusalem, threatening to expose the ambassador's behind-the-scenes attempts at interference, if they did not stop him.

On Saturday morning, a man barged his way through the front door of our office building and headed for the elevator without bothering to identify himself. When a security guard challenged him, he cursed the wary sentinel in three or four different languages and demanded access to Rosenbaum. The guard called me, and by the time I arrived in the lobby, the two men had almost come to blows.

Although the football jersey Stephen Katich was wearing struck me as out of place on a man of his age, it revealed a physique that appeared surprisingly athletic for a senior citizen who walked with a cane. Nevertheless, by the time I straightened out the confusion and took him up to my office, Katich was red-faced and out of breath.

Soon, Newell and Valyi arrived for the joint briefing. All three of my listeners were amazed at the amount of information that had been compiled in such a short time.

Our session was interrupted by a phone call from Florida. The *Bon Chance*'s on-board generator had suddenly quit and former commando James Doughty had brought his boat in at Nassau for repairs. When he used the downtime to check in by phone with his lawyer, he was astonished to learn that he was the subject of a hunt by the WJC, Reuters, and the *New York Times* in connection with an investigation regarding the former Secretary-General of the United Nations. As I suspected, Doughty and his wife were among the few Americans who were unaware of the Waldheim story.

Vance called me right away. The lawyer said that Doughty's first reaction had been to quip, "I guess my past is catching up with me." When Vance asked Doughty what he remembered of his interrogation forty-one years earlier, Doughty recalled that he had been taken to Salonika and was questioned "intensively" by several officers, one of whom he described as "a tall, lanky German." Vance asked if it could possibly have been Waldheim. Doughty thought it over and responded: perhaps, perhaps not. None of the Germans had given their names. He had not been mistreated by his interrogators, evidently out of deference to the fact that he had served solely as a medic. He had no firsthand knowledge of the fate that befell fellow commando Sergeant John Dryden, destined, according to one of the captured documents, to be "handed over to the SD in compliance with the Fuehrer Order."

Although we had hoped for more, this was probably the most we could realistically have expected. And one important point had been verified: Doughty confirmed that his interrogation had been conducted *at Salonika*.

I stayed awake for the next forty-five hours straight, working with Cathy Valyi to prepare the report that Bronfman had demanded "immediately." At the same time, I managed to steal a few minutes now and again to keep abreast of developments on the investigative front.

Willi Korte relayed some disappointing information. I had asked him to try to locate Waldheim's Wehrmacht personnel file, and he had enlisted the assistance of George Wagner at the National Archives, who now faced the task of picking up where the late John Mendelsohn had left off. Wagner knew that the U.S. government had microfilmed the files of German nationals before it returned the original documents to the Bonn government. But the files on Austrians had apparently been returned to Vienna *without* making microfilm copies—on the premise that Austria was a victim of the Nazis. Wagner said that in the decades he had been working with the Wehrmacht records at the Archives, he had "never seen" the personnel file of an Austrian officer. Wagner and Korte found that they were able to retrieve copies of the voluminous personnel files of some of Waldheim's German comrades, including Herbert Warnstorff, Helmut Poliza, Friedrich Stahl, and others, but there was not a trace of the personnel file on the Austrian *Oberleutnant* himself.

Just great, I muttered to myself. "We've got the file on Waldheim's immediate superior and we've got the file on his top deputy. There's just one file that can't be found—Waldheim's."

It appeared that our only source for the Waldheim personnel file was the government of Austria, which now seemed likely to be headed soon by Waldheim himself.

The news from Korte was followed by an equally dismaying report from Steinberg. He had just met with some officials of Yugoslavia's U.N. mission, who told him directly that their government would not be releasing its Waldheim files.

*   *   *

On completing the report ordered by Bronfman (and after catching up on lost sleep), I turned my attention to several hundred pages of captured Army Group E documents that I had copied during my research trip to the National Archives a month earlier but had not yet studied. I had made a special effort to copy all the intelligence reports I could find that had been authored and certified "copy correct" by *Oberleutnant* Waldheim.

Reviewing these documents was a tedious process, partly because my limited facility with German necessitated frequent resort to a dictionary—especially for the more complicated military expressions—and partly because I was hunting for so many different types of information.

One of the subjects I most wanted to pursue was the 1944 massacre on the road between the towns of Stip and Kocane that reportedly constituted part of the Yugoslav indictment of Waldheim.

The original March 26 report in the Belgrade newspaper *Vecernje Novosti* had contained only the barest of details:

> According to the testimony of the war criminal Egbert Hilker, Kurt Waldheim was responsible for the reprisal committed on the road between Kocane and Stip in late October 1944, when three villages were burned and 114 people killed.

The report left so many unanswered questions. What were the names of the three villages? Precisely when in October 1944 had the crimes occurred? Who was Egbert Hilker? What was the connection that made Waldheim "responsible?"

In his April 6 defense memo, Waldheim had vigorously denied any involvement in the atrocities. The killings took place "around October 20," he said, "according to army records." Waldheim claimed that he was nowhere near Stip and Kocane at that time. On October 13, he asserted, he had flown with other officers from Arsakli/Salonika to Army Group E's new headquarters in Mitrovica, Yugoslavia. This, said Waldheim, was confirmed by the pilot, one Captain Prem, and by his log book "and witnesses." In any event, "Captain Egberts [*sic*] . . . seems to have given [the] order for this event."

It was difficult enough to find an atlas that referenced the small Macedonian towns of Stip and Kocane; I could find none showing the tiny villages *between* the two towns. In desperation, I turned to the Cartographic Section of the Library of Congress. A researcher there was able to find a map of the Stip area, and he read into the

Kurt Waldheim, in an official portrait photographed during his tenure as U.N. Secretary-General.
Courtesy of United Nations

The SS photograph that destroyed Waldheim's forty-year deception: 1st Lieutenant Kurt Waldheim (second from left) at the airstrip in Podgorica, Montenegro (Yugoslavia), on May 22, 1943, with (from left) Italian General Escola Roncaglia, Wehrmacht Colonel Herbert Macholz and Waffen-SS *Obergruppenfuehrer* Artur Phleps, commander of the infamous "Prinz Eugen" Division of the Waffen-SS.
Courtesy of World Jewish Congress

A close-up view of *Oberleutnant* Waldheim at the May 22, 1943, meeting at the Podgorica airstrip. *Courtesy of World Jewish Congress*

Waldheim (top right) as depicted on the front page of the December 3, 1944, issue of the Wehrmacht newspaper *Wacht im Suedosten,* poring over military maps with General Alexander Loehr (center), who was hanged as a war criminal in 1947.

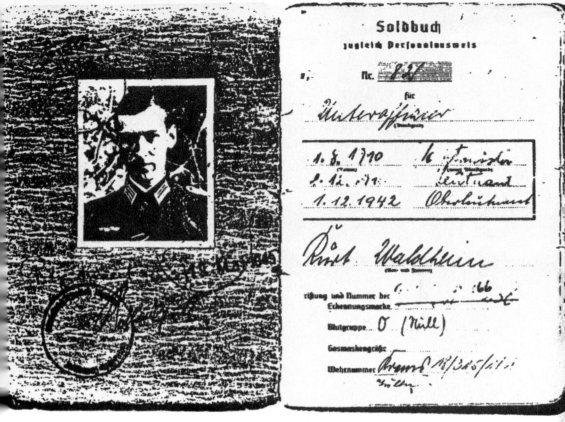

The cover and front page of 1st Lieutenant Kurt Waldheim's military pay book.

Combative campaign poster created in reponse to the revelations about Waldheim's Nazi-era past. It reads: WE AUSTRIANS WILL ELECT WHOM *WE* WANT! NOW MORE THAN EVER—WALDHEIM.
Courtesy of Profil/*Walter Wobrazek*

top left: Michael Graff, the controversial General Secretary of the Austrian People's Party.
Courtesy of Profil/*Walter Wobrazek*
top right: Renowned Vienna-based Nazi-hunter Simon Wiesenthal.
below: Paris-based Nazi-hunter Beate Klarsfeld, who braved detention by the Austrian police to stage public protests against Waldheim during the election campaign.
Courtesy of Shelly Shapiro

Juden-Musterung in Saloniki

Wie wir vor einigen Tage meldeten, mussten sich etwa 12.000 Juden am Kai von Saloniki melden, um registriert und einer natzbringenden Arbeit zugeführt zu werden   Aufn.: Kriegsberichter Dick

The Germans were anything but secretive about their persecution of the Jews of Salonika, Greece. This photo, shown as published in the July 26, 1942 issue of the German government–sponsored newspaper *Donauzeitung,* is headlined JEW-INSPECTION IN SALONIKA and bears the caption "As we reported a few days ago, some 12,000 Jews were ordered to report to the wharf in Salonika, in order to register so that they can be directed to useful work."

The Auschwitz concentration camp in Nazi-occupied Poland, final destination for most of the Jews deported from Greece. Nearly all were gassed immediately upon arrival, in the words of camp commandant Rudolf Hoess, "because of their poor quality." *Auschwitz State Museum, courtesy of U.S. Holocaust Memorial Museum*

above and below: Survivors of the Kozara "operation" being marched off to concentration camps. Nearly 70,000 people, including some 23,000 children, were killed or deported during this "cleansing" action.

German soldiers preparing to hang a captured Yugoslav partisan.

A Yugoslav village being burned to the ground by German soldiers.

Three of the young British servicemen murdered in 1944 after falling into the hands of Kurt Waldheim's Army Group E intelligence/counterintelligence branch: (above left) Sub-lieutenant Allan Lane Tuckey, Royal Naval Volunteer Reserve; (above right) Gunner Raymond Jones, Royal Artillery; (below right) Captain David Allen LaTouche "Bunny" Warren, Royal Northumberland Fusiliers and British Special Operations Executive in photograph held by his brother, Charles Warren, of Sydney, Australia.
Courtesy of News Limited of Australia

(Below left) Barbara Cruxton of Birmingham, England, and husband Sidney holding military mementos of her brother, Raymond Jones.
Courtesy of News Team International Ltd.

right: Edgar M. Bronfman, President of the World Jewish Congress (WJC).

below left: Elan Steinberg, Executive Director of the WJC.

below right: WJC Secretary General Israel Singer.

The "honor list" attached to the gory 1942 Wehrmacht report on the "final liquidation of the bandit [partisan] plague" in the Kozara region of western Bosnia. Major General Friedrich Stahl is first on the list. Lieutenant Kurt Waldheim is the twenty-fifth name.
Courtesy of U.S. National Archives

GENERALMAJOR STAHL
MAJOR i. G. GEHM
OBERSTARZT Dr. WEBER
MAJOR FUNKE
MAJOR HERBST
HAUPTMANN PLUME
HAUPTMANN KONOPATZKI
KRIEGSGERICHTSRAT Dr. MAIERHÖFER
KRIEGSVERWALTUNGSRAT PATZSCHKE
STABSZAHLMEISTER MEYER
OBERLEUTNANT URBACH
OBERLEUTNANT STRNAD
OBERLEUTNANT SAUER
OBERLEUTNANT Dr. WURIANEK
OBERLEUTNANT KITTEL
OBERLEUTNANT DEEPEN
OBERLEUTNANT KREUZPAINTNER
OBERZAHLMEISTER BLEIDISTEL
HEERESJUSTIZINSPEKTOR POLASEK
LEUTNANT HÄHNEL
LEUTNANT LIPPERT
LEUTNANT HEIL
LEUTNANT BUMB
LEUTNANT LOCKEMANN
LEUTNANT WALDHEIM
LEUTNANT BÖTTCHER
ASSISTENZARZT Dr. ENGELBERG
KRIEGSPFARRER BRAUN
SONDERFÜHRER (Z) MATERN

MINISTER TURINA
MAJOR i. G. BESTALL
RITTMEISTER GOVEDIĆ
OBERLEUTNANT RITTER ULLISPERGER v. DONAUTRAU
LEUTNANT z. See VESELINOVIĆ

The cover of the United Nations War Crimes Commission file on mass-murder suspect Kurt Waldheim.

7744/Y/G/557   1 9 FEB 1948

UNITED NATIONS WAR CRIMES COMMISSION

YUGOSLAV   CHARGES AGAINST   GERMAN   WAR CRIMINALS

0240 4/14   CASE No. R/N/684.*

Name of accused, his rank and unit, or official position. (Not to be translated.)

Kurt(?) WALDHEIM, Oberleutnant, Abwehroffizier with the Ic - Abteilung des Generalstabes der Heeresgruppe E from April 1944 until the capitulation of Germany.
(P.29572)

Date and place of commission of alleged crime.

From April 1944 - May 1945.
All parts of Yugoslavia.

Number and description of crime in war crimes list.

II. Putting Hostages to Death   I. Murder.

References to relevant provisions of national law.

Violation of Articles 23 b & c, 46 and 50, of the Hague Regulations, 1907, and Article 3, para. 3 of the Law concerning Crimes against the People and the State, 1945.

SHORT STATEMENT OF FACTS.

Oberleutnant WALDHEIM, the German Abwehroffizier with the Ic staff of the "Heeresgruppe E", headed by General LÖHR, is responsible for the retaliation actions carried out by the Wehrmacht units in Yugoslavia, inasmuch as the "Heeresgruppe E" was involved in directing the retaliation orders issued by the OKW. Thus the Ic staff of the "Heeresgruppe E" were the means for the massacre of numerous sections of the Serb population.

THE CENTRAL REGISTRY
OF WAR CRIMINALS
AND SECURITY SUSPECTS

FINAL
CONSOLIDATED WANTED LIST
PART 1
M - Z

GERMANS ONLY

NOTE: ALL PREVIOUS CROWCASS WANTED LISTS
SHOULD BE DESTROYED

JUNE 1948

The cover of the U.S. Army–prepared wanted list on which the name of murder suspect Kurt Waldheim appears.

F BROJ 25572

FEDERATIVNA NARODNA REPUBLIKA JUGOSLAVIJA
DRŽAVNA KOMISIJA
ZA UTVRDIVANJE ZLOČINA
OKUPATORA I NJIHOVIH POMAGAČA

O D L U K A
o utvrdivanju zločina okupatora i njihovih pomagača

ZLOČINAC:

Prezime i ime: ____W A L D H E I M (KURT?)____

Približna starost: _____

Narodnost: _____ Austrijanac _____

Jedinica, zvanični položaj i čin: Oberleutnant, Abwehroffizier na službi u Ic-Abteilung des Generalstabes der Heeresgruppe E, u aprilu 1944 do kapitulacije Nemačke.

Poslednje boravište: _____

Ostali lični podaci: sada u bekstvu _____

ZRTVE ZLOČINA (OŠTEĆENICI):
(sa ličnim podacima)

KRATAK OPIS I KVALIFIKACIJA ZLOČINA:

Ubistva i pokolji.= Streljanja taleca.= Namerno rušenje i puno= šenje imovine.= paležem naselja i sl.= (čl.3 tač. 3 jugoslovenskog Zakona o krivičnim delima protiv naroda i države u vezi sa odredbama čl.23 b), c), i g), 46 i 50 Haškog Reglmana od 1907 god., i sa od= redbama čl. II tač. 1 b) Zakona br. X Kontrolnog Saveta za Nemačku od 20.12.1945 god.)

The cover of the 1947 Yugoslav indictment of *Oberleutnant* Kurt Waldheim on charges of "Murders and exterminations—hostage executions—deliberate destruction of property by setting settlements on fire, etc."

Aktenzeichen des RJM.: 1 p —

1. Vor- und Zuname: (akademischer Grad)	Dr.Kurt Waldheim Dipl.cons.Akad.
2. Geburtstag und -ort:	21.12.1918.St.André-Wördern
3. Deutschblütige Abstammung: (wodurch nachgewiesen ?)	ja,durch Ahnenpaß
4. Glaubensbekenntnis:	röm.kath.
5. Beruf des Vaters:	Bezirksschulinspektor i.R.
6. Vermögensverhältnisse des Beamten:	kein Vermögen
7. Frühere Zugehörigkeit (mit genauer Zeitangabe) a) zu politischen Parteien:	./.
b) zu politischen Verbänden:	./.
c) zu Freimaurerlogen: (mit Angabe des Grades)	./.

d) zu politischen oder
    konfessionellen Beamten-
    vereinen:
	./.

8. Zugehörigkeit
  (mit genauer Zeitangabe)
  a) zur NSDAP.:
    (Mitgliedsnummer, Amt ?)
  b) zu einer Gliederung:
    (Dienstrang und Führerstelle ?)
	SA.Reiterstandarte 5/90 SA-Mann seit 18.11.1938
	NS.Studentenbund seit 1.4.1938

c) zu einem angeschlossenen
    Verband :
    (Amt ?)	

d) zum NS-Fliegerkorps, NS-
    Reichskriegerbund, Reichs-
    kolonialbund, Reichsluft-
    schutzbund, DDA., Alt-
    Herrenbund der Deutschen
    Studenten und sonstigen
    Verbänden, soweit die Zu-
    gehörigkeit zu den Personal-
    akten anzuzeigen ist:
    (Ämter ?)	

Vordruck Nr. 148. Personalbogen   Queen

Excerpt from a 1940 judicial service application showing
Waldheim as an "SA-man since November 18, 1938" and as a member of the Nazi
Student Union "since April 1, 1938."

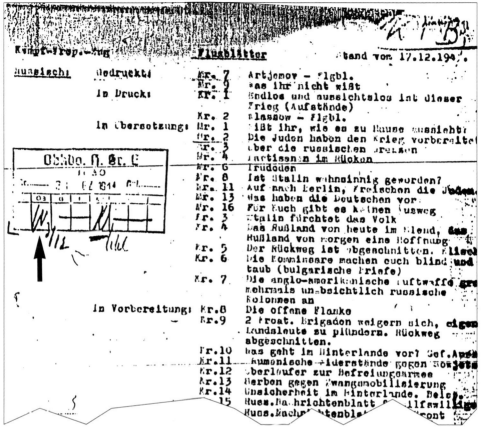

Kurt Waldheim's handwritten "W" in the box (note arrow, middle left), that was reserved for him as Army Group E's "O3" (third special missions staff officer). This is a list that accompanied a December 1944 package of propaganda leaflets designed to be dropped behind enemy lines in hopes of persuading Allied soldiers to desert to the German side. Among the draft leaflets reviewed by Waldheim prior to their translation into Russian were ones with such titles as THE JEWS PREPARED THIS WAR (sixth from top) and LET'S GO TO BERLIN, SHRIEK YOUR JEWS (eleventh from top). The former concludes with the exhortation, "enough of the Jewish war, kill the Jews, come over."
Courtesy of National Archives

SOME WHO FOLLOWED WALDHEIM'S LABYRINTHINE EVIDENTIARY TRAIL:

left: Reporter Hubertus Czernin of the Vienna weekly magazine *Profil*.
Courtesy of Profil/*Peter Lehner*

below left: Austrian historian Georg Tidl.
Courtesy of Profil/*Walter Wobrazek*

below right: Neal M. Sher, Director of the U.S. Justice Department's Nazi-hunting Office of Special Investigations (OSI).

above left: U.S. Justice Department senior historian Patrick J. Treanor.
Courtesy of Virginia C. Treanor
above right: The late Stephen Katich.
below: Researcher Willi Korte at left, with author.

The late Stephen Katich (far right) with U.N. Secretary-General Kurt Waldheim in New York, 1977.

Anton Kolendic, the former Yugoslav intelligence agent whose allegations caused an international furor in 1986.
Courtesy of Profil/*Hubertus Czernin*

phone the names of the villages on either side of the road between Stip and Kocane. In all, there were more than a dozen.

I turned next to Stephen Katich for help. He scanned the most readily available Yugoslav books on the history of the war, but could find no October 1944 references to Stip, Kocane, or any of the villages between them. Katich reminded me that there had been *thousands* of such crimes committed by German forces. "It would take a damn encyclopedia to tell the whole story," he complained. "I'm afraid that by the standards of what happened in my country during the war, the murder of a hundred people was not so newsworthy an event."

Ana Marija Bešker, a press counselor at the Yugoslav Embassy in Washington, checked some other volumes in the embassy's library, but she had no luck either.

The break we needed came when *Newsweek's* David Newell put his colleague Andrew Nagorski on the trail. Nagorski and another of the magazine's staffers traveled to Macedonia and were soon directed to the three villages: Krupiste, Gorni Balvan, and Dolnyi Balvan. Nagorski wrote a moving article for *Newsweek,* quoting the recollections of three of the survivors. Each of them recalled that the massacres occurred on October 14—not October 20, as Waldheim insisted.[7] Newell put me in touch with Nagorski, who assured me over the phone that the witnesses were "absolutely certain" of the date. One of them, who survived when dead bodies fell on top of him and shielded him from the Germans' bullets, had explained in tears, "For me, October fourteenth is my second birthday. It was the beginning of my second life."

Profil's Hubertus Czernin was on the trail as well. In an obscure postwar book on the history of the Wehrmacht's 22nd Infantry Division, he found references to a certain Karl-Heinz Egberts-Hilker, the commander of one of the division's armored reconnaissance units. He was clearly the "Egbert [*sic*] Hilker" quoted in the Yugoslav file, for he had been executed in Yugoslavia in December 1947, for his role in the massacres between Stip and Kocane.

The book disclosed that all males in the villages between the ages of sixteen and fifty had been ordered killed in "reprisal" for the destruction of a bridge by the Yugoslav resistance. Czernin also learned that, pleading for his life to be spared, the Wehrmacht officer apparently pointed out to a Yugoslav court that he had confessed to full responsibility for the killings and had not sought to shift blame onto anyone else. This seemed to contradict the Yugoslav claim that Egberts-Hilker had implicated Waldheim in these killings, and it lent further support to the suspicion that the *Odluka* was a less than completely honest indictment.

Profil managed to track down Josef Prem, the pilot whom Waldheim said had flown him from Arsakli to Mitrovica around the time
in question. Prem told the magazine that it was quite possible that
Waldheim was among those he had carried that day; but he refuted
Waldheim's claim of documentation, saying that he no longer had
his flight logs, and adding that it was impossible to remember who
his passengers had been.

Nevertheless, Czernin observed that if Waldheim really had flown
to Mitrovica, "rather than travel by train or car," then "he could not
have ordered the massacre between Stip and Kocane," as he would
have remained at all times at a considerable distance from the towns.[8]

Czernin's analysis infuriated me. The Yugoslavs had not, so far as
we knew, accused Waldheim of ordering the killings, but rather of
being "responsible" for them. And there were any number of ways
for an officer, operating from a great distance, to participate in the
process of recommending, authorizing, or otherwise facilitating such
a "reprisal" action—particularly in a war in which radio and telegraphic equipment played such an important role.

At least we now had the correct date for the massacres, and the
names of the villages. I began to search through my bulging folders
of National Archives printouts, looking for pertinent references.

I was alone in the office one evening around eight o'clock when
I was finally able to begin to put the chronology together. The coffee
had run out hours earlier. I thought about quitting for the day and
heading for the subway. Suddenly, I came across a reference that
stopped me cold. Before me lay a faded copy of Waldheim's *Mor-
genmeldung* ("morning report") of October 12, 1944, just two days
before the killings. Stamped *Geheim* ("Secret"), it bore Waldheim's
distinctive signature. In it, the "O3" officer summarized for General
Loehr, Lieutenant Colonel Warnstorff, Major Hammer, and several
other listed officers the most important new developments in the
Balkan theater of operations. Waldheim's single-page report was divided into three underlined geographical headings: Eastern front,
Greece, and Macedonia. In each category, the developments were
listed in descending order of importance, as was standard practice.
The first words of Waldheim's intelligence update on Macedonia
were unforgettable:

> *Macedonia:* Additional bandit forces (probably IIe. V. Prilep
> Brigade) approaching the Stip-Kocane road.[9]

When he wrote these words, I told myself, Waldheim surely was
already on notice that, if he identified an area of partisan activity,
atrocities were a potential consequence; he had already seen such

crimes ensue on at least one other occasion. *It's just like what happened in Karpenission, on Crete,* I said to myself. Sure enough, less than forty-eight hours after Waldheim pinpointed the road between Stip and Kocane as the site of the most important buildup of partisan strength in Macedonia, Wehrmacht forces moved in, set fire to three villages, and murdered 114 of their inhabitants.

There was more. The report bore the "received" stamp of Army Group E's Operations ("Ia") Branch—and Waldheim had already admitted that this was the very unit that made "the operational decisions" based on his own reports. Furthermore, if Johann Mayer's testimony, quoted in the UNWCC files, was reliable, it had been one of Waldheim's responsibilities "to bring up suggestions concerning reprisal actions" for the approval of his superiors. Finally, it dovetailed with Franz von Harling's testimony at Nuremberg that reprisals were an "Ia responsibility" in the Balkans.

Continuing to dig through my microfilm printouts, I soon came upon a *second* October 12 report, issued near day's end, in which Waldheim again warned of the threat posed by Yugoslav resistance forces on the road between Stip and Kocane.

As I thought about the grisly pattern, the October date gnawed at me. I was almost sure that I had encountered something else concerning October 1944, but I could not bring it to mind. What was it? I asked myself repeatedly.

Suddenly, I remembered: The original "disparity document"— that was it! I jumped up from my desk and threw open the middle drawer of my main file cabinet. Racing through the folders, I found the old *Wochenpresse* story from early March, which had reproduced a portion of Waldheim's summary of operations *for October 1944.* The report listed 739 "bandit" dead and ninety-four taken prisoner, but only sixty-three weapons captured. Clearly, the 114 civilians murdered on the road between Stip and Kocane were part of Waldheim's "tally." He knew exactly what was going on!

Although, as in the Iraklion episode, actual proof of a go-ahead to the killers in the field was nowhere to be found, a strong argument could be made that what Waldheim had done, at a minimum, was to recklessly endanger scores of innocent civilians by reporting information to his superiors that he had every reason to know might result in atrocities of the kind that soon ensued.

After we released the Stip-Kocane documents to the press, the *New York Times* sought out Bob Herzstein's comment on the new evidence. Reached at the University of South Carolina, Herzstein observed that although Waldheim had neither ordered nor carried out the killings, the documents suggested that he "supplied the information on which massacres were based."

Waldheim's denial came later that day. "It's just another effort of the Jewish Congress to vilify me," he told reporters who found him on a campaign stop. "I haven't even seen a partisan, as I said repeatedly." The information passed on in his reports, Waldheim explained, "came in from the subordinated units—divisions, regiments, for instance." What others might have done with the information that he relayed was not his responsibility.[10]

What seemed like an interminable quest for Waldheim's UNWCC file finally came to an end when a contact in New England obtained a photocopy of the file from his own Israeli sources and sent it to me by courier. The surreptitious release of the file by the Israelis indicated that the present government in Jerusalem had no desire to protect the former U.N. Secretary-General. I was sure that Jerusalem, by now, regretted the interference that its U.N. mission had run for Waldheim years earlier.

Although we already knew its contents, Singer, Steinberg, and I stared at the remarkable cover sheet: UNITED NATIONS WAR CRIMES COMMISSION: Yugoslav Charges Against German War Criminals.

To the right of the preprinted words "Name of the Accused" was the typewritten entry: Kurt (?) WALDHEIM. The specification of crimes consisted of two entries: "Murder" and "Putting Hostages to Death." The cover sheet concluded with a "Short Statement of Facts" regarding the man who, decades later, would win election as U.N. Secretary General:

> Oberleutnant WALDHEIM, the German Abwehrofficier with Ic. staff of the "Heeresgruppe [Army Group] E," headed by General LOEHR, is responsible for the retaliation actions carried out by the Wehrmacht units in Yugoslavia, inasmuch as the "Heeresgruppe E" was involved in directing the retaliation orders issued by the OKW [Wehrmacht High Command]. Thus the Ic. staff of the "Heeresgruppe E" was the means for the massacre of numerous sections of the Serb population.

Some Hebrew lettering had been penned into the margins of the material. In order to avoid unnecessarily embarrassing the Israelis, I deleted the scribblings when I made copies.

In the interim between the first presidential election and the runoff, Simon Wiesenthal launched another media offensive against us. His attack was again embraced eagerly by the Austrian press, but received only limited attention elsewhere.

Should Waldheim win the presidency, the Nazi-hunter charged, observers would say it was "because of the Jews." On the other hand, if he lost, they would say "the Jews have killed off our candidate."[11]

Although Wiesenthal continued to complain that the WJC's accusations were made "without evidence,"[12] he admitted to one American journalist that he had not seen "all of the documents" that we had amassed.[13]

A few Jewish leaders were finally willing to admit publicly that they were baffled by Wiesenthal's behavior in the Waldheim affair, particularly his off-repeated condemnation of the WJC. Elie Wiesel, the Auschwitz survivor and Nobel Peace Prize winner who, a year earlier, had bravely confronted President Reagan on live national television over his decision to visit the German military cemetery at Bitburg, was among them. "How do you explain that? I am puzzled by it," Wiesel told one reporter. Sam Bloch, vice president of the American Gathering and Federation of Jewish Holocaust Survivors, told the same journalist that Wiesenthal's comments sounded "like an exoneration of Waldheim. I am dismayed."[14]

Meanwhile, the chasm between the U.S.-based Simon Wiesenthal Center and Wiesenthal himself continued to widen. On May 16, the Center issued a press release on the Waldheim controversy, expressing its "strong support for the recommendation made by Neal Sher, Director of the OSI, that Waldheim be barred from entry into the U.S. based on existing charges." The release added that the Center "applauds all those committed to the investigation, including the World Jewish Congress, whose initial release of the documents sparked this long-overdue inquiry."

22

Following leads I had provided during my Saturday briefing, David Newell and his *Newsweek* colleagues dug into the story of the British commandos captured on Alimnia Island. The result was a remarkable investigative report, published in the magazine's May 26 issue, concerning the men who had been turned over to the SD "for final special treatment" after Waldheim's Intelligence/Counterintelligence Branch in Salonika requested the authorization to do so, on the grounds that further interrogations were "fruitless."

The magazine had managed to locate the mother of Royal Navy Sub-Lieutenant Allen Lane Tuckey in the London suburb of St. Albans. Forty years after the young commando disappeared, Cicely Tuckey Clark broke down when *Newsweek*'s Debbie Seward appeared at her home to inquire about her son. Mrs. Clark showed the reporter a photograph taken of Allen Tuckey shortly before he went to war. *Newsweek* used it to illustrate its story. Seeing the handsome, doe-eyed young man, barely twenty-one years of age, served as a grim reminder that, amid all the intricate and often dreary paperwork, we were tracking the fate of real people, who had families and friends and dreams for the future. The last word Mrs. Tuckey had of her son came, she said, in a June 1944 letter from a British military officer informing her: "We have had indirect news to say that he is a P.O.W. He is very fit and well. We have heard nothing official, but this news is quite reliable." After the war, the Tuckey family waited with ever-decreasing anticipation for their son's return. Confidence steadily dissolved, replaced by a growing sense of dread, until at last a horrible realization struck: Allen would never be coming home. Forty-one years later, they still did not know the circumstances of his presumed death. For years, *Newsweek* learned, Allen's brother Henry and his stepfather, Albert Clark, had pressed the British government to determine precisely what had happened to the Alimnia prisoners, to no avail.

The magazine also interviewed Herbert Warnstorff, Waldheim's immediate superior in Army Group E, at his home in West Germany.

Warnstorff recalled that Waldheim always "did what he was supposed to do—very correct work." I was fascinated by his disclosure that Waldheim took occasional trips into the field with Army Group E's commanding officer, General Loehr himself.[1]

On May 28, I made another brief trip to Washington, where Stephen Katich kept his promise to introduce me to Ambassador John Scanlan. The career diplomat met us outside the main State Department building, on C Street Northwest, opposite the old wartime headquarters of the OSS. Scanlan was friendly and sympathetic, but he was pessimistic about the odds of persuading the Yugoslav authorities to make public Belgrade's indictment and underlying evidence against Waldheim. He spoke candidly of the embarrassment that the affair was causing the authorities there. Still, he promised to try.

Katich was not satisfied with the conversation. Shortly after my return to New York, he called to announce that he had decided to journey to Yugoslavia to see if he could get the *Odluka* himself. I was surprised, but pleased that someone with Katich's determination was going to try where others had failed.

We worked out a simple telephone code, so that he could report on his progress without arousing suspicions. I knew that he had friends and family whom he wished to visit in Yugoslavia, but I suggested that if he did manage to obtain any new material, he should bring it back immediately. "Catch the first flight to the States," I advised, and "I'll get you another ticket to go back later to visit." I added, more as an expression of friendship than of real concern, "Be careful."

We were on the paper trail of a number of important episodes in Waldheim's wartime years, and the picture was becoming incrementally clearer with each new discovery. At the National Archives, Willi Korte was searching for additional details concerning the response of the German General Staff in Athens to directives concerning the partisans. We had already seen how, on August 8, 1943, Waldheim noted in the Athens headquarters war diary that the 1st Mountain Division was being apprised of Hitler's new order that captured partisans be killed and suspects be deported en masse to Germany for slave labor. Exactly one week later, the 1st Mountain Division requested authority to deport "all male civilians" from the area of Arta in northern Greece. (In the same message, it warned the General Staff about the "resistance movement" threat posed by the Jewish leadership of Ioannina.) Waldheim had passed on this criminal request to his Athens commander, General Heinz von Gyldenfeldt. Korte's task was to find out what happened next.

Korte found messages dated August 25 and 29, 1943, that indicated growing tension between German and Italian forces. The original request to deport "all male civilians" was amended to include only men aged eighteen to fifty. But the commander of the Italian 11th Army, General Vecchiarelli, objected even to this less extensive plan, and told his troops not to obey the criminal order. (This was consistent with what we knew of the prevalent Italian attitude toward German excesses, and it contradicted the Nuremberg testimony of Major Hammer, who tried to blame the Italian 11th Army for German atrocities.)

Most importantly, Korte found von Gyldenfeldt's signed but undated response to the 1st Mountain Division request that had been passed on by Waldheim. The response revealed that the Germans had no intention of letting the Italians stand in their way. Von Gyldenfeldt noted tersely that such matters were "clarified" by General Loehr's "recent order."[2] The reference was to the directive we had already seen in which Loehr had declared that "it may be necessary to seize the entire male population, insofar as it does not have to be shot or hanged . . . for further transport into the Reich."

Korte searched for a key that might link Waldheim even more directly to the Arta/Ioannina episode. We could already prove that the criminal request was received and signed "copy certified correct" by Waldheim; we could prove that it was passed on by Waldheim to von Gyldenfeldt, who wholeheartedly approved it; but Korte could find no record of who had transmitted von Gyldenfeldt's response to the 1st Mountain Division.

I pointed out to Korte that the most important gap in our knowledge was that we did not know what, if anything, the 1st Mountain Division actually did after receiving von Gyldenfeldt's blanket approval. Had male civilians in the Arta area actually been deported? And what of the Jewish leadership in Ioannina?

As I was pondering this gap, a large bundle of documents arrived in the mail from Hans Safrian in Vienna. The "New Austria" group had copied them at the West German Military Archives in Freiburg. The materials came to me without explanation, and I had to translate and study them word by word.

Several of the documents added to our knowledge of the Arta/ Ioannina episode. One seemed to indicate that the Italian surrender had disrupted German plans. This was a telex from Waldheim's Ia Branch in Athens to Army Group E headquarters in Arsakli/Salonika, dated September 30, 1943, approximately three weeks after the Italian army's capitulation. The telex declared that, concerning Arta and Ioannina, large-scale evacuation measures were impractical at the moment because sufficient forces to carry them out were not available. Instead, it recommended small-scale evacuations, to be decided on a case-by-case basis.

Another group of reports confirmed what we already knew from the history books, that it was not until six months later, on March 25, 1944 (by which time Waldheim had long since returned to Army Group E headquarters), that the 1,725 Jews of Ioannina were deported. I still felt that the extended time lag made it difficult to ascribe any culpability to Waldheim for certifying the report that depicted the Jewish leadership there as being at the heart of an embryonic resistance movement.

One of the Ionnina-related documents in Safrian's package, a March 27, 1944, report of a Secret Field Police detachment serving with the 22nd Mountain Corps, was identical to a report that was part of a Nuremberg document I had found and copied on my initial visit to the National Archives during the first week of April.[3] The report was a blow-by-blow account of the "evacuation" of the "1,725 racial Jews" of Ioannina in a seven-hour operation carried out between 3 A.M. and 10 A.M. on March 25. Because the crime had occurred so long after Waldheim departed from Athens, I had not yet devoted much time to analyzing the report. But now that I scrutinized it thoroughly, I realized that it contained extraordinarily damning information. First, it disclosed that men of the 22nd Mountain Corps had taken part in the operation. These, I knew, were Wehrmacht forces directly subordinated to Army Group E headquarters.[4] That was bad enough. But the report also noted that the removal of the Jews had involved the "collaboration" (*Mitwirkung*) of the Ioannina detachment of Secret Field Police Detachment 621— a German Army unit that was abbreviated "GFP 621" in the document. I raced to my files to see if my recollection about GFP 621 was correct. It was: *GFP 621 took its instructions from Waldheim's own intelligence section (Ic) in Arsakli/Salonika.*[5]

Many of the papers sent to me in this package from Vienna related to a series of incidents that occurred during Waldheim's stay in Athens. Some were initialed *W* and others were initialed *Wa*, and I conjectured that the *W* signified Bruno Willers, chief of the Operations Branch (Ia), and that the *Wa* was probably the designation that his deputy Waldheim adopted in Athens to distinguish his own mark from Willers's; they were the only two officers assigned to the operations unit.

We knew that on August 8, 1943, the same day Waldheim recorded in the Athens war diary the fact that Hitler's criminal order commanding the killing of captured partisans had been transmitted to the 1st Mountain Division, he also reported that the division was heading for the area of Gliki-Parga to conduct a "cleansing operation." But until now, we did not know what, if any, consequences had ensued. One of the "New Austria" documents gave us the answer. Initialed *Wa,* the classified Ia report, dated August 13, 1943, contained a curt summary of the 1st Mountain Division's murderous operations during the preceding twenty-four hours:

> Enemy in Parga, Gliki, Renatia withdrew before our forces. Numerous villages cleared of inhabitants. Little enemy resistance. Complete results up to the present: 80–100 enemy dead, 50 prisoners, 30 rifles. Abundant livestock. Kukleski (17 km. north of Filippias) burned down, ammunition detonated at same time. 10 bandit suspects shot.[6]

Here again we saw the enormous imbalance between supposed partisans killed or captured—130 to 150 as reported by *Wa*—and the number of firearms seized—just thirty. What's more, the German troops appeared to have exceeded their already criminal instructions: According to Hitler's order, partisan *suspects* were to be deported, not shot.

Two of the documents in Safrian's package demonstrated advance knowledge of atrocities. The first, dated August 29, 1943, and stamped "Secret," advised Army Group E that three Greek villages were going to be erased:

> Chostia, Thisbe, Domvrena evacuated. Villages are to be *zerstoert* ("destroyed").[7]

The second document, an October 4, 1943, report by Waldheim's Ia Branch, informed Army Group E how the 68th Army Corps was planning to send hostages to makeshift gallows in order to deal with a problem of missing weapons:

> Unless missing weapons are handed over by 4 October, 5 hostages from Limnos will be hanged.[8]

Although the *W* on these documents probably signified Willers, Lieutenant Waldheim, as his deputy, surely had been privy to the information.

Safrian's package also contained copies of other Wehrmacht documents covering the later period when Waldheim was stationed at Army Group E headquarters in Arsakli/Salonika. These documents recorded the direct involvement of Waldheim's Ic/AO Branch in the decision-making process regarding a spring 1944 proposal to deport all of the British and Maltese citizens on the island of Corfu to the Reich as slave laborers.

An April 13 telex from Ic/AO Branch to *Korpsgruppe* Ioannina demanded the necessary information:

> There are still British subjects among the persons on Corfu. Age, nationality are to be reported here. It is intended by the SD to transfer them to Athens for the purpose of transportation to the Reich, for military and security reasons. A brief commentary is requested.

The following day, the Ic section of *Korpsgruppe* Ioannina provided the requested data, noting that eight Britons were currently in custody on Corfu, including one Chaime Miseraki, whose religion— noted as *Jude*—obviously merited special mention.

Two weeks later, on May 1, Waldheim's Ic/AO Branch advised the Ic section of *Korpsgruppe* Ioannina that extreme measures were in the works for Corfu's Maltese population as well:

> It is being proposed that able-bodied Maltese on Corfu should be deported to the Reich for labor service. At the same time, important Maltese are to be arrested as hostages to assure trustworthy attitude toward the German occupying troops.[9]

Finally, Safrian's material served as an introduction to two previously unknown Allied commando episodes. A "Secret" three-page report from Waldheim's Ic/AO Branch at Army Group E, dated May 8, 1944, put us on the trail of an only partly identifiable prisoner. Most of the document's title had been blacked out by censors, along with several of the names and a number of sentences. Clearly visible, however, was the signature of Major Hammer, as well as a pointed *W* at the end of the text, reflecting authorship either by Warnstoff or Waldheim. Directed to the High Command of Army Group F, the report summarized what had been learned from interrogating prisoners captured in a Greek boat off the coast of the Greek island of Cephalonia (in the Ionian Sea, west of the mainland) on March 26. Among the prisoners were Britons, Americans, Poles, and fifteen Russian deserters from German military service. The surname of one of the British prisoners could be made out: "Warren." The report included a summary of "Warren's" interrogation:

> Warren did not consider it practical to entrust the execution of sabotage operations to the Greeks on their own because of their limited reliability. He would not give an account of his own

activity, even though the interrogator assured him that he need not disclose anything about his comrades.[10]

Despite the seemingly prosaic language employed, these were frightening words indeed: In light of the requirements of Hitler's Commando Order, the use of the term "sabotage" in this report had very likely sealed Warren's fate. Had "Warren" really confessed to participating in "sabotage" missions despite the knowledge he surely had of the fatal consequences likely to flow from such a confession?

How would we ever find out what had happened to this man for whom we had neither a first name nor a date of birth? I decided to circulate the document to reporters, especially in Britain, in the hope that someone might be able to unearth answers.

The tale of yet another captured commando group emerged from other documents in Safrian's package. This story began with a May 6, 1944, message from the Ic Branch of the General Command of the 22nd Mountain Corps, addressed to the High Command of Army Group E. It reported on the capture of four British soldiers twenty kilometers northwest of Ioannina, and it identified them by name:

> Captain Bluett. Born 14 June 1903. Active officer. Originally from Williamstown (South Africa).
> Captain Hamilton. Born 21 Sept. 1919 in Calcutta. Civilian profession: student of philology in Oxford. Actual origin Scotland. Speaks relatively good German.
> Soldier Davies, cavalry. Unit No.: 7942 601. 21 years old, originally from England. Civilian profession: mechanical engineer.
> Soldier Benett,* artillery. Born 14 April 1920 in London. Orderly to Capt. Bluett, was in Egypt. Civilian profession: business employee.

The report noted that the prisoners refused to provide information beyond their basic identifying data.[11]

A companion report was sent the same day from the Ic Branch at the headquarters of the 22nd Mountain Corps to Field Gendarmerie Troop 422:

> The English prisoners, Captain Bluett, Captain Hamelton [sic], soldier Davies, and soldier Benet [sic], are to be transferred to Army Group E/Section Ic in Salonika.[12]

The four prisoners thus were sent not merely to Army Group E headquarters, but *directly to Waldheim's unit*. The document certainly

*The correct spelling was later verified as "Bennett."

gave the lie to Waldheim's public insistence that prisoners were never interrogated by Army Group E headquarters personnel.

I passed a copy of the document on to Neal Sher at OSI, and sent another copy to Michael May in London, so that he could forward it to Greville Janner in the House of Commons. Janner was a former war crimes investigator for the British army. Recently, the London M.P. had organized the House of Commons' "All-Party Parliamentary War Crimes Group," with the goal of enacting legislation enabling the prosecution of Nazi war criminals who had found sanctuary in Great Britain. He was our best hope for prodding the Thatcher government to provide information about the fate of Bluett and all the other Allied prisoners.

Even to those of us on the inside of the investigation, the trail of Waldheim's wartime activities was still maddeningly difficult to follow. What, I wondered, must it be like for the casual observer? In an attempt to bring some order to the intricate story, the WJC released, initially in London, the sixty-six page report, *Kurt Waldheim's Hidden Past,* which Cathy Valyi and I had completed in two nonstop, sleepless days of composition. It was designated an "interim" report because, as I wrote in the introduction, "there is an enormous volume of documentary evidence that has not yet been reviewed."

I reiterated that our major quest was to see the truth emerge, whatever it might be. The reason for Waldheim's evasions, I wrote, was becoming increasingly clear: "Waldheim's principal accuser continues to be the one that he is least able to refute: his own name and signature on a host of incriminating documents."

I attempted to provide the first English-language summary chronology of Waldheim's Wehrmacht service, beginning with his assignment to Reconnaissance Branch 45 on the Russian front in 1941. From there, we now knew, he went to the Bader Combat Group in Montenegro in March 1942 and then, in the spring/summer of 1942, to Stahl's West Bosnia Combat Group in the Kozara region of western Bosnia. He next showed up at Loehr's headquarters in Arsakli around August 31 and then at the Podgorica airstrip in Montenegro in May 1943 in the middle of "Operation Black." During the summer of 1943, Waldheim was stationed in Athens, where, among other duties, he kept the daily war journal. He spent the bulk of 1944 assigned to the Ic/AO Branch at the High Command of Army Group E at Arsakli/Salonika, during a time when his commander, General Alexander Loehr, was implicated in wholesale atrocities against Greek and Yugoslav partisans, Allied commandos, and Jewish civilians. Late in the war, during the frantic German retreat across Yugoslavia, Waldheim himself, according to the Yugoslav War Crimes

Commission, was implicated in murders and other atrocities. The duration and scope of his wartime activities, when compared with his traditional, bland autobiographical accounts, were staggering.

"Is Kurt Waldheim a war criminal?" our report asked. I tried to answer the question:

> Documentary evidence and witness testimony have implicated Waldheim in crimes committed in the Balkans against partisans, Jewish and non-Jewish civilians and prisoners of war, and in the deportation of thousands of Italian soldiers to forced labor. The World Jewish Congress is neither a government prosecutor nor a court of law and hence has no authority to "charge" any individual with crimes. Kurt Waldheim does, however, bear the opprobrious designation of accused Nazi war criminal.

I cited the CROWCASS and UNWCC listings, then asked another, more basic rhetorical question: "Why did Waldheim lie about his past?" This, the report noted, "is the question that Waldheim has steadfastly refused to answer."[13]

One month after we filed suit to compel the State Department to release to us any materials in its possession concerning Waldheim's prewar affiliations or wartime military service, State complied by sending us a brief, and very curious, one-page capsule biography, prepared in 1952 by reporting clerk Dorothy L. Ault on behalf of Walter Dowling, acting U.S. high commissioner in Vienna. The first four entries covered the years in question, albeit in skeletal fashion:

May 25, 1940	Court Official
January 21, 1944	Assistant Judge
August 30, 1945	Law Graduate in Professional Training
November 26, 1945	Entrance into Foreign Service

The report concluded: "As Dr. Waldheim has had little contact with the members of the Embassy, there is no additional biographic data to report at this time."

Incredibly, the State Department report made no mention whatsoever of Waldheim's wartime military service.

I studied the document for some time before the impact hit me. At the end of the terse "Confidential" report, the author listed the source of its biographical information. The entry read: "Austrian Foreign Ministry." But the same report noted that, as of its writing, Waldheim was chief of the *Personnel Division* of the Austrian Foreign Ministry. Thus, the State Department's request for information on

Waldheim had in all likelihood been routed *to Waldheim himself,* who then provided this "abridged" biography!*

As the June 8 runoff election approached, relations between Austria and Israel grew increasingly strained, especially after Israeli Justice Minister Yitzhak Moda'i's announced, "There is a basis for putting Waldheim on trial, if he were in Israel, for involvement in war crimes." He added that Israel had "enough proof" (largely supplied to it by the WJC) to indicate that Waldheim had passed on information that led "to liquidation actions."

A Waldheim aide responded by accusing Israel of being on a "witchhunt," and People's Party General Secretary Graff declared that "Israeli politicians" had been "roped into the slander campaign of the World Jewish Congress."[14]

Waldheim himself took the offensive by addressing the Arab world directly. He may have thought that no one in the West would ever read the contents of an interview that he gave to Beirut's *Usbu' al-'Arabi* ("Arabweek"), but the WJC's London research unit spotted the story and forwarded it to me, complete with a skillfully rendered English translation. Here, Waldheim explained to a presumably sympathetic audience that Austrians would vote for him because they are Austrians, not "Jewish cadres of the Socialist Party and their extensions in the United States and Israel." Then he suggested a reason for the "Jewish attack on me"—the fact that Austria had never paid war reparations to the Jews. "Jewish leaders want Austria to pay," he declared, "and they are serving notice . . ." Carrying his invocation of the old stereotype of Jewish fixation on money still further, Waldheim suggested that economic interests were a motivation of the WJC because Edgar Bronfman "is a businessman and owner of Seagram's whiskey firm."

The same issue of the Beirut weekly carried a rare interview with Waldheim's wife, Sissy. She was even less subtle than her husband had been, blaming all of her husband's troubles on "world Zionism."[15]

Back in Vienna, meanwhile, *Profil* published a list of more than two hundred Austrian writers, artists, and scientists who urged their countrymen not to vote for Waldheim.[16] But Michael Elizur, the Israeli ambassador to Austria, who had twice tried to pressure us into stopping our exposure of Waldheim, promptly dispatched a "Secret" cable to his superiors at the Israeli Foreign Ministry in Jerusalem, cautioning that he "did not find among them the names of any people of stature or of intellectual prominence."

*The careful reader may also recall that Waldheim's 1971 official U.N. biography stated that he "was head of the personnel department of the Ministry for Foreign Affairs in Vienna from 1951 to 1955."

The *Kultesgemeinde,* the central organization of Vienna's Jewish community, now held a press conference to express the "indignation and bitterness" that Austrian Jewry felt over the People's Party's use of unabashedly anti-Semitic themes in the Waldheim campaign. Chairman Ivan Hacker called the tactic "Lueger-type political anti-Semitism," a reference to the anti-Jewish mayor of turn-of-the-century Vienna, Karl Lueger. His colleague Ariel Muzicant went further still, naming names; he singled out for blame party leaders Michael Graff and Alois Mock. As if to prove the point, Graff responded by denouncing "the Mafia methods of the slanderers of the World Jewish Congress."[17]

These ugly developments also had a more direct impact on us. Singer told me that his elderly mother, herself a refugee from German-annexed Austria, had received a series of threatening late-night phone calls from someone who spoke fluent German. I had been plagued recently by phone calls at my apartment that featured only silence on the other end, usually against the telltale whirring and clicking of an international connection.

Meanwhile, a steady stream of hate letters arrived at our office, most of them with variations on one theme: "You Jews are going to die." More than half bore Austrian postmarks. And one night, all four tires on Singer's car were slashed as it sat unattended in his driveway.

Information—some of it reliable, some of it of questionable reliability, some of it obviously fraudulent—continued to inundate us from all sides.

In the "reliable" category was a series of reports that gave a sharp focus to the Yugoslav story—and with it, the Soviet aspect of the affair. The latest issue of the Yugoslav magazine *Duga* contained the first report, an article by Milomir Maric, on the extraordinary claims of Anton Kolendic, a former partisan fighter with Tito, who served as head of the Yugoslav military mission in Vienna after the war. According to this account, in 1947 or 1948, Kolendic's assistant, Vasilije Kovacevic, had shown him a list of some thirty names of war criminals, forwarded by Belgrade. Kurt Waldheim's name had leapt from the list, since Kolendic and his deputy knew that he was the assistant to Austrian Foreign Minister Karl Gruber. Kovacevic proposed that it would be more feasible to "work" Waldheim in co-operation with the Soviets, rather than attempt it alone, and Kolendic agreed. One of them then showed the list to a senior Soviet operative in Vienna, a Colonel Gonda. In an interview with the magazine, Kolendic noted that, only shortly after this incident, Tito broke with the Soviets. As a result, he recalled for *Duga,* the "joint enterprise was quickly forgotten."[18]

Here was our first direct testimony that the Soviets were alerted to Yugoslavia's indictment of Waldheim, almost from the start.

The *New York Times*'s John Tagliabue obtained his own interview with Kolendic, who repeated the account. The *Times* version, however, differed slightly from *Duga's*. *Duga* had quoted him as saying that he knew the Soviets would seek to blackmail Waldheim on their own, even without their former Yugoslav partners. But in the *Times,* Kolendic was reported as saying only that he understood that the Soviets would "initiate a search" for the persons on the list. When asked directly what, if anything, the Soviets had done with the list, Kolendic told Tagliabue, "We never received an answer."[19]

A short time later, the Austrian Socialist Party newspaper, *Arbeiter Zeitung,* published reporter Georg Hoffmann's interview with Professor Vladimir Dedijer, a former Yugoslav partisan leader, now a member of the Serbian Academy of Sciences and Arts. Dedijer, who was in the process of writing an encyclopedic biography of his old friend Marshal Tito, said that Waldheim's name had surfaced "hundreds" of times in the background documents that he had assembled, and they made one thing clear: "Waldheim is a war criminal. There is sufficient material for the Greek and Yugoslav governments to request his extradition on the basis of international law."

But Dedijer was interested less in Waldheim's wartime role than in the aftermath of the war. He saw the postwar Waldheim as a victim of the machinations of the world powers. "Waldheim," he alleged without elaboration, "was blackmailed by several states."

In the "Questionable" category of information, regrettably, were allegations such as those made by Moshe Mayuni, a Greek Jew now living in Israel, who was present in Ioannina during the March 1944 deportation of the Jews. Mayuni claimed that, on March 24 of that year, he had seen Waldheim administer a beating to his brother. This clashed with Waldheim's claim that he was in Vienna on leave during the Ioannina deportations.

I found it difficult to credit Mayuni's dramatic (and no doubt sincerely made) charge, especially in the absence of documentary evidence proving that Waldheim had been on duty in Greece at the time. Why had Mayuni never leveled the charge during Waldheim's ten years at the U.N.?

This was only one of several "eyewitness" accounts of Holocaust survivors and former British P.O.W.'s that had surfaced, and I was wary. Hearing my reservations, Singer and Steinberg yielded to my pleas that the WJC keep a respectable distance from these remembrances. It was of paramount importance for the WJC to maintain the integrity of its investigation. Even one tiny mistake would give Waldheim's supporters all the ammunition they needed to discredit everything we had done and still hoped to do.

Indeed, as I had feared, the Mayuni allegation soon proved to be in error. *Stern* quickly tracked down medical records confirming that Waldheim was in a hospital at Semmering, Austria, from March 2 to March 29 of that year. I took little comfort in the knowledge that I had repeatedly (if unsuccessfully) warned reporters about going into print with this story before it was verified. Their impatience gave Waldheim's supporters the opportunity to use the Mayuni episode as "proof" that all of Waldheim's accusers lacked credibility.

But there was good news as well in the *Stern* article. The German weekly found and reprinted a March 26, 1944, report addressed to both Ia *and* Ic at Army Group E headquarters, declaring that the Jewish deportations in the Ioannina area had been completed "without incident." The receipt of this report meant that Waldheim's immediate superior, Colonel Warnstorff, knew about the fate of the Ioannina Jews and that, when Waldheim returned from the hospital a few days later, he almost surely had found out also.[20]

The provably "fraudulent" category of reporting, meanwhile, came directly from Austria. Five days before the runoff election, *Wochenpresse* reported that the WJC had attempted to bribe a former Greek partisan named Socrates Chatzisvangelis with $150,000 if he would falsely implicate Waldheim in war crimes. The rest of the Austrian press picked up the charge and the story became front-page news throughout the country. People's Party General Secretary Michael Graff exploited it to the hilt. He fired off an indignant telex to Bronfman, which he immediately circulated to the media, declaring, "I never believed that you would go so far. . . . In the absence of a satisfactory explanation in due time, I must assume that the World Jewish Council [*sic*] has really attempted to bribe a witness, and the Austrian people will draw the appropriate conclusions."

The bribery charge had, of course, been invented from whole cloth. We had never even heard of Chatzisvangelis, much less offered money to him, yet the fabricated story was reported in Austria as if it were a confirmed fact. The Austrian press assault on us had reached a new low. In my official capacity as attorney for the WJC, I cabled *Wochenpresse*, demanding a retraction, threatening a lawsuit, and calling for a fair hearing on the episode—something that, I realized now, we would never get in Austria, before or even after the election.

Wochenpresse ignored my telex; the magazine did not bother even to acknowledge its receipt. However, an enterprising UPI reporter managed to track down Chatzisvangelis, who told the news agency a surprising story. He confided that he had indeed been offered money—*by someone who identified himself as a Waldheim backer*—if he would *exonerate* the candidate. Of course, *Wochenpresse* ignored the UPI story, too.

The Simon Wiesenthal Center desperately wanted to play a role in the Waldheim drama, to be seen as aggressively pursuing Waldheim's exposure. The Los Angeles–based organization's leadership knew that its thousands of contributors expected no less. The Center also worried that Simon Wiesenthal's behavior might be mistakenly attributed to the Center, leading to a potentially serious loss of both financial support and credibility. The Center finally found an opportunity when it was able to obtain a copy of the same one-page WASt document that *Profil* had published weeks earlier, in late April—the page that confirmed that during Waldheim's tenure at the U.N., someone had gained possession of the war chronology that revealed his war cover-up. The *Profil* piece had gone largely unnoticed outside Austria, and now the Center, with its well-developed public relations capabilities, was able to disseminate the "news" to a worldwide audience. The Center also passed on to the media a rumor that the 1979 Berlin records check was conducted in connection with French President Valery Giscard d'Estaing's plan to confer the Medal of the Legion of Honor on the U.N. Secretary-General. If that was true, charged the Center's dean, Rabbi Marvin Hier, then the French government was partially responsible for the cover-up.

The Center's accusation spawned a brief investigation by the government of France, which soon reported that both former President Giscard d'Estaing and his Foreign Minister, Jean François-Poncet, denied that they had ordered—or even seen—the report on Waldheim. A spokesman for sitting Prime Minister Jacques Chirac, however, confirmed that the French report had been prepared in 1979, and that it revealed Waldheim's oft-repeated account of his war service to be a fabrication. The spokesman added that the French government was attempting to ascertain why the records were checked, who had ordered the report, and why the government had never publicly challenged Waldheim on the discrepancies that the report revealed. For now, Chirac's office could say only that the 1979 inspection was performed by an unnamed "junior French official in West Berlin." His spokesman added the intriguing comment that he believed that the report was prepared, not for any branch of the French government, but for some, as yet unknown, third party or parties. Privately, the man who had headed French intelligence throughout the 1970s told intimates that his agency had never been asked to investigate Waldheim and that he had never seen the Berlin file.* The French government promised to continue probing the matter.[21]

In a telephone interview, an angry Hier told the *Washington Post*'s Michael Dobbs that the French statement was entirely unsatisfactory, as it failed to reveal "why Paris became interested in Waldheim in 1979 or who ordered the inquiry." Hier noted that "someone was suspicious of Kurt Waldheim" years ago, and he wanted to know who that someone was. If those answers were not forthcoming from the Elysée Palace, Hier said, then it was obvious to him that the French authorities "have something to hide." In its newsletter to contributors, the Wiesenthal Center again demanded to know "which French government agency requested this memo." Hier's organization bitterly denounced France and other governments that "had access to this incredible information and then did nothing to see to it that the world's foremost human rights officer be held accountable for his trail of deceit and lies."[22]

In these last days before the election, the man after whom Marvin Hier's organization was named was continuing to take a radically different approach to the Waldheim controversy. He chose this decisive moment to escalate the rhetoric against the World Jewish Congress to new heights of angry hyperbole. Charging again that we had "accused Waldheim of war crimes without evidence," Wiesenthal portrayed the WJC as engaging in "a sort of sadism." This, he told one interviewer, "is the same as killing somebody. You can also kill morally."

So *we* were the murderers. What, then, was Waldheim? In the same interview, Wiesenthal raised the question on his own. After asserting that "there is no evidence" against Waldheim and then claiming that the former U.N. chief had been involved solely in intelligence gathering and reporting, the Nazi-hunter posed a question that went even beyond the issue of what Waldheim had already been proved to have done. "What *could* he have done?" Wiesenthal demanded. Immediately, he provided his own categorical answer: *"Nothing!"* Wiesenthal's "explanation": Waldheim "could not make decisions because he was merely a lieutenant sitting at a desk." In a second interview a few days later, Wiesenthal went even further. Now it was not just the (supposed) impossibility of Waldheim making decisions. Waldheim, he said, could not even generate *recommendations:* "His rank was so low that he could not make any recommen-

*The retired official, Count de Marenches, subsequently made the same assertions publicly, in his 1992 book *The Fourth World War* (New York: Morrow), pp. 136–37.

dations. So he cannot be responsible for what his superiors decided."[23]

I was as surprised by the explanation as I was angered by the Nazi-hunter's unqualified exoneration of Waldheim. As Wiesenthal well knew, some of the very worst Nazi war criminals (Eichmann among them) had perpetrated their crimes from inside comfortable offices. And it was simply ludicrous to assert that someone in Waldheim's position was somehow barred even from making recommendations to his immediate superior in Salonika, the chief of intelligence/counterintelligence. Moreover, it had already been proved conclusively that Waldheim had been an *operations*—not intelligence—officer at at least one of his postings (Athens). In addition, following up on my father's comment that German military intelligence personnel were commonly given, for security and other reasons, ranks that were considerably lower than their authority and responsibilities would otherwise have indicated, I had established that Waldheim's intelligence position in Arsakli/Salonika was one that was customarily filled by a lieutenant colonel or a major.*

One thing, at least, was clear: If there had ever been any hope, however slim, of moderating Wiesenthal's behavior in the Waldheim matter, it now had evaporated completely.

I had often referred to Beate Klarsfeld, a German non-Jew married to a French Jew, as "the real Simon Wiesenthal," because she had repeatedly had the courage to put her life on the line in the pursuit of justice in Nazi cases. Back in the sixties, after it was disclosed that then–West German Chancellor Kurt Georg Kiesinger had a Nazi past, she rushed toward him on the floor of the West German Parliament and slapped him in the face, making a moral statement captured for posterity by a lucky photographer. Since that time, Klarsfeld, who was just six years old when the war ended, had devoted her life to tracking down Nazi war criminals. She had been arrested and briefly imprisoned in Syria while agitating for the apprehension of Alois Brunner, who had worked as an aide to Adolf Eichmann, helping to plan and execute the deportation of Jews from, among other locations, Salonika. She had survived car bombings and numerous other arrests, particularly in South America. Only three years earlier, she had journeyed to Chile to demonstrate publicly

---

*Indeed, Wiesenthal would later make virtually the same point in responding to a claim by a Wehrmacht counterintelligence suspect that his lowly rank of *private* made it impossible for him to have been responsible for the criminal roundup of more than a thousand Jews in Belgrade. The Nazi-hunter pointed out that low ranks were not uncommon in Wehrmacht counterintelligence units. See Marta Halpert, "Dentist Facing Charges in Austria for Alleged War Crimes in Belgrade," Jewish Telegraphic Agency *Daily News Bulletin,* October 14, 1992.

against the Pinochet government's failure to arrest fugitive Nazi war criminal Walter Rauff, the designer of the Nazis' mobile gas chambers, an act of valor that promptly landed her in a Chilean jail.

Now the redoubtable Klarsfeld took her courage to the front lines in Austria. As a local politician addressed a Waldheim rally in Vienna's St. Stephan's Square, proclaiming that the election must be decided by the people of Austria, rather than foreign accusers who were waging a "campaign against Austria," three clusters of balloons were released from the edge of the crowd; one of them carried a sign bearing the inscription: WALDHEIM LIAR.

Then, as Waldheim himself rose to speak, Klarsfeld led a group of about twenty protestors into the crowd, chanting, "Waldheim, Nein!" and displaying a banner that declared: "Anti-Semitism must not pay—Waldheim NO." Police officers and Waldheim supporters ripped the banner from the hands of the protestors and threw it to the ground. Vienna's Finest then began to haul away Klarsfeld and her allies. Gesturing toward the scene as police dragged the protestors out of the square, Waldheim stepped closer to his microphone. The Austrian people, he bellowed, wished to use Western-style freedom "in a constructive way, not like that." The crowd cheered.

Following Waldheim's speech, Andreas Forst, a twenty-nine-year-old student, shouted out a question, asking Waldheim whether he would agree to a televised debate with his opponent, Kurt Steyrer. Within seconds, Forst was attacked by about twenty bystanders, who ripped his shirt, punched him, and spat at him. Not one of his attackers was arrested by the Austrian police who stood nearby.

In an interview after the incident, Klarsfeld noted that in 1938 the Austrians "freely opened the door to Hitler. Today they closed it to us." Forst echoed her sentiments. "You saw the way they reacted," he sighed. "That was Austrian fascism 1986."[24]

Less than a week later, Klarsfeld was again taken into custody by the Austrian police, this time ostensibly to check the renowned Nazi-hunter's "personal documents," when she led a peaceful protest at a Waldheim rally in Linz.

Two days prior to the election, the scene was repeated yet again. Waldheim appeared at a campaign rally in the main square in Amstetten, in northern Austria. An impressively large crowd of supporters roared its approval—and Waldheim beamed—as an overeager local official shouted into a microphone, *"Oesterreich {Austria} ueber Alles!"*

Waldheim launched into his stump speech, drawing on some of his most provocative routines. "Enough of the past!" he demanded, to the cheers of the crowd. He railed at the leaders of the WJC, intoning the distinctly Jewish-sounding names of its key officials in New York with emphasis. Again the crowd cheered.

Suddenly, a group of sixteen black-clad protestors, led by Klarsfeld, rounded a corner and approached the edge of the crowd. One of them carried a placard declaring: "Waldheim is a liar." Within moments, a group of burly Waldheim supporters descended on them, yelling curses and striking them with their fists. Standing before the microphone on the platform, Waldheim pointed in the direction of the small band of demonstrators and, even as they were being assaulted, derided them as "an example of the abuse of Western democratic liberties!"

The police quickly approached the fracas and detained the members of the Klarsfeld group briefly, recording their names. They took no action against the goons who had beaten the protestors. The *New York Times* printed an extraordinary photo of Klarsfeld herself being dragged away by the police.[25]

On the following day, election eve, a People's Party official used a public appearance to continue the offensive. "All good Austrians should vote for Waldheim," he declared, "and so should our Jewish citizens." In German (as in English translation), the choice of words clearly separated "good Austrians" and Jews into different classes of citizens.[26]

On awakening the morning of June 8, I trudged to the door of my apartment and dragged in the massive Sunday edition of the *New York Times*. A front-page story brought the nightmare of the past four months to its anticipated denouement. I grimaced as I read the headline at the top of the page: POLLS SHOW WALDHEIM WILL WIN PRESIDENCY TODAY.

23

Nightfall in Vienna saw People's Party headquarters filled to capacity with well-dressed revelers, young and old, ecstatic at the prospect of Waldheim's imminent triumph. Devouring frankfurters as they viewed television reports of province after province going for Waldheim, the crowd grew ever more boisterous. After it became clear that Waldheim's margin of victory was going to be larger than had been anticipated, the celebration, punctuated continuously by loud cries of adoration for the candidate, began to turn into a frenzy of mass-rapture. The bizarre scene was captured in this vignette recorded by one observer:

> As the evening wore on and it emerged that Waldheim's majority had risen to 7.7 percent, strikingly dressed girls mingled with the crowds, hungry for adventure. Rich women appeared in expensive dirndls, and a sprinkling of chic girls wore the latest fashions. One statuesque blonde beauty suddenly appeared in a dark-blue mackintosh asking to see Alois Mock, the leader of the People's Party. While an eager, if inebriated, aide went off in search of the worthy but lacklustre Herr Mock, the girl confided that this was the greatest day of her life and that she was keen to—as she put it—"rape handsome Herr Mock." Under her mackintosh she wore only black suspenders and a long black sweater.[1]

When, at last, victory was assured, the candidate himself was ushered in for a brief address to his supporters. A band that had been playing military marches stopped abruptly. As dozens of plainclothes police officers looked on, Waldheim declared that the election result was his countrymen's response to his call for a return to "fairness, morality, and Christian values."

It was a dejected Elan Steinberg who presented the WJC's initial reaction to the press. "In a perfect world," he said with a sigh, "a man like Waldheim would be put on trial. In a less-than-perfect world, he would just go away. In the *very* imperfect world in which we live, he has been elected president of Austria."

It was true. Waldheim had received 2,460,203 votes (53.89 percent), compared to 2,105,118 for Steyrer. Nearly 54 percent of the Austrian electorate had voted into office an accused Nazi war criminal, after a campaign fueled by overt appeals to anti-Semitic and xenophobic sentiments.

Schuller was morose, and offered his postmortem analysis to me over the phone: We had gone up against "too many interests," he declared. In addition to the People's Party and the Austrian press, we battled the Soviets, the Croatian faction of the Yugoslav government, perhaps the U.S. government, perhaps the British, perhaps the French. And we found ourselves battling the legendary Simon Wiesenthal.

"I am not so much in a bad mood," Schuller said unconvincingly. "Mostly I am ashamed that we have such a bad press."

Die Presse characterized Waldheim's election as "the first expression of Austrian national pride in many years."

Congratulatory messages were sent to Waldheim by several world leaders, among them British Prime Minister Margaret Thatcher, Libya's Muammar Qadaffi and Egyptian President Hosni Mubarak. Lebanese President Bashir Gemayel telephoned his best wishes. The governments of Kuwait, the USSR, Poland, Bulgaria, and Czechoslovakia sent their formal compliments to Waldheim. One Kuwaiti newspaper declared that Waldheim's election "disposed of Zionist propaganda," and the Libyan news agency exulted that this was an expression of the determination of the Austrian people to "get rid of the dirt that Zionism threw on Austrian history."

An exuberant Waldheim told reporters that he was confident that his victory would put the allegations to rest and leave open the doors to the U.S. and the rest of the world.

He could hardly have been more wrong.

Neighboring Yugoslavia, still openly ambivalent, balked at sending a congratulatory note. Soon thereafter, *Vecernje Novosti* openly criticized the Belgrade government for its continuing silence concerning Waldheim's actions during the war.

Upset by Prime Minister Thatcher's formal note of congratulations, British Labor Party officials called on her to bar Waldheim from entry into the United Kingdom. M.P. Greville Janner provided the Thatcher government with a copy of the document from the Freiburg archives that stated that the four Allied commandos captured near Ioannina were to be taken to Waldheim's branch at Army Group E headquarters, and he demanded information about the ultimate fate of Bluett, Hamilton, Davies, and Bennett.

The European Community's Executive Commission declined to congratulate the election victor.

One of Holland's biggest newspapers termed Waldheim's election "a disgrace."

The government of Israel announced its "deep regret" and "sorrow" over Waldheim's election. An Israeli official declared the election "a nightmare for every Jew." On the floor of the Knesset, an enraged Rabbi Meir Kahane ripped apart a large Austrian flag. Israel formally recalled its ambassador to Austria, Michael Elizur, the man who had urged Jerusalem to pressure Bronfman to stop our exposure of Waldheim.

Canadian External Affairs Minister Joe Clark announced that his government would seek more information on Waldheim's war record.

Edgar Bronfman issued a prepared statement reflecting the WJC's official stand. It was anything but conciliatory:

> Even though Mr. Waldheim will take office, this is not the end of the affair. The representatives of moral conscience will continue to dig into his past, to explore his wartime conduct, to bring to public attention everything that can be gathered and that, in fairness, warrants attention. It is crucial to do so. Otherwise, the motto "Never again"—as it applies not only to Jews but to all victims of totalitarianism—will become meaningless, and such horrors may well recur.

Rabbi Marvin Hier of the Simon Wiesenthal Center announced that he was "appalled." The election of a man who "deliberately lied about his past," Hier said, "is an indictment of the Austrian people's unwillingness to squarely face up to their past." Kurt Waldheim, he added, "could not have been elected the president of any other country." Hier urged other nations not to congratulate Waldheim. "The Austrian people wanted Waldheim," he commented ruefully. "They can have him."[2]

Anthony Lewis, writing in the *New York Times,* declared that the Austrian electorate had "significantly advanced . . . the process of making forgetfulness acceptable."[3] A *Times* editorial noted that the Austrian presidency was largely symbolic, "but," it observed, "what a symbol!"[4]

Senator Daniel Moynihan declared that Waldheim's election

amounted to an act of symbolic amnesty for the Holocaust. One hundred and eleven members of Congress petitioned President Reagan to boycott the July 8 inauguration in Vienna.

But the signals from the executive branch were mixed. Presidential spokesman Larry Speakes provided the White House's official reaction: "The people of Austria have made their choice in a free democratic election. The President will be sending the usual diplomatic letter to the new president of Austria later today."⁵ The statement sounded to me as though Speakes could not bring himself to utter the name "Waldheim."

Responding to a reporter's question, Speakes made the disconcerting assertion that Waldheim could not be barred from visiting the U.S. in an official capacity, but only as a private tourist. U.S. Department of Justice spokesman Pat Korten was quoted in a similar vein, declaring that immigration laws do not apply to official visits; accordingly, Waldheim could enter and leave the U.S. in his presidential capacity "as he pleases." Learning of Korten's statement, I immediately phoned him; he insisted that he had been misquoted. As far as official visits were concerned, Korten told me, Waldheim could not come unless he received an invitation. And consideration by the Administration of any such gesture would be postponed until Attorney General Meese decided whether or not to place him on the watchlist. In effect, Austria's new president was barred from the United States pending completion of the watchlist inquiry.

The morning after the election, I was in a New York broadcast studio, ready to appear via satellite link on the "AM Canada" television program. I had just learned that the Soviet news agency Tass had finally lifted the Soviet veil of silence on the Waldheim case, but only to denounce what it termed the "U.S.-Zionist plot" that had attempted to interfere with the elections of a free country. Tass characterized the charges against Waldheim, whom it praised as an accomplished statesman, as "unjust and slanderous," the product of an "unseemly undertaking of the Zionists and their patrons in the Washington administration."

A few minutes later, the "AM Canada" interviewer asked me how I felt about the fact that the Kremlin had congratulated Waldheim. I responded testily. "Considering the fact that the Soviets recently congratulated Ferdinand Marcos on his supposed reelection only weeks before he was forced to flee the Philippines, I don't think too much of it." Then I predicted that, as far as the free world was concerned, Waldheim would become "a prisoner of his presidential palace."

Despite the confident nature of my responses, I was, in fact, deeply discouraged. I tried to buoy my spirits by reminding myself that the typical Austrian voter had possessed little objective information on which to base his decision. An old friend, Professor Charles Sydnor of Virginia's Emory and Henry College, had been in Austria during the last days of the campaign. On his return, he commented that the average Austrian did not understand "what the fuss is all about." He complained, "I would ask people what the charges were about Waldheim's war record, and they didn't even know." He wrote of having interviewed a "stout, red-cheeked" People's Party campaign worker whom he encountered at Branau am Inn, Hitler's birthplace. The campaigner had explained away the Waldheim controversy: "The whole thing has been financed by Jewish big business in America."[6] Given the tenor of the local reporting, I realized, what else was the Austrian man-on-the-street supposed to believe? I reminded myself that, despite Waldheim's win, more than 46 percent of the Austrian electorate had voted against him.

Indeed, quite a number of influential Austrians took a principled stand. Among them was Chancellor Fred Sinowatz, who tendered his resignation in protest of Waldheim's election (though he actually had little chance of keeping the post). Several cabinet ministers followed suit, including Foreign Minister Leopold Gratz, who later delivered a speech denouncing the People's Party for having "consciously made use of anti-Semitism and xenophobia" during the campaign and for its efforts "to incite Austrian internal hatred."[7]

Finance Minister Franz Vranitsky, an articulate, conservative Socialist banker with a TV-anchorman's good looks and the reserved demeanor that is a financier's stock-in-trade, was named as interim chancellor, and he succeeded in forging a ruling coalition with the tiny, but notoriously reactionary, Freedom Party. Vranitsky was undoubtedly a good choice for a tough task. His disdain for Waldheim was well known. He spoke English well, and he effectively communicated his message to the U.S. in a series of high-profile appearances on American television: We have more in common than the recent differences created by this Waldheim story. We should try to move forward.

But Austria's ambassador to the U.S., Thomas Klestil, who had helped fight Waldheim's battle in Washington, was as confrontational as Vranitsky was conciliatory. Klestil warned publicly that if Meese decided to place Waldheim on the watchlist, the action could lead to a retreat from Austria's traditional pro-American attitude.

During a press conference two days after the election, Waldheim again portrayed the presidential vote as an acquittal. The controversy concerning his wartime activities would now disappear, he said, and the doors to the U.S. and other countries would be opened to him. He shrugged off the war years with the declaration, "I was a third *Ordonnanz* officer—a sort of secretary and nothing more." And he offered yet another preposterous claim: "There was absolutely no anti-Semitism in my election campaign" because, he declared, he "wouldn't have tolerated it."

A reporter took exception, suggesting to Waldheim that "the whole world" had witnessed how the People's Party had employed anti-Semitic appeals.

"What is the whole world?" Waldheim fired back. "If you think that the whole world is certain circles in New York, that may be true." It was obvious that Waldheim was growing increasingly comfortable with the anti-Semitic code words that had proved so useful in his campaign.[8]

This same day, Elisabeth "Sissy" Waldheim finally admitted that she had been a member of the Nazi Party. But she insisted that she had dropped out of the Party, at Waldheim's request, when they were engaged in 1943.*

Also this day, Gerhard Waldheim and two attorneys turned over a three-inch-thick sheaf of documents to the U.S. Department of Justice, constituting yet another written counterattack against the mounting evidence against President-elect Waldheim. I longed to see the material. But access was limited to Justice Department personnel.

We had so much, and yet so little. We had the proof that Waldheim had covered up his prewar and war record and even that he was continuing to dissemble. We could place him in one location after another where atrocities were committed by the invariably small units in which he served in important capacities. In some instances—most notably in the Allied commando cases—we could prove that Waldheim was personally involved. But the extent of that involvement was nearly impossible to pin down with certainty, especially since we could not prove the state of Waldheim's knowledge regarding the likely consequences of his reports and requests. There were, moreover, questions that were still unanswered about the precise routing of Waldheim's communications. And we could not be sure whose *W* initial appeared on some key documents.

*The withdrawal claim was later proved false. See "Mrs. Waldheim Was a Nazi," *New York Times,* June 12, 1986; Ilona Henry, "Waldheim's Wife Never Left Nazi Party," *Jerusalem Post,* December 17, 1986.

Nearly every aspect of the case seemed to have a missing link. We could prove that General Stahl himself had nominated Waldheim for a medal for his performance during the Kozara campaign, but we could not determine precisely what Waldheim had done to earn the honor. The Yugoslav charges were important, to be sure, particularly Johann Mayer's claim that Waldheim was responsible for reprisal killings and the destruction of villages. But Mayer was dead, we still had not seen a copy of his actual testimony, and the UNWCC file's quotation of it left the impression that Mayer had provided no specifics concerning dates, places, or incidents. Nor could we definitively disprove the claim of Waldheim's defenders that Mayer had concocted the charges in order to satisfy his Yugoslav captors.

In sum, we still lacked the proverbial smoking gun, the direct and incontrovertible link that proved Waldheim's personal and willful complicity in a war crime. Sometimes it seemed as if the only thing that was certain any longer was that Waldheim was lying about nearly every stage of his war record. Just how far we could take the investigation and how long we could continue were difficult questions. I worried that we might already have seen all of the most important documents that lay in Western archives.

Perhaps more than anything, we needed the Yugoslav files. These, after all, were the documents that had landed Waldheim on the CROWCASS list, that caused him to be placed in the top category of wanted war criminals by the U.N. War Crimes Commission. What did they say? What proof could they add to what we already had?

On June 23, I was sitting at my desk, trying to make sense of it all, when Neal Sher called from OSI. "I just got word from Yugoslavia," he said. "Better brace yourself, Eli."

"Okay," I replied. "What's up?"

"Remember Stephen Katich?"

"Yeah, of course. In fact, he's in Yugoslavia for us right now."

"Well, he just *died* there."

For a few moments I was too stunned to say anything. Finally, I stammered, "What? How?"

"He was hospitalized about ten days ago and then . . . he died." Sher speculated that Katich may have known he was dying, and may have wanted to finish his days in the old country.

I could not accept that scenario. I filled Sher in on why Katich had gone to Yugoslavia. I recalled his enthusiasm for the prospect of retrieving the Waldheim files.

I yearned for more details. How did Katich die? What had really happened to the old Library of Congress researcher? Had he perhaps sacrificed his life in the attempt to uncover the truth about Waldheim?*

---

*On July 31, 1986, I met with Katich's sister, who lived in Canada. By now, we knew that Katich had suddenly fallen ill during his trip to Yugoslavia; Ambassador Scanlan arranged for him to be hospitalized in Belgrade. After a week in the hospital, Katich suffered a massive stroke and died.

I asked his sister bluntly, "Do you suspect any foul play in Stephen's death?"

"To tell you the truth, I'm not sure," she replied. "I don't know what to think anymore." She explained that, on hearing the news, she had flown to Yugoslavia, where she discovered to her consternation that no autopsy had been performed. Her brother was simply dead and buried. "It was all very strange," she said, her eyes welling with tears.

As of this writing, the authors have been unable to learn anything more concerning Katich's death.

24

Simon Wiesenthal continued to be the moat that surrounded Castle Waldheim. The man whose photograph and quotes had appeared so prominently in Waldheim's campaign literature told reporters that he did not vote for *either* candidate in the Austrian presidential race "because this election really upset me."

Writing in the June issue of the Vienna Jewish newspaper *Ausweg* ("Alternative"), Wiesenthal suggested sarcastically that the whole controversy began when Israel Singer had a bad dream about Waldheim, and upon awakening, decided to check into the candidate's past. Echoing a favorite People's Party line, Wiesenthal declared that Singer first accused Waldheim of being a war criminal and only later began searching for "relevant substantiating documents."

Wiesenthal added a bizarre twist to his earlier theme of characterizing the destruction of the Jews of Salonika as solely an SS operation. He wrote that the WJC "campaign" had raised the "question" of whether or not the Wehrmacht was involved in the Salonika deportations. Indeed it was, he decided, but the German army did not assume the sinister role that others attempted to attribute to it; to the contrary, he said, the Wehrmacht had "provided food for the deportees." 1 could hardly believe what I was reading: Wiesenthal was portraying the Wehrmacht, on whose trains some forty-six thousand Jews had been carried from Salonika to Auschwitz, as a purely benign force in the tragedy. Nor did Wiesenthal make any mention of General Loehr's personal involvement in the process of removing the Jews from throughout occupied Greece.[1]

Wiesenthal again heaped invective on anyone who had joined in the exposure and denunciation of Waldheim, including the WJC, the Socialist Party, his old nemesis Bruno Kreisky and resigning Chancellor Fred Sinowatz, and he offered a unique theory to explain why the accusations against Waldheim received so much attention in the U.S. Charging that American Jews harbor a collective sense of guilt because they "did not act strongly enough against the Nazis," he explained that Singer and the WJC had offered them an opportunity to purge this guilt; thus was Waldheim "demonized."

The Nazi-hunter unashamedly appropriated some of the most effective themes from the Waldheim campaign, charging the WJC had intervened in internal Austrian affairs and that our efforts to expose Waldheim "practically became a campaign against Austria." The WJC's tactics, he added, had provided "ammunition" to anti-Semites in Austria.

Wiesenthal conceded in his article that Waldheim's defense was "clumsy" and that the People's Party had responded in "an inadequate fashion," but he scrupulously avoided upbraiding either the candidate or the party for its anti-Semitic appeals. Nor did he call on Waldheim to offer some *explanation* for his extraordinary deception, something to dispel the notion that if Waldheim's wartime activities were so innocent, then there would have been no need for a cover-up. Of the outrageously anti-Semitic and deceptive (but pro-Waldheim) reporting of the Austrian press, he could bring himself to offer only the belittling comment that "obviously we do not find philo-Semites on every editorial board." Instead, he directed all of his ire at Waldheim's pursuers, especially the WJC. It was *they* who were responsible for the resurgent anti-Semitism in Austria.

Addressing the issue of whether or not he was defending Waldheim, Wiesenthal claimed again that he was not. He said that this misperception came from the fact that Waldheim's accusers did not meet his high standards. Presuming that his Viennese readers would be unaware of his record of publicly accusing innocent men of being Nazi war criminals, Wiesenthal declared that throughout his forty years of Nazi-hunting, he had never leveled accusations "without having sound and watertight proof."[2] Concerning Waldheim, he said, "I saw no document which, in my view, would constitute proof."[3]

Finally, adopting the persona of a benevolent arbiter, he called for a panel of experts from seven nations—the U.S., Israel, Great Britain, Yugoslavia, Greece, Austria, and Germany—to examine the war record of the president-elect. Wiesenthal predicted that in a mere two weeks these experts could examine all the relevant evidence and come to "the right conclusions." Waldheim immediately accepted the idea. In a French radio interview, he added, "Wiesenthal has always acted very correctly toward me."[4]

I noticed that Wiesenthal had been careful in his article to avoid alienating the man who headed the Los Angeles center bearing his own name. His piece did not place Rabbi Marvin Hier on the list of misguided attackers, even though Hier had repeatedly joined us in denouncing Waldheim. But privately, Wiesenthal told an acquaintance that Hier, along with Singer and Steinberg, were, among Jewish leaders, "the three most dangerous people for the Jews."

Wiesenthal's article was the final straw for Steinberg. With Singer's reluctant assent, Steinberg began to take on Wiesenthal publicly. He complained to the *New York Daily News* that Wiesenthal "has yet to explain his motives for whitewashing Waldheim's past."[5]

Next, Steinberg asked me to prepare for Singer's signature a response to the *Ausweg* article. Entitled "Sorrow for Wiesenthal," my four-page draft attempted to focus primary attention not on the WJC's actions but on those of the self-styled Nazi-hunter:

> The recent election of Kurt Waldheim as president of Austria has shocked the conscience of the entire civilized world. Nearly as shocking has been the unpardonable behavior of Simon Wiesenthal. . . .
>
> There can be little doubt that it was Mr. Wiesenthal who ensured the electoral victory of Dr. Waldheim. Each and every time that damning evidence regarding Waldheim's lies and his activities in Hitler's armed forces was brought forward by the World Jewish Congress or by others, the world's most famous Nazi-hunter was there with one or another unlikely "explanation" . . .
>
> Wiesenthal never joined in the international demand for an explanation from Waldheim, and he does not do so even now. Instead, like Waldheim himself, he remains silent on the subject of Waldheim's deception, insisting that the Waldheim question is a matter of "Austrian internal affairs." It is as though Austria never sent Waldheim to New York, where he headed (and deceived) the United Nations for fully ten years. Suddenly disowned by Mr. Wiesenthal, moreover, is the commonsense principle that one who goes to great lengths to conceal something must have some *reason* for doing so. . . .
>
> Perhaps Mr. Wiesenthal can explain why he actually rejected the offer I made . . . of an opportunity to examine our documentation. I invited him to read through our entire file on Waldheim. But he declined. Almost defiantly, he admitted to the *New York Times* in late May that he had not seen our documentation. What he did not tell the *Times,* of course, was that he had *chosen* not to look at the evidence. . . .
>
> Where, Mr. Wiesenthal's critics ask, was Wiesenthal's own investigation of Kurt Waldheim? Where were his documents, his witnesses? Why, they ask, did he not have the courage to join Beate Klarsfeld in the streets of Vienna—where, as Kurt Waldheim looked on silently, she was viciously attacked by Waldheim supporters? And why, they ask, did Mr. Wiesenthal

not have the decency to denounce a political campaign fueled
by the very anti-Semitism he professes to fight? His whitewashing of Kurt Waldheim will long be a stain upon his reputation.
He has humiliated himself and embarrassed the Jewish world.
For Simon Wiesenthal, we have only pity.

Steinberg toned down my draft considerably, and we sent the
manuscript to *Ausweg.* It was never published. Although we could
not prove the point, we had no reason to disbelieve a source in
Vienna who told us that Wiesenthal had managed to get it killed.

In truth, publication of our response would have been a Pyrrhic
victory, for it would have done nothing to ease the pain that Wiesenthal's betrayal had caused us. For me, that pain was especially
acute; it was impossible to forget how Wiesenthal had been the hero
of my youth.

Visitors to the Simon Wiesenthal Center in Los Angeles invariably
see Wiesenthal's self-tribute, engraved on parchment in large letters
and encased in protective glass. It declares:

> When each of us comes before the Six Million, we will be asked
> what we did with our lives. One will say that he became a
> watchmaker and another will say that he became a tailor . . . but
> I will be able to say, I DID NOT FORGET YOU.[6]

These are the most famous words of the legendary Nazi-hunter.
His 1967 autobiography had been my introduction to the subject of
bringing fugitive Nazi war criminals to justice. He could not know
it, but he became something of a mentor to me through that book.
I read it enough times to commit whole paragraphs to memory. Much
later, during my law school years, stealing time from my studies, I
organized a nationwide campaign to obtain the signatures of prominent American law professors on a petition addressed to the West
German government, demanding that Bonn extend indefinitely the
statute of limitations on Nazi war crimes prosecutions. Afterward, I
received a letter from Wiesenthal himself, thanking me for my efforts
and offering the grandfatherly encouragement that he had "no doubt"
that I would have a "fine" career as an attorney. I treasured that
letter. I even became an annual contributor to Wiesenthal's Vienna
operation.

But subsequent events had tempered the hero worship of my
youth. Reality began to intrude in 1979 when I worked at OSI as a
Justice Department summer intern. One of our most sensitive cases
concerned Otto Albrecht von Bolschwing, a former top-level aide

to Adolf Eichmann whom we had found in California. OSI investi-gated the case quietly, so as not to alert von Bolschwing, who had moved to the U.S. in 1954 (after several years of service to U.S. intelligence). It was one of the Justice Department's most important and aggressively pursued investigations. In the fall, when I returned to law school, my mother sent me a clipping from the *Jerusalem Post,* containing a story based on an interview with Wiesenthal, wherein the Nazi-hunter disclosed that von Bolschwing was living in the United States. The reader was left with the impression that it was Wiesenthal who had found him. Surprised that so sensitive a matter was now being discussed publicly, I called my former boss at OSI and asked if he had gone public. No, he replied, the von Bolschwing affair was still hush-hush. He was horrified, and furious, when he learned from me that Wiesenthal had spoken to the press about it. "Dammit, I told him about the case in the strictest confidence," he complained. It appeared that Wiesenthal was trying to take credit for OSI's extraordinary discovery. Fortunately, the story was not picked up outside Israel; but I learned a sad lesson from that episode about Wiesenthal's willingness to violate a confidence.*

More recently, I had become aware of several disturbing problems in Wiesenthal's autobiographical accounts. Perhaps the most extraor-dinary example was the story, told in his 1967 book *The Murderers Among Us,* of his initial arrest during the war. According to the book, he was taken into custody at his house at 4 P.M. on July 6, 1941, by "an auxiliary Ukrainian policeman" who took him to Brigidki Prison in Lvov. Wiesenthal describes in detail how he and about forty other Jews were thereupon lined up against a wall inside the prison court-yard and ordered to cross their arms behind them. One by one, the doomed men were shot in the back of the neck. Each body was thrown into a wooden crate and hauled off. Wiesenthal wrote that after every few shots, the executioner "would step back to the table and have a swig of vodka and some *zakusky* (Polish hors d'oeuvres) while another man handed him another gun." According to the ac-count, about twenty Jews had already been killed and the executioner was drawing close to Wiesenthal when church bells sounded and a Ukrainian voice suddenly shouted, "Enough! Evening mass!" Wie-senthal had been miraculously spared. With the help of a Ukrainian acquaintance, he managed to escape that night and "reached home the next morning."[7]

---

*Eventually, von Bolschwing was prosecuted by OSI, but because he was in ill health, he was not deported; he died soon thereafter in California. For Wiesenthal's disclosure, see Alan Elsner, "Canada Shelters Ex-Nazis, Wiesenthal Says," *Jerusalem Post International Edition,* October 15, 1979. He repeated the offense in his January 31, 1980, annual report to his contributors.

The scene is arguably the most harrowing in the entire book. Unfortunately, however, it differs rather remarkably from the account that Wiesenthal gave when he was questioned as a prospective witness at Nuremberg in 1948. In the formerly classified Nuremberg transcript, which I had copied, out of idle curiosity, during one of my Waldheim research trips to the National Archives, Wiesenthal declared under oath that he was arrested at his apartment by "two Germans and a Ukrainian" and was taken to perform forced labor in the local railway yards. Now, when I at last found the time to read what I had copied, I was stunned to find that he made no mention of Brigidki Prison, shootings, vodka, *zakusky,* or bells signaling evening mass.[8]

It was an unforgettable episode. While I was certainly aware of many cases in which Jews had effected near-miraculous last-moment escapes from Nazi execution squads, never before had I heard of an instance in which the killers, having rounded up their intended victims and begun shooting them, allowed something so prosaic (and unrelated to the "logistics" of genocide) as the tolling of church bells to interrupt them in what might be termed "mid-murder."

In his 1948 account, moreover, he gave the date of his initial arrest during the Second World War as July *eight*—not, as his book says, July *six*. As I read the Nuremberg transcript against the text of the book, it took some moments (and recourse to a 1941 calendar) before I realized what the change of date had accomplished. With the arrest date two days earlier—on a *Sunday* instead of a Tuesday—the whole astounding new story about being arrested, being saved at the last minute from execution by church bells tolling "evening mass," and escaping from Brigidki Prison that very night, neatly fits Ukrainian Catholic religious practice (Orthodox, Roman Catholic, and Uniate). The problem is, according to his own sworn testimony behind closed doors in 1948, Wiesenthal was still a free man when all of this was supposed to have been happening!* Perhaps he had not realized that his confidential testimony could one day be made public.

I was struck by a pathetic irony: Simon Wiesenthal and Kurt Waldheim were two Austrians who shared at least one fault: an inability to tell a consistent story about their wartime experiences.

I had long had questions as well about Wiesenthal's oft-repeated claim to fame, the one story that vaulted him into international prominence and kept him there—namely, the contention that he pinpointed Adolf Eichmann's whereabouts in Argentina, enabling Israeli

---

*The story is repeated—with the July 6 date intact and the word "vespers" substituted for "mass"—in Wiesenthal's 1989 book, *Justice Not Vengeance* (London: Weidenfeld & Nicolson; see pp. 7–8.) As with mass, communal attendance at vespers was traditional on the sabbath and holy days only.

agents to effect his daring apprehension in 1960. A simple sampling of material from the pages and dustjackets of Wiesenthal's books illustrates the claim:

"Wiesenthal is best known for his discovery of Adolf Eichmann's South American hideout. . . ."[9]

"Mr. Wiesenthal was the man most responsible for finding Adolf Eichmann and approximately 1,000 other Nazi criminals. . . ."[10]

As Wiesenthal's story goes, in 1953 he became acquainted in Austria with someone he refers to only as Baron M., a fellow stamp collector, who showed him a letter he had received from an ex–Wehrmacht officer who wrote of having met "this awful swine Eichmann" in Buenos Aires. This, Wiesenthal said, is what ultimately led him to tip the Israelis to Eichmann's presence in Argentina. In his 1974 book *Aftermath,* the late Ladislas Farago had relegated Wiesenthal to a footnote in which he charged that the Nazi-hunter had falsely taken credit for the tip, which, he wrote, the Israelis had actually received from Dr. Fritz Bauer, public prosecutor for the state of Hesse in West Germany. The fact that Wiesenthal's name appeared nowhere in the 1975 account of the Eichmann mission by former Mossad chief Isser Harel (who personally directed the project) had long ago led me to conclude that Farago's otherwise largely unreliable book was probably correct on this one point.[11]

What did it all mean? Had Wiesenthal played loosely with the facts of his background solely in order to build a reputation for himself, or did the embellishments serve the larger, humanitarian purpose of positioning him to accomplish great things? Did the end justify the means? I agonized over the proper use of the information I had. Those of us who had actually prosecuted Nazi criminals knew that the myth of the man was far larger than his life. But who was daring—or foolish—enough to stand up and say so?

As I pondered this issue privately, Gerald L. Posner and John Ware made a bold attempt to bring a fragment of the information into the open. Their book, *Mengele: The Complete Story,* was published shortly after Waldheim's election. Although Wiesenthal was certainly not the subject of their book, the two writers were quite willing to take on the celebrated Nazi-hunter in print.

Posner and Ware repeated the account given by Mossad chief Harel in his 1975 book about the mission, *The House on Garibaldi Street:* A blind German Jew named Lothar Hermann, who lived in the Argentine town of Coronel Suarez, wrote a series of letters to prosecutor Bauer in Hesse, claiming that Eichmann was living nearby.

Bauer, believing that neither the Bonn nor Buenos Aires governments would genuinely attempt to apprehend Eichmann, passed the
information secretly to Israeli authorities, who pursued the matter
and ultimately brought Eichmann to face justice in a Jerusalem court-
room. Posner and Ware stated directly what Harel had only seemed
to imply: Wiesenthal had taken credit all these years for something
in which he had no part.

The problem with the Posner and Ware conclusion, as with Ladislas
Farago's similar assertion twelve years earlier, was that neither account was supported by any real *proof.* Where was the explicit confirmation by the Israeli government that Wiesenthal had played no
role whatsoever? And what of Wiesenthal's claim in his 1961 book
Ich jagte Eichmann (I Hunted Eichmann) that he had traced the Eichmann family to Argentina based on statements that the arch-Nazi's
children had made before the family vanished from Austria? Still,
Posner and Ware had renewed my curiosity about the authenticity
of the seminal accomplishment that had made Wiesenthal a house-
hold name.

With the apprehension of Eichmann in 1960, Josef Mengele came
to be considered by many the most notorious Nazi war criminal still
at large. Wiesenthal methodically set up Mengele as a classic "opposite number," much like the role Professor Moriarity played for
Sherlock Holmes. The Nazi-hunter thereafter spent more than two
decades proclaiming that the ghoulish selector and experimenter of
Auschwitz infamy was living in opulence, protected by the secret
police and military of Paraguay's then–dictator Alfredo Stroessner.
He portrayed Mengele as a regular patron of the best restaurants in
Asunción, who traveled, accompanied by bodyguards, in a sleek black
Mercedes 280SL.

In numerous "sightings" and "close calls" over the years, Wiesenthal placed Mengele in Paraguay, Bolivia, Uruguay, Chile, Argentina,
Spain, and Germany. For twenty years, Wiesenthal could get international press headlines almost at will by announcing another Mengele "sighting." I had long marveled at the way the international
media gave credence to these reports despite the fact that Mengele
never turned up at any of the places to which Wiesenthal dispatched
them. In truth, as the world would not learn until much later, Mengele was living in near-squalor in a tiny, ramshackle house in Brazil—
ironically, the one reputed Nazi haven where Wiesenthal never had
Mengele living.

With the discovery of Mengele's remains at a cemetery in Embu,
Brazil, in 1985, and the determination that he had died while swim-
ming in 1979, the ultimate incompetence of Wiesenthal's Mengele
hunt became pathetically clear. Wiesenthal had persisted in his Men-

gele "sightings" for six years after Mengele's death and burial! The book by Posner and Ware added some details of Wiesenthal's escapades that, in a less serious matter, would have been hilarious.

There was, for example, the time (in 1961) Mengele supposedly had tried to find a Middle East hideout. According to Wiesenthal, Mengele and his wife sought refuge in Egypt, but were barred from entry by President Gamal Abdel Nasser. Mengele was then taken on a chartered yacht by a former SS-*Obersturmbannfuehrer* named Schwarz to the Greek island of Kythnos. Wiesenthal learned of this, he said, as he was about to leave for Jerusalem for the Eichmann trial. Fearing that "several weeks would be lost" if he utilized "normal diplomatic channels," Wiesenthal said he called the editor of a German magazine: "The magazine wanted the story. I wanted the man." (Why Wiesenthal would have chosen to risk frightening Mengele away by going to the press rather than to, say, the Israelis, who had only recently captured Eichmann, is beyond comprehension.) In his autobiography, Wiesenthal recalled that the magazine sent a reporter, who arrived on the island "twelve hours" after Mengele had left. "We had lost another round," wrote Wiesenthal. Not so, according to the magazine's writer, Ottmar Katz, who told Posner and Ware that "not a single detail" of Wiesenthal's tip was correct. He said he spent four or five days on Kythnos and found no trace of Mengele. "I did explain to Wiesenthal that it was all wrong," he said, "and then seven years later I read his book and he said we'd missed Mengele by a few hours."[12]

Wiesenthal also claimed that in March 1964, a dozen Auschwitz survivors who called themselves "The Committee of Twelve" pursued Mengele to the Paraguayan jungle. Repeating a story that he had been told, Wiesenthal described the resulting scene in the Hotel Tirol, near Hohenau in eastern Paraguay. The Committee of Twelve entered the hotel lobby shortly before 1 A.M. on "a hot dark night." According to Wiesenthal, they "ran up the stairway, and broke open the door of bedroom No. 26" only to find it empty. The hotel owner told them that the lodger—clad in his pajamas—had rushed off ten minutes earlier after receiving a phone call.

The problem with this account is that the Hotel Tirol had no second floor and no Room 26. Nor was there a telephone through which Mengele could have received a warning![13]

Wiesenthal was later quoted as saying that the "Committee of Twelve" had "planned to kidnap Mengele to take him to a yacht and judge him when out at sea." This amplified version of the story seemed to overlook the fact that Paraguay is a landlocked country. As Posner and Ware noted sarcastically, "The possibility of an escape by yacht to the open sea" was "somewhat ambitious."[14]

The "close calls" continued at regular intervals, as Posner and Ware documented. In November 1968, for example, Wiesenthal claimed that his "agents" had snapped photos of Mengele on the streets of Asunción, but within twenty-four hours he admitted that he was mistaken. In a 1970 television interview, Wiesenthal announced that he had "new information that Dr. Mengele is in Puerto San Vincente in Paraguay," in the military zone of Alta Paraña. Paraguayan authorities responded, correctly, that no location known as Puerto San Vincente existed in Alta Paraña.[15] In March 1971, Wiesenthal said that he had just missed catching Mengele in Spain, where he had been spotted driving a car.

The numerous Mengele "sightings" attracted the attention of Horst von Glasenapp, a German investigative judge, who arranged for Wiesenthal to appear before a Vienna court in a special session. Von Glasenapp reported that Wiesenthal "refused to answer" questions about Mengele, claiming that he had to protect the confidentiality of his informants. Von Glasenapp appreciated that concern, but concluded, "I left feeling he was eager to convey that he was leading the field on this question, that he was the man out in the front. Perhaps behind his refusal to answer the questions was a feeling that the people he had in mind were not so reliable after all."[16]

In September 1977, Wiesenthal told *Time* magazine that Mengele owned two elegant homes in Asunción and was surrounded by bodyguards. He wore dark glasses when he went out and was active in "a surviving network of Nazi bigwigs known as *Die Spinne* [The Spider]." Mengele, according to Wiesenthal, was a frequent visitor to the German Club in Asunción, where he liked to impress others by slamming his pistol onto the bar.[17]

A Wiesenthal bulletin, mailed to his financial supporters in 1978, declared that Mengele was "living in Paraguay, where he is protected by the local junta." He noted pointedly that his monitoring of Mengele's activities "has cost us a lot of money."[18] Indeed, the Nazi-hunter's fund-raising goals seemed to be the primary motivators of his myriad public pronouncements. For, had the objective of actually apprehending Mengele instead been the principal consideration, then the information should have been given quietly to those who could take him into custody. Had Wiesenthal really known where Mengele was living, the fame that the Nazi-hunter gained in the course of publicizing these "sightings" would almost certainly have come at the terrible price of providing Mengele and his protectors with timely warning that the Nazi doctor's hideout had been discovered.

The Nazi-hunter's reports became increasingly bizarre: Mengele was ensconced amid a colony of Nazis in Chile; he had recently purchased a phony passport of a Central American country "from a private agency in Washington" that was selling them for $20,000 apiece; he was in Uruguay; suffering from heart disease, he was ready to surrender to a West German Embassy; he had been seen "five times recently . . . his capture could happen in the next several weeks."[19] Of course, these reports were every bit as baseless as the Paraguay tales that Wiesenthal had supplied to the media for years. But the more sensational the reports became, the more the press devoured them. Now that it was known, however, that Mengele had died in Brazil in 1979, Wiesenthal's January 1981 annual report, placing him in Rio Negro, Uruguay, four months earlier, looked almost like gallows humor. "As we are told, his state of health is not at all good," Wiesenthal had written his contributors.

The Mengele case even created a curious tie between Wiesenthal and Kurt Waldheim. Under the Freedom of Information Act, I obtained from the U.S. State Department a May 17, 1979, letter from Wiesenthal to U.N. Secretary-General Waldheim, informing Waldheim that Paraguayan authorities were tracking Mengele's "frequently changing" residences. (Mengele had died in Brazil three months earlier, unbeknownst to his pursuers.) Wiesenthal implored Waldheim to use his influence to convince Paraguay to issue an arrest warrant for Mengele.[20]

The following year, after Paraguay issued the warrant, Wiesenthal was eager to share the credit. He told reporters that Waldheim played "a decisive part" in convincing Paraguay to act. This was an invaluable testimonial from the great Nazi-hunter, for this was the very time when questions were being asked about Waldheim's prewar affiliations and wartime record.

In a 1984 letter to the editor of the New York Times, Wiesenthal again praised Waldheim for his assistance in the Mengele case.[21] In retrospect, the picture was absurd: There was Wiesenthal heaping praise on Waldheim for his role in aiding the hunt for a nonexistent Nazi war criminal in the wrong country!

Posner and Ware conjectured that "financial constraints" plus "a knack of playing to the gallery" were responsible for the plethora of groundless "sightings." "The truth," they said, "was that Wiesenthal's file on Mengele was "a potpourri of information," which "only sustained his self-confirmatory myths."[22]

After Mengele's remains were found in Brazil in 1985, an initially skeptical (not to mention embarrassed) Simon Wiesenthal acknowledged that Mengele had, indeed, died years earlier. A top forensic specialist engaged by the Wiesenthal Center had already concurred in the identification of the skeleton as Mengele's.

Wiesenthal moved quickly to create the vague impression that he too had suspected in the late 1970s that Mengele was hiding out in

Brazil (even though his annual reports through 1985 had placed Mengele's South American residences solely in Argentina, Paraguay, Chile, Bolivia and Uruguay). In January 1986, following documented media disclosures that Mengele's son Rolf had secretly visited his father in Brazil in 1977, Wiesenthal wrote in his annual report to contributors that he had learned in 1977 from "a reliable source" that Rolf was "about to travel to Brazil." In this new account, the Nazi-hunter claimed that he had hoped to dispatch two people to trail Rolf but lacked the eight thousand dollars needed to fund the operation. According to Wiesenthal, he therefore approached "a popular Dutch newspaper" and offered it the "exclusive rights to the manhunt story" in return for its agreement to pay the expenses of the mission. The newspaper declined, he said, viewing the expenditure as "too risky." As a result, Wiesenthal wrote, "[t]he operation had to be called off." Left unaddressed in the Nazi-hunter's report, however, is why Wiesenthal should have deemed it appropriate to go to the media—rather than to the Israeli, German or Brazilian government—with sensitive information that, with careful police and diplomatic work, could have led to the apprehension of the most notorious of all fugitive Nazi criminals. Even more inexplicable is Wiesenthal's failure, *after* having been turned down by the unnamed Dutch newspaper, to turn the matter over to governmental authorities rather than simply "calling off" the "operation." Later, however, Wiesenthal offered a dramatically different account that conveniently cured some of the embarrassing weaknesses of the first version.*

A few knowledgeable people—such as Israel's former ambassador to Paraguay, Benjamin Weiser Varon—sought to take Wiesenthal to task publicly for his misdirection over the years, but the criticisms were either unnoticed or else demolished by vitriolic letters to the editor from Wiesenthal supporters who typically accused the critics of defaming one of the great figures of Jewish history. (Varon even charged that Wiesenthal's oft-repeated claims that Mengele was protected by an impenetrable phalanx of Paraguayan soldiers, police officers, and bodyguards naturally dissuaded would-be pursuers of the notorious war criminal from attempting a seemingly "foolish"

*In his 1989 book *Justice Not Vengeance* (London: Weidenfeld & Nicolson), Wiesenthal repeats the claim that he had learned of a trip to Brazil by Rolf Mengele. This time, however, the date is inexplicably changed by two crucial years. In the 1989 account, Wiesenthal writes (at page 111) that he learned of a then-impending trip by Rolf Mengele in the spring of *1979*, several months after Josef Mengele had, unbeknownst to his pursuers, died. Proof that the new version is not the result of a typographical error lies in the book's explicit questioning of why Rolf would have made such a trip "to see a dead man" who drowned "[o]n 7 February 1979. . . ." Curiously, Wiesenthal's new version makes no reference to any plan to trail Rolf Mengele. The 1979 version has an obvious advantage over its 1977 predecessor: it transforms Wiesenthal's failure to pass the supposed tip on to the proper authorities into an error of no practical consequence (since Mengele had died earlier that year).

mission to capture the purportedly "untouchable" Mengele at a time when he, in fact, "lived alone and unprotected in a shack in Brazil with a single Mauser near his bed."[23]) However, now that Posner and Ware's detailed accounts added bits of color to what insiders already knew concerning Wiesenthal's Keystone Kops–style performance in the Mengele case, I thought that the Wiesenthal myth might at last explode. When, however, it did not, I hypothesized explanations. Posner and Ware had interspersed the Wiesenthal material throughout their book, making it difficult to follow the thread of his actions over the years. And they had not attempted a broader debunking of the myth of Wiesenthal as the great hunter of Nazis, as they could have done by, for example, highlighting his false sightings of other notorious Nazis (such as Lyons Gestapo chief Klaus Barbie, whom he reported in 1971 to be living in Egypt, although he had actually been residing in Lima, Peru, for twenty years.*) Reviewers of the book, apparently unwilling to join in questioning the Wiesenthal legend, tended to ignore his role in the Mengele story. The media, after all, had been something of a co-conspirator in creating the irresistible legend of the cloak-and-dagger-equipped survivor who used a secret international network of well-placed informants to bring to justice the arch-villains of the century. Moreover, the Mengele case was old news by now—Waldheim was the current news concerning ex-Nazis. Thus, the book languished on bookstore shelves and its cataloging of what Ambassador Varon derisively termed "The Great Nazi Hunt That Never Was" essentially evaporated in the mist of history, doubtless to Wiesenthal's great relief.†[24]

Still, Posner and Ware had taken a bold step, and I wondered if it was time for me to add another part of the story. Over the years, I had collected a large stack of materials regarding Wiesenthal's role in the fiasco over Martin Bormann, former chief of the Nazi Party chancellory, who had vanished in Berlin during the final hours of the Third Reich. At Nuremberg, Hitler's deputy was convicted *in absentia* and sentenced to death. For more than thirty years there-

---

*See Wiesenthal's annual report of January 31, 1984 (in which he also refers to Barbie solely as one who committed crimes against French Resistance members, making no mention of his role in crimes against Jews, such as his responsibility for the deportation of Jewish children from France to their deaths in Poland). For background on Barbie, see Tom Bower, *Klaus Barbie: The Butcher of Lyons* (New York: Pantheon, 1984).

†Nevertheless, Wiesenthal was clearly stung by these criticisms. By 1989, he retracted his opinion that Mengele was dead, and resumed his campaign of announcing Mengele "sightings" in South America. I was appalled by the resumption of this practice, which cruelly tormented survivors of Auschwitz by suggesting that the man who helped send so many of their loved ones to the gas chambers might be alive, well, and laughing at them from a new safe haven. In 1992, a DNA analysis commissioned by the German government confirmed that the Embu remains were those of Josef Mengele and Wiesenthal finally agreed that Mengele was indeed dead.

after, he was the central figure in most media accounts regarding the pursuit of fugitive Nazi war criminals. Newspaper articles, magazine stories, and even entire books were devoted to fantastic accounts of his "Fourth Reich" activities in various South American countries.

Wiesenthal had long claimed to be in the vanguard of the Bormann search. For example, his May 1965 letter addressed to the "Dear Friends of the Documentation Center" disclosed that he had obtained confidential information indicating "that Martin Bormann is still alive." He claimed to have a witness who saw Bormann with Mengele in 1961 and identified him from a photograph. After assuring his contributors that "the matter was *verified*," Wiesenthal appealed "to our friends to help us and to support us in order to continue this work."[25]

In *The Murderers Among Us,* Wiesenthal "disclosed" that Hitler's ex-confidant was, in 1966, living in South America, where he was "well protected" by virtue of his "money and a network of fanatically devoted helpers."[26]

In 1968, Wiesenthal told a Swedish newspaper that his coworkers had tracked Bormann to a place called the "Waldner Kolonie" in southern Brazil, near the Paraguayan border.[27]

A January 31, 1969, letter to "Friends of the Documentation Center" continued the theme, reporting on "tangible statements" from a Wiesenthal informant proving that Bormann had been in Brazil, at least "for the past year." Wiesenthal closed this latest note to his contributors with the plea, "We hope to continue our activity with your help."[28]

In a 1970 interview, Wiesenthal announced that Bormann had lived the previous year in Dribura, a German "colony" in the Brazilian state of Rio Grande do Sul, bordering on Paraguay. He made a point of noting that the pastor of this colony was named "Himmler."[29] The German Embassy in Rio de Janeiro took note of this report and pointed out key errors: The town was called Ibiruba; it was on the Argentine border; the pastor's name was Huemmler. And there was no trace of Bormann's ever having set foot there.

On September 29, 1970, Wiesenthal was summoned before the Criminal Investigation Division of the Provincial Court in Vienna, where officials took sworn testimony regarding his numerous statements about Bormann. Under oath, Wiesenthal said:

> It is true that until very recently I have made statements to several journalists regarding the conjectural whereabouts of Martin Bormann. In this representation I could admittedly only make statements on a locale of residence where in my opinion Bormann could conceivably have been some time ago.

Wiesenthal hedged the accuracy of quotes attributed to him, complaining that "things I mentioned as being believable were presented . . . as facts."

But his sworn protestation that in his statements to reporters he had been referring only to "conjectural" whereabouts was directly contradicted by the unequivocal statements made in his letters to his financial contributors, which he personally signed.

In truth, throughout this entire period of Wiesenthal's "sightings," Bormann's bones lay under German soil. German authorities ultimately verified the remains, which were unearthed in Berlin in 1972, proving that Bormann died while fleeing from Hitler's bunker *in 1945,* shortly after his Fuehrer had committed suicide. Wiesenthal was, at first, dubious of the claim, but eventually even he agreed with the conclusion.[30] Bormann had been dead all along!

In his 1973 final report on the Bormann matter, First State Prosecutor Joachim Richter of the Frankfurt State Prosecution Office declared that he had taken "special notice" of Wiesenthal's statements over the years. The recent Wiesenthal material in particular, the report charged, "contained predominantly anonymous and frivolous-sounding letters."[31] As I read these words, I was reminded of how I had concluded years earlier that Wiesenthal's cavalier dissemination of unevaluated, anonymous "tips" had likely endeared him to Nazi *protectors* as a disseminator of disinformation that would send law enforcement authorities onto false trails.

In sum, Wiesenthal's roles in the biggest Nazi cases of all—Mengele, Bormann, and, in all likelihood, Eichmann as well—were studies in ineptitude, exaggeration, and self-glorification. But few were willing to tell these tales, and it seemed that even fewer wanted to hear them. Meanwhile, Wiesenthal's fame grew with each passing year, as did the list of international honors bestowed upon him (including the Congressional Medal, personally conferred by President Reagan in a 1980 White House ceremony, and his first Nobel Peace Prize nomination, in 1983).

Like Singer and Steinberg, I was more than ready to take on Wiesenthal: He had gone far beyond the buffoonery and false boasts of prior years; his behavior during the unfolding of the Waldheim scandal had been truly reprehensible.

I made a first attempt to address the Wiesenthal question during a speech at the Stephen Wise Free Synagogue in Manhattan. In the course of my remarks, I quoted a litany of crudely anti-Semitic statements that had emanated from Austria, especially from People's Party spokesmen, the Austrian press, and Waldheim himself. Then I added a postscript, one that I thought was temperate under the circumstances. I made a single-sentence reference to my "disappointment" that "the renowned Nazi-hunter Simon Wiesenthal, who lives in Vienna, has seen fit to blame the World Jewish Congress—not Waldheim and his supporters—for this outpouring of hatred." My attempt to cite examples of Wiesenthal's charges, his inexcusable defending of Waldheim and his distorting the history of the Holocaust in Greece was immediately interrupted.

"No!" someone shouted from the audience.

"How dare you!" yelled another.

A third person rose and lectured me about Wiesenthal's many achievements, such as his role in capturing Eichmann.

The room reverberated with the sounds of shocked, angry voices.

I leaned close to the microphone and tried to explain: "I'm just telling you what has happened in Austria this year." But no one seemed to hear.

My speech was over. I never got to confess my bewilderment as to the *motivation* behind Wiesenthal's unprecedented behavior. Instead, I retreated from the pandemonium and managed to hail a cab outside the synagogue. As the taxi sped downtown, Steinberg's admonition, "You can't do battle with a legend and hope to win," dominated my thoughts. I could almost hear him reproaching me with some variation on the theme "I told you so."

25

I answered the knock on my Washington hotel room door and accepted the package that was thrust at me by a bicycle-helmeted courier. I ordered a pot of coffee from room service, kicked off my shoes, and sat down to study forty-nine pages of typewritten text entitled, *In the Matter of Kurt Waldheim*. It was a partial copy of Waldheim's defensive submission to Attorney General Meese, dated June 11, 1986. No one outside of the Justice Department was supposed to see this material, but here it was, lent to me for the day by someone who, like myself, had served several years at OSI and then left government service. My former colleague said he was merely an intermediary; he explained that "a mutual friend at Justice" wanted to get my thoughts on Waldheim's submission. Since I had been immersed for months in the nearly Byzantine details of "Waldheim's war," and since I was also one of OSI's sources, someone at the Department evidently felt that it was both desirable and appropriate to solicit my analysis of Waldheim's most detailed defense to date. For once, I was happy to disengage my inquisitive instincts: If I did not know the identity of my Justice Department "contact," then I could not get him or her into trouble. Since I saw nothing wrong with the Department soliciting my help in analyzing Waldheim's complex submission, I found the plan a tad silly. Still, the intermediary arrangement suited me just fine; at the end of this day, I was to give my analysis to my former colleague and he would pass it on to our "mutual friend," whoever that was.

I set to work. There were many points of interest, covered by Waldheim's lawyers in chronological order, beginning with 1938. They continued to deny Waldheim's prewar memberships in Nazi organizations. "Any fair examination of the record quickly reveals the fallacy of these allegations," the brief stated. Whatever meetings young Waldheim may have attended were "for the purpose of disguising his resistance to enrollment in the organization." This was a most inventive explanation: He participated in Nazi meetings so as to conceal his personal revulsion at formally enrolling as a member!

Here, too, was another intriguing clue concerning one of the mysterious handwritten dates in Waldheim's WASt records. Waldheim's brief claimed that, in early 1979, the U.S.-run Berlin Document Center, at the request of French authorities, reviewed its records to determine whether Waldheim had ever been a member of any of the Nazi organizations whose surviving records are stored there. The Berlin Document Center responded on March 3, 1979, indicating "negative findings." What interested me was not the negative report, but the fact that once again the French were implicated. The check was conducted less than three weeks prior to one of the handwritten dates on the relevant records at the French-run WASt archive in the same city.

There were repeated assertions by Waldheim's lawyers that his posting in western Bosnia was merely a paper assignment and that he was 120 miles away during the Kozara massacres, serving on the Bader Combat Group's liaison staff attached to the Italian "Pusteria" Division in Plevlje, Montenegro, where he remained until the Pusteria Division withdrew west toward the Dalmatian coast, on July 11, 1942. Waldheim explained that his previous confusion on this point resulted from the fact that there was a mountain pass near Plevlje known as the "Kozara Saddle." The brief stated that the existence of this "other" Kozara was confirmed by "contemporary maps." Thus, the report declared, "it is almost certain" that Waldheim was not involved in the Kozara campaign. What strange language, I thought. Here were Waldheim's attorneys, attempting to defend their client, and they were finding it necessary to resort to qualifying words such as "it is almost certain." This was simply *not* the way American defense lawyers were accustomed to speaking.

In reality, it was "almost certain" that he *was* involved, for we had already seen documents establishing that the Bader Combat Group was dissolved and Waldheim was sent back to western Bosnia long before July—indeed, during the last week of *May,* on the eve of the Kozara campaign. Either Waldheim's people were unaware of the new proof on this point, or else they were hoping that the Justice Department was unaware of it. Waldheim was probably having as much difficulty as the rest of the world in keeping track of the piecemeal disclosures and discoveries.

The report summarily dismissed the charge that Waldheim (although supposedly not there) was decorated for the Kozara campaign and was listed on the "honor roll" appended to the Kozara report-cum-prose poem. It quoted Waldheim's explanation that King Zvonimir Medals were "handed out like chocolates." The "medal award process," Waldheim's lawyers argued, was "unrelated to reality" and "rife with irregularities and inaccuracies."

However long Waldheim had really remained in Montenegro before heading north to Bosnia, his lawyers made an enormous slip on page 22 of their presentation, conclusively confirming my suspicion that he was *the* liaison there between the Bader Combat Group and the Italian Division "Pusteria." The memo stated: "D.V.K.5 [Waldheim's liaison unit in Plevlje] consisted of an interpreter, Dr. Waldheim, and a Signal Corps team with a radio truck, which was to provide a communications link between the Italian Divisional Command and the German command of *Kampfgruppe* Bader." This held the potential to be a critical admission, for if we discovered any criminal involvement on the part of this D.V.K.5 unit, we now could pin it directly onto Waldheim. For once, we had him *in charge* of something, not just second-in-command. And this time, he also did not have any subordinates onto whom he could try to shift blame. He was "it," *the* liaison between the Germans and the "Pusteria" Division.

Waldheim claimed that he remained in Montenegro until the Italians pulled out on July 11, and then arrived in the Salonika area in "mid-July 1942." This outdated defense at first appeared to throw Waldheim from the kettle straight to the flames, for while this chronology kept him conveniently away from Kozara, it placed him in Salonika, Greece, just as the German actions against the Jews were beginning.* Waldheim's brief countered this dilemma with an apparently legitimate claim that he was away on study leave and other assignments when the actual Salonika deportations took place (namely, March through May 1943 and again in August 1943). Nevertheless, this latest chronology brought Waldheim "briefly" back to Salonika in July 1942. This was when the final phase of the deportation of the Jewish population was being planned. Waldheim's brief also brought him back yet again in early October 1943, less than two months after the city was completely depopulated of Jews— a dramatic development that could not have gone unnoticed by such a well-informed intelligence officer. Despite this, Waldheim continued to deny that he had learned of the deportations before this year, forty-three years after the fact. He doth protest too much, I said to myself. There had to be a reason.

Regarding the "Black Operation," the topic of conversation at the meeting memorialized in the now-famous Podgorica airstrip photograph, Waldheim's presentation repeated an old refrain, declaring

---

*On July 13, 1942, between six thousand and seven thousand Jewish males, ranging in age from eighteen to forty-eight, were assembled in Salonika's main square and registered for the Nazi slave labor system. Almost immediately, the Germans began assigning the Jews to forced labor sites.

that "atrocities were perpetrated by both sides" in Yugoslavia, by both the Germans and Tito's partisans. The brief contended that, in any event, Waldheim's only role at the meeting was that of a simple interpreter. Attached as an exhibit was a letter from one of the officers in the photograph, *Oberleutnant* Joachim Macholz, declaring as much. It also included a copy of a page purporting to come from the wartime diary of General Artur Phleps, "recently made available" by Phleps's son Reinhard, stating that the subject of the meeting was the chain of command between German and Italian forces in the Balkans. In Waldheim's view, this (supposed) fact rendered the meeting innocuous. *Right,* I scoffed silently, it was an innocent discussion of division of authority among the perpetrators of a massacre. We knew from the book by Phleps' second-in-command, Otto Kumm, that the "chain of command" discussion was, in fact, a dispute between the German commander, Lueters, and the Italian commander, Roncaglia, over which of them was in charge of carrying out *the Black Operation.* The gruesome campaign had been commenced just a week earlier, and it was inconceivable to me that the airstrip meeting did not include some discussion of strategy and tactics for its continuation. Waldheim's brief derided that notion, questioning why a "planning session" would have been held for "[an] operation already in progress." It occurred to me that, in order to find the brief persuasive on this point, one would have to conclude that this was the only large-scale, protracted military operation of the Second World War in which strategic plans were not modified and updated, even once, during its implementation. That possibility, ludicrous on its face, was in any event conclusively disproved by National Archives documentation we had seen months earlier, proving that revised instructions were indeed issued as the operation progressed.

The brief next moved on to a detailed discussion of Waldheim's role in the Ic/AO Branch at Salonika, and I realized with a start that it completely ignored his Athens assignment. Waldheim's brief was silent on the subject of the deportation of the once-allied Italian soldiers and the targeting of partisans at Arta and the Jewish leadership of Ioannina. In Athens (unlike Salonika), Waldheim had been assigned to *Operations* rather than Intelligence, and this fact made the "omission" all the more frustrating.

Regarding the interrogation and disposition of captured Allied commandos, Waldheim's attorneys acknowledged that criminal abuses occurred. But they relied on the argument that "there was a distinct division of labor between the Ic section [Intelligence] and the AO [Counterintelligence] section" in order to distance Waldheim from any of the crimes. They employed additional curious language, writing "it must be assumed" that "all such activities were handled by the AO section, and not Dr. Waldheim's Ic section." *Nonsense,* I said to myself. There was no completely separate unit known as Ic. Warnstorff, as chief of the entire Ic/AO Branch, supervised *both* Ic *and* AO—and Lt. Waldheim was his principal aide. Indeed, Army Group E's organizational table gave Warnstorff, not Hammer, primary responsibility for such "AO" tasks as cooperation with the SD and issuing command and disciplinary instructions to the Abwehr troops. This defense also conveniently ignored the fact that a broad range of classified documents addressed to the Ic/AO Branch was received and read by Waldheim in his capacity as the special missions staff officer who served as the branch chief's principal aide. Some of the supposed "exclusively AO" documents even bore his initials or signature.* Many documents we had already found demonstrated that the Ic and AO functions often overlapped and that Waldheim was thoroughly familiar with the latter. Most importantly, documents proving that Waldheim was personally involved in some of the Allied commando incidents were already a matter of public record. Perhaps recognizing the weakness of the argument, the report added a chilling disclaimer. It pointed out that any mistreatment of commando prisoners "would constitute a war crime, as opposed to a persecution or crime against humanity." But U.S. immigration law, they noted, covered only the latter two categories of crimes, *not* war crimes. Thus, Waldheim's brief argued, even if his involvement in the commando episodes made him a Nazi war criminal, such a fact would still not satisfy the narrow provisions of the Holtzman Amendment; he could not be barred from the U.S. on the basis of any actions against British and American commandos. I penned a sarcastic comment in the margin: "Ah, the wondrous legal technicality—ever the villain's refuge!" How humiliating, I thought, for the president of Austria to be trying to squeeze through a "Nazi war criminal loophole" in the law.

As far as Jewish deportations from southern Greece were concerned, the brief declared that, during a portion of this period, Waldheim was home in Vienna, being treated for a thyroid condition, completing his doctoral dissertation, and receiving his law degree. On other occasions, Waldheim's attorneys wrote, he was simply busy with his own intelligence-gathering activities in Salonika and knew

---

*In an affidavit later provided for Waldheim's use and released by the Austrian Foreign Ministry in 1987, Waldheim's immediate superior, Col. Herbert Warnstorff, noted that Waldheim was responsible for "the registering of incoming confidential matters with a short description." For examples of "AO" documents initialed "received" by Waldheim but *not* by the "AO" (Major Hammer), see USNA T311/179/958 and T311/285/1114–15.

nothing of the genocide of the Jewish communities on the Greek islands. The brief argued that captured documents explicitly referencing Ic/AO involvement in these crimes actually implicated only the AO section. Waldheim was never even informed, much less involved. The documents, in other words, should not be read as written—even though Waldheim's lawyers were unable to cite so much as a shred of evidence establishing that only AO personnel were involved in the Jewish deportations.

I sat bolt upright when I reached the portion of Waldheim's defense memo that dismissed the *Odluka*. Apparently, Waldheim and his lawyers had obtained a copy of the Yugoslav indictment! The brief attacked the testimony of the two key witnesses, Major Klaus Mellinghoff and Johann Mayer. It noted the disturbing—if it was true—information that, "as opposed to all other documents, the complete protocols of these testimonies no longer exist according to the responsible Yugoslav archivists." Waldheim's brief said that only selected fragments of the witnesses' statements remained.

Mayer's testimony was subjected to a full frontal attack. The brief charged that the *Odluka* version differed significantly from the UNWCC version, and it quoted excerpts from the two versions to prove the contention:

MAYER'S ODLUKA TESTIMONY
I am aware that on one occasion in Sarajevo certain civilians were killed; though it was a question of German soldiers who had deserted and who had created an antifascist organization, orders for shooting them were issued by Section Ic, according to an information from the Gestapo. . . . This order was issued by the chief of the General Staff and the Commander of the Army Group. This was in November/December 1944.

MAYER'S UNWCC TESTIMONY
I remember certain persons having been murdered at Sarajevo in November, 1944. They were executed according to the order given by Waldheim in retaliation for desertion from the German army of some other persons.

"This discrepancy," Waldheim's brief charged, "shows clearly the negligence, or otherwise the bad faith, in which this file was put together."

If the comparison was legitimate, it was more imperative than ever that we get our hands on the *Odluka*. I had to study these apparent inconsistencies for myself, to see how carefully or haphazardly the

UNWCC committee had summarized the Yugoslav evidence. Had the purported distortion of Mayer's testimony occurred at the hands of the UNWCC—or of the Yugoslav authorities?

Mayer was described in the brief as a man with a reputation among his fellow P.O.W.'s as a collaborator with their Yugoslav captors. Waldheim's report attached an affidavit from Mayer's widow repeating assertions she had made to the Austrian press.

She declared:

> My husband according to his narratives was repeatedly interrogated about different staff officers of Army Group E. After the war he told me that he and his co-prisoners at that time made incriminating testimony only against those comrades who had died or whom one thought to be in safety.

But how would Mayer have had any reason to know that Waldheim was "in safety"? And what of all the other troubling aspects of Frau Mayer's previous statement? I reread the quote and was struck by another point. Mayer's widow characterized the testimony as "incriminating." Surely, I thought, after Waldheim's people had gone to the trouble of tracking this woman and obtaining a sworn statement, they would have tried everything short of torture to get her to characterize her husband's testimony as "false"or "falsely incriminating," but she did not do so. The careful reader was left with the impression that Johann Mayer's testimony, whether self-serving or not, likely was *truly* "incriminating."

The brief charged that popular press coverage of the *Odluka* material ignored the fact that it contained testimony from other witnesses who upheld Waldheim's version of his Wehrmacht responsibilities and his underlying anti-Nazi attitude. The brief claimed that the *Odluka* quoted one German P.O.W. as commenting, "He rejected National Socialism, not so much for social or scientific reasons, but much more for reasons of faith and conservatism." I chuckled when I read another portion of this testimony, which described the young Waldheim as "not much liked" by his comrades "due to his flighty, unrestrained, and somewhat haughty nature."

There was another snippet of *Odluka* testimony presented here that the Waldheim people found to their liking, because it parroted Waldheim's claim that there was a brick-wall separation between the duties of Ic and AO. But it also contained some compelling and quite damning information. The brief said that one witness (unnamed) stated that the chief of Ic (Warnstorff) was "the aide to the Ia." That confirmed what we had seen in the Army Group E organizational chart at the National Archives: Warnstorff was not only the number-one man in Intelligence, but also the number-two man in Operations. The witness said that Warnstorff was responsible "for presenting an all-encompassing picture of the enemy situation, which constituted the basis for the operational plans." Here was straightforward confirmation of our thesis that Ic reports *resulted in Wehrmacht actions.* And what was Waldheim's role? According to this witness, Waldheim was Warnstorff's "representative in the Ic area," whose duties included preparing the morning and evening reports and the weekly situation reports as well as preparing and presenting "graphic situation outlines for the meetings of the Chief of the General Staff." The brief said that Waldheim's primary duty with Army Group E was to prepare twice-daily summaries of enemy activities; in the performance of this duty, he "gathered *and evaluated* information regarding all aspects of hostile action. . . ." (Emphasis added.) Could anyone imagine that the chief of the General Staff had never taken *action* on the basis of Waldheim's briefings? Or that Waldheim did not understand that he was providing the informational ammunition for these decisions? Or that in "evaluating" enemy information, Waldheim was not performing the classic function of an intelligence officer? "But, of course," I muttered under my breath, "he was not responsible for how the information and 'evaluations' he provided were used."

Moments later, I found Waldheim's lawyers addressing that very subject. I could hardly believe my eyes as I read their analysis. They *conceded* that Nazi crimes might have resulted from Waldheim's reports, but insisted that such "misuse" of his reports was not Waldheim's responsibility:

> That German military field commanders, acting on the basis of military information contained in Dr. Waldheim's reports, may have committed war crimes, or even crimes against humanity, does not in any way invalidate the legitimate military purpose of Dr. Waldheim's reports. Almost any information is subject to misuse, often with disastrous results. Such results, however, are not the fault of the information or the preparer of the information.

Left unmentioned by Waldheim's brief was the question of how many instances of such "misuse" of his reports might reasonably have been expected to put the gifted intelligence officer *on notice* of what he was helping to perpetrate. Surely, I told myself, he had a duty at *some* point to at least try to extricate himself from this machinery of death and destruction. Other Germans *did* say "no," *without*

322   ELI M. ROSENBAUM

coming to harm.* Moreover, as the former Waffen-SS General Eric von dem Bach-Zelewski testified in an affidavit read at the Eichmann trial, the possibility of escaping a morally objectionable assignment "by applying for a transfer was open" and "certainly [posed] no jeopardy to life."

The brief attempted to obscure Egberts-Hilker's purported testimony that Waldheim was responsible for the 1944 massacres in the villages between Stip and Kocane. The attorneys acknowledged that killings had taken place, but declared that Yugoslav accounts depicted the casualties as "innocent civilians," whereas German documents described them as "partisan attackers." In a self-righteous tone, the brief asserted that the German army was harassed by Yugoslav partisans, who blew up a bridge and then sniped at German repair crews. Not only did Egberts-Hilker admit to his Yugoslav captors that he had taken it upon himself to deal with the situation, the brief said, but "it would appear" that his actions "were lawful."

I felt a knot form in my stomach. I thought about the repeated warnings Waldheim prepared concerning partisan activity on the Stip-Kocane road, and the "disparity document," in which he reported on the killings of hundreds of obviously unarmed "bandits" during the very month that the Stip-Kocane murders occurred. I recalled the gruesome eyewitness accounts gathered by *Newsweek*'s Andrew Nagorski. It was one thing for Waldheim to try to deny responsibility for the massacres. But the attempt to justify the killings as "lawful" had brought the Waldheim affair to a moral nadir. The fact that Waldheim's brief had been submitted by two well-connected Washington attorneys—one of whom, Donald Santarelli, served as an associate deputy attorney general in the Nixon Administration— made the document even more contemptible.

I found it fascinating that Waldheim did not yet have the audacity to include this revolting characterization of the Stip-Kocane murders in any of his public statements.†

On June 24, Ronald Lauder, U.S. ambassador to Austria, announced that he would miss the Waldheim inauguration. Lauder explained

---

*An official West German inquiry found no case in which a refusal by German personnel to obey a criminal order posed "an objective danger" to life or limb. Indeed, individuals—and even entire units—refused such orders without harm. See Adalbert Rueckerl, *The Investigation of Nazi Crimes 1945–1978* (Heidelberg, 1979), pp. 80, 141–42; Daniel Goldhagen, "The 'Cowardly' Executioner: On Disobedience in the SS," *Patterns of Prejudice*, Vol. 19, No. 2 (April 1985), pp. 19–31; and David H. Kitterman, "Those Who Said 'No!': Germans Who Refused to Execute Civilians During World War II," *German Studies Review*, Vol XI, No. 2 (May 1988), pp. 241–54..

†He never did. See, for example, the July 1987 "White Book" issued on President Waldheim's behalf by the Austrian Foreign Ministry, which contains a two-page denial of responsibility for the Stip-Kocane killings that is devoid of any hint that they might have been "lawful."[1]

that he had prior plans to be away on personal business. It was an obvious ruse (as he later admitted). Several other nations, including the Israelis and the Yugoslavs, joined in the boycott.

One day later, the *Salzburger Volkszeitung,* commenting on the unprecedented diplomatic snub, informed its readers that Ambassador Lauder was descended from "kosher immigrants from Europe." The newspaper then posed a rhetorical question: Does an American ambassador serve "the interests of his country or those of an ethnic power lobby"?[2]

The Simon Wiesenthal Center in Los Angeles soon disseminated in full the story that *Profil* had carried in Austria the previous year (albeit without hard documentation), and that Rabbi Hier had presented in summary form to Congress in April. Here at last was the complete verbatim text of Waldheim's 1944 doctoral dissertation, extolling the theories of Konstantin Frantz and his concept of a "Greater Reich," which, Frantz proclaimed, should encompass all German-speaking peoples, notably including those in Austria, Switzerland, Luxembourg, Belgium, and Holland. Although the doctoral candidate had not cited any of the anti-Jewish pronouncements of the notorious nineteenth-century anti-Semite, who had made it clear that there was no room in the Greater Reich for Jews, neither had the young Waldheim hesitated to praise Frantz as a man ahead of his time. Forty-two years later, Waldheim's feeble response was that he wrote the dissertation under severe time constraints and political pressures. And at any rate, he said, he had only espoused the idea of "voluntary" union.

Disclosure of the full text of Waldheim's dissertation touched off a fresh outpouring of anti-Waldheim sentiment in Switzerland and Holland. But there was barely a ripple of criticism in Austria.

Profil, however, was determined to keep the Waldheim controversy alive within the president-elect's home country. Its June 30 issue featured a remarkable piece claiming that the CIA had penetrated the Austrian Security Service, or HNA, during the postwar years. Reporter Hubertus Czernin said that, although he was unable to obtain a copy of the HNA file on Waldheim, he had it on good authority that the file had branded its subject a *Schreibtischtaeter* ("desk-perpetrator"), someone who, in effect, committed crimes with a pen. This seemed to me a fair characterization. Unfortunately, however, *Profil* never was able to obtain documentation to support its claim.

The same article reported that while Waldheim was at the U.N., the Israelis had tried to get information on his Nazi-era activities. Both the Austrian Chancellory and the Austrian Security Service turned them down, the magazine claimed.

I thought long and hard on this point. Obviously, Jerusalem was satisfied with whatever background information its agents ultimately were able to find, since the Israelis assured the *New York Times* in 1981 that they had, in effect, "cleared" Waldheim of the "Nazi" rumors. They surely would not have done so without checking as thoroughly as possible.

One sentence in the *Profil* piece could be read as suggesting that it was Simon Wiesenthal who had checked out Waldheim for the Israelis, but the scenario was limited to the issue of whether Waldheim had ever been a member of the Nazi Party (which he had *not*). The piece quoted Wiesenthal: "Yes, I had been asked, in the seventies, whether Waldheim was a Nazi. . . . I checked and then replied, negative, there's nothing."[3]

Mark Wurm, a German-speaking Los Angeles businessman and Wiesenthal Center volunteer, sent me a copy of a story from the April 11 issue of *National Zeitung,* a neo-Nazi newspaper published in West Germany. The piece was typical of the "journalism" in that execrable rag, defending Waldheim against the vicious Jewish attacks to which he was being subjected. But the article made one interesting, albeit unsupported, claim: Lieutenant Waldheim, the paper asserted, was the representative of the German Foreign Office at Army Group E. This was enormously intriguing, because the Foreign Office had played an important role in formulating German "reprisal" strategies and in executing Hitler's "final solution to the Jewish Problem."

The assertion seemed plausible enough. Waldheim had appropriate credentials, having already received a degree from the Consular Academy in Vienna. Moreover, the Foreign Office's special envoy to the Balkans was someone with whom Waldheim, as a Viennese with diplomatic training, would have had a natural affinity: Hermann Neubacher, the former mayor of Vienna.*

We never were able to verify the surprising (and probably incorrect) claim, and I could only conjecture why the neo-Nazi newspaper would publish an item that was so distinctly unhelpful to Waldheim. The paper specialized in revisionist history, claiming that the Nazis were falsely maligned, that the Holocaust was a Zionist hoax, and that the Allies were the "real" war criminals. But its Nazi apologist publishers also had a pronounced dislike for "closet" Nazis; in their view, one should take pride in one's Nazi past. Waldheim clearly fit

---

*Neubacher was personally entrusted by Hitler on October 29, 1943, with responsibility for planning *Suehnemassnahmen* ("reprisal measures") in collaboration with the military. After the war, he was tried, convicted, and sentenced to twenty years at hard labor in Yugoslavia. The Ic "Activity Report" for August 1944, signed by Hammer and initialed by Waldheim, notes a "service trip of Ic to Athens for talks with Minister Neubacher, General Felmy, and General Scheuerlen—Abwehr discussions."

the definition of a "closet Nazi," and thus attracted their ire. Waldheim, I imagined, must feel besieged from all sides now.

As a tribute to the Austrian president-elect, the June 30 issue of the Soviet English-language propaganda "news magazine" *New Times* printed an old U.N. photograph of Waldheim accompanied by a "People on the World Scene" biographical sketch that began by informing its readers that the former U.N. chief had just been elected Federal President of Austria.* No reference of any kind was made to the global controversy that surrounded Waldheim and his campaign. More remarkable than this omission, however, was the article's account of Waldheim's early life:

> A lawyer by education, he graduated from the law school of Vienna University and studied at the Vienna Consular Academy. Kurt Waldheim embarked on a diplomatic career in 1945.[4]

I marveled. Even Waldheim was never so audacious as to "forget" World War II in its entirety! The deletion was especially outlandish in light of Moscow's obsession with reminding the world of Nazi atrocities and of the Soviet people's suffering and heroism in "The Great Patriotic War." This was the same government that, only six months earlier, had so vehemently protested the Austrian government's plan to memorialize Alexander Loehr! The article provided disheartening evidence that Moscow was going to stand by the man who, by acceding to their wishes for a substantial increase in Soviet-filled Secretariat posts in New York, had served their espionage interests so well at the U.N. It also meant the death of what little hope we had of receiving documents from the U.S.S.R. or its East German satellite state. Whatever hidden information lay buried in the secret archives in East Berlin, Potsdam, and Moscow would remain, it seemed, permanently beyond our grasp.

The New Yorker's Jane Kramer shared our appraisal of Waldheim's relationship with Moscow. In an incisive overview of the affair, she opined that Waldheim was never a Soviet spy in the conventional cloak-and-dagger sense, but that he had possessed a secret and very embarrassing past that had forced him to be, at a minimum, obliging. She quoted Singer, at his most outrageous, saying that Waldheim "is like the girl who takes a quarter here, a quarter there, and builds a clientele that way, with two-bit favors that add up to a lot of time in bed."[5]

The Soviets appeared to have set their course, but it was increas-

---

*This publication is not to be confused with the American magazine of the same name.

ingly apparent that many other governments were confused about how best to deal with Waldheim's election. Nowhere was this more apparent than in Yugoslavia. On July 2, Austria's new Foreign Minister, Peter Jankowitsch, who had declared that his first task was to polish the nation's tarnished image, arrived in Belgrade for the first official visit by an Austrian government representative since the election. Together with the Yugoslav foreign minister, he announced an expansion of relations, declaring that all was well between the two countries. Both men later told a disbelieving press corps that the Waldheim matter did not even come up during their private talks.

The statement came as no surprise to us. Yugoslavia desperately needed Austrian cooperation to prevent its teetering economy from collapsing. And Waldheim was going to be president for six long years.

The Yugoslavs had always been reluctant to provide information about Waldheim, and what little they had released came through nominally unofficial channels, such as the newspapers. But these tidbits, infrequent as they were, showed that at least some Yugoslav officials wanted the full story to come out, and an extraordinary issue of *NIN* confirmed that suspicion. The Yugoslav magazine reported that there had been heated debate within the Yugoslav government concerning the release of additional evidence against Waldheim; ultimately, the decision had been made not to do so, because the material was "under special regimen." Writer Milos Vasic pluckily took issue with the government's decision, declaring that the public "cannot be left scratching its head." How can the state be quiet, he asked, "while everyone else is talking, providing evidence, and shouting?"[6]

Belgrade had company. Washington too was waffling. President Reagan caused a panic in our office when he responded to a *USA Today* reporter's unexpected question by stating that he had seen no conclusive evidence that Waldheim took part in Nazi crimes.[7] We worried that this was a signal that Attorney General Meese had decided to reject—or table—OSI's recommendation that Waldheim be barred from the U.S. Reacting swiftly, Steinberg distributed to the press documents showing that Waldheim's Ic/AO Branch had ordered the deportation of more than two thousand Greek Jews from the islands of Crete and Rhodes. This was actually a re-release of material previously issued by us or published in *Profil,* but Steinberg knew that the information was little known outside Austria, and he saw the opportunity to place some "fresh" evidence on the table at a time when the U.S. government seemed ambivalent. Steinberg's gambit, born of desperation, worked; the Washington press corps turned up the heat on Meese, barraging the Justice Department with inquiries about the status of the Waldheim "watchlist" probe.

On July 8, 1986, Kurt Waldheim was inaugurated as president of Austria. The highest ranking U.S. official to attend was Felix Bloch, an Austrian-born diplomat who was deputy chief of mission at the U.S. Embassy in Vienna and a close friend of Waldheim's campaign manager.* Even the Soviets, perhaps concerned because the U.S. and the Yugoslavs were snubbing Waldheim, sent only a deputy to represent Soviet Ambassador Mikhail Yefremov, who, like Ambassador Lauder, managed to "have to" be home at the time; it was a pleasant surprise for us.

Austrian Socialists in attendance wore black ties in protest and gave an at best muted reception to the incoming president.

The crowd of uninvited spectators included a group of protestors led by Beate Klarsfeld, Rabbi Avi Weiss of New York, and Sister Rose Thering, a Dominican nun and professor of education at Seton Hall University in New Jersey.

President Waldheim appeared haggard and drawn; it was rumored that he had suffered from a bowel infection for the past few weeks. In an inaugural speech suffused with irony, he declared that the rallying cry "Never Again" must be directed "not only at the horror of the Holocaust, but also at the terrible mentality which caused it: anti-Semitism." Daily, he said, Austrians must "renew our readiness to accept and treat all our fellow citizens—of whatever race, creed, and conviction—as brothers and sisters."[8] Some parliamentarians openly shook their heads in disbelief at Waldheim's invocation of the postwar Jewish world's "Never Again" vow.

Following the speech, a formal procession took the presidential party to Heroes' Square. Waldheim had a special duty to perform there, one that derived from the fact that, as the new president of Austria, he was also supreme commander of the Austrian armed forces. With the declaration that "the army is not merely an instrument of the state, but also a document of the whole Austrian people's will to self-assertion," he formally assumed command. It had taken forty-one years, I mused, but at last Lieutenant Waldheim had worked his way to the top.

Waldheim proceeded from Heroes' Square to his new residence,

*Three years later, Bloch was suspended by the State Department on suspicion of being one of the most damaging Soviet agents of the past four decades. As of this writing, although the government has taken the highly unusual step of publicly branding him a suspected traitor, he has not been charged with any offense. According to press accounts, the government has concluded that it lacks sufficient evidence to indict Bloch on espionage charges.

the Hofburg Palace, ironically the very place from which Hitler, following the *Anschluss*, acknowledged the cheers of his new Austrian subjects.

Across the street, Klarsfeld and Weiss unfurled a banner emblazoned with a stark message: NO TO THE WAR CRIMINAL PRESIDENT.

Security men pulled down the offending banner.

Waldheim attempted to ignore the scene, but others did not. A group of Waldheim supporters shouted, "Get out of Austria!" and hurled anti-Semitic curses at Klarsfeld and Weiss. A line of police kept the two groups separated.

Undeterred, the demonstrators clambered onto chairs and displayed posters of Waldheim in Wehrmacht uniform, along with a facsimile of the UNWCC war crimes file cover page.

"You dirty red!" someone called out.

"Go back to your *Fuehrer!*" one of the protestors responded.

A brief scuffle ensued, which police soon broke up.

Later, as Sister Rose prepared to return to the U.S., she was detained at the Vienna airport and subjected to a demeaning strip-search. Although her American passport identified her as a nun and she wore a large cross pendant (dramatically interwoven with a Star of David), she was the only person on the flight who was strip-searched. Interviewed upon her return to the United States, she characterized Austrian security personnel as "rude and totally de-humanizing, with no humaneness and no apologies." The search, she declared, was "a last harassment by the Austrian government before I left Austria."[9]

Television coverage of Waldheim's inaugural depicted a spectacle with all the splendor and trappings of a regal coronation. "Just great," Singer muttered. "Just great. *I'm* getting ulcers. But Waldheim, that *momser* [a Yiddish expletive meaning "bastard"], *he's* sleeping in the Kaiser's bed."

26

In the course of an interview for the July 21 issue of *Profil,* People's Party General Secretary Michael Graff called accusations of anti-Semitism in the Waldheim campaign "a grotesque reversal of facts." He praised Simon Wiesenthal's "balanced and nuanced position," which he contrasted with the "despicable" one of "people like Mr. Singer."

Graff, a veteran backer of the candidate who regularly rewrote World War II history, now tried his own hand at revising more recent history: "I was pleasantly surprised that no anti-Semitic utterances were heard during the campaign," he calmly told the magazine's incredulous reporter. He conceded that there was "a reserve of anti-Semitism in Austria," which, he said, everyone should strive to overcome. But he warned, "This will be more difficult as Mr. Singer continues his campaign of lies." Graff had a remarkable penchant for issuing new threats even as he denied making the old ones.

Nowhere were Graff's statements greeted with more skepticism— and alarm—than in Israel. The *Jerusalem Post*'s Reuven Koret characterized Waldheim's campaign as one that utilized "the worst Jew-baiting of the postwar period." Waldheim, the *Post* editorialized, had risen to power "on a wave of anti-Semitic froth."[1] On August 8, the paper reported a disturbing new development: Incidents of Austrian police harassment of Jews, particularly in Vienna, had escalated. The paper lamented the fact that these events had received "little or no press coverage locally."

Shortly thereafter, a remarkable document arrived in the mail from one of my contacts in Austria. It contained the confidential minutes of the first meeting, held on July 31 in Vienna, of the newly formed "Austria's Image Abroad Group." Eight prominent Austrians had joined forces to plan a course of action to counter the devastating impact of the Waldheim affair on the country's international reputation. Three of the founding members were Cardinal Franz Koenig, the Archbishop of Vienna; *Profil* editor-in-chief Peter Michael Lingens; and Lingens's longtime mentor, Simon Wiesenthal. According to the minutes, the participants agreed that Lingens would write to important foreign journalists, inviting them to visit Austria. Other Austrian personalities would submit articles to foreign newspapers.

Wiesenthal spoke of his impression that the American public's view of Austria was extremely negative. The Nazi-hunter stressed that, in whatever ameliorative steps the group might take, they must speak with a single voice.[2]

Events increasingly indicated that the concern was justified; perhaps worst of all, the country was burdened with a pariah president. After a Waldheim spokesman announced that the new president's first foreign trip would be to Ireland, Irish officials declared that he was not welcome. When the Finnish press speculated that Waldheim might attend the funeral of former president Urho Kekkonen, it was quickly denied by Finnish authorities. Next, the Dutch government refused to allow the Austrian president to attend the formal opening of its "Delta" flood defense system, an event to which every other European head of state was invited. The embarrassing list of official snubs grew steadily as the weeks passed.

In my occasional speeches, I began to refer mockingly to Waldheim as a prisoner of the Hofburg Palace and as "the Maytag repairman of the planet Earth—the loneliest guy on the planet."

Throughout the summer, when I could get away from the office, I made brief trips to Washington, to dig further into the World War II documents at the National Archives. Many of the new finds added only small pieces to various aspects of the Waldheim puzzle, but they were encouraging, for their discovery confirmed our belief that U.S. and foreign archives held documentary riches that were as yet unfound and unexploited.

In a July trip, I located, for example, the 1946 Nuremberg interrogation of Loehr's chief of staff, General August Winter, which confirmed that Secret Field Police Detachment 621 took orders directly from "the Ic" at Army Group E headquarters.[3] Bob Herzstein had found the first suggestion of this fact four months earlier, but now we knew with certainty that the detachment, which was heavily involved in the deportation of the Jews of Ioannina in March 1944, came under the direct operational control of Waldheim's unit.

One discovery was as fascinating as it was frustrating. This was a "Secret" order dated February 15, 1944, from Winter, altering the work allocation plan. The final change, recorded in a footnote, was a directive that, henceforth, the "O3" officer, Waldheim, was charged with maintaining Army Group E's *V.S. Brieftagebuch*.[4] When I compared this notation with the listing of Ic responsibilities that Herzstein had discovered here in March, I realized that this was the illegible handwritten entry that we had been unable to decipher; the fact that it was a change in the orders explained why it prompted a handwritten addition to the organizational chart. Some quick research revealed what this assignment entailed. The *Verschluss Sachen Brieftagebuch* (literally, "journal of documents to be kept under lock and key") collected Army Group E's most highly sensitive classified materials. In addition to classified military plans, this would likely have included supersecret orders relating to reprisals and Jewish deportations. And the whole thing had been in Waldheim's care!

Minutes later, I found a companion document that further elucidated the nature of Waldheim's responsibility. This was a January 4, 1944, order from Winter, entitled "Security of Documents Kept Under Lock and Key." It explained:

> Lately, attacks against couriers and messengers conveying official mail have multiplied. Repeatedly, the enemy has succeeded despite all security measures (escort, sufficient weapons, preparation for speedy destruction), to obtain V.S. documents during attacks by bandit groups. . . . Above all, the *destruction* of courier mail must be foreseen in such a way that it can be effective in case of need within an instant. Experience has proven that the availability of gasoline and matches is not enough. In principle, an early destruction is better than a belated one.

The document rambled on, but made it clear that the custodian of the *V.S. Brieftagebuch* had to be prepared to destroy it "in an instant," should it appear that the material was in danger of falling into enemy hands.[5] The document brought to mind Major Hammer's 1944 order directing the destruction of all Army Group E documents concerning Allied commandos; that order had deprived us of key documents that would have identified the individual officers at Ic/AO Branch involved in the various commando incidents.

When I showed these finds to Robert Wolfe, head of the Archives' Military Reference Branch, he blanched. Wolfe told me that in almost every case, the Germans had indeed torched the V.S. documents, and that, said Wolfe, was certainly true in the case of Army Group E. In all likelihood, therefore, Waldheim or a colleague of his had performed this particular duty effectively. This was the man who claimed total ignorance of hostage reprisal killings and Jewish deportations; yet Army Group E forces were guilty of both, and now we knew that it was Waldheim himself who was charged with custody of—and had quite possibly been the one who destroyed—the most sensitive records at Army Group E headquarters, records that might have shed considerable light on those very matters.

On learning of this latest discovery, British war historian Gerald Fleming added several important points to our knowledge. He told us that the supersensitive "V.S." collection was deemed so important by the Germans that a special comptroller made spot checks to ensure that it was locked up as ordered. In a letter to the WJC, Fleming noted that the V.S. journal "would include *all* recorded secret orders . . ." and that maintaining it was *"the most confidential task* in the whole Ic/AO Army Group E setup." Not surprisingly, he said, the *V.S. Brieftagebuch* was kept by "the most trustworthy officer, who was invariably very carefully selected." The fact that Waldheim was given this responsibility indicated, he wrote, "the High Command's complete proven trust in him." Finally, he confirmed Wolfe's recollection: "There is no knowledge of any such record surviving."[6]

And so, we had traced what might have been the ultimate evidentiary treasure trove right to Lieutenant Waldheim's hands, only to see it, quite literally, go up in smoke.

This went a long way toward explaining our continuing difficulties in attempting to ascertain the workings of Ic/AO Branch at Army Group E. Too often, when one or another sinister report was originated at or "cc'd" to Army Group E, copies did not show up in the surviving records of the army group. It now seemed likely that they were destroyed in the "V.S. bonfires" at war's end, perhaps even by Waldheim himself.

Returning to the National Archives on August 6, I decided to check the surviving records of all the units subordinate to Army Group E headquarters, in the hope that other critical documents had escaped destruction at these lower commands. I focused first on the fate of the Jews of the northwestern Greek city of Ioannina. The document that *Stern* had published, showing that Waldheim's intelligence unit in Salonika was informed of the roundup and deportation of the Ioannina Jews the day after it happened (March 25, 1944), proved little. Waldheim's subsequent unearthing of proof that he was far away at the time, receiving medical treatment for a thyroid condition, had taken the wind out of the German newsweekly's sails. We needed to learn if there were other communications concerning the Jews of Ioannina—specifically, communications sent when Waldheim was *on* station.

I began with the records of *Korpsgruppe* Ioannina. As I scanned the microfilm frames, a clear pattern emerged: The *Korpsgruppe* routinely sent copies of its own "Ic Situation Reports" to Army Group E headquarters, where they were passed to Waldheim's Intelligence section. The *Korpsgruppe*'s Ic Situation Report of April 9, 1944 (which Hans Safrian had already found during his own research), reported what had happened in late March:

In the course of the raids against Jews in Ioannina, Arta, and Prewese on March 25, 1,725 Jews were evacuated.[7]

Had Waldheim returned from medical leave by the time this report came in? He had been discharged from the hospital on March 29, so in all probability the answer was yes.

But "in all probability" was not good enough. After nearly three more hours of manual scrolling through microfilms, I finally found the proof we needed, in the "Activity Report of Department Ic" of the headquarters of the 22nd Mountain Corps for the period January 1 to June 30, 1944. On page 7, the destruction of several thousand Jewish lives was noted by this Army Group E component in a single, unambiguous sentence:

> The Jewish population of Ioannina and Corfu was deported by the SD.[8]

The report, which clearly was transmitted to Army Group E headquarters (where, as an "Ic" document, it would have been directed to Waldheim's section), was dated September 15, 1944—when Waldheim was, by his own admission, back from his wedding leave (which had ended September 3). His continuing protestations of ignorance, absurd from the start, were becoming even more disgraceful.

The further I waded into the archives, the deeper my outrage grew. Among the more horrific discoveries were eighty-five daily reports of the Ia (Operations) Section of Army Group E headquarters in Arsakli/Salonika, covering the period from May 2, 1943, through the end of that year. They contained numerous explicit accounts of grisly reprisals perpetrated in Greece and Serbia by forces under Army Group E's command, such as: the "burning" and "leveling to the ground" of "bandit villages," reprisal shootings of hostages, deportations of entire populations to concentration camps, and "evacuation" of women and children from "bandit villages." The October 5 report, for example, noted that "the village of Akmotopak has been completely destroyed and its entire population shot" by the 22nd Mountain Corps, in retaliation for the killing of a single German regimental commander and the sabotage of telephone lines.[9]

A July 29, 1943, cable from the operations staff of the 68th Army Corps passed on to subordinate divisions new instructions concerning the treatment of captured partisans. Hitler had decreed that such prisoners were now to be put to use as slave laborers in order to ensure the Germans' coal supply. The cable noted that the Quartermaster Branch of Army Group E headquarters had "ordered the inclusion of bandit group members between 16 and 55 years of age at P.O.W. collection points." Lest the lower commands misinterpret the modified orders as anything other than a bow to military and economic necessity, the telex stressed that reprisal actions "are not affected by this" and that "action against bandits is required as heretofore."[10]

Also of interest was a document pertaining to Waldheim's posting in Athens. It was a handwritten draft of a September 14, 1943, message sent from Waldheim's Ia unit in Athens to Army Group E headquarters in Arsakli/Salonika. It reported:

> With the exception of smaller energetic reconnaissance operations, *no cleansing operations* are intended in the foreseeable future. Initiatives on a larger scale can be undertaken only after the *Abschub* ["deportation"] of the Italians. Even then, though, the troops will be quite busy with the Italian equipment. [Emphasis in original.][11]

The report was initialed with a single *W*. Although this probably signified Waldheim's boss Bruno Willers rather than Waldheim himself, there could be little doubt that Waldheim, as second-in-command of Willers's Operations section, had seen it. It was highly significant for its use of the word *Abschub* in regard to the Italian troops, rather than the euphemisms "evacuation" and "departure" applied elsewhere. When first confronted with documentation of his role in the betrayal of his erstwhile Italian comrades-in-arms, Waldheim had insisted that the men were returned to their homeland. When this claim could no longer be sustained, Waldheim had argued that *he thought* the Italians were being sent home. But the word "deportation" in the Ia report left no room for ambiguity.

An electrifying moment came for me when I came across a secret September 10, 1944, single-page directive of the High Command of Army Group E, issued over the name of Loehr's new chief of staff, General Schmidt-Richberg. Titled "Bandit Situation Mainland," its second paragraph presaged some of the worst Nazi viciousness of the war:

> It should be pointed out . . . that severe and active measures produce the best results, especially since these bandit groups are forced to leave their bases and are not sufficiently trained in large-scale mobile warfare.[12]

This command to employ "severe" measures against the partisans was issued just as Army Group E's retreat was about to begin, a journey that was frequently punctuated by large-scale atrocities as the Germans fought a desperate rear-guard action against Yugoslav partisans. (The Stip-Kocane killings, for example, took place just a month later.) It seemed likely that this directive helped set the stage for the atrocities to follow. The last word of the German text was initialed by Major Hammer and by a W. *But was it Waldheim?* Or Warnstorff? Or someone else? There seemed to be no way to tell.

Another frightening report, dated March 8, 1944 (at a time when Waldheim was on medical leave), was signed by Colonel Warnstorff and sent to the High Command of Army Group F. The report presented a profile of the population of Greece. Warnstorff noted that the country was currently made up of 7,061,360 Greeks, 133,400 Turks, and a smattering of Armenians and Albanians. Under the category *Juden* ("Jews"), Warnstorff reported "22,770 (?)." The confusion indicated by the typed question mark was accentuated by a handwritten note in the right margin, where an unidentifiable German wrote, "In Salonika alone in 1940 there were more than 60,000."[13] What did the annotation mean? Was it a self-congratulatory note, or was it written in order to indicate that there was yet more deportation work to do? At any rate, the document proved that Waldheim's unit was kept well informed on the fate of the Jewish population of Greece.

I also found an important new document pertaining to the deportation of the Jews of Corfu. It originated with the Corfu station of Secret Field Police Detachment 621, which, we had confirmed, answered directly to Warnstorff. On April 27, 1944, that unit sent a message to the intelligence section of *Korpsgruppe* Ioannina, agitating vigorously for the deportation of the Corfu Jews. Noting that the commander of the island, a certain Jaeger, was opposed to this, the writer of the report suggested that Jaeger's opinion be disregarded. The only possible problem, he cautioned, was "the lack of ships."[14]

To try to put this new document in context, I turned to my notes on the Corfu tragedy. The first thing that I noticed was that this report had somehow escaped the attention of the prosecution team at Nuremberg, for it was not part of the extensive Nuremberg series of documents concerning the Corfu deportation. Probably for that reason, it was not referenced in any of the basic works on the Holocaust.

We had previously seen a Nuremberg document showing that on April 28, 1944, the Ic section of *Korpsgruppe* Ioannina wrote to the Ic/AO Branch of Army Group E asking it to "effect implementation measures with the SD for the purpose of settling the Jewish question." This request was consistent with the Army Group E organizational table, which stated that Waldheim's branch—Ic/AO—was responsible for "cooperation with SD" (and that this was a function specifically entrusted to Waldheim's immediate superior, Col. Warnstorff, the Ic officer).

Checking the dates, I realized that the new document preceded this criminal request to Waldheim's unit by just one day. It was, in a sense, the missing link, the document that *explained* that fateful request—for it transmitted the recommendation from Secret Field Police Detachment 621 to the *Korpsgruppe* Ioannina that led, the very next day, to the *Korpsgruppe's* request to Waldheim's Ic/AO Branch that it take steps to "settle" the "Jewish question" on Corfu. Now we knew that the request had its origin in a unit—Secret Field Police Detachment 621—that was directly subordinated to Waldheim's immediate superior, Col Warnstorff.

For a moment, I found myself feeling quite pleased to see how neatly all the pieces of the investigative puzzle fit together. I heard myself whisper, "It's *perfect!*"

Only a few seconds later, however, I plunged from that investigative "high" to the depressing memory of what it all *meant:* one thousand, seven hundred, and ninety-five innocent human beings— fathers and sons, mothers and daughters, old people and children and babies—all were shipped, by boat and then railroad cattle cars, to the Auschwitz death factory. Only 112 survived, the last remnant of a Jewish community founded 975 years earlier, during the reign of the Roman emperor Titus.* I thought of so many survivors I had interviewed from other towns and cities, weeping still at the loss of parents, siblings, and, worst of all, children.

Eli, I lectured myself, if you let this get to you, you won't get any work done. But it was hard to continue.

I glanced at my watch and was relieved to see that it was nearly closing time at the Archives. I packed up my notes, my dictionaries, my microfilm indices, and my newly made photocopies and exited onto Pennsylvania Avenue, where the damp, sweltering air of an August evening in Washington seemed, for once, only the most trifling of annoyances.

The Simon Wiesenthal Center continued its highwire act of trying to distance itself, ever-so-quietly, from the man for whom it was named. The August 1986 issue of its newsletter, *Response,* included a reproduction of a postcard the Center had printed for readers to use in order to petition the Canadian government to refuse Wald-

---

*As of 1990, there were just eighty Jews remaining in Ioannina. The historic Old Synagogue, though little used now, has been restored at the initiative of the New York–based Sisterhood of Janina.

heim permission to enter that country. It was a follow-up to a previous distribution by the Center of one million "No to Waldheim!" postcards urging President Reagan to put Waldheim on the U.S. watchlist.

In a story entitled "French Waldheim Investigation Revealed," the Center's newsletter expanded on its previous demand that the French authorities explain why they had checked Waldheim's Wehrmacht records seven years earlier. Readers were reminded that the French government had confirmed "Wiesenthal Center allegations" that one of its "junior officials" in West Berlin had prepared a memo on Waldheim in 1979 that covered his military career from 1939 through 1944—"and includes specific reference to his assignment to Wehrmacht Gruppe E, which was under the command of General Alexander von [*sic*] Loehr, who was executed for war crimes after WW II." The Center's associate dean, Rabbi Abraham Cooper, declared that "the world needs to know" who in France "requested this memo." Quoted in boldface type, Cooper charged that "the Center now knows" that Yugoslavia, the U.S.S.R., West Germany and Austria, as well as France, "had access to this incredible information," and he demanded to know why they "did nothing" to hold Waldheim accountable for his decades-long "trail of deceit and lies."[15]

The Center was asking *precisely* the right questions. If only Wiesenthal himself were doing the same, I lamented.

As summer yielded to fall, the WJC found itself once again under attack. In a September 1986 address to a Jewish audience in Rockland County, New York, Yehuda Blum, who, as Israeli representative to the U.N. in 1981, had defended Waldheim to the *New York Times* against rumors that he had supported the Nazis, charged that "the World Jewish Congress got him [Waldheim] elected." It was a low blow. Waldheim's election was a foregone conclusion before the revelations about his past. In fact, the exposure of his cover-up had arguably helped turn a predicted landslide victory into a squeaker.[16]

Blum's accusation stung, but I was relieved to see that he was willing to concede that he too had been duped during his tour of duty at the U.N. During his U.N. tenure, he said, "everyone accepted" the conventional account of Waldheim's service. Blum disclosed that Waldheim himself, "in private conversations as late as 1981," had told Blum "that he was injured in 1941 and went back to practice law in Vienna."[17]

Willi Korte, now on our payroll, called from Washington in mid-September to report a striking new find in the Archives. He had unearthed microfilm copies of a package of drafts of what he characterized in his low-key way as "interesting" German propaganda leaflets. These were designed to be air-dropped behind Red Army lines in an attempt to get Soviet soldiers to defect to the German side.

When I received the material from Korte the next day, I saw immediately why he had phoned me as soon as he found the documents. Some of the leaflets contained raw anti-Semitic invective about "the accursed Jews" and "blood-sucking Jews." The most repulsive of the lot declared: "*The Jews* prepared this war. *Jews* hung it around our necks. *Jews* do not want it to end." (Emphasis in the original.) The leaflet closed by urging Red Army soldiers to join with the Nazis: "Enough of the Jewish war. Come over. Kill the Jews." Those last three words, *Erschlagt die Juden,* were an explicit incitement to mass murder.

But it was the cover memo on the package that made it unforgettable. Addressed to "Ic/AO" at Army Group E, it explained that the enclosed pamphlets had been prepared by Propaganda Company 690 in Russian, and were provided to Waldheim's branch in German translation, "with request that you be aware of it." The memo said that "for the time being" such flyers were being printed "in 80,000 copies," but that "repeat printings are planned."[18]

The cover memo bore the "received" stamp of Army Group E's Ic/AO Branch, dated December 3, 1944. And the "O3" box within that stamp held the handwritten *W* and the handwritten date "3/12" (3 December). This time, there could be no doubt that the *W* was Waldheim's, for it was in the box reserved for the "O3" officer.

The index to the enclosed pamphlets—which listed, near the top, such venomous titles as "The Jews Prepared This War" and " 'Let's Go to Berlin,' Shriek Your Jews"—was also stamped "received" by Waldheim's branch, and here again was his handwritten *W* and "3/12" in the "O3" box. Both stamps featured a similar handwritten *W* in the "AO" box as well, raising the intriguing possibility that Waldheim was filling in for the branch's Abwehr officer, Major Hammer; indeed, it appeared that Waldheim might have been the *only* officer to review the leaflets.

Both Korte and I felt that this was, at a minimum, a case of "bad atmospherics"; it plainly reeked. Why did Waldheim sign off on a package of materials that urged Soviet soldiers to "Kill the Jews"? How did that fit into the matrix of Waldheim's known activities? Why had this vicious material crossed Waldheim's desk in the first place? Had he initialed it merely to "certify copy correct," which seemed awful enough—especially for someone who still claimed he knew nothing of the fate of Jews during these years—or did its significance run deeper?

"It's juicy *New York Post*–type stuff," I told Korte over the phone. "It's fascinating that Waldheim even *saw* leaflets like these, but what does it prove beyond 'knowledge'? Does it mean that he had anything to do with actually disseminating this stuff or authorizing its dissemination behind Soviet lines? What does it *mean,* Willi?"

Korte had no answer. Neither did I.

I decided not to show this new find to Singer and Steinberg until I had a chance to analyze it further. They would want to release it to the press immediately. But releasing the documents before we understood their actual significance could be a terrible waste of evidentiary "ammunition." We would get an easy, top-of-the-fold headline—"Kill the Jews" would ensure that—but we would perhaps prove nothing of substance.

Singer poked his head into my office a few hours later. As usual, he found me poring over some captured documents.

"Got anything good, Rosenbaum?" His impatience was obvious.

"I'm working on something that might be good," I replied. "We'll see where it goes."

"Okay. We need the document that shows Waldheim giving the order to kill Jews" was Singer's facetious response.

And then he disappeared, never seeing the look of utter astonishment on my face.

In a dramatic Saturday night surprise in Innsbruck, the right wing Freedom Party, allied with the Socialist Party in a fragile governing coalition, elected Joerg Haider as its new national chairman, reflecting a further lurch to the right in Austrian political life. The thirty-six-year-old Haider had gained worldwide notoriety the previous year when he termed convicted Nazi war criminal Walter Reder "a soldier who had done his duty."

In response to this embarrassing development, Austria's interim chancellor, Socialist Franz Vranitsky, immediately announced the termination of the Socialist/Freedom coalition and informed President Waldheim that elections would be held in November, six months early. Vranitsky and Waldheim agreed to dissolve Austria's parliament the following week.

Austria's government had collapsed.

On the heels of this political breakdown, the September 15 issue of *Profil* carried Hubertus Czernin's unabashed hatchet-job on the World Jewish Congress, entitled "The Hanging Party." *Profil* was still anti-Waldheim, but once more seemed desperate to prove that it was also anti-WJC and, hence, patriotic.

Czernin accused the WJC of being interested in Kurt Waldheim's past "not only for lofty purposes," but also "to make its mark in

American public opinion" and thus enhance its influence relative to other Jewish organizations. Czernin informed his readers that at the WJC the "real Waldheim-hunter" was not the "omnipresent Israel Singer," despite his "almost messianic zeal," but rather Eli Rosenbaum, who "searched for material" and "meticulously prepared each attack" against Waldheim. Czernin mentioned my two February trips to Vienna, and clearly was still pained by his inability to identify my "source."

Czernin mocked the WJC as "calling for an ersatz war against Hitler forty years after Hitler." In Czernin's view, we at the WJC had "aimed at Hitler and hit Waldheim," with the result that "the best-known Austrian in the U.S.A., with the exception of Arnold Schwarzenegger, is suddenly a suspected war criminal." He quoted an unnamed "American journalist" as surmising that our zeal could be explained in part by "the guilt complex of many American Jews, because they did not help their co-religionists in the concentration camps. . . ." (This was actually a nearly verbatim recitation of one of Simon Wiesenthal's more odious contentions.)

A U.S. government decision to place President Waldheim on the watchlist of excludable aliens "would automatically provoke serious bilateral tensions," Czernin warned. And he painted a pessimistic picture of Waldheim's chances of avoiding that fate, charging that U.S. law on the issue was imprecise enough so that "with some bad will or lack of historical knowledge, one can ensnare anyone ever connected with the Nazis." Czernin declared that the outlook for Waldheim was made more dismal because of what "some people in Washington" viewed as an "evil game" between the WJC and the Justice Department's OSI—especially visible in the "personally close relationship" between the WJC's Rosenbaum and OSI Director Neal Sher.

"Now it is Kurt Waldheim's turn" to succumb to the U.S. exclusion law, Czernin predicted. He then quoted the unnamed "skeptical U.S. journalist" as complaining: "Just because someone tells an untruth, that is not sufficient reason to deny him entry."[19]

I speculated that this heavy-handed attack was the opening salvo of the "Austria's Image Abroad Group," perhaps instigated by *Profil* editor-in-chief Peter Michael Lingens, a charter member of the group and a longtime collaborator of Simon Wiesenthal's. If so, it was a clever gambit, for *Profil* had earned considerable respect among foreign journalists for its role as the only significant Austrian publication to pursue aggressively the facts of Waldheim's secret past.

For me, the article removed any remaining doubt as to whether Czernin, Lingens, and *Profil* were "friend or foe." Still, I resolved to maintain a cordial relationship with Czernin; the contact might yet prove useful again someday. I laughed out loud as Don Corleone's injunction in *The Godfather* came to mind: "Keep your friends close. And your enemies closer."

However much the WJC was coming to be associated in the public's mind with the Waldheim affair, in truth we continued to grapple with a broad array of issues and challenges. Some of those were, quite literally, matters of life and death, requiring us to drop everything else to deal with them on an emergency basis.

One such situation developed unexpectedly on the morning of September 11, when our telex machine suddenly came to life, clacking out a sixteen-line message, in Spanish, from Manolo Tenenbaum, the head of the WJC's Latin American Branch, in Buenos Aires, Argentina.

The first line contained only a single word: *"URGENTE."* It was not an opening that Tenenbaum used cavalierly. Indeed, I had not seen him employ it before.

The telex message advised that an ominous report had come in from Paraguay. Tenenbaum's source had phoned him, "in a state of great emotion," to tell him that anti-Jewish posters and graffiti had appeared throughout the main streets of Asunción, the capital, accusing the country's Jews of "robbing the country and sending the money to Tel Aviv and Moscow." One poster was entitled "Jews— Wanted Dead or Alive," and it blamed the Jews for everything from the killing of Christ to "planning World War III."

Paraguay's tiny Jewish community was terrified, and for good reason. Paraguay was a police state, run with an iron fist by General Alfredo Stroessner, a brutal dictator who reveled in his German ancestry and seemed little troubled by his country's reputation as a haven for fugitive Nazi war criminals. Indeed, the Jewish leadership there had been warned repeatedly over the years that the Jews of Paraguay would pay a steep price—in lives—if any attempt were made to apprehend Nazi criminals hiding in the country.

If anti-Jewish outrages were going on in public now, it could only be happening with the connivance, or at least the tacit approval, of Stroessner's dreaded secret police. It was this element that made the situation truly desperate.

Tenenbaum implored us to send a cable to Stroessner as soon as possible, signed by Edgar Bronfman, appealing to the Paraguayan president to take steps to halt these abominations.

We moved swiftly to draft a carefully worded telegram to Stroessner, and after Bronfman approved it, we dispatched it to the *Casa Presidencial* in Asunción. "Jews have suffered much in this generation," the cable pointed out. It made emotional reference to the ongoing escalation in terror attacks against Jews around the world, including the massacre earlier that year in the main synagogue in Ankara, Turkey. "Often the Jews are first," Bronfman's cable warned, "but the rest of society crumbles rapidly thereafter." Bronfman pleaded with Stroessner to "ensure the Jewish community of Paraguay of that safety they so direly need and that peace of mind which they seek along with all other Paraguayan citizens."

Twelve days later, Tenenbaum telexed us again, this time to relay the happy news that "Stroessner personally gave orders to put an end to the anti-Semitic wave," and that Tenenbaum's contact in Asunción "is grateful for the WJC intervention, which he considers decisive." According to the contact in Asunción, Tenenbaum reported, "Stroessner enormously fears being accused of being an anti-Semite, because of the repercussions in the United States."

Later, we learned from one of our South American representatives that what Stroessner had in mind was the possibility that, as our contact put it, "Bronfman would do to him what he has done to Waldheim."

Dusko Doder of the *Washington Post* called me on September 19 to report that he had completed the job that Stephen Katich was trying to accomplish when he died. A Serb himself who had also served as the *Post*'s Moscow bureau chief, Doder had his own well-placed sources in Yugoslavia, who had finally provided him with a copy of the *Odluka*. On his own, Doder had spirited it out of Yugoslavia. He said that he would dispatch a duplicate to me by overnight courier, on the condition that the WJC not release it until after he published his scoop in the *Post*. I readily agreed.

While he was in Yugoslavia, Doder told me, he had spoken to several former intelligence agents who disclosed that Tito had known of Waldheim's past all along. They went even further than Anton Kolendic had gone a few months earlier, asserting not only that the Soviets had approached Waldheim but that they had actually compromised him.

Doder was full of news. He said that in the course of writing his story, he had been careful to give Waldheim a chance to attempt to refute his material point by point. In the process of responding, he said, a Waldheim spokesperson declared that "additional research" had shown that Waldheim's previous statements about Kozara were incorrect, and the spokesman admitted to Doder that Waldheim had, indeed, been stationed in western Bosnia during the Kozara campaign; Waldheim now was admitting that, yes, he had served in Stahl's West Bosnia Combat Group. This dramatic reversal was accompanied, however, by an odd claim, namely that Waldheim's specific assignment in Stahl's unit had been in the Quartermaster Department. Neither Doder nor I knew what, if any, significance there was to this job assignment. On the one hand, it sounded, at first hearing, like pretty tame stuff: In most armies of the world, quartermaster units order and keep track of supplies. On the other hand, a month earlier, I had found a document showing that the Quartermaster Branch at *another* of Waldheim's postings (Army Group E's High Command) gave orders to round up captured partisans for deportation to slave labor. If the Quartermaster Department in Stahl's West Bosnia Combat Group was involved in deportations, then we might at last be on the verge of solving the riddle of Waldheim's actual role at Kozara. But that was a very big "if."

At the least, however, this latest change in Waldheim's Kozara account showed that the Austrian president finally realized that he could no longer sustain the lie that he had only had a "paper assignment" to Stahl's infamous unit, or that he had served only as an interpreter.

A package from Doder arrived at my home by Federal Express the next morning, a Saturday. As I held the ten-page *Odluka* in my hands at last, I was surprised to find my mood turn melancholy. I thought of Katich, and wished that he could share this moment.

I sat down with the file, prepared to race through it. But I stared at alien words and realized: I don't have a bloody idea what it says! The *Odluka,* of course, was written in Serbo-Croatian.

I rushed the package over to Dusan Tatomirovic, the man who handled such translations for us. There was nothing to do now but wait.

At the WJC offices, I was still the late-night Phantom of the Xerox, copying and recopying anything with potential relevance and cross-filing it all in folders representing every conceivable subject. Here, for example, was a Secret Field Police document referring to propaganda activities and a "cleansing operation" on the island of Rhodes. I jammed copies of it into seven separate files, marked SECRET FIELD POLICE, PROPAGANDA ACTIVITIES, CLEANSING OPERATIONS, ANTI-PARTISAN WARFARE, GREECE, and RHODES. By now, I had a pair of four-drawer file cabinets overflowing with Waldheim documents.

On evenings and weekends, I tried to plunge into some of those files. Working on hands and knees on the floor of my apartment, I spread out innumerable pages and arranged them by topic, then rearranged them by date, then by unit. I stared at them for hours, searching for patterns and links.

It was on one such evening in mid-September, when I was reviewing the Nuremberg documents I had copied during my first research trip to the National Archives, that I noticed that General Loehr's order of August 10, 1943, commanded that directives regarding "propaganda for deserters" were to "come from [the] Commander-in-Chief Southeast" (that is, Loehr himself).[20] The order made specific reference to successes already registered in attracting deserters in Russia. Back in April when I found this document, the subject of deserter propaganda had meant nothing to us; but now I thought at once of the "Kill the Jews" package of deserter propaganda leaflets. Was there a connection?

I will never know what impelled me that night to go past the official Nuremberg prosecution staff translation to the original German text of Loehr's order,* but when I did so, I was stunned by what I saw. The original German text ended with three words that had been inexplicably *deleted* from the staff translation: *"Branch Ic/AO."* Thus, the correct translation of this sentence within Loehr's order was: "Directives regarding propaganda for deserters will come from Commander-in-Chief Southeast, Branch Ic/AO."

So Waldheim's Intelligence/Counterintelligence Branch was in charge of deserter propaganda! Everything was beginning to make sense. I checked the Army Group E organizational chart and, sure enough, one of the functions listed under "AO" was "Authorization for own propaganda and initiatives for counter-propaganda" to Propaganda Company 690. I had seen that unit mentioned somewhere, I was sure of it. I scrambled to find my copy of the leaflet package that Korte had discovered. The top page, initialed by Waldheim, stated that the enclosed leaflets were prepared by the First Combat Propaganda Troop of *Propaganda Company 690.* The leaflets—or at least some of them—had evidently been sent to Waldheim and his cohorts for clearance!

An alarm bell rang in my mind. I suddenly remembered another tidbit, found by Herzstein during his March search at the National Archives. My fingers raced through file folders until I found the document that confirmed my memory. Herzstein had determined that the Wehrmacht newspaper *Wacht im Suedosten*—the paper that displayed the front-page photo of Waldheim with General Loehr—was published by Propaganda Company 690. I checked the date on the Wehrmacht newspaper and whispered, "Good God!" The newspaper photo was published *the very same day* that Waldheim initialed the propaganda package: December 3, 1944. And there was more: I noticed for the first time that the "Kill the Jews" leaflet was one of those in the package that was listed as still being in German—

*The prosecution staff translation is contained within the "Staff Evidence Analysis" of NOKW-155, prepared by the Office of U.S. Chief Counsel for War Crimes.

that is, it had not yet been translated into Russian. Waldheim had received it and initialed it while it was still in draft form.

Now I had a clear chain of facts: (1) It was the responsibility of Waldheim's unit to clear and supervise Propaganda Company 690's dissemination of "deserter" propaganda; (2) a particularly vile propaganda package, including an explicit exhortation, still in draft, to "Kill the Jews," was initialed by Waldheim as the "O3" officer; (3) this seemed to reflect approval of the leaflets by Waldheim and his colleagues; at least there was no indication that anyone at Army Group E had *objected* to any of the text;* and (4) the very same day, Waldheim received the honor of being pictured in a front-page photograph alongside General Loehr, printed in a newspaper published by the very same propaganda company that produced the hideous series of pamphlets. It seemed that the newspaper's editors were "sucking up" to the lieutenant who helped approve their work.

First thing the next morning, I showed a stunned Singer and Steinberg what we had, and I shipped all the latest documents down to Neal Sher at OSI. In a phone conversation, Sher told me that he thought this was "the closest thing anybody's found to a smoking gun." Although plainly unwilling to be drawn into a discussion on the specifics of his appraisal, Sher did not disagree with my suggestion that the documents, in addition to their immediate significance, demonstrated again the bankruptcy of Waldheim's claim that Ic and AO had separate responsiblities (deserter propaganda was clearly supposed to be a counterintelligence, or AO, activity) and his contention that he had no inkling of the homicidal campaign against the Jews.

We released the story to the press on September 23. As I expected, it made headlines around the world. The barometer of Big Apple emotion, the *New York Post* front page, featured a headline, printed in bright red above the masthead, that screamed: NEW WALDHEIM "KILL JEWS" SHOCKER.

In Vienna, President Waldheim responded tersely that our allegations were "without foundation."

This same day, the government of Israel announced that it would not replace its ambassador to Austria until such time as Waldheim

---

*The absence of any indication of objection to the murderous texts of the leaflets is especially interesting in light of the fact that, *more than two years earlier*, the German Armed Forces Propaganda Office had been informed that Wehrmacht leaflets containing "invitations to violence" against the Jews had *backfired* with the target audience of Soviet soldiers. Leaflets "which called for the killing and murder [*sic*] of Jews" were seen, in one captured 1942 German analysis, as "correct" in their "anti-Semitic tendency," but as "misdirecting the primitive mind of the Russian soldier, who will infer from them that Germans are inclined towards violence and for that very reason will be afraid to surrender" (August 2, 1942 report signed by 2nd Lt. Tietze, reprinted in Raul Hilberg, *Documents of Destruction* [Chicago: Quadrangle, 1971], p. 84).

left office. Jerusalem's reasoning was that diplomatic protocol obliges an ambassador to present his credentials to the president, and the Israelis were not about to instruct any diplomat of theirs to do so. Ambassador Elizur was supplanted by Gideon Yarden, a lower-level official who did not have to present himself to Waldheim.

On Sunday morning, September 28, I met Dusan Tatomirovic at Caffe Reggio, a block away from Washington Square, to receive his "rush" translation of Doder's Yugoslav haul. Then I raced home to study it.

Finally, I had a readable version of the *Odluka* in my hands. I could hardly wait to get home and dive into the text.

But it soon became apparent that reading the *Odluka* was something of an anticlimax. There was little of significance in it that we had not already learned by way of the Yugoslav press and the UNWCC file. Worse still, the eleven items of evidence listed on the last page—captured German documents and reports on the interrogations of Mayer, Egberts-Hilker, and four other witnesses—did not accompany the copy Doder had retrieved.

The indictment was full of conclusory language that usually was unaccompanied by hard evidence. Much of it was a rough patchwork of facts about Nazi crimes in Yugoslavia, the structure and operations of Army Group E, the duties of Ic personnel, and recollections of German P.O.W.'s. Time and again, it detailed an atrocity, only to close the discussion with the unsupported words "for which Waldheim can also be held responsible." Egberts-Hilker's quoted testimony made *no* reference to Waldheim—or even to Waldheim's intelligence branch at Army Group E. Instead, it spoke only of reprisal orders from Hitler.

Only Johann Mayer's testimony, which, in the main, was logically consistent with what we had documented on our own, seemed to have the potential of directly implicating Waldheim. The *Odluka* provided a lengthier series of quotations than we had previously seen from Mayer's testimony. Until now, we had only seen snippets, as quoted or paraphrased in the Yugoslav press and in the UNWCC file. It was true, I now saw, as Waldheim's submission to the Justice Department claimed, that the UNWCC committee had paraphrased and shortened Mayer's testimony, and perhaps the example that Waldheim's brief cited was indeed unfair to the Austrian president. But, on balance, I found that the committee had done a fair job of summarizing. For example, here was another textual comparison:

MAYER'S TESTIMONY AS QUOTED IN THE ODLUKA
I was assigned as a clerk in the personnel section. At that time

the following were assigned in the command: Lt. Col. Warnstorff of the General Staff, who was the Ic officer of the Army Group (the third ranking officer in the General Staff). Lt. Waldheim, whose Christian name so far as I recall was Kurt, was attached to his section, officially an aide-de-camp (O3), but in fact he performed the duties of an Ic officer for espionage. . . . Lt. Waldheim's job was to propose to his superior, Lt. Col. Warnstorff, all actions of Ic and to prepare all the written reports for that purpose. These reports dealt with the question of hostages, retaliation measures, and behavior with regard to war prisoners and the civilian population.

MAYER'S TESTIMONY AS REFERENCED IN THE UNWCC FILE

I joined the Heeresgruppe on 3rd April 1944 as a personnel division clerk. The commander was Lieut. Col. Warnstorff and his deputy was Waldheim. He was an *Ordonnanzoffizier*. His duties were those of an intelligence officer. It was up to him to bring up suggestions concerning reprisal actions, treatment of prisoners of war and civilian internees. . . .

What we had here was consistent with what we already knew about the Allied commando episodes and about Stip-Kocane and other incidents involving the retreating forces of Army Group E. Mayer, moreover, depicted Waldheim as a facilitator of war crimes, a "desk-murderer," rather than a hands-on perpetrator. This, too, was in harmony with the results of the modern-day investigation of Waldheim. Once you put aside its hyperbolic conclusions, the *Odluka* was at bottom a measured, moderate document. For example, it did not quote Mayer as saying that Waldheim actually gave the orders to commit specific atrocities; instead, it generally implicated Waldheim in a chain of command that was responsible for the crimes. It seemed to me that if the Yugoslavs had decided to create phony charges against Waldheim, as Waldheim now contended, they would have put even more forceful words into Mayer's (or Egberts-Hilker's) mouth. Trumped-up evidence would have been a great deal more damning than what this particular *Odluka* contained.

In light of the December 1947 internal Yugoslav correspondence that *Vecernje Novosti* had previously disclosed—in which Yugoslav authorities candidly referred to the "possible use" of their information on Waldheim's war record—I should not have been surprised to see that the *Odluka* appeared driven more by conclusions than by facts. Still, it was a disappointment to verify that the Yugoslavs seemed to have been more interested in compromising Waldheim than in actually proving a war crimes case against him. Their failure to list Waldheim's immediate superior, Herbert Warnstorff, with the UNWCC—despite his having been frequently mentioned in Waldheim's *Odluka* as being responsible for reprisals—was a painful reminder of what Belgrade's priorities had been.

Nevertheless, it was remarkable how close the Yugoslavs had come to properly making a case against Waldheim. Based on what we now knew, the *Odluka*'s focus on reprisal killings, mass terror measures against civilian populations, and treatment of P.O.W.'s was largely on target. Waldheim's current pursuers had unearthed a veritable mountain of evidence placing Waldheim in the vortex of criminal activities at Army Group E headquarters. (It appeared that Belgrade had been unaware of Waldheim's assignments in Bosnia and elsewhere, perhaps owing to the confused state of their holdings of captured documents in the immediate postwar years.) If nothing else, Belgrade had built what we at OSI used to call a "status" case: The Yugoslavs had correctly identified Waldheim as a key member of a demonstrably criminal unit. Indeed, if Mayer's specific testimony was accurate, then Waldheim had participated actively in the formulation of gruesome reprisal strategies.

It was certainly easy to see why a seasoned Yugoslav intelligence officer like Anton Kolendic had been so tantalized, forty years earlier, by the prospect of using this file as a blackmail device. However poorly (or even disingenuously) researched and written the *Odluka* was, there could be no denying that once it was "validated" by the United Nations War Crimes Commission, it would have given the Yugoslavs a powerful weapon with which to compromise Waldheim. To an up-and-coming young diplomat in postwar Austria, it would have been nothing less than the atomic bomb of blackmail devices.

27

Autumn found Simon Wiesenthal still fuming, complaining to a reporter that the Waldheim accusations "were completely unfounded and organized from abroad." The words "organized from abroad" were virtually identical to the ones that the People's Party had used nearly every day during the election campaign to appeal to Austrians' xenophobic and anti-Semitic sentiments. And "abroad" was the People's Party code word for "Jews." Wiesenthal piled absurdity on top of nonsense, insisting to his interviewer that there were "no more anti-Semites in Austria than in other countries."

The article reported that Wiesenthal had "indirectly" criticized Israel for its decision not to replace Michael Elizur as its ambassador to Austria, stressing that the Jewish state needed "friends more than any other country." If it maintained relations with such "fascist" nations as South Africa and Chile, he said, there was no "rhyme or reason" for shunning Austria.[1]

Over a transatlantic telephone connection, Leon Zelman, the survivor who had first led us to the case, declared to me that he was "demolished" by the Wiesenthal interview, and never wanted to see Wiesenthal—"or even to hear his name"—again.

Two days later, People's Party General Secretary Michael Graff met with visiting representatives of the American Jewish Committee and acceded to their entreaty that he publicly denounce anti-Semitism. But he did not apologize for the People's Party outrages that had shocked the world, among them some of his own statements.

Within the month, Graff was again being quoted on the subject of anti-Semitism: "The People's Party never argued in an anti-Semitic way; we did not hit hard—if we wanted to do that, we could do a lot more."[2] Presumably, the Jews were to take comfort in the thought that Graff and his colleagues had spared them from having to endure "a lot more." Viktor Reiman, a columnist for Vienna's mass-circulation daily *Kronenzeitung,* returned to the subject in his own way. He repeated the calumny that "it was not the Austrians" who revived anti-Semitic feelings, but the WJC, because it behaves "like masters with regard to Austria." Reiman accused the WJC of "culminating" its campaign of "unfounded accusations against Waldheim" by calling Waldheim "the butcher from Austria," and by claiming that "all Austrians are Nazi pigs." None of this was true, but it presumably found a receptive audience in Austria.

I met in New York on October 23 with Hans-Peter Martin of Hamburg's *Der Spiegel,* who passed on several new pieces of information. He had learned that when members of Waldheim's campaign staff realized that accounts the candidate had given them about his wartime activities were incorrect, they decided that they could not trust him and would have to conduct their own research into the candidate's background.

Martin also disclosed that Brian Urquhart, the distinguished former Under Secretary-General of the U.N., had wanted to resign his post in 1971 when Waldheim was elected. According to Martin, Urquhart never cared for Waldheim and the thought of working under any former Wehrmacht soldier was repugnant to him, but U.N. colleagues convinced Urquhart that he was desperately needed. Before making a decision, Urquhart had asked Waldheim for details concerning his wartime service. Not surprisingly, Waldheim replied that he had been wounded in 1941 and spent the remainder of the war completing his law studies. Hearing this, Urquhart decided to stay. Now, Martin said, Urquhart felt betrayed.*

On October 30, the front page of the *Washington Post* carried Dusko Doder's story about the *Odluka,* disclosing as well Waldheim's startling admission that he really was at Stahl's headquarters in western Bosnia during the time of the Kozara massacres, if only as a quartermaster officer. The subtitle of the story was a bit of a leap, declaring: "He Concedes Role in '42 Massacre of Yugoslav Citizens." Waldheim's new story—his sixth completely changed version in seven months—placed him in the Kozara area in the summer of 1942, but only in a supposedly innocuous job that gave him "the duties of a supply officer."†

---

*Urquhart eventually confirmed all of this in his 1987 book, *A Life in Peace and War* (New York: Harper & Row).

†The reader will recall the following major permutations of Waldheim's claims regarding his whereabouts and activities during June and July 1942: (1) During 1942 and 1943, he served in Salonika, Belgrade, Podgorica, and Tirana (making no mention of Kozara or any other area of Bosnia); (2) he was stationed in Salonika throughout the summer of 1942; (3) he was in fact at Kozara, but only as an interpreter, and it was "nonsense" to say that a massacre took place there; (4) he understood that atrocities were indeed committed at Kozara by General Stahl's forces, but he only had a "paper assignment" to Stahl's command and "made a mistake" when he said he was at Kozara; in fact, he was 120 miles away, near Plevlje, in another area that happened also to have the name "Kozara"; and (5) he did indeed report—briefly—to General Stahl's headquarters, but was immediately detailed to Plevlje, Montenegro.

Doder's article also discussed his extraordinary confirmation of Anton Kolendic's account of how the Yugoslavs had alerted the Soviets to Waldheim's war record. The *Post* reporter recounted how several former Yugoslav intelligence and government officials had confirmed to him, in separate interviews, that the Yugoslavs had compiled a secret dossier on Waldheim's war record in the immediate postwar years for the purpose of blackmailing him, and had shared the material with the Soviets. Kolendic himself repeated that he was "absolutely certain" that the Russians had used the material to approach Waldheim.

A number of former Yugoslav intelligence operatives, "now all comfortably retired," were able "to recall vividly" the details of the Waldheim operation. One former senior intelligence officer (whom Doder promised anonymity) went further, confiding that he had been told by a colleague that the Soviets had informed him "in early 1948" that Waldheim had been successfully "recruited" and that the Yugoslavs should "stop their interference." A second former official, who had been an aide to Tito, explained to Doder, "We had to give him to the Russians. We were an appendage of the Soviet Union at the time. . . ." A third ex-agent told Doder that Yugoslav secret policy chief Alexander Rankovic "decided to try to recruit" Waldheim. He continued:

> That was not difficult in those days. You show your victim the document but then you tell him everything would be fine, you'd protect him provided he would do something for you in return. And that was 1947. You have to feel the atmosphere of that year. War crime trials were still going on, people were afraid.

The agent recalled seeing memos prepared by Kolendic concerning his discussions with Waldheim and with the Soviet agent Gonda. Kolendic, who had previously denied that the Yugoslav side attempted to recruit Waldheim on its own, refused to meet Doder a second time to respond to his former colleagues' recollections.

Mirko Milutinovic, Tito's former chief of staff, told Doder, "I knew that Waldheim had been compromised." But the operation's success had not necessarily been predicated on hard information. Milutinovic confirmed that the Yugoslavs, at the time, did not know about Waldheim's involvement in the Kozara campaign, and he claimed that Tito did not feel that the available evidence sufficed to prove him a full-fledged war criminal. This account left little room for doubt that the *Odluka* was a hastily prepared indictment, aimed far more at blackmail than conviction.

Still another Tito confidant told Doder that the Yugoslav dictator viewed Waldheim as a "Soviet man" who might also have links to the American side. Doder's sources quoted Tito's view that Waldheim was a "pliable" man, a convenient choice for the top position at the U.N.

I was especially intrigued by Doder's assertion that "present and former" U.S. intelligence officials had told him that Waldheim had long been suspected of having what Doder termed "a special relationship" with the Soviets, but that the proof had always been elusive.[3]

Waldheim spokesman Gerold Christian responded to Doder's journalistic tour de force by talking to Reuters and to the *Post*'s arch rival, the *New York Times,* maintaining that the *Post* story had nothing new, that Waldheim had acknowledged his 1942 participation in Wehrmacht operations in the Kozara area way back on April 1, in an interview published in the *Salzburger Nachtrichten* newspaper. I marveled at Christian's bravado. Waldheim's statement to the Austrian newspaper—similar to one he had made in late March on Austrian radio in the immediate aftermath of the WJC press conference at which we revealed the National Archives documentation placing him at Kozara—had been retracted *the very next day* in his interview published in the April 2 issues of the Yugoslav newspapers *Vecernje Novosti* and *Politika Svet.* He told those papers that he "made a mistake" when he admitted he had been in the Kozara area; in reality, he claimed, he had been in Plevlje, Montenegro, and had received only a "paper assignment" to General Stahl's forces in Western Bosnia. Moreover, in his April 12 defense memo, Waldheim wrote that "witnesses in Plevlje, Montenegro, have meanwhile confirmed that I was in that town, more than 200 km south of Banja Luka and 'Kozara area' . . ." during the Kozara operation.

Christian also denied the claims that Waldheim was compromised by the Soviets. And, in what surely was one of the most counterproductive (and, however unintentionally, hilarious) testimonials ever offered by any politician's spokesperson, Christian declared that "all things that Mr. Waldheim said were not incorrect."

Suddenly, however, a most unlikely white knight came to Waldheim's rescue: Anton Kolendic told a Reuters reporter that he "categorically" denied saying to "Dusko Doder or anyone else" that the Soviet or Yugoslav intelligence services had actually tried to recruit Waldheim. Stranger still, Kolendic charged in another interview that it was "an absolute lie" that he had told Doder that the Soviets approached Waldheim. But he stuck to his assertion that he had handed the Waldheim file to the Soviets.

It appeared that enormous pressure was being put on the former head of Yugoslav intelligence in postwar Vienna to retract portions of the statements he had made to Dusko Doder and other journalists. This was tortuous Yugoslav intrigue at its worst.

Here was Kolendic's new account: Waldheim's name was one on a list of forty thousand persons wanted for war crimes, and it was Kolendic's job to pass this information on to the Allied forces in Austria. Because Waldheim was living in the Soviet zone at the time, Kolendic said, his dossier went to "Tovarich Gonda." And that, he said, was pretty much the end of the matter, for soon afterward the Soviets and Yugoslavs broke relations. Kolendic said he "never heard" of anyone trying to blackmail Waldheim.[4]

Even as Kolendic was doing his renunciation dance for the press, President Waldheim formally received the credentials of Gennady Shikin, newly appointed Soviet ambassador to Austria. Shikin went through the customary diplomatic motions with no hint of embarrassment.

On October 31, Waldheim sent a lengthy report on his war record to British M.P. Robert Rhodes James, which, by virtue of its dating, I came to refer to as Waldheim's "Halloween Memo." Rhodes James had worked at the U.N. under Waldheim from 1972 through 1976 and disliked him intensely. (In a later interview, Rhodes James said that he and his U.N. colleagues found Waldheim to be a "ranting, rude, bullying egomaniac."[5])

Rhodes James, like his House of Commons colleague Greville Janner, was pressing the Thatcher government to bar Waldheim from entry into Britain and demanding that the government release whatever documents it had concerning Austria's new president. It was in apparent response to these initiatives that Waldheim sent Rhodes James the Halloween Memo. Curiously composed in the third person, it covered most topics in well-rehearsed fashion. But it added a few new twists.

One of these concerned the Podgorica photo. Previously, Waldheim had maintained that he was present at the 1943 airstrip meeting during the "Black Operation" merely to act as an interpreter. To Rhodes James, however, he said that he was there as an interpreter *and* liaison officer. It was a passing detail, a change that was impossible to catch unless one followed every nuance of the story. Waldheim had just added another small fact to his wartime record, surrendering further evidence to refute his claim that he knew nothing about the atrocities that were happening at this terrible time.

On the subject of the Allied commandos, the memo attempted to counter the charges with general denials: Waldheim "was never involved in the handling of prisoners . . . and of captured commandos"; none of the commando documents "originated with, were

directed to, were received by, or were acted upon by Dr. Waldheim"; no commando document "refers to Dr. Waldheim"; Waldheim held "no responsibility" for interrogating prisoners.[6] Most
of these denials, however, had already been exposed as lies by captured documents previously provided to the media by the WJC and
others.

At least he now conceded formally what had been obvious ever
since we found Army Group E's organizational chart, which listed
Waldheim by name, as the officer responsible for the Intelligence/
Counterintelligence Branch's "progress reports" and the "Ic Morning and Evening reports" on the enemy situation: These reports
were *his own,* even though they went out over Colonel Warnstorff's name with Waldheim technically signing only for their "correctness."

On this same Halloween day, the *Washington Times* carried a routine Reuters story on Waldheim's continuing travails. But buried
within the piece, separated from the remainder of the text by brack-
ets, were several remarkable paragraphs based on an interview conducted, not by Reuters, but by the newspaper's editor-in-chief,
Arnaud de Borchgrave. The former *Newsweek* senior correspondent
had spoken with Alexandre de Marenches, who had directed the
French external intelligence service from 1970 to 1981. As early as
1978, de Marenches asserted, French intelligence had concluded that
Waldheim was "an agent of influence under Soviet control." That
appraisal was made, according to de Marenches, partly on the basis
of statements from Romanian and other Eastern Bloc defectors, who
contended that Waldheim's Soviet ties were "well-known among East
European intelligence services."

I was especially struck by de Marenche's implication that his people
were investigating Waldheim in the late seventies, and I wondered
if this was another clue to the mysterious 1979 inspection of Waldheim's French-held WASt file in Berlin.

The paper cited examples of how Waldheim might have repaid
his debt. There was, for example, the case of Geli A. Dneprovsky,
whose 1979 appointment as head of U.N. personnel in Geneva was
angrily opposed by the U.S. mission, which advised Waldheim that
Dneprovsky was a KGB colonel. According to the paper, when U.S.
Ambassador William Vanden Heuvel conveyed Washington's stren-
uous objections to Waldheim's representative in Geneva, he was
told, "Mind your own business."[7]

OSI's Neal Sher, concerned about the escalating feud within the
ranks of those who had always supported OSI's work, helped arrange

a "peace breakfast" on November 2 at the Doral Park Hotel in New York City. It brought together Simon Wiesenthal and his U.S. lawyer, Martin Mendelsohn, along with Singer, Steinberg, and Sher; I was not there. Mendelsohn brought a cassette recorder, with which he taped part of the discussion.

Steinberg reported to me afterward that the meeting was generally amicable, although he thought Wiesenthal appeared somewhat nervous.

As we suspected all along, Wiesenthal said that he was angry at me for not contacting him when I first came to Vienna; Steinberg took the heat on that issue, protecting Schuller by claiming that he, Steinberg, had instructed me "not to tell anyone" about the reason for my trip.

Bitterly, and with surprising candor, Wiesenthal expressed his disappointment that Auschwitz survivor and author Elie Wiesel had won the Nobel Peace Prize a month earlier, and he did not; Wiesenthal claimed that the Nobel Committee had planned to make it a joint prize, but said he had heard that a letter to the Prize Committee from the WJC had effectively killed his candidacy. We had done nothing of the sort. Steinberg denied that the WJC had sent any such letter and pledged that he would sue anyone who masqueraded as a WJC representative to attack Wiesenthal.*

Steinberg returned to the office optimistic that the "war" with "that louse Wiesenthal" was over at last.

But two days later, the *International Herald Tribune* quoted Wiesenthal as saying that the WJC's charges against Waldheim were "unsustained" and "unfounded." The Nazi-hunter repeated his outrageous allegation that the WJC did not know how to read German war documents.† "In 40 years of working on 1,100 cases of Nazi crimes," he asserted, "I have never made a charge that I could not sustain through witnesses or documents." The WJC's actions had "provoked resentment against all Jews."

Taking another tack, Wiesenthal again attacked his old enemy, Socialist Party leader Bruno Kreisky, for having had Nazis in his cabinet. Once more, there was no sign in the article of Wiesenthal

---

*So confident was Wiesenthal that he would be sharing the prize with Wiesel that he later disclosed that he had contacted a lawyer to have papers drafted conveying his share of the prize money to charity.
†Wiesenthal explained that none of the reports signed by Waldheim showed him ordering or approving actions. But the Nazi-hunter was only knocking down a straw man; we had made no such characterization of the documents. More importantly, Wiesenthal's argument sidestepped the weightiest accusations against Waldheim—namely, that he communicated criminal orders, provided information and analyses upon which such orders were based, and assisted in the implementation of criminal orders.

criticizing the People's Party and its leaders, Graff, Mock, and Waldheim (or, for that matter, the Austrian press), for the pervasive anti-Semitism of the election campaign.[8]

The early November meeting of the Jewish organizations possessing "nongovernmental organization" (NGO) observer status at the United Nations was ordinarily the type of gathering that I would have paid good money to *avoid* attending. Held this time at the impressive headquarters of the Anti-Defamation League of B'nai B'rith—literally across the street from U.N. headquarters—these meetings were typically little more than a succession of pretentious presentations by one after another representative of a major Jewish organization boasting of his or her supposed success in getting the group's views taken seriously by this or that U.N. delegation, official, or agency. In truth, however, with few exceptions, the work that all of us did at the U.N. was little more than tilting at windmills, our accomplishments more imagined than real; for the world body was still overwhelmingly and implacably hostile to Israel and other Jewish interests. The General Assembly had even voted to declare Zionism—the national liberation movement of the Jewish People—"a form of racism."

The latest conclave of more than a dozen Jewish NGOs turned out to be no different from its predecessors—except that I had asked for and been granted time to address my counterparts on the subject of Kurt Waldheim. When at last my turn came, I placed before the assembled delegates a very modest proposal: I asked that we agree as a group to seek a meeting with Vernon Walters, the U.S. representative to the United Nations. The purpose of the meeting would be to press Ambassador Walters to take concrete action to carry out the provision (Section 1303) of the Anti-Terrorism Act of 1986 calling for the U.S. government to attempt to build a consensus among the member nations for the termination of Kurt Waldheim's $81,000 U.N. annual pension.

The proposal seemed so unremarkable that I had assumed that any discussion of it would revolve solely around agreeing upon a few convenient dates to propose to Walters's office for the requested meeting.

I could not have been more wrong. To my astonishment, my proposal was met with dour looks and almost universal antipathy.* One, then another, Jewish representative complained about the fact

---

*The one exception was Women's International Zionist Organization (WIZO) representative Evelyn Sommer, who enthusiastically supported the proposal.

that Jewish organizational activitism in the Waldheim case was, as one of them put it, "making it look like Waldheim is just a Jewish issue." Someone *else* should carry the ball this time, I was reproached. All around me, heads nodded approval of the rebuff.

"All I'm asking for is a joint approach for a single private meeting," I pleaded, "to try to get the government to enforce its own federal statute. Is that so radical an idea?"

"But why does it always have to be *Jewish* groups?" was one representative's immediate rejoinder, delivered with a scowl. "Yes," said another, "why is it always *Jewish* organizations?"

I could not resist a sarcastic response. "The Anti-Terrorism Act was passed by both houses of Congress—and the last time *I* looked, the U.S. Congress was not 'a Jewish organization.'"

I was chagrined to find that I was winning no converts to my position. Again I was lectured about the importance of other— that is, non-Jewish—groups taking the lead on the Waldheim matter. Once again, bobbing heads communicated approval by acclamation.

My blood was boiling by now. Despair, exasperation, and ire combined to create a fury that frightened even me. I felt a tingling sensation as my face flushed red with anger.

"I hear what I am being told," I said as calmly as I could. "But I cannot believe that I have to remind *this* group that it has become part of the fate of our people to be the world's collective memory of the Holocaust and all the crimes of the Nazis."

This time it was my turn to do the lecturing. "As little as the world cared to stop the Holocaust while it was taking place," I declared, "it cares even less to be reminded of it now. If you are waiting for the rest of the world to come to the rescue now, you will be waiting at least until the Messiah comes, my friends. *All* of you know that if *we* don't go to see Walters, no one else will do it."

There was silence. As I glanced around the room, people looked down at the papers they had brought with them or found other ways of averting their eyes. No minds had been changed.

I felt a throbbing pain in my stomach, as if I had been at the receiving end of a roundhouse punch to the solar plexus.

Silently, I gathered my papers together and rose to leave. It was the only time in my life that I had ever walked out of a meeting in protest. A few minutes later, as I stood at curbside trying to hail a cab, I thought of the complaints I had heard my former law school professor Alan Dershowitz voice about the persistent timidity and "ghetto mentality" of much of the Jewish "leadership" in the United

States. Dershowitz had always made plain his disdain as he emphasized the word "leadership." I needed no further convincing now.*

The significance, if any, of Waldheim's new version of his Kozara story, according to which he was assigned to the Quartermaster Department of General Stahl's West Bosnia Combat Group as an *Ordonnanzoffizier* having "the duties of a supply officer," remained a frustrating mystery to Bob Herzstein. He lamented to one interviewer that Waldheim's statement "does not further my knowledge of what he was specifically doing. He has not told us what he was doing in Kozara to deserve the [King Zvonimir] medal."[9]

Herzstein's statement surprised me. Had he not seen during his own research the document I had seen at the National Archives in August—the one that showed that the Quartermaster Branch at another of Waldheim's postings (Army Group E's High Command) gave orders to round up captured partisans for deportation to slave labor? Surely that document provided a strong basis to suspect that we might at last be on the trail of Waldheim's actual deeds at Kozara during the summer of 1942.[10] It took little effort to convince Singer and Steinberg that another trip to the National Archives was in order.

The expedition paid off almost immediately. A sympathetic staffer at the Archives led me to three extraordinary documents that, he confided, OSI's Pat Treanor had recently discovered in the microfilmed Wehrmacht records. The documents were all classified "secret" and bore dates from the first week of June 1942. And they confirmed our worst suspicions.

The first was a June 2 order to Stahl's West Bosnia Combat Group from Colonel Munckel, the General Quartermaster on the staff of the Wehrmacht's Commanding General for Serbia. It instructed Stahl's headquarters to "reach agreement with the Croatian government" concerning "deportation of prisoners" to "Croatian camps" and elsewhere. "Anticipated arrival dates and numbers are to be reported by phone before each transport leaves," to the Quartermaster Branch of the Commanding General for Serbia.[11]

The second document, dated June 4, was a six-page order from Stahl entitled, "Guidelines for the Operations in West Bosnia." It made it clear that the "deportation" of prisoners was a "Supply" function, to be handled by quartermaster personnel. And it left no

*A month later, I went alone to meet with two members of Walters's staff at the U.S. mission. They told me that the mission had not received any instructions from the State Department on the section of the Anti-Terrorism Act pertaining to Waldheim's U.N. pension. In fact, they had not even been aware of that provision, they said, until I brought it to their attention. At this writing, the United States still has taken no action to mobilize opposition at the U.N. to continuing Waldheim's pension.

doubt that the "prisoners" to be "deported" were *civilians,* not Yugoslav partisans: The same order, signed by Stahl himself, commanded that "whoever fights or is found with a weapon" and whoever "supported such persons" was "to be shot."[12] This meant that the deportees had to be persons *other* than partisans and their supporters.

The final document, dated June 5, relayed "changed instructions" to Stahl's headquarters from General Quartermaster Munckel. It commanded that "Deportation of prisoners to Croatian concentration camps is to be handled by the Combat Group itself."[13]

I was stunned. It was suddenly clear what Waldheim's recent admission of service in the Quartermaster Department *meant:* He was an officer in the detachment within the command staff of General Stahl's infamous West Bosnia Combat Group that was directly responsible for the deportation of more than sixty-eight thousand Yugoslav civilians, over a third of them *children.* Thousands had died in the forced marches and most of the remaining deportees died at the Croatian death camps.

Was Waldheim a minor cog in this gruesome machine, or was he a critical component? What I needed was a personnel roster of the Quartermaster unit at Stahl's headquarters. But after several fruitless hours scouring the microfilms, I reluctantly concluded that it was doubtful that any had survived the war. Another dead end! But perhaps there was one way to solve the mystery. I decided to compare what little we knew about this unit to a similar unit about which we had more facts: the supply unit of the Bader Combat Group in eastern Bosnia. That unit was designated Qu ("Quartermaster Department")—a *corps*-level designation—while the supply unit of Stahl's West Bosnia Combat Group was designated Ib (roughly, "Quartermaster section")—a *division*-level designation.[14] The obvious inference was that the Quartermaster section at Kozara was *smaller* than the one in eastern Bosnia—which, according to National Archives documents we already possessed, had *only four* officers assigned to it! Thus, it could be deduced that Waldheim was one of only a very few officers in the Kozara unit that handled the critical aspects of the criminal Kozara deportations.

As I stared at the documents and realized their full significance, I instinctively covered my mouth with my right hand. It had taken more than half a year to get from the Yugoslav news agency's original Kozara allegation to this moment. During these months, Waldheim had changed his basic story so many times that I had nearly lost count: He wasn't there; he was there but it wasn't a massacre; he was at a "different Kozara" and it was just a "paper assignment" anyway; and then finally he was indeed there but "only" in the quartermaster unit at Stahl's headquarters. At long last it all made sense.

No longer was it hard to understand why Stahl had personally nominated Waldheim for the Croatian government's Zvonimir Medal for "heroic bravery in the battle against the insurgents in the spring and summer of 1942" and why Waldheim's name had been included on the "honor roll" appended to the gory Kozara prose poem.

For once, I thought, let's not give the Waldheim people the opportunity to blame "the Jews" for the latest disclosure. I phoned Dusko Doder at the *Washington Post* on November 5 and told him I was returning the favor for his supplying me with a copy of the *Odluka*. I briefed the startled reporter on the new documents. "I'm going to Fed-Ex the documents to you," I assured him, "along with draft translations. I'll write the National Archives microfilm citations on the pages; you can walk down the street to the Archives and check the films yourself, so that you don't have to take my word for it." My one condition was that the WJC not be identified as the source. Doder readily agreed.

The *Post* published Doder's front-page world exclusive on November 7. The headline: NAZI DATA TIES WALDHEIM UNIT TO MASS BALKAN DEPORTATION—CIVILIANS SHIPPED TO CONCENTRATION CAMPS.

As he had promised, Doder kept the WJC out of the story, noting only that the documents were "held in the U.S. National Archives and made available to the *Washington Post* yesterday."

Waldheim responded to this latest damning disclosure by issuing a tersely worded denial of involvement in any "handling of P.O.W.'s or civilians."

A more aggressive reaction came from Simon Wiesenthal. He phoned Neal Sher in response to the *Post* story. Incredibly, the Nazi-hunter insisted that the Kozara deportees had been *soldiers,* and, hence, in his view, no crime had been committed! Wiesenthal warned Sher about continuing to pursue Waldheim. "Stay away from this, Neal. It will burn you."

The publication of Doder's sensational article happened to take place just as Vienna was about to host the third Helsinki Review Conference to discuss international compliance with the human rights provisions of the Helsinki Accords; it was the largest gathering of foreign ministers in the Austrian capital since the fabled Congress of Vienna in 1915. A key question for us was: How would the foreign ministers of the various nations deal with the fact that there was a controversial new president in the host country? Would they follow the dictates of protocol, which required that they pay courtesy calls on Waldheim?

Privately, the chief U.S. delegate, Ambassador Warren Zimmerman, had assured me before his departure that the American side intended to avoid Waldheim at all costs. Still, I was worried that the Reagan Administration lacked the will to carry out what would amount to an unprecedented diplomatic snub. So I was greatly relieved when the State Department announced, shortly before the conference, that Secretary of State George Shultz would meet privately during the conference with Soviet Foreign Minister Eduard Shevardnadze and with Shultz's fellow NATO foreign ministers, but would *not* meet with President Waldheim. The Yugoslav Foreign Minister also refused to pay his respects.

The Soviets, however, soon showed that they were suffering no such squeamishness. On the eve of the conference, Shevardnadze paid a surprise courtesy call on Waldheim, becoming the very first senior official of a major foreign power to do so.[15]

A *Washington Post* reporter covering the conference discovered, quite involuntarily, that the domestic press was still defending Waldheim. As Doder related it to me later, at one point his colleague found herself surrounded by irate Austrian journalists who berated her about her paper's latest story. She was told that the *Post* printed Doder's piece only because it was a "Jewish" paper, and because Doder himself was Jewish. (He is a non-Jewish Serbian-American.)

And so my attempt to keep the WJC out of the story went for naught in Austria. "The Jews" were blamed anyway. As usual.

On November 15, I met with Doder at his comfortable home in northwestern Washington to discuss a variety of issues, including the relationship between Waldheim and the U.S.S.R. Doder said that he had asked former CIA Director Richard Helms about the possibility that the Soviets had compromised Waldheim. Helms replied that there had been rumors at Langley to that effect, but never any hard evidence. (A Helms intimate later told me that the former CIA chief had said the same thing to him.)

Doder told me that the *Post* had received a letter from former Austrian Foreign Minister Karl Gruber, in which Gruber declared that he had "proof" that Waldheim did nothing nefarious during the war: When Waldheim accompanied him to Moscow after the war to negotiate the State Treaty, the Soviets objected to two members of the Austrian delegation because of their Nazi pasts, but, Gruber's letter noted, they did not object to Waldheim.* Doder agreed with

---

*A "white book" later coauthored by Gruber, *Kurt Waldheim's Wartime Years: A Documentation* (Vienna, 1987), makes a similar allegation about the *Yugoslav* government. The authors assert that during the 1947 Austro-Yugoslav negotiations in London, in which Gruber and Waldheim participated, "the Yugoslav side objected to some members of the Austrian delegation because of their alleged Nazi past, but never raised any questions about Dr. Waldheim" (p. 17).

me that Moscow's behavior could just as easily "prove" that the Kremlin had incriminating information but was using it (or planning to use it) to blackmail him.

Regarding Yugoslavia, Doder was dismayed, but not greatly surprised, by the split within the government along ethnic lines, Serb versus Croat. He suspected that disgruntled Serbian elements in the government had arranged for the Belgrade newspapers to gain access to the Waldheim information they had reported in the first few weeks of the scandal.

Doder was struck by the fact that after the Yugoslav president made a state visit to Austria in April, the revelations suddenly ceased. The journalist also believed that former Yugoslav intelligence official Anton Kolendic had been ordered to recant his story about Soviet intelligence having approached Waldheim. Doder said that he had never been especially alarmed by Kolendic's waffling, however, since the essential elements of the former spy's tale had been confirmed to Doder by other intelligence and government sources in Yugoslavia.

A few days before my meeting with Doder, President Waldheim had sat down with another American journalist. On returning from Washington, I was able to read the results of what had obviously been a somewhat awkward encounter. "My family doctor in New York was a Jew," Waldheim explained to *New York Times* Bonn bureau chief James Markham. "I attended Jewish weddings. . . ." As president, he would use his "whole moral authority" to "fight anti-Semitism," Waldheim declared.

In his interview with Markham, Waldheim repeated his longstanding claim that he had never sought to hide the details of his war record, particularly his service in the Balkans; rather, he had just left it out of his accounts. "I have not really done anything wrong," he assured his interviewer.[16]

Waldheim's variation on the timeworn some-of-my-best-friends-are-Jews theme sent Neal Sher to the books to track down a favorite passage. "Take a look at the Heinrich Himmler quote on page 660 of Hilberg's book," he urged me over the phone. I headed for the bookshelf. The Gestapo chief's statement, part of a 1943 diatribe on the subject of Jewish "evacuations," did indeed make for an incisive, if, by Sher's own admission, not entirely fair, comparison:

> And then they come, our 80,000,000 good Germans, and each one has his decent Jew. It is clear, the others are swine (*Schweine*), but this one is a first-class Jew. Of all those who speak thus, no one has seen it, no one has gone through it.[17]

*   *   *

Shortly before the autumn 1986 parliamentary election, the People's Party and the Austrian press again resorted to heavy-handed attempts to stir up anti-Semitic sentiments, this time by exploiting Israel's decision not to replace its ambassador in Vienna. A *Kronenzeitung* editorial warned that if Israel and the WJC continued to "interfere so massively" in Austria's domestic affairs, they will "achieve only the opposite results from what they want."[18] Alois Mock issued a denunciation of Israel's attitude; it was, he declared, unacceptable, reflecting the view only of fanatics. "Austria must not accept any recipe from Israel," he told his countrymen.[19]

Austrians went to the polls on Sunday, November 23, under overcast skies. The surprise result was that *both* the Socialist Party and the People's Party lost seats in the National Assembly; neither party won a majority. The big gainer was the small Freedom Party under the leadership of the controversial Joerg Haider, described, however exaggeratedly, by Austrian parliament member (and former Waldheim campaign manager) Heribert Steinbauer as a man who "can out-Nazi the Nazis when he chooses." The People's Party floated a trial balloon, briefly suggesting a coalition government with the outrageous Haider; but the two parties were unable to reach an accord.*

Lacking a majority, Chancellor Franz Vranitsky promptly tendered his resignation to Waldheim, but the president asked the Socialist leader to attempt to form a new Socialist/People's Party coalition. A deal was soon struck between the two parties that kept Vranitsky in office but installed the dreadful Alois Mock as Vice-Chancellor and Foreign Minister. Austria's foreign policy would now be shaped by the same man who headed the People's Party during the frightfully ugly Waldheim presidential campaign. Bruno Kreisky promptly resigned his longtime honorary chairmanship of the Socialist Party, specifically in protest of the Mock appointment.

As November drew to a close, British M.P. Greville Janner finally received a substantive response from British Foreign Secretary Sir Geoffrey Howe concerning the Ioannina-area commandos. Howe's letter of November 26 reported that all four men had survived the

---

*Haider has always denied that he is a Nazi, and it cannot fairly be said that he is a proponent of Hitlerian ideology. But he has invited criticism through both deed and word. His regular appearances before Waffen-SS veterans' organizations, his description of convicted Nazi war criminal Walter Reder as a soldier who "only did his duty," his claim that the Reagan Administration was cowed by the "powerful lobby" of the World Jewish Congress, and his assertion, during a debate, that the Third Reich's "orderly" employment program was superior to Austria's current program, have made Haider internationally notorious. The employment program remark led to his ouster as governor of the Austrian province of Carinthia in 1990.

war. It also revealed that the Britons had been abused by their captors:

> They were held in a Gestapo gaol [jail] in Salonika before being sent to Germany for internment. The records suggest that they were interrogated by Gestapo rather than the Wehrmacht, and that they suffered ill treatment at the hands of Gestapo personnel.

Howe added that no "evidence was found that Dr. Waldheim was involved with the men."

The letter raised more questions than it answered. According to one of Hans Safrian's documents, the men—Bluett, Hamilton, Davies, and Bennett—were initially to be delivered to "Dept. Ic" (Waldheim's intelligence unit) at the High Command of Army Group E in Salonika. If, as Howe's letter stated, the commandos were held and interrogated by the Gestapo, did that mean that Waldheim's unit handed them over? And what exactly did Howe mean by "ill treatment"?

The answers were not forthcoming from the Foreign Office: Howe adamantly rejected Janner's repeated pleas that the documentation be made public. I suddenly found myself recalling that the U.N. War Crimes Commission files—including the long-secret file on mass murder suspect Kurt Waldheim—had not always reposed in Manhattan. For many years, they had been stored in London in the custody of Her Majesty's government.

Janner aide Philip Rubenstein sounded tired and angry on the phone as he relayed word of Howe's refusal to disclose any details of the British government's evidence.

"It's another brick wall, I'm afraid, Eli. Sorry. Thatcher's people won't budge."

A few weeks earlier, President Waldheim had appeared, unannounced, at a lecture being given in Vienna by Simon Wiesenthal. Wiesenthal, to everyone's surprise, abandoned the remainder of his presentation and walked out of the room.

When asked why, he explained that it was wrong for the president of a country to enter a meeting "through the back door." He tried to pass off the affair as a protocol lapse, but he was obviously embarrassed by the public display of appreciation from a man for whom he had battled these many months. Reading the press accounts of the Wiesenthal walkout, I allowed myself to hope that the Waldheim/Wiesenthal connection might at last be growing tenuous.

Any fantasies I might have entertained about a change of heart on Wiesenthal's part were almost immediately dispelled, however. Later in the month, some three weeks after the world was apprised of our Kozara findings, the Nazi-hunter announced that he had "seen no evidence" that Waldheim was "involved in a crime. . . . If I did, I as an Austrian citizen would ask him to resign."[20]

Long ago I had resolved to stop being surprised by Wiesenthal's words, but I did a double take when I read this report. It would be more understandable if Wiesenthal said, perhaps, that he remained unconvinced that Waldheim was guilty of war crimes. But how could he claim with a straight face that there was *"no* evidence"? One could perhaps argue whether there was enough actually to convict Waldheim "beyond a reasonable doubt" in a court of law, but the evidence implicating him in Nazi crimes was by now both voluminous and compelling.

In Los Angeles, Simon Wiesenthal Center dean Marvin Hier was reduced to assuring the press that "Simon Wiesenthal's views on Waldheim are not the views of the Simon Wiesenthal Center." It was an awkward and painful disclaimer for the embattled Hier.

The *Jewish Heritage,* a small Los Angeles weekly in Hier's backyard, was one of the few voices in the Jewish world to speak out candidly. The paper editorialized that Wiesenthal "has given the authority of his position as a Nazi-hunter to the cause of Waldheim. . . . But Simon Wiesenthal is wrong. Deadly wrong."[21]

28

Thanksgiving 1986 brought a surprise that seemed to presage a breakthrough in Yugoslavia. After months of silence on the Waldheim affair, the Yugoslav government quietly sent letters to Hans Safrian of the "New Austria" group; Dorothy Reitman, president of the WJC's Canadian affiliate, the Canadian Jewish Congress; and others who had been involved in pursuing the truth about Waldheim. The letters all conveyed the same unexpected invitation:

> We wish to inform you that the Archives of Yugoslavia . . . and the Military Historical Institute . . . are now open . . . in respect to Kurt Waldheim.

OSI had obviously received a similar invitation, for Neal Sher and Pat Treanor soon hopped a plane to Belgrade. So did Safrian, who was convinced that the Yugoslav archives, largely unindexed and unstudied, would prove to be a goldmine of captured documents. We all believed there were valuable nuggets to be had there, including some that were perhaps unknown even to the Yugoslavs.

But our newfound optimism soon waned. A disturbing report appeared in *Die Presse* on December 6, claiming that sources had revealed to the Vienna daily that the U.S. Justice Department would refuse to place Waldheim on the watchlist and would drop its Waldheim probe before Christmas. The report alarmed us. It was certainly true that Meese was taking his time making a decision on OSI's seven-month-old recommendation and we worried that this was an ominous sign—especially when a Justice Department spokesman said he could not comment on the Austrian newspaper's claim. Immediately I checked with one of my own sources in Washington.

"No such thing," he said curtly. "Meese really hasn't decided yet. He wants to give the Waldheim people every possible opportunity to respond to whatever it is that OSI's got."

The story, it turned out, was simply another baseless reassurance served up to the Austrian public by the domestic press.

Meanwhile, Avi Beker in the WJC's Jerusalem office reported that he had reliable information that Waldheim had personally approached an official of the U.S. Embassy in Vienna in a last-ditch effort to prevent his name from being placed on the watchlist. The State Department man supposedly replied that he had no input in the decision: It was strictly Justice Department business.

On December 10, I plodded again through National Archives microfilm records, only occasionally finding another piece of evidence. Although these were mostly modest additions to the growing, already horrible picture, there were a few moments of significant success. For example, I located the "Secret" daily report of the Intelligence section of the Athens staff, dated August 27, 1943. Paragraph "f" noted, matter-of-factly, that four Jewish of Ioannina were to be brought before a firing squad:

> In Ioannina, 4 Jews found guilty of trading gold with bandits. Intention: Shoot them for having facilitated the bandits.[1]

This was an operational matter, so this "intention" was likely one that had originated or been approved at Ia, the Operations section—where Waldheim was second in authority at the time. Whether or not the Jews were shot was not disclosed by the documents, but the order was curiously harsh. According to the Hitler order we had already seen recorded by Lieutenant Waldheim in the Athens headquarters war diary just three weeks earlier (August 8, 1943), execution was a partisan warfare measure reserved at that time for captured partisans; other troublesome elements ("suspects, etc.") were to be deported to the Reich for slave labor. The death sentence contained in this daily report illustrated the increasing cruelty with which the German army operated in the Balkans. I reviewed my notes and confirmed that, only twelve days prior to this report, Waldheim had helped alert his superiors to the 1st Mountain Division's warning concerning the threat posed by "the Jewish Committee" in Ioannina. I could only wonder whether the warning had caused a lethal (but certainly predictable from Waldheim's vantage point) overreaction.*

I also came across a September 9, 1943, document that *Profil* had mentioned, but not reproduced, in its April 21 issue, reporting that the disarmament of Italian soldiers in Greece "is running as planned."

---

*This document was a particularly surprising find, as it is extremely unusual to encounter a document from the National Archives microfilm collection that deals so explicitly with killing Jews and yet was not made part of the Nuremberg evidence set; it is presumably for this reason that the document is not cited in the major reference works on the Holocaust.

I immediately realized that the Austrian magazine, which described it solely as a "report," had missed a key point: The document was a *telex.* More importantly, it had actually been *transmitted by Waldheim,* as the text at the bottom of the telex proved:

> *Transmitted:* Waldheim, 1st Lt.   11.50 hours.
> *Received:* 1st Lt. Zag

Voilà! I heard myself whisper. At last we had proof—incontrovertible proof at that—to confirm my suspicion that Waldheim had been personally involved in the transmission of operational dispatches for the Ia section during his Athens assignment.[2] Here was a development of enormous importance. We already knew that the tiny Ia section—in which, as the Athens headquarters' "O1" officer, Waldheim was second-in-command—had only weeks earlier telexed two vicious, criminal orders to the 1st Mountain Division, one, from the Fuehrer, directing them to kill captured resistance fighters and to deport "suspects, etc.," and the other giving them the go-ahead to seize and deport the entire male population in areas of northern Greece in which the division was facing unusually stiff resistance. We already knew that Waldheim had recorded Hitler's murderous order in the Athens command's war diary and that he had relayed to his superiors the 1st Mountain Division's mass-deportation request, but we did not know whether he was personally involved in the *transmission* of the two criminal orders—an act that clearly would constitute a war crime. Since the Athens unit's "transmission" copies of the telexes had apparently not survived the war, there seemed to be little hope of getting to the truth; but now the discovery that Waldheim did, on at least some occasions, transmit Ia telegraphic messages from the Athens headquarters instantly propelled him to the top of the suspect list. My gut feeling now was that it was significantly more likely than not that he was involved in the criminal transmission of one or both of the unlawful commands.

Turning my research sights on Waldheim's service in Salonika, I found a November 5, 1943, report on Italian "Fascists in Athens" that neatly refuted one of Waldheim's key defenses. The report was written by *Fuehrung Abwehr Truppe 390* and addressed to the Ic/AO Branch in Salonika, some weeks after Waldheim's arrival there upon the successful completion of his Athens assignment. Warnstorff's initial was in the "Ic" box and a *W* initial appeared in the "O3" box reserved for Lt. Waldheim.[3] Waldheim had gone to great lengths to separate himself from any Abwehr activities, contending that Ic and AO were completely separate sections and that all of the criminal actions of Ic/AO Branch were exclusively the responsibility of the

"Abwehr side," headed by Major Hammer. But this document showed Waldheim acknowledging receipt and review of a report from an Abwehr unit, one that plainly involved *political*—not military— matters. The document brought to mind another "Abwehr side" responsibility in which we had already demonstrated Waldheim's involvement: "deserter propaganda."

Finally, I found one of the more dramatic documents yet unearthed concerning Waldheim's P.O.W.–related activities while serving on General Loehr's staff. It was a portion of the war diary of the Operations Branch (Ia) of Army Group E, dated October 17, 1943. The diary presented a minute-by-minute account of the key occurrences of the day, in chronological order. It revealed the following events that began in the afternoon of October 17 on the Dodecanese island of Levitha:

16.40   *First Lt. Waldheim* informs Head of General Staff that, according to news from the Air Force, our shipwrecked [men] who found safety on Levitha imprisoned and disarmed the Englishmen on the island. Major General Winter: Please radio immediately to Lt. General Mueller: according to information as yet not confirmed, German shipwrecked who landed on Levitha are said to have disarmed the English occupying force. Further information will follow as soon as news comes in.

16.43   Major General Winter advises the Supreme Commander Southeast [Maximilian von Weichs] concerning above conversation. Air Force informs that German shipwrecked on Levitha disarmed English occupiers. I had this forwarded as still unconfirmed information. Air Force could pick up the prisoners and convey weapons and the necessary ammunition to our occupying force.

16.50   Major General Winter gives instructions to *1st Lt. Waldheim* for transmittal to the Air Force that Army Group E requests to have the prisoners of Levitha picked up by Junkers plane and to provide the German occupation force with weapons and instruments and whatever else they need. [Emphasis added.][4]

The references to Waldheim's role in the removal of the British prisoners of war were unequivocal: When Loehr's chief of staff, General Winter, was confronted with newly captured British prisoners, to whom did he turn in order to have something done about them? None other than First Lieutenant Waldheim. Yet Waldheim was continuing to maintain that he had absolutely nothing to do with P.O.W.'s. Only about six weeks earlier, in his "Halloween Memo," he had declared that he "was never involved in the handling of prisoners generally, and of captured commandos in particular."

At the time of the Levitha incident, Waldheim had been at his post for less than two weeks. Already, however, he held a position that gave him responsibility for personally apprising Army Group E's chief of staff of important military developments and was entrusted with the additional responsibility of communicating to another branch of the German military (in this case, the Luftwaffe) the operational requests of the second-in-command of an army group that controlled more than four hundred thousand Wehrmacht troops.

The telephonic inquiry "Roosevelt?" signaled me that Neal Sher had returned my call. Newly returned from Yugoslavia, he sounded exhausted and, I thought, downcast. Indelicately, I asked him about what, in a telephone call only a few hours earlier, Karl Schuller had termed "some disturbing reports from Yugoslavia": Documents of Freidrich Stahl's West Bosnia Combat Group were nowhere to be found in the Yugoslav files. Sher deflected my question. "I can't talk about the trip, I'm afraid." His evident unhappiness, however, left me persuaded that Schuller's tip had been, as usual, on the money.

Schuller had also heard that Sher, Treanor, and the other researchers had not been allowed into the important Zagreb archives. This was especially disappointing in light of the fact that, eight months earlier, when Martin Mendelsohn had traveled to Yugoslavia for the Artukovic trial, he had been assured that those Zagreb files held incriminating documentation on Waldheim. According to Schuller, the newly returned researchers had also verified that Johann Mayer's full testimony was missing. Sher did not deny or confirm any of these reports, but his mood spoke volumes.

Sher's spirits needed some lifting. By coincidence, I was ready to pass on to OSI my discovery about the Levitha prisoners. I summarized the information for him.

"Does the document have his *name* on it?" Sher asked, suddenly animated.

"In black and white, Chief."

"It actually says, '*Waldheim*'?"

"Sure does."

"*Nailed again!*" Sher exclaimed. "Do you see it? It means he was *known to be* someone you'd call on for that sort of thing."

"And it catches him in yet another lie—but I guess that's a pretty cheap thrill by now."

"Listen, Eli, can you overnight it to my office?"

"I've already prepared the envelope."

We released the Levitha documents to the press on December 29. Steinberg wrote the release, which concluded with our by-now standard plea to Attorney General Meese:

> The WJC called on Attorney General Meese to "finally implement the findings of the Justice Department's Office of Special Investigations and bar Waldheim from entering the United States." In April, the Office of Special Investigations found Waldheim to be excludable as a "Nazi persecutor."[5]

In Britain, the Levitha disclosure caused a new uproar and gave the tabloids yet another field day at Waldheim's expense. M.P. Robert Rhodes James charged that the new documents were proof that Waldheim's denial of involvement in the handling of prisoners "is totally untrue."

The response from Waldheim's office was predictable. Spokesman Ralph Schieder declared that the allegations "must be old and completely unfounded."[6] This was a new variation on the line previously favored by President Waldheim's handlers. Most often, they denounced WJC disclosures as being based on what they dismissed as rehashings of "old documents"—that is, documents that had been made public previously. Steinberg always saw that as a fat pitch, for it gave him the opportunity to bellow to the press a favorite retort that threatened to carry from our offices all the way to the Hofburg Palace: "Of *course* they're old documents—they're from *1943!*"

On December 30, the Canadian government's Commission of Inquiry on War Criminals submitted to the country's Governor General a 966-page final report, nearly two years in the making, on its investigation into allegations that Nazi war criminals had found safe haven in Canada after the war. The commission, headed by Justice Jules Deschênes of the Superior Court of Quebec, concluded that at least scores of suspected Nazi criminals were in fact still living in Canada and that legal action could be taken against them.*

To my surprise, the commission's report criticized Simon Wiesenthal quite candidly. Noting that Wiesenthal had, over the years, publicly estimated the number of Nazi war criminals in Canada as,

---

*The report led ultimately to the belated passage of war crimes legislation and the commencement of a war crimes prosecution program in Canada.

variously, "several hundred" and fully six thousand, the commission charged that he (and others) had purveyed "grossly exaggerated figures as to their number." In its analyses of 217 of the 219 suspect names given by Wiesenthal to the Canadian government, the commission complained that it had "tried repeatedly to obtain the incriminating evidence allegedly in Mr. Wiesenthal's possession, through various written and oral communications with Mr. Wiesenthal himself and with his solicitor . . . but to no avail." In presenting the results of its own inquiry into Wiesenthal's targets (six of whom he had gone so far as to name publicly[7]), the commission left little doubt of its disdain for Wiesenthal:

> Of the 217 officers . . . , 187 (i.e., 86 percent of the list) never set foot in Canada, 11 have died in Canada, 2 have left for another country, no *prima facie* case has ben established against 16 and the last one could not be located. . . . It is obvious that the list of 217 . . . furnished by Mr. Wiesenthal was nearly totally useless and put the Canadian government, through the RCMP and this Commission, to a considerable amount of purposeless work.[8]

Although the Canadian press treated the report as befitted a major news story, it almost completely ignored the commission's withering verdict on the work-product of the "world's foremost Nazi-hunter." I realized again that the media lacked the stomach (or was it the heart?) to report the truth about Wiesenthal. It was a phenomenon upon which he had successfully relied for decades.

Year-end reviews of the biggest news stories of 1986 put the Waldheim exposé alongside the Soviet nuclear power plant tragedy at Chernobyl, the explosion of the space shuttle *Challenger,* the exposure of the Iran/*Contra* affair, and, most ironically, the awarding of the Nobel Peace Prize to Auschwitz survivor Elie Wiesel. Yet, despite our success in helping to unmask Waldheim, we remained disheartened. The bottom line, after a year of exhausting work by the WJC and others, was that a suspected Nazi war criminal, listed by the UNWCC and CROWCASS as wanted for mass murder, was still president of Austria.

And prospects for the future were gloomy. Yugoslavia had sealed off the Zagreb archives and had seemingly "lost" Johann Mayer's testimony, potentially the single most damaging item underlying the *Odluka.* The Soviet and East German archives remained closed to us. The Austrian government refused to make public Waldheim's official Wehrmacht personnel file, which had been returned to Austria by the U.S. National Archives without microfilming and now might even be missing from government archives in Vienna. The French government had fallen silent, providing no additional information concerning the 1979 check of Waldheim's WASt records in Berlin. Even the governments of Greece and the United Kingdom were reluctant to cooperate. And we still could not answer the most oft-asked question of all: How had Waldheim managed to carry off such an audacious cover-up for a full decade at the U.N.?

Somehow, we had to bring an end to the matter, or at least to our involvement in it. The tumultuous year had drained the WJC's limited resources, both physically and financially. People for whom I had the greatest respect (such as Rabbi Arthur Hertzberg of Dartmouth College) were warning us that the WJC was getting permanently mired in this depressing affair. Singer, Steinberg, and I decided to direct the major part of our efforts in the Waldheim case toward convincing Attorney General Meese to place Waldheim on the watchlist. Meese was reportedly still mulling it over, reviewing volumes of evidence as well as Waldheim's increasingly desperate rebuttals. We decided that if we could achieve this goal of official censure by the U.S. government, we could, in good conscience, leave the remainder of the task to the next generation of historians and investigators.

Yes, it was still important to unearth the full truth about Waldheim's past, just as it was important to pursue, relentlessly, any other suspected war criminal, no matter how long ago the crime, no matter how difficult the investigation. But *another* investigation beckoned, too: To me it was becoming almost as important now to learn precisely how and why the truth had been suppressed for so long, especially during Waldheim's tenure at the U.N. Whoever participated in the cover-up had not only betrayed Hitler's victims, but had exploited and perhaps profited from that betrayal. Increasingly, it was this thought that kept me awake at night.

Again and again my thoughts returned to the same line of questions: Who had checked the WASt records, in 1972 and again in 1979, and why had they kept silent about what they had found in Berlin? Whoever they were, the inquirers probably were *not* agents acting for the Soviet Union or Yugoslavia, neither of which had front-door access to the French-run WASt archive. At any rate, these two countries undoubtedly knew a great deal about Waldheim almost immediately after the war, and they almost surely had enough information to satisfy their needs before and during Waldheim's decade at the U.N.; they had no urgent need to check further, especially since doing so might alert the French or American authorities to their activities.

Then who was it? Most mystifying—and troubling—was the possibility that the Israelis were somehow involved. Of all the nations on the planet, Israel clearly had the most incentive to investigate the openly hostile Secretary-General Waldheim from every conceivable angle. It also possessed one of the world's most highly regarded intelligence services. How could the consummately proficient Mossad have failed to use its French contacts to obtain the information in Waldheim's WASt file? Worse yet, what if the Israelis *had* gotten their hands on the information but either did not understand its significance or—and I dreaded this possibility most of all—*did* understand exactly what it meant but decided for some reason to remain silent? But why would the Israelis, of all people, cover up Waldheim's Nazi past?

Nothing seemed to make sense anymore.

29

Once again I answered a knock on a Washington hotel room door, accepted a thick envelope that was thrust at me, and sat down to spend the day studying. Inside the envelope were Kurt Waldheim's second and third submissions to the U.S. Justice Department, the texts of which disclosed that they had been delivered to Justice on August 1 and November 24, respectively.

The introduction to Waldheim's second defensive submission stated that the document was being submitted in response to a request from the Justice Department that he address eight broad subject areas. Waldheim's attorneys had responded with a ninety-seven-page report, proffered, they said, "with full knowledge of the nature of the campaigns being waged against him and his reputation. . . ." The report charged that the Justice Department was attempting to go beyond the narrow "persecution" provisions of the Holtzman Amendment to conduct "a full-blown war crimes investigation," for which it had no statutory authority. Matters such as the Kozara campaign, the Black Operation, the fate of the Allied commandos, and the Stip-Kocane reprisal killings did not involve questions of participation in "persecution" based on race, religion, national origin, or political opinion, but rather of participation in *war crimes;* hence, the brief declared, the Justice Department's consideration of these matters was "not appropriate."

This is truly pathetic, I said to myself as I read the paragraph in which Waldheim again posited the notion of a war crimes loophole in U.S. immigration law. I mockingly paraphrased Waldheim's argument: "Look, even if I *am* a Nazi war criminal, you can't bar me from coming to the United States—because war crimes are legally irrelevant under the American statute." What a humiliating posture to be taken by the president of a country, the former Secretary-General of the United Nations!

Between the date of Waldheim's first submission to Meese and this one, much had been discovered, and there were, accordingly, several important new issues for him to address. First, he admitted now that he had indeed served on General Stahl's staff in western Bosnia during the Kozara offensive. Confronted with the evidence that the Bader Combat Group, headquartered in eastern Bosnia, was disbanded before the Kozara massacres, Waldheim's report conceded that the earlier submission had made a "substantial factual error" in claiming that he was still serving as the Bader Group's liaison in Plevlje, Montenegro, at the time that the Kozara atrocities were taking place in western Bosnia. The error was caught, the brief asserted, when Gerhard Waldheim found, "among intimate family correspondence," a notation indicating that his father was in Sarajevo on Pentecost Sunday, May 24, 1942, and would be involved there for a week with personnel administration matters until he reported to his new assignment in Banja Luka, the headquarters location for Stahl's West Bosnia Combat Group. The brief deadpanned, "Research efforts were somewhat hampered by the unavailability of contemporaneous division records" for the West Bosnia Combat Group. Supposedly as a result of his son's serendipitous find (rather than as a result of the carefully documented challenges to his previous Kozara alibis), Waldheim, who earlier had said that he was 120 miles away from Kozara, at another place called Kozara (this one in Montenegro), and even had claimed to have located confirming witnesses, requested that his defenders reexamine certain documents, which were discovered to have been mistranslated the first time around. Now, I chuckled, the documents reigned supreme and his purported "witnesses" inexplicably did not count.

In this latest version of his Kozara alibi, Waldheim could not claim to have been an interpreter, for we had proved that no Italian units arrived at Banja Luka. Instead, he said (as his spokesman would tell Dusko Doder after this brief was submitted) that he was "only" in "Ib," the Quartermaster Department, as the number-two man under a certain Captain Plume. There were also three clerks assigned to them. The brief asserted that Waldheim "simply performed the functions of a supply officer."

I was stunned again. The quartermaster unit of Stahl's headquarters was even smaller than I had supposed; it had just *two* officers! And, of course, one of them was Waldheim.

The brief said that the nature of his duties was accurately reflected in Waldheim's "contemporaneous notations," sporadic though they were. The moment I read this, I realized that "contemporaneous notations" was a euphemism for a diary, and I found it profoundly galling that Waldheim suddenly claimed to be in possession of personal war diaries—from which, moreover, he would now selectively quote, but would not submit in their entirety. It struck me at once that those notes—the existence of which had been a carefully guarded secret all these months—could be the most important documents in the whole affair. I imagined that this was rather like learning that Richard Nixon had taped his Oval Office conversations. But the Justice Department was evidently going to have to settle for what Waldheim *said* was in those diaries, with no way for anyone to check those claims for accuracy.

And yet, even in Waldheim's own guarded words, there was a spectacular admission contained in his description of one series of diary entries. In his attempt to prove that he was assigned to the Quartermaster Department, Waldheim said that his diaries mentioned:

> . . . the arrival, or expected arrival, of a Pioneer (Engineer) Company and a truck column in Banja Luka on June 4, 1942. This notation correlates with a June 2, 1942, order from the Quartermaster Department of the Commanding General in Serbia wherein a truck column is ordered dispatched for arrival in Banja Luka on June 4, 1942. . . . That order further specifies that the column is to report to the Ib [officer] in Banja Luka, Captain Plume, Dr. Waldheim's immediate superior. On the basis of these comparisons, it appears that Dr. Waldheim's contemporaneous notations accurately reflect his activities, and the activities surrounding him.

According to his lawyers' brief, Waldheim's "contemporaneous notations" even showed him personally receiving a visit from Colonel Munckel, the quartermaster for all of Serbia, on August 12, 1942.

As I read the brief's statement that Waldheim's service in the Quartermaster Department at Stahl's headquarters had involved him in transportation matters, I could hardly believe my eyes. I had to remind myself that this brief was submitted on August 1, nearly three months *before* Waldheim learned, through the *Washington Post,* that documents had survived the war showing that the Quartermaster Department at Stahl's headquarters was assigned responsibility for transporting prisoners en masse to Croatian concentration camps. Moreover, thanks to Pat Treanor's find at the National Archives, we knew that the visitor Waldheim "received"—Colonel Munckel—was the very man who had ordered the Quartermaster Department to handle the deportation of prisoners to concentration camps. And Waldheim's reference to the truck column *proved* that he was involved in *transportation matters* handled by the Quartermaster Department! I laughed out loud at the thought of how he had to be regretting these admissions now.

When I turned the page to the last portion of the Waldheim brief's response to the Kozara allegations, I was surprised to find a small yellow Post-it self-stick note attached near the top of the page. On the tiny sheet was an annotation of sorts, the only one I would encounter in the two briefs. Since the words were typed, I was unable to discern who had authored them. It seemed obvious, however, that *someone* wanted me to know about some apparently new evidence in the case.

The tersely worded note consisted of three words that plainly referred to Waldheim's pre-Kozara service in Montenegro with the Bader Combat Group, followed by two code numbers immediately recognizable to me as National Archives microfilm citations:

KAMPFGRUPPE BADER DEPORTATIONS
T501/250/382-393
T501/250/935-65

I was tempted to race over to the microfilm reading room at the National Archives, but I had given my word that I would complete my review of the Waldheim briefs by five o'clock, and time was running short already. I copied the text of the note onto an index card and slipped the card into my shirt pocket. There would still be time this evening to hit the Archives; I could always catch a late shuttle back to La Guardia.

Although the distraction of the anonymous clue momentarily weakened my powers of concentration, I pressed ahead with my reading of Waldheim's brief.

Turning their attention to Waldheim's Athens assignment, his attorneys addressed an issue that the first submission had ignored, the disarming and deportation of the Italian 11th Army. The memo declared that Waldheim was "actually participating in what can be characterized as military chivalry," the objective having been to send the Italian troops in Greece to their homeland. Having defined one of the cruelest betrayals of the war as "chivalry," Waldheim's lawyers then asserted that the return to Italy was effected "peacefully and without incident." Waldheim's audacity still seemed to know no bounds. As any good World War II book would confirm, the Italians had *not* been returned "to their homeland," as promised; they were instead shipped to the Reich as slave laborers.

Regarding the assignment at Army Group E headquarters in Arsakli/Salonika, the brief described Waldheim as " 'O3' officer (Assistant Adjutant to Intelligence Officer)." This was the first time I had seen Waldheim actually admitting formally to having been an intelligence officer; it certainly clashed with his previous statements that he was merely an interpreter and liaison officer—"just a sort of secretary." Waldheim had come a long way since his March 5 interview with Jane Pauley of NBC, in which he had insisted, "I was an interpreter in [the] German High Command in the Balkans, and that was it."

While it continued to maintain that Waldheim had had nothing to do with the interrogation of captured Allied commandos, the brief allowed that it had been his responsibility "to report information from interrogations conducted by others." The brief further conceded that it was "possible" that "the SD's treatment of captured commandos could constitute war crimes," but it asserted that Waldheim was never involved in transferring prisoners to the SD and declared it "unlikely" that his intelligence section was involved. It added a fallback argument, claiming that, even if Waldheim *had* been involved, this would be insufficient justification under U.S. law for placing him on the watchlist, since the German response to commando raids had been born of purely military—not "persecutory"—motives. Once again, Waldheim was relying on the ugly proposition that complicity solely in Nazi war crimes was a defense under U.S. law.

As far as the deportation of the Salonika Jews was concerned, the brief made a subtle but interesting alteration to previous defenses. It declared again that Waldheim did not assist in the deportations and added—here was more curious wording from Waldheim's own attorneys—that it was "likely" that he did not know of them.

The memo, for the first time, conceded that the AO "section" of his Ic/AO branch at Arsakli was involved in atrocities—specifically including Jewish deportations and the handing over of captured commandos to the SD—but it continued to maintain that Ic and AO were totally separate units.

Waldheim submitted to the Justice Department a statement from Herbert Warnstorff in which his former immediate superior carried the argument to its ludicrous extreme, contending that even he, as chief of the Ic/AO Branch, was not fully aware of the branch's AO activities. Everything was blamed on the dead Major Hammer, who headed a "separate staff performing separate and distinct functions." Thus, Waldheim's brief contended, it was Hammer who was responsible for the "order . . . from Ic/AO Branch" that "represents the beginning of the southern [Greek] islands Jewish deportations" to Auschwitz, and Hammer who would have handled any delivery to the SD of the captured Allied P.O.W.'s "for treatment, which may have included execution . . ." and "could constitute war crimes."

These, the brief asserted, were matters of liaison with the SD, and hence solely within the province of the AO section, under Major Hammer.

If Waldheim's continued dependence on the fiction that there was a strict separation between the activities of the intelligence (Ic) and counterintelligence (AO) sections of the small Ic/AO Branch in which he served as first assistant to the chief was an exercise in futility, his attempt to distance himself from these atrocities of his branch by stressing (quite accurately) that they were SD liaison matters was, to put it mildly, counterproductive. For, as the organizational table of Army Group E expressly stated, "cooperation with SD" (*zusammenarbeit mit SD*) was a responsibility of Col. Warnstorff as Ic officer, *not* of Hammer as AO officer![1] Hence, there was no reason to suppose that Warnstorff's principal assistant—the "third special missions staff officer" Lt. Waldheim—was not similarly involved in SD "cooperation" matters handled by his branch.

Actually, the brief's discussion of the Jewish deportations—specifically its explicit reference to the Ic/AO order regarding Jewish deportations from the Greek islands—let slip an equally damning admission, namely that Ic/AO Branch *issued orders.* Until now, Waldheim had insisted that his branch was simply an intelligence-*gathering* unit, and that operational orders were drafted and issued only by other components of Army Group E headquarters, principally the Ia (Operations) Branch. This new admission effectively undercut another line of defense consistently pursued in Waldheim's brief: that he had, as the brief put it, "no command authority." That argument was always a straw man anyway—the Nuremberg trials confirmed that it was sufficient under international law for one to make recommendations for unlawful orders, formulate drafts of such orders, or communicate within the chain of command criminal orders issued by others.[2] Moreover, the second title borne by his immediate superior, Col. Warnstorff—deputy to the Chief of Operations—left no doubt that, like all military intelligence operations, Waldheim's branch had been involved in proposing operational actions. (Indeed, there was no shortage at the National Archives of draft orders prepared by Ic/AO Branch, including some signed by Waldheim himself.[3] Still, this latest admission was a helpful confirmation.)

Waldheim's brief attempted to deal with the testimony in Yugoslav captivity of Johann Mayer by hurling a series of ill-considered epithets at his late accuser. Waldheim's lawyers argued that Mayer should not be believed because he had been a "collaborator" with his captors and had been referred to by his fellow prisoners by the term "Antifa," an abbreviation for "anti-Fascist" prisoner, "a term of derision signifying abandonment of loyalty and principals [sic]." Left unmentioned by Waldheim's tactful lawyers was the fact that what Mayer supposedly had abandoned was loyalty to *the Nazis* and fidelity to *Nazi* principles. After the war, they asserted, he had been "shunned as a collaborator" by his "former comrades-in-arms" because he had cleverly made "false charges" against other Germans. But the brief repeated the claim that Mayer's allegations were made solely against personnel of Army Group E "whom he knew to have escaped captivity by the Yugoslavs," and Waldheim's attorneys made no attempt to deal with the question of why Mayer should have been ostracized if he had cleverly managed to spare all of his comrades who were most in harm's way.

On the subject of the 1944 Stip-Kocane massacres, *presto!*, "through a fortuitous set of circumstances," the brief announced, Waldheim had tracked down copies of the last letters, written to his mother and friends, of Captain Karl-Heinz Egberts-Hilker, the field commander executed by the Yugoslavs for carrying out the killings. On the eve of his execution, Egberts-Hilker supposedly declared to his family and friends that the actions in the villages on the road between Stip and Kocane were undertaken on his initiative, and his alone.

Waldheim's brief again made the extraordinary concession that Nazi war crimes and crimes against humanity might have been repeatedly perpetrated "on the basis" of *his own reports:*

> That German military field commanders, acting on the basis of military information contained in Dr. Waldheim's reports, may have committed war crimes, or even crimes against humanity, does not in any way invalidate the legitimate military objectives of Dr. Waldheim's reports. Almost any information is subject to misuse, often with disastrous results. Such misuse and ensuing results, however, are not the fault of either the information or the preparer of the information.

"The first time, maybe not," I replied in a stage whisper appropriate to my hotel surroundings. "But what about the *second* time? What about the *third* time? Come on, Waldheim: You *knew* that retaliation against civilian villages was standard operating procedure for dealing with partisan activity."

Near its end, the brief dealt with the subject of "Dr. Waldheim's credibility," an expression that I had thought was long ago relegated to oxymoron status. Waldheim's attorneys took pains to point out that the Holtzman Amendment does not allow the U.S. government to ban someone merely "because of any statements he may have made, even if they are found to be false, inaccurate, incomplete, or misleading":

> None of the alleged misrepresentations attributed to Dr. Wald-heim occurred in the context of his seeking a visa. . . . Accordingly, the statements which Dr. Waldheim has made to the media or the public cannot provide a cognizable basis for his exclusion from the United States, even if they are proved to be indisputably false.

Aha, I thought, here's the "Mere Liar" defense, prudently added to back up the "Mere War Criminal" defense of an earlier portion of the brief.

The Waldheim package also included a purportedly professional handwriting analysis of various documents containing *W*'s and partial signatures of assorted types. The handwriting analyst had no choice but to concede that any document signed "Waldheim" was actually signed by Kurt Waldheim. However, he was reluctant to say the same for the ubiquitous *W* in the "O3" box of so many key reports. He declared that "unexplained differences" between the initial *W* and the *W* in Waldheim's full signature "prevent his being identified as the writer of the initials. It appears likely that they were written by another person or persons." Coyly, however, the "expert" refrained from delineating the supposedly "unexplained differences."

Such was Waldheim's pitiful defense to our discovery of his initial in the "O3" box of the "received" stamp on the "Kill the Jews" package of propaganda leaflets. The "handwriting analysis" was shockingly bogus. The American expert's "unexplained differences" were, of course, readily explained by the fact that Waldheim, like many other people (then as now), signed his full name one way and styled his initials another way. The telltale clue that exposed the bankruptcy of the analysis was that Waldheim's expert had not compared the *W* initials in question with even one *W* initial that Waldheim would concede was his own. Clearly, Waldheim did not dare allow such a comparison, for the inescapable fact was that he was *the* "O3" officer at Loehr's Army Group E headquarters, and hence the "O3" box was reserved for *his* scrawled *W*.

I had often seen litigants in the United States resort to hired-gun experts who would tailor their "expert opinions" to suit their clients' needs. But rarely had I seen the gambit executed with such little subtlety. Even Mr. Magoo could see through this one, I mused.

Waldheim's third submission to Meese, dated November 24 and also brought to my hotel room this day, added comparatively little to the saga. There was, however, one truly unforgettable passage. In responding to "the claimed 'revelations' published by the media in recent weeks," Waldheim's latest submission portrayed the Kozara massacres as purely "military operations" having no "persecutory objectives." "No actions" at Kozara, it asserted, "were undertaken on the basis of any person's race, religion, national origin, or political beliefs." And then it took the presentation one final nauseating step further:

> ... operations of the German Army in the Kozara region had purely military objectives. All "actions" were taken *against persons perceived to be members of or supporters of hostile forces.* [Emphasis added.]

"Sure," I heard myself reply testily, "*twenty-three thousand children* were 'members of or supporters of hostile forces.' What utter obscenity, 'President' Waldheim!"

For nearly a minute, I continued to stare at the words. Waldheim and his "respectable Washington lawyers" had reached a new, depraved low.

On completing my reading of the two Waldheim submissions, I returned them to the envelope in which they had been delivered to me. With them, I enclosed several pages of notes I had written on various assertions made in the Waldheim briefs.

At five o'clock, almost to the minute, a messenger appeared at my hotel room door, just as my former Justice Department colleague and I had agreed. I handed him the envelope.

It was almost time to head back to New York. But there was one item of unfinished business that required my attention first.

Although it was rush hour, finding a cab proved surprisingly easy. I asked the driver to take me to Ninth and Pennsylvania: the National Archives.

As I rode the elevator to the fourth-floor microfilm reading room, I removed from my shirt pocket the index card on which I had jotted down the tip that had been left for me inside Waldheim's second brief. I quickly retrieved from the microfilm storage room roll number 250 of microfilm series T501. Anxiously, I slipped it out of its light blue National Archives box and loaded it onto a reader-printer.

It took only a few minutes of studying the German text to realize that someone—and I presumed that it was once again OSI's Pat Treanor—had made a truly momentous discovery.

30

As I stared at the forty-four-year-old images on the screen (and later, on the plane trip home, at the copies I printed out), their full significance became clear. These two documents were a direct link between Kurt Waldheim and the 1942 deportation of hundreds of Yugoslav civilians sent from eastern Bosnia to slave labor in Norway, when Waldheim was serving with the Bader Combat Group. The action was unquestionably a Nazi war crime under the terms of Article 6 of the Charter of the International Military Tribunal.*

The crime occurred during the spring of 1942, while Waldheim was serving as the Bader Combat Group's one-and-only German liaison officer to the Italian Division "Pusteria." Waldheim had effectively admitted in his first brief to the Justice Department (June 11, 1986) that he was *the* liaison officer and interpreter to the Italian division, assisted only by a signal corps team. He had stated that his assignment "was to provide communications between an Italian division command" in Plevlje, Montenegro, "and German headquarters" in eastern Bosnia.

One of the documents found by OSI was an April 10, 1942, order from General Bader himself entitled "Guidelines for the Operations in Bosnia." It set out directives on how German and Italian forces were to deal with the civilian population: Civilians who aided the resistance were to be shot; towns that supported the resistance or in which weapons were found were to be "burned to the ground"; and civilians suspected of favoring the resistance were to be interned in "internment camps"; the removal of the civilian population of the area was listed as an option as well, albeit only with authorization from the Bader Combat Group's command staff. The guidelines added: "Civilians in the operations area of the Italian divisions who violate given orders are to be delivered by the Italian military au-

*The Nuremberg Charter (adopted by the U.S., the United Kingdom, France, and the Soviet Union in 1945) defined "war crime" to include, among other offenses, "ill treatment or deportation to slave labor or for any other purpose of civilian population of or in occupied territory. . . ."

384

thorities to the General Bader Combat Group's command staff."[1]

The second document was dated forty days later, May 20, 1942. It proved that General Bader's orders were in fact carried out by the Italian division to which Waldheim was dispatched as liaison officer and interpreter. The document was a review of the joint German-Italian-Croatian encirclement operations in the area of Rogatica and Foca, two Bosnian communities held by the partisans. On page 5, under the heading "Prisoners," the Germans reported that the "Pusteria" Division had taken 488 prisoners who "were handed over to the Higher SS & Police Leader Belgrade for forced labor in Norway."[2]

Several factors, considered in combination, left virtually no doubt that Waldheim had been personally involved in this delivery of nearly five hundred people to the SS for slave labor: (1) Waldheim was *the* German liaison officer with the "Pusteria" Division; (2) this mass deportation was carried out on the orders of Waldheim's combat group; and (3) General Bader's instructions required the Italians to turn over all such prisoners to *his* command staff.

I was impressed. This was a truly spectacular find OSI had made.

Still, the documents left me curious on two counts. First, it was logical to presume that Waldheim was involved, as sole liaison to the "Pusteria" Division, but what was his *exact* role in this terrible crime? Second, what was the ultimate fate of those nearly five hundred deportees? During the flight back to New York, it occurred to me that those poor souls had doubtless been as anonymous to Lieutenant Waldheim then as they were, four decades later, to me. The thought brought to mind a moving photograph I had once seen of a stone cross in Karlshagen, Germany, erected at the mass grave of several hundred civilians who had been deported from various countries to toil as slave laborers there for the Nazi V-rocket program. Efforts to identify the remains after the war had been unsuccessful, so the cross was inscribed with a simple, moving legend: GOD SAYS, "I KNOW THEIR NAMES."

Back in New York, I telephoned Ana Marija Bešker, a Yugoslav Embassy official who had been very helpful on several previous occasions. She informed me that there was a society in Norway that "keeps alive the memory of the cooperation" between Yugoslav prisoners deported there and the Norwegian resistance. "We are very grateful to the Norwegians," she told me. "They helped our people a lot." Bešker promised to try to supply me with the address of the Norwegian organization.

Next, I wrote to a Serbian scholar in Cleveland who had also helped me in the past, explaining, "I am trying to learn whatever I can about these prisoners—who they were, the conditions under which they were transported and housed, the places at which they were put to work in Norway, and the conditions to which they were subjected there."

Eventually, although all attempts to ascertain the fate of the 488 deportees were unsuccessful, I learned that the Yugoslav War Crimes Commission estimated that, of nine thousand Yugoslavs deported to slave labor in Norway, only two thousand survived the war.

"In the more recent past, the Austrians have had to learn to bear more international criticism than they were accustomed to," President Waldheim conceded during a speech at a January 13, 1987, New Year's reception for those members of the Vienna diplomatic corps who were willing to attend a function at which he presided. Perhaps his international isolation had provoked some introspection. He added, "Much of what we had endeavored to suppress over the past decades returned with a vengeance." Austria, he declared, was "burdened with a common legacy that nobody can escape."[3]

Shortly after my return to New York, University of Vienna Professor Maximilian Gottschlich and a colleague, Karl Obermair, released a disturbing study of anti-Semitism in the Austrian media's coverage of the Waldheim campaign. Gottschlich (a non-Jew) concluded that the worst culprit was *Kronenzeitung,* the mass-circulation Viennese daily, read by 2.5 million Austrians—over 40 percent of the country's population. Of 176 *Kronenzeitung* articles concerning the Waldheim controversy, Gottschlich found that more than one-third contained anti-Semitic elements. The report listed three of the most frequently appearing mass-media stereotypes of Jews:

- Jews know how to make capital by constantly digging up certain events from the past.
- Jews have always had an ambiguous attitude toward the truth.
- Jews are always interfering in things that do not concern them.

Gottschlich charged that the People's Party and the Austrian press jointly "created a climate of opinion" that made it acceptable to speak openly against Jews. "The floodgates have been opened," he warned.[4]

On February 7, a strange item arrived in the mail at the WJC offices. Inside an envelope bearing a London postmark, unaccompanied by any explanation, was a copy of a December 15 letter, typed on People's Party stationery, purportedly sent from Austria's new Vice-

Chancellor and Foreign Minister, Alois Mock, to British Prime Minister Margaret Thatcher.

The key paragraph of the "Dear Mrs. Thatcher" letter ostensibly disclosed a nascent plot by Mock and others to induce President Waldheim to resign, using health considerations as a pretext:

> I found your proposal in connection with President Waldheim reasonable. It is to be regretted that on nominating him, the People's Party could not take into account the political campaign that was launched against him later. Analyzing the situation now, I share your opinion, that in the field of foreign policy the person of Mr. Waldheim exerts a detrimental effect on the international Conservative movement and isolates Austria from our Western friends. This isolation may result in a more vigorous orientation of the country towards the Soviet Bloc. Therefor [*sic*] I regard the resolving of the issue opportune. In this way, it seems to be advisable to persuade President Waldheim to resign in the cours [*sic*] of 1987 citing health reasons.

The letter seemed almost too good to be true; here was "the man who invented Waldheim" abandoning his creation.

"Check it out, Eli," Steinberg instructed. "If this thing is legit, we've got to release it as soon as possible."

I telephoned Michael May in London. An hour later, he phoned back with disheartening news: The London return address on the envelope was a phony. There was no such street address in London. Now believing the letter to be a probable forgery, we theorized that it might have been circulated by Waldheim *supporters* in the hope that it would be publicized by Waldheim's enemies and then proved false, thereby thwarting any possibility that he would use health reasons as a pretext for resigning. It was convoluted double- and triple-think reasoning, but we were beginning to understand how some of these Austrian intrigues worked. We put the letter in our files, content to have avoided disaster.

Unfortunately, the *Jerusalem Post,* which received its own anonymous copy, fell for the trap. On February 10, it ran Mock's letter to Thatcher as a front-page world exclusive. The People's Party Press Service immediately issued a hysterical release criticizing *us:*

> This is the latest outrage of the anti-Waldheim Mafia. . . . This is OVP [People's Party] General Secretary Dr. Michael Graff's reaction to the false information in the *Jerusalem Post* . . .
> "The baseness of the Waldheim enemies at the World Jewish Congress and in Israel knows no bounds. Now that it is general

knowledge that all the accusations against Federal President Dr. Waldheim are without any basis in fact, the campaign of libel is being continued through false information and fake letters."

Later, upon examining the letter, Mock's own cabinet chief declared that because of the use of People's Party stationery and the style of writing the address, the forger was likely to have been an Austrian. All that really mattered, however, was that the hoax had worked, thanks to a careless *Jerusalem Post.* As a *Die Presse* editorial snickered, "Waldheim looks stronger now than ever before."

Late February found me once again ensconced in a Washington hotel room, this time to read Waldheim's final, obviously desperate submission to the U.S. Justice Department, dated December 19, 1986. As I skimmed the document, I suddenly realized that although the four briefs incorporated numerous sworn statements from Waldheim's war comrades, there was not even a single statement *from Waldheim himself.* Every assertion and denial was instead made by his Washington attorneys. What gutlessness, I said to myself.

In this last plea to Attorney General Meese, Waldheim attempted to deal with the disclosure that it was the Quartermaster Department—*his* small department—at General Stahl's headquarters that was responsible for the mass deportations to the Croatian concentration camps during the Kozara offensive.

After conceding that transportation functions "traditionally reported to the supply or quartermaster officer," Waldheim's brief asserted that they did not, in fact, do so at Stahl's headquarters. An attached affidavit from an old war comrade, Ernst Wiesinger, contended that there had been a special "transportation officer" who was "temporarily" assigned to Stahl's combat group and who "reported directly" to Stahl's chief operations (Ia) officer.

This was nonsense. There was not a single document so much as suggesting that such a person had ever existed. And it had taken the Waldheim forces nearly a year of dramatic flips and flops about Kozara before they came up with this latest notion. Neither Waldheim nor Wiesinger produced a *name* for this convenient, phantom officer. More importantly, the documents we had provided to the *Washington Post* clearly showed that Colonel Munckel, the quartermaster for all of Serbia, assigned the Quartermaster Department (Ib) at Stahl's headquarters the responsibility for transporting prisoners to the concentration camps. All of the documents identified this, quite explicitly, as an Ib function; not one supported Wiesinger's claim that it was an Ia function. Moreover, Wiesinger even got the designation of the office in which he supposedly worked wrong, repeatedly referring to it as "IVa" rather than Ib. Actually, Wiesinger's affidavit *hurt* Waldheim, first when it confirmed that Waldheim was the number-two man in that department, and then when it disclosed that Waldheim had even shared an office with the department's chief, Captain Plume.

Waldheim's attorneys resorted to the same type of strange language they had used in their earlier submissions, concluding that "it would appear" that Waldheim had no involvement with prisoners at Kozara. And they reiterated that the Quartermaster Department "did not perform any duties relating to transportation."

But it was far too late for such denials. Waldheim was now entangled in his own web of deception: In his second submission to Meese, back in August, he had disclosed that his own notes from 1942 reflected not only that he had personally met with Colonel Munckel, but also that he expected the arrival of "a truck column . . . to report to the Ib [quartermaster] in Banja Luka, Captain Plume, Dr. Waldheim's immediate superior." Waldheim had made these disclosures regarding his involvement in transportation matters before he realized how they could provide the key pieces to the Kozara puzzle. And since these admissions were purportedly based on his own contemporaneous wartime notes, he would be unable now either to disavow them or blame "faulty memory" as he had on so many other occasions during the past year. This time, he was *trapped.* I paused to relish the thought for a moment before continuing my reading of Waldheim's brief.

Faced with this dreadful predicament, his lawyers opted for a strategy of excision. They simply made no mention of the previous references to Munckel and the truck column and pinned their hopes on the possibility that OSI would fail to notice the omission. I could not know whether OSI had detected the ploy, so I detailed it in the handwritten notes I sent back with Waldheim's brief.

In late February, King Hussein of Jordan became the first head of state to meet with Waldheim. The Austrian president greeted the king at the Vienna airport as he arrived on February 21 with Queen Noor for a skiing holiday in the Austrian Alps.

Waldheim's office announced soon thereafter that the president had, at last, received an invitation to visit a foreign country—Jordan. Following that, Egypt and communist Hungary were added to the list.

Encouraged by these developments, Alois Mock launched an outrageous, high-profile campaign to demonstrate his supposed sensitivity to Jewish causes. The Zurich newspaper *Neue Zuericher Zeitung* speculated that Mock's actions were the result of a belated recognition by the People's Party that, despite its anger at the WJC, Austria's image could not be improved without Mock making some "gestures" toward the Jews. The paper reported that Mock was "planning a Jewish museum in Vienna and a symposium with representatives of various religions."

On March 11, the Belgrade daily *Vecernje Novosti* unexpectedly threw Waldheim's pursuers another crumb, reporting tersely and without real explanation that, on November 20, 1952, the Yugoslav government had put Waldheim on a list of thousands of former German officers who were to be barred from entering the country. This was five years after the Yugoslav War Crimes Commission indicted Waldheim as a Nazi criminal, wanted for mass murder. The Yugoslav newspaper did not divulge the source of its information, nor did it comment on the peculiar fact that, in the decades following his inclusion on this list of "undesirable foreigners," Waldheim visited Yugoslavia several times as the personal guest of President Tito.[5]

On March 15, Cynthia and I were wed in Houston. We left for a honeymoon at the Las Brisas resort in Acapulco.

As we basked in the bright sunlight at poolside, the pressures of the past year seemed to fade away like a bad dream. Smiles came easily to my face again. Now it was the time to think of the future, not the past.

But my rapture was abruptly interrupted when I made the mistake of buying an English-language newspaper published in Mexico City. Here, I read that Simon Wiesenthal was once again a candidate for the Nobel Peace Prize. I marveled at how little known (or else little understood) his actions of the past year appeared to be outside Austria.

I decided to forgo newspapers for the remainder of our time in Mexico.

I returned from Acapulco to find that Waldheim could still count on support from the Kremlin. On April 9, Tass quoted, with obvious approval, the text of Waldheim's "call for broader cooperation and international détente." There was no mention of the controversy that still dogged him.

Meanwhile, pressure was building on Attorney General Meese from all sides. Jewish and Greek organizations, joined by some high-profile members of Congress, urged him to bar Waldheim forthwith. An informant at the State Department told us that the Austrian ambassador to the U.S., Thomas Klestil, was pleading desperately with the Administration to make the opposite determination.

On Saturday, April 25, the wire services reported that Meese would confer with Austrian Interior Minister Karl Blecha in Brussels on Monday, at an international conference hosted by the European Community's justice and interior ministers. Their topic ostensibly would be transatlantic cooperation in the fight against terrorism. There was no indication that the two men would discuss Waldheim.

Schuller telephoned me at home to discuss the upcoming meeting. It would have been good to hear his voice after all these months, except that it immediately became clear that he was deeply depressed. "So many terrible things are still happening here," he complained. "This is not the Austria I used to love." He told me again that he was seriously thinking of leaving his homeland, forever. I assured him that I would try to help him settle in the United States, if that was what he really wanted.

Schuller switched topics. He wondered whether Meese might bring to Brussels some news about Waldheim. Schuller said that he was heartened by some German press reports forecasting that Meese was, indeed, going to place Waldheim on the watchlist. He predicted that many of his countrymen would try to explain away the action by citing the "fact" that "the Jews control the U.S. government," but he believed that the unprecedented decision—if Meese really made it—would force Waldheim to resign at last. On the other hand, he worried that something untoward might result from the upcoming Meese/Blecha meeting, even an announcement by Meese that Waldheim would *not* be barred from the U.S. "You know," he lamented, "it is hard to stop thinking about all these claims that our friend worked for the American OSS after the war, and that the CIA was protecting him after that." Schuller added that if there were any truth to these allegations, "then all is lost, because Mr. Reagan's closest adviser is Mr. Casey, who holds all the secrets from *both* agencies." My reminder that William Casey had just resigned his CIA director's post for health reasons changed nothing, as far as Schuller was concerned. "If Waldheim was the U.S.A.'s asset, then Casey will protect him—and he would have *already* told Mr. Reagan what has to be done. You can be sure of that!"*

That night, I met Neal Sher at the Plaza Hotel. In perfect springtime weather, we walked off to Smith & Wollensky's steakhouse for dinner. I handed my old friend a congratulatory cigar in celebration

---

*William Casey resigned as Director of Central Intelligence on February 2, 1987. He died three months later, on May 6, 1987.

of OSI's landmark deportation, the previous Monday, of Karl Linnas, the former chief of the Nazi concentration camp at Tartu, Estonia. Sher puffed on the cigar with pleasure, until a waiter asked him to extinguish it. Sher made it clear that there was little he could say about the Waldheim matter, but he did express the belief that "a decision is probably imminent."

Sher had no reading of Meese's inclinations. And he, too, was unsure what might come of the Brussels meeting two days hence, but he agreed with me that it was hard to believe that Waldheim would not be on their agenda on Monday. He told me that a copy of OSI's final report had gone to State Department Legal Adviser Abraham Sofaer. I informed Sher that I had been told by someone at State "who was in a position to know" that Judge Sofaer agreed with OSI's conclusions and had sent Meese a memo saying so. My former boss smiled and put down his fork. "My lips are sealed, Roosevelt."

"Eli—quickly—are you sitting down?" The voice on the phone came from the same friend at the State Department who had told me of Judge Sofaer's reaction to OSI's Waldheim report.

"Uh, yeah," I replied groggily. "Actually, I'm lying down." It was early on Monday morning, April 27, and I was still in bed. "What's up?" I asked.

"They told me I can't tell anyone. But I'm telling you. Waldheim is being put on the watchlist, *today.* It's being announced at 11:30."

"*Holy* . . . I mean, uh, that's great!"

"Total victory. Congratulations. It was your letter to Meese that prompted the whole thing. But, Eli—"

"Yeah?"

"You can't tell *anyone.*"

Not tell anyone? That was the least of my problems. This morning I was supposed to prepare a package of documents for a *New York Times* reporter on the subject of the "Pusteria" Division's deportation of 488 Yugoslavs to Norway. Then I had to catch the shuttle to Washington to attend oral arguments at the Supreme Court in an OSI case, *United States* v. *Kungys,* for which I had submitted an *amicus* brief on behalf of the WJC. How on earth could I concentrate on any of this *now?*

I ditched the idea of passing the Pusteria bombshell on to the *Times,* but I could not get out of the trip to Washington for the *Kungys* argument. The Justice Department had charged that Juozas Kungys was one of a band of Lithuanians who rounded up hundreds of Jewish men, women, and children—people who were their neighbors in the town of Kedainiai—and shot them to death. After the war, by lying to American immigration authorities, Kungys obtained a U.S. immigration visa. He was living in New Jersey when OSI located him. Because the trial judge refused to credit any of the eyewitnesses (on the basis that they still resided in Soviet-controlled Lithuania, and hence might have been subject to KGB intimidation to testify "correctly"), the issue before the Supreme Court concerned an esoteric but crucial detail: whether Kungys's misrepresentation of his wartime residence was "material" enough to justify revoking his citizenship.

My heart pounded in anticipation as I arrived at the U.S. Supreme Court building. I really don't want to go into this hearing, I thought. But I took my front-row seat and tried to focus on the arguments.

The highlight of the hearing occurred when Justice Thurgood Marshall, one of American history's towering champions of human and civil rights, leaned over the bench and demanded of Kungys's attorney, "Isn't it a fact that the reason that your client lied was because he was involved in these mass killings and he was trying to conceal it?" The lawyer, clearly startled by the unexpected question, denied the charge.

Finally the hearings were over* and I scrambled for information. I found several OSI staffers waiting in the foyer of the Supreme Court building. They broke the news that Meese had announced the decision at a press conference in Brussels. I feigned surprise, but had no need to contain my excitement.

It was official. For the first time in its history, the U.S. had formally barred the democratically elected head of state of a friendly nation from entering this country. In Brussels, Meese explained that he had no choice—the law and the facts compelled the decision. He added, reportedly without even a hint of incredulity, that he hoped that the excellent relationship between the U.S. and Austria would not be damaged by the fact that the U.S. had barred the Austrian president from setting foot in our country!

A short while later, in the Justice Department's amphitheater-like Washington press briefing room, Department spokesperson Terry Eastland stood behind a lectern nearly buried in microphones and audio cables and prepared to address a standing-room-only crowd of reporters. The Justice Department, he announced, had collected and analyzed evidence of Waldheim's wartime activities and had concluded that Kurt Waldheim "assisted or otherwise participated in" Nazi-sponsored acts of persecution "because of race, religion, na-

---

*The Supreme Court ultimately decided against Kungys on technical legal grounds, and he later surrendered his U.S. citizenship in return for the government's agreement not to seek to deport him. There has never been an adjudication of guilt on the allegations of involvement in mass killings.

tional origin, or political opinion." In a less-than-subtle reference to Waldheim's intricate patchwork of lies and half-truths, Eastland noted dryly that "efforts by a person to hide or otherwise distort potentially improper activities have routinely been regarded as significant" in making watchlist decisions. Should Waldheim attempt to enter the U.S., another Justice Department official explained to reporters, he would be detained and either returned home immediately or offered the opportunity for an exclusion hearing before a U.S. immigration judge.

There was to be one disappointment for the press this extraordinary day: Eastland reminded the media that it was longstanding Justice Department policy not to release "internal investigative reports." Thus, OSI's accumulation of evidence would remain inaccessible to the public.*

However, one important new piece of evidence came to light at the press conference. Sher disclosed the previously unpublicized episode concerning the Yugoslav prisoners captured by the "Pusteria" Division and turned over to the Germans, presumably with the aid of liaison officer Waldheim, to be sent to Norway for slave labor. This was the very scoop I had been preparing for the *New York Times*. To my amazement, however, Sher's disclosure went almost unnoticed by the assembled reporters.† It was an almost comical reminder of the media's inability to follow the intricacies of the Waldheim case. The press could not even recognize a new disclosure when it was handed to them! Similarly unnoticed was Sher's disclosure that OSI had ascertained that Waldheim was stationed in Banja Luka (where General Stahl's headquarters were located) when the local Jews were arrested and deported—yet another fact that clashed with his repeated protestations of total ignorance regarding such matters. Based on Waldheim's position and responsibilities in the quartermaster unit there, moreover, OSI had concluded that Waldheim was actually *involved personally* in the removal of the town's Jews—an action that sent them to their deaths.

John McCaslin of the *Washington Times* learned that Meese had made his final decision on Saturday, before leaving for Brussels, after an hour-long meeting with U.S. Secretary of State George Shultz. I found out on my own that there was a third man at the meeting, State Department Legal Adviser Abraham Sofaer. Thus, the decision

---

*As of this writing, OSI's final report has still not been released. Having disqualified myself from the Waldheim case upon returning to Justice in May 1988, I have not seen it either. As of April 1993, the issue of whether the report's release could be compelled under the Freedom of Information Act was still under consideration by the U.S. Court of Appeals in Washington, D.C.

†The *New York Times* reported this story, nearly a year later, as a new development.[6]

had already been made by the time Sher and I had dinner on Saturday night and worried over the issue.

I called Steinberg in New York and we congratulated one another. We had traveled a long road since receiving the initial tip in January 1986 in Jerusalem, and we shared feelings of both elation and relief.

By the time I arrived back at the office, the WJC had already issued Edgar Bronfman's official reaction: "Attorney General Meese has acted in a courageous manner and has sent a clear message: Nazis are not welcome here."

Once more, our tiny office was crowded with reporters and camera crews. As usual, Steinberg handled most of the interviews, but the *New York Times* quote the next morning was mine: "History has at last caught up with Kurt Waldheim."

International reaction was both varied and largely predictable.

Asked whether Waldheim would be welcome in his country, Canadian Prime Minister Brian Mulroney replied, "No, not at all."

The British government said that it was not convinced that there was sufficient evidence against Waldheim to support the watchlist decision. A spokesperson for Prime Minister Thatcher declared that Waldheim "is democratically elected and as such we would afford him every courtesy." However, the spokesperson added pointedly, "There are no plans to invite him at the moment."

Israeli Prime Minister Yitzhak Shamir said that the U.S. had acted correctly.

In Los Angeles, the Simon Wiesenthal Center said that it too applauded the Attorney General's decision. The American press overwhelmingly welcomed the decision, with the *Washington Post* using the opportunity to wonder aloud how Austria "somehow elected as its head of state a man who—virtually no one in Austria now disputes—lied about his wartime service and whose best defense is that he 'merely belonged to a military unit' that committed terrible atrocities."

The Soviet Union condemned the watchlist decision as an "unfriendly act" and declared that "American Zionist circles" were behind it. An angry *Izvestia* piece asked, "How is the fever pitch of political passions around this topic to be explained?" and cited the explanation given by Franz Muri, chairman of the Austrian Communist Party: The U.S., which "year after year and day after day invites fascist dictators for official visits and supports their regimes," was attempting to settle accounts with Waldheim for his Middle East policies of the past. Perhaps the most incredible note sounded by the Soviets was Radio Moscow's citation of the Kremlin's heretofore archenemy Simon Wiesenthal: "Mr. Wiesenthal . . . said that according to the historical documents he had examined, there are no grounds to indict Mr. Waldheim for war crimes."[7]

In Austria, the U.S. announcement came as a colossal surprise, in part because the domestic press had been confidently predicting that OSI's recommendation would be rejected by Meese. "Almost all Austrians reacted with shock and anger," reported one journalist on the scene. Support for Waldheim was widespread, this time even among Socialist politicians. The People's Party fired off a barrage of press releases, defending Waldheim and attacking Meese's decision. The party's press service said that the decision was forced by "Jewish backers" and/or a "worldwide conspiracy" engaged in a "campaign" against "our democratically elected head of state." One People's Party functionary publicly urged Waldheim to sue Meese, for at least $1 million in damages.

Most of the Austrian press continued to defend Waldheim, employing some of the most outrageous headlines yet, such as the one on the front page of *Kronenzeitung:* USA PUTS WALDHEIM ON THE "BLACKLIST" WITHOUT PROOF!

The accompanying story declared that a poll of Austrians showed that a mere 19 percent felt that Waldheim should resign. On the following day, *Kronenzeitung* crudely denounced the U.S. decision as "reminiscent of the Inquisition in the darkest Middle Ages."[8]

The *Salzburger Nachrichten,* one of the few newspapers that had opposed Waldheim's bid for the presidency, predicted that the decision would have a "catastrophic" effect for "the whole of Austria."

The "class" daily *Die Presse* charged that the Justice Department announcement was "some kind of advance payment" to Edgar Bronfman and the WJC before the 1988 presidential elections. The paper purported to soften its tone a few days later when it editorialized: "We are asking God in the name of his son Jesus that he shall forgive all those who spoke and decided wrongly."[9] *Kurier* deputy editor Hans Rauscher wrote that U.S. officials had "allowed themselves to be misled" by "a few fanatics."[10]

The schizophrenic *Profil* jumped on the crowded bandwagon of Austrian publications working overtime to show, in effect, that "our accusers are no better than we are." The magazine's May 25 cover drawing depicted a Hasidic (and manifestly unsympathetic-looking) Jew dressed as Uncle Sam, grinning and thrusting his forefinger out toward the (Austrian) reader. The drawing promoted an off-target cover story entitled "Anti-Semitism in the USA" (as though Austria's rampant anti-Semitism, displayed most notoriously in the pages of its biggest daily newspapers and in its political discourse, had some sort of analog in the United States).* In an accompanying article, Hubertus Czernin derided the U.S. decision, pointing out "errors" in the Justice Department's conclusions. Although the reporter had no way of knowing what was in OSI's report to Meese, he declared that U.S. investigators placed too much credence in the testimony of Johann Mayer. Czernin also denounced the Justice Department's "grotesque formulation" of U.S. law, under which Waldheim was condemned because he did not avail himself of his "only . . . chance to escape his place on the watchlist" under the Justice Department interpretation—namely, to join "the resistance in the Balkans."[11]

Foreign Minister Alois Mock immediately announced that Austria was recalling its ambassador to the U.S. for "consultations." He also summoned U.S. Ambassador Ronald Lauder and forced him to listen to a hyperbolic lecture masquerading as a formal protest. The watchlist decision was "categorically rejected," Mock fumed. The American action was a "medieval" injustice.

In an interview over German radio, Mock was asked whether Waldheim should resign. "I see no reason for that," he responded coolly. "He was elected with an unusually large majority and only Austrians— no one else—determine who is head of state in Austria." In a formal statement released by the People's Party, Mock continued his histrionics. "I speak of a campaign which is still being carried on by certain foreign groups against the head of state. . . ." In reality, he declared, it was "a defamation campaign against our homeland Austria."

Austrian Chancellor Franz Vranitsky, after a three-hour meeting with his ministers, expressed "shock" at the decision, but he refused to say whether he would postpone a long-planned official visit to Washington. "The federal government will take all steps to protect the head of state from unjustified accusations," he said in a prepared statement. "The known charges against President Kurt Waldheim are not proven and are therefore rejected," the Socialist added. The decision-making process utilized by the U.S., said the chancellor, was "incomprehensible."[12]

Former Chancellor Bruno Kreisky, the éminence grise of Austrian politics, bemoaned the fact that the Waldheim scandal had robbed Austria of its international reputation. "I stand," he said bitterly, "before the rubble of my life's work."

---

*A poll taken during June through August 1991 by the Gallup Institute of Austria is instructive. It found that 37 percent of Austrians felt that Jews have too much power in the world, 28 percent believed Jews had too much influence in Austria, 20 percent wanted the entry of Jews into influential positions limited numerically, and 19 percent said it would be better for Austria to have no Jews living in the country at all.

Simon Wiesenthal too made his views known to the media, asserting that, according to the evidence he had seen, "there are no grounds to indict Mr. Waldheim for war crimes."[13] Wiesenthal even charged again that Waldheim's pursuers had misinterpreted his "copy certified correct" signature.[14] In Wiesenthal's view, Waldheim's error was that he failed to sue his accusers for libel when the charges were first made the previous year. "An innocent victim of slander has the right and the duty to go to court," he declared. Wiesenthal disclosed that he had recommended this very strategy to Waldheim's son, Gerhard, a year earlier. A lawsuit "would have stopped everything," he explained.[15]

Surely, I said to myself, "stopping everything" concerning an investigation into alleged war crimes was the most inappropriate of goals for someone in Wiesenthal's profession. But the Wiesenthal remark that most angered me concerned the *impact* of the U.S. decision. The man who, by fighting us every step of the way, probably had done more than anyone else to elect Kurt Waldheim to the presidency, charged that the Reagan Administration's action was likely to produce increased anti-Semitism in Austria.[16] So now, as I read Wiesenthal, it was not only the WJC that caused anti-Semitism in Austria—the U.S. government was to blame, too!

Still, the Nazi-hunter saw a way for Waldheim to extricate himself from the predicament he was in: Allow an international commission to, in effect, redo OSI's investigation. And if the allegations could not be substantiated, then the U.S. would have to remove his name from the watchlist. "I have talked it over with Waldheim," Wiesenthal announced, "and he agrees that it is a good idea." Wiesenthal allowed that if the proposed commission confirmed OSI's findings, then Waldheim should resign. Still, it did not appear that the Nazi-hunter had a particularly thorough probe in mind, for, in reviving his "commission" idea, he declared again that the historians would need to be given only a few weeks to conduct their inquiry.[17]

The daily *Kronenzeitung* exulted at Wiesenthal's solution. ONLY AN HISTORIAN-COMMISSION CAN EXONERATE WALDHEIM, blared the paper's May 6 front-page headline. It was followed by the subheading: "Conversation with Eichmann-Hunter Simon Wiesenthal."

Waldheim's own reaction was to denounce Meese's watchlist decision as "grotesque."

Later, in a nationally televised speech to his countrymen, a shaken Waldheim declared that the watchlist decision was "dismaying and incomprehensible. . . . Let me assure all of you once again: You can trust me." He said that Meese's decision violated the principle that a person is innocent until proven guilty, and he reminded his countrymen that his predecessor, Rudolf Kirchschlaeger, had reviewed archival material and had found no proof of guilt.

He then announced that the government would rush the publication of a "White Book" that would successfully refute all charges. Declaring that "truth and justice" would win out, he vowed to appeal the Justice Department decision.

At the WJC, we fervently hoped that he would do just that. He could initiate the procedure simply by applying for a visa and, after being denied one, exercising his right to an exclusion hearing. The reason we wanted him to force a hearing was, however, the very reason he was almost certainly going to *refrain* from doing so: At an exclusion hearing, all of OSI's evidence would be placed on the public record. And Waldheim would have to testify—under oath.

Although Waldheim took great pains in his televised address to appear conciliatory and "presidential," his private comments dripped with anti-Semitic venom. He was overheard telling a group of World War II veterans that "the lobby of the American East Coast" was behind the U.S. decision. It was, he added, a "terribly brutal and ruthless" group. And in a meeting with a delegation of the World Citizens Council, a U.S.–based Christian organization, he attacked Edgar Bronfman and Israel Singer by name, and complained bitterly that the U.S. Attorney General "must have been placed under extreme pressure" to have acted as he had. "The leaders of the World Jewish Congress," he charged, "have shown no respect for the Austrian people."[18] It was as though the WJC—not the U.S. government—had placed him on the watchlist, and as though all Austrians—not just Waldheim—had been barred from the U.S.

University of Vienna researchers Maximilian Gottschlich and Karl Obermair, shocked by the domestic media's vituperative reaction to the watchlist announcement, raced to complete a scientific survey of the manner in which the decision had been reported. The study found that dozens of articles in the country's two biggest newspapers (*Kronenzeitung* and *Kurier*), and some in its most prestigious ones as well (*Die Presse* and *Salzburger Nachrichten*), contained "significantly" anti-Semitic and anti-American assertions. Fully a third of the 177 sampled articles from the mass-circulation *Kronenzeitung* and the "quality" daily *Die Presse* were marred by anti-Jewish statements. Even *Profil* was censured, for publishing anti-American material. Not surprisingly, the official press service of the People's Party was found to have sounded anti-Semitic themes in more than a quarter of its releases, but this time even the Socialist Party's press service was caught, on two occasions, doing likewise.[19]

Neal Sher, Deputy Assistant Attorney General Mark M Richard, and State Department attorney Mary Mochary were hastily dispatched to Vienna to explain to Austrian government officials the basis for the watchlist decision. Upon his return, Sher told me that, in a Vienna coffeehouse, a corpulent woman, recognizing him from newspaper photos, called him a *"Judenschwein"* ("Jewish swine") as she walked by his table.

Meanwhile, a U.S. official disclosed that the U.S. Embassy in Austria had been deluged with calls accusing the U.S. of cooperation with the "Jewish Mafia" and of being "a mouthpiece for world Jewry."

On May 5, at a WJC meeting in Budapest (the first major Jewish convocation held behind the Iron Curtain in more than twenty years), Edgar Bronfman declared that the Waldheim affair was "over," and he called for reconciliation between Austrians and Jews. But Bronfman's definition of "over" did not preclude a parting shot at Austria's president. Characterizing Waldheim as having been "part and parcel of the Nazi killing machine," he declared that it was time for the president of Austria to resign.

The "killing machine" characterization infuriated Waldheim's supporters anew. This time, they succeeded in persuading Waldheim to file libel charges against Bronfman in an Austrian court. The WJC president, ignoring the pleas and dire warnings of his personal attorneys, bravely announced his willingness to travel to Austria to confront President Waldheim in open court. The high-stakes game of "chicken" ended a few months later when Waldheim withdrew the lawsuit.

The WJC's formal role was over, as Bronfman had declared, and the results were bittersweet at best. Although it was apparent that Waldheim would not follow Bronfman's advice and bail out of his six-year presidential term, we had met our goal of at least beginning to expose his past. The WJC and a handful of like-minded pursuers had accomplished something wholly unprecedented. No one outside a government prosecutor's office had ever before dared to attempt to build a complex war crimes case from scratch purely through archival research, without the benefit of subpoena power. The minimal resources at our collective disposal notwithstanding, we had succeeded.

I was mentally and physically exhausted. It was time to move on.

At the end of June, after nearly a year and a half of working on the Waldheim investigation, I resigned my post at the WJC. I moved back to Washington to pursue other projects and, more importantly, to join my wife of three months; a New York–Washington "commuter marriage" was no way to start a lifetime together.

I told myself that I was through with Kurt Waldheim.

31

An early summer business trip to Germany provided me with an opportunity to rendezvous with Karl Schuller in Hamburg. He was waiting for my arrival and threw open the door as I approached his hotel room. "Eli, Eli!" he exclaimed, embracing me with a hearty bear hug. It was an emotional moment for both of us. Schuller and I had not seen one another since the public exposure of Waldheim's cover-up began nearly a year and a half earlier. We adjourned to the hotel bar and shared a few drinks. His pipe smoke curled toward the ceiling and I thought: *déjà vu.*

Except for his warm-weather attire, Schuller looked much as he had when I first met him in February 1986. But his enthusiasm was supplanted now by despondency. He told me again that he was so disgusted with his homeland that he wanted to move to America. "Austria," he moaned, "is just a *terrible* country. You can't imagine." The sadness was contagious. Here was a man beaten down by his revulsion with Austrian politicians and the domestic press and, worse still, by what he viewed as repugnant behavior on the part of a shockingly large percentage of his countrymen. He had seen his country transformed, almost overnight, from a successful neutral nation with a reputation for magnanimity toward refugees, a country known for its genial people and its happy music, into one with a reputation for bigotry and an identification with Nazism.

When I had first met Schuller in Vienna, I retained a reservoir of skepticism about his motivations; as a Socialist, he had a vested interest in "getting" the People's Party candidate. But I had long ago become convinced that he was driven far more by moral and ethical considerations than political ones. He was a Socialist in the purest sense: He had an idealistic vision of a utopian society in which the nation is one big family. Now he discovered that the real problem was that he really did not care much for his family.

He was also afraid. He disclosed that a friend had been physically attacked by a Waldheim supporter who suspected him of being involved in the exposure campaign. He himself was plagued by late-night telephone callers who hung up when he answered. He suspected that his house was being watched and he even worried that his phone might be tapped.

I was deeply dismayed to learn that Leon Zelman had also been adversely affected, even more than Schuller. I had told Schuller about Zelman's role in bringing me to Vienna. He knew Zelman by reputation and had received some disquieting information lately from an acquaintance of the big-hearted survivor. Zelman, he had heard, was "near suicide." (Fortunately, Schuller's informant turned out to be prone to exaggeration.)

We moved on to other topics. Schuller had learned that during the recent visit to the U.S. of Austrian Chancellor Vranitsky, what Schuller called "a meeting for four eyes only" (that is, not even interpreters were present) had taken place between Vranitsky and U.S. Secretary of State George Shultz. Schuller had learned that Shultz confided to Vranitsky his strong belief that the Soviets had used knowledge of Waldheim's wartime activities to pressure him over the years.* However, Schuller had received no information as to when the U.S. purportedly became aware of that alleged pressure, nor any details of just what sort of "pressure" it was, or how it had been applied.

Schuller and I spoke for hours, well into the evening, sharing our regrets about the way things had gone. At the same time, we shared a fantasy: If, by some miracle, way back in March of the previous year when we first took our story to the public, we had known everything that we now knew, the affair would surely have turned out very differently. Instead, the convoluted nature of the Waldheim story and the difficulties of the investigative process had forced the facts out in bits and pieces, thereby diminishing greatly their collective impact.

"If we had known it all in the beginning," Schuller averred, "Waldheim would have been gone in days. But at least we did the morally correct thing."

I suddenly realized that I had never told him how deeply skeptical—indeed, well-nigh incredulous—I had been in January 1986 when Israel Singer dispatched me from Jerusalem to Vienna to pur-

---

*Years later, in a letter to one of the authors of this book, Shultz wrote that he had "speculated in private that it was very likely that the Soviets had kept their knowledge quiet, while letting Waldheim know they knew, in order to cast a cloud of blackmail over him all through his U.N. tenure, with the aim of getting a Waldheim 'tilt' toward Moscow." Although the former Secretary of State wrote that he could no longer recall with certainty whether he made this comment to Vranitsky, he added that "it is likely that I *did* say something along the lines that you describe." (Emphasis in original.)

sue a seemingly bizarre rumor. Schuller admitted that he, too, had
been a doubter at first

We spent the next several days together, our conversations typically reaching into the morning hours.* Inevitably, we found ourselves once again drawn to the Waldheim puzzle, to continuing the
effort to unlock all the secrets. We brainstormed, and once again
allowed the discoveries to evolve from fragments of information and
assorted hypotheses.

Schuller told me an extraordinary story of how an acquaintance
of his had intercepted a letter to Waldheim, written after Waldheim completed his U.N. stint, from an old war comrade who
said that while he had always wanted to contact Waldheim at the
U.N., he had realized that it would have been dangerous to do
so. The episode was a reminder of how precarious a proposition
Waldheim's cover-up had always been—and especially of how, in
the late 1970s, when "Nazi" rumors began to encircle Waldheim
in New York and *someone* (but *who?*) had checked his military records in Berlin, his entire, elaborately constructed house of cards
had come within a hairsbreadth of collapsing. Whoever the "someone" was, Waldheim owed him a great debt of gratitude for keeping
silent.

Now it was my turn to share my biggest remaining leads with
Schuller. Thanks to OSI's research, we had learned that Waldheim
almost certainly had played a role in transferring prisoners from the
Italian "Pusteria" Division to Nazi slave labor camps in Norway. I
showed Schuller the pertinent documents from the National Archives. He pored over them anxiously, at last looking up and giving
me an appreciative smile. "*Ja,* this is our friend, no question! It is
perfect, Ja."

A second line of discussion was prompted by an entry in Waldheim's *Soldbuch,* the service record that each German soldier carried
with him. I had seen a portion of it appended as an exhibit to one
of Waldheim's submissions to the Justice Department. It revealed a
previously unknown assignment, to something called the 438th "Special Administrative Division," which, in late 1943, became responsible for antipartisan operations in the southeastern part of what
used to be portions of Yugoslavia, but which had been designated
by the Germans as the XVIII Military District. We really knew
nothing about this period of Waldheim's service, other than the key

---

*To my relief, there was no repetition of the hard drinking that had characterized the first
meeting with Schuller. I eventually came to the conclusion that his surprising behavior during
that first clandestine encounter was a product of his initial nervousness about meeting with
me.

fact that it was, obviously, something he was still attempting to conceal.

I informed Schuller that there was another mysterious entry in Waldheim's *Soldbuch*, recording his assignment to something called the "von Schultz Brigade" on May 18, 1945—several days *after* the German surrender. Schuller speculated that this might reflect the date that the assignment was entered into the *Soldbuch*, for such things sometimes happened in the frenetic days after the German capitulation. This was the only assignment listed in Waldheim's *Soldbuch* for 1945, and quite likely referenced the previously unidentified "infantry division" to which Waldheim said he was transferred late in the war but supposedly failed to reach. Schuller had no more idea than I what this von Schultz Brigade was. But he was sure that the name "von Schultz" had come to his attention before, perhaps in connection with Waldheim's early assignments under General von Pannwitz. The mystery gnawed at Schuller, and finally he persuaded me to join him in making "one quick investigation."

In Hamburg, Schuller and I had little trouble hunting up a copy of Erich Kern's *General von Pannwitz and His Cossacks,* one of the volumes he had shown me during our initial meeting in Vienna. There, we found references to *Oberstleutnant* [Lieutenant Colonel] Hans-Joachim von Schultz as von Pannwitz's top deputy and head of operations. After a promotion to *Oberst* ("Colonel"), von Schultz served, as of February 1945, as commander of the *2.Kosaken-kavalleriedivision*, reporting directly to von Pannwitz.[1] If this was identical to the von Schultz Brigade referenced in Waldheim's *Soldbuch*, it was evidence supporting one of our more speculative theories. One of Schuller's sources had contended that Waldheim rejoined the infamous von Pannwitz—his earlier commander (1941) on the Russian front—in the final year of the war. Further research revealed that, by this late hour of the war, von Pannwitz's Cavalry Corps was officially designated as a *Waffen-SS* unit.[2] That gave rise to the tantalizing possibility that Waldheim, by war's end, was an SS officer!

The possible SS connection was of no great moment in and of itself, of course. What really mattered was the answer to the difficult question: What did the von Schultz Brigade actually *do?* We knew that, near the end of the war, von Pannwitz's units were sent into northern Yugoslavia to battle Tito's partisans. One historian reported that they acquired a reputation for leveling villages "with fire and sword." The Cossacks themselves claimed that the unusually brutal measures they used there were the result of "the baleful influence of the Nazi German SS."[3] Schuller and I could only speculate that this was why Waldheim was so careful to say that he had never actually managed to link up with his new infantry unit billeted near Trieste.

Waldheim had long claimed that, failing to reach his final assignment, he returned instead "to the area of Villach via Udine." If this version was true, it opened yet another avenue for conjecture. With the aid of an atlas in a Hamburg city library, Schuller pointed out that, because of the mountains, the only navigable land route from Udine to Villach passes through the village of Tolmezzo—the very place where the Cossack units had established an extraordinary encampment, stocked with valuables and war booty. They had with them their families and, of course, their horses. Schuller had read that Tolmezzo was the storehouse for the legendary Cossack treasure—vast amounts of gold and jewels that were never traced after the war. My Austrian friend's imagination ran wild: Waldheim would have been a logical choice to undertake the special mission of spiriting the Cossack treasure off to safety. The Austrian-born lieutenant knew von Pannwitz, the commander of the Cossack unit, and he was an expert horseman.

Schuller and I both knew that we were well into the realm of speculation now, but we could not stop. With a start, I realized that I was as hooked as I had ever been on this ever-expanding mystery story.

We agreed that, no matter what, the research had to continue. It would be impossible to pursue Waldheim as aggressively as before, but we would carry on as best we could. "I don't care if it takes the rest of my life," Schuller declared. "As long as there is a possibility of getting the complete truth, I am not going to drop it." He said that he would keep me informed of any new discoveries by mail. His letters would be unsigned.

His last words to me in Germany, delivered as I prepared to board a flight from Hamburg, were: "We will get everything. In two weeks. In four weeks. In six months. But we will get it all. Of this I am sure, Eli."

Back home, I managed to find evening and weekend time to continue my research, quietly putting together more pieces of the puzzle. Living in Washington afforded me convenient access to the National Archives. My recently won freedom from the pressure-cooker atmosphere of the WJC, with its insistence on immediately publicizing every discovery, permitted a more thoughtful approach.

Before I plunged too deeply into my private research, I decided that I had to try to ascertain with certainty the author of the pointed W that appeared on so many important documents. I needed to establish at last whether or not that nearly ubiquitous initial really belonged to Waldheim, as so many students of the Waldheim case blithely assumed.

I dove back into the files and microfilms, and my excitement grew the more I studied. I found that the pointed *W* appeared, disappeared, and reappeared in a pattern that neatly tracked Waldheim's movements. For example, we knew that Waldheim finished his assignment at Athens and returned to Army Group E headquarters at Arsakli/Salonika early in October 1943. By checking captured Army Group E documents, I ascertained that October 8, 1943, was the earliest date that the pointed *W* appeared on an Ic/AO report.[4]

Similarly, we knew that Waldheim was on hospital leave at Semmering from February 25, 1944, until about April 16. I found that neither his signature nor the pointed *W* appeared on any surviving Army Group E documents during that period. The initial last appeared in a February 18 document and then magically reappeared on April 21. We also knew that Waldheim had been on leave again from August 15 to September 3, 1944. Sure enough, the microfilms showed the initial last appearing on August 13 and then reappearing on September 4.

Finally, according to information that had been released by the Austrian government in defense of Waldheim, he left Arsakli/Salonika for a trip to Vienna "towards the end of July" 1944, departing Vienna on the last day of the month to return to duty. The Austrian government provided no documentation of this absence, nor did it give an explanation for the leave; the claim was obviously intended to place Waldheim away from the Salonika area at least for a portion of the critical time during the final phase of the deportation of the Jews. But the information proved a great help to me in tracking the man who penned the pointed *W*. Poring over the surviving records from Army Group E, I saw, first of all, that the *W* last appeared on a document dated July 19, and did not reappear until August 3. Thus, the paperwork helped to corroborate Waldheim's leave. But what was more important now, for my purposes, was the fact that the pointed *W* also disappeared from Army Group E documents during precisely this same period.

The difficulties of the analysis were compounded by the fact that I had to sort through three different *W* possibilities in the Army Group E records, signifying either Waldheim or his boss Warnstorff or perhaps even Loehr's chief of staff, August Winter. The situation cleared a bit by the middle of 1944, when Winter was replaced by Schmidt-Richberg; during the months of August and September, the assignment charts listed only Waldheim and Warnstorff as officers whose last names began with the letter *W* and who were in a position to have initialed the documents in question. But how to rule out categorically the possibility that Warnstorff, not Waldheim, was the author of the pointed *W?* I was reluctant to pin everything on the way that the crucial initial followed a pattern that meshed with Waldheim's movements in and out of Arsakli/Salonika—no matter how remarkable the association was.

The last piece of the "*W*" puzzle fell into place when I noticed that the monthly "Ic and AO" activity report of Army Group E for September 1944 disclosed that Colonel Warnstorff was away in Athens from September 14 through September 27. I hopped a cab to the National Archives, where I quickly found a series of Ic/AO documents covering that very period *and* bearing the pointed *W* initial. These, then, could *only* be Waldheim's.[5]

The correlation was exact. When Waldheim was on duty at Army Group E headquarters, the pointed *W* appeared on reports emanating from the Intelligence/Counterintelligence Branch, even when Colonel Warnstorff was away. When Waldheim was away, the pointed *W* disappeared. There could no longer be any doubt. The pointed *W* did not signify Warnstorff or Winter. Or anyone else. It was Waldheim!

That long-awaited confirmation made me dive again into the boxes I had filled to near-bursting with the accumulated documents of the past year and a half. The doubts that had lingered for so long were now dispelled. It really *was* Waldheim's *W* on Major Hammer's "AO Activity Report for the Month of July 1944"—the counterintelligence document that Willi Korte had found in that first spring of the Waldheim affair.[6] Contrary to Waldheim's protestations of ignorance about the Abwehr section's "wholly separate" activities, then, he had actually been informed about these secret operations in minute detail.

And it was also Waldheim's *W* on the ominous September 10, 1944, directive from Loehr's chief of staff, General Schmidt-Richberg, that "severe, active measures" against the partisans "produce the best results."[7] These chilling instructions had been transmitted only weeks before the massacres in the three villages along the Stip-Kocane road in Macedonia, just as Army Group E's bloody retreat was about to begin. In light of the murderous actions that had *already* been authorized—and taken—by the Germans in waging war against the resistance, no one reading the words "severe, active measures," would have failed to discern their criminal import.

Now we knew too that it really was Waldheim's *W* on the May 8,

1944, report on the interrogation of the Cephalonia prisoners—the report that, by declaring the prisoner "Warren" to have been a member of a *Sabotagetrupp,* had all but guaranteed that Hitler's "Commando Order" for the "special handling" of Allied commandos would be triggered, with fatal consequences for Warren, whoever the poor fellow was.[8] Based on the placement of Waldheim's lone *W* immediately after the last word of text, we also could now safely conclude that the three-page report had actually been *written* by Waldheim. The fact that it was strangely devoid of any solid proof to support the deadly conclusion that Warren actually had been part of a *Sabotagetrupp* only made it all the more damning.[9]

An entirely different mystery cleared almost concurrently that summer when I obtained a copy of an obscure 1984 article from the *Journal of Modern Greek Studies* on the subject of the destruction of the Jewish community in Ioannina. Author Rachel Dalven based her study in part on her interviews with some of the few Jews of Ioannina who had survived the war. Their accounts made fascinating, if depressing, reading. I had always wondered whether the message transcribed by Waldheim on August 15, 1943, and sent on to his Athens superiors—warning that the "Jewish Committee" in Ioannina "must be regarded as center of preparations for a resistance movement"—had precipitated any *action* by Germans. I remained skeptical of Bob Herzstein's theory that Waldheim's report made him co-responsible for the Germans' mass removal and deportation to Auschwitz of Ioannina's more than seventeen hundred Jews, because that criminal operation was not carried out until more than seven months later, in late March 1944. In the absence of additional evidence, the time lag was just too great to hold Waldheim responsible.

But buried in Dalven's 1984 article was the nucleus of the solution that had eluded everyone. She reported that the Germans had first acted against the Jews of Ioannina during the late afternoon hours of Saturday, *August 20, 1943.* It was no accident that the Germans waited until the Sabbath, for this was a favorite Nazi tactic, designed to catch the Jews with their guard down. Dalven's article recounted how a contingent of Germans swept into Ioannina and surrounded the area in which the "New Synagogue," the Jewish school, and the homes of the city's wealthiest Jews were located. The Germans took two of the most prominent Jews away and terrorized them, but did not physically harm them. On this occasion, the Germans allowed their Jewish victims to return to their homes—after what Dalven described as two hours of "maddening agony" for "the whole community"—undoubtedly to spread the word about the perils of displeasing the German authorities.[10] And all of this had happened just *five days* (and on the *first* Sabbath) after Waldheim had helped target the "Jewish Committee" in Ioannina! The following month, Dalven's article disclosed, the Germans returned; this time they arrested two Jews—Nissim Batash and his son-in-law—and hanged them on suspicion of aiding the partisans (a charge that had already been rejected by their Italian allies). The Jews were now living in abject fear, precisely as their German masters wished.

This burst of Nazi terror on the heels of one of Waldheim's reports was eerily reminiscent of the timing disclosed in the documents I had found concerning the destruction of Karpenission (on Crete) and the massacres on the Stip-Kocane road. The Ioannina episode also served to remind me how very fragmentary were the surviving records of the Nazis, for neither the arrest and terrorization of the two prominent Jews nor the subsequent hanging of Batash and his son-in-law was reflected in any of the captured German reports yet unearthed.

At the same time that I was immersing myself anew in the Waldheim documents, an especially dramatic find was being made by Swiss journalist Hanspeter Born. Working in the West German Military Archives in Freiburg, he located a document reporting that on April 14, 1944, a First Lieutenant Heinicke of Army Group F instructed a certain *Sonderfuehrer* Paschiera to place a call to Army Group E in Arsakli/Salonika to inquire about the status of the commando prisoners captured on Alimnia Island. Paschiera did as he was told and spoke with First Lieutenants Helmut Poliza and Ludwig Krohne—Kurt Waldheim's immediate subordinates.

Paschiera asked where the men were.

The document recorded the response: "The men are at E."

Heinicke asked if the interrogations had been completed.

As noted in the report, the reply from Poliza and Krohne was, "Interrogation not completed (very stubborn)."

Paschiera asked when the commandos would be ready for "special handling."

The answer to that grim question: "The time of special handling will be decided by the SD."[11] The document thus conclusively established the involvement of Waldheim's subordinates in the homicidal "processing" of Allan Tuckey and the other young Britons.

Two related "Alimnia" documents found by the Swiss journalist were of even greater importance. The first was the set of original interrogation reports on Michele Lisgaris and the other two Greek sailors captured along with the British commandos. The reports were signed by Poliza as "Interrogator"—the officer who had personally supervised the interrogation—and by an interpreter who had evidently served as the actual interrogator.

So now it was at last indisputable that conducting prisoner interrogations was a responsibility of Waldheim's men.*

But it was a final document found by the Swiss writer that provided
the long-sought evidence that irrefutably implicated Waldheim in the
murder of the Alimnia prisoners. Willi Korte had discovered, more
than a year earlier, that Waldheim had reviewed a report on the
Alimnia interrogations and that Ic/AO Branch at Arsakli/Salonika
had cabled Army Group F on April 26, 1944, that "further interrogation of English Alimnia commandos [is] fruitless" and requested
a decision on handing them over to the SD. However, because the
only surviving copy of the cable was the one received by Army Group
F (rather than Army Group E's *transmission* draft), we had never
been able to link Waldheim—or any other named individual at Ic/
AO Branch—to this lethal notification and request. But now, thanks
to Born's research, we had an Alimnia document that Waldheim
could not escape: a cover letter dated April 21, 1944, transmitting
to Army Group F Poliza's interrogation reports on three Greeks who
had "participated" in a "commando raid" against the island of Alimnia. The letter was signed by the "AO," Major Hammer (in place
of Colonel Warnstorff, who was evidently absent), and it bore what
I had now confirmed to be Waldheim's telltale *W,* along with the
initials of his subordinate, Lt. Poliza. The initials identified Poliza as
author of the enclosed reports *and Waldheim as author of the letter of
transmittal.*† Thus, Waldheim was a party to the notification of Army
Group F that the Greek prisoners had been conclusively determined
to be "commandos"—a characterization that not only is unproven
by the Greek prisoners' interrogation reports but, in light of Hitler's
"Commando Order," effectively doomed them to torture and death
at the hands of the SD. Indeed, we already knew that just six days
later, Army Group F cabled Waldheim's branch with instructions to
hand over eight of the ten British and Greek prisoners "to SD for
possible interrogation . . . and final special treatment pursuant to the
Fuehrer Order." It would have taken no particular bravery for Waldheim to point out in his transmittal that the Greek sailors had per-

*Copies of these documents are in the authors' possession. During taping of a 1988 Thames
Television (U.K.) program on the Waldheim case, Helmut Poliza confirmed that he had
overseen the interrogation of the Greek prisoners. Although he admitted that he and Krohne
decided on the lines of questioning to be used by their subordinates who conducted interrogations, and although he admitted personally attending interrogations on occasion, when
asked whether he had interrogated any of the British Alimnia prisoners, he replied, "I couldn't
remember."
†The British government eventually concurred in this assessment of the reports and cover
letter. See Ministry of Defence, *Review of the Results of Investigations Carried Out by the Ministry
of Defence in 1986 into the Fate of British Servicemen Captured in Greece and the Greek Islands*
(London:HMSO, 1989), pp. 53 and 96 (discussion of "Annex 85"). See also page 20.

formed only a transportation function for the British personnel, and to propose that they therefore be spared, as non-commandos.[12]

Waldheim really *had* played a central role in the fatal "handling" of the Alimnia prisoners. The thought that he was comfortably ensconced in the Hofburg Palace, from which he was continuing to deny any wartime involvement with prisoners, was infuriating. Reviewing the Alimnia documents again, I felt the kind of rage I had not experienced since the first months of the campaign.

The rage gave way to nausea a few months later when, following the death of Cicely Tuckey Clark—mother of Alimnia prisoner Allan Lane Tuckey—British journalist Tom Bower was granted access to the family's papers. Among them was a large collection of correspondence and other documents generated during the family's decades-long postwar struggle to find out what had happened to the young Special Boat Squadron officer. A November 2, 1950, letter to his mother from the British Foreign Office had advised her that the last trace of her son was six years earlier, in April 1944, when, according to a "final" British investigation, he was taken, with most of his captured comrades, "by air to Salonika" and there "handed over to representatives of Lt. Colonel Warnstorff, Chief Intelligence Officer of Army Group E."[13]

In the same London *Times* article in which he disclosed the Foreign Office correspondence with the Tuckey family, Bower revealed another official letter, this one from the Ministry of Defence, to the brother-in-law of Alimnia prisoner Raymond Jones. The MoD letter was of decidedly recent vintage—March 26, 1986—and it was sent in response to an inquiry from Jones's family that had obviously been prompted by the initial exposure earlier that month of the Waldheim cover-up. Although the letter, signed by Lord Trefgarne, the Minister of State for Defence Support, said that the men died in "unknown circumstances," it suggested the possibility that SBS gunner Jones and his comrades "had been lost in attempts to swim [from Alimnia Island] to the mainland"—a theory that the British government had obviously known for decades was completely wrong.[14]

Something smelled very bad in London. That impression was strengthened still further a short time later when M.P. Robert Rhodes James revealed that Her Majesty's government had mysteriously *shredded* some of its files on the fate of the Alimnia prisoners. Worse yet, the documents had been destroyed in 1978, while Waldheim was still Secretary-General of the U.N. Newspapers on both sides of the Atlantic reported on suspicions harbored by some observers that the destruction might have been the handiwork of Soviet "moles" inside the British government who, the speculation continued, were trying to protect the KGB's most valuable asset in New York, Secretary-General Waldheim. The scenario seemed far-fetched. But one had to admit that stranger things had already been documented in the evolving story of the Waldheim cover-up.*

The issues still spinning through my mind went well beyond the jumble of dates and locations of Waldheim's war years. I was still unable to provide a satisfactory answer to the burning question: Why had the truth not come out during Waldheim's U.N. tenure? Who had known what about Waldheim and when had they known it? Even more important, what had they *done* with this information? Who was responsible for aiding and abetting the most audacious and successful Nazi cover-up in history?

Clues existed in abundance, especially when one reviewed the reactions of various governments, first to our investigation, then to Waldheim's election as president of Austria, and, finally, to the decision to place Waldheim on the U.S. watchlist.

The British response could best be characterized as tepid. On the one hand, Prime Minister Margaret Thatcher's private secretary declared that ". . . in the absence of proof of criminal activity on the part of Dr. Waldheim, the Government takes the view that he is entitled to the courtesies due to a democratically elected Head of State of a friendly country." And London was still refusing to make public its files on the case. On the other hand, Prince Charles had openly snubbed Waldheim during a visit to Vienna with Princess Diana. More importantly, Britain had also initially vetoed Waldheim's nomination to the Secretary-General's post. Perhaps British actions, or the lack thereof, spoke louder than words in this case for, in December 1987, the British press quoted unnamed sources in the Foreign Office as saying that it had been made clear "unofficially" that Waldheim would not be welcome in the United Kingdom. (At this writing, Waldheim has not set foot in the U.K.)

France was something of a wild card in the deck. Paris had said little throughout the affair and its aftermath. But clearly some French official had compiled the politically explosive 1979 report on Wald-

---

*The British aspect of the affair became still more confounding when, in October 1989, the British Ministry of Defence issued a report summarizing its renewed inquiry into the fate of British servicemen captured in Army Group E's field of operations during 1943–1944. The disappointing report, which curiously failed, time and again, to ask (much less answer) the ultimate questions, omitted crucial pieces of evidence previously made public elsewhere, and relied on a number of demonstrably flawed interpretations of evidence, concluded that the MoD found "no grounds" for trying Kurt Waldheim on war crimes charges in connection with the murdered British servicemen. The report offered no judgment, however, on responsibility for the deaths of the Greek sailors.

heim's war assignments as reflected in documents held in the French-run WASt archive in Berlin. But why was this done, and for whom? The answer from Paris: no answer.

Circumstantial evidence argued against official Israeli knowledge of Waldheim's past. The Israeli Embassy official who reviewed my early evidence had been deeply—and, it appeared, genuinely—shocked. And Israeli U.N. representative Benjamin Netanyahu had publicly called the Yugoslav charges grave ones after he reviewed the UNWCC file. Moreover, Jerusalem had ignored the attempts of its ambassador to Austria to squelch our efforts. Indeed, it was the Israelis who were responsible for the surreptitious release of the UNWCC file. Clearly, the Israeli govenment was not trying to protect Waldheim. Former Israeli Justice Minister Yitzhak Moda'i had declared, "There is a basis for putting Waldheim on trial, if he were in Israel, for involvement in war crimes." Following Waldheim's election, the government of Israel announced its "deep regret" and "sorrow," and recalled Ambassador Elizur. After the watchlist decision, Prime Minister Yitzhak Shamir declared that the U.S. had acted correctly. On the other hand, there was still no explanation on record for why the Israeli U.N. representative had publicly cleared Waldheim, during a 1981 *New York Times* interview, of having supported the Nazis. Whatever the explanation, I simply could not believe that Jerusalem had knowingly participated in a Nazi cover-up. Yes, Israel's obsession with the practice of *Realpolitik* sometimes seemed to draw the Jewish state into an endless series of awkward alliances and controversial intrigues. But involvement in a Nazi cover-up was, I was sure, a profanity that no Israeli government could have stomached.

Nor could I readily buy the contention that Waldheim was a U.S. asset, despite Waldheim's own statement that he "could very well imagine" that the U.S. knew about his wartime activities. Had he been "American property," surely someone would have come forward by now—as had happened immediately in the case of the far more notorious Klaus Barbie—to say, "When I worked in U.S. intelligence, I was involved with Waldheim." But not even a phony claimant of that ilk had surfaced. To believe the "American asset" hypothesis, one had to conclude that the operation had been executed flawlessly *and* that our government had, in this case, proved uncharacteristically leakproof over a period not just of years, but decades. Moreover, of all the world's major governments, it was the U.S. alone that vigorously pursued the Waldheim investigation and *only* the United States that formally condemned him. Attorney General Meese certainly did not act to place Waldheim on the watchlist as a "Nazi persecutor" until he had cleared the decision with the

White House—where, quite obviously, no countervailing instructions were issued by the president or by then–Vice President George Bush, who was the U.S. representative to the U.N. who voted for Waldheim's initial election—and who later headed the CIA. Nor had CIA Director and former OSS official William Casey—perhaps President Reagan's most trusted adviser—used his influence to block the watchlisting of Waldheim (or at least delay it indefinitely), as he would certainly have done had Waldheim been on the U.S. payroll. Finally, after the watchlist decision was announced, Vice President Bush's office took the unusual step of issuing a statement declaring that Bush believed the action "is correct and he fully supports it."[15]

My analysis of the American angle soon found support in the recollections of two former U.S. officials, Professor Seymour Maxwell Finger and William Safire, both of whom denied that there had been any suspicion on the part of U.S. authorities that Waldheim had a secret Nazi past. Finger, who had been a senior official in the U.S. mission to the U.N., disclosed that the State Department's instructions to then–Ambassador Bush in December 1971 had been to vote for Max Jakobson of Finland and Prince Sadruddin Aga Khan of Pakistan (the U.N. High Commissioner for Refugees), but to *abstain* on Waldheim. Safire, a White House speechwriter at the time, recalled that the U.S. position of ambivalence on Waldheim had actually changed to opposition during the selection process, which involved three rounds of voting over the five-day period from December 17 to 21. During a December 21 summit conference in Bermuda between Secretary of State William P. Rogers and British Foreign Secretary Sir Alec Douglas-Home (President Nixon and Prime Minister Heath were conferring there at the same time), a discussion was had on the question of who should be the replacement for U Thant. Douglas-Home's government had already vetoed Waldheim in the first round. By the end of the discussion, which Safire witnessed, Rogers agreed that Waldheim should not get the post. But it was too late: An aide soon walked in with the news that the third (and, as it happened, final) vote had just been taken in New York, and Waldheim had won before the U.S. delegation could be apprised of Rogers's opposition to Waldheim. The Soviets had vetoed the other two finalists.[16]

Had Waldheim been an American intelligence asset, a decidedly different scenario would almost certainly have played out, especially since the fact of his candidacy for the top U.N. post was known within the U.S. intelligence community (it had been repeatedly disclosed in press reports on the U.N. succession question for more than seven months).[17] Secretary of State Rogers would have been informed, long before the Bermuda summit, that Waldheim was

"U.S. property" (and hence a truly superb choice for U.N. Secretary-General).

The Yugoslav government's response was nothing short of schizoid, probably reflecting, more than anything else, the internal struggles between the Serbs and Croats, which seemed to be pushing the country toward the brink of civil war.* Yugoslav support for Waldheim ebbed and flowed throughout the months prior to the Austrian presidential election, and continued to do so afterward. Quite clearly, the Yugoslavs did not wish to harm their vital trade relationship with their all-important neighbor Austria, nor did they wish to risk eroding the image of Tito—an unavoidable consequence of the disclosures concerning the charges that the Belgrade authorities had filed against Waldheim in 1948 but which Tito made certain were never seriously pursued. Just as clearly, however, elements within the Yugoslav government were unwilling to ignore the issue of the Kozara massacres, the "Black Operation" atrocities and so many other crimes committed in Yugoslavia by components of Army Group E.

Most fascinating of all was the Soviet reaction to our investigation. In early 1987, the Soviets had issued an angry protest over the Austrian attempt to memorialize General Loehr, but they seemed to grow deaf, dumb, and blind just a few weeks later when the Waldheim scandal broke and it was disclosed that Waldheim had served on the war criminal's staff. The Soviet press blackout on the Waldheim scandal was so total that they even remained silent concerning a possible CIA cover-up of Waldheim's past, as hinted at by the CIA's 1980 letter to Representative Solarz. Never before, in my memory, had the Soviets passed up such a spectacular propaganda opportunity. They could have accused the U.S. of withholding from them the information that Waldheim was listed on CROWCASS, for the Soviets were not a party to it or to the UNWCC. Their silence was anything but subtle. And, of course, Moscow did not release a single piece of paper from its vast collections of captured German war documents. It was inconceivable that the Soviets had not bothered to search their files—or that, upon conducting such a search, they had not found a single document of relevance. No, the Soviets were sticking by the man whose ascent to the top of the U.N. hierarchy they had plainly engineered—and whose personnel practices had been so very accommodating of their espionage interests in New York City.

---

*Full-fledged civil war did indeed ensue, in 1991. At this writing, the war is still raging. Tragically, the people of Bosnia are once again being subjected to gruesome "cleansing actions," this time not at the hands of Germans and Croats but rather Serbs intent on the "ethnic cleansing" of Bosnia to remove Moslems and other non-Serbs. The Croats, too, invaded Bosnia, in hopes of acquiring some of its territory for the newly reestablished Croatian nation.

This became even clearer once Waldheim was elected president of Austria. The Soviets were among the first to send their congratulations, and their "news" accounts omitted any reference to his war service—or to the controversy that surrounded that service. When the U.S. announced that it was barring Waldheim, a Tass dispatch, issued from Washington, condemned the watchlist decision as "an unfriendly act" resulting from "a provocative campaign" against Waldheim by "the Zionists in the U.S.A."[18] Quickly, Soviet Premier Nikolai Ryzhkov became the first foreign head of government to visit President Waldheim in Vienna.

The Soviets had to have known a great deal about Waldheim's vulnerability to exposure of his wartime affiliations and assignments. And I had to agree with Charles Lichenstein, former deputy U.S. representative at the U.N., who posited that if the Yugoslavs knew about Waldheim before Tito split with Stalin (as they clearly did), "then you can be sure the KGB knew everything."[19] The interviews conducted in Yugoslavia by *Washington Post* correspondent Dusko Doder had confirmed that the information had indeed been shared with the Soviets. British M.P. Rhodes James bluntly charged that "Waldheim was 'created' by the Russians. He was their man."[20]

Most unsettling of all was my realization that, fully two years into the public exposure of Waldheim's Nazi past, after we had disclosed Waldheim's listing on CROWCASS and the UNWCC, after we and others had detailed his service with criminal units throughout Yugoslavia and Greece, and even after the U.S. government placed him on the watchlist, crucial files in the Soviet Union, Austria, Greece, France, and elsewhere remained beyond the reach of those of us who wanted the full truth to come out. *The cover-up was still under way.*

32

I made many trips back to the National Archives, working on my own time and at my own expense. I carried on a fairly ambitious international correspondence as well, seeking every available morsel of additional information, however inconsequential it might appear at first glance. My files became a private monster that threatened to take over our Washington town house.

Often I studied late into the night, relishing the solitude of the small hours. Yet, for a time, the major product of my research was the generation of still more unanswered questions.

It was on one such late-night immersion in my boxes of photocopies, books, and microfilm printouts that I was able to piece together a chain of National Archives documents that convincingly implicated Waldheim in the transmission of homicidally criminal orders—an act that itself constitutes a war crime under international law.

The criminal order in question was General Bader's "secret" command of April 10, 1942, explicitly ordering German and Italian forces to execute prisoners: "Captured rebels caught with weapons in their hands, or whoever helps them, should be shot" (sind zu erschiessen). The order added that localities that supported the resistance or in which weapons were found were to be "burned to the ground."[1]

The order itself was not a new discovery; OSI had found it sometime earlier, and I had been tipped off to its existence by the anonymous Post-it attached to the copy of Waldheim's August 1, 1986, brief that I had been asked to examine. But a second look at the order only now made its full significance apparent.

Crucial to evaluating the document was the fact that Waldheim had admitted, in his August 1, 1986, submission to Attorney General Meese, that he was the German liaison to the Italian Division "Pusteria." As he was the only person in D.V.K.5 ("German Liaison Unit No. 5") who could interpret and translate between German and

Italian, Waldheim's role had included translating orders from General Bader's headquarters into Italian and transmitting them to the "Pusteria" Division in Montenegro; messages from the Italian division were translated by Waldheim into German and transmitted to Bader's headquarters in eastern Bosnia.[2] The only other men in D.V.K.5 were mere "signal" personnel—radio/teletype technicians.

What all of this meant was that for the one and only time in the investigation of his war career, Waldheim could be held responsible for *everything* his "unit" did. He could not cast the blame on his superiors or his subordinates (or, for that matter, on officers of equal rank); he had none.

The significance of this understanding was enormous, especially with respect to General Bader's murderous order of April 10, 1942. That latter fact became apparent to me this evening only when I looked at the distribution list attached to Bader's order, which disclosed that twenty copies of the order were to be distributed, to sixteen offices and units, including two copies to the 718th Infantry Division (one of which was to go to its "Croatian Liaison Officer"), one to the "Italian 5th Mountain Division 'Pusteria,' " and one each to the two other Italian divisions engaged with Bader's combat group. Neither Waldheim's D.V.K.5 nor any of the other German liaison units were on the distribution list, however.

As I studied the distribution list, I suddenly realized that the absence of an overt reference to D.V.K.5 had an explanation. Obviously, the German liaison units had to be apprised of the operational orders being disseminated from German headquarters to "their" Italian units. Moreover, in all likelihood, the German liaison units, which received such orders by radio and by courier, had to provide the Italian divisions with an Italian translation of this particular order (or at least a summary in Italian). Why then were they not listed on the distribution? The explanation was one that plainly incriminated Waldheim: Each Italian division was to receive its copy *through the German liaison unit* that was its link to General Bader's headquarters. Thus, no separate entry was necessary.[3] This meant that it was *Lieutenant Waldheim* who passed on Bader's lethal instructions to the "Pusteria" Division.[4]

And that, by Nuremberg's definition, made Waldheim a war criminal.

I realized now that General Bader's order also linked Waldheim to what likely was the planning that preceded the "Pusteria" Division's subsequent transfer to German hands of 488 civilians for deportation to slave labor in Norway. The document advised that logistical instructions for placing civilians in camps would be forthcoming:

Civilians who are thought to be helping the rebels must be interned. You will receive orders regarding how to get them into the internment camps.

All of this reminded me of something Waldheim had said about his service in Yugoslavia during his March 3, 1986, interview with John Tagliabue of the *New York Times,* when then-candidate Waldheim was first confronted with our original evidence of his cover-up. I pulled the yellowed press clip from one of my folders, to reread his exact words. They seemed ancient and eerie now:

Someone with bad intentions might conclude because partisans were there, Waldheim must have committed war crimes. That is pure nonsense.

After U.S. Attorney General Meese announced the U.S. government's decision to place the Austrian president on the watchlist, Waldheim had assured his countrymen that the Austrian government would rush the publication of a "White Book" that would successfully refute all charges. A hastily assembled three-man "Archive Mission" of Austrians quickly responded to an official invitation from Belgrade to study the Waldheim records in the Yugoslav archives. The team spent a mere three days in Yugoslavia, then announced that it had found "no indications of Dr. Waldheim's participation in . . . actions of retribution in the fight against the partisans, or in measures against Jews, prisoners of war, or deserters." The statement added that the "delegation was assured by the representatives of the Yugoslav archive that it had looked at all documents of possible relevance."[5]

With the completion of this initial publicity stunt, a task force of politican/authors, including former Foreign Minister Karl Gruber and Drs. Ralph Scheide and Ferdinand Trauttmansdorff of the Austrian Ministry of Foreign Affairs, made use of the "Archive Mission's" report in the preparation of the promised White Book. They noted that Gerhard Waldheim had also provided personal papers from his father.

By the late summer of 1987, the White Book was ready for publication, but an internal argument reportedly raged over its distribution. The Socialist Party resisted the attempts of the People's Party to have the White Book printed as an official government document. Finally, it was published and distributed independently by Foreign Minister Alois Mock and was sent by the Austrian Foreign Ministry to all Austrian embassies abroad.[6]

The exposition, composed of 67 pages of text and 230 pages of mostly familiar exhibits, was entitled *Kurt Waldheim's Wartime Years:*

A Documentation.[7] Its cover was, indeed, white; in some circles, it
soon became known as the "Whitewash Book," and when I received
my copy I immediately understood why. For example, the White
Book declared that the deportation of civilians captured by the Italian
Division "Pusteria" was "not known to Dr. Waldheim and bore no
relevance whatsoever to his duty in Plevlje as a German-Italian interpreter. Allegations along these lines are therefore false." With a
stroke of the pen, the White Book's authors had converted Waldheim
from *the German liaison officer* between the Wehrmacht forces and
the "Pusteria" Division into simply "an interpreter." No explanation
of *how* Waldheim—as the liaison between the German command
that ordered the mass deportation and the Italian division that actually captured the prisoners and delivered them to the Germans—
could possibly have been unaware of this episode was even attempted. Such was the character of Waldheim's "official" refutation.[8]

The White Book blithely ignored entire subject areas in which
Waldheim had been implicated in criminal conduct. Others received
patently disingenuous treatment, with the authors repeatedly setting
up and knocking down straw-men arguments misrepresented to be
those of Waldheim's accusers. Discussing Waldheim's role in preparing the now-infamous Athens war diary entries about the orders
to kill captured partisans, the White Book continued to avoid discussion of the possibility that Waldheim had taken part in actually
transmitting the criminal instructions:

> The fact is that these entries do not indicate the initiating or
> implementing of any order or action, but merely show instead
> the recording by the German liaison staff of orders given to a
> German unit by a higher command. Because Dr. Waldheim had
> no role in the formulation, drafting, or issuance of these orders,
> he was in no position to modify their directives or to prevent
> their implementation. Accordingly, he was not involved, either
> directly or indirectly, in any impropriety that may have arisen
> out of the orders of the ensuing dispatch of German troops.

On Waldheim's role in the disarmament and deportation of the
Italian troops in Greece, Waldheim's people were finally forced to
admit that the end result was not what Waldheim's attorneys had
previously characterized as "chivalry." Through his Foreign Ministry
surrogates, Waldheim now admitted that he had personally participated (as an "interpreter") in the surrender negotiations with the
Italian General Vecchiarelli, and further admitted that the Germans
had promised the general that his men could go home to Italy once
they surrendered their arms. Without so much as a hint that Wald-

heim had ever contended otherwise, the report noted dryly, "Records indicate that most of the Italians were subsequently brought to Germany." The White Book dismissed Waldheim's role with the declaration that the decision to deport the Italians to slave labor in Germany (where the conditions were so brutal that the Italians lodged a formal protest with Hitler) was made at a higher level. Twice before, in June and October of the previous year, Waldheim had contended that the Italian troops were shipped "to their homeland and thereby to liberty." Now he had changed his story completely, in effect admitting that his previous statements were false. But as had happened so often in similar instances of Waldheim reversals, the press—still hopelessly overwhelmed—took no notice.

The Foreign Ministry's official defense of President Waldheim parroted his long since disproved claims about the supposedly inviolable separation in the duties of the "Ic" and "AO" personnel in Army Group E's Ic/AO Branch. It painted a fanciful picture in which the AO staff, under Major Hammer, was responsible for any and all atrocities, whereas Waldheim worked strictly in the comparatively pristine Ic section, not only uninvolved in what the AO men in his small branch were doing, but blissfully ignorant of those activities as well.

An affidavit from Colonel Warnstorff, reprinted as an exhibit, recalled that Waldheim was his "regular aide" in Arsakli/Salonika. This characterization was not particularly helpful to Waldheim, especially in light of the fact that Warnstorff was not only Chief of Intelligence, but was also the number-two man in Operations for Army Group E. The Warnstorff affidavit even confirmed that Waldheim was responsible for "the registering of the incoming confidential matter[s] with a short description." Thus, Waldheim did not merely log in the most sensitive messages; he had to read them, understand them, and summarize them—yet he still professed ignorance of anything sinister that was going on!

On the subject of the Allied commandos, the White Book declared, "Unprecedented research efforts failed to yield any evidence whatsoever linking Dr. Waldheim to the conducting of prisoner interrogations." It was a clever attempt to divert attention from the proof that had been unearthed of Waldheim's role in the lethal process of *evaluating* the results of such interrogations, and of his service as immediate superior of officers who did conduct the interrogations.

When it addressed the contents of the *Odluka,* the White Book noted that "the protocol of the only testimony supposedly burdening Dr. Waldheim, that of Johann Mayer, could not be located." Indeed, it was either lost or (as I later confirmed) the Yugoslavs were holding it back from everyone. It was fascinating to compare this news with the previous announcement that the three-man Austrian team had seen "all" the Yugoslav documents "of possible relevance."

On page after page, the White Book sounded the same weak refrain: Yes, the facts *look* bad, but actually there's an explanation. . . .

In sum, there was nothing in the White Book to alter a knowledgeable reader's view of Waldheim's war years.

Outside Austria, the White Book and its sophomoric reasoning were largely ignored. Waldheim quickly decided that he had to go further in his defense. He seized on a proposal advanced by Simon Wiesenthal.

Wiesenthal had made an effort, shortly after Waldheim's election, to regain credibility by calling for a panel of historians from seven nations—the U.S., Israel, Great Britain, Yugoslavia, Greece, Austria, and Germany—to be assembled to examine the war record of the president-elect. Following the watchlist decision, he had renewed that call, once again with the assertion that the team could perform its assignment in only a few weeks (even though it had taken OSI many months of research to conclude its Waldheim inquiry). With Waldheim's blessing, Austrian officials now persuaded Professor Hans Rudolf Kurz of Switzerland to head such a group. Kurz immediately set out to recruit others. The Austrian government invited the Yugoslavs to place a historian on the commission, but the Yugoslavs, perhaps wary of a trap, did not respond.

The "International Commission of Historians Designated to Establish the Military Service of Lt. Kurt Waldheim" began its probe in August 1987. I and many other observers were skeptical, because of the unimpressive composition of the panel (with two notable exceptions); its meager resources; its lack of subpoena power; the failure to appoint even a single prosecutor, attorney, or investigator; and the absence of a written assurance from Waldheim that he would testify *under oath*. The commission held its meetings in quarters provided by the Austrian Foreign Ministry, which aroused suspicion when it refused to sweep the room for electronic listening devices. Schuller told me, although he could offer no proof, that Waldheim's people had, indeed, bugged the room. The U.S. Department of Justice refused to supply information to the commission, declaring that if Waldheim wanted access to the U.S. government's evidence, all he had to do was apply for a visa and, upon receiving notice that his application was denied, insist on his right to a hearing.

Each of the commission members was to concentrate on a specific aspect of the allegations. The British member, historian Gerald Fleming, studied Waldheim's role in the treatment of Allied commandos. Dr. Yehuda Wallach, a professor at Tel Aviv University, concentrated on the subject of Jewish deportations. Dr. Manfred Messerschmidt, head of the West German Military Archive in Freiburg, studied Kozara. Brigadier General (retired) James L. Collins, Jr., the American representative, was tasked with the assignment of tracking down information in the possession of the U.S. government, including the files of the former OSS. Dr. Jean Vanwelkenhuyzen of Belgium studied other matters, including Waldheim's alleged prewar affiliations with Nazi-sponsored groups. Professor Hagen Fleischer of Greece, the man who had alerted the world to Waldheim's Athens assignment via the April 1986 *To Vima* article, was to focus on the subject of atrocities against Greek partisans.

As the historians were preparing to tackle their assignment, historian Robert Herzstein was putting the finishing touches on a book about Waldheim. He had obtained at least one significant piece of new information about the Austrian president's postwar vulnerability to blackmail.

Although Yugoslav sources had told the *Washington Post*'s Dusko Doder that Yugoslav intelligence had used its war dossier on Waldheim to compromise him, Waldheim had always denied even knowing that the Yugoslavs possessed compromising information about him. But Fritz Molden, the former OSS agent who became an assistant to Foreign Minister Karl Gruber after the war now disclosed to Herzstein that in 1951 or 1952 a Yugoslav diplomat and Tito intimate named Vladimir Velebit had quietly asked Molden "whether or not this Waldheim had relatives living in Yugoslavia." As Herzstein noted, the "clear implication" was that Belgrade "had something on the rising young foreign service officer." And Molden, the man who had first recommended Waldheim to Gruber, could hardly have failed to relay to his young protégé the news of this remarkable inquiry by a senior Yugoslav official.

Having been thusly made aware that Belgrade was on his trail, Waldheim would have had a powerful incentive to accommodate the Tito regime's wishes from that time forward.

The early autumn arrival of a thick envelope bearing a Vienna postmark and addressed to me in Schuller's familiar handwriting brought the welcome news that Karl had been as serious as I had been when we vowed at our Hamburg meeting to continue the research.

The envelope was jam-packed with copies of captured documents Schuller had recently obtained from the Freiburg military archive. They were accompanied by Schuller's handwritten analyses. For the most part, Schuller's latest discoveries added still more small pieces to the puzzle. Many of the documents punched holes in Waldheim's claims and denials, especially his insistence that he was uninvolved in "AO" activities. Schuller took particular delight in methodically demolishing some of the more outlandish assertions made in the "White Book."

One of Schuller's new finds clearly stood out in significance from the others. It was an October 30, 1944, report, signed by Colonel Warnstorff.[9] In the document, the man who had characterized Waldheim as "my regular aide" reported on a conversation he had held the preceding day with one SS-*Oberfuehrer* Gstoettenbauer.

Warnstorff, like Waldheim, had insisted throughout the Waldheim controversy that he had known nothing of deportations or concentration camps. But Schuller's new document demolished that lie. In it, Warnstorff reported having spoken with *Oberfuehrer* Gstoettenbauer about the fate of concentration camp inmates. The explicit language used in Warnstorff's report made it clear that he was well acquainted not only with the fact of the existence of the Nazi camps, but also with the mass murders being perpetrated there. Warnstorff suggested to his SS contact that, in order to obtain "good behavior" from Albanian troops on the Eastern Front, it might be advisable, in the event that "German concentration camps" holding Albanian prisoners are closed, "not to liquidate" *(nicht liquidieren)* the inmates, but rather to hand them over to the Albanian government. A handwritten addition implied that sparing the Albanians would yield propaganda benefits as well.

So Warnstorff not only knew about the camps and what happened in them, but he was personally involved in deliberations regarding the fate of the inmates! Although it was impossible to ascertain from the document whether Waldheim too had been involved in the life-or-death discussion with the SS officer, another document in Schuller's "package"—showing Waldheim joining Warnstorff and an Abwehr captain named Fuhrmann just two weeks later in negotiations with the legendary Cetnik partisan leader Draga Mihailovic about cooperating with the Germans—strongly suggested that this was precisely the type of discussion to which the intelligence officer who insisted he had been "only a sort of secretary" might indeed have been a party.[10]

Interestingly, the report on the discussions concerning the fate of Albanians in German concentration camps was denominated an "Ic"—not an "AO"—document, further blurring the supposed "line" between these two sections of Waldheim's branch.

Pursuing the question of Albanian prisoners, I found at the Library of Congress the memoirs of Hermann Neubacher, the German Foreign Office's Plenipotentiary for the Southeast. In the book, Neubacher claimed that Gstoettenbauer did indeed spare the lives of two thousand Albanian prisoners (though Neubacher credited his own intervention with the SS officer and made no mention of Warnstorff).[11]

I immediately passed on the new documents to Neal Sher. The concentration camp incident had not been discovered by OSI in its own research. I gave the materials to *Newsweek* as well, which published their contents in its issue of January 4, 1988.

The *Newsweek* publication prompted the historians commission to make several "urgent" appeals to me to share with them any new documentation in my possession. The fact that the commission had not found the concentration camp document on its own—even though commission member Manfred Messerschmidt headed the Freiburg archive in which the original reposed—confirmed my fears about the quality and thoroughness of the commission's inquiry. I advised the commission that I was concerned that the panel lacked even a single investigator or prosecutor, had no subpoena power, and, worst of all, had agreed to allow Waldheim to examine its evidence *prior* to any interview of the Austrian president. Although I immediately provided the commission with copies of the documents I had given to *Newsweek,* the historians had already questioned Herbert Warnstorff, and hence could not confront him with the concentration camp incident. I declined to surrender to the commission any nonpublic evidence in my possession, in part (as I explained to one of the historians) because I had a request pending with Waldheim's office for my own interview of the former U.N. chief; if I gave my documents to the commission, the historians would be duty-bound to share them with Waldheim, who would then be able to tailor his answers to the evidence when questioned.*

As the commission bent to its task, Simon Wiesenthal found himself in the spotlight once more. Schuller called me from Vienna in late September with the details. He reported that *Epoca,* an Italian magazine, had published an article alleging that a full year earlier, Gerald Fleming (now a member of the historians commission) had sent Wiesenthal certain documents pertaining to the role of Waldheim's unit in interrogating the Alimnia prisoners, but that Wiesenthal had failed to make them public in Austria. Although the documents were ones that we and others had already disclosed, the charge seemed to refute Wiesenthal's chronic complaint that he had seen no documentary evidence to support the published charges against Waldheim.

An obviously shaken Wiesenthal called a press conference. He said that Fleming had asked him *not* to publish the documents, for

---

*My interview request was subsequently denied by Waldheim.

fear of stirring up additional anti-Semitic outbursts in Austria. Predictably, he further denied that the evidence proved Waldheim's direct involvement in war crimes. But the Nazi-hunter made an unexpected and dramatic move. For the first time, he called on Waldheim to resign the Austrian presidency. If the commission found Waldheim "guilty," Wiesenthal said, he would have to resign. And even if the commission cleared Waldheim, Weisenthal said, he would still be "a burden for Austria," and should step down anyway.[12]

What lay behind this sudden turnabout? According to Schuller, Wiesenthal was in a tight spot, because one of his staff members had quit in protest over his role in the Waldheim affair, and was telling reporters that, during the 1970s, Wiesenthal had received a letter from "an American Jew" inquiring about Waldheim and had replied that the U.N. diplomat's past was unmarred by serious blemishes. She also recalled how Wiesenthal had prominently displayed on his office wall a commendatory letter signed by Secretary-General Waldheim.* Schuller had learned that another one of Wiesenthal's assistants had spirited away copies of critical correspondence, including a letter from Wiesenthal to West German Chancellor Helmut Kohl, which Schuller characterized as "outrageous," although he could not provide full details. Was the great Nazi-hunter finally running scared? If so, why?

A few days later, thanks to a source in Vienna, I had the letter in hand, along with a second Wiesenthal letter to Cardinal Koenig, the top Catholic prelate in Vienna. The contents of Wiesenthal's private correspondence were even more distasteful than I had expected.

In a December 12, 1986, letter, the Nazi-hunter had advised the West German chancellor that he should ignore the (relatively mild) criticisms leveled at him by Edgar Bronfman in a recent West German newsmagazine interview. Bronfman had opined that Kohl, while not a hater of Jews, lacked the sensitivity and understanding of the past that his predecessor, Helmut Schmidt, had displayed. "He could even propose a Bitburg," Bronfman remarked, in pained reference to Kohl's successful effort the previous year to pressure President Reagan into paying respects at a German war cemetery that included the graves of SS men. Bronfman had also been critical of Kohl's record, unique among western leaders, of lavishing praise on the disgraced Kurt Waldheim.[13] In Wiesenthal's private letter to Kohl, the Nazi-hunter complained that Bronfman's ascendancy to the WJC presidency reflected the replacement in world Jewish leadership of the pre-Hitler "aristocracy of ideas" with a postwar "aristocracy of money" (a theme he also sounded in the letter to Cardinal Koenig).

---

*The former Wiesenthal staffer later reported these same two recollections in a letter to me.

For Kohl, however, Wiesenthal had only worshipful praise. Bronfman, he wrote, "will not succeed" in his attempt to portray Chancellor
Kohl as an "enemy" of Israel and the Jews. The German chancellor,
he continued, had proved, both by words and deeds, to be "just the
opposite."[14]

A short time later, OSI's Neal Sher, along with U.S. Ambassador to
Austria Ronald Lauder, encountered Wiesenthal at a B'nai B'rith
dinner in New York. The two American officials saw their chance
to urge him to expand on his new position that Waldheim should
resign. They proposed a statement for Wiesenthal to issue, denouncing Waldheim. A participant in the conversation called me on October 31, two days after the dinner. "Simon wouldn't budge," he
reported. "He won't do anything that might make it look like the
WJC was right."

As the commission's work continued, Waldheim's increasingly jittery
allies suddenly went on the rampage again. One of the first salvos
in this ferocious new round of assaults was a letter from Carl Hoedel,
deputy mayor of Linz, who wrote to Edgar Bronfman and copied his
message to Ambassador Lauder.
    Hoedel, of the People's Party, wrote that the WJC's claims con-
cerning Waldheim were "worth as much as those of your fellow
believers . . . who had Jesus Christ condemned to death . . . because
he did not fit into the schemes of the gentlemen of Jerusalem . . ."[15]
    Lauder paraphrased the contents of the letter for an American
reporter: "You Jews got Christ, but you're not going to get Waldheim. . . ." The ambassador complained bitterly that neither the government nor the People's Party had taken any action against Hoedel,
nor was there any public clamor for his removal. "This would not
have happened anyplace in the Western world," Lauder complained,
courageously abandoning the diplomatic niceties ordered by his State
Department superiors. "The deputy mayor of Linz would not have
lasted fifteen minutes anyplace in the Western world. He is still in
office today." When Lauder was replaced shortly thereafter by Henry
A. Grunwald, who had escaped the Holocaust by fleeing Austria as
a young man, *Kronenzeitung* foreign editor Kurt Seinitz remarked,
"We think maybe better an old Jew than a new Jew."[16]
    Almost simultaneously, Alois Mock struck his cruelest blow yet
against Jewish interests. Speaking at the U.N. in New York, the
Austrian Foreign Minister and engineer of Waldheim's candidacy
disclosed publicly that Iranian Jews were fleeing the tortures of the
Khomeini regime in a secret rescue effort to which the Austrian and
Pakistani governments were providing support. He even opined that

the Jewish escape program had the tacit approval of Iranian authorities.[17]

Israeli officials and Jewish leaders familiar with the secret rescue mission were mortified. They could hardly conceive of disclosures more likely to embarrass the intolerant mullahs ruling Iran into terminating this life-or-death program. This was, after all, precisely the disaster that had befallen the desperate effort to spirit the endangered black Jews of Ethiopia to safety in Israel a few years earlier, after the operation was prematurely disclosed in the American press. Fearful of giving Mock's disclosures any further publicity, Jewish organizations said nothing publicly and Jewish newspapers were asked to refrain from reporting Mock's statement. Although Jewish leaders could not know whether he had somehow failed to appreciate the obvious danger in his revelation, privately the incident became known as "Mock's Revenge."

A month later, People's Party General Secretary Michael Graff went completely off the deep end. He told the Paris newsweekly *L'Express* that Waldheim need not worry about his war past "as long as it is not proven that he strangled six Jews with his own hands."[18] Graff immediately apologized for his facetious suggestion of a six-Jew minimum, but was forced to resign his party post over the ugly quip. That same day, Hoedel announced his resignation as deputy mayor of Linz.

The resignations did little to calm Austria's frightened Jewish community. "This is the first time since 1945 that anti-Semitism from the top has been introduced on the Austrian scene," one community leader complained to an American reporter. "It is not a pogrom, but the feeling is conveyed," he lamented.[19]

In late November, *Profil* published a report by Hubertus Czernin charging that the International Historians Commission was thoroughly infiltrated by operatives from Mock's Foreign Ministry. Czernin said that one of Mock's deputies sat in the room next to the commission's meeting quarters and that the secretary who typed the minutes was a staff member of the Foreign Ministry.

Nevertheless, according to Czernin, the commission had, from Mock's point of view, "gone out of control," moving toward the same conclusion as the one reached by the U.S. Justice Department. Czernin reported that, during an interview, Mock vented his rage that the commission was going beyond its mandate; instead of merely studying the available evidence, it was looking for *new* evidence!

By phone, Schuller confirmed rumors that the commission seemed to be ready to condemn Waldheim. "I don't know if I should laugh or cry," he said. "It's too crazy."

*   *   *

On January 28, 1988, the president of Austria received the historian commissioners at his residence, in order to respond to a provisional list of questions. Two presidential advisers were also present, as well as Gerhard Waldheim. Hours after it ended, I received a confidential telephonic report that the session was an unpleasant experience for all concerned.

When Waldheim admitted to his prewar affiliation with Nazi organizations, Dr. Vanwelkenhuyzen asked whether membership in the Nazi Student Union was a prerequisite to being allowed to prepare his doctoral dissertation—the one that praised the concept of a unified nation of Germanic-speaking peoples. Waldheim replied that it was not an absolute requirement; but if he had not joined, he said, there might have been difficulties.

Kurz asked whether or not Waldheim had passed on orders to the Italian "Pusteria" Division to turn over prisoners to the Germans for deportation to slave labor in Norway. Waldheim acknowledged that his position at the time had been intended for a colonel and that, since the colonel never showed up, he, as a lieutenant, had the responsibilities of a colonel. He explained his duties: "I passed on reports from the Combat Group Bader to the 'Pusteria' Division, and such reports also came to me in reverse." The admission meshed perfectly with my analysis of General Bader's order to kill armed partisan prisoners and those who aided them, and to prepare to send civilians suspected of favoring the resistance to "internment camps." Despite the fact that he was *the* liaison officer, Waldheim said that he had only recently learned of the prisoner transfers. He claimed that his unit was not involved; he had passed on no such instructions.

Messerschmidt noted: "The prisoners were handed over either by you or by the Italian liaison staff. The U.S.A. states that the Pusteria handed over prisoners to the SS through your agency . . ."

"Our staff was not involved in that," Waldheim replied. "We dealt with tactical procedures. I am convinced that prisoner transportations were not arranged through us."

As far as western Bosnia was concerned, Waldheim referred to (but did not produce) pages from his notebook which, he said, proved that his duties concerned only matters such as rationing, fuel, and ammunition. (He was careful not to disclose that he had told the U.S. Justice Department that his "contemporaneous notes" proved that he *was* involved in transportation matters.) As further proof of his noninvolvement in transportation, Waldheim referred to the affidavit of his witness, Ernst Wiesinger, who claimed that General Stahl's combat group had a special "transportation officer" assigned to it.

Messerschmidt uttered the names of several Balkan villages: Klissura, Kalavrita, Dostomon, Striri, Kalamata—all were sites of reprisal atrocities. Waldheim denied knowledge of any atrocities in these locations, despite the fact that he once initialed a report that explicitly detailed the setting afire of Kalavrita "from one end to the other," and the slaughtering of women and children in other Greek towns and cities.

When the commission moved on to the subject of prisoner interrogations, Waldheim was forced into an about-face, since the world had now seen a report proving that *his deputy,* Poliza, had supervised the interrogation of the Alimnia Island commando prisoners. In the second version of his defense memo, Waldhcim had claimed that prisoner interrogations were conducted "at the corps and division levels, and not at the command of Army Group E." In his first submission to the U.S. Justice Department, his lawyers had retreated brilliantly, writing that ". . . all such activities were handled by the AO section, and not Dr. Waldheim's section." Now, however, in typical fashion, Waldheim casually offered yet another version, admitting that "rather infrequent interrogations of prisoners . . . were the responsibility of Poliza and Krohne." But, he claimed, "I never interrogated a prisoner or partisan personally myself."

One of the commissioners pressed further on the Alimnia commandos: "It has been said that the sailor Lisgaris was to be exempted from special treatment because he had been forced to participate in the commando operation. Who originated this suggestion to Army Group F?"

Waldheim replied, "I no longer recall who *in the Ic section* made this recommendation."

The commissioner responded, "I assume that this matter [of the commandos] crossed your desk."

"Perhaps," Waldheim acknowledged.

At this late date, Waldheim still claimed not to know what, in Singer's words, "every dog in Salonika" knew. He repeated that he was not stationed in Salonika during the time when fifty thousand Jews were deported. He said that he went downtown very seldom and therefore did not notice, even after the fact, the disappearance of one-fifth of the population and the evaporation of much of the city's merchant class. "Mr. Wiesenthal has spoken to me about this," Waldheim noted, "and has said you were neither a war criminal nor a Nazi but admit that you knew about the Jewish population being taken away. I honestly did not know about it." My source told me that at least some of the commission members were as incredulous as we were when they heard this.

One especially tense encounter took place when Messerschmidt, clearly referring to the newly discovered document on Albanian prisoners in Nazi concentration camps, quizzed Waldheim about his purported ignorance regarding the concentration camps:

> Messerschmidt: In the Intelligence section, it was known that there were concentration camps and that liquidations were in progress there. The question is: What did "O3" know? *Warnstorff has stated that you knew whatever he knew.*
>
> Waldheim: I assure you that I did not know anything of these things. In fact, I knew only a fraction of whatever it is that Warnstorff knew.

The meeting ended with a terse comment from commission president Kurz: "Thank you for talking to us. We have not spared you. We will inform the press that the discussion was useful, nothing more."[20]

It was an extraordinary lie that brought out more of the shocking truth concerning Waldheim's actions at Kozara. Ironically, however, this time the lie was not Waldheim's. In late January 1988, just as the historians commission was moving toward the completion of its assignment, two Yugoslavs, historian Dusan Plenca and sportswriter Danko Vasovic, announced that they had found a sensational document that proved Waldheim's direct involvement in the Kozara deportations. It was purported to be a July 22, 1942, Croatian telex in which "Lieutenant Kurt Waldheim" demanded transportation to ship 4,224 Serbs, "mostly" women and children, "on their way" to two camps near Belgrade. Here, at last, was the ultimate smoking gun, explicitly showing Waldheim shipping innocents off, very likely to their deaths!

Though I hoped that the document was authentic, I was immediately suspicious. It is highly unusual for a military report to reference an officer's first name. Contributing to my skepticism was the fact that the two Yugoslavs were being coy about actually showing the document to anyone, and even gave conflicting accounts of the current whereabouts of the original.

Plenca and Vasovic quickly sold the document to the highest bidder, the German magazine *Der Spiegel,* which published it in its February 1, 1988, issue. The magazine's world exclusive was accompanied by much editorial crowing about how it had done what no one else (supposedly) could do—prove conclusively that Waldheim was guilty of a Nazi crime. Plenca told reporters that although the document did not show Waldheim killing people himself, it proved something equally sinister: "He prepared them for death."²¹

The telex published by *Der Spiegel,* if genuine, was indeed the most sensational single piece of evidence yet to emerge. Translated from Serbo-Croatian, the key text read:

> Very urgent. Lieutenant Kurt Waldheim from the staff of General Stahl demands that 4,224 prisoners from Kozara, most of them women and children and approximately 15 percent older men, be sent on their way: 3,514 to Grubisino Polje and 730 to Zemun.*

Even as doubts were growing everywhere about the authenticity of the new document, Waldheim now made perhaps the biggest mistake of his entire defensive campaign. Unexpectedly, he conceded that he *might* have been involved in the civilian deportations from Kozara, including those of women and children. In an interview with the Vienna newspaper *Kurier,* published in the February 3, 1987, issue, Waldheim complained that "after 46 years, I can say with good will that I cannot remember." But Waldheim had an "explanation," even for the Kozara abomination. "In every war there are prisoners and refugees," he said. Civilians who "fled from the fighting" in the Kozara region were sent to "transit" camps, and even if he did participate in arranging such human shipments, this, he claimed, was not "a close connection to war crimes."²² Waldheim seemed to expect the newspaper's readership to believe that he was blissfully unaware of the fate that awaited the deportees—namely, transfer to almost certain death in Croatia's Jasenovac death camp or in the inhuman Nazi labor camps in Germany and occupied Norway.

Schuller reported to me by phone that Waldheim's latest statements had exasperated some of the president's most solid supporters. Such things simply did not happen "in every war." And those who were deported had not been, as Waldheim claimed, assisted by the Germans in "fleeing from the fighting." Transporting men, women, and children to concentration camps was a war crime. But Waldheim was portraying it as an act of chivalry—much as he had done in defending his role in the 1943 "repatriation" of the Italian soldiers to Italy, when in fact they were deported to slave labor in Germany.

Waldheim's shocking response to the *Der Spiegel* document turned out to be spectacularly ill-timed on his part. For, even while Waldheim was being interviewed, the document was being forensically examined by West German authorities. And within days, they concluded

---

*The alert reader will notice the numerical irregularity: 3,514 plus 730 totals 4,244, not 4,224.

that it was a patent forgery; the typewriter that was used to prepare the document was not available until four years after the war. *Der Spiegel* apologized in print.

Nevertheless, Waldheim was now on record with a most remarkable incriminating statement, and all of us who were working on the investigation were dumbfounded. Why had Waldheim rushed his response? Perhaps he was merely careless; perhaps he was growing overly confident of the security of his position as president; or perhaps he knew that, somewhere, a document such as this really did exist.

If overconfidence was the explanation, it actually appeared to be a justifiable emotion for Waldheim. His countrymen were rallying around him ever more enthusiastically. A Gallup Poll released a few days after Waldheim confessed that he "cannot remember" whether he helped deport civilians during the Kozara bloodbath found that 72 percent of the Austrian public felt that he should not resign.[23]

"Who could remember everything from the war period?" Waldheim had asked rhetorically, near the beginning of our investigation. One obvious answer was: Certainly not Kurt Waldheim. The still-growing list of memory lapses and claims of ignorance by this former intelligence officer (who had been well enough informed to be called upon to brief General Loehr's chief of staff on developments throughout Europe and the Mediterranean) was breathtaking, as I fully realized only when I spent an afternoon compiling a partial list of them:

He did not know why documents (at least one of which he signed) listed him as a prewar member of various Nazi organizations.

He did not know that Yugoslav prisoners captured by the Italian Division "Pusteria"—to which he was the *sole* German liaison officer—were handed over to the Germans, much less that this was done in order to effect their deportation to slave labor in Norway.

He did not know that Kozara was a massacre site, nor that civilians were deported en masse to their deaths; indeed, for some time, he could not remember that he was even at Kozara. Finally, he contended that he "cannot remember" whether he was involved in the deportation of women and children from Kozara.

He never saw any Jews in Salonika wearing the Star of David. He never even heard about the deportation of Jews from Salonika and the Greek islands. He did not know that 20 percent of Salonika's population had disappeared, that Jewish businesses were shuttered, nor that the Jewish cemetery was destroyed. Although he cited Gerald Rietlinger's landmark book on the Holocaust in one of his own books, he had never noticed the pages about the destruction of

Salonika's Jews, those about the deportation of Jews from the Greek islands, or those about Loehr's involvement in the Jewish deportations to Auschwitz.

He did not know that the deportation of Jews from his home city of Vienna "was such a mass affair," even though he claimed to have spent much of the war there, studying law.

The "Black Operation" in Montenegro was "not in my memory," nor had he ever heard of General Lueters, the man whose arrival he was awaiting when he was photographed at the airstrip in Podgorica.

He did not know that the Italian soldiers whose surrender he helped to negotiate—and whose removal from Greece he helped carry out—were not repatriated as they had been promised, but instead were shipped to forced labor camps in Germany.

"Nothing like" Hitler's order to kill captured partisans (which, it was later established, he recorded in the Athens command's war diary) ever came to his attention.

Regarding the document, found for us by Bob Herzstein so long ago, showing that Waldheim had briefed Loehr's chief of staff during a meeting at which the use of hostages as human shields against partisan attacks on German locomotives was discussed, Waldheim was unsure "to what extent this matter was actually implemented." Anyway, he speculated, perhaps he left the meeting early.[24]

He never saw a British officer. At first, he was sure that no one in the Ic section ever interrogated prisoners; only when documentary proof surfaced did he "remember" that his two deputies conducted interrogations. He recalled nothing of the fate of any of the commandos, nor could he recall who "in the Ic section" made recommendations as to the fate of the Alimnia prisoners. "It is, of course," he moaned, "difficult to remember something which happened over forty years ago."

He could not recall the 1943 Kalavrita atrocity, even though he had initialed a report on it.

He "had no idea" that he was accused of Nazi crimes by Yugoslavia and was listed as wanted by the UNWCC. He never heard of the Yugoslav witness, Johann Mayer, although they were almost certainly in contact at Army Group E headquarters on personnel matters.*

When first confronted with allegations regarding the 1968 "Prague telex" (months before an actual copy surfaced), he could not recall issuing the inhumane order.

---

*For example, the reader will recall that Mayer worked in the personnel department at Army Group E headquarters and that the army group's organizational table disclosed that Waldheim was the officer assigned responsibility for, among other things, "personnel matters of Ic/AO Branch." A direct denial of knowledge of the UNWCC listing was made by Waldheim in an interview aired by Britain's Channel 4 on March 6, 1988.

He had "no recollection" of discussing his wartime activities with Brian Urquhart or anyone else at the U.N.

After filling five pages of a legal pad with more than thirty other examples, I abandoned the effort. But I began to suspect that the "Ic" designation for Waldheim's Army Group E intelligence assignment actually denoted "Ignorance Chief." The wonder was that the apparently deaf, dumb, blind—and now amnesiac—Waldheim had never been court-martialed by General Loehr.

I thought that the essence of Waldheim's deception had actually been captured best by Lars-Erik Nelson in a New York *Daily News* column on the subject of the U.S. decision to place Waldheim on the watchlist:

> Austrian President Kurt Waldheim spent World War II in the midst of horrendous crimes, of which he has said:
>
> 1. He wasn't in the German army.
>
> 2. If you can prove he was in the German army, he wasn't anywhere near the war crimes.
>
> 3. If you can prove he was near the war crimes, he didn't know about them.
>
> 4. If you can prove he knew about them, he didn't take part in them.[25]

33

The 202-page *Report of the International Commission of Historians Designated to Establish the Military Service of Lieutenant Kurt Waldheim* was released to the government of Austria on February 8, 1988, and distributed to the press the following day.

It used a glut of surprisingly impolitic words to call the Austrian president a liar:

> In many areas, Waldheim's version of his military past does not accord with the results of the commission's work. He made an effort to forget his military past, and as soon as this became possible no longer, he tried to make it appear harmless. In the opinion of the commission, it has been forgotten so completely that they were unable to take from Waldheim any evidence or clues which might have assisted in clarifying their work.

The commission noted Waldheim's numerous denials that he had ever been a member of Nazi organizations, then documented its finding that he was "unquestionably" a member and speculated that this was "yet another gesture of conformity with the Nazi regime."

In analyzing Waldheim's military service under the Third Reich, the commission's research proved spotty at best, plainly incompetent at worst. I was, for example, flabbergasted to see that, in the section on the deportation of Greek Jewry, the historians had somehow overlooked the single most powerful document linking Waldheim's Ic/AO Branch to Jewish deportations—the captured document that reported the accomplishment of the deportation of the Jews from the East Aegean islands "at instruction of High Command of Army Group E, Ic/AO." The document—a Nuremberg exhibit—had been publicly utilized in the Waldheim affair nearly two years earlier!

But although the historians commission made numerous such mistakes, and although the members, to my mind, resolved far too many doubts in Waldheim's favor—including many that were artificial products of highly improbable notions advanced by the former U.N.

437

chief—the bottom line was that the report contained enough accusatory findings to justify characterizing Waldheim at least as an accessory to the perpetration of Nazi war crimes.

The commission found that Waldheim was aware of the severe measures implemented against partisans, noting that, as early as Waldheim's 1941 service on the Russian front, the "partisan phenomenon was a familiar one and considered dangerous. Warnings to the troops were issued." By the spring of 1942, when he finished his convalescent leave and joined the Bader Combat Group in Yugoslavia, the commission concluded, Waldheim "would have become familiar with questions of the 'combatting of resistance groups,' the treatment of prisoners, and reprisal practice."

The commission was equivocal concerning Waldheim's possible involvement in Montenegro in the transfer of partisan prisoners to slave labor in Norway. While conceding that it had not been able to review the U.S. Justice Department's evidence on this point, the commission declared that the available information "allows the interpretation" that Waldheim was not involved.

Which version of Waldheim's Kozara story was closest to reality? The commission recalled that Waldheim had "repeatedly stated that he did not take part" in the deportations of civilians in western Bosnia, but concluded that the contrary was probably true, as documentary evidence established that Waldheim's quartermaster unit "was involved not only in supplying the German troops, as Waldheim has stated, but also with transportation of prisoners." (The commissioners did not, of course, know about Waldheim's "contemporaneous notes"—disclosed only to the U.S. Justice Department— proving his personal high-level involvement in transportation matters while serving on General Stahl's staff.)

On the question of whether or not Waldheim had advance knowledge of the ultimate destiny of the Italian troops whose surrender he helped negotiate and whom he helped transport from Greece, the commission concluded that "the German authorities in Athens and Salonika knew . . . before the handover of weapons by the 11th Army, that not a single Italian soldier would be returned to his country. . . . Waldheim was fully briefed on the disbandment and removal of the Italian 11th Army . . . hardly a single German soldier believed that the Italians were to be transported back to their homeland."

As "O3" at Arsakli/Salonika, the commission declared, Waldheim's duties "extended far beyond the mere gathering of intelligence data." For example, the "O3" (Waldheim) "could be brought in to work as a specialist" on Army Group E *operational* orders for fighting a war "by means of 'reprisals' and 'cleansing operations.' " In discussing

Waldheim's "O3" responsibilities, the commission also confirmed what we had been saying about the daily and evening intelligence reports that Waldheim had signed "for correctness"—namely, that not only had he certified them in this fashion, but he frequently was also their *author* (as Army Group E's organizational chart had disclosed all along). I wondered whether Wiesenthal would now charge that these eminent war historians were—like the WJC—"misreading" the German military text in this connection.

Warnstorff, Poliza, and Waldheim all gave the commissioners essentially the same story. Warnstorff conceded that the section had a "general knowledge" of reprisal activities, but denied that either he or Waldheim knew about the specific orders. Poliza declared that any material addressed to Ic/AO went directly to the AO Branch. Waldheim said that he knew only "a fraction of what Warnstorff knew." But the commission discerned a different message in the paperwork trail, confirming that Waldheim had "knowledge of numerous 'reprisal and cleansing' actions." The commissioners concluded that while "he had no part in the decision-making process," he "was certainly party to what was afoot." Antipartisan warfare, they emphasized, was *"the* issue in the South East." (Emphasis in original.)

In connection with the commando incidents, the commission noted that Waldheim had "consistently rejected allegations that he was involved." Then, after disclosing that Warnstorff admitted to the commission that "I certainly read" Hitler's Commando Order, the historians stated their own standard for judging complicity in these war crimes:

> The transmission of records of the interrogation of Allied commandos was directly related to their eventual fate. . . . Involvement of this type qualifies as the obeying of orders in full knowledge of the fact that the order was criminal in intent.

The commission observed that, in passing on the commando interrogation transcripts despite his own knowledge of Hitler's order, "it could be argued that" Waldheim "was effectively giving orders, in clear knowledge that the orders would lead to criminal acts."

The commission noted that executions of commandos were usually carried out "in the dead of night," a fact, it said, that indicated "intensified consciousness of wrongdoing." While some German officers had saved prisoners from *Sonderbehandlung* by passing the names of captured soldiers to the Red Cross, Waldheim admitted to the commission that he had never done so. The commission noted pointedly that others who refused to take part in Nazi crimes had not even received serious punishment.

The report confirmed that the Greek sailor Lisgaris, captured on Alimnia Island and temporarily spared as a potential witness to present to the Turkish government, was eventually delivered to the SD and executed like the others. Before his death, another prisoner recalled seeing him "with one leg half rotted away." The commission noted that this was "obviously . . . a consequence of 'stringent interrogation' by the SD."

Who then was it at Ic/AO who initiated and transmitted the telex that, in the commission's words, "accelerat[ed] the expected fatal outcome of the prisoners' treatment"? The commissioners acknowledged that it was a mystery that probably could never be solved. But they were, at least, able to eliminate one prime suspect. Noting that the matter had been declared "exclusively Ic's task," they ruled out the Abwehr officer, Major Hammer. This left only Warnstorff, Waldheim, and, possibly, Waldheim's deputies Poliza and Krohne. In any event, there was the April 21, 1944, cover letter, clearly initialed by Waldheim, transmitting to Army Group F Poliza's interrogation reports on the "commandos."

The report's conclusion on the commando question found that President Waldheim was indeed criminally implicated in "the anticipated fatal series of events":

> After the Commando Order [by Hitler] of 18 October 1942, any report which said "We have commando prisoners here" meant that the fate of such men was as good as sealed . . .
>
> It emerges from this course of events that Waldheim knew precisely what was going on with regard to the commandos, since several of those papers that survived, concerning commando prisoners, interrogations, and the handing over of such prisoners to the SD, passed across his desk. *By initialing such documents, First Lieutenant Waldheim was involved [eingeschaltet] in the knowledge of and the chain of events . . .* [Emphasis added.]

Did Waldheim know about Jewish deportations from Greece? The commission first quoted from numerous Waldheim statements that he was ignorant of the fate of the Jews, such as the declaration in his March 1986 telex to Edgar Bronfman that he had "never" been involved or even "informed about" the deportation of Jews from Greece. The commission reported that Waldheim repeated this denial to them, and declared flatly that it "is unbelievable. As we know from many statements given under oath, this was common knowledge."

The historians further took issue with Waldheim's assertion that the Wehrmacht was not involved in these deportations, declaring, "There is ample proof that the Wehrmacht in general and Army Group E in particular was involved in deportation of Jews."

The commission also was sharply critical of the "White Book" that the Austrian Foreign Ministry had issued the preceding year to defend President Waldheim against the Nazi charges. The report noted, for example, that the White Book's compilers were "at pains to prove . . . that a strict division of the functions of AO and Ic was in force, and that therefore Waldheim could not have any knowledge of the activities of AO in his branch. . . ." The commission's response: Both documentary evidence and witness testimony "contradicted" and "refuted" this claim.

After considering the mass of evidence, the commissioners concluded with an indictment that must have shaken the former U.N. chief to the depth of his being:

> The resulting picture is one of varying proximity to criminal measures and orders under the rules of war. . . . In general, some guilt must arise simply from knowledge of violation of human rights, when the person concerned—through lack of personal strength or courage—neglects his duty as a human being in intervening against injustices. . . .
>
> The Commission has received no indication of any case in which Waldheim raised objection to, protested at, or took steps against an order for an injustice of which he was certainly aware, in order to prevent or at least hinder the realization of the injustice. On the contrary, he repeatedly assisted in connection with illegal actions and thereby facilitated their perpetration.

Two sources reported privately that Waldheim, during a meeting with Chancellor Vranitsky and Vice-Chancellor Mock, declared that he was not surprised by the commission's conclusion, because three of its members were Jews.[1] The charge was not only despicable, it was incorrect; only two of the seven historians were Jewish.

"He repeatedly assisted in connection with illegal actions and thereby facilitated their perpetration."

Those concluding words by the historians commission should have been the end of it. Labeled by the commission as a Nazi war crimes facilitator and a liar, Waldheim surely would now have to resign the presidency in disgrace, much like the far less seriously implicated Richard Nixon. The Austrian government would certainly never prosecute him for war crimes; the Israelis might make some noise about pressing for extradition and trial, but nothing was likely to come of it. Most likely, Waldheim would retire into the netherworld of defrocked politicians and live out the remainder of his years in acrimony and anger. Perhaps, like Nixon, he would receive a multimillion-dollar book contract.

I knew that I would be satisfied if he just went away. That was all I had wanted from the very start.

But now Waldheim and the People's Party, once again aided and abetted by the friendly Austrian press, pulled off perhaps their greatest and most audacious coup, quite possibly the most unlikely gambit in what was now a forty-three-year-old cover-up. One day *before* the commission's report was released to the media, the Austrian Press Service, the official press arm of Waldheim's government, was allowed an exclusive on the story. And the story that was put out that day should serve as a case study for would-be "spin-doctors" the world over. The Austrian Press Service declared that the commission had "found no evidence" that Waldheim took part in war crimes. Foreign Minister Alois Mock weighed in immediately as well, crowing that it was now clear that Waldheim had no personal culpability in crimes. Waldheim himself added that his role in the war "was the normal fate of a young Austrian."

Quite naturally, the story dominated the domestic press and was picked up by newspapers and television networks around the world, which dutifully put out the "shock" story of Waldheim's innocence before they had a chance to see the commission's full report.

The impotent commissioners were caught completely by surprise. Too late, they staged their own press offensive, angrily denying the accuracy of the story released by the Austrian Press Service. When asked by a BBC reporter whether Waldheim should resign, Manfred Messerschmidt, who had initially been thought to be "in Waldheim's pocket," discarded his previous reluctance to render any "political" verdicts. "Yes. I think so. Yes." Waldheim, he asserted, had not only a general knowledge of war crimes "but a certain kind of involvement."[2]

During the historians' ninety-minute press conference, commission historian Yehuda Wallach came close to shouting as he excoriated the Austrian newspapers for printing headlines that misrepresented what the commission had done. Once again, the domestic press had embraced an utterly bogus pro-Waldheim story. *Kronenzeitung,* the country's largest paper, had run a banner headline, "Historians Found No Personal Guilt on Waldheim's Part"—with the word "No" underlined in red. *Kurier,* the second largest paper, weighed in with "Waldheim Is No War Criminal!" The headline in *Neues Volksblatt,* the People's Party newspaper, boomed "All the

Facts Exonerate Waldheim!" Wallach was furious. "That simply isn't in our report," he declared. "That stands in starkest contrast to our findings." Fellow commission member Messerschmidt made the same point in his remarks.

In Washington, a U.S. Justice Department spokesperson stated that the findings demonstrated that Waldheim was complicit in war crimes under the Nuremberg standards. In Moscow, by contrast, First Deputy Foreign Minister Anatoly G. Kovalev said that the report demonstrated that "Waldheim was not an accessory to the crimes charged against him" and added, "We regard Mr. Kurt Waldheim as the president of Austria." In Vienna, former Austrian Chancellor Bruno Kreisky's reaction to the commission's report was to call for Waldheim to step down. It was "not good for Austria," he declared, "to have a liar on the top of the state." Fellow Austrian Simon Wiesenthal for once agreed with his old nemesis Kreisky—but with a different explanation. Four months earlier, when the historians were just beginning their work, the Nazi-hunter had stated that if the commission cleared Waldheim, he could then resign (in the interest of restoring Austria's international image) without the departure being interpreted as an admission of guilt. Now that the results were in, Wiesenthal told reporters that Waldheim should be "persuaded to resign." Wiesenthal explained that Waldheim could now give up his post as head of state "without loss of face." The Nazi-hunter's explanation was nearly as fatuous as the conclusion it was supposed to justify. "[T]he worst accusation, that of war crimes, is over with the report," Wiesenthal declared.[3]

Professor Wallach, the Israeli member of the commission, wrote in the *Washington Post* a few days later that the "dubious attempts" of Waldheim, his political allies, and the Austrian press to interpret the commission's report as an acquittal "were short-lived." Anyone who reads the report, he declared, "understands that the findings of the commission by no means rehabilitate Waldheim. Quite the opposite is true."[4]

In the court of world opinion, however, such statements came far too late. It is an unfortunate truth of the news business that the first story is almost always the one that sticks. Indeed, in the days that followed, although some press coverage was finally given to the damning conclusions reached by the commission, I discovered that most people, including the majority of the free world's reporters and editors, tended to remember only the first story—*the big lie*—that Waldheim was "exonerated."

To my astonishment and dismay, I saw that lie persist and gain near-universal acceptance.

444 ELI M. ROSENBAUM

Waldheim remained in office.
Incredibly, the gambit had *worked*.

Proof, as if more was needed, of the extent to which the Waldheim affair had corrupted Austrian life was visible on American television screens within days of the release of the historians commission report, when former Austrian resistance figure Fritz Molden appeared on ABC's "Nightline" program to discuss the case. Held out by his countrymen for decades, however ridiculously, as "proof" of the supposedly vigorous opposition to the Nazis within wartime Austria, Molden was also a longtime patron and friend of Waldheim. But whatever credibility he might have had was destroyed when he informed his American viewers that not only was Kurt Waldheim blameless vis-à-vis the Jews of Greece, but the whole German army was as well:

> Neither his [Waldheim's] commanding officers or anybody in the German Army in Greece had the slightest thing to do with these [Jewish] deportations. This was not their business. It was the business of the SS and of the Nazi police.[5]

Former Foreign Minister Karl Gruber, Waldheim's steadfast supporter and onetime boss, descended even further into the gutter. He attributed the report's harsh criticism of Waldheim to the (supposed) fact that it was authored by a Socialist and by Jews who were indignant that Austria had not paid war reparations. A short time later, in an interview with a French journalist, Waldheim's daughter, Christa Karas-Waldheim, blamed her father's woes on the Socialists, the World Jewish Congress (which "used my father" for "the sole aim of getting into the news"), and the media. "One must not forget that the press is in Jewish hands, particularly in the United States," the young attorney explained.[6]

No sooner had the historians commission report been released in Vienna than Waldheim found himself having to confront evidence newly discovered in Vienna and far from home, in London and Johannesburg.

First, Richard Mitten, an American writer living in Vienna, and Hans Schafranek, an Austrian writer, made a remarkable discovery about Waldheim's prewar Nazi affiliations. Poring over the records of the old Consular Academy, they caught Waldheim in yet another audacious lie, this one more than forty years old. As *Profil* had disclosed shortly after the Waldheim affair began, Waldheim, on January 25, 1946, filed with the Provincial High Court in Vienna a formal explanation of his prewar activities. In his court paper, filed for "denazification" purposes, he insisted that he had never actually been a "member" of the SA, as his SA cavalry organization was "of a purely sporting nature" and his "affiliation" with the Nazi Student Union was similarly without real substance. To bolster his case, he added that because of his and his family's hostility to the Nazis, "the scholarship granted to me prior to March 1938 by the Austrian Chamber of Commerce and Industry to study at the Consular Academy was cancelled . . . so that I had great difficulty in finishing my studies."

The new documents shattered Waldheim's story completely. They showed not only that Waldheim did not receive his scholarship from the ardently pro-Nazi Chamber of Commerce until May 25, 1938—that is, two months *after* Nazi Germany's March 1938 annexation of Austria—but also that it was awarded only upon Waldheim's presentation of proof of his "pure Aryan descent" (four Aryan grandparents) and upon submission of a May 18, 1938, letter from Friedrich Hlavac von Rechtwall, the Director of the Academy, attesting to Waldheim's attachment to Nazi ideology. Hlavac assured the Chamber that Waldheim "has been a convinced Nazi for years."[7]

As Mitten and Schafranek pointed out, Hlavac was almost surely exaggerating when he wrote of Waldheim's having been a committed Nazi "for years." But the documents suggested that a strong motive for Waldheim's having sought to join Nazi organizations was (as it was for so many other Austrians and Germans) his belief that it would advance his career. The documents also indicated, Mitten and Schafranek wrote, that "Waldheim's readiness to accommodate, his nearly instinctive penchant for ingratiating himself with anyone who might advance his career, seem to have begun early."[8]

President Waldheim responded to the revelation by resorting to a time-tested tactic: professing ignorance. "I did not know that," he insisted. "I had no idea of this exchange of correspondence. This is the first time I was informed of it."[9]

But there was no way Waldheim could explain his way out of the fact that his story about the cancellation of his scholarship after the *Anschluss* was, as Mitten put it, "a fairy tale."

Austria's embattled president was facing crisis after crisis now. Even while Mitten and his collaborators were digging into the Consular Academy records, British journalists at last were able to trace the British prisoners captured in the Ioannina area on May 6, 1944—Captain Bluett, Captain Hamilton, Soldier Davies, and Soldier Bennett. We had seen, almost two years earlier, the captured document reporting that the four men "are to be transferred to Army Group E/Dept. Ic in Salonika." Foreign Secretary Howe had advised M.P. Greville Janner in November 1986 that while the Ministry of Defence determined that all four men had survived the war, they had "suffered ill treatment" while held captive in Salonika. Howe's refusal to elaborate or to release the government's documentation had prevented us from pursuing the matter further.

Until now. With the discovery of Captain Bluett—Charles Bluett—in Johannesburg, it was at last possible to learn the key details. During his first interrogation in Salonika, in which an interpreter in Wehrmacht uniform participated, he was beaten with rubber truncheons by two SS men for a half hour. Later, he was lined up with other prisoners before a Wehrmacht firing squad, which actually fired, striking at least one prisoner. He was then taken away and questioned again by the same people as before, an interrogation that ended with the arrival of a tall, slim Wehrmacht officer who spoke to his questioners in German. But he did not get a clear look at the officer's face, and hence was unable to say whether or not it was Waldheim.[10]

But even as Bluett was sharing his recollections with a Thames Television producer, a far more serious assault on Waldheim's past was taking place back in London.

Nearly a year earlier, we had begun circulating to journalists, especially in the U.K., the "Warren" document that Hans Safrian had found for us—the secret May 8, 1944, report, heavily censored after the war (apparently by U.S. authorities), concerning the interrogation of a group of prisoners captured in March 1944 off the coast of the Greek island of Cephalonia. Most importantly, the report, which was signed by Major Hammer and initialed with the W that I now knew with certainty to be Waldheim's, described one of the prisoners—a man whose identifying data had been concealed with black tape prior to microfilming, all save his last name, "Warren"—as a member of a *"Sabotagetrupp."* The report, clearly written by Waldheim himself, was addressed to Army Group F, and seemed likely to have doomed Warren—whoever he was—to a gruesome fate under the terms of the Fuehrer's Commando Order.

We had circulated the document worldwide in the desperate hope that somone somewhere would be able to trace Warren and ascertain both his fate and the veracity of Waldheim's 1944 intelligence analysis—strangely devoid of supporting evidence—that Warren was on a "sabotage" assignment.

Suddenly, on March 11, 1988, all the answers poured forth. Robert Fisk, of the *Times* of London, had found Warren's family, in Australia. "Warren" was Captain David Allan La Touche Warren, a shy but dashingly handsome Brisbane-born volunteer in the Royal Northumberland Fusiliers who had been recruited by Britain's legendary Special Operations Executive (SOE) to be infiltrated into Greece as a liaison with the partisans. He was twenty-nine years old at the time of his capture off Cephalonia. As I had feared, Captain Warren vanished in German captivity after Waldheim labeled him a saboteur. His family had labored in vain to trace him after the war.

But the key to the mystery was back in London, in the person of Warren's SOE commanding officer, Colonel Christopher M. ("Monty") Woodhouse. When the *Times* found him, he was serving as visiting professor in the Department of Byzantine and Modern Greek Studies at King's College, University of London. Shown Waldheim's report for the first time, a shocked Woodhouse was at last learning the particulars of the fate that had befallen the young officer he had sent on what turned out to be his final mission, forty-two years earlier.

As he read Waldheim's intelligence analysis, Woodhouse went from sadness to surprise, and then to rage. It was, he declared, "nonsensical" to conclude that "Bunny" Warren had been on any kind of "sabotage" mission. Woodhouse revealed to the *Times* that all Warren had been doing at the time of his capture was trying to help a tiny group of escapees *get to freedom* in Italy: a U.S. Air Force P.O.W., three Poles, and fifteen Russian deserters from German military service. He was on a *mission of mercy* to rescue escaped prisoners of war![11]

Woodhouse, the author of numerous books on Greece, immediately set out to put his thoughts on paper, and by August he had prepared a draft article on the Warren case for Britain's *Encounter* magazine. A friend in London faxed a copy of the draft to me. In it, Woodhouse described Bunny Warren as "one of the nicest" of his wartime officers. Kurt Waldheim, he declared, "being no fool, could not possibly have derived such nonsensical conclusions in good faith from properly and honestly conducted interrogations." But by labeling Warren part of a *Sabotagetrupp,* Waldheim "brought Warren inexorably within the scope of Hitler's Commando Order." That, in turn, was "equivalent to a sentence of death."

Woodhouse had now learned that Captain Warren was executed "on or soon after 15 May"—the day after Waldheim's intelligence report was received at command headquarters.

The Austrian president, the old SOE commander concluded bitterly, was "an accessory in the murder of my friend."

The charge elicited no response from the Hofburg Palace.[12]

34

The Simon Wiesenthal legend continued to flourish. Represented by a premier New York speakers' bureau, he was able to charge $17,000 per lecture; the promotional literature distributed by the bureau to prospective sponsors of Wiesenthal's lectures continued to describe him as the man who helped apprehend "nearly 1,100 Nazi criminals" and who made possible Israel's 1960 apprehension of Adolf Eichmann. He published an updated version of his memoirs, with the opening biographical sketch authored by *Profil* publisher Peter Michael Lingens. In the book, Wiesenthal refers to Lingens—whose opening sentence calls Wiesenthal "the 'Eichmann hunter' "—as his "friend of many decades" who "has worked for some time in my office."[1] Lingens's prefatory contribution to the book repeated the story of Wiesenthal's miraculous "Sunday evening mass" escape from certain death in 1941. Referring to the millions who had not managed to escape the ghettos and death camps, Wiesenthal declared in an afterword, "I want to be their mouthpiece. . . ."

Appalled by Sir Laurence Olivier's fictional cinematic portrayal of him as a bumbler in *The Boys from Brazil,* Wiesenthal had long refused to sell the motion picture rights to his life story unless he was guaranteed creative control. Finally, the Home Box Office cable network agreed, and *The Murderers Among Us—The Simon Wiesenthal Story,* went into production. The film repeated all the standard Wiesenthal tales, including his purported role in the capture of Eichmann and others. It said nothing, however, about Waldheim. Ben Kingsley, who had won an Oscar for his portrayal of Gandhi in the film of the same name, played Wiesenthal. The film received the Emmy award for "Best Writing—Miniseries or Special."

In November 1988, Wiesenthal celebrated his eightieth birthday with a gala dinner at New York's Marriott Marquis Hotel. I received an invitation, indicating that the Wiesenthal Center, which sponsored the dinner, had not done a very good job of culling its mailing list. The keynote speech was delivered by none other than German Chancellor Helmut Kohl. A few Jewish activists protested Kohl's participation (emphasizing his support of Kurt Waldheim and his role in the Bitburg affair), but Wiesenthal and the Los Angeles organization bearing his name would not be deterred.

That same month, Wiesenthal received the Jabotinsky Award from the Anti-Defamation League of B'nai B'rith for "courageous Jewish leadership." A League official, in presenting the award, lauded Wiesenthal for his role in the Eichmann capture.

One had to be impressed with the ability of the carefully cultivated Wiesenthal legend to survive his many mistakes, embarrassments, and false claims. He had no equal as a self-promoter.

Privately, even Wiesenthal Center officials confessed to me their skepticism of Wiesenthal's claimed prowess. A 1974 analysis of Wiesenthal's Nazi-hunting career by one writer had concluded, perhaps a bit too harshly, that "he was personally responsible for the eventual downfall of only two." Embarrassingly for the man who has long taken credit for bringing to justice no less than eleven hundred Nazi criminals, one Wiesenthal Center official asserted that the Nazi-hunters actual tally was in the "tens."[2]

This theme had actually been debated in a series of letters to the editor of the *Jerusalem Post* back in the spring and summer of 1986, prompted by Wiesenthal's strange behavior in those early months of the Waldheim affair. Avner Less, who had interrogated Eichmann for the Israeli police, angrily challenged Wiesenthal's "claim to be the world's foremost Nazi-hunter," raising questions about his involvement in the Eichmann and Mengele cases, among others. His letter to the editor laid down the gauntlet:

> I think that we, the survivors of the extermination of our people by the Nazi mass-murderers, have the right to request a fully balanced statement from Mr. Wiesenthal of his Nazi-hunting activities during these many years.[3]

Israeli writer Wim van Leer, shocked by Wiesenthal's conduct in the Waldheim affair, related in the same newspaper that he had once asked West Germany's chief war crimes prosecutor what Wiesenthal had contributed to the pursuit of justice in Nazi cases. The man had smiled and replied, "Mr. Wiesenthal is a Nazi *hunter,* not a Nazi *finder."* After van Leer's charge was published, the official in question, Alfred Streim, was beseeched to come to Wiesenthal's defense. However, the best that Streim could say was that information supplied by Wiesenthal had led to court action in "a few cases."[4]

OSI Director Neal Sher had received a similar plea from Wiesenthal. Dutifully, Sher wrote a letter to the *Jerusalem Post.* "I have come to know and work closely with Mr. Wiesenthal and his office in Vienna," Sher wrote. "I can attest to the fact that Mr. Wiesenthal and his archives have been relied upon frequently by this office. . . . [H]e has been and continues to be an invaluable source of information and sound counsel."[5]

The words would soon come back to haunt the Justice Department prosecutor, especially after he and Wiesenthal had a falling out over the Waldheim case. Later, in a private letter to Wiesenthal (indiscreetly shared by the Vienna Nazi-hunter with a New York acquaintance he hoped would rise to his defense),* Sher bluntly told Wiesenthal what he *really* thought of him—and his "information":

> In general, I can tell you that a few of your allegations have resulted in active, ongoing investigations. The vast majority, however, were of little value: many "suspects" had long been dead; in many instances, you did not furnish basic identifying data, thus rendering the allegations virtually useless; as to others, there is no record of entry into the United States; in some cases, you have identified the wrong person; in other cases, you have not even provided what could fairly be termed an "allegation"; and, in many instances, we could uncover no incriminating evidence. In this regard it is important to note that you have not provided OSI with any concrete *evidence* against the individuals named in your correspondence. Moreover, several specific requests to you seeking such evidence have gone unanswered.

And then Sher delivered his coup de grâce:

> The "bottom line" is that, to my knowledge, for at least the time that I have served as Director, no allegation which has originated from your office has resulted in a court filing by OSI.[6]

One of the unpredictable results of the Waldhcim affair was to bring to the surface the documentation that would at last prove the utter falsity of Wiesenthal's claims regarding his role in the Eichmann case. Ironically, it was the idolizing HBO film that finally proved Wiesenthal's undoing. Isser Harel, shown promotional material for the film during a visit to New York in 1988, could contain his disgust no longer. Upon his return to Israel, the former Mossad chief methodically set to work assembling a full record of the Vienna avenger's involvement in the case. A copy of the 278-page package made its way to me.

Harel minced no words in stating categorically that "in the matter

---

*The acquaintance passed copies of the letter on to many others, including the World Jewish Congress, which made it public.

of the capture-operation [of Eichmann in 1960] he [Wiesenthal] had played no part." Harel derided Wiesenthal's various claims, from the "Baron M." episode to the claimed importance of his purported role in blocking a postwar attempt by Vera Eichmann to have her husband declared dead. Of a meeting between Wiesenthal and Israeli agents "Michael and Meir" at which, according to Wiesenthal's 1967 *The Murderers Among Us* memoirs, he turned over photographs of Eichmann, Harel declared that "no such meeting ever took place."

The information that Eichmann was hiding in Argentina had come from German prosecutor Fritz Bauer, Harel emphasized, not from Wiesenthal. In one remarkable passage, Harel quoted from Wiesenthal's book *I Hunted Eichmann*—published in Germany in 1961, a year *after* Eichmann's apprehension by Harel's hand-picked team of Mossad agents. In the book, Wiesenthal claimed that something that Eichmann's children had said after the war, before the family vanished from Austria, had clued him in to the fact that their destination was Argentina:

> According to the story told by Eichmann's children before they left, it seemed likely that they had gone to live somewhere out in the Argentinian pampas, since they said they would be going to a big farm, where they could ride horses and would have an "uncle."[7]

In writing these words, Wiesenthal had presumably calculated that no one would ever disclose the contents of a September 23, 1959, letter he wrote to the Israeli ambassador in Vienna. But here, in Harel's package, was a photocopy of that very letter, written eight months *before* Eichmann's apprehension. In it, Wiesenthal had expressed the view that the children's words indicated that the family was bound for *Germany:*

> The children's school friends say that Eichmann's three sons had told them—before leaving school—that they will be going to a property with vast lands, where one can also do horseriding. Due to still additional ways of expressing themselves, the impression was that they might be talking about Northern Germany.[8]

"A minor bit of touching up," wrote Harel, tongue firmly in cheek. "Northern Germany instead of the Argentinian pampas."

Harel also did a thorough job of debunking Wiesenthal's oft-repeated claim to having just missed capturing Eichmann in Austria in 1949. Wiesenthal's 1967 book, *The Murderers Among Us,* contains a breathless account of a daring mission to which, he writes, he was a party on December 31, 1949, to capture Eichmann. The plan was to apprehend the fugitive Nazi as he stole away from his hideout in the vicinity of the Austrian Alpine village of Grundslee to pay a surreptitious New Year's Eve visit to his wife in the nearby town of Altaussee. Wiesenthal's description of the mission, which ended in failure when, according to the book, Eichmann fled back to Grundslee after receiving an apparent warning, is nothing short of high drama.[9] But, as Harel documented, it is (to use the former Mossad chief's words) "pure fantasy" to claim a near-miss in capturing Eichmann. The key to Harel's analysis: a confidential June 1, 1960, letter from Wiesenthal to the Israeli ambassador in Vienna that Harel's manuscript reproduces as an exhibit. In that letter, written seven years *before* the worldwide publication of Wiesenthal's account of the 1949 close call in the Austrian Alps, the Nazi-hunter wrote that "rumors" that Eichmann had been sighted in the late 1940s in the Aussee region of Austria were incorrect. Wiesenthal actually conceded in his letter to the Israeli ambassador that, since 1945, Eichmann had "never again" set foot in Austria! (Indeed, at the time of the nonexistent close call, Eichmann was hiding out in Germany, and was only months away from making his escape, via Italy, to Argentina.)

Harel's dissection of Wiesenthal's claims, while confirming what I had long believed to be the truth, was nonetheless something of a shock to read. It really *was* true, then, that the arrest that had made Wiesenthal famous around the world was an accomplishment that owed, in Harel's words, "precisely nil" to the Nazi-hunter's investigative efforts. The memory of how, as a youngster, I had thrilled to Wiesenthal's heroic account in *The Murderers Among Us* now served only to heighten the sense of betrayal I felt as a result of his conduct in the Waldheim affair.*

Wiesenthal's behavior remained arguably the most baffling part of the entire Waldheim episode. Despite Schuller's early warning, and

---

*In 1989, when Harel's material was made available to the Jewish Telegraphic Agency, the Simon Wiesenthal Center responded in part by providing JTA reporter Susan Birnbaum with an incorrect translation of a November 10, 1959, letter to Wiesenthal from Yecheskel Sachar, the Israeli ambassador to Austria. In the letter, Sachar advises Wiesenthal that he had discussed the Eichmann case with "our people" in Israel and that "according to the last reports that are in their possession, the Eichmann family is in Argentina." The Wiesenthal Center translation, however, makes it appear that these reports were instead in *Wiesenthal's* possession and that Ambassador Sachar, rather than informing Wiesenthal that the Eichmanns were in Argentina, was telling him that the Israelis had confirmed Wiesenthal's information: "As per the last memos, which *you* have, the Eichmann family is in Argentina." (Emphasis added.) When reporter Birnbaum tried to report on what she had received from the Wiesenthal Center, the JTA refused to transmit her story. That same cancelled dispatch was to report on the JTA's telephone interview with Rafi Eitan, the Mossad agent who was the first to physically capture Eichmann. Eitan confirmed Harel's claim that Wiesenthal had played no role in locating Eichmann.

my own realistic view of Wiesenthal, I never dreamed that he would attempt to assist Waldheim in any way. Once we revealed what Waldheim had concealed, there was no doubt in my mind that Wiesenthal would, as he had done in other cases involving less serious Nazi cover-ups, call for an immediate inquiry and full disclosure—or at least for Waldheim to explain why he had lied all these years. Instead, he had fought us every step of the way, using tactics completely at odds with his own *modus operandi,* developed over four decades.

He refused to examine our evidence, yet criticized our conclusions. He repeatedly rejected charges that Waldheim was a war criminal (as though he had the means to adjudge such questions), insisting that there was "no evidence," and indicted the Austrian president only for his professed ignorance of Jewish deportations. He even accused us (and the U.S. government)—rather than the Waldheim campaign and the country's biggest newspapers—of inciting anti-Semitism in Austria, and he contrived bogus defenses for Waldheim.* He condemned us for using the fact of Waldheim's indictment by Tito's Yugoslavia and for interfering in another country's "internal politics"—even though he himself had combined these same two elements in a successful 1979 effort to destroy the political career of a leading official of the Australian Liberal Party.† In the 1970s, moreover, he had written proudly of having denounced a top political ally of the Socialists for having served in a German *unit* that committed crimes; and he had boasted of helping force the (long overdue) resignation of Germany's ambassador to New Zealand for having served in an *organization* (the Waffen-SS)—not even a unit—that took part in crimes. But somehow *Waldheim's* service in demonstrably criminal units was insufficient justification for similar action.‡

---

*The reader will recall such Wiesenthal "explanations" as his claim that the Wehrmacht was not involved in Jewish deportations from Salonika, his characterization of the Kozara deportees as "soldiers," his assertion that the Soviets and Yugoslavs would not have voted for Waldheim at the U.N. if they believed he was implicated in Nazi crimes, his declaration that the Historians Commission report meant that the war crimes accusations "are over" (and that Waldheim could resign "without losing face"), his charge that the WJC had accused Waldheim, from the start, of being a Nazi war criminal and his insistence that Waldheim was not the author of (and could not be blamed for) documents he had signed "for correctness."
†See Wiesenthal's January 31, 1980, annual report, in which he boasts that his allegations against the man, who "was on the verge of a political career . . . struck like a bomb," forcing him "to resign from all his political functions." On October 8, 1992, the Associated Press reported that Wiesenthal was again citing a Yugoslav indictment in exposing an alleged Nazi criminal, this time wartime Belgrade's "Commissioner for Jews."
‡See Wiesenthal's January 31, 1978, annual report, in which he discusses the case of Friedrich Peter, noting that the evidence implicated "not only the 1.SS Infantry Brigade, to which Peter belonged, but specifically his own company . . ." and Wiesenthal's January 31, 1980, annual report, in which he discusses the case of Karl Doering. Doering, denounced by Wiesenthal solely as a former "captain in the SS," had actually been found not guilty of any illegal actions by a de-Nazification court in 1948.

And he had pointed to the Kremlin's backing of Waldheim as ex-culpatory evidence, even though Wiesenthal was on record con-demning the Soviet puppet regime in East Germany for placing former Nazis in important positions and had denounced Moscow for branding him a Gestapo collaborator. On the plus side, it was Wie-senthal who proposed the establishment of the International His-torians Commission; on the minus side, he had falsely proclaimed that the commission's damning report exonerated Waldheim of war crimes.

It was still hard to believe that so bizarre—and prolonged—a reaction could have been provoked either by the damage to his ego caused by the WJC's having helped expose a Nazi "right under his nose in Vienna" or by the strength of his desire to avenge himself against the Austrian Socialist Party for the disparaging remarks that Bruno Kreisky had made about him years earlier. Even Wiesenthal's confidants seemed clueless. "I'm as mystified as you are," one of them told me.

I stared at my voluminous files and hoped that, just as they held the key to Waldheim's war years, so, too, might they one day help to explain the mysterious behavior of "the Avenger of the Six Million."

As I continued to research Kurt Waldheim's war record, I tried to remain alert for every possible connection between Wiesenthal and Waldheim.

I already knew that Wiesenthal had, on a number of occasions prior to our 1986 exposure of Waldheim's cover-up, vouched for the irreproachability of his record during the Nazi era. The *Wash-ington Post*'s John Goshko had told me of his experience in 1971, when then–Foreign Minister Waldheim was waging an ultimately unsuccessful campaign for Austria's presidency and Wiesenthal re-sponded to Goshko's inquiry by assuring the reporter that he had already checked Waldheim's record and found nothing worth pur-suing. A disenchanted former Wiesenthal collaborator had disclosed that the Nazi-hunter had given a similar response to "an American Jew" who had written to him during the 1970s inquiring about Wald-heim. Then, in 1980, there was the matter of Wiesenthal's effusive public praise of Waldheim in a letter to the *New York Times* for providing assistance in the Mengele hunt, at the very time that serious questions were being raised in New York (and then dropped as inconclusive) about Waldheim's record during the Nazi era. And I had in my files a memo on Leon Zelman's call to our offices on March 24, 1986, after we had disclosed the fact of Waldheim's CROWCASS and UNWCC listings, in which the survivor had played an audio recording of a Wiesenthal press conference that day—a press conference at which Wiesenthal revealed that when "some people came to me in the fall of 1985 and they were looking for material against him [Waldheim]. . . . I told them I had nothing of the sort . . ."*

In those last months preceding my initial visit to Vienna, the most tenacious of these pursuers, it had since been revealed, was Austrian historian Georg Tidl. In December 1985, Tidl, who had begun his quiet investigation of presidential candidate Waldheim, telephoned fellow Austrian Simon Wiesenthal. If anyone should know about Waldheim, Tidl had reasoned, it would be Wiesenthal. In response to Tidl's general inquiry, Wiesenthal replied that he had already checked the files and had concluded that everything was in order as far as the candidate's prewar and wartime records were concerned. Wiesenthal conceded that, prior to his service in the Wehrmacht, Waldheim might have been a member of a Nazi-sponsored riding unit, but said there was no proof of this.

Tidl asked Wiesenthal if he was aware of any evidence that Waldheim was still assigned to von Pannwitz's unit when it was absorbed into the infamous 15th SS Cossack Division, thereby, as Tidl put it, automatically making Waldheim an SS officer.

Wiesenthal responded that Waldheim had had nothing to do with that SS division and asked, somewhat sarcastically, "whether anyone in 1945 could have resisted the confederation of a Wehrmacht unit with the SS."

That was hardly the issue, Tidl replied.

Wiesenthal countered with a second hostile question: Was any of this really important?

Tidl certainly thought so, and he was confused by Wiesenthal's ease in issuing a clearance.[10]

But the most tantalizing of all the Wiesenthal links to Waldheim was not to become apparent until the autumn of 1987.

It must have been about 3 A.M. I sat at my desk in the upstairs study of my rented Washington town house. My eyes protested at the attempt to focus upon yet another piece of paper. Why was I pushing so? I had done my job. Waldheim was exposed and so what if much of the world did not want to hear any more about it? When could I give up this quest for—what?

Only idly did I peruse the pages in front of me. I was flipping

*Wiesenthal's statement was also mentioned in a story in the March 25, 1986, edition of the German daily *Die Welt*. In his angry piece in the June 1986 issue of *Ausweg*, Wiesenthal again noted that "last year already various people showed up in our office, called me on the phone, wrote me letters or looked me up, in order to get information on Dr. Waldheim." In the August 17 and August 24, 1987, issues of *Profil*, it was disclosed that two of those who queried Wiesenthal in 1985 were Johannes Fischer of Austrian television and Austrian historian Georg Tidl.

through the August 24 issue of *Profil,* which I had only recently received. A letter to the editor from Simon Wiesenthal immediately caught my attention. In his letter, the Nazi-hunter replied to a *Profil* story that detailed Wiesenthal's telephone conversation with Tidl in December 1985. The letter sought to justify Wiesenthal's answers to Tidl's inquiries about the possibility of Waldheim's having become an SS officer in the closing months of the war. His answers, Wiesenthal wrote, were based on information he had obtained *in 1979 from Berlin*—a "no records on file" response regarding Waldheim from the Berlin Document Center, *"and from the Wehrmachtauskunftstelle (WASt) a summary of Waldheim's war service."*

A sudden surge of adrenaline instantly banished my drowsiness. I was sitting ramrod straight now, my eyes riveted to the text of the letter that lay before me on the desk. There, at long last, was the beginning of the answer to the last unresolved mystery of the Waldheim affair, in cold black-and-white print, seemingly unnoticed by the rest of the world. Here, in an uncharacteristically quiet letter authored by Wiesenthal, was the piece that nearly completed the puzzle.

I was flabbergasted. *No wonder* the French government had been silent for the past year about the reason it had checked Waldheim's WASt file in 1979: Wiesenthal, as a nongovernment inquirer, was not supposed to be allowed access to those French-administered records. Now I knew why the French Prime Ministerial spokesman's explanation—that a junior official had written the WASt summary in 1979 but "apparently" not for any branch of the French government—had been so strange and incomplete. Some "junior French official" had, it was now obvious, performed an unauthorized favor, checking Waldheim's Wehrmacht service record and preparing a summary that made its way to Wiesenthal.

More importantly, it was now clear that Wiesenthal had the proof of the cover-up in his hands, way back in 1979— definitive proof that Waldheim had not, in fact, spent the midwar years studying law in Vienna, but instead had served in the Balkans with Army Group E. Why had he not made this astounding information public *then?* Indeed, what reason did he have in 1979 to persuade someone to copy the record for him?

Equally baffling was why he had continued to sit on the information years later, when he knew that others were checking on Waldheim.

Suddenly, a torrent of memories was unleashed. I could almost see Karl Schuller handing me, during my second and final trip to Vienna in February 1986, copies of Waldheim's WASt Wehrmacht records and directing my attention to the handwritten annotations that meant that "someone—but who?" had checked the then–

Secretary-General's records *in 1979*. Now we *knew* who, even if we still did not know *why*.

And I could not stop thinking about the irony that it had been the Los Angeles–based institution bearing Wiesenthal's name that had most aggressively pursued the "French" angle of the Waldheim story. How Wiesenthal must have cringed when he saw the Center's dean, Marvin Hier, complain to the press that the French government's explanation was unsatisfactory because it did not disclose why the French authorities had become interested in Waldheim in 1979 *or who ordered the records-check*.[11] Even more alarming to Wiesenthal must have been the charge by the Center's associate dean, Abraham Cooper, that "the central question" was "which French government agency or official requested this memo" and Cooper's angry denunciation of whoever "had access to this incredible information and did nothing then to see to it that the world's foremost human rights officer be held accountable for his trail of deceit and lies."[12]

I *had* to have the answer to the final questions: Why had Wiesenthal checked Waldheim's Wehrmacht records in 1979 and why had he kept silent all these years about the astounding cover-up that those documents plainly disclosed? And there was only one person who could answer those questions: Wiesenthal himself.

On December 9, 1987, I had dinner with Martin Mendelsohn, who, among his many other duties, was Wiesenthal's Washington lawyer. Choosing my moment, I said, "I want to speak with Simon."

Mendelsohn agreed to contact Wiesenthal. The word that came back from Vienna, however, was discouraging: Wiesenthal had no interest in speaking with me, either in person or by telephone.

"He won't talk to you," Mendelsohn reported. "Why don't you write him a letter, and I'll pass it on."

Having no other options, I accepted Mendelsohn's proposal. I labored on a five-page missive, which ultimately contained thirty-two questions, and dispatched it to Mendelsohn on January 4, 1989.*

Did Wiesenthal agree, I asked, that the Ic/AO Branch of Army Group E's High Command was "a criminal unit"? (I repeated the question for each of the principal units in which Waldheim served while in the Balkans.) Did he agree that Waldheim participated in Nazi-sponsored acts of persecution? Did he agree that the passing on of criminal orders "is itself a criminal act, as adjudged at Nuremberg?" Some of the questions concerned Wiesenthal's own conduct. "Have you ever publicly decried the anti-Semitism in Kurt Waldheim's election campaign?" And: "When did you learn of [General

---

*The full text of the letter is reprinted in the appendix.

Alexander] Loehr's involvement in crimes against Jews?" Then: "When did you first learn that Waldheim had served on Loehr's staff?" I even asked Wiesenthal whether, if *he* had been president of the WJC in March 1986, when we learned of Waldheim's listing by the U.N. War Crimes Commission on murder charges, "would you have withheld this information from public disclosure?" If so, "when, if ever, would you have revealed it?"

On and on went my questions. For me, the key question was number 29, on the last page, in which I directly asked Wiesenthal *why* he had reviewed Waldheim's Berlin files in 1979:

> In your letter published in the August 24, 1987, issue of *Profil,* you wrote that you had checked for records on Waldheim at the Berlin Document Center in 1979 and that you had received in the same year a copy of Waldheim's Wermachtauskunftstelle [WASt] file. I have several questions to ask in this connection.
>
> (a) Did this information come to you unsolicited or instead in response to your own inquiries?
>
> (b) If your answer to (a) was that you pursued this information on your own initiative, what prompted your investigation?[13]

Wiesenthal's response was not long in coming, although he declined to address himself directly to me. In a January 22, 1988, letter to Mendelsohn, whom he authorized to share it with me, the Nazi-hunter did everything *except* answer my questions. The questions, he complained, made it appear that I considered *him,* not just Waldheim, to be an "accused person." He added that he viewed "most" of my questions as "offending."

The Nazi-hunter recalled that he had met me while I was still at OSI and that I had "made a favorable impression" on him. OSI Director Neal Sher, he continued, "always spoke highly" of me.

With that preamble completed, Wiesenthal vented his spleen in the remaining six pages, attacking the Socialist Party (but, again, not the People's Party), Singer, Steinberg, another WJC official (a Holocaust survivor, in fact—whom he derided as "a sick man"), and, of course, me. The reason I had not contacted him during my trips to Vienna, wrote Wiesenthal, was that the WJC's principal goal was not pursuing justice; rather, it was facilitating the election of the Socialist candidate for president.

On finishing the letter, I could not help but admire, however begrudgingly, Wiesenthal's continuing mastery of the art of self-preservation, even in this eightieth year of his life. Many of my questions (such as the ones on "criminal units") were no-win propositions for him: Any conceivable answer he could give would be susceptible to a negative interpretation. His best strategy really was just to ignore the questions. And that was precisely what he did.

I was less angry about Wiesenthal's "nonresponsive response" than I was frustrated by my inability to obtain the answer to the riddle of his 1979 inquiries in Berlin. But by now, frustration seemed a normal state of affairs in the Waldheim matter.

Still, this time it was different. The final element of the Waldheim mystery seemed ever so slightly beyond my grasp.

Nothing about Sunday, May 8, 1988, appeared even remotely exceptional. I planned a quiet day at home, beginning with a couple of hours relaxing with the Sunday morning newspapers.

I found nothing of great interest in the *Washington Post*. Nor, at first, was I especially tempted to linger over anything I found in that day's massive *New York Times*. Eventually, I made my way to the *Times* Book Review Section. And then, without warning, I found myself reading the same passage over and over again. I felt a chill, as though the blood had suddenly drained from my face. Here was the answer I thought I would never see!

It was buried in a letter from Simon Wiesenthal to the editor of the Book Review. Had he slipped? If so, why? Perhaps he had tired of the battle. Perhaps he had grown careless in his old age, but I doubted this; he seemed to be as shrewd as ever. Perhaps he thought no one would realize the significance of his admission. Perhaps he feared that his former associate, who was now disseminating to me and others copies of papers from his office files, was about to disclose it independently. Or perhaps he surmised from my letter that I already knew the answer and was going to disclose it publicly. If so, by going on record, in a comparatively unlikely forum (where, moreover, few, if any, readers would possess the familiarity with the intricacies of the Waldheim case necessary to understand the true significance of Wiesenthal's words), he could later, if necessary, show that he had "never" hidden anything. It was even possible that he had somehow convinced himself by now that Waldheim's deception was a matter of small moment.

In his letter, Wiesenthal commented on writer Shirley Hazzard's criticism of Bob Herzstein's recently published book on Waldheim. Hazzard (the author of the *New Republic* piece in 1980 that had caused Congressman Stephen Solarz to check on Waldheim) had written in an earlier letter to the Book Review that, to her, it seemed doubtful that, as Herzstein claimed, Wiesenthal "had no reason to be suspicious" about Waldheim's war activities, a fact that Herzstein predicated on the assertion that the Nazi-hunter had been "unaware" that Waldheim had concealed his service with several units in the Balkans.*[14] Wiesenthal evidently could not resist a retort. While his letter undoubtedly seemed of only nit-picking significance to nearly all who read it, upon close examination, it held the elusive key to the greatest mystery of all: How had Waldheim managed to carry on his cover-up for so many years?

Wiesenthal's letter stated again that he had had the French report on Waldheim in his hands in 1979. But this time he disclosed his *reason* for checking on Waldheim that year: *The government of Israel,* he wrote, alarmed by Waldheim's hostile stance on Middle East questions, had asked him to do so.[15]

So there it was: He had done it for the Israelis! Wiesenthal added that he had acted on Jerusalem's request by having a "friend" make cursory inquiries in Berlin. (Obviously, a "junior French official" had helped.) Had Wiesenthal somehow missed the significance of the French data? Was this just another, albeit perhaps the worst, case of incompetence on his part? Wiesenthal provided his own answer in the letter, asserting that, in 1979, "I did not know he had not mentioned his Balkan years."

In mock self-punishment, I pretended to slap myself on the forehead as I realized what had happened: *The truth never came out while Waldheim was still at the U.N. because Wiesenthal had steered Israel— the only government in the world with both the incentive and the willingness to expose Waldheim—off the trail!* He had issued a clean bill of health for Waldheim, and the Israelis handling the matter, evidently having the same image of Wiesenthal-the-infallible-Nazi-hunter held by most of the rest of the world, had swallowed it.†[16]

So many things made sense now! I grabbed a pen and furiously began to make notes, spelling it out for myself. It was almost as though I feared that I needed to reduce it all to writing lest all that had been learned would somehow evaporate. And the more notes I made, the more everything began to fall into place.

Clearly, the major keepers of Waldheim's secret for the first twenty-five years of the cover-up were the Soviets and the Yugoslavs; their behavior as the disclosures surfaced these past two years reinforced that conclusion. For decades, both governments had possessed sufficient ammunition to destroy Waldheim's diplomatic career at

---

*At the time, Herzstein's publisher was also promoting his Waldheim book with advertisements that contained but a single testimonial: " 'Absolutely brilliant.'—Simon Wiesenthal."
†I asked contacts in Israel to seek out further details. They were able to confirm that Wiesenthal had, indeed, reported to the Israelis in 1979 that Waldheim was free of Nazi affiliations and that Jerusalem had foolishly relied on this assurance. Perhaps if Isser Harel had not resigned from the Mossad in the mid-sixties, a more realistic appraisal of Wiesenthal's abilities might have led Jerusalem to refrain from relying on the seal of approval he conferred on Waldheim.

will, but had refrained from using it. The Soviets, in particular, had benefited handsomely from Waldheim's actions over the years. The Kremlin surely could not have imagined, however, that the success of the cover-up would be ensured in its latter years by the man celebrated the world over as the greatest Nazi-hunter of them all (but openly reviled by the Soviet government for his statements in support of Jewish refuseniks and dissidents in the U.S.S.R.).*

Now it was at last obvious why Israel's U.N. ambassador, Yehuda Blum, had assured the *New York Times* in 1980 that the Israeli government was confident that Waldheim had not been a Nazi: The legendary Simon Wiesenthal had "cleared" him for Jerusalem. (The longstanding rumors that the handwritten dates in Waldheim's Berlin records reflected "Israeli inquiries" also made sense now.)

It seemed similarly clear to me why Wiesenthal had fought so frantically to shield Waldheim in the face of our disclosures, why he had attacked us at every opportunity, and why he had warned both the *New York Times* and OSI's Neal Sher against continuing to pursue Waldheim as they had been doing. Yes, he was doubtlessly embarrassed and angered by the WJC's encroachment on his "turf." And he certainly had his political reasons to support Waldheim, especially his hatred of Bruno Kreisky's Socialist Party. But there was something much more powerful at work, too. Having previously absolved Waldheim, Wiesenthal's reputation as the world's all-knowing authority on Nazi war criminals was now bound inextricably with Waldheim's desperate struggle to protect the secrets of his Nazi past. If Wiesenthal backtracked, or if Waldheim's pursuers succeeded independently, the Nazi-hunter would be forced to face the humiliation of having the Israelis know—and perhaps even make public— the fact that he had failed so horribly. Wiesenthal and Waldheim each had a secret, and their secrets would have to share the same destiny.

Now, too, it was clear why Wiesenthal had turned the *Kinder und Frauen* victims of Kozara into "soldiers"—and even more why he had stooped to denying the role of Army Group E in the Salonika Jewish deportations. The WASt document he had received way back in 1979 disclosed not only the fact that Waldheim served in Army Group E, but that he served in its High Command (*Oberkommando*), and not just briefly, but for *years* during the war. Had Wiesenthal

*Curiously, in July 1990, Wiesenthal—who had repeatedly asserted that Soviet support for Waldheim at the U.N. was strong evidence of his non-involvement in Nazi crimes—accused the U.S.S.R's puppet regime in the then–German Democratic Republic of having "blackmailed a variety of people" in the West with information about their Nazi pasts. See "East Germany's Stasi Blackmailed Nazis, Wiesenthal Says," Reuters dispatch, July 16, 1990.

not realized that Loehr's command was perpetrating crimes against Jews and others in tandem with the SS? At any rate, he must have been mortified when the WJC began to point out (and to document) the culpability of Army Group E's High Command, for it made him appear monumentally incompetent in the eyes of Israeli intelligence. It was bad enough if, in examining the WASt report in 1979, Wiesenthal had failed to deduce that it meant that Waldheim had covered up entire years of the war. But it was immeasurably worse if Wiesenthal had failed to realize the potentially sinister significance of a Wehrmacht assignment so clearly set forth in the document. And if Wiesenthal's ultimate incompetence ever became known to the general public, his reputation would be ruined.

I was struck by the thought of how he must have panicked when he realized that both *Profil* and the WJC had based some of their initial accusations on that very same WASt file! No wonder he declared, on the very first day of Waldheim's exposure, that there was "nothing at all incriminating" in the allegations against the former U.N. chief and insisted that the Soviets would never have voted for Waldheim had there been any evidence of wartime wrongdoing. And after offering this public exoneration—one that he could not have been in a position to prove—Wiesenthal had to hope against hope that no one would find hard evidence of Waldheim's own involvement in war crimes. His predicament had turned increasingly awkward as additional evidence against Waldheim came out, week after week. It was no longer surprising that Wiesenthal had not wanted to see what we had found, or that he had worked so tirelessly to discredit the WJC in the media and on Capitol Hill and to persuade the Justice Department to lay off Waldheim.

As detail after detail tumbled into the public arena, Wiesenthal was ever more hopelessly mired on the wrong side of one of the most sensational Nazi scandals of all time. But with his and Waldheim's reputations now linked forever, the man whose Congressional Gold Medal declares him "keeper of the flame of the conscience of mankind" had defiantly begun to take one position after another that was contrary to everything he had ever espoused before.

His bizarre conduct became fully understandable only now when I realized that he was not just defending Waldheim; he was defending *Wiesenthal!*

As I sat, all alone in the living room, brooding over what had become of my boyhood hero, I thought again of a related, almost equally improbable irony: It had been the *Simon Wiesenthal Center* that leveled the charge that whoever saw the WASt document and did not tell the world of its contents was covering up for Waldheim!

*   *   *

If one can be guilty of malpractice in the field of Nazi-hunting, this was surely it. Actually, the atrocious error that Wiesenthal had made in 1979 when he cleared Waldheim for the Israelis was hardly very surprising, given the extraordinary incompetence that has characterized the Nazi-hunter's biggest cases (and countless smaller ones) since the war. Indeed, if this blunder had been Wiesenthal's only offense in the Waldheim affair, it might have been forgivable.

But Wiesenthal's subsequent actions, at least those that followed Waldheim's initial exposure, were unpardonable, indeed unconscionable. He had used his "mandate" to help elect to Austria's presidency an accused Nazi war criminal—one whose campaign, moreover, reintroduced overt anti-Semitic parlance to the lexicon of major-party European politics for the first time since the Nazi era. He had given aid and comfort to some of the vilest hate-mongers in Austria, even adopting some of their code words in attacking the World Jewish Congress. By mid-1988, he was denouncing the WJC leadership in the Austrian press as "some psychopaths in America," telling an Austrian reporter that he had delivered the following condemnation to Singer and Steinberg in person: "When I look at you and see that you dare speak on behalf of world Jewry, I see what Hitler did to us."[17] Worst of all, he had resorted to the basest tactic of all: denying undeniable facts about the Holocaust and other Nazi barbarities. This act of utter indecency—the ultimate betrayal of Hitler's victims—is one that none of us, even those who knew the truth about Wiesenthal's Nazi-hunting "record," could ever have imagined him capable of committing. But how *could* anyone ever have predicted that, in order to protect his *own* reputation, Wiesenthal would sink to embracing the hideous syllogism at the heart of Waldheim's campaign of lies: If there were *no crimes,* then there was no cover-up.

At last I had the answers, even if they gave me no real comfort. The nightmare of the past two years was finally over. Or *was* it? I knew now that I had to see to it that the truth came out. That, however, would be a new and different kind of nightmare. It was one thing to take on Kurt Waldheim, a man who, in the words of WJC president Edgar Bronfman, had been part and parcel of the Nazi killing machine. But it was quite another to tell the truth about Simon Wiesenthal. Not only would the Nazi-hunter's many influential associates surely respond with rhetorical daggers drawn, but there would also be no joy for me in exposing the revered idol of my youth. Millions of people the world over—myself among them— had found great comfort in the thought that Hitler's surviving minions were being successfully pursued, to the farthest corners of the earth when necessary, by this nearly superhuman avenger. How reassuring it had been to know that the Nazis had not gotten away scot-free.

Tragically, *both* of these notions were at least 95 percent myth. And therein lies the continuing nightmare—of which men like Kurt Waldheim remain enduring symbols.

35

In mid-1989, America's dozen-year-old *Voyager 2* space probe completed its exploration of Neptune and embarked on a journey beyond our solar system. On its endless expedition into uncharted outer space, *Voyager* carries with it a twelve-inch-diameter gold-coated phonograph record encased in a protective aluminum jacket. Entitled *Sounds of Earth,* it was the brainchild of astronomer Carl Sagan, whose idea was to cast a bottle into the "cosmic ocean," in the event that some extraterrestrial society should intercept the space probe.

Included in the two-hour recording is an excerpt from Beethoven's Fifth Symphony; greetings in fifty-seven human languages; Chuck Berry's rendition of "Johnny B. Goode"; a message from the President of the United States in 1977, Jimmy Carter; and another from the Secretary-General of the United Nations that year, Kurt Waldheim.

In his 1978 book *Murmurs of Earth,* Sagan disclosed how Waldheim's message came to be included. One day in 1977, unannounced and wholly unsolicited, a tape-recorded statement arrived in the scientist's office. It was from Waldheim, who had learned of Sagan's invitation to President Carter and had brazenly decided to submit his own message as well, "on behalf of the people on our planet." The *Voyager* team decided that a message from the "chief human rights officer of the planet Earth" was indeed appropriate, so they included it.

On that disc that is now soaring silently through outer space, Waldheim's voice, in heavily-accented English, speaks for us all, assuring unknown intelligences in galaxies equally unknown that the people of Earth seek "only peace and friendship":

> As the Secretary-General of the United Nations, an organization of 147 member states who represent almost all of the human inhabitants of the planet Earth, I send greetings on behalf of the people of our planet. We step out of our solar system into the

universe seeking only peace and friendship, to teach if we are
called upon, to be taught if we are fortunate.

Sagan estimates that the recording of Waldheim as leader of the
human race will survive in outer space for more than one billion
years.[1]

On Earth, the notion of Waldheim as representative of the people
of our planet now seems as preposterous as his 1977 plaint to *The
Times* of London, "All I have is moral power." The revelations about
his past made it impossible for him to serve effectively even as
representative of the people of Austria. At this writing, he has recently completed his six-year term as president. Throughout, he
remained largely a prisoner of the Hofburg Palace, an increasingly
broken and embittered man given to ever less-subtle anti-Jewish
invective. Not once did he admit to so much as a single lie, much
less offer an explanation for the forty-six-year deception that finally
proved his undoing. His humiliating six-year quest for official invitations abroad succeeded only in a few Arab and Moslem countries,
and in tiny Lichtenstein. Not one major Western leader visited Vienna during Waldheim's term of office, so fearful were they of having
to decide whether to meet or snub him. Waldheim has been compared to Richard Nixon in the final weeks before the Watergate
scandal drove him from the White House; both men seemed oblivious to the consequences of what they had done. The comparison
fails, however, in part because there was never any public consensus
in Austria that Waldheim should resign. And he never did, although
he did announce in June 1991 that he would not seek reelection.
But even his belated withdrawal from public life will not end the
misery of never knowing when the next document will surface, what
it will reveal, or what additional revisions it will require in his ever-
changing story.

Der Spiegel characterized President Waldheim as a man who
"crosse[d] Austria back and forth," appearing at minor functions to
deliver "empty discourses." Manchester's *Guardian* newspaper
termed Waldheim a "spectre in the palace" who appeared "visibly
shaken" during his public appearances, and who "resemble[d] one
of those *Thunderbirds* [television show] puppets, with a bizarre habit
of extending his arms like a wraith." One of his few notable public
meetings was with Austrian-born bodybuilder-turned-actor Arnold
Schwarzenegger, who posed, grinning, with Waldheim, whom he
called "my president." Waldheim spokesman Gerold Christian reported that the two men were natural allies because "Waldheim is a
political bodybuilder."[2]

The closest Waldheim came to an official reception in a major foreign country was a visit he made to Bavaria in late March 1992. Invited to Germany by the conservative Peutinger Collegium Foundation to receive an award for his "contributions to world peace and freedom," Waldheim was met at a red-carpet ceremony at Munich's airport by an old friend, German Chancellor Helmut Kohl. Although the visit was technically "unofficial," Kohl's involvement—which marked the first (and, ultimately, only) time a Western leader met Waldheim outside Austria—was widely viewed as a calculated move specifically intended to destroy Waldheim's pariah status while there was still time; just twenty-nine days remained before elections in Austria to choose a successor to Waldheim.

Kohl's reception of Waldheim was followed by an elegant luncheon cohosted by the premier of Bavaria. The episode generated an outpouring of criticism that was even more abusive than that to which Kohl had been subjected during the Bitburg affair in 1985. The *Washington Post* accused the German chancellor of having "sought to draw a veil of silence over the past by honoring Waldheim," and it openly asked whether Kohl had been motivated by a desire to "appease" the growing number of anti-immigrant and neo-Nazi voters in the German electorate.[3] Other newspapers in the U.S. and abroad were even more caustic in their criticism of Kohl.[4] Munich's *Sueddeutsche Zeitung* called Kohl's behavior "a signal: Look here, we are somebody again! Take note, dear right-wing voters!"[5] The Israeli government was especially alarmed, with a spokesman for Prime Minister Yitzhak Shamir referring to "sinister winds now blowing through Europe" and the presidium of Israel's parliament calling a special session to denounce Kohl.[6] The meeting with Waldheim further damaged Kohl's already wretched standing in the Jewish world, especially as it took place on the heels of what columnist William Safire had dubbed the "Auschwitz-in-the-sand" scandal—the sensational disclosure by the German media that Kohl's government had stood idly by while a veritable legion of German companies helped Libyan madman Muammar Qadaffi develop a poison gas manufacturing capability.

Two weeks later, however, Kohl was treated to a spirited defense, in an op-ed piece in the *Jerusalem Post*. "Was Kohl trying to attract the right-wing vote by receiving Waldheim?" the piece asked. "Not at all," it assured the paper's readers. "German right-wingers never cared much about the Waldheim controversy, as Kohl, a political professional, was well aware." Anyway, there had never been any "concrete evidence" to "substantiate" the charges against Waldheim.

The author of the piece was Simon Wiesenthal.[7]

*   *   *

There is no chance that Kurt Waldheim will ever be brought to trial for war crimes. The Austrian government continues to defend him, as did *both* the Socialist Party and People's Party candidates in the 1992 election to succeed him.*[8] In any event, not since the 1970s has a suspected war criminal been tried in Austria. The United States has no criminal jurisdiction over Waldheim. Yugoslavia, ripped apart by a fratricidal civil war that broke out in 1991, is preoccupied with its own ongoing misery; in what is surely the most monstrous development in the Balkans since the end of the Second World War, 1992 saw the return of civilian detention camps to Bosnia, this time set up not by the Germans and Croats, but by Serbs bent on the systematic perpetration of murder, rape, deportation, and other crimes of mass terror in order to "ethnically cleanse" Bosnia of Moslems and other non-Serbs. Greek authorities have consistently kept a healthy distance from the Waldheim controversy. Even in the most unlikely event that Waldheim should find himself in Israel (Austria does not extradite its own citizens), trial would be difficult, for Israeli law focuses primarily on Nazi crimes against Jews, and the most damning and extensive evidence against Waldheim concerns crimes against non-Jews.

Nor, despite the dramatic and unexpected breakup of the U.S.S.R. in 1991, should one hold out much hope that additional fragments of the truth will emerge from Soviet archives. The Russian government has evidenced little, if any, appetite for making major public disclosures of intelligence data or for authorizing significant revelations about Soviet overseas intelligence operations. By early 1993, moreover, Russian officials were conceding their inability even to identify all former Soviet intelligence assets abroad, complaining publicly that "many" documents in the Soviet intelligence archives might have been destroyed by communist operatives in the last months before the dissolution of the Soviet Union.[9]

Regrettably, the labyrinthine complexity of the Waldheim story enabled the former U.N. chief and his allies to outmaneuver the media throughout his tenure as Austria's president. A September 19, 1990,

---

*That election was won in May 1992 by People's Party candidate Thomas Klestil, who, while serving as Austria's ambassador to the U.S., had fought so tenaciously to block Waldheim's placement on the U.S. watchlist. In the final days of the campaign, Klestil attempted to appeal to Waldheim's constituency by telling a rally that it was "finally time to stop transforming the generation that lived through the war into devils." The remark was also seen as a pointed reference to criticism that had been leveled a few weeks earlier at People's Party officials who accepted invitations to address a group of Waffen-SS veterans and at a *Kronenzeitung* columnist who wrote that fewer Jews were killed at Auschwitz by gassing than by other means.

story in the *Los Angeles Times,* for example, indicated that the Austrian Press Service's concocted claim that the International Historians Commission found Waldheim innocent continued to serve him well. The *Times* reporter, who interviewed Waldheim in a reception room of the Hofburg Palace that once served as the boudoir of Empress Maria Theresa, noted unquestioningly that Waldheim "refers questioners to reports of international commissions that found no evidence of his involvement in war crimes."

In this same story, Waldheim also sang a favorite old refrain. I did not volunteer to go to war; I was drafted. If you blame me, you have to blame "a whole generation" of Austrians. The campaign against me was waged by "certain quarters" and "certain parties."

He quoted Simon Wiesenthal in his defense.

Asked whether he would ever resign, Waldheim countered: "Why should I? I haven't done anything wrong. I have a clean conscience."[10]

A mutual acquaintance arranged a lunch meeting for me with retired Admiral Stansfield Turner at his magnificent home in one of Washington's more expensive suburbs. Turner was CIA director from 1977 to 1980—serving under President Carter, his classmate at the U.S. Naval Academy—and held that post when the Agency's Frederick Hitz wrote his letter to Congressman Solarz, in effect repeating Waldheim's misleading account of his war years. Turner had met Waldheim once, in the mid-eighties, when they both served as judges for an essay contest on international peace.

I showed him the Hitz letter, and he studied it carefully. He first mentioned that Solarz was and is a close personal friend (and I wondered whether the fact of this friendship helped explain the usually media-savvy Solarz's low-keyed reaction to our early disclosures about Waldheim, which included a reference to the Hitz letter). Turner said that he had no specific recollection of the letter, and speculated that Hitz and his associates probably would have conducted little research before drafting what Turner would have viewed then as an unremarkable response to Solarz's inquiry.

We moved on to other topics. Turner said he was previously unaware of the "Prague telex," in which Foreign Minister Waldheim ordered the Austrian Embassy closed to Czech nationals during the ill-fated anti-Communist uprising, and he eagerly accepted my offer of a photocopy. Turner recalled no suspicions concerning Waldheim and the Soviets during his CIA years. But he seemed inclined to agree with the deductive conclusion, which I explained at some length, that Waldheim was a longtime Soviet "asset." And he confirmed that espionage activity by Soviet nationals employed at the

U.N. Secretariat was a thorny problem during Waldheim's tenure, noting with a mixture of anguish and satisfaction, "We caught some of 'em red-handed while I was at the Agency."

Turner later wrote a brief letter to me, reiterating his assertions about what had transpired at the CIA. He had never been aware that the Agency's biography of Waldheim was incorrect. However, he wrote, had he been apprised of that fact, he would "certainly" have seen to it that the biography was "corrected."

Turner's account matched the one that his predecessor, Richard Helms, had given to an intimate who had, in turn, shared it with me (except that Helms said that there *had* been suspicions of Soviet influence over Waldheim during his own time at the CIA; Helms, like Turner, adamantly denied that the CIA had known of or covered up Waldheim's true past). Although it was certainly clear to me that the CIA *could* have discovered that Waldheim was playing fast and loose with his personal history—the Agency doubtless had access to and even possession of the appropriate OSS and captured German records—my belief, which was strengthened by the meeting with Turner, remains that the CIA never bothered to conduct a serious background check or, even if it did, never understood the intelligence significance of what it might have found.* The reason for this failure is hinted at in Turner's letter. Presidents and CIA directors, he wrote, "weren't spending their time" studying the personal history of the U.N. Secretary-General.

The endless speculations of the conspiracy theorists notwithstanding, Turner's explanation has the ring of truth. The key to that view lies in the fact that the United Nations, at the time of Waldheim's election and tenure, was viewed in Washington as the ultimate empty gesture, a toothless, spineless anachronism that was hopelessly paralyzed by the rivalry between the two great superpowers of the Cold War era. Indeed, that perception of the U.N. was on target for the most part. But it appears to have produced a logical "disconnect" that resulted in one of this country's greatest postwar intelligence

---

*In response to a Freedom of Information Act request, the CIA wrote to me on June 9, 1987, that it was in possession of "an OSS report [on Waldheim] dated 26 April 1945," but would not release it to the public. It was later established that the report was actually a *British* summary of an April 26, 1945, interrogation of a German prisoner. The British Defence Ministry released the report in 1989. In it, an "Oblt. [First Lieutenant] Waldheim" is described tersely as "Subordinate officer to Warnstorff in Salonika." Warnstorff, in turn, is listed as chief of intelligence at "Army Group" in Salonika. In a June 3, 1988, letter (copy in authors' possession) to Congressman Stephen Solarz, John L. Helgerson, the CIA's Director of Congressional Affairs, wrote that in 1972, "after initial allegations of Mr. Waldheim's Nazi past surfaced at the United Nations," the CIA requested a records check at the State Department–run Berlin Document Center. The BDC, however, had no records on Waldheim. According to Helgerson's letter, the CIA did *not* check any "foreign file holdings," such as the French-run WASt archive in Berlin (which did, of course, house records on Waldheim).

failures. The fundamental mistake was in thinking that because the institution itself was of little consequence in world affairs, and because the position of Secretary-General was invested (especially then) with virtually no geopolitical clout, the selection of the person to fill that post was similarly inconsequential. Missing at Langley was the foresight to predict how even a politically powerless head of an impotent international organization could provide important *intelligence* assistance to this country's foreign adversaries. The failure to appreciate this possibility inevitably led the U.S. to acquiescence in the Soviet delegation's campaign to engineer the installation of Waldheim. A known commodity to Washington as a longtime official and diplomat of a neutral but Western-oriented European nation, Waldheim must have seemed harmless enough to the American side, even though he was anything but their first choice for the post. Had a proper background check been seen as necessary, however, it would have disclosed at a minimum that Waldheim was an easy target for Soviet intelligence, because he had a hidden (and extremely awkward) past that the Soviets in all likelihood had already discovered—and had used to "compromise" him—or else that Waldheim might *assume* that they had discovered and would tailor his actions accordingly. The result was the installation of a Secretary-General whose "most conspicuous—and, on occasion, preposterous—gestures" were made to Soviet needs during the ten years of his tenure[11]— a decade, moreover, marked by a dangerous escalation in Cold War hostilities and a dramatic increase in Soviet espionage operations in the West.

The full cost of this U.S. intelligence failure is still impossible to calculate.

In the end, one should search for some meaning in this sordid affair, some lessons that might have value for the future. In a sense, Waldheim was an unimportant man, who had distinguished himself at the U.N. more by his mediocrity than anything else. He had eased into diplomatic semiretirement and then won the largely ceremonial post of president of a small European nation that was comparatively unimportant politically, economically, and militarily.

But in another sense, he was a vital symbol. The crimes of the Nazis were not accomplished by a mere handful of evil leaders like Hitler, Eichmann, and the Berlin-based commanders. The execution of those ghastly crimes, on an unparalleled scale, required the complicity of many thousands of people. They were the essential gears in a giant criminal machine. Waldheim was such a gear, a component in a horrific, lawless enterprise that brought devastation, misery, and tragedy to vast areas of Europe. His postwar career was, therefore, an intolerable affront to human decency—as was the conduct of those governments and individuals who had enabled his deception to succeed and who had aided him even after he was exposed.

This tragic outcome should serve as a timely reminder that the backgrounds and true intentions of those who, in offering themselves as champions of human rights, aspire to leadership positions—either by election (Waldheim) or by acclamation (Wiesenthal)—must be carefully scrutinized in every instance. Such positions are *never* so "unimportant," "ceremonial," or "powerless" that nonchalance about who fills them is an acceptable risk to take. U.S. intelligence learned that lesson the hard way. By mistakenly thinking that the identity of the occupant of the Secretary-General's post at the then-impotent United Nations was of so little consequence that a full-scale background check was unnecessary, the U.S. suffered a major intelligence defeat in the seventies: a ten-year reign on the part of a U.N. chief whose checkered past likely required him to accommodate the U.S.S.R.'s most cherished intelligence goals.

For those who have felt most deeply the imperative of seeing the perpetrators of Nazi war crimes brought to justice, a tragic blunder was also made in the case of Simon Wiesenthal. There were many— myself among them—who knew for years that Wiesenthal was pathetically ineffective as a Nazi-hunter. Those of us who kept secret our knowledge that Wiesenthal's most spectacular and celebrated claims could not withstand close scrutiny justified our inaction with the belief that his courtship of the ever-gullible media "at least kept alive the issue" of unpunished Nazi criminals. But in the end, that silence helped create the Simon Wiesenthal whose "living legend" status enabled his clearance of Kurt Waldheim to shield the then– Secretary-General from exposure. Wiesenthal's fame also empowered him to play a major role both in accomplishing Waldheim's election as president of Austria and in stoking the fires of anti-Jewish hatred in that country, especially by legitimizing the ugly, nonstop attacks on the WJC and others (such as the Israeli and American governments) who dared to pursue the truth about Waldheim; Wiesenthal had even used some of the same hate-filled phrases that blackened Waldheim's campaign. Our silence also allowed this self-styled Nazi-hunter to persist for so many years in making public accusations of heinous criminality against individuals who were either innocent or at least unimplicated by any credible evidence. All of this, moreover, has dishonored the memory of those who were murdered—among them fully one-third of all the Jews in the world at that time.

The Waldheim affair also has something to say about the perilous consequences of a nation's turning a blind eye to its true history.

Widespread self-delusion about the history of their country during the Nazi era helped create the psychological atmosphere in which the xenophobic and anti-Semitic appeals of the Waldheim campaign were favorably received by enough Austrians to propel Waldheim to electoral victory—and to simultaneously wreak havoc with Austria's international reputation. Contributing to the incendiary mixture that made these results possible was the failure of Austria's educational system to counter these tendencies with balanced teaching, and also the rather remarkable concentration of the country's major media in the hands of conservative business interests.*

That the shock treatment of the Waldheim affair was anything but a full cure for what ails Austria may be seen in the pandemic anti-Semitism that produced seventy-two desecrations of Jewish cemeteries there in 1990–1991 and in the 1990 report by Amnesty International documenting scores of recent instances, some of them racially motivated, in which the Austrian police tortured people taken into custody. It is also evident in the fact that, fully six years after "law student" Waldheim's initial exposure, an Austrian ambassador had no qualms about writing to an American newspaper to, in his words, "offer a correction" to a fellow European diplomat who had written of having personally fought "Germans, Austrians and Italians" during World War II. The ambassador's "correction": Yes, some Austrians "had been drafted" into the German army (as though thousands upon thousands had not volunteered enthusiastically for the army as well as for the SS and other instrumentalities of Nazi terror). But, the ambassador stressed, it had to be remembered that there was no "Austria" extant at the time, as the country had been "wiped off the map" by Hitler. [12]

It would be wrong, however, to conclude smugly that "only in Austria" is such self-delusion possible. We Americans need not even look beyond our borders for other examples. Have we taught our own schoolchildren what our forebears *really* did to the Native Americans who settled this land long before Columbus "discovered" it? Have we impressed upon them the responsibility that the nation owes to the descendants of these "Indians" who were dispossessed, demonized, and even murdered en masse in the name of "progress"? Have we dealt honestly with the lingering consequences of the slavery system that destroyed much of the social fabric of our African-American population, tearing families asunder and then "freeing" them into a society unprepared to accept them into its factories, neighborhoods, or schools? We have, of course, done none of these

*Some fascinating details on this concentration of ownership may be found in Jane Kramer, "Letter From Europe," *The New Yorker,* June 30, 1986, p. 74.

things. The full price for this abdication of responsibility has yet to be paid, especially if we continue to countenance the so-called playing of the "race card" in American politics and remain silent while our television networks and newspapers provide a daily forum for merchants of racial and religious hatred like Patrick Buchanan.

Forty-nine years ago, on July 24, 1944, the more than 1,700 Jews living on the island of Rhodes were deported en masse to the Nazi death camp complex at Auschwitz, Poland. Upon arrival, most of them were immediately murdered in the gas chambers, their bodies promptly incinerated in the ovens and cremation pits. Neither infant nor invalid was spared.

Today, that terrible time is but a dim memory to the island's inhabitants. Miraculously, the twelfth-century synagogue still stands, rising above the cobblestone-paved streets of the old Jewish quarter in the town of Rhodes. Just thirty-five Jewish families are left to use it, however. The only other visible sign of the once-flourishing Jewish community is the main street, a short walk from the synagogue. Now designated the "Street of the Hebrew Martyrs," its name memorializes the spot on which the Jews of Rhodes were assembled by the Germans. From there, they were marched to the waiting coal barges that took them away—forever—"at instruction of High Command of Army Group E, Ic/AO."

At Jerusalem's Yad Vashem Holocaust memorial, the single most overwhelming sight for me has always been the "Hall of Names," the product of the Israeli government's continuing effort to record the name of every Jew who perished at the hands of the Nazis. The exhibit includes a display of "passports" issued by the Third Reich to two of those six million innocents. One was issued to Etylda Berkowitz. From her passport photograph, it is immediately obvious that she was no more than six or seven years old. The German official who dutifully prepared her passport was careful to enter a response to *every* preprinted question. Thus, little Etylda Berkowitz even had an "occupation." The single-word entry: "Child."

Only at our peril do we allow ourselves to suppose that the kind of evil that killed Etylda Berkowitz was destroyed forever with the defeat of Hitler's armies. The virus of hatred that can erupt again into the nightmare of genocide lives on, in varying states of dormancy, in depraved minds and cold hearts in every nation. And those who harbor such pernicious desires know that there will always be legions of "Lieutenant Waldheims" willing, or even eager, to play their necessary roles. It is for that reason, above all others, that men and women who seek to prevent such catastrophes in the future must insist on the painstaking study of the history of Nazi inhumanity, on the credible pursuit of those who took part in the monstrous crimes of that era, and on proof of the integrity and good faith of anyone who would present himself as a champion of human rights—or as "representative of the Six Million."

APPENDIX 1

June – Dec. 1941   Second Lieutenant Kurt Waldheim
is transported by train from France
(where he had taken part in the
German occupation) to the Soviet
Union, where he leads the 1st unit
of the Mounted Reconnaissance
Squadron of the Wehrmacht's 45th
Infantry Division during the invasion of the U.S.S.R., for which he
wins the Iron Cross II Class, Assault Badge, Eastern Medal. Commander: Helmuth von Pannwitz.

October 8, 1941: Placed in charge
of a cavalry squadron.

December 1941: Wounded near
Orel, Russia, and evacuated to
Frankfurt, then home to Vienna.

Dec. 1941 – Apr. 7, 1942   Recuperation leave, mostly at
Baden, near Vienna.

March 6, 1942: Declared once again
fit for service.

March 14, 1942: Assigned (while
still on leave) to the High Com-

mand of the 12th Army ("AOK 12").

March 22, 1942: Assigned (while still on leave) to the Bader Combat Group (a component of AOK 12).

April 7, 1942: Convalescent leave ends.

Apr. 7/8 – end May 1942   Serves with the General Bader Combat Group *(Kampfgruppe General Bader,* part of AOK 12) as the liaison officer ("D.V.K.5") attached to the Italian 5th Mountain ("Pusteria") Division, stationed at Pusteria Division headquarters in Plevlje, Montenegro, Yugoslavia, while that division is engaged with the Germans in the brutal suppression of partisans in eastern Bosnia (by such means as mass deportations to slave labor in occupied Norway). Commander: General Paul Bader. Commander of Pusteria Division: General Giovanni Esposito. Waldheim is photographed with Esposito.

May 28, 1942: The Bader Combat Group is dissolved.

May 24, 1942   Reports to Sarajevo, Yugoslavia, to join staff of the West Bosnian Combat Group *(Kampfgruppe Westbosnien,* also part of AOK 12), commanded by General Friedrich Stahl. Position: "O2" in the Ib (Quartermaster) section, as deputy to Capt. Plume, the combat group's Quartermaster.

end May 1942 – Aug. 28, 1942	West Bosnian Combat Group staff (including Waldheim) moves to new headquarters in Banja Luka, a resort town in western Bosnia. The combat group is engaged in the brutal suppression of resistance in western Bosnia, most notably in the Kozara area.
	On July 22, 1942, receives King Zvonimir medal w/ Oak Leaves "for bravery under fire" from Croatian Ustashi regime of Ante Pavelic, on General Stahl's recommendation.
	July 30/31, 1942: West Bosnian Combat Group moves to Kostajnica, on River Una (40 miles NW of Banja Luka).
	August 14, 1942: West Bosnian Combat Group staff moves again, this time to Novska, north of the Sava River.
	August 28, 1942: The West Bosnian Combat Group is dissolved.
by Aug. 31, 1942	Assigned to the headquarters staff of the High Command of Army Group 12 (AOK 12), at Arsakli, near Salonika, in northern Greece, initially as an interpreter assigned to the Intelligence/Counterintelligence ("Ic/AO") Branch. Commander: General Alexander Loehr. (Note: Exact date of arrival is unknown.)
Nov. 19, 1942–Mar. 31, 1943	On study leave in Austria.
	December 1942: Receives promotion to First Lieutenant while on leave.

January 1, 1943: AOK 12 in effect "becomes" Army Group E.

Apr. 2, 1943   Pay entry in Waldheim's paybook reflects payments to him at *Frontleitnebenstelle-187* (Field Office for Staff in Transit-187), in Belgrade, supposedly "indicating that Dr. Waldheim was in transit to a temporary duty station rather than returning to his permanent assignment with Army Group E in Arsakli, Greece" (per July 1987 Austrian Foreign Ministry "White Book"). (Note: It is unclear whether he first returned to Arsakli/Salonika before reporting to his next duty station, in Tirana, Albania [see below]).

Apr. – July 1943   Assigned temporarily to the German liaison staff attached to the Italian 9th Army, stationed in Tirana, Albania. Position: Interpreter and liaison officer. Immediate superior: Col. Joachim Macholz. Responsibilities include occasional assignments in such places as Podgorica, Yugoslavia and Athens, Greece.

May 22, 1943: Photographed with Waffen-SS General Artur Phleps, Italian General Escola Roncaglia and his own superior, Col. Macholz, waiting at an airstrip in Podgorica, Yugoslavia, for the arrival of General Rudolf Lueters, in midst of the "Black Operation" antipartisan campaign.

July 1943   Returns briefly to the High Command of Army Group E in Arsakli/Salonika for reassignment (see next entry).

July 19 – Oct. 4, 1943   Serves as the "O1" officer (deputy to the chief of operations) in the "Ia" (Operations) Branch of the German General Staff attached to Italian 11th Army in Athens, Greece (renamed the Army Group Southern Greece after Italian capitulation on September 8, 1943). Immediate superior: Lt. Col. Bruno Willers. Commander: Major General Heinz von Gyldenfeldt, until September 9 (then, with change to full-fledged Army Group, General Helmut Felmy). The Athens command is responsible supervising antipartisan warfare, combatting the resistance, and, after the Italian capitulation, disarming Italian forces and deporting them to slave labor in Germany.

October 4, 1943: Waldheim is photographed at the Army Group Southern Greece farewell party (with Major General von Gyldenfeldt, Lt. Col. Willers, General Heinz Felmy, and others) at the Hotel Grande Bretagne, Athens.

early Oct. 1943 – Apr. 1945   Serves as the "O3" Officer in the "Ic/AO" (Intelligence/Counterintelligence) Branch of the High Command of Army Group E, headquartered initially in Arsakli/Salonika, Greece. Commander: General Alexander Loehr. Immediate superior: Col. Herbert Warnstorff. Immediate subordinates: Lt. Helmut Poliza and Lt. Krohne

November 23–December 25, 1943: On leave (rest/recuperation) at home in Baden, Austria.

January 1944: Receives War Merit Cross 2nd Class with Swords.

February 25 to mid-April 1944: On leave in Austria (thyroid treatment and then recuperation at Semmering).

April 14, 1944: Receives law doctorate.

End of July–August 3, 1944: On a "trip to Vienna" (reason unknown; perhaps for service with the "438th Division for Special Purposes").

August 15–September 3, 1944: On special leave, presumably to marry (weds Elisabeth Ritschel on August 19).

October 13, 1944: With Army Group E now in retreat, Waldheim claims he flew from Arsakli, Greece, to Pristina, Yugoslavia, and then travelled by road to Stari Trg, near Mitrovica, Yugoslavia.

October 14, 1944: Army Group E High Command staff arrives at its new headquarters in Mitrovica (on a Danubian island near Belgrade).

November 15–18, 1944: Loehr and some aides fly on November 15 from Mitrovica to still another new headquarters, in Sarajevo (Bosnia), Yugoslavia. Waldheim and the rest of the Ic/AO Branch staff depart by car the night of November 15 and travel to the new headquarters in Sarajevo, according to Waldheim, by way of Visegrad and Ucice, and then a plane trip from Kraljevo, arriving at Sarajevo on November 18.

December 3, 1944: Waldheim is pictured, with General Loehr, atop the front page of the Wehrmacht newspaper *Wacht im Suedosten;* he initials an anti-Semitic propaganda package the same day.

February 1945: Army Group E staff retreats by road from Sarajevo to Nova Gradiska, Yugoslavia (Croatia).

March 1945: Army Group E staff retreats by road from Nova Gradiska to Zagreb, Yugoslavia (Croatia).

Late March/Early April 1945: On leave (claimed), to move pregnant wife from Vienna to mountains near Schladming. (This claim is not documented in leave record.)

Apr. 1945   Waldheim is transferred from the High Command of Army Group E staff in Zagreb to "an infantry division in the area of Trieste," which he claims he was never able to reach. Waldheim has *never* identified this "infantry" unit although he has often addressed at length the subject of his having failed to reach it.

Apr. 20, 1945   Receives War Merit Cross First Class with Swords.

May 7, 1945   Nazi Germany surrenders at Rheims. Capitulation ratified in Berlin on May 8 (VE-Day).

May 9, 1945   Demobilized in Austrian province of Styria, effective this date. Then joins wife and newborn daughter in Ramsau, and registers at the village administrative office.

May 18, 1945   "Officially discharged" by Allied authorities with final entry for this date in his military paybook: 3rd Battalion, 1st March Regiment, 1st March Brigade von Schultz. He is subsequently transported in a truck column to a U.S. P.O.W. camp in Bad Toelz, Bavaria.

June 1945   Released from custody by U.S. authorities.

APPENDIX 2

1. Are you aware of any case in which the Soviet Union has used an individual's prior Nazi affiliations to blackmail, "oblige," or "encourage" him into serving Soviet interests? If so, when did you first encounter such a case?

   Are you aware of any case in which the Soviet Union disregarded an individual's Nazi past and used that person as an operational or intelligence asset? If so, when did you first encounter such a case?

2. Same questions as in paragraph number 1., but asked with respect to the United States government.

3. With which of the following statements, if any, do you agree (any explanations you might care to provide with your responses would be greatly appreciated):
   (a) Kurt Waldheim has lied about his prewar past.
   (b) Kurt Waldheim has lied about his wartime whereabouts and activities.
   (c) Kurt Waldheim deliberately concealed his prewar affiliations with Nazi organizations.
   (d) Before the war, Kurt Waldheim was a member of one or more Nazi organizations.
   (e) Kurt Waldheim has lied about his contemporaneous knowledge of Nazi atrocities against Jews.
   (f) The Ic/AO Gruppe of the High Command of Army Group E was a criminal unit (that is, it participated in the planning, facilitating, or carrying out of one or more Nazi crimes against Jews or non-Jews).

(g) The Quartiermeister section of the Kampfgruppe Westbosnien was a criminal unit.

(h) The Operations section (Ia) of the German General Staff
attached to the Italian 11th Army (later Armeegruppe Sud-
griechenland) was a criminal unit.

(i) The "D.V.K. 5" of the Kampfgruppe General Bader was a
criminal unit.

(j) Army Group South East's liaison detachment to the Italian
9th Army High Command and Command Montenegro (stationed in Tirana) was a criminal unit.

(j) Kurt Waldheim was an accessory to Nazi war crimes during
the Second World War.

(k) Kurt Waldheim participated in the commission of Nazi-
sponsored acts of persecution during the Second World War.

(l) Kurt Waldheim committed one or more war crimes during
the Second World War.

(m) Kurt Waldheim committed one or more crimes against humanity during the Second World War.

(n) The passing on of criminal orders drafted by others is itself
a criminal act, as was adjudged at the Nuremberg trials?

4. To what extent, if any, do you hold the following responsible
for the upsurge in anti-Semitism that began in March 1986? I
would appreciate your "ranking" these persons and entities as
well (with "1" being most responsible and higher numbers reflecting lesser responsibility; you may simply cross out those
persons/entities, if any, which you feel bear no responsibility):

(a) Kurt Waldheim
(b) Michael Graff
(c) Alois Mock
(d) The OVP [People's Party]
(e) The SPO [Socialist Party]
(f) Elements within the Austrian press
(g) The World Jewish Congress
(h) The U.S. Department of Justice
(i) The U.S. Office of Special Investigations
(j) Neal Sher
(k) The U.S. Department of State
(l) Elements within the U.S. mass media
(m) Others (please identify)

5. Have you ever exposed or denounced publicly former Nazis or
Nazi criminals in the OVP? If so, would you be so kind as to

identify those persons and provide documentation reflecting such public exposure or denunciation.

6. *Prior* to 1986, did you ever discuss Waldheim's war record with him? If so, when did you do so, what prompted the discussion(s), and what did Waldheim tell you?

7. Have you ever publicly decried the anti-Semitism in Kurt Waldheim's election campaign? If so, please provide documentation reflecting any such public statement. I am especially interested in any such statements made before the May 4 and June 8, 1986 presidential elections.

8. Do you in fact agree that Waldheim's campaign had a blatantly anti-Semitic component?

9. Do you agree with the proposition that, during 1986, the OVP became the first major political party in postwar European history to use overt anti-Semitism as a political tool? If you do not agree, please explain. Do you at least agree that the party did use anti-Semitism as a vote-getting device? If you agree with this proposition, how do you justify your continued close association with the OVP?

10. Are you, as a formal matter, a member of the OVP? If not, would you please describe your past and current relationship with that party.

11. Please provide details of conversations and meetings you had with OVP officials and members of Waldheim's campaign team prior to the June 8, 1986 presidential election.

12. *Before* March 1986, what, if anything, did you know about Waldheim's military service: (1) in the U.S.S.R. in 1941; and (2) in Yugoslavia, Albania, and Greece during the period 1942–45? If you knew anything of these matters, when and how did you gain this knowledge?

13. When did you first learn that Waldheim was trying to conceal from the public the fact of his wartime service in Greece and Yugoslavia? If you learned this prior to March 1986, why did you not speak out publicly?

14. Did you publicly protest the emplacement of the Loehr me-

morial plaque? If so, please provide documentation reflecting
such protest. If you did not publicly protest, why not? Did the
Anti-Defamation League of B'nai B'rith err in protesting the
decision to honor Loehr?

15. When did you learn of Loehr's involvement in crimes against
    Jews? When did you first learn that Waldheim had served on
    Loehr's staff?

16. What do you know about *Ausweg*'s decision not to publish Elan
    Steinberg's response to your June 1986 front-page attack on
    the World Jewish Congress?

17. What is your evaluation of Johann Mayer's testimony as quoted
    in the Yugoslav 1947 Odluka?

18. If *you* had been the President of the World Jewish Congress
    in March 1986, when the organization learned that Kurt Wald-
    heim had been listed by the United Nation War Crimes Com-
    mission as wanted for murder, would you have withheld this
    information from public disclosure? If so, when, if ever, would
    you have revealed it? If you had been unable to obtain the
    underlying documentation from Yugoslavia, would you have
    withheld from disclosure the fact of Waldheim's U.N.W.C.C.
    listing until after the presidential election?

19. In your estimation, how complete (in percentage terms) are
    Berlin Document Center membership records of: (1) the
    NSDAP; (2) the SA; (3) the SA-Reitersturm; (4) the NS-
    Studentenbund; and (5) the NS-Reiterkorps?

20. If you agree that Kurt Waldheim served in one or more criminal
    units during World War II, how would you distinguish his case
    from that of Friedrich Peter (*aside* from the formality of Peter's
    unit having been part of the Waffen-SS)?
    Do you feel that Peter's *personal* complicity in Nazi crimes
    was ever established? If so, why do you not campaign for him
    to be placed on trial?

21. How do you respond to those who charge that your repeated
    public assurances that accusations made against Waldheim were
    without foundation contributed significantly to his election?

22. Does the Dokumentationszentrum possess a copy of the final

CROWCASS list? If so, when did your office first obtain this list?

23. Please state whether you have publicly denounced the anti-Semitic material published since March 1986 in the following publications (and if you have done so, please provide documentation of same; if you have not done so, please explain why you refrained):
    (a) *Volksblatt* (official OVP newspaper)
    (b) *Kronenzeitung*
    (c) *Kurier*
    (d) *Die Presse*
    (e) *Wochenpresse*

24. Do you agree that many of the reports that bear Waldheim's signature under the "F.d.R." notation were in fact *authored* by Waldheim as well, even though the nominal signatory was Herbert Warnstorff or some other superior of Waldheim's?

25 Do you agree with Kurt Waldheim's argument that Ic and AO at Army Group E were "strictly separate entities"?

26. Why have you never spoken out publicly against *Wochenpresse*'s false and libelous charge that the WJC offered money to a former Greek partisan to get him to make an incriminating statement against Kurt Waldheim?

27. Based on what you now know about Kurt Waldheim, do you feel that he was morally qualified to serve as Secretary-General of the United Nations? Whatever your answer, please explain.

28. Have you formulated a theory of why Kurt Waldheim concealed and lied about his whereabouts and activities during World War II? If so, would you be so kind as to state that theory.

29. In your letter published in the August 24, 1987 issue of *Profil*, you wrote that you had checked for records on Waldheim at the Berlin Document Center in 1979 and that you had received in the same year a copy of Waldheim's Wermachtauskunftstelle [WASt] file. I have several questions to ask in this connection.
    (a) Did this information come to you unsolicited or instead in response to your own inquiries?
    (b) If your answer to (a) was that you pursued this information

on your own initiative, what prompted your investigation?

(c) Did you also receive the documents on Waldheim in the files of the Krankenbuchlager? If you have *ever* seen these documents, when did you first do so?

30. Do you possess copies of any of the following documents (and if not, have you ever seen copies of them):

(a) Kurt Waldheim's Wehrmacht personnel file (Personalakten).

(b) The reports and other materials on Waldheim assembled by the Heeresnachrichtenamt as alleged in the June 30, 1986 issue of *Profil.*

(c) The "personal notes" made by Dr. Waldheim during the war (which are frequently cited by Waldheim's defenders).

31. When Georg Tidl and others contacted you in 1985 seeking information about Kurt Waldheim's prewar and wartime past, what did you tell the Waldheim team about these inquiries?

32. Do you agree that the Austrian Foreign Ministry's so-called "White Book" of July 1987 contains false statements of fact made in support of Kurt Waldheim?

NOTES

CHAPTER ONE

1. See "Research Circular No. 26," United Nations War Crimes Commission (Research Office), September 1947, Record Group 153, Records of the Judge Advocate General, International Affairs Division, War Crimes Office, 1944–49.

2. See U.S. Department of the Army, *German Anti-Guerilla Operations in the Balkans (1941–1944)*, DA Pamphlet 20–243, Washington, DC: 1954; Milt Copulos, "State Shuns Heroic Ally," *Washington Times*, June 11, 1985, p. D1; William L. Shirer, *The Rise and Fall of the Third Reich*, New York: Simon & Schuster, 1960, pp. 823–24.

3. See, for example, *Vjesnik*, Zagreb: January 17, 1986; *Borba*, Belgrade: January 17, 1986; *Neue AZ*, Vienna: January 16, 1986 (quoting the Soviet army newspaper *Krasnaja Swesda*).

4. Otmar Lahodynsky, "Lance fuer Loehr," *Profil*, Vienna: January 27, 1986.

5. See Jewish Telegraphic Agency, *Daily News Bulletin*, August 31, 1973. See also the interview of Elisabeth Waldheim in *al- Usbu' al- 'Arabi* ("Arabweek"), Beirut: no. 1390, June 2, 1986. For a criticism of Waldheim's stance on Israeli issues, see former U.S. representative to the U.N. Jeanne Kirkpatrick's "What Waldheim Didn't Do," *Washington Post*, April 13, 1986, p. C7.

6. The *New York Times Magazine*, September 13, 1981, p. 70.

7. For more on the Arthur Rudolph case, see Linda Hunt, *Secret Agenda*, New York: St. Martin's Press, 1991; and Tom Bower, *The Paperclip Conspiracy*, Boston: Little Brown & Co., 1989.

CHAPTER TWO

1. Nahum Goldmann, *The Autobiography of Nahum Goldmann*, New York: Holt, Rinehart and Winston, 1969.

2. See Shirley Hazzard, "The League of Frightened Men," *The New Republic*, January 19, 1980, pp. 17–20. The "Nazi youth movement" charge and Soviet invasion suspicions were angrily repeated, albeit to little notice, during 1980–82 by Hillel Seidman, a longtime New York correspondent for Jewish newspapers. See "Waldheim Challenged by Seidman on Nazi Youth Activities," *Jewish Press*, Brooklyn, N.Y.: October 24, 1980; Hillel Seidman, *United Nations Perfidy and Perversion*, New York: M.P. Press, 1982, pp. 31–69 and 147–50.

3. Solarz's letter was not made public at the time of its writing. The text was first published in *Profil*, Vienna: March 14, 1988, p. 33.

4. Waldheim's letter of December 19, 1980, copy in authors' possession.

5. Hitz's letter of December 31, 1980, copy in authors' possession.

CHAPTER THREE

1. Kurt Waldheim, *Im Glaspalast der Weltpolitik,* Dusseldorf and Vienna: Econ Verlag, 1985, p. 38. English-language version: *In the Eye of the Storm: A Memoir,* London: Weidenfeld & Nicholson, 1986; Bethesda, MD: Adler & Adler, 1986.

2. *Tagebuch in dem Verfahren* of Dr. Kurt Waldheim, copy in authors' possession.

3. National Socialist German Workers Party, *Gau* Leadership of the Lower Danube, Personnel Office, Political Evaluation Section, to President of the Superior Provincial Court, August 2, 1940, reproduced in *Wochenpresse,* Vienna: March 11, 1986.

4. The "sporting activities" characterization came from a January 25, 1946, letter written by Waldheim and filed with the Provincial High Court in Vienna; see *Profil,* Vienna: March 24, 1986, p. 22.

5. Kurt Waldheim, *op. cit.,* p. 41.

6. Rudolf Gschopf, *Mein Weg mit der 45.Inf.Div.* ("My Way with the 45th Infantry Division"), Linz, Austria: Oberoesterreichischer Landesverlag, 1955.

7. *Unsere Ehre heisst Treue* ("Our Honor Is Loyalty"), Vienna: Europa Verlag, 1965. The former Czech intelligence agent who supervised the release of these documents and later defected to the U.S. has confirmed their authenticity; see Ladislaw Bittman, *Geheimwaffe D,* Bern: S01 Verlag, 1973, pp. 59ff. The former head of the West German Central Office of Land Judicial Authorities for the Investigation of National-Socialist Crimes was also convinced that the documents were "undoubtedly genuine"; see Adalbert Rueckerl, *The Investigation of Nazi Crimes 1945–1978: A Documentation,* Heidelberg: C.F. Mueller, 1979, p. 139.

8. Nikolay Krasnov, *Nyezabyvayemoye* ("The Unforgettable"), San Francisco: Russkaya Zhizn, 1957.

9. Erich Kern, *General von Pannwitz und seine Kosaken* ("General von Pannwitz and His Cossacks"), Goettingen: Plesse-Verlag, 1963. See also George Stein, *The Waffen-SS 1939–1945,* Ithaca: Cornell University Press, 1966, pp. 188–89.

10. Waldheim campaign brochure, *Die Bundespraesidentwahl am 25.April ist eine Persoenlichkeitswahl.* Other brochures from Waldheim's first presidential campaign were similarly close-mouthed concerning the candidate's military service. See *Werben fuer Waldheim: Handbuch fuer die Bundespraesidentenwahl 1971,* Vienna: 1971; and Waldheim Press Service, *Lebenslauf,* Vienna: February 1, 1971.

11. United Nations Press Section, Office of Public Information, "Biographical Note: Kurt Waldheim of Austria Appointed Secretary-General of the United Nations for a Five-Year Term Beginning on 1 January 1972," New York: Press Release SG/1765, December 22, 1971. The U.N. press release on Waldheim's reelection to a second five-year term is similarly worded; see Press Release SG/1774/Rev.5-BIO/1028/Rev.5, January 31, 1978.

12. Waldheim campaign brochure, *Portrait aus dem Inhalt: Dr. Kurt Waldheim,* Vienna: 1986. Waldheim's official curriculum vitae, available from the Austrian Press Service, was even more vague; see Bundespressdienst, Republik Oesterreich, "Dr. Kurt Waldheim," Vienna (n.d.).

13. Kurt Waldheim, *Im Glaspalast . . . , supra,* pp. 42–44.

CHAPTER FOUR

1. Otto Kumm, *Vorwaerts Prinz Eugen!* ("Forward Prince Eugen!"), Osnabrueck, West Germany: Munin Verlag, 1978, p. 76.

2. Yugoslav War Crimes Commission, *Report on the Crimes of Austria and the Austrians Against Yugoslavia and Her Peoples,* Belgrade: 1947, p. 32.

3. A captured German order conveying identical instructions the next day was later found in the collection of the U.S. National Archives. See USNA (United States National Archives document) T314/1244/325.

4. *Wacht im Suedosten* (subhead: "Deutsche Frontzeitung fuer alle Wehrmachtstelle"), December 3, 1944, issue number 1562.

5. D. J. Diakow, *Generaloberst Alexander Loehr: Ein Lebensbild,* Freiburg, West Germany: Verlag Herder, 1964, p. 115.

6. See U Thant, *View from the United Nations,* Garden City, NY: Doubleday, 1978, pp. 437–38; see also Brian Urquhart, *A Life in Peace and War,* New York: Harper & Row, 1987, p. 332.

7. Kurt Waldheim, *In the Eye of the Storm, op. cit.,* p. 31.

8. See Hubertus Czernin, "Geschichten vom Doktor W.," *Profil,* Vienna: October 14, 1985, pp. 12–13.

9. See Robert Knight, "The Waldheim Context: Austria and Nazism," *Times Literary Supplement,* October 3, 1986; Max E. Riedlsperger, *The Lingering Shadow of Nazism: The Austrian Independent Party Movement Since 1945,* Boulder, CO: East European Quarterly/Columbia University Press, 1978, pp. 23, 42, 63–64, 121; Donald R. Whitnah and Edgar L. Erickson, *The American Occupation of Austria: Planning and Early Years,* Westport, CT: Greenwood Press, 1985, p. 238; and "Austria" entry, *Encyclopedia Judaica,* Jerusalem, 1972.

10. See, for example, Kurt Steiner, *Modern Austria,* Palo Alto: SPOSS, 1987, p. 116.

CHAPTER FIVE

1. Patrick Dean in a February 5, 1947, British Foreign Office report, quoted in Tom Bower, *The Pledge Betrayed,* Garden City, NY: Doubleday, 1982, p. 417.

2. George H. Stein, *The Waffen-SS: Hitler's Elite Guard at War 1939–1945,* Ithaca: Cornell University Press, 1966, pp. 273–74.

3. Heinz Hoehne, *The Order of the Death's Head: The Story of Hitler's SS,* New York: Ballantine ed., 1971, pp. 530–32 and notes 209 and 218.

4. NOKW-066-UK.

5. Gerald Reitlinger, *The Final Solution: The Attempt to Exterminate the Jews of Europe 1939–1945,* New York: A.S. Barnes & Company, 1961 ed., pp. 373, 376n.

6. Affidavit of Dieter Wisliceny, November 29, 1945, Nuremberg, Germany: reprinted in *Red Series,* Volume VIII, pp. 606ff.

7. Raul Hilberg, *The Destruction of the European Jews,* New York: Harper ed., 1979, p. 451 (citing NOKW-1885); Gerald Reitlinger, *The Final Solution, op. cit.,* p. 375n.

8. Jacob Robinson and Henry Sachs, *The Holocaust: The Nuremberg Evidence,* Jerusalem: Yad Vashem Martyrs' and Heroes' Memorial Authority/YIVO Institute for Jewish Research, 1976.

9. " 'Ich stecke meinen Kopf nicht in den Sand': Der neue Uno-Generalsekretaer Kurt Waldheim ueber sein Programm" (" 'I Do Not Stick My Head in the Sand': The New U.N. Secretary-General on His Program"), *Der Spiegel,* Hamburg: January 3, 1972.

10. Jane Rosen, "The U.N.'s Man in the Middle," the *New York Times Magazine,* September 13, 1981, pp. 68, 70.

11. Kurt Waldheim, *The Austrian Example,* New York: Macmillan, 1973 (originally *Der Oesterreichische Weg,* Vienna: Verlag Fritz Modlen, 1971), p. 45.

12. Kurt Waldheim, *The Challenge of Peace,* New York: Rawson, Wade Pub-

lishers, 1977 (originally published in France as *Un metier unique au monde,* Editions Stock, 1977), pp. 24–26.

CHAPTER SIX

1. USNA T501/250/274.

2. Jozo Tomasevich, *The Chetniks: War and Revolution in Yugoslavia, 1941–1945,* Stanford, CA: Stanford University Press, 1975, p. 252, n. 152.

3. Crown's technical analysis is summarized in Dr. David A. Crown, "Laboratory Report in re: Photograph—May 22, 1943, Dr. Kurt Waldheim," Fairfax, VA: Crown Forensic Laboratories, Inc., February 27, 1986; copy in authors' possession.

4. Kurt Waldheim, *Im Glaspalast . . . , op. cit.,* pp. 19–20.

5. Hugh Gibson quoted in Donald R. Whitnah and Edgar L. Erickson, *The American Occupation of Austria: Planning and Early Years,* Westport, CT: Greenwood Press, 1985, pp. 219–20.

6. Heinz Hoehne and Hermann Zolling, *Network,* London: Secker & Warburg, 1972, pp. 139–41. On the KGB's continued activity in Vienna, see, for example, "Bonn's Superspy," *Insight* Magazine, March 16, 1987, p. 41.

7. Former Austrian Foreign Minister Karl Gruber quoted in Robert Knight, "The Waldheim Context: Austria and Nazism," *Times Literary Supplement,* London: October 3, 1986.

8. Karl Gruber, *Between Liberation and Liberty,* New York: Praeger, 1955, p. 212.

9. Kurt Waldheim, *The Austrian Example, op. cit.,* pp. 55–56.

10. Kurt Waldheim, *Im Glaspalast . . . , op. cit.,* p. 36.

11. Text of Statement by Mr. Adam Malik, Permanent Representative of the Union of Soviet Socialist Republics to the United Nations, at the closing of the 26th Session of the General Assembly, December 22, 1971 (United Nations Office of Public Information, Press Release GA/4546).

12. Kurt Waldheim, *op. cit.,* p. 125.

13. Arkady N. Shevchenko, *Breaking with Moscow,* New York: Ballantine ed., 1985, pp. 316–18.

14. See Juliana G. Pilon, "Moscow's U.N. Outpost," Washington: The Heritage Foundation, Background Report No. 307, November 22, 1983, pp. 3–4. In 1985, the Roth-Hyde Amendment to the Foreign Missions Act of 1982 closed this loophole by extending existing travel restrictions on Soviet and Soviet-bloc U.N. diplomatic missions to U.N. Secretariat officials of those countries.

15. See, for example, the statement of Charles Lichenstein, former political officer of the U.S. delegation at the U.N., quoted in a UPI dispatch of May 3, 1987: "Several hundred Russian and Eastern Bloc agents were given responsibility for the day-to-day operation of the United Nations. . . . Waldheim did not have to make pro-Russian speeches. It was more effective to have him just look the other way and allow KGB infiltration."

16. This criticism was repeated in Juliana G. Pilon and Ralph Kinney Bennett, *The UN: Assessing Soviet Abuses,* London: Institute for European Defence and Strategic Studies, 1988, pp. 10, 28–29.

17. Arkady N. Shevchenko, *op. cit.,* pp. 395–96.

18. See Shirley Hazzard, "The Guest Word," the *New York Times Book Review,* August 25, 1974. Hazzard later authored an excellent analysis of Waldheim's "conspicuous . . . partiality" to "Soviet requirements" at the U.N. See Shirley Hazzard, *Countenance of Truth,* New York: Viking, 1990, pp. 65, 89–94.

19. Arkady N. Shevchenko, *op. cit.,* p. 396.

20. Arkady N. Shevchenko, *op. cit.,* pp. 406–07; see also "Kurt Waldheim in

Moscow," *News from Ukraine*, Kiev: September 1977, p. 2; and Hillel Seidman, *United Nations: Perfidy and Perversion*, New York: M.P. Press, 1982, pp. 105–06.

21. Arkady N. Shevchenko, *op. cit.*, pp. 392–94.

22. Shirley Hazzard, "The League of Frightened Men," *The New Republic*, January 19, 1980, pp. 17–20; see also Hazzard's Letter to the Editor, *New York Times*, April 16, 1986.

23. Martin Mayer, *The Diplomats*, Garden City, NY: Doubleday, 1983; see also Martin Mayer, "Waldheim: Portrait of a Skilled Opportunist," *The Wall Street Journal*, April 23, 1986, p. 31.

24. Brian Urquhart, *op. cit.*, pp. 228, 268.

25. Robert Rhodes James, "A UN Enemy Within," *The Guardian*, Manchester, England: October 10, 1987; and Robert Rhodes James quoted on BBC World Service Programme "Outlook," February 22, 1988.

26. See James M. Markham, "A Reporter's Notebook: In Austria, Silence Louder than Oom-Pah-Pah," *New York Times*, June 8, 1986, p. 16; Russell Watson, Scott Sullivan, and Andrew Nagorski, "Waldheim Under Seige," *Newsweek*, June 9, 1986, p. 32; and "Like a Beggar," *Der Spiegel*, Hamburg: nr. 41/1986, October 8, 1986, p. 170.

CHAPTER SEVEN

1. See Vlado Strugar, *Der jugoslawische Volksbefreiungskrieg 1941–45* (translated by M. Zoellner), Berlin: Deutscher Militaerverlag, 1969.

2. *Fuer Tapferkeit und Verdienst*, Munich, Germany: Schild Verlag, n.d. [1955], p. 51. For participants in actual combat, another medal (the so-called "3-leaf" medal) was preferred, according to a July 1942 captured Wehrmacht document.

3. Kurt Waldheim, *Im Glaspalast . . .* , *op. cit.*, p. 42.

4. See Hubertus Czernin, "Waldheim und die SA," *Profil*, Vienna: March 3, 1986. The article quotes Waldheim's *"Notiz"* of February 23, 1986.

CHAPTER EIGHT

1. See Summary Record of the 40th Meeting, United Nations Commission on Human Rights, March 3, 1986, U.N. Document E/CN.4/1986/SR.40.

2. "Former U.N. Secretary Denies Being in Hitler's Storm Troops," AP dispatch, March 3, 1986, AM cycle.

3. John Tagliabue, "Files Show Kurt Waldheim Served Under War Criminal," *New York Times*, March 4, 1986, pp. A1, A6.

4. See Summary Record of the 41st Meeting, United Nations Commission on Human Rights, March 4, 1986, U.N. Document E/CN.4/1986/SR.41.

5. Patrick Blum, "Waldheim Denies He Was a Nazi," *Financial Times*, London: March 4, 1986, p. 2.

6. V. Aparin and T. Redkin, "A Defamatory Furor Fails," *Izvestia*, January 7, 1979 (English-language excerpts reprinted in *The Current Digest of the Soviet Press*, Vol. XXX, no. 1, February 1, 1979, p. 10. For Wiesenthal charges regarding Nazis working for the East German and Polish governments, see, for example, Simon Wiesenthal, *Die Gleiche Sprache: Erst fuer Hitler—jetzt fuer Ulbricht* (The Same Language: First for Hitler—Now for Ulbricht), Bonn: Deutschlandberichte, 1968; Simon Wiesenthal, *Anti-Jewish Agitation in Poland*, Bonn: Rolf Vogel [n.d.—1969?].

7. See Simon Wiesenthal, *Dokumentationszentrum Bulletin of Information No. 25*, January 31, 1985, p. 5. Hoefer finally resigned in December 1987. See Robert J. McCartney, "W. German TV Host Quits After Charges of Nazi Past," *Washington Post*, December 23, 1987.

8. "Austrian Magazine Accuses Waldheim of Nazi Past," Reuters dispatch, March 3, 1986, AM cycle.

9. "Wiesenthal: Sowjets fanden nichts Belastendes ueber Kurt Waldheim," *Neue Kronenzeitung*, Vienna: March 3, 1986, p. 4.

CHAPTER NINE

1. "Waldheim Denies Knowledge of Atrocities During War Service," AP dispatch, March 5, 1986, PM cycle.

2. "Ex–UN Chief Accused by Jews," *The Times*, London: March 5, 1986, p. 1.

3. Tanjug News Agency, "Zagreb Vjesnik: Documents on Waldheim Decoration," Belgrade: dispatch of March 5, 1986.

4. See, for example, "Veterans Day Marked in Yugoslavia," Xinhua General Overseas News Service, Beijing: July 5, 1982; Dragoje Lukic, "The Children of Kozara," *Yugoslav Life*, Belgrade: April–May 1986, p. 3; Ahmet Donlagic, Zarko Atanackovic and Dusan Plenca, *Yugoslavia in the Second World War*, Belgrade: Medunarodna Stampa Interpress, 1967, pp. 86–93.

5. "Mock: 'Gelenkte Verleumdungskampagne,'" *Wiener Zeitung*, Vienna: March 6, 1986.

6. Reuters dispatch quoting *Newsday* columnist Ken Gross, March 7, 1986.

7. David Remick, "Book Controversy—Publisher May Recall Waldheim's Memoirs," *Washington Post*, March 6, 1986, p. B2.

8. "Waldheim Was Not 'Cleared' When He Joined the Public Service," *Jerusalem Post*, March 7, 1986, p. 1.

9. See Raul Hilberg, *op. cit.*, pp. 434, 442–47.

CHAPTER TEN

1. Peter Michael Lingens, "Ich weiss, dass es unwahrscheinlich klingt," *Profil*, Vienna: March 10, 1986, pp. 13–15.

2. Otto Kumm, *7. SS-Gebirgs-Division "Prinz Eugen" im Bild* ("7th SS Mountain Division 'Prince Eugen' in Photographs"), Osnabrueck, Germany: Munin-Verlag G.m.b.H., 1983, p. 116.

3. USNA T311/184/0582.

4. See Lucien O. Meysels, "Die Akte Waldheim—Der 14. Mann," *Wochenpresse*, Vienna: March 11, 1986; the November 7, 1944, "Daily Report" is reproduced as U.S. National Archives microfilm frame T311/184/0582.

5. "Dr. Waldheim's Local Difficulty," *The Guardian*, Manchester, England: March 11, 1986.

6. William Drodziak, "Waldheim Defends Wartime Record; Surge of Popular Sympathy Bolsters His Presidential Campaign," *Washington Post*, March 12, 1986, p. A25.

7. Raul Hilberg, *op. cit.*, p. 443, fn. 460.

8. Paul N. Hehn, *The German Struggle Against Yugoslav Guerillas in World War II*, Boulder, CO: East European Quarterly/Columbia University Press, 1979.

CHAPTER ELEVEN

1. Paul N. Hehn, *op. cit.*, pp. 133, 136.

2. Office of U.S. Chief of Counsel for War Crimes, Interrogations of Albert Gottfried Friedrich Stahl, June 10 and 13, 1947, USNA Record Group 238. Affidavit of Albert Gottfried Friedrich Stahl, June 12, 1947, Nuremberg document NOKW-1714.

3. Report of the *Wehrmachtbefehlshaber Suedost* (12th Army), Dept. Ia, *Activity Report for the Period from July 1–31, 1942*, July 31, 1942; USNA T311/175/0312.

4. Kurt Neher (714th Infantry Division war reporter), *Divisionsgeschichte in Versen* ("History of the Division in Verse"), 1942; USNA T315/2258/1441 ff. See section entitled *Kampf in der Kozara*.

5. *Taetigkeitsbericht fuer Juli 1942* ("Activity Report for July 1942"), USNA T315/2258/0739,0748.

6. High Command of Army Group E, *Arbeitseinteilung Stand 1 Dezember 1943*, USNA T311/181/0003-0036.

7. USNA T501/267/0033, also designated as Nuremberg document NOKW-172.

8. The Waldheim briefings are referenced in the following captured documents in the holdings of the U.S. National Archives: T311/175/0988 (deployment of a "hostage railcar" has "proved useful"); T311/175/0933 (civilian slave labor in Greece); T311/178/0793-94 ("Operation Viper"); T311/0175-0176 (Winter's talks with Heinrich Himmler on coordination of security measures; July 20, 1944, attempt on Hitler's life involved "only a very small nucleus of officers").

9. *Handbuch fuer den Generalstabsdienst im Kriege* ("Handbook for the General Staff Service in War"), Berlin: Reichsdruckerei, 1938, pp. 23–26.

10. Harry Sauerkopf quoted in *Allgemeine Juedische Wochenzeitung*, Dusseldorf, Germany: March 21, 1986.

11. *Der Stern*, Hamburg: March 20, 1986; reprinted in *Profil*, Vienna: March 24, 1986.

12. Allan A. Ryan, Jr., *Klaus Barbie and the United States Government: A Report to the Attorney General of the United States*, Frederick, MD: University Publications of America ed., 1984 (originally published by the United States Department of Justice, 1983), p. 69.

13. See, for example, United States General Accounting Office, Report by the Comptroller General of the United States, "Nazis and Axis Collaborators Were Used to Further U.S. Anti-Communist Objectives in Europe—Some Immigrated to the United States," Washington: U.S. Government Printing Office, no. GAO/GGD-85-86, June 28, 1985; see also Charles Thayer (former chief of the U.S. Office of Strategic Services), *Bears in the Caviar*, Philadelphia: J.B. Lippincott, 1951; Charles Thayer, *Hands Across the Caviar*, Philadelphia: J.B. Lippincott, 1952; and Christopher Simpson, *Blowback*, New York: Weidenfeld & Nicolson, 1988.

14. William R. Corson, *The Armies of Ignorance: The Rise of the American Intelligence Empire*, New York: Dial, 1977, pp. 87–88. Corson's account is marred by his erroneous statement that CROWCASS was an acronym for Central Repository [sic] of War Criminals and Security Suspects.

CHAPTER TWELVE

1. See the 1979 annual report of Simon Wiesenthal's Documentation Center, Vienna: January 31, 1980, p. 8.

2. "Waldheim Denies He Was Suspected of Murder," UPI dispatch, March 23, 1986, AM cycle.

3. Jan Krcmar, "Former U.N. Chief Rejects Renewed War Crimes Allegations," Reuters dispatch, March 23, 1986; AM cycle; see also Arthur Spiegelman, "Jewish Group Says Waldheim Once Listed as War Crimes Suspect," Reuters dispatch, March 23, 1986, BC cycle.

4. Editorial in the *Salzburger Nachrichten*, Salzburg, Austria: March 24, 1986.

5. David Lewis, "Nazi-Hunter Calls on Yugoslavia to Clear Up Waldheim Charges," Reuters dispatch, March 24, 1986.

6. *Die Presse,* Vienna: March 24, 1986.

7. Peter Sichrovsky, "Soll ein ehemaliger Nazi und Luegner Vertreter Oesterrichs sein?," *Profil,* Vienna: March 24, 1986, pp. 24–26.

8. *Wochenpresse,* Vienna: March 25, 1986.

9. Ilse Leitenberger in *Die Presse,* Vienna: March 25, 1986.

10. Planinc's statement is quoted in David Lewis, *op. cit.*

11. Sources on the Wiesenthal press conference include an audio recording; "Kriegsverbrecherliste: Wiesenthal skeptisch," *Kurier,* Vienna: March 25, 1986; "Wiesenthal to Give the SS Briefing on Waldheim Scandal," Reuters dispatch, March 24, 1986, PM Cycle; David Lewis, "Nazi-Hunter Calls on Yugoslavia to Clear Up Waldheim Charges," Reuters dispatch, March 24, 1986; and "Jewish Congress Says Army Document Listed Waldheim as Wanted," AP dispatch, March 24, 1986, PM cycle.

12. See "This is Our Man, Says Nazi-Hunter," *The Sun,* Vancouver, B.C., Canada: March 11, 1971, p. 1; *ibid.,* March 12, 1971; and Supreme Court of British Columbia, File No. 7659/71 (copy in authors' possession).

13. According to Wiesenthal's report (pp. 5–6), his testimony was intended to contradict Merten's claim that he had tried in vain to block the deportation of the Greek Jews—a crime for which, the report notes, he had already been convicted in Greece. On the central role of Merten, who was the *Kriegsverwaltungsrat* (Chief of Military Administration) in Salonika (a civilian employee of the Wehrmacht who reported to the Wehrmacht Commander Salonika-Aegean, who, in turn, reported to General Loehr), see especially Raul Hilberg, *The Destruction of the European Jews, op. cit.,* pp. 434 and 443–47. Professor Hilberg's book, which has been the preeminent reference work on the Holocaust for more than thirty years, documents the orders issued by Merten to prepare the way for the Jews' deportation (for example, directives requiring Salonika's Jews to be marked and to move into a ghetto, and warning the Jews that escapees from the ghetto would be shot on sight) and his tragically successful efforts to persuade the doomed Jews that no harm would come to them in Poland. Hilberg also notes that the Jews of Salonika were removed to Auschwitz on Wehrmacht trains. See also Gerald Reitlinger, *The Final Solution, op. cit.,* pp. 370–76, which contains further details of Merten's sinister orders and other deeds in Salonika. Reitlinger confirms that transportation for the deportees was "provided by the Transport Command of the Wehrmacht" (citing the Nuremberg testimony of SS-*Hauptsturmfuehrer* Dieter Wisliceny, one of Adolf Eichmann's minions). Reitlinger adds the important detail that, at the beginning of the deportation process, General Loehr himself implored the Italian General Carlo Geloso (Italian 11th Army) to assist in the deportation of the Jews from occupied Greece. Geloso resisted Loehr's entreaties, and evidently refused to block an escape route being used by Salonika Jews hoping to flee to Athens via Plati (where the Italian Zone began). Wisliceny's January 3, 1946, Nuremberg affidavit (reprinted in Vol. VIII of *Nazi Conspiracy and Aggression,* U.S. Government Printing Office, 1950) contains numerous references to his cooperation with "Dr. Merten" and "the military administration" to evacuate the Jews of Salonika to Auschwitz. "Dr. Merten," he declared, "was the decisive authority and said he wished the Jews in Salonika first be concentrated in certain areas of the city." Wisliceny confirmed that Salonika's Jews were swiftly forced into ghettos "without difficulty," in order to facilitate their eventual removal *en masse*—a criminal operation to which "Dr. Merten agreed," asking only that a small number of Jews be left behind to work as slave laborers on a rail construction project. In July 1944, Wisliceny added, "Hoess, Commandant of Auschwitz, told Eichmann in my presence in Budapest that all of the Greek Jews had been exterminated because of their poor quality."

14. Israel Singer's cable to Rabbi Marvin Hier, March 24, 1986, copy in authors' possession.

CHAPTER THIRTEEN

1. Kurt Waldheim interview on Austrian Hoerfunk radio program "Abend-journal," March 25, 1986; interview on Austrian television program "Zeit im Bild," March 25, 1986; both interviews are quoted in "Waldheims Darstellung seines Einsatzes in Zitaten," *Salzburger Nachrichten,* Salzburg, Austria: April 1, 1986, p. 2.

2. Alois Mock quoted in *Die Welt,* Bonn, Germany: March 26, 1986, and "No Intervention in Waldheim Affair, Chancellor Says," Reuters dispatch, March 26, 1986, AM cycle.

3. "Kultesgemeinde fuerchtet neuen Antisemitismus," *Die Presse,* Vienna: March 26, 1986, p. 1.

4. See *Profil,* Vienna: April 21, 1986.

5. See *New York Times,* June 12, 1986.

6. Kurt Waldheim interview in *Vecernje Novosti,* Belgrade: March 26, 1986.

7. Kurt Waldheim and Heribert Steinbauer quoted in Roland Prinz, "Waldheim Calls Nazi Charges Conspiracy Against Him," AP dispatch, March 27, 1986, AM cycle.

8. Peter Humphrey, "Yugoslavia Under Pressure to Speak Out on Waldheim," Reuters dispatch, March 27, 1986, PM cycle.

9. Kurt Waldheim interview in *Vecernje Novosti* as quoted in "Kurt Waldheim Was on Mt. Kozara as Wehrmacht Officer," Tanjug dispatch, Belgrade: March 27, 1986.

10. Alexander Stanic quoted in "Yugoslavia Breaks Silence on Waldheim Affair," Reuters dispatch, March 28, 1986, AM cycle; and Roland Prinz, "Nazi Hunter Has No Evidence Waldheim Was War Criminal," AP dispatch, March 28, 1986, AM cycle.

11. Manfred Maurer, "Offenbar kein Thema fuer den Juedischen Weltcongress: Das Blut an den Fingern israelischer Politiker!," *Neues Volksblatt,* Vienna and Linz: March 28, 1986.

12. See Jan Krcmar, "Yugoslav Documents on Former U.N. Chief Fail to Show Up," Reuters dispatch, March 28, 1986, AM cycle.

CHAPTER FOURTEEN

1. *Kronenzeitung,* Vienna: March 30, 1986; editorial quoted in "Peres Calls for Answers About Waldheim's Past," AP dispatch, March 30, 1986, AM cycle; and *The Jerusalem Post,* Jerusalem: April 1, 1986.

2. Joerg Haider quoted in James M. Markham, "A Handshake Awakens Austria's Wartime Pain," *New York Times,* March 6, 1985.

3. *Wochenpresse,* Vienna: April 1, 1986.

4. "War Criminal File No. F-25572," *Vecernje Novosti,* Belgrade: March 26, 1986; "Intelligence Officer '07,' " *Vecernje Novosti,* Belgrade: March 31, 1986.

5. "Svjedocanstvo iz Stipa" ("Testimony from Stip"), *Danas,* Belgrade: April 1, 1986.

6. UPI dispatch, April 2, 1986.

CHAPTER FIFTEEN

1. See Roland Prinz, "Waldheim: Nine People Exonerate Him; Police Detain Demonstrators," AP dispatch, April 3, 1986; "Waldheim's Wartime Colleagues Vouch for Him," UPI dispatch, April 3, 1986, AM cycle; and "Ex-Soldiers Defend Waldheim," *The Financial Times,* London: April 4, 1986, p. 3.

2. *Vecernje Novosti,* Belgrade: April 2, 1986, and *Politika Svet,* Belgrade: April 2, 1986, both cited in Tanjug dispatch of April 2, 1986.

3. "Extra Ausgabe: Die Verleumdungskampagne—So wollten sie Kurt Waldheim fertigmachen!" Vienna: April 1986.

4. "Le Congres juif mondial transmettre le dossier Waldheim president de la Republique autrichienne," *Le Monde,* Paris: April 3, 1986.

5. David Lewis, "Waldheim Says Allegations Collapsed Like a Pack of Cards," Reuters dispatch, April 4, 1986.

6. Stephanie Nebehay, "Waldheim Says He Has No Fears About His U.N. File," Reuters dispatch, April 4, 1986, PM cycle.

7. Kurt Waldheim and Julian O'Halloran quoted from BBC-TV interview broadcast in the United Kingdom on April 4, 1986.

8. For Waldheim's claims regarding the "other Kozara" and the witness who remembers him, see *NIN* magazine, Belgrade: April 4, 1986; "Ich fuehle mich dafuer nicht verantwortlich," *Der Spiegel,* Hamburg: April 14, 1986; and Kurt Waldheim, "Memorandum: Position of Dr. Kurt Waldheim on Recent Allegations Levied Against Him," Vienna: April 6, 1986, p. 2.

CHAPTER SIXTEEN

1. David Kahn, *Hitler's Spies,* New York: Collier Books, 1978, p. 407.

2. German Military Documents Section, Military Intelligence Division, United States Department of War, "German Operational Intelligence," 1946 (reprinted in *German Military Intelligence, 1939–1945,* Frederick, MD: University Publications of America, 1984).

3. *Trials of War Criminals Before the Nuernberg Military Tribunals Under Control Council Law No. 10,* Washington: U.S. Government Printing Office, 1950, Vol. X, p. 1169 (NOKW-473).

4. Christian Strait, *Keine Kameraden: Die Wehrmacht und die sowietischen Kriegsgefangen, 1941–1945,* Stuttgart, Germany: Deutsche Verlagsanstalt, 1978, p. 34.

5. David Lewis, "Waldheim Exudes Confidence in the Eye of the Storm," Reuters dispatch, April 6, 1986, BC cycle.

6. Kurt Waldheim, "Memorandum: Position of Dr. Kurt Waldheim on Recent Allegations Levied Against Him," Vienna: April 6, 1986, p. 8.

7. Dept. Ic, Kommandant Ost-Aegaeis, "Activity Report for the Period from 1 July to 15 September 1944" (dated September 22, 1944), Bundesarchiv-Militaerarchiv, Freiburg, RH26-1007/25 (also USNA T501/260/0443-0512); cited in Hubertus Czernin and Nikos Chilas, "Im Walzertakt verpruegeln," *Profil,* Vienna: April 7, 1986.

8. Dept. Ic, Kommandant Ost-Aegaeis, to Ic/AO Branch, High Command of Army Group E, August 11, 1944. Cited in Hubertus Czernin and Nikos Chilas, *op. cit.,* and Raul Hilberg, *op. cit.* (1985 edition), Vol. 2, p. 708, fn. 74.

9. Hubertus Czernin, "Mayer, Nicht Meier," *Profil,* Vienna: April 7, 1986, p. 18.

10. NOKW-155.

11. NOKW-923 and NOKW-885.

12. Nuremberg document C-81 (also 498-PS).

13. Quoted in *Trials of War Criminals . . . op. cit.,* Vol. XI, p. 342.

14. Monthly activity report, July 1944, for Ic/AO Branch, High Command of Army Group E, USNA T311/186/0341–42.

15. USNA T311/186/0343–44.

16. NOKW-935, read into the record August 14, 1947.

17. USNA T314/1458/55.

18. NOKW-1985.

19. USNA T311/175/0987.
20. NOKW-885.
21. USNA T311/175/0488.
22. USNA T314/1458/69.
23. See, for example, NOKW-1915 and NOKW-1997.
24. USNA T311/175/0977.

CHAPTER SEVENTEEN

1. Elaine Sciolino, "U.S. to Request Access to U.N. File on Waldheim," *New York Times,* April 9, 1986, p. A8; see also Deborah Orin, "Blackmail Theory on Waldheim," *New York Post,* March 8, 1986.

2. The earlier and later versions of Waldheim's campaign biographies are reprinted in Peter Handke, *Pflichterfuellung: Ein Bericht ueber Kurt Waldheim,* Vienna: Gruppe "Neues Oesterreich," May 1986, pp. 46–47.

3. *Time,* April 7, 1986.

4. See Nick Ludington, "Israeli Envoy Says Waldheim Case Should Not Be Closed," AP dispatch, April 9, 1986, AM cycle; and Michael Littlejohns, "Waldheim File Turned Over to Austria, Israel by U.N.," Reuters dispatch, April 9, 1986, AM cycle.

5. See Michael Littlejohns, *op. cit.;* and Elizabeth Pond, "Former U.N. Head Kurt Waldheim in the Eye of the Storm," *Christian Science Monitor,* April 9, 1986. Wiesenthal repeated the charge nearly a year later, asserting that Waldheim might have signed as a kind of notary, without giving his approval. See "A Former Architect Who Builds a Lot More than Physical Things," *The Pennsylvania Gazette,* Philadelphia (University of Pennsylvania): February 1987, p. 19.

6. In a subsequent interview, Wiesenthal admitted to delivering this warning. See Lars-Erik Nelson, "Nazi-Hunter and Nazi-Haters," *New York Daily News,* May 16, 1986. After the *Daily News* reported that in an interview with the paper, Wiesenthal had spoken of giving the warning to the *Times* about its reputation, Wiesenthal gave an interview to the latter newspaper's Bonn bureau chief, James Markham, in which he denied having given any such warning (though he complained to Markham that his paper seemed to be "following the conclusions of the World Jewish Congress" regarding Waldheim). Wiesenthal claimed that the *Daily News* correspondent had never identified himself as such and had only broached the subject of the Waldheim case at the conclusion of a discussion about Ukrainian anti-Semitism. *Daily News* foreign editor Jon Sims responded for his paper, asserting that "we stand by the account and all the quotes" in the article. He insisted that his reporter had indeed identified himself to Wiesenthal as a *Daily News* correspondent. See James M. Markham, "Wiesenthal Faults Jewish Congress on Waldheim," *New York Times,* May 17, 1986.

7. See Simon Wiesenthal and Joseph Wechsberg, *The Murderers Among Us,* New York: McGraw-Hill, 1967, p. 57.

8. USNA M1019/24/0612ff.

9. "Waldheim's Superior Denies He Was War Criminal," UPI dispatch, March 28, 1986, PM cycle.

10. USNA T311/285/1131.
11. USNA T311/285/1114.
12. USNA T311/285/1182.
13. The April 26 and April 27, 1944, orders are both reproduced in NOKW-227; also USNA T311/285/1181 and 1182.
14. The June 5, 1944, order is reproduced in NOKW-227. It can also be found at USNA T311/285/1183.
15. NOKW-1791.

16. "Kreisky Says Waldheim Affair Is Catastrophe for Austria," Reuters dispatch, April 11, 1986, AM cycle.

17. "Wiesenthal: Some Evidence Tends to Exonerate Waldheim," A.P. dispatch, April 11, 1986, PM cycle; Harry Rabinowicz, "WJC 'Moved Too Fast,' " *Jewish Chronicle,* London, April 11, 1986.

18. For example, the reader will recall that at the March 25, 1986, press conference at which the WJC presented Bob Herzstein's research findings, I responded to a reporter's question as to whether Waldheim was a war criminal by saying that we could not say that, that this was a matter for the authorities in the countries directly affected, and that, "in the end, only a court of law can decide the question." Later, when I testified before a House of Representatives subcommittee on April 22, 1986, I made a similar statement, noting that although he had been accused by the Yugoslav government, "[w]hether Dr. Waldheim is actually guilty of Nazi war crimes is something that can be determined only by a court of law." Israel Singer took a slightly different tack in an April 8, 1986, Reuters interview, declaring that he was not interested in seeing Waldheim put on trial. Instead, he asked only that Waldheim "go back and quietly live his life out."

CHAPTER EIGHTEEN

1. "Wir Oesterreicher waehlen, wen wir wollen," and "Ich fuhle mich dafur nicht verantwortlich," *Der Spiegel,* Hamburg: no. 16/1986, April 14, 1986.

2. "Staberl" column, *Kronenzeitung,* Vienna: April 16, 1986.

3. USNA T501/331/125 and 129.

4. Wehrmacht organizational tables, such as the one for Army Group E, identify this responsibility as an Ia function. With regard to Waldheim, Dr. Gerard Schreiber, a historian at the German Military Archive in Freiburg, "testified" on this point during the filming of a Thames Television (U.K.) mock "trial" of Waldheim in 1988: "As O1, he was the one who was drafting the tactical operations for the German units as the right hand of the Ia." See Jack Saltman, *Kurt Waldheim: A Case to Answer?* (London: Robson, 1988), p. 258.

5. USNA T501/331/129.

6. Freiburg file # RH 31-10/3.

7. NOKW-755 and NOKW-1104.

8. The document is included in NOKW-1887 (also USNA T315/65/743-44).

9. USNA T311/179/1409-11.

10. USNA T501/330/1108.

11. USNA T501/330/1066.

12. USNA T311/179/844-46.

13. USNA T311/179/1259-62.

14. USNA T311/179/1256-58.

15. Kurt Waldheim quoted in *La Repubblica* (Rome), as reported in Kurt Andrich, "Die Spuren von Banja Luka," *Wochenpresse,* Vienna: April 15, 1986, p. 22. See also David Binder, "Waldheim Placed in Town of Reprisals," *New York Times,* February 8, 1988.

16. UPI dispatch, April 15, 1986, PM cycle.

17. Rod Nordland, Andrew Nagorski and Steven Shabad, "Waldheim: A Nazi Past?," *Newsweek,* March 17, 1986, p. 14.

18. Simon Wiesenthal, Letter to the Editor, *Newsweek,* April 7, 1986.

19. "The Past Stalks a Statesman," *U.S. News & World Report,* issue of April 28, 1986 (released April 19, 1986).

20. See United Nations War Crimes Commission, *History of the United Nations War Crimes Commission,* London: 1948, p. 485. The minutes of the February 26,

1948, meeting are on file at the U.S. National Archives. Waldheim was assigned the "A" rating.

21. "Prominent American Lawyer to Study Waldheim Documents," Reuters dispatch, April 17, 1986, PM cycle; see also "Waldheim Files," *The Financial Times,* London, April 18, 1986, p. 1.

22. James M. Markham, "Waldheim Rejects Ending Candidacy," *New York Times,* April 17, 1986, p. A9.

23. Elizabeth Pond, "Waldheim Asserts Nazi-free Past—Interview," *Christian Science Monitor,* April 17, 1986, p. 1.

24. Quotations from Uteschill and Perez de Cuellar are taken from "Comments by Leading Politicians and Witnesses of Dr. Waldheim's Performance from 1937–1947," report distributed in New York City by Gerhard Waldheim, beginning April 17, 1986.

25. Mitja Ribicic interview in the April 20, 1986, issue of *Kurier* (Vienna), quoted in "Aide Says Tito Probably Knew of Waldheim's Role in Yugoslavia," Reuters dispatch, April 19, 1986, AM cycle; and British Broadcasting Corporation, "The Waldheim Affair," *Summary of World Broadcasts,* April 23, 1986.

26. Cables between Israeli Ambassador Michael Elizur and the Israeli Foreign Ministry in Jerusalem, copies in authors' possession.

CHAPTER NINETEEN

1. Televised address of President Rudolf Kirchschlaeger, April 22, 1986 (transcription provided by Austrian Radio & TV, Washington, D.C.).

2. Waldheim quoted in Patrick Blum, "President's Verdict Unlikely to Quell Waldheim Storm," *The Financial Times,* London: April 24, 1986.

3. "U.N. Chief and Wiesenthal Deny Defending Waldheim," *New York Times,* April 22, 1986, p. A4.

4. David Holmberg, "Kurt Waldheim a 'Liar,' Says Sen. Moynihan," *New York Newsday,* April 22, 1986, p. 3.

5. Gerhard Waldheim quoted in "Spectre in the Palace," *The Guardian,* Manchester, England: April 29, 1987.

6. All quotations from the hearings are taken from "Allegations Concerning Dr. Kurt Waldheim: Hearing Before the Subcommittee on Human Rights and International Organizations of the Committee on Foreign Affairs, House of Representatives, Ninety-ninth Congress, Second Session, April 22, 1986," Washington: U.S. Government Printing Office, 1986.

7. "Kirchschlaegers 'Urteil' ueber Waldheim ist fertig," *Die Presse,* Vienna: April 22, 1986, p. 1.

8. "Yugoslavia Says West Germany and Allies Hold Waldheim Key," Reuters dispatch, April 22, 1986, PM cycle.

CHAPTER TWENTY

1. John M. Goshko, "Waldheim Accused by U.N. in 1948," *Washington Post,* April 23, 1986, p. A1.

2. Skok's protest was finally disclosed publicly in "Question and Answer," *NIN,* Belgrade: July 6, 1986.

3. OSI report quoted in Philip Shenon, "Justice Official Urges Waldheim Be Barred from U.S.," *New York Times,* April 25, 1986, p. A1.

4. See "Waldheim Criticizes Any U.S. Move to Bar Him," Reuters dispatch, April 25, 1986, AM cycle; "Says U.S. Memo Based on Unfounded Allegations," AP dispatch, April 25, 1986, AM cycle; and William Drozdiak, "Waldheim Plays

Down U.S. Memo on Nazi Past; Vienna Asks Washington for Clarification," *Washington Post*, April 26, 1986, p. A17.

5. See "Candidate Waldheim Convinced Nazi Scandal Will Blow Over," AP dispatch, April 27, 1986, PM cycle; and "Waldheim Under Siege," *Newsweek*, June 9, 1986, p. 30. The "100,000 Waldheims" analysis was given by Esther Ben Chur, as noted in the *Philadelphia Inquirer*, December 20, 1987.

6. Flora Lewis, "Austria, Look at Yourself," *New York Times*, April 24, 1986, p. A23.

7. USNA T501/250/401.

8. USNA T315/2268/783.

9. USNA T312/465/3541.

10. Vojin Hadistevic, "Waldheim on Kozara," *NIN*, Belgrade: April 27, 1986.

11. Polish newspapers as quoted in "West German Chancellor Praises Waldheim," AP dispatch, April 26, 1986, AM cycle, and "Polish Papers Assail Waldheim," *New York Times*, April 27, 1986.

12. Elaine Sciolino, "Austrian Says Waldheim Got Only Cursory Check," *New York Times*, April 26, 1986, p. 28.

13. "Kohl Defends Waldheim, Saying Critics Are Arrogant," *New York Times*, April 27, 1986, p. 3 (from Reuters).

14. UPI dispatch, April 27, 1986, BC cycle.

15. James M. Markham, "Austrians Examine Their Past Along with Waldheim's," *New York Times*, April 27, 1986, p. E2.

16. Allan A. Ryan, Jr., "Waldheim May Be Innocent: But Why Is He Acting Like So Many Nazi War Criminals Have?," *Washington Post*, April 27, 1986, p. C6.

17. Hubertus Czernin, " 'Extrem labiles Meinungsklima,' " *Profil*, Vienna: April 28, 1986, pp. 24–26.

CHAPTER TWENTY-ONE

1. *Neue Vorarlberger Tageszeitung*, Bregenz, Austria: May 1, 1986, as quoted in Richard Grunberger, "Waldheim in the Press: A Selected Survey," *Patterns of Prejudice*, London: Vol. 21, no. 1, Spring 1987, p. 11.

2. *Die Presse*, Vienna: May 2, 1986, quoted in Grunberger, *op. cit.*, p. 11.

3. Misha Glenny, "Austria Cushions Waldheim," *The New Statesman*, London: May 2, 1986.

4. Waldheim quoted in *Le Monde*, Paris: May 3, 1986.

5. May 2, 1986, letter from Silvana Konieczny-Origlia to Israel Singer, copy in authors' possession.

6. Nemerovsky and Waldheim quotations taken from transcription generously made available by reporter Steven Nemerovsky.

7. Andrew Nagorski and Nancy Cooper, "Waldheim on the 'A' List," *Newsweek*, April 21, 1986.

8. Hubertus Czernin, "Der Mitwisser," *Profil*, Vienna: April 21, 1986, citing Friedrich-August von Metzsch, *Die Geschichte der 22. Infanterie-Division*, Kiel, West Germany: Verlag Hans-Henning Podzu, 1952.

9. USNA T311/183/630.

10. For coverage of the Stip/Kocane story, see Elaine Sciolino, "New Papers Issued on Waldheim Case," *New York Times*, May 15, 1986; John M. Goshko, "Waldheim Linked to Reprisals," *Washington Post*, May 15, 1986; Deborah Orin, "Waldheim Signed Death Warrant For 114 Yugoslavs," *New York Post*, May 15, 1986; and "Waldheim Says He Certified Reports, But Was Not Involved," AP dispatch, May 15, 1986, PM cycle.

11. Lars-Erik Nelson, "Kurt Foes Lashed," *New York Daily News*, May 16, 1986, p. 7.

12. "Waldheim Wiesenthal," UPI dispatch, April 15, 1986, PM cycle.

13. James M. Markham, "Wiesenthal Faults Jewish Congress on Waldheim," *New York Times,* May 17, 1986.

14. Joseph Berger, "Some U.S. Jews Surprised," *New York Times,* May 17, 1986.

CHAPTER TWENTY-TWO

1. Russell Watson and David Newell, "Opening Waldheim's File," *Newsweek,* May 26, 1986, pp. 24–25; see also Tom Bower, "The Heroes the World Forgot," *The Times,* London: February 5, 1988.

2. USNA T311/179/1407–8.

3. Nuremberg document NOKW-1915.

4. This was confirmed by Army Group E's Chief of Staff, General August Winter, in the course of his June 13, 1947, interrogation at Nuremberg, in which he stated that Army Group E consisted of only two corps staffs, the 22nd Mountain Corps and the 68th Army Corps (USNA M1019/80/0087ff).

5. Confirmation that GFP 621 was subordinate to Waldheim's Ic/AO Branch may be found in the following documents, among others: organizational table of Army Group E as of December 1, 1943 (listing Waldheim's immediate superior, the headquarters "Ic" officer Col. Warnstorff, as bearing primary responsibility for "technical and activity orders to the Abwehr troops and the Secret Field Police" and for "[d]isciplinary matters for officers and men of the Abwehr troops and Secret Field Police Group 621" [USNA T311/181/0007]; a July 23, 1944 Ic/AO order to "members of GFP groups," signed by Warnstorff [USNA T501/260/445]; the transcript of the February 10, 1947 Nuremberg interrogation of Lt. Col. Roman Loos of the Secret Field Police (which includes his statement that he reported to Lt. Col. Behle, Col. Warnstorff's predecessor under General Loehr) [USNA M1019/43/0926ff]; the transcript of the February 13, 1947, Nuremberg interrogation of Loos (which includes his statement that the duties of the Secret Field Police groups were "decided upon by the respective Ic") [USNA M1019/43/0920]; and the transcript of the November 19, 1946, Nuremberg interrogation of Loehr's Chief of Staff, General August Winter (which includes his statement that Secret Field Police units were subordinate to Ic/AO Branch at Army Group E) [USNA M1019/80/77-83]. The Secret Field Police also had an internal hierarchy (headed by a Field Police Commissioner) responsible for day-to-day administration.

6. Freiburg file #RH 31-10/3.

7. Ibid.

8. Ibid.

9. Freiburg file #RH24-22/23.

10. Freiburg file #24-22/21; also USNA T314/673/723–25.

11. USNA T314/673/727.

12. Freiburg file #RH24-22/22.

13. World Jewish Congress, *Kurt Waldheim's Hidden Past: An Interim Report to the President,* New York: World Jewish Congress, June 2, 1986.

14. See *New York Times,* May 23, 1986.

15. *Al- Usbu' al- 'Arabi* ("Arabweek"), Beirut: no. 1390, June 2, 1986.

16. *Profil,* Vienna: June 4, 1986.

17. Reuters dispatch, May 31, 1986.

18. Milomir Maric, "Rane Iz Lova U Mutnom," *Duga,* Belgrade: June 13, 1986, pp. 45–47.

19. John Tagliabue, "Soviet Was Reportedly Told About Waldheim," *New York Times,* June 7, 1986.

20. USNA T314/673/346, as reported in *Stern,* June 5, 1986.

21. See Paul Lewis, "Inspections of Waldheim Files in 1970s Reported," *New York Times*, June 5, 1986; "France Says Aide Saw Waldheim Records in '79," *New York Times*, June 6, 1986; "French Discuss 1979 Report," *New York Times*, June 7, 1986.

22. *Simon Wiesenthal Center RESPONSE*, August 1986, p. 3.

23. Wiesenthal quoted in Jane Biberman, "Wiesenthal Decries Waldheim War Crimes Charge," *Long Island Jewish World*, June 6–12, 1986, p. 10 (emphasis added), and Robert Mackay, "Nazi Hunter Calls for Study of Waldheim Records," UPI dispatch of June 9, 1986, PM cycle.

24. See David Storey, "Police Prevent Protest Led by Nazi-Hunter at Waldheim Rally," Reuters dispatch, May 24, 1986, AM cycle; and Larry Gerber, "Police Break up Protest in Downtown Vienna," AP dispatch, May 24, 1986, AM cycle.

25. See Reuters dispatch, June 7, 1986; *New York Times*, June 7, 8, and 12, 1986; and *Newsweek*, June 9, 1986. See also Jane Kramer, "Letter from Europe," *The New Yorker*, June 30, 1986.

26. See Laurie Stone in *The Village Voice*, New York: August 12, 1986.

CHAPTER TWENTY-THREE

1. The account of the election-day festivities in People's Party headquarters is taken from Richard Bassett, *Waldheim & Austria* (New York: Viking, 1988), pp. 144-46.

2. "Holocaust Center 'Appalled' by Waldheim Election," AP dispatch, June 9, 1986, AM cycle.

3. Anthony Lewis, "Message to Austria," *New York Times*, June 12, 1986, p. 31.

4. Editorial, "Dutiful in Austria," *New York Times*, June 10, 1986, p. A-26.

5. Reuters dispatch, June 9, 1986.

6. Charles W. Sydnor, Jr., "Over Waldheim's Triumph Looms Nazi Legacy," *Newsday*, June 10, 1986; Sydnor quoted in Chris Criscione, "Waldheim Rode a Backlash to Presidency, Expert Says," Bristol (Virginia) *Herald-Courier*, p. 14A.

7. From address by Leopold Gratz, June 21, 1986 (translated excerpts in authors' possession).

8. Robert Mackay, "Waldheim: 100 Years of Investigations Will Not Show Me a Nazi," UPI dispatch, June 11, 1986.

CHAPTER TWENTY-FOUR

1. See, for example, Gerald Reitlinger, *The Final Solution* (New York: Perpetua edition, 1961), pp. 375–76, in which Loehr's personal intervention on this subject with the Italian General Carlo Geloso is recounted.

2. A leading example of Wiesenthal's falsely accusing a U.S. resident is the case of Frank Walus of Chicago, Illinois. In his January 31, 1975, annual report to his contributors, Wiesenthal declared that he had "succeeded in tracing a Pole in Chicago who performed his duties with the Gestapo in the ghettos of Czentstochau [sic] and Kielce [Poland] and handed over a number of Jews to the Gestapo. His name was Frank Walus." Wiesenthal disclosed that he had informed the U.S. authorities of Walus's past as a "Gestapo secret police agent." There were at least two problems with this charge: First, the Gestapo, a component of Hitler's elite SS, was for members of the master race, not Poles and others deemed by the Nazis to be *Untermenschen* ("sub-humans"). Second, Walus was innocent: he had spent the war as a forced laborer in Germany, hundreds of miles from Kielce and Czestochowa. (A detailed account of how OSI confirmed Walus's innocence may be found in

Allan A. Ryan, Jr., *Quiet Neighbors: Prosecuting Nazi War Criminals in America*, New York: Harcourt, 1984, pp. 210–217.) An instructive Canadian example is the case of Ivan Chrabatyn, a Vancouver janitor whom Wiesenthal publicly "exposed" as a mass murderer in 1971. See "This Is Our Man, Say Nazi-Hunters," *Vancouver Sun*, March 11, 1971, p. 1. However, the witness identified by Wiesenthal told reporters that he knew absolutely nothing of Chrabatyn's wartime activities. See "Witness 'Never Knew' City Janitor—Wrong Man Accused in Massacre?" *Vancouver Sun*, March 12, 1971, p. 1. In a May 10, 1972, letter of apology to Chrabatyn (copy in authors' possession), *Sun* attorney Peter W. Butler conceded that the paper's "investigations" had confirmed that the charges made against Chrabatyn "were untrue." A libel suit brought by Chrabatyn against the newspaper was settled for $11,000. Although the suit named Wiesenthal as a co-defendant, Chrabatyn was never able to serve the Nazi-hunter with legal process. In his January 31, 1972, annual report to contributors, Wiesenthal defiantly declared, "There are no doubts concerning this man's identity."

3. Simon Wiesenthal, "Waldheim Wahl und die Folgen," *Ausweg* ("Alternative"), Vienna: June 1986. See also "Wiesenthal Says Austria and Its Jews Are Election Losers," Reuters dispatch, June 8, 1986, AM cycle.

4. Kurt Waldheim quoted in Reuters dispatch, June 17, 1986.

5. Lars-Erik Nelson, "Wiesenthal Scored by Jewish Congress," *New York Daily News*, June 12, 1986, p. 10.

6. The display is pictured in Rhonda Barad (ed.), *The Liberators: The Simon Wiesenthal Center Honors the American Soldiers Who Liberated European Jewry*, Los Angeles: Simon Wiesenthal Center, 1975.

7. Simon Wiesenthal and Joseph Wechsberg, *The Murderers Among Us*, New York: McGraw-Hill, 1967, p. 28.

8. See transcripts of interrogations of Simon Wiesenthal, May 27 and 28, 1948 (Nuremberg Interrogation no. 2820, USNA M1019/79/460–476). In an August 24, 1954 sworn statement (copy in authors' possession) filed with German authorities, Wiesenthal tells a different story, claiming that his initial confinement lasted for "a few days." Once again, he makes no mention of any firing squad episode.

9. Simon Wiesenthal and Joseph Wechsberg, *op. cit.*, dustjacket and pp. 123–28. The book's jacket copy credits Wiesenthal for his "discovery of Adolf Eichmann's South American hideout" and his "tireless sifting through every clue, rumor and scrap of information that finally led to the capture of the man responsible for the deaths of thousands."

10. Simon Wiesenthal, *Sails of Hope*, 1973 (dustjacket text).

11. See, for example, Gerald L. Posner and John Ware, *Mengele: The Complete Story*, New York: McGraw-Hill, 1986, p. 136. See also Ladislas Farago, *Aftermath*, New York: Simon & Schuster, 1974, p. 70n.; letter to the editor from Avner Less (who interrogated Eichmann for the Israeli National Police), *Jerusalem Post*, August 20, 1986; and Isser Harel's own account of the Eichmann operation, *The House on Garibaldi Street*, New York: Viking, 1975.

12. Simon Wiesenthal and Joseph Wechsberg, *op. cit.*, pp. 161–62.

13. *Ibid.*, p. 213. Wiesenthal's account of the Hotel Tirol episode may be found in Simon Wiesenthal and Joseph Wechsberg, *op. cit.*, pp. 168–69. Note: The hotel added a second floor (but not a Room 26) years later.

14. *Ibid.*, pp. 213, 214.

15. *Ibid.*, p. 246.

16. *Ibid.*, pp. 251, 252.

17. "Wiesenthal's Last Hunt," *Time*, September 26, 1977.

18. Simon Wiesenthal quoted in Gerald L. Posner and John Ware, *op. cit.*, pp. 207, 208.

19. *Ibid.*, p. 299; Simon Wiesenthal, Dokumentationszentrum Annual Report, January 31, 1983, p. 4.

20. May 17, 1979, letter from Simon Wiesenthal to Kurt Waldheim, obtained by the authors from the U.S. Department of State, under the provisions of the Freedom of Information Act.

21. Letter to the editor from Simon Wiesenthal, *New York Times*, March 13, 1984.

22. Gerald Posner and John Ware, *op. cit.*, p. 209 (citing *The Times* of London).

23. Varon's most recent reiteration of this charge appeared in his biweekly column in the October 15, 1992, issue of the *Boston Jewish Times*.

24. For an example of Wiesenthal's renewal of Mengele sightings, see Tom Tugend, "Four Years after Mengele Inquiry, Some Still Doubt Ex-Nazi Is Dead," *Jewish Telegraphic Agency Daily News Bulletin*, March 6, 1989. Wiesenthal's belated concession that Mengele is dead was reported in Terrence Perry, "Mengele," AP dispatch, April 8, 1992.

25. Letter from Simon Wiesenthal to Friends of the Documentation Center (emphasis added), Dokumentationszentrum, Vienna: May 1965, copy in authors' possession.

26. Simon Wiesenthal and Joseph Wechsberg, *op. cit.*, p. 332.

27. Account of a Simon Wiesenthal interview with the Swedish newspaper *Dagens Nyheter*, as reported in a UPI dispatch of March 13, 1968, published in *Neue Zuericher Zeitung*, March 15, 1968.

28. Letter from Simon Wiesenthal to Friends of the Dokumentationszentrum, Vienna: January 31, 1969, copy in authors' possession.

29. See the Italian magazine *Epoca*, no. 1029, June 14, 1970.

30. See, for example, letter from Simon Wiesenthal to Friends of the Dokumentationszentrum, Vienna: January 31, 1975, wherein he reported his successful attempts to persuade West German Chancellor Willy Brandt not to hand over Bormann's skeleton to his family, lest the burial site become a sort of Nazi shrine. See also AP dispatch of August 14, 1991, quoting Rabbi Abraham Cooper of the Simon Wiesenthal Center acknowledging that Wiesenthal "is in agreement with German authorities that he [Bormann] died in 1945." Similarly, see Simon Wiesenthal, *Justice Not Vengeance* (London: Weidenfeld & Nicolson, 1989), p. 105 (conceding that Bormann died in 1945).

31. See Excerpts from Final Report of the Frankfurt State Prosecution Office under File Index No. Js 11/61 (GStA Ffm.) in "Criminal Action Against Martin Bormann on Charge of Murder," dated April 4, 1973, as quoted in Jochen von Lang, *The Secretary—Martin Bormann: The Man Who Manipulated Hitler* (U.S. edition), New York: Random House, 1979, pp. 355, 356.

CHAPTER TWENTY-FIVE

1. *Kurt Waldheim's Wartime Years: A Documentation*, Vienna: Carl Gerold's Sohn Verlagsbuchhandlung K.G., 1987.

2. The *Salzburger Volkszeitung*, issue of June 25, 1986, quoted in Richard Grunberger, *op. cit.*, p. 12.

3. "W. dem, der leugt," *Profil*, Vienna: June 30, 1986, p. 16.

4. "People on the World Scene" column, *New York Times*, June 30, 1986.

5. Jane Kramer, "Letter from Europe," *The New Yorker*, June 30, 1986, p. 68.

6. *NIN*, Belgrade: July 6, 1986, p. 4.

7. *USA Today*, July 4, 1986.

8. Kurt Waldheim's inauguration speech is quoted in *Kurt Waldheim's Wartime Years: A Documentation, op. cit.*, p. 71.

9. Mel Juffe, "Strip-Searched Nun Vows More Waldheim Protests," *New York Post*, July 12, 1986, p. 10.

CHAPTER TWENTY-SIX

1. Reuven J. Koret in the *Jerusalem Post,* July 28, 1986.
2. "Report on the First Meeting of the 'Austria's Image Abroad Group' on 31 July 1986," copy in authors' possession.
3. USNA M1019/80/0077-80.
4. USNA T311/181/28.
5. USNA T311/178/342.
6. See World Jewish Congress press release, July 31, 1986.
7. USNA T314/673/641–50.
8. USNA T314/673/32–40.
9. NOKW-755.
10. USNA T314/1539/462.
11. USNA T501/330/1113.
12. USNA T311/181/966.
13. USNA T311/286/256.
14. USNA T314/673/630–634.
15. Simon Wiesenthal Center, *Simon Wiesenthal Center RESPONSE,* August 1986. See also Don Shannon, "Waldheim Data Known in Paris in '79, Hier Says," *Los Angeles Times,* June 4, 1986, p. A5.
16. In a letter published in the September 19, 1986, issue of Los Angeles's *Jewish Journal,* Nikolaus Scherk, the consul general of Austria in Los Angeles, pointed out that Waldheim "was far ahead in the polls from the very beginning of the campaign," indeed by, "for Austria, unprecedented margins."
17. Dan Rosenbaum, "Blum: Terrorists Show True Colors as Anti-Semites," *The Jewish Tribune,* Spring Valley, NY: October 3, 1986, p. 9.
18. The propaganda leaflets and the cover memo are found in USNA T311/180/382–415.
19. Hubertus Czernin, "The Hanging Party," *Profil,* Vienna: September 15, 1986.
20. NOKW-155.

CHAPTER TWENTY-SEVEN

1. Jola Zalud, "Deep Rift Divides Austria's Jews Over Waldheim," Reuters dispatch, October 12, 1986.
2. Michael Graff quoted in *Die Presse,* Vienna: October 29, 1986; in the November 17, 1986, issue of *Profil,* Graff claimed that *Die Presse* had misquoted him.
3. Dusko Doder, "New Charges, Admission on Waldheim's Record," *Washington Post,* October 30, 1986, p. A1.
4. See "Washington Post Report on Waldheim Untrue, Spokesman Says," Reuters dispatch, October 30, 1986, AM cycle; and James M. Markham, "Waldheim Denying Blackmail by Soviet in the Postwar Years," *New York Times,* October 31, 1986.
5. David Horovitz, "Waldheim Had Pro-Arab Bias During '73 War," *Jerusalem Post,* May 3, 1987.
6. Kurt Waldheim, "Information in the Matter of Dr. Kurt Waldheim," memorandum sent to British M.P. Robert Rhodes James, October 31, 1986, p. 4.
7. See "Meese Weighing Waldheim Status After Reports of Soviet Blackmail," *Washington Times,* October 31, 1986, p. 7A.
8. Henry Tanner, "Waldheim: In Vienna, Lingering Bitterness," *International Herald Tribune,* November 4, 1986.

9. Richard Bono, "Historian: Waldheim Facilitated Deportations," *The South-ern Israelite,* November 7, 1986, p. 3.

10. The explanation may lie partly in the fact that Herzstein was now preoc-cupied with attempting to prove that Kurt Waldheim had been a U.S. intelligence asset after the war and that the OSS and CIA consequently worked to ensure the success of his cover-up of his Nazi past. In a lengthy analysis published under his byline in the *Boston Globe* on May 1, 1988, Herzstein referenced a remarkable array of famous American officials—past and present—in describing a CIA cover-up of mammoth proportions. George Bush, Ronald Reagan, William Casey and Admiral Stansfield Turner were among those who figured in Herzstein's fantastic account. Unfortunately, Herzstein's inexperience in matters of U.S. intelligence betrayed him. For example, his *Globe* piece cites as a key element of proof in his conspiracy theory the fact that, "By 1948, he [Waldheim] turned up in the S.I. files of U.S. Army counterintelligence." Herzstein explains that "S.I." was an acronym for *"source of information or intelligence."* In fact, as the authors have confirmed via documents obtained from the Army under the Freedom of Information Act, "S.I." was the CIC's categorization for a routine series of files on individuals who, for various reasons (in Waldheim's case, his postwar service in senior posts in the Austrian Foreign Ministry), had come to CIC's attention. "S.I." is an abbreviation simply for *"special investigation,"* not "source of intelligence." In a 1988 book, *Waldheim: The Missing Years* (New York: Arbor House), Herzstein sought to develop the U.S. cover-up theme more fully, by weaving a tapestry of extraordinary hypotheses presented as fact, albeit again with scant success (such as when he awkwardly at-tempted to "explain" how the U.S., under Ronald Reagan, and with the CIA headed by former OSS official William Casey, should still be seen as Waldheim's longtime protector, notwithstanding the fact that the U.S. is the *only* country on the globe that has publicly branded Waldheim as a Nazi criminal and barred him from entry; after making the preposterous assertion that Waldheim's status as a U.S. intelligence asset may be seen in the "remarkable calm self-assurance" with which the "unruffled" Waldheim met the unfolding scandal in 1986–87 (Herzstein must have been watch-ing some *other* Kurt Waldheim), he contends that the Reagan-Meese watchlist "surprise" for Waldheim was the product of their having "bowed to political pres-sure" (pp. 257–259). Regrettably, the book—advertised by its publisher as written by the man who was "the first to uncover evidence of Waldheim's hidden war record"—also misrepresents Herzstein's role in the exposure of Waldheim's past. (See page 22, in which Herzstein implies that, when first contacted by the WJC in mid-March 1986, the focus to that point had been on Waldheim's "prewar Nazi background," but that he entered the case in order to research Waldheim's "wartime career"; of course, these assertions are belied by even a cursory review of the press stories in the weeks that preceded Herzstein's engagement by the WJC, beginning with the very first *New York Times* story, on March 4, 1986, headlined "Files Show Kurt Waldheim Served Under War Criminal," and accompanied by the dramatic Podgorica airstrip photograph.) Herzstein's book omits important facts about the Soviet and Yugoslav governments' respective roles in Waldheim's postwar life, and even goes so far as to claim that Waldheim had the support of the two NATO members of the U.N. Security Council (the U.S. and the United Kingdom) when he sought, and won, the U.N. Secretary-General's post in December 1971 (p. 225). In fact, the U.K.—America's closest military and intelligence ally—*vetoed* Wald-heim's nomination in the first round and the U.S. abstained, favoring two other candidates. Waldheim won at the third and final meeting, but only because the *Soviet Union* vetoed the other two remaining finalists and the State Department's oppo-sition to Waldheim was not communicated to the U.S. Mission in time to affect the final vote. Most troubling of all in Herzstein's 1988 book are the evidentiary gym-nastics in which the author engages in order to arrive at the torturously irresolute conclusion that, while Waldheim was a "facilitator" of Nazi war crimes and an

"accessory" to their perpetration (p. 254), he is "a well-meaning, ambitious man" whose "nonguilt" would have spared him a trip to the dock at Nuremberg, but "must not be confused with innocence" (pp. 254, 260). For example, Herzstein cites a May 25, 1944, document prepared by Waldheim (and first disclosed by Swiss journalist Hanspeter Born in 1987) as evidence of a "protest" against German reprisal policy, "moral in inspiration" (pp. 122, 123). As the International Historians Commission noted in its February 1988 report, however, it was nothing of the sort:

> Even the document dated May 25, 1944, cited in the press and quite familiar to the Commission, in which Waldheim is supposed to have protested against excessive reprisals (this involved a monthly "Enemy Situation Intelligence Report—Greece") does not contain any protest against the use of such measures. Rather, there are only pragmatic remarks regarding the "dosage" of such measures. There is no "criticism of the atrocities in the Balkans," as was stated in several press reports. Such an "Enemy Situation Intelligence Report" was, in any case, not the proper place for "protests." Moreover, criticism of excessive, counterproductive punitive measures had already been expressed in terms of a military order (dated December 22, 1943), and also expressly stated by General Speidel, on the occasion of the massacre at Kalavrita in December 1943.
>
> This document, by the way, is once again proof that Waldheim was well aware of punitive measures of reprisal.

In the final analysis, the Herzstein book may perhaps best be appraised by reference to the fact that advertisements for it highlighted the following endorsement: " 'Absolutely brilliant.'—Simon Wiesenthal."

11. USNA T501/249/1238–43.
12. USNA T501/249/1216–22.
13. USNA T501/249/1244–45.
14. See USNA T501/250/411; T501/250/60; and T501/250/415.
15. "Shevardnadze Meets Waldheim on Eve of Security Conference," Reuters dispatch, November 3, 1986, AM cycle.
16. James Markham, "Waldheim, Ostracized, Cuts Lonely Figure in Presidency," *New York Times,* November 12, 1986, p. A1.
17. October 4, 1943, speech by Heinrich Himmler, contained in Nuremberg document PS-1919 and quoted in Raoul Hilberg, *op. cit.,* p. 660.
18. See report on *Kronenzeitung* editorial in Eric Bourne, "Austria: Waldheim Affair Lingers," *Christian Science Monitor,* November 20, 1986, p. 22.
19. Jewish Telegraphic Agency *Daily News Bulletin,* October 21, 1986.
20. Wiesenthal quoted in William Tuohy, "Waldheim's Shadow Looms Over Austrian Parliament Elections," *The Los Angeles Times,* November 22, 1986, p. 34.
21. Herb Brin, "Waldheim Issue Splits Center and Wiesenthal," and "Wiesenthal's Wrong" (editorial), *Jewish Heritage,* Los Angeles: November 28, 1986.

CHAPTER TWENTY-EIGHT

1. USNA T501/331/378.
2. USNA T501/331/313–314.
3. USNA T501/259/642–645.
4. USNA T311/175/755–756.
5. World Jewish Congress, "Nazi Document Reveals Waldheim Role in Handling British Prisoners," press release of December 29, 1986.
6. Robert Rhodes James and Ralph Schieder quoted in Alan Travis and Mischa

Glenny, "Documents Revive Call for Waldheim Inquiry," *The Guardian,* Manchester, England: December 31, 1986.

7. See Simon Wiesenthal's annual report of January 31, 1985, p. 1.

8. Commission of Inquiry on War Criminals, *Report—Part I: Public,* Ottawa: Canadian Government Publishing Centre, 1986. For comments on Simon Wiesenthal, see especially pp. 245–261. The Commission's reference was to 217 alleged officers of the "Galicia" ("Halychyna" in Ukrainian) Division of the Waffen-SS identified by Wiesenthal. The Commission added pointedly (p. 261) that "[c]harges of war crimes against members of the Galicia Division have never been substantiated, either in 1950, when they were first preferred, or in 1984, when they were renewed, or before this Commission." For at least a decade, Wiesenthal had demanded that U.S. and Canadian authorities investigate the "Nazi pasts" of these "SS officers" who "in the employ of the Germans committed horrible crimes" (see, for example, his annual reports, issued each January, for 1977, 1983, 1984, 1985, 1986, and 1987). After being humiliated by the Canadian commission he had previously described, in his 1986 annual report, as being headed by "one of the highest and most esteemed judicial personalities in Canada," Wiesenthal suddenly started claiming in his annual reports that what was of interest was what the members of the Division had done *before* they joined it. Some, he said, were ex-members of the Ukrainian police units that had participated in the mass murder of Jews. But, he wrote in his 1988 annual report, the fact that it is (in Wiesenthal's estimation) "virtually impossible" to "find out which members of the SS-Division 'Galicia' belonged to the police regiments and committed the heinous crimes" did not overcome the fact that "each young Ukrainian who joined" the Division "must have *known about* the activities of the SS, because the population witnessed their activities daily." In the Waldheim affair, of course, Wiesenthal had repeatedly stressed that "mere knowledge" of crimes was not itself criminal. Nor, it appeared, did the supposed "impossibility" of identifying Division members who might have taken part in crimes suggest to Wiesenthal that there was anything unfair about publicly disclosing the names and residences of suspected Division veterans, as he had repeatedly done in his annual reports of 1983, 1984, and 1985.

CHAPTER TWENTY-NINE

1. According to the Army Group E organizational table, Major Hammer could be involved in such matters as well, but only in his alternate capacity as deputy Ic officer, not as AO officer. For an example of a document evidencing Warnstorff's personal involvement in cooperation with the SD (and the SS), see a September 7, 1944, document of Army Group E, signed by Warnstorff (NA T311/181/1072) (proposal to the SS to "Withdraw the SD from the Greek Area").

2. See, for example, the decision of the International Military Tribunal at Nuremberg in Case No. 12 (the "High Command Case"), in which it held that "the staff officer who puts that [criminal] idea into the form of a military order, either himself or through subordinates under him, or takes personal action to see that it is properly distributed to those units where it becomes effective, commits a criminal act under international law" (*Trials of War Criminals Before the Nuernberg Military Tribunals under Control Council Law No. 10,* Vol. XI [Washington: U.S. Government Printing Office, 1950], p. 513).

3. For an example of a draft order prepared at Ic/AO Branch and signed by Waldheim, see NA T311/181/1114 (September 7, 1944).

CHAPTER THIRTY

1. USNA T501/250/382–393.

2. USNA T501/250/935–65; see also USNA T501/250/145–147, which makes it clear that the 488 deported persons were prisoners of the Pusteria Division.

3. Kurt Waldheim quoted in *Kurt Waldheim's Wartime Years: A Documentation, op. cit.,* p. 71.

4. The results of Gottschlich's study were reported in David Lewis, "Academic Says Waldheim Campaign Boosted Austrian Anti-Semitism," Reuters dispatch of February 2, 1987.

5. *Vecernje Novosti,* Belgrade: March 11, 1987 (cited in "Waldheim Was Made Persona Non Grata in 1952," AP dispatch, March 11, 1987, AM cycle).

6. See David Binder, "Waldheim Linked to Nazi Roundup," *New York Times,* February 18, 1988.

7. See "Angry Austria Urges Waldheim to Sue Meese for a Million," *Washington Times,* April 29, 1987; "Diplomacy of 'Blacklists,' " *Izvestia,* May 1, 1987; and "Reaction to US Decision to Bar Entry to Waldheim," text of Radio Moscow commentary, April 28, 1987, reprinted in BBC, *Summary of World Broadcasts,* May 1, 1987.

8. "USA setzen Waldheim ohne Beweise auf die 'schwarze Liste'!" ("USA Puts Waldheim on the 'Blacklist' Without Proof!"), *Kronenzeitung,* Vienna: April 28, 1987; see also "Inquisition" in the issue of April 29, 1987.

9. *Die Presse,* Vienna: April 29/30, 1987, and May 3, 1987.

10. David Lewis, "My Conscience Is Clear, Waldheim Tells Austrians of U.S. Ban," Reuters dispatch of April 29, 1987.

11. Hubertus Czernin, "Schreckliche Maschine," *Profil,* Vienna: May 25, 1987.

12. Alison Smale, "Waldheim Says His Conscience Is Clear," AP dispatch of April 28, 1987.

13. See, for example, Peter Hoffer, "Austria Rallies Behind 'Clean' Kurt Waldheim," *Daily Telegraph,* London: April 29, 1987.

14. Peter Gnam, "Wiesenthal: Waldheim bisher zu stolz, um Verleumder vor Gericht zu Klagen," *Kronenzeitung,* Vienna: April 29, 1987.

15. "Nazihunter Says Waldheim Should Have Taken Accusers to Court," Reuters dispatch, April 28, 1987; Peter Hoffer, "Austria Rallies Behind 'Clean' Kurt Waldheim," *Daily Telegraph,* London: April 29, 1987.

16. Alison Smale, "Furor Around Waldheim Shows Austrians Sensitive About Past," AP dispatch, May 2, 1987.

17. "Nazi Hunter Says Waldheim Agrees to Probe," UPI dispatch, May 4, 1987; "Austria to Set Up Panel to Probe Waldheim's Wartime Activities," Jewish Telegraphic Agency *Daily News Bulletin,* May 5, 1987; "Angry Austria Urges Waldheim to Sue Meese for a Million," *The Washington Times,* April 29, 1987.

18. See Michael Doan and Charles Fenyvesi, "Kurt Waldheim: Persona Non Grata," *U.S. News & World Report,* May 11, 1987; Peter Hoffer, "Waldheim Attack on U.S. Jews," *Sunday Telegraph,* London: May 3, 1987; and Peter Hoffer, "Waldheim Vows Move to Counter U.S. Action," *The Washington Post,* May 5, 1987.

19. Maximilian Gottschlich and Karl Obermair, "Waldheim and the Watch List Decision: Anti-American and Anti-Semitic Reporting in the Austrian Print-Media" (Vienna: University of Vienna/Anti-Defamation League of B'nai B'rith, June 1987).

CHAPTER THIRTY-ONE

1. Erich Kern, *General von Pannwitz und seine Kosaken* ("General von Pannwitz and His Cossacks"), Goettingen, Germany: Plesse Verlag, 1963; see pp. 201 and 204.

2. See George H. Stein, *The Waffen-SS 1939–1945*, Ithaca: Cornell University Press, 1966, p. 188; and Jurgen Thorwald, *The Illusion: Soviet Soldiers in Hitler's Armies*, New York: Harcourt Brace Jovanovich, p. 309.

3. Nicholas Bethell, *The Last Secret*, New York: Basic Books, 1974, pp. 77–78.

4. See USNA T311/179/1117.

5. See, for example, USNA T311/179/265–70, 407, 426–29.

6. USNA T311/186/347.

7. USNA T311/181/466.

8. USNA T314/673/723–725. The report is initialed "W" and signed by Major Hammer.

9. Any lingering suspicion that such proof might have been present in portions of the document censored after the war by American authorities was eliminated in 1989, when the British Defence Ministry released an almost fully reconstructed version of the report.

10. Rachel Dalven, "The Holocaust in Janina [Ioannina]," *Journal of Modern Greek Studies*, 1984.

11. April 14, 1944, report, signed by Paschiera (copy in authors' possession).

12. The reader will recall that Army Group E did suggest to Army Group F that the Greek sailors be spared "since [they were] compelled to participate." Whoever may have been responsible for this (ultimately unsuccessful) act of decency, it is clear that Waldheim was not: When asked, during his January 28, 1988, meeting with the International Historians Commission who had made this suggestion, Waldheim stated that he did not know.

13. Letter of November 2, 1950, from M.L. Priss, Foreign Office, to Allan Tuckey's stepfather, Col. Albert Clark (copy in authors' possession).

14. Tom Bower, "The Heroes the World Forgot," *The Times* (London), February 5, 1988.

15. Letter of June 23, 1988, sent on behalf of Vice President George Bush by Donald P. Gregg, Assistant to the Vice President for National Security Affairs, to Gordon Zacks, co-chairman of the National Jewish Coalition.

16. See Seymour Maxwell Finger and Arnold A. Saltzman, *Bending with the Winds* (New York: Praeger, 1990), pp. 25–29; and William Safire, "Reviving the U.N.," *New York Times*, March 21, 1991, p. A23. In a conversation with one of the authors of this book, Safire stated that he could not recall specifically why Waldheim was not Douglas-Home's and Rogers's preferred candidate. But nothing sensational (wartime or otherwise) was involved according to Safire, who added that had anything potentially scandalous been raised, he would surely remember it. According to Safire, the two foreign ministers simply felt that Waldheim "wasn't a very good man for the job." What the columnist does recall vividly is "the feeling of 'Ugh!' in the room" when the aide came in and said that it was too late to block Waldheim's election.

17. See, for example, articles published in the *New York Times* on May 4, 1971 (p. A9), October 4, 1971 (p. A12), October 6, 1971 (p. A14), and November 13, 1971 (p. A13).

18. "Diplomacy of 'Blacklists,' " *Izvestia*, May 1, 1987.

19. Ken Gross, "His Nazi Past Rises to Haunt Former U.N. Chief Kurt Waldheim," *People*, May 19, 1986, p. 51.

20. Robert Rhodes James, "A U.N. Enemy Within," *The Guardian*, Manchester, England: October 30, 1987.

CHAPTER THIRTY-TWO

1. USNA T501/250/382–393.

2. In his January 28, 1988, interview with the "Historians Commission" *(infra)*, Waldheim similarly stated, "I passed on reports [sic] from the Bader Combat Group to the Pusteria [Division] and such reports also came to me in reverse." Of course, what Waldheim relayed from Bader's headquarters to the Italians were *orders*, not mere reports ("reports" travelled in the opposite direction, from the Pusteria Division to German headquarters).

3. It is instructive to compare the April 10 order to others in this respect. For example, an order of March 22, 1942 (USNA T501/250/410), which was *not* circulated to the Italians, explicitly references the D.V.K. units (including D.V.K.5) on its distribution list. In any event, orders would not have gone directly from Bader Combat Group headquarters to the Pusteria Division in Plevlje. For example, a courier dispatched to Plevlje with such an order would have delivered it to the D.K.V.5 officer there (Waldheim), who would have been responsible for passing it on to the Italians.

4. It may be asked whether Waldheim was in place as the liaison officer with the Pusteria Division in time to transmit Bader's April 10 order. Waldheim was in fact assigned to D.V.K.5 in a *March 22, 1942,* order of the Bader Combat Group (USNA T501/250/410–412), at which time he was evidently still on medical leave as a result of the injuries he sustained in the Soviet Union the previous year. But his medical leave ended by April 7, and according to the Austrian Foreign Ministry's 1987 "White Book" *(infra)*, Waldheim's D.V.K.5 assignment "immediately followed upon the termination of his recuperation leave" (p. 64). Wehrmacht policy, as reflected, for example, in Waldheim's movements during and after subsequent leaves, required him to be at his duty station as soon as his leave ended—in this case by April 8, 1942.

5. "Government Researchers Say Yugoslav Documents Do Not Implicate Waldheim," AP dispatch, May 15, 1987, PM cycle.

6. See Serge Schmemann, "Kohl and Waldheim Meet Privately," *New York Times,* August 15, 1987.

7. *Kurt Waldheim's Wartime Years: A Documentation, op. cit.*

8. *Ibid.,* pp. 38, 41.

9. The document may also be found in USNA T311/186/778.

10. The Mihailovic meeting is reported in a November 3, 1944, "Ic" report signed by Warnstorff (copy in authors' possession).

11. Hermann Neubacher, *Sonderauftrag Suedost 1940–45* (W. Berlin, 1956), p. 189.

12. See Daniel Johnson, "Waldheim's Alleged Nazi Crimes Stirred Anew," *Daily Telegraph* article reprinted in *The Washington Times,* October 6, 1987, p. A10; and "Wiesenthal Denies Holding Waldheim Data," *Baltimore Jewish Times,* October 9, 1987.

13. Edgar Bronfman, quoted in the December 1, 1986, issue of *Der Spiegel* (issue nr. 49).

14. December 12, 1986, letter from Simon Wiesenthal to West German Chancellor Helmut Kohl and July 1, 1985, letter from Wiesenthal to Cardinal Koenig (copies in authors' possession).

15. Hoedel letter (copy in authors' possession) quoted in Daniel Johnson, "Austria Today: Why Jews Are Living in Fear," *Daily Telegraph,* London: October 5, 1987.

16. Henry Kamm, "Vienna Journal: A New Yorker's Anguish in the Land of Waldheim," *New York Times,* October 9, 1987.

17. "Austria Helps Iranian Jews," AP dispatch of October 2, 1987.

18. *L'Express,* Paris: November 17–18, 1987.

19. Paul Grosz quoted in Mike Leary, "Waldheim's Woes are Austria's Too," *The Philadelphia Inquirer,* December 21, 1987.

20. *Report of the International Commission Designated to Establish the Military Service of Lieutenant Kurt Waldheim,* Vienna: February 8, 1988.

21. "Yugoslav's Data Link Waldheim to Atrocities," *New York Times,* January 24, 1988.

22. Kurt Waldhcim quoted in *Kurier,* Vienna: February 3, 1987.

23. Peter Hoffer, "Waldheim Says He Can't Recall Wartime Telegram," *The Washington Post,* February 6, 1988, p. A24.

24. *Report of the International Commission . . . , op cit.*

25. Lars-Erik Nelson, "Making Waldheim a Martyr," *The Daily News* (New York), April 29, 1987, p. 33.

CHAPTER THIRTY-THREE

1. See Robert J. McCartney, "Waldheim Statement on Jews Cited," *The Washington Post,* February 14, 1988.

2. "The World This Week," BBC Television, February 21, 1988.

3. Daniel Johnson, "Waldheim's Alleged Nazi Crimes Stirred Anew," *Daily Telegraph* article reprinted in *Washington Times,* October 6, 1987, p. A10; John Holland, "Historians Say Waldheim Not Vindicated," UPI dispatch of February 9, 1988; "Waldheim Not Exonerated?" AP dispatch, February 9, 1988; Serge Schmemann, "Waldheim Report Leaves Austria as Divided as Before," *New York Times,* February 10, 1988, p. A10; Susan Bloch, "Waldheim Stonewalls, Refuses to Resign, Asks for Compassion," *The Boston Jewish Times,* February 18, 1988, p. 1. In the fearless style that is a trademark of the smaller of Boston's two Jewish papers, its article referred to the Vienna Nazi-hunter as "long-time Waldheim apologist Simon Wiesenthal."

4. Jehuda Wallach, "Waldheim: What We Found," *The Washington Post,* March 6, 1988.

5. Fritz Molden, interviewed on the ABC television program "Nightline," February 15, 1988.

6. Karl Gruber's remarks are reported in "Austria's Leader Asserts Waldheim Imperils Coalition," *New York Times* (Reuters dispatch), February 15, 1988, p. A1. The interview with Christa Karas-Waldheim was published in *L'Evenement du Jeudi* (Paris), issue of July 14–20, 1988, p. 30.

7. May 18, 1938, letter from Consular Academy Director Friedrich Hlavac von Rechtwall to the Presidium of the Chamber of Commerce (copy in authors' possession). The letter also notes that Waldheim and three other applicants "have brought proof of Aryan descent [four Aryan grandparents] and were described by student leaders at the Consular Academy as completely suitable with regard to their political attitude."

8. From Richard Mitten's translation of his article (co-authored by Hans Schafranek) in the Zurich weekly *Die Weltwoche,* November 8, 1988.

9. Waldheim quoted by Hubertus Czernin in the November 14, 1988, issue of *Profil.* Waldheim's 1946 court filing was first reprinted in that magazine's March 24, 1986, issue.

10. Bluett's recollections, given to Thames Television, are summarized in the Ministry of Defence's 1989 report on its investigation into Kurt Waldheim's alleged involvement with captured British servicemen.

11. Robert Fisk, "Mystery of Censored Report," and "Officer's Fight to Escape the Inevitable," *The Times* (London), March 11, 1988.

12. Woodhouse's article, "The Case of Captain Warren," was published in the September/October 1988 issue of *Encounter.* The British Defence Ministry reacted

to these disclosures by reopening its decades-old inquiries into the fate of *all* the missing British servicemen now linked to the wartime activities of Kurt Waldheim. After more than a year of investigation, the British government later (in October 1989) issued an apologetic announcement: "It is very much regretted that, in spite of extensive research . . . it has not proved possible to obtain any definite evidence as to the final fate of the missing men."

CHAPTER THIRTY-FOUR

1. Simon Wiesenthal, *Justice Not Vengeance,* London: Weidenfeld & Nicolson, 1988, p. 2.

2. Ladislas Farago, *Aftermath,* New York: Simon & Schuster, 1974, p. 70n; Letter to the Editor of Efraim Zuroff (Simon Wiesenthal Center), *The Jerusalem Post,* April 22, 1986.

3. Letter to the Editor from Avner Less, *The Jerusalem Post,* August 20, 1986.

4. See the Letters to the Editor of Wim van Leer, *The Jerusalem Post,* May 20, 1986, and July 14, 1986, and Letter to the Editor of Alfred Streim, *The Jerusalem Post,* June 29, 1986.

5. Letter to the Editor from OSI Director Neal M. Sher, *The Jerusalem Post,* May 11, 1986.

6. April 18, 1990 letter from OSI Director Neal M. Sher to Simon Wiesenthal (copy in authors' possession, provided by the World Jewish Congress).

7. Simon Wiesenthal, *Ich jagte Eichmann,* Guetersloh, Germany: Sigbert Mohn Verlag, 1961, p. 220.

8. September 23, 1959, letter from Simon Wiesenthal to Ambassador Yecheskel Sachar (copy in authors' possession).

9. Simon Wiesenthal, *The Murderers Among Us* (New York: McGraw-Hill, 1967), pp. 116–120.

10. See Christoph Kotanko, "Biedermaenner und Brandstifter," *Profil,* Vienna: August 17, 1987, p. 10.

11. Michael Dobbs, "French Had Waldheim File in '79," *The Washington Post,* June 7, 1986, p. A12.

12. "French Waldheim Investigation Revealed," Simon Wiesenthal Center, *Simon Wiesenthal Center RESPONSE,* August 1986, p. 3.

13. The final part of question number 29 was: Did you also receive the documents on Waldheim in the files of the Krankenbuchlager? If you have *ever* seen these documents, when did you first do so?

14. Shirley Hazzard, "Chaos Was His Opportunity," *New York Times Book Review,* March 27, 1988, p. 47.

15. Letter to the Editor from Simon Wiesenthal, published in the *New York Times Book Review* of May 8, 1988.

16. Another largely unnoticed confirmation comes from the unlikely source of Robert Herzstein. In a June 16, 1989, postscript to the paperback version of his book, *Waldheim: The Missing Years,* Herzstein, arguing for his theory that Waldheim was a U.S. asset, cavalierly dismissed the suggestion that the CIA did not check Waldheim's military record in the WASt archives. "This is peculiar," Herzstein wrote, "since all investigative bodies, *including the Wiesenthal Documentation Center in Vienna,* routinely check WASt in cases of individuals accused of criminal conduct on behalf of the Nazi regime."[emphasis added] In an endnote, Herzstein disclosed that "Simon Wiesenthal supplied this information to the author in June, 1987." See Robert M. Herzstein, *Waldheim: The Missing Years,* New York: Paragon House Publishers, 1989, pp. 266 and 304.

17. Simon Wiesenthal quoted in an interview by Robert Buchacher, published in the July 25, 1988, issue of *Profil.*

CHAPTER THIRTY-FIVE

1. Carl Sagan, *et. al., Murmurs of Earth: The Voyager Interstellar Record,* New York: Random House, 1978, pp. 25–29.

2. "Like a Beggar," *Der Spiegel,* no. 41/1986, October 6, 1986, pp. 170, 171. Waldheim's "moral power" quote was reported in *The Times* (London), July 9, 1977.

3. "Kurt Waldheim's German Visit," *The Washington Post* (editorial), March 29, 1992.

4. See, for example, an April 1, 1992, *New York Post* editorial ("Chancellor Kohl's Willful Insult"), in which Kohl was accused of "revolting behavior" intended "to shore up his image as a German nationalist in Bavaria." The editorial ended with this warning: "This episode will not be forgotten by anyone who remembers Germany's attempt to wipe the Jewish people from the face of the earth."

5. *Sueddeutsche Zeitung* editorial, quoted in Marc Fisher, "Germany Facing Harsher Criticism," *The Washington Post,* March 31, 1992.

6. *Ibid.*

7. Op-ed piece, "Just Who Are Our Jewish Leaders?" *The Jerusalem Post,* April 16, 1992. Wiesenthal's bylined coauthors were Michael Wolffsohn and Lord (George) Weidenfeld.

8. See, for example, Austrian ambassador Friedrich Hoess's April 6, 1992, letter to the editor of the *New York Times* (published on April 13, 1992). On the promises by the Socialist and People's Party candidates to work to remove Waldheim's name from the watchlist, see Michael Z. Wise, "Austrians Waltz Toward Polls," *The Washington Post,* April 24, 1992.

9. See *e.g.,* George Will, " 'Exoneration' of Alger Hiss," *Newsweek,* January 11, 1993, p. 66 (noting senior Russian official's retreat from previous statement that his research had shown that accusations against an American accused of espionage were "groundless").

10. Rone Tempest, "Waldheim, Despite Hostage Trip, Gets No Respect on Global Stage," *Los Angeles Times,* September 19, 1990, page A6.

11. Shirley Hazzard, *Countenance of Truth, op. cit.,* p. 65. See also pp. 89–94.

12. The Amnesty International report is described in a Reuters dispatch reprinted in the *Washington Times* on January 9, 1990. The letter to the editor regarding the service of Austrians in the armed forces of Nazi Germany was penned by Friedrich Hoess, ambassador of Austria to the United States, and was published in the *Washington Post* on April 1, 1992.

GLOSSARY AND ABBREVIATIONS

Abwehr The counter-intelligence and espionage service of the German High Command.

Anschluss Literally, "connection"; the annexation of Austria by Nazi Germany in 1938.

AO *"Abwehr-Offizier"* (counter-intelligence officer in a German army unit).

AOK 12 *Armeeoberkommando 12* (High Command of the 12th [German] Army).

BDC Berlin Document Center (U.S. State Department—run repository of captured Nazi-era German records, located in Berlin).

CIA (United States) Central Intelligence Agency.

CIC (U.S. Army) Counter Intelligence Corps.

CROWCASS Central Registry of War Criminals and Security Suspects, initially issued in 1945 by SHAEF (Supreme Headquarters, Allied Expeditionary Force, commanded by General Dwight D. Eisenhower) and updated periodically under the principal supervision of U.S. military personnel. CROWCASS was intended to serve as a "wanted list" of persons being sought by various governments.

D.V.K. *Deutsche Verbindungskommando* (German Liaison Detachment), German army liaison to other Axis commands (Croatian, Italian, etc.).

Einsatzgruppen Special mobile SS and police units created for special missions in occupied territories (particularly the liquidation of Jews, communists and partisans in Eastern Europe).

F.d.R. *Fuer die Richtigkeit* (after a signature, attested to the accuracy of a document; not to be confused with **F.d.R.A.**, which denoted "certified true *copy*").

Gestapo *Geheime Staatspolizei* (Secret State Police of the Nazi government of Germany).

GFP *Geheime Feldpolizei* (Secret Field Police).

Ia Operations unit or senior operations officer in a German army headquarters.

Ib Quartermaster/supply department, unit or officer.

Ic Intelligence section or senior intelligence officer in a German army unit. At the High Command of Army Group E, the Ic headed the Ic/AO Branch.

Ic/AO Combined intelligence (Ic) and counter-intelligence (AO) branch of a German army group, under the command of the Ic officer.

Kampfgruppe Literally, combat group, an assemblage of German and often other Axis military units, under unified German command.

KGB *Komitat Gosudarstvennoy Bezopasnosti* (Committee of State Security), the principal espionage and counter-espionage service of the former Soviet Union.

Luftwaffe German air force.

Mossad Principal foreign intelligence service of the State of Israel.

NA U.S. National Archives (Washington, D.C.).

NOKW- One of the designations given to documents assembled for the postwar Nuremberg trials.

NS- *Nationalsozialistische* (National-Socialist, "Nazi"), prefix that forms the first part of the names of many Nazi organizations, such as *NSDAP* (Nazi Party—National-Socialist German Workers Party), *NS-Reiterkorps* (Nazi Rider [Cavalry] Corps) and *NS-Studentenbund* (Nazi Student Union).

O1 First Special Missions Staff Officer (*Ordonnanzoffizier*), principal assistant to the chief of operations in a German army unit.

O2	Second Special Missions Staff Officer *(Ordonnanzoffizier),* principal assistant to the quartermaster in a German army unit.
O3	Third Special Missions Staff Officer *(Ordonnanzoffizier),* principal assistant to the chief of intelligence in a German army unit.
Odluka	Yugoslav criminal indictment (literally, "decision" in Serbo-Croatian).
Ordonnanzoffizier	Special Missions Staff Officer, principal deputy or aide to a branch chief (see "O1," "O2" and "O3").
OSI	Office of Special Investigations, the U.S. Justice Department's Nazi war crimes prosecution unit.
OSS	(U.S.) Office of Strategic Services, American wartime intelligence organization.
POW	Prisoner of War.
SA	*Sturmabteilung* (storm troopers), the "Brownshirts," originally the shock troops of the Nazi Party.
SBS	(British) Special Boat Squadron/Service.
SD	*Sicherheitsdienst,* the Security Service of the Reich Security Head Office (RSHA), originally the intelligence service of the SS and Nazi Party.
SOE	(British) Special Operations Executive, secret wartime organization that trained and dispatched agents to assist resistance forces in Nazi-occupied Europe.
Soldbuch	German soldier's paybook.
Sonderbehandlung	Literally "special treatment," infamous SS and SD euphemism for execution, often preceded by torture.
Special Treatment	See *Sonderbehandlung.*
SS	*Schutzstaffel* (literally "protection detachment"), the elite uniformed para-military arm of the Nazi Party. Under the leadership of *SS-Reichsfuehrer* Heinrich Himmler, it became the dominant instrument of Nazi tyranny and mass murder.
T	Designates a U.S. National Archives Microcopy series (for example, T501).

TASS   *Telegravnoye Agentstvo Sovietskovo Soyuza,* Telegraphic Agency of the Soviet Union (the official "news" agency of the former Soviet Union).

U.N.   United Nations.

UNWCC   United Nations War Crimes Commission, international agency created to facilitate the apprehension of persons suspected of committing war crimes and crimes against humanity during the Second World War. It predates the creation of the United Nations organization.

USNA   U.S. National Archives (Washington, D.C.)

VS   *"Verschluss sache"* (literally, articles to be kept under lock and key), highly classified documents, subject to special safeguarding and to registration and summarization in the *VS-Brieftagebuch,* the classified documents logbook.

Waffen-SS   Combat units of the SS. Waffen-SS personnel also served as guards (and in other capacities) at Nazi concentration and death camps.

WASt   *Wehrmachtauskunftstelle* (Wehrmacht Information Office), the then-French-run repository of old Wehrmacht records, located in Berlin.

Wehrmacht   German armed forces (army, navy and air force), although the term is often used to refer solely to the German army.

WJC   World Jewish Congress.

ABOUT
THE AUTHORS

Eli M. Rosenbaum is a graduate of the Wharton School of the University of Pennsylvania (MBA 1977) and of the Harvard Law School (JD 1980). From 1980 to 1984, he served in Washington, D.C., as a trial attorney with the U.S. Justice Department's Office of Special Investigations (OSI), the federal government's special task force for the investigation and prosecution of Nazi war criminals.

During 1984 and 1985, Rosenbaum was a corporate litigator with the Manhattan law firm of Simpson Thacher & Bartlett.

In November 1985, he was appointed General Counsel of the World Jewish Congress.

In May 1988, Rosenbaum returned to the U.S. Department of Justice, where he now serves as Principal Deputy Director of OSI, in which capacity he is responsible for overseeing all federal investigations of suspected Nazi war criminals. (Upon rejoining the Department of Justice, Rosenbaum disqualified himself from involvement in all federal investigative and other official aspects of the Waldheim case.)

He lives in Washington, D.C., with his wife Cynthia and their two daughters.

William Hoffer is the author or coauthor of seventeen nonfiction books, including the international bestsellers *Midnight Express* and *Not Without My Daughter*. He lives in Virginia with his wife, author Marilyn Hoffer.

INDEX

ABC "Nightline," 444
Abendjournal (Austria), 153
Ackerman, Gary, 232–33, 235, 240–41
Adler & Adler (James & Esthy)
  Waldheim's books, 105, 128–29
Aftermath (Farago), 304–05
Albania
  Jews, deportation of, 54
  prisoners of, 425–27, 432
Alimnia Island (Dodecaneses), prisoners of, 190, 203–04, 205, 207, 272, 410–12, 431, 440
Allied commandos & other Allied prisoners
  Commando Order (Hitler), 190–92, 202–07, 218–19, 273–75, 278, 367–68, 409, 411, 422–23, 439–40, 446, 447
  See also Prisoners
Ankara (Turkey), massacre at, 342
Anti-Defamation League of B'nai B'rith
  NGO meeting, 356–58
  and Wiesenthal, 449
Anti-foreigner sentiment, 175, 291, 294
Anti-partisan actions. *See* Resistance movement; War crimes
Anti-Semitism, 299
  in Germany, 338–39
  in Paraguay, 341–42
  in U.S., 396–97
Anti-Semitism (Austrian)
  People's Party, 12, 141–42, 145, 156, 160, 329, 349–50, 363, 386–87, 399–400, 427–28
  postwar, 66–67, 163–64, 175–76, 230, 323, 327–28, 349–50, 398, 427–28, 466, 473

press, 142, 143, 145, 161, 164–65, 215, 299, 349–50, 362–63, 386, 399–400
prewar, 234, 256
World War II, 11
Anti-Semitism (& Waldheim)
  election campaign, *xvii*, 155–56, 253, 281, 282, 291, 294–95, 329, 356, 457
  family & supporters, statements by, 155, 214
  Waldheim, statements by, 156–57, 226–27, 362–63, 399, 441–42
Arafat, Yasir, 6, 92
Arbeiter Zeitung (Austria), 283
Archive Mission, 420–21
Arta. *See* Ault, Dorothy L., 280
Artukovic, Andrija, 162, 176
Arthur Ui (Brecht), 141–42
Athens
  Waldheim in, 113, 129, 209–10, 216–18, 220–21, 334, 407, 421
  wartime events in, 193, 216–19, 221
Auschwitz. *See* Death camps
Austria, 10–11
  Jewish community of, 2, 11–12, 48, 92, 155–56, 215, 229, 282, 298, 390, 429
  NAZI past, non-acknowledgment of, 213, 246
  postwar government & Waldheim, 22–23, 42–43, 44, 66–67, 75–76, 81, 84, 102, 106, 133
  public relations, 329–30, 340
  reparations, 11–12, 66–67, 281
  U.S., relations with, 396, 400
  World War II atrocities, involvement in, 11
  Yugoslavia, treaty negotiations, 262
  See also Vienna

523